Preface

The European Community Legal System is a new and intimidating prospect for Irish Lawyers educated in the traditional mould. The Community system has its origins in Civil Law and it is based on Civil Law concepts. It abounds with strange terminology for the Common Law lawyer: phrases like Competition Law and Economic Law do not possess a familiar ring for lawyers in these islands. 'Direct Applicability' and 'Direct Effect' strike unease into the breasts of many a fearless courtroom warrior. Moreover, the subject matter of Community Law, which relates primarily to commercial, economic and trade matters, ushers us into a strange environment where, in the absence of specialist training, comprehending the facts which create the legal problem can present an almost insurmountable obstacle for the ordinary practitioner. The nature of the European Community's legal system is by definition inter-disciplinary: economics, law and politics frequently overlap and theoretical and idealistic aspirations are often tempered by realistic and pragmatic solutions. The multi-lingual forum gives the polyglot an advantage. The rapidly changing nature of the system, reflecting, as it necessarily must, economic policies and preoccupations means that its institutions must be flexible and adaptable. Principles emphasising the long term must be distinguished from short term rules which can and must change frequently. Timetables and schedules introduce an inevitable element of dynamism. Legal and economic instruments must be at hand to allow for swift action in crisis conditions; regular institution adjustment is frequently compelled by traders' ingenuity, by currency fluctuations or by quota allocations. In these circumstances, expediency ceases to carry pejorative connotations. Even retroactivity must be viewed differently in such a rapidly altering landscape.

And, *mirabile dictu*, the system is scarcely thirty years old! In our approach to legal history we are wont to look at patterns and trends in time spans measured in centuries. Here, however, Community developments have occurred in mere decades. In contrast with the oft invoked institutional and legislative paralysis the jurisprudential basis of the Community has been firmly articulated and established in little over a generation. Most of the familiar legal systems have taken centuries to develop but the European Community presents us with a structure which

v

had developed rapidly, not in a slow methodical evolution. And paradoxically, for a system created by Civilians, the structure owes much of its design to judicial rather than legislative genius. This is all the more extraordinary when it is remembered that the Court of Justice is dependent on the presentation of suitable cases for determination. Its clear teleological approach to the interpretation of the Treaties has ensured that precedents have significance beyond the immediate fact pattern which calls for resolution.

For the Irish lawyer the initial approach to the Community system may be less intimidating than for the true Common Law practitioner. If we look at the Foundation Treaties as a written constitution constraining the governing institutions and furnishing the Court of Justice with the power of judicial review, strong parallels with the Irish legal system can be identified. Moreover, the creation of a Community theory of Human Rights from scant legal bases by an activist judiciary is remarkably reminiscent of Irish constitutional developments since the early 1960s.

Although the Irish legal system has adapted well to the Community presence, Irish lawyers in general have been slow in their recognition of the new system. Perhaps this is understandable. Most successful practitioners have been too busy to take time off to be re-schooled, the familiarisation process was inevitably slow. One of the present authors, Bryan McMahon, studied 'Common Market' law more than twenty five years ago in the United States at a time when there were no courses in EEC Law in Irish universities and very few in the United Kingdom. He began teaching the subject for the first time in Ireland more than twenty years ago at University College, Cork—five years before Ireland joined the Community. One of his earliest pupils (his co-author in this venture) went on to study in Europe and returned to teach the subject at University College, Dublin where he was involved in the re-establishment of the Diploma in European Law. Mary Robinson, SC also dipped into the same US well and introduced the subject to the law programme in Trinity College, Dublin where she has acted as a catalyst in promoting the subject over the years. And before this, Dr. John Temple Lane, whose name has been so intimately linked with the whole area for the past three decades, had studied in Chicago and had written seminally on the subject. He has acted as a guiding figure to both practising and academic lawyers over the past two decades. Mr. Justice Brian Walsh, combining his European vision and experience with his juristic appreciation and true feeling for the Civil Law, was also truly inspirational in promoting European Law and establishing the Irish Society for the Study and Practice of European Law, later the Irish Society for European Law.

Recently, more and more students have been exposed to Community law at under-graduate level and many have gone on at post-graduate level to study in Amsterdam, in Bruges, in Brussels and in Florence. Some notable practitioners have also emerged in the field in recent years reflecting the growing demand for professional expertise in this area. '1992' has created an urgency for greater familiarity with Community Law. Most Irish lawyers, even of the older generation, now realise that they must familiarise themselves at least with the basics of the Community's legal system before '1992'. Promotional efforts associated with the slogan have

European Community Law in Ireland

Bryan M.E. McMahon

B.C.L. LL.B. (NUI), LL.M. (Harvard), PhD. (NUI), Solicitor,
currently in practice with
I.M. Houlihan & Sons, Solicitors,
Ennis, Co. Clare,
Professor of Law, University College, Galway

Finbarr Murphy

B.C.L. LL.B. (NUI), Dip. I.C.E.I. (Amsterdam),
Barrister-at-Law (King's Inns),
Group Legal Adviser, Bank of Ireland,
formerly of the Faculty of Law,
University College, Dublin

Butterworth (Ireland) Ltd
Dublin 1989

Republic of Ireland	Butterworth (Ireland) Ltd, Dublin and Abingdon (UK)
United Kingdom	Butterworth & Co (Publishers) Ltd, 88 Kingsway, London WC2B 61A North Castle Street, Edinburgh EH2 3LJ
Australia	Butterworths Pty Ltd, Sydney, Melbourne, Brisbane, Adelaide, Perth, Canberra and Hobart
Canada	Butterworths. A division of Reed Inc., Toronto and Vancouver
New Zealand	Butterworths of New Zealand Ltd, Wellington and Auckland
Singapore	Butterworth & Co (Asia) Pte Ltd, Singapore
USA	Butterworths Legal Publishers, St Paul, Minnesota, Seattle, Washington, Boston, Massachusetts, Austin, Texas and D & S Publishers, Clearwater, Florida

ISBN 1 85475 000 3

Typeset by Opus, Oxford
Printed and bound by Billing & Sons Ltd, Worcester

heightened professional awareness and have renewed the tempo of the integration process. Even in the United States, where familiarity with the significance of European developments has been extremely limited, commentators are now sitting up and taking notice of the renewed impetus in European integration. It is rare indeed that a legal text should be launched in an atmosphere of heightened interest in the subject matter.

The book we have written attempts to introduce the Irish lawyer to the Community's legal system. It also traces and outlines the impact which the Community's legal system has had on the national system and it focuses on the adjustments and the responses that were required of Ireland because of its accession to the Community. Finally, it outlines the substantive law on the major areas concerned such as The Free Movement of Goods, Persons, Services and Capital. Comment and exposition is also made on selected policies of the Community. In this regard, it has not been possible to cover every Community policy and the authors have been somewhat selective. Ireland's lack of coal deposits and its marginal steel industry, combined with significant public opposition to nuclear energy, means that the law of the European Coal and Steel Community and the law of Euratom receive only a passing mention. Other Community policies, either because of their novelty or their underdevelopment, have been sacrificed to the dictates of space; the common transport policy is a case in point. It may be possible to include these topics in a further edition of this book. But the reader should not imagine that simply because a topic is not covered in the present text, that it lacks significance or importance.

So many thanks and acknowledgements are due to various people that we have listed them on a separate page. To each and every one mentioned we acknowledge our indebtedness. What errors remain are attributable to our own fallibility. In this connection, in a time of increasing litigation, we have to state that while every effort is made to present the law accurately as it appeared on 1 September 1988 we cannot accept any liability for any inaccuracies or mis-statements contained herein.

Bryan M.E. McMahon
Finbarr Murphy

The Arthur Cox Foundation

Arthur Cox, solicitor, classical scholar and former President of the Incorporated Law Society of Ireland, was associated with the setting up of many Irish Companies, not least the E.S.B. he was a specialist in company law and was a member of the Company Law Reform Committee which sat from 1951 and reported to the Government in 1958, ultimately giving rise to the Companies Act, 1963. When he decided to retire from practice as a solicitor in 1961 a number of his clients, professional colleagues and other friends, in recognition of his outstanding contribution to Ireland and his profession, thought that a fund should be established as a tribute to him which fund would subsidise the publication of legal text books. There was a generous response to this appeal.

After this retirement he studied for the priesthood and was ordained in 1963. He went to Zambia to do missionary work. He died there in 1965 as a result of a car accident.

The Foundation was established to honour Arthur Cox and was for many years administered by Mr. Justice John Kenny in conjunction with the Law Society. In paying tribute to the memory of Arthur Cox it is appropriate that tribute should also be paid to Mr. Justice John Kenny, who died on 25 March, 1987. John Kenny was a close personal friend of Arthur Cox and, like Arthur Cox, graced with distinction his own barristers' profession, as a chancery practitioner, and both the High Court and Supreme Court, as a judge. John Kenny was the encouraging force behind the publication of a number of Irish legal textbooks. Without his quiet drive and enthusiasm there would have been no Foundation. To both Arthur Cox and John Kenny we pay tribute.

The Law Society, as the continuing trustee of the Foundation, is pleased to have been able to assist in the publication of this book by Professor Bryan McMahon and Mr Finbarr Murphy.

Maurice R. Curren
President,
The Incorporated Law Society of Ireland,
February 1989.

Contents

Contents

Contents

Table of Statutes

Table of Statutory Instruments

Table of European Communities Legislation

Treaties

Secondary Legislation

Table of Treaties and Conventions

Table of Treaties and Conventions

Table of Other Enactments

Table of Cases

Decisions of the European Court of Justice are listed both alphabetically and numerically. The numerical Table follows the alphabetical.

A

C

D

E

xlii

L

M

Table of Cases

l

Decisions of the European Court of Justice are listed below numerically. These decisions are
also included in the preceding alphabetical Table.

liv

Foreword

In April 1951 the Treaty of Paris was signed. This marked the creation of the first of the three Communities which today institutionalise distinct aspects of European economic cooperation. This first step—the creation of the European Coal and Steel Community—resulted from the untiring efforts of a few men of great idealism, courage and integrity such as Schuman, de Gasperi, Monnet and Hallstein. These men shared a vision of a Europe bound together by economic and social ties instead of being divided into competing and often hostile groups easily angered by trade rivalries. They realised how terrible the cost had been to ordinary people who had witnessed two terrible wars in the first half of this century. They realised also how deeply men yearned for peace—for a peace that would endure. But such a peace had to be based on something more lasting than one generation's memories of its own suffering. Such memories would pass and fade with the rebirth of national rivalries and pride. To Schuman and his colleagues the basis for such an enduring peace lay in economic cooperation amongst European states persuaded to share their resources and to trade freely with one another. Cooperation in coal and steel was the first step. This was followed by the creation of Euratom ensuring cooperation in the field of atomic energy. However, the real advance was achieved with the signing of the Treaty of Rome in 1957. This set European states on the road to economic and social unity and has made the possibility of war between them utterly inconceivable. Now more than thirty years on the European Economic Community which this Treaty brought into being has become an accepted fact. What the future has in store is a matter of conjecture. It may be that a movement towards closer political union has already commenced. On the other hand it may be that Member States will say 'thus far and no further'. In either event it is important for us, in Ireland, to know our Community and to appreciate the role it can play in our internal affairs both now and in the future.

In this book the authors set themselves the task of examining, in an Irish dimension, the legal aspects of membership, how it has effected and will effect the national legal system and whether and to what extent emerging new principles of law may be relied upon in Irish courts. This requires an understanding of how the Community is organised and of the competence and powers of its institutions. To this end this book contains adequate information not only as to the Treaty provisions but also as to the manner in which, in practice, the various institutions have operated and the extent to which the checks and balances provided by the Treaty have been successful. The authors display a first class knowledge of the legal order in the Community and also a sound practical knowledge of how particular powers are exercised. This combination has added considerably to the usefulness of this book as an Irish lawyer's guide-book to the Community, and, to an understanding of how the functioning of the Community effects the Irish legal system.

The Community which the Treaty of Rome brought into being was not a mere alliance of states banded together for the achievement of some common purpose. If it were such then the achievement of the stated purpose would have been part of the foreign policy of the State but could have had no effect, as such, on the internal or national law. Here however, was something different and new. This Treaty created an entirely separate and distinct legal entity to which each acceding State surrendered portion of its national sovereignty. A form of super-state came into being which was armed with the necessary competence and power to achieve the purposes for which it was created and the over-lordship of which, in matters pertaining to such achievement, was freely accepted by each Member State. This super-state is however an entity subject to law in the sense that it is bound by the Treaty, by which it was created, in the same way as Ireland, as a State, is bound by the Constitution, which brought it into being. But it is also a Community which, under the Treaty, has a legislature empowered to make laws consonant with its terms and designed to further the achievement of the purposes for which it was established. So the creation of the Community saw the emergence of a new and autonomous legal order, now called European law, which had to be recognised as having supremacy over national law if the Community was to function as the Treaty intended. This was something entirely strange to the Irish legal system. Under the Constitution, Irish law stemmed from the Constitution itself and from laws duly made by the national legislature. No executive act would make applicable in Ireland rules, regulations, or principles emanating from an outside law-making authority. Nor could an Irish statute so provide because such would be contrary to the Constitution. The problem was, of course, solved by the Third Amendment to the Constitution which was enacted by the people on the 10 May, 1972 authorising the State to join the Communities and providing

'No provision of this Constitution invalidates laws enacted, acts done or measures adopted by the State necessitated by the obligations of membership of the Communities or prevents laws enacted, acts done or measures adopted by the communities, or institutions thereof, from having the force of law in the State.'

It was by means of this Constitutional provision that European law became applicable within the State and obtained the necessary supremacy over national law.

The authors classify European law according to its sources. In the first category are the principles and concepts contained in the Treaty itself. These of course are dominant rules to which may be added the basic principles of the laws of Member States as elaborated in the jurisprudence of the Court of Justice. These Treaty provisions and basic principles may be regarded as comprising the constitutional law of the Community to which all other law must conform. Next, there is the vast field of secondary legislation which consists of Regulations, Directives and Decisions. These come from the Council or the Commission and must be within the powers of the enacting Institution and conform with the Treaty and the basic principles. All such legislative acts are subject to judicial review in much the same way as statutes or statutory orders may be challenged in Irish Courts either on constitutional grounds or as being *ultra vires* the enabling statute. Readers will follow with interest the differences, which the authors discuss, between Regulations and Directives and, of course, Decisions which stand on their own. To understand these differences is to understand the circumstances in which a provision of European law is directly effective in Irish Courts. It may be that such a provision can confer rights either unknown to or expressly denied by national law.

This book underlines the message that European law is now part and parcel of our legal system. No longer can lawyers shrug it off as something which only assumes importance when one goes to continental Europe. The fact is that this new system of law, derived from the treaties and the basic principles common to the laws of Member States as well as European legislative acts, is no longer distant from the Irish scene. It has come to Ireland, and, what is more, its coming results, not from the leave and licence of a Parliamentary Statute which could be altered or repealed at Parliament's will, but, from a provision of Ireland's Constitution which can only be changed by the people.

It is with great pleasure that I recommend this book to lawyers and students in Ireland.

T.F. O'Higgins
Judge at the Court of Justice
of the European Communities

Acknowledgements

The Authors would both like to thank, in the first instance, Valerie Hill of the Department of Law, UCC, Ann Kelliher, Bernadette Bradley and Patricia Garland of the Faculty of Law, UCD and Maria Blaney of the Group Legal Adviser's Office, Bank of Ireland, whose skill and patience translated various hand-written and dictated first drafts into workable manuscripts of the various chapters of this book.

The Authors also gratefully acknowledge the assistance received from the Arthur Cox Foundation. Professor McMahon would especially like to record his thanks and appreciation to the Management Fund, University College, Cork, which partly supported his studies and to Worcester College, Oxford and Temple Law School, Philadelphia for research facilities when earlier drafts were being written. Finbarr Murphy would like to thank the Court of Justice of the European Communities and Judge T.F. O'Higgins for sponsoring a research visit the Court of Justice in September, 1986.

It would not have been possible to write this book without the cooperation of many officials of the European Communities. The Authors would like to record their gratitude to Terry Stewart, Director of the Office of the Commission in Molesworth Street, Dublin and his predecessors, Conor Maguire and Denis Corboy. Friendly assistance was also forthcoming from Mary O'Connor and Carol Guinan; but our greatest thanks must be reserved for a small corps of persons—extraordinarily well versed in Community affairs—in the library and information service of the Dublin Office: Tim Kelly, Rosemary McCarthy, Lynette Fegen, and Johanna Finnerty. Down the road in Molesworth Street the Dublin based officials of the European Parliament were equally helpful; our thanks must go to Joe Fahy, Dermot Scott, Nancy Mullins and Mary Killoran. In Luxembourg the Irish member of the Court of Justice has always been of great assistance and we would like to record our thanks to Mr. Justice Andreas O'Keeffe and his successor Judge T.F. O'Higgins as well as their legal secretaries Philippa Watson, David O'Keeffe and Deirdre Curtin.

Considerable assistance was also procured from a variety of persons in the service of the State. In this connection we would like to thank John Mahon of the Supreme Court Office, Seamus Phelan, Clerk of the Oireachtas Joint Committee on the secondary legislation of the European

Acknowledgements

Communities, Derek Mockler, Marion Byrne and Colm Gaynor of the Department of Agriculture, Sean O hEigeartigh, Wally Kirwan and Frank Murray of the Department of the Taoiseach, Barry Robinson and Declan Kelliher of the Department of Foreign Affairs, Rory Greer and Pascal Leonard of the Department of Labour, Mary Morrissey of the Department of Finance, Colm McCashin of the Central Bank, Arthur Plunkett of the Office of the Attorney General, and Michael Liddy of the Office of the Director of Public Prosecutions.

Our families and friends, who remained mercifully silent as projected completion dates came and went, cannot be adequately thanked but we would like to put on record our special appreciation of the support given by Mary McMahon and Maire Darby.

Larry Ennis and Finola O'Sullivan of Butterworth (Ireland) Limited and their silent, suffering colleagues at Abingdon have been immensely helpful and forgiving. If they have learned anything from this project it is that 'nearly finished' means just that.

Finally, we would like to thank successive generations of students in the Faculties of Law at UCC and UCD. Many of the chapters in this book were worked out and elaborated in lectures given in the context of under-graduate and post-graduate courses in European Community law. It is hard to envisage a more receptive or critical audience.

Part I

Overview and introduction

Chapter 1

Introduction

Background[1]

1.1 Immediately after World War II, Europe in the main and not only Germany, lay in ruins. Germany had lost the War and as a result was inflicted with heavy penalties by way of reparation payments. But neither did victory come cheaply to the Allies; in truth, after full stock was taken, the victory was seen to be little short of Pyrrhic. In the six years of the War tanks had rolled across the European land mass and the areas of Africa bordering on Europe. For six years the young men of Europe had gone out to be killed or wounded in history's most horrific war. For six years the economies of the European countries had tried to cope with the vital problems of arming, fighting, healing and rebuilding. When the war was ended large parts of Europe literally had to be rebuilt.

1 See generally Stein, Hay and Waelbroeck, *European Community Law and Institutions in Perspective: Text, Cases and Readings*, pp. 1–9 (1976); D. Lasok and J. W. Bridge, *Law and Institutions of the European Communities*, Fourth Edition (1987), Chapter 1; P. J. G. Kapteyn and P. Verloren van Themaat, *Introduction to the Law of the European Communities* (1973) Chapter 1.

1.2 As victors, the Allies faced two immediate problems. How could Germany be prevented from rising to power again? And how could the economy of Europe be re-constructed? The latter problem was brought about by the havoc wreaked by six years of war; the former by the real fear that Germany, having invaded France three times in seventy years, would not easily surrender its Master-race aspirations.

1.3 The Allies, however, had learned a lesson from the Treaty of Versailles in 1918, and were determined that although Germany was certainly to be punished, its punishment must not be so severe as to embitter it and spur it again to seek revenge. It was proposed that, as well as any repayments that Germany was to make, its war resources, the coal and steel of the Ruhr valley, should also be placed under international control. The European Coal and Steel Community was established in 1951. This move it was hoped as well as rendering Germany powerless, would also greatly help the economic recovery of Europe. In addition to this, however, it is fair to stress that there were other factors which favoured a cooperative approach in political and economic matters in the Europe of the time.

1.4 Firstly, with the defeat of Nazism in Germany, the concept of the nation state as a political unit of organisation fell into disrepute. The idea of the nation state which thrived and blossomed in the nineteenth century, became warped into a form of racialism under Hitler and as a result went into serious decline. After the war Western Europe concluded that the nation state as a principle of political organisation was becoming obsolete, especially when it considered the recent and rapid developments in technology, transport and communication generated in the war effort. With the advent of intercontinental missiles the nation as a unit of international politics seemed unreal; moreover, Eastern Europe was already talking and thinking in larger terms—in terms of international Communism. The trend towards bloc politics became clear. The war had dramatically changed the world power scale.

Before the war, in 1939, a count of the major powers would certainly have included France, Germany, Great Britain and Japan; after the war, when the dust had settled, there seemed to be only two powers: the United States of America and Russia. The emerging scene suggested that in the future a share of world political power might also go to China and Africa. In any event, it was clear that the scale of things had changed and if the countries of Western Europe were to maintain status then they would have to bind themselves into some kind of comparable bloc of continental dimension. As early as 1946 in Zurich, Churchill was already declaring the need for 'a kind of United States of Europe'.

1.5 But what form was the grouping of Western Europe to take? It was clear that whatever form it ultimately settled for, the old *entente* method of international accommodation was inadequate. Such treaties depended too much on the retention of the *status quo* economically and politically. A change in government might mean a different foreign policy, and a political or an economic crisis frequently caused such treaties to be revoked at the very time when the need was most pressing. Something more permanent, more stable was needed. Something more resistant to immediate and economic pressures was required. Whether the ultimate form of friendship would emerge as a federation or a confederation, would only be determined by subsequent events. What was clear was that the form of cooperation would have to be a more intense form of integration than had been previously adopted by States in their search for international harmony.

1.6 Secondly, the increasing military threat from Eastern Europe served to band the Western Europeans into a kind of defence comradeship of necessity. The power and intention of the Soviet Union was clearly seen in Czechoslovakia in 1948, and the first chilling breezes of the Cold War began to be felt almost immediately. The ruthless suppression of the

Hungarian people in 1956 confirmed for many the suspicions about post-war Russian ambitions and it became clear that Western Europe, unless it was to remain easy prey to the Soviet Union, had to combine and organise itself. The United States of America was also quick to recognise the threat from the Soviet Union and the consequent need for a strong, united Europe. Thus not altogether altruistically, but nevertheless in a manner deserving of praise, the US poured money into Europe in the form of Marshall Aid. A condition imposed by the USA was that the fund had to be administered and distributed by the Europeans themselves. The Organisation for European Economic Cooperation was established and the reconstruction was begun.

The immediate military reaction to the Russian annexation of Czechoslovakia in 1948 was the signing of the Brussels Treaty by the United Kingdom, France and the Benelux Countries. This Treaty, however, although principally a defence alliance, was much more. It also contained provisions for economic, social and cultural cooperation and heralded significant developments to come.

1.7 Thirdly, the economic arguments for large-scale cooperation were undeniable.[1] The advantages of groups of countries cooperating and forming an expanded market were known in theory ever since Adam Smith wrote *The Wealth of Nations* in the nineteenth century, and indeed there were many efforts previous to 1950 to put the basic principles of free trade into operation. The United States of America in the late eighteenth century, the Zollverein in nineteenth-century Germany, and the Benelux in the 1940s are all examples of this free trade theory being successfully implemented in practice. There had been notable failures too; a survey of these failures leads one to believe that before the ideals of free trade can be fully realised it is necessary that there be a favourable combination of political as well as economic factors. There must be, it seems, a political willingness, to some extent, before the economic advantages follow. Such a willingness certainly emerged in post-war Western Europe and it ultimately led to the signing of the Treaty of Rome.

1 For general introduction to economics of international trade see J. Viner, *International Economics* (1951); R.E. Caves, *World Trade and Payments: an Introduction* (1973); C.P. Kindleberger, *International Economics* (5th ed. 1973); R.M. Stern in Stein, Hay and Waelbroeck, *supra*. pp. 311–316.

1.8 Finally, in spite of what has already been said about social, political and economic circumstances being favourable in post-war Europe for an international cooperative movement, it must not be thought that the EEC was an historical inevitability. Few things in history are inevitable. Conditions were certainly conducive to cooperative efforts in European politics and economics in the late 1940s and early 1950s, but one wonders whether the European movement would have been so successful had it not been for the untiring individual efforts of, among others, men like Schuman, Gaspari, Monet and Hallstein. Their contribution in any rehearsal of relevant causes, should not be underestimated. The burning conviction of these individuals and their energetic and sustained efforts, contributed much to the eventual formulation and implementation of the European ideal.

1.9 It was against this background that the European Coal and Steel Community (ECSC) was established in 1951. It proved to be an immediate success. Encouraged by the development, plans for more ambitious integration were quickly formulated. In 1953 a treaty establishing a European Defence Community (EDC) was a signed but was rejected by the French Assembly in 1954. A proposal from the European Assembly for a European Political Community was also abandoned at the same time. Ambitions for European integration went underground and sought another outlet; they surfaced three years later in the form of proposals to establish a European Atomic Energy Community (Euratom) and a European Economic Community (EEC). It is with this last Community that this book is primarily concerned.

ECSC

1.10 As indicated already the first of the three Communities to be established was the ECSC. This was established by the Treaty of Paris in April 1951. The treaty purported to cover a narrow sector of the economy only, namely coal and steel, and its novel features may be better appreciated when this is borne in mind. In particular the willingness of the signatory states to transfer some of their sovereignty to an independent autonomous Community, the willingness to vest in the High Authority (the executive body of the new Community) such strong powers of decision making and the whole intensity of the integrative process associated with the establishing treaty can only be understood when the limited (though important) sphere of activities covered by the treaty is borne in mind. When later forms of integration began to be mooted subsequently on a wider level, the Member States were not so generous in transferring their sovereign powers. In 1950, however, the sap was rising and the Member States were willing to make the required act of faith.

1.11 Institutionally, the ECSC was to be administered by the Council of Ministers, the High Authority, the Parliamentary Assembly and the Court of Justice. The Court was to apply the law and administer justice and the Assembly was to provide an institutional outlet for the voice of democracy. Real decision-making power was to be divided between the Council of Ministers and the High Authority, with many independent decision making initiatives being vested, seemingly irrevocably, in the High Authority.

The principal functions of the ECSC are to supervise the formation of prices and to fix maximum or minimum prices, if necessary, to control and stimulate investment in the coal and steel sector.[1] A free market within the Community is established and all tariffs and quantitative restrictions between the Member States are outlawed. A common tariff *vis-à-vis* non-Member countries was to be established. Equal access to the sources of production is guaranteed and discriminatory measures and other practices are outlawed. Apart from the transfer of power by the Member

States to the Community the other novel feature worth noting at this stage was the recognition that, in addition to the signatory States, individuals and enterprises also had enforceable rights under the treaty.

The success of the ECSC served as an inspiration to the European minded federalists when renewed efforts were being made in 1957 to re-float the European concept in other fields in the wake of the aborted EDC (*supra*). The determination not to be defeated by the EDC experience, but to learn from it, was greatly assisted by the success story of the ECSC. In 1957, in Rome, the treaties establishing the EEC and Euratom were signed. Euratom seeks to create 'the conditions necessary for the speedy establishment and growth of nuclear industries'.[2] Because of the narrow area of interest it need only concern us incidentally in the present study.

1 See ECSC Treaty, art.s 1–6.
2 Euratom Treaty, art. 1.

The European Economic Community

1.12 In contrast to the ECSC and Euratom, the EEC is much more comprehensive in the area of activity it purports to cover. Unlike the treaties establishing the ECSC and Euratom, the treaty establishing the EEC embraces the whole economy.[1] Simply put, it envisages the creation of a single market between the Member States where goods can move freely and without restriction within the defined market. It provides for the erection of a common-tariff *vis-à-vis* non-member countries and a method of collecting and transferring such Community tariffs to Community coffers. But the EEC is much more than a Customs Union in that it also makes provision for the free movement of persons (including business enterprises), the free movement of services and the free movement of capital. Moreover, the integration process is carried further by Member States agreeing that the Community should also be responsible for the creation, elaboration and implementation of common policies in various areas such as agriculture (including fisheries), conjunctural (short-term) policies, competition matters, transport, etc. Provision is also made for the harmonisation and co-ordination of laws.

1 See EEC Treaty, art.s 2 and 3 for a summary of tasks and activities of the Community. See *infra*. These articles are not comprehensive as they make no reference to the Community's social policy or to the programme for the harmonisation of indirect taxes. See Hans Smit and Peter E. Herzog *The Law of the European Community* (1982), para. 3.03.

Economic rationale of EEC[1]

1.13 The economic rationale underlying the EEC Treaty can be briefly put, at the risk of oversimplification, in the following way. The establishment of a large single market in Europe means that the advantages associated with large scale production—the economies of the 'long pull'—can be more readily achieved. The producer who has goods to trade can do so more easily in a large market than in a small one. If his productivity is high, the larger trading area gives him the opportunity to trade, indirectly or directly, for other goods overproduced in other markets. He may optimise his trading opportunities. Moreover, by concentrating on his own skill he can maximise his production. When one specialises in what one is good at, one wastes less time. Specialisation inevitably means increased output and less waste.

In such a large market what should happen therefore is that good efficient producers should expand with the expanding market, and bad inefficient producers should suffer in the increased competitive situation. The expanding industries will require more labour and the contracting industries will create more unemployment. It is important, therefore, in this situation that the newly unemployed should be able to move to where the new job opportunities are created. Hence not only must one provide for free movement of goods, but also one must make provision for the free movement of persons. Moreover, if persons are to be allowed to move freely within the market, they must also be permitted to take their capital with them to make full use of the economic advantages which their new destination offers. It is of little use to permit free movement of persons if one does not also permit the person to take with him his 'stake' which enables him to exploit the economic advantage newly created in the wider market. Thus, one should, if one is really intent on creating a large market in the full sense, make provision for free movement of goods, persons, services and capital. (The 'four freedoms'.)

Of course if one is attempting to ensure that the advantage of free trade will follow one may also have to ensure that distortions and imbalances are not re-introduced by other means. This may lead to a commitment in the elaboration of various *common* policies. Within the EEC, common policies have been adopted in such areas as agriculture, fisheries, competition matters (restrictive practices and monopolies), and transport.[2] Lastly, the advantages of the larger free market may be obstructed by different laws in the Member States, so harmonisation programmes in legal matters ought also to be provided for.

1 See literature cited *supra* fn. 1 para. 1.7
2 In 1986 new titles have been added to the EEC Treaty dealing with Economic and Social Cohesion (Regional Policy), Research and Technological Development, and the Environment. See Single European Act, Section II, art.s 23–25. Supplement 2/86—Bull. E.C.

1.14 With this simple background we can now more readily appreciate Articles 2 and 3 of the EEC Treaty. Article 2 sets out the *general aims and objectives* of the Community; Article 3 sets out *the means or methods* to be used to achieve the Community ends.

Article 2
'The Community shall have as its task, by establishing a common market and progressively approximating the economic policies of Member States, to promote throughout the Community a harmonious development of economic activities, a continuous and balanced expansion, an increase in stability, an

accelerated raising of the standard of living and closer relations between the States belonging to it.'

Article 3 summarises the operative parts of the treaty and can be looked at as an index of what the Treaty in fact subsequently deals with in greater detail. It is reproduced here to indicate to the reader in a summary fashion what the Treaty is really about.

Article 3
'For the purposes set out in Article 2, the activities of the Community shall include, as provided in this Treaty and in accordance with the timetable set out therein:
(a) the elimination, as between Member States, of customs duties and of quantitative restrictions on the import and export of goods, and of all other measures having equivalent effect;
(b) the establishment of a common customs tariff and of a common commercial policy towards third countries;
(c) the abolition, as between Member States, of obstacles to freedom of movement for persons, services and capital;
(d) the adoption of a common policy in the sphere of agriculture;
(e) the adoption of a common policy in the sphere of transport;
(f) the institution of a system ensuring that competition in the common market is not distorted;
(g) the application of procedures by which the economic policies of Member States can be co-ordinated and disequilibria in their balances of payments remedied;
(h) the approximation of the laws of Member States to the extent required for the proper functioning of the common market;
(i) the creation of a European Social Fund in order to improve employment opportunities for workers and to contribute to the raising of their standard of living;
(j) the establishment of a European Investment Bank to facilitate the economic expansion of the Community by opening up fresh resources;
(k) the association of the overseas countries and territories in order to increase trade and to promote jointly economic and social development.'

General features of the establishing Treaty

1.15 At this juncture it might be appropriate to make some general comments about some notable features of the EEC Treaty. First, it is worth noting that the Treaty is in many respects a framework treaty (*traité câdre*) only, in that in many areas the Treaty merely provides general principles as guidelines for the attainment of Community objectives. The details are left to be worked out by the institutions at a later date. In this respect too it should be noted that the Treaty is not consistent in the level of treatment it gives to every subject. In some parts an effort is made to provide for a topic in some considerable detail, whereas in other parts only the most general indications are provided.

1.16 Second, the EEC Treaty is much more comprehensive than the traditional forms of cooperation at international level in the range of topics it embraces. It applies to all branches of the economy and while particular exceptions and escape clauses are provided for—for example on grounds of public morality, safety, life or health (art. 36), capital movements (art. 73), balance of payment difficulties (art.s 104, 108, 109), changes in rates of exchange (art. 107) deflection of trade (art.s 115, 134) and defence against state trading monopolies (art. 37(3), 2nd para.)—the total picture is of a comprehensive attempt to embrace all branches of the economy. In particular, the Treaty is not confined to industrial goods; it also extends, for example to agriculture (including fisheries) an area which traditionally proved to be not amenable to international cooperation because of the unpredictabilities and the strong national interests associated with that sector. Because of the comprehensive nature of the Treaty the areas *not* covered by the treaties are worth noting. In particular military and defence matters, and human rights are not mentioned. With regard to military matters it is understandable that those should be omitted in view of the failure to launch successfully the EDC in 1954 (see EEC Treaty, art. 223). In any event the immediate defence problems of western Europe were already catered for, albeit in the traditional way, by the Western European Union and by NATO.[1] Likewise the omission of a charter of Fundamental Human Rights in the Treaty was somewhat acceptable in view of the existence of the European Convention on Human Rights, since 1950, with its own implementing institutions, including a European Commission and a Court of Human Rights. In any event significant developments in the area of human rights have taken place in recent years within the Community, through the judicial initiative of the Court of Justice. These developments will be dealt with later. Finally, in this context it should be mentioned that while many matters are dealt with in the Treaty progress has not been equally rapid in all areas. Advances in some areas have been particularly difficult while in other areas progress has been less than spectacular (for example the establishment of a fisheries policy and progress towards EMU). In approaching Community law one must learn to live with unevenness in the level of performance.

1 See A. H. Robertson, *The Creation of Western European Union*, 2 EUR. Yearbook 125 (1956). See now, however, Provisions on European Co-operation in the sphere of foreign policy, in Single European Act, Title III, *supra* para. 1.13 fn. 2

1.17 Third, in the Community legal system the provisions of the Treaties are more important than the provisions of secondary legislation such as regulations, directives and decisions. In fact all such subordinate legislation must conform to the Treaties in much the same way as acts of the Oireachtas and Ministerial Orders must conform to the Constitution (Bunreacht) within the Irish domestic legal system. In the Community legal system the Treaty provisions are of a higher order of things than secondary legislation and possess an invalidatory effect on such subordinate legislation.

1.18 Fourth, even from a cursory reading of the Treaty one is struck by the intensity of the integrative process to which the Member States commit themselves. In contrast to traditional conventions and treaties there is a willingness on the part of the signatory states to shed sovereignty, to establish autonomous supra-national institutions, apparently on an irrevocable basis, and to transfer substantial powers of decision-making to the institutions of the new Community. The commitment towards the welding of the economies, although somewhat less than the commitment under the ECSC, was nevertheless quite remarkable, especially when one remembers that the commitment was not to a static Community but to an evolving one. The Treaties themselves, however, cannot be changed by the normal legislative process provided for in Article 189 of the EEC Treaty, but require the consent of all Member States.

1.19 Lastly, and not unrelated to the previous point, attention should be drawn to the dynamic nature of the Community. When one reads through the treaty one is struck by the provision at many points of timetables, programmes and schedules which have to be achieved within given time constraints. The picture one takes from such a reading is that of a Community moving, progressing, continuously evolving towards ultimate goals. Customs duties must be dismantled within given time schedules; new members must adapt by specified dates; directives must be implemented in national law by given deadlines. It should not, however, be imagined that all these deadlines are always met. In many cases adjustments must be made and postponements must be tolerated. But the picture remains the same; that of a dynamic Community moving inexorably on schedules towards more or less well defined goals.

Members of the Community

1.20 The original members of the European Community were France, Germany, Italy and the Benelux countries that is Belgium, the Netherlands and Luxembourg. In 1973, the UK, Ireland and Denmark joined. The Community was further extended by the accession of Greece in 1981 and of Spain and Portugal in 1986 bringing the total membership now to twelve.[1]

1 Turkey and Morocco have also applied for membership. It might also be noted that the EEC can make 'association agreements' with third countries. These agreements establish a special relationship, short of full membership, between the signatory state and the Community. See for these and other trade agreements D. Lasok and J. W. Bridge, *Law and Institutions of the European Communities*, Fourth Edition (1987) 59 *et seq*.

1.21 Treaties of accession were signed for each of the new members and while these Treaties were very detailed and made some concessions to the individual circumstances of each applicant country, they were characterised by three principles in particular.[1] First, the new members had to accept the original Treaty without any basic amendment and had to join the Community at the stage of development at which they found it. The new members were jumping on a moving train. Second, certain institutional adaptations to the Treaty were accepted, those related to such things as the number of seats in Parliament allocated to the new member states, the number of votes they were to have in the Council's weighted voting system, and alteration in the numbers of Commissioners and Judges. These adaptations, however, were in the nature of consequential adjustments rather than fundamental amendments. Third, transitional arrangements were agreed which laid down timetables to give the new members time to adapt to the full rigours of the Community order. In the case of Ireland, the transitional period was five years, so that by 1978 the adjustment period was over, and full Community obligations applied.

1 See G. Olmi, Introduction in *Thirty Years of Community Law* ed. by Commission of European Communities, Luxembourg (1983), at p. 7.

Chapter 2

Profile of the European Communities

2.1 The legislative, executive and judicial functions of the EEC are principally entrusted to four institutions:

The Council

The Commission

The Assembly (Parliament)

The Court of Justice

Each of the institutions represents values which might be regarded as fairly basic pre-conditions of any political organisation in the Western European tradition. In so far as the Court of Justice is entrusted with the interpretation and the application of the law it reflects the ideal of justice. The Assembly (Parliament) is the institutional expression of the fundamental concept of democracy. The Commission was designed to express the new supra-national ideal whereas the Council of Ministers is the body which preserves the old idea of nationalism. The Commission might be described as the executive of the Community and is responsible for new initiatives and the formulation of proposals and policies as well as for their implementation. The Council of Ministers, where each Member State has equal representation, (although provision is made for a weighted voting system), has the final say, however, in most cases. A fuller description of the composition and the function of each of these institutions will be given at a later point.[1]

1 See *infra* Chapter 4. Other institutions of minor importance can also be noted: the Economic and Social Committee (Article 4) and the Court of Auditors.

2.2 Although those institutions now service all three Communities (ECSC, EEC and Euratom) it can be noted from an historical point of view that this was not always the situation. When the ECSC was established in 1951, it was serviced by four institutions: the Council of Ministers, the High Authority, the Assembly and the Court of Justice. When the EEC and Euratom were established in 1957 it was considered that it would be wasteful and unduly cumbersome to have three Assemblies and three Courts. Accordingly, it was decided that the Assembly and the Court of Justice would service all three Communities. There would, however, continue to be separate Councils of Ministers and separate Commissions.

The final stage in the rationalisation of the administration was taken in 1965 when it was decided to merge the executives.[1] The position now is that while there are three distinct communities governed by three separate treaties, they are administered by one set of institutions. The term 'the European Community' is now used as a collective designation for the institutions created by the treaties and for the grouping formed by its Members States.[2]

1 Treaty establishing 'a Single Council and a Single Commission of the European Communities' commonly referred to as the 'Merger Treaty'. 8 April 1965, effective from 1 July 1967.
2 O.J. C 63 See: Gordon Weil, *The Merger of the Institutions of the European Communities* (1967) 61 A.J.I.L. 57. 13.3.78, p. 36. See also G. Olmi, Introduction, in *Thirty Years of Community Law*, (1981), at p. 3.

2.3 One further institutional development has to be mentioned. Since 1961 the Heads of Government of the Member States together with their Foreign Ministers, have begun to meet on a regular basis in what are now known as Summit Conferences (three times a year) to discuss Community matters and in particular, Community problems which are proving intractable. Although no provision is made for this new development in the treaty and although there exists a danger of confusion between the functions of the Council of European Communities as set up by the treaties and the new unscheduled development of what became known as the European Council, the new institutional development has been beneficial in adopting guideline policies and freeing political blockages. Its importance was a well-established fact of political life before its position in the institutional framework of things was fully confirmed in Article 2 of the Single European Act signed in 1986. This article provides as follows:

'The European Council shall bring together the Heads of State or of Government of the Member States and the President of the Commission of the European Communities. They shall be assisted by the Ministers for Foreign Affairs and by a Member of the Commission.
The European Council shall meet at least twice a year'.[1]

1 See *infra* para. 4.17.

The Single European Act

2.4 In June 1985, the European Council, meeting in Milan, convoked the first Inter Governmental Conference since the signing of the EEC and Euratom Treaties in March 1957. The task of the Conference was two-fold:

– to propose certain amendments to the EEC Treaty;
– to draft a treaty on political cooperation and European security.

The conclusions of the conference, which took place under the Presidency of Luxembourg, were approved by the European Council at its meeting of 2–3 December, 1985 and the texts prepared by the Conference were consolidated and formally adopted as 'the Single European Act' on 17 and 28 February 1986. It entered into force on 1 July 1987.

2.5 The Single European Act did not, however, come on the scene unexpectedly. In fact, it is the culmination of a process of reform which had been in train for at least a decade and a half, a process of reform which received boosts from time to time from various initiatives which were taken during that period and which were designed to address perceived problems encountered in the inexorable move towards further integration. These initiatives identified a stagnation in the federalisation process, a weakness in the powers of Parliament, a failure to complete the internal market, a disappointment in progress towards economic and monetary union and a tentative ambiguity with regard to political cooperation, as the principal problems facing the Community in the mid-1980s.

2.6 The Single European Act, which was ratified by the Parliaments of the twelve Member States, introduced several changes at the institutional level to provide solutions to these problems.[1] It provided for a move from unanimity to qualified majority voting in matters concerning the completion of the internal market. The role of the European Parliament (the new name formally adopted instead of 'the Assembly') was strengthened in the decision-making process by the establishment of a 'cooperation procedure' in many cases instead of the old consultative role cast for it under the original EEC Treaty. On the political front, the practice of the Member States with regard to European Political Cooperation (EPC) was put into Treaty form and provision was made for the establishment of a small administrative secretariat located in Brussels, to handle matters related to this. The Act also introduced into the EEC Treaty new articles on monetary cooperation, social policy, 'economic and social cohesion' (regional policy), research and technological development, and environment policy. The increased case load in the Court of Justice of the Communities was also recognised by the Single European Act, which allowed for the establishment of any inferior tribunal for the trial of certain categories of cases with a right of appeal on points of law to the Court of Justice. Further, in formally recognising the European Council the Single European Act put an end to the anomalous existence of this institution in recent years. Finally, the Act adopted the year 1992 as the latest date for the attainment of the free internal market in goods, persons, services and capital.

These matters will be noted in greater detail in their appropriate contexts below.

1 See F. Murphy, *The Single European Act* XX Ir. Jur. (n.s.) Pt. 1, pp. 17–42 and pp. 240–263.

Chapter 3

The Legal System: Community Law

3.1 Under the present heading we are concerned with introducing the Irish lawyer to some unfamiliar and fairly basic concepts that arise in the Community system, with defining some terms and relationships that occur in Community law and with indicating, in a general way, what are the peculiar features of this new legal system.

International law, national law and Community law

3.2 Before accession to the EEC in 1973 the Irish lawyer was theoretically only concerned with two legal systems: international law and national law. In fact, unless the Irish lawyer had an international practice he was concerned only with domestic national law as it applied within the jurisdiction of the state. The separate spheres of operation meant that the points of intersection between international law and national law was a matter of little concern to the vast majority of practising lawyers. International law, after all, for the most part concerned the regulation of the State in its relations with other States. International law was, and still is, primarily concerned with the making and enforcement of treaties, the rules in relation to diplomats, envoys and the like, and the rules relating to international conflicts and wars. Not the stuff that finds its way on to the normal practising lawyer's desk. Moreover, because of Ireland's attitude to international law (the 'dualist' approach—see *infra*), international commitments made no impact in Irish domestic law until a separate piece of Irish legislation was adopted. The Irish lawyer in these circumstances could as far as domestic practice was concerned feel quite secure in simply monitoring domestic legislation only. If international commitments were to impact on his practice they would have to manifest themselves in an Irish legal measure first.

3.3 Although the Irish lawyer's preoccupation with international law did not have to be great before accession to the European Communities an appreciation of the relationship between international law and national law was essential for a complete understanding of his own legal system. To be confident of his own competence the Irish lawyer had to define and determine this relationship between international law and Irish domestic law. In particular he had to answer the following questions.

(1) What is the effect of international commitments undertaken by the Irish Government
    (a) at the international level and
    (b) in the domestic legal system?
(2) Do commitments at international level require transformation before they have legal significance in the internal legal system?
(3) Can an individual within the Irish legal system rely on international commitments binding on Ireland and the Irish Government, as giving him rights in the national courts?

3.4 The answers to these questions in the Irish legal system are fairly straightforward, but before they are briefly outlined the theory of international law as it impacts on national legal systems must be adverted to. There are two approaches to this problem. First of all, one might say that international obligations and national rights operate in two separate spheres and that obligations incurred by a State do not necessarily have any immediate legal impact within the national system. Thus, if the Irish Government signs a convention with other States this may create obligations for the State in the international arena and such sanctions as are available at international law may be applied if Ireland does not fulfil its obligations under the treaty. But, of itself, the signing of the treaty does not have any impact in domestic Irish law. This approach maintains that before such an international commitment has any effect within the legal system of the signatory State a separate and *second* legal act must be taken by the signatory State. For this reason the approach is known as the *dualist approach* to international law. In the example given above before the Irish commitment would have an effect within the national system it would have to be the subject of a separate legal act (an act of the Oireachtas). Technically what one would say is that the international commitment would have to be 'received' or 'incorporated' by separate legal act to have any effect within the legal system.

The Irish Constitution clearly opted for this view of international law when in Article 29 it declares:

'No international agreement shall be part of the domestic law of the State save as may be determined by the Oireachtas'.[1]

Thus, to give a recent example of the rule operating in practice, when Ireland signed the Tokyo Convention on Hijacking (1963) it accepted an international commitment, but to give this commitment a significance at national level it had to pass subsequently the Air Navigation and Transport Act, 1973.

---

1 Apart from treaty obligations just mentioned the Constitution at Article 29.3 gives recognition to the general principles of international law. See John Temple Lang, *Legal and Constitutional Implications for Ireland of Accession to the EEC Treaty* 9 C.M.L. Rev. 1972, pp. 167–8. See also *Re O Laighleis* [1960] I.R. 93.

3.5 In contrast to the dualist approach to international law is the '*monist theory*' of international law. As its name indicates this theory declares that for international commitments to impact within the signatory State's legal system no separate legal act is required. The international commitment, once undertaken, immediately and without any further or additional act flows directly into the national system. Only one (monist) act is required to create obligations at both the international and national levels. Countries which subscribe to this theory see international law as being of a superior order and in some respect possessing an invalidatory effect on national law. Countries subscribing to the dualist philosophy, on the other hand, see international law as totally dependent on the wills of the signatory states and having no independent existence without the creative act of the states. From this point of view international commitments only enter the domestic legal system when separately authorised to do so.

Against this theoretical backdrop we may now answer the questions relating to the relationship between international commitments and Irish domestic law posed earlier.

3.6 As already noted Ireland subscribes to the dualist theory of international law. International treaties subscribed to by Ireland, therefore, may create obligations for Ireland at international level, but do not have any legal effect in the domestic scene until 'incorporated' into the Irish legal system by way of a separate Act of Oireachtas. If no such incorporating act has been passed no individual within its State may rely on the international obligations before national courts. If an incorporating measure has been adopted then the impact which this has and the rights it gives are to be determined from this Act rather than from the international convention which inspired it. Whether an individual has rights under this legislation which he may maintain before the national courts will therefore depend, as it does in any piece of national legislation, on the terms of the incorporating Act itself. In short, it will be a question of statutory interpretation for the national courts.

After accession in 1973: International law, Community law and Irish law

3.7 After accession to the European Community in 1973 this fairly straightforward picture became somewhat more complex. After 1973 the Irish lawyer was now faced with three separate legal systems: the international order, the Community system and the national system. The province of each system had to be determined and the relationship of the legal systems *inter se* had also to be defined. From an Irish point of view we can say that the relationship between international law and national law remained the same as it had been up to 1973 and as previously outlined. What remains, therefore, to outline here is (i) the relationship between Community law and international law and (ii) the relationship between Community law and national law.

(i) *Relationship between Community law and international law*
3.8 Before addressing the more complex question posed at (ii) it is appropriate to remark on the relationship between Community law and international law. This of course, is a matter to be determined by the institutions (and particularly by the Court of Justice) of the Community. Although *not entirely free from doubts* it would appear that the Community now sees the relationship between its law and international law in monist terms. In appropriate circumstances, therefore, international law comes into the Communities' legal system without the need for an independent act of incorporation or reception.[1] Moreover, treaties validly concluded by the Communities with third countries, while subordinate to the ECSC, EEC and Euratom Treaties, take precedence over secondary legislation such as regulations or decisions (with regard to 'mixed agreements', see post 7.8).

1   H.G. Schermers, 'The Community's Relations under Public International Law', in *Thirty Years of Community Law*, ed. by Commission of European Communities, Luxembourg. (1983) at pp. 230–231.

(ii) *The relationship between Community law and the National Legal System*
3.9 To understand the nature of the relationship between Community law and the National Legal System a general word must be said, at the outset, about the nature of Community law and the legal system established by the ECSC, EEC and Euratom Treaties.

The nature of the Community legal system

3.10 It must not be thought that the legal effects created by the Treaties establishing the European Community are comparable to the legal effects created by traditional international treaties or conventions. The ECSC, EEC and Euratom Treaties did much more than create mutual obligations between the signatory states at the international level. They created a whole new legal order, a whole new legal system which could not be properly analysed or appreciated in the traditional concepts associated with the international legal system. Undoubtedly, the characteristics and phenomena of this new legal system were not fully perceived from the beginning and indeed were eventually elaborated, not always without difficulty, by the Court of Justice of the European Community. By now, however, many of the features have been established and so generally accepted by the Member States as to admit of fairly simple statement and elaboration. In brief one can with some degree of confidence now make the following assertions as to the nature of Community law and its relationship with the legal systems of the Member States.

(1) The EEC Treaty established a new and autonomous legal order which Ireland accepted on acceding to the European Community in 1973. This legal order has independent institutions which have wide (and still expanding) powers conferred upon them.[1]

(2) This legal order is separate and distinct from the international legal order and from the national legal system.[2]

(3) This new legal order declares that Community measures can penetrate into the national legal system without a separate incorporating act on the part of the Member State. Neither can Community measures be kept out of the national legal system by acts or omissions of the Member States. In terms of traditional terminology the relationship between Community law and national law is monist.[3]

(4) In the event of a conflict between Community law and national law, Community law is supreme.[4] Indeed, in this matter because of the 3rd Amendment to the Constitution, Community law is free from the accusation or challenge that it is contrary to the Constitution. In this sense Community law is superior even to the Constitution.

(5) Individuals may, in appropriate cases, rely on Community law before their national courts. In so far as traditional international law considered only nations as being the proper subjects of rights and duties, Community law in recognising as proper subjects, individuals and enterprises, introduces an important change in this matter.[5]

(6) Finally, the subjects of Community law have their relations regulated by the rule of law. Obligatory procedures are provided and the administration of these procedures and the application of Community rules are entrusted to institutions which are themselves subject to the rule of law.

1 See Dagtaglou, in *Thirty Years of Community Law Development of Judicial Control in the European Communities* (1981), p. 40.
2 See Bebr (1983) 549 *et seq.*
3 *Infra.* chapter 13.7.
4 *Infra.* chapter 13.21.
5 *Infra.* chapter 13.10. Nowadays it is true there is an emerging trend in international law to the effect that individuals may be the subjects of duties.

3.11 As already mentioned this position was not arrived at without some difficulty and with some serious reservations by some Member States. By now, however, it can be said with some confidence that it clearly represents the Community view on the matter and most Member States have accepted these basic precepts with greater or lesser enthusiasm.

In Ireland's case, too, it can be said that we have accepted these propositions and a description of the technical measures required to enable this position to prevail can be postponed until a later chapter. Suffice to note at this juncture that Community measures do not now require special acts of incorporation to create effects in Irish law; that Community measures prevail over Irish laws to the contrary; and that the individual has rights under Community law which he may maintain in the Irish courts. All of these clearly indicate how different, and how much more important than traditional international law, Community law is for the Irish legal system.

Part II

Community Institutions

Chapter 4

The Institutions of the Communities

Introduction

4.1 One commentator has observed that the authors of the ECSC Treaty deliberately discarded the tripartite scheme of government which was espoused by Montesquieu in the 18th century and which has been implemented in one form or another by a variety of states.[1] Instead, the ECSC Treaty of 1951 and the EEC and Euratom Treaties of 1957 adopted a quadripartite institutional structure in which the traditional tripartite legislative, executive and judicial powers were represented by the Assembly, the Council and the Court of Justice respectively, but to which was added the Commission, a new entity charged with the protection of the Community interest. This remains the basic institutional framework for the Community but in the meantime significant modifications have taken place.

First, the Assembly—or Parliament as it is now called—possessed none of the real attributes of a parliament: it had no taxing power, no legislative power and its members were selected, not elected. Second, the Council, which is the body in which national interests are represented, exercises the greater part of the legislative power in the modern Community although it had been consigned to a back seat role in the ECSC Treaty. The Commission—now incorporating the High Authority of the ECSC—was envisaged as the executive body, with a virtual monopoly of legislative initiative; it has seen this position of eminence whittled away during the past two decades by changes not all of which were anticipated by the treaties. As envisaged by the treaties, the Parliament is now a directly elected body with much greater powers. But the developments not foreseen by the treaty authors are those which have more fundamentally altered the institutional balance. These include the emergence of COREPER, the development of European Political Cooperation and the institutionalisation of the European Council. The significance of these developments is outlined below.

1 Guy Schrans, in *Thirty Years of Community Law* (1983), Part 1, Chapter 2, p. 18.

The European Parliament

4.2 Relevant Treaty provisions:

ECSC Treaty	Articles 20–25
EEC Treaty	Articles 137–144
Euratom Treaty	Articles 107–114
Convention on Institutions Common to the European Communities	Articles 1–2
First Act of Accession	Article 10
Adaptation Decision	Article 4
Council Decision 76/787 ECSC, EEC, Euratom and annexed Act	*passim.*
Second Act of Accession	Article 10
Third Act of Accession	Article 10
Single European Act	Articles 3, 6–9

4.3 The Parliament is the institution designed to give democratic legitimacy to the Communities. According to the basic treaty provisions it consists of the representatives of the peoples of the Member States brought together in the Community. Since 1 January 1959, the 'Assembly' provided for in each of the basic treaties has functioned as a single institution pursuant to the terms of the Convention on Institutions Common to the European Communities.

In March 1962 the Assembly (or Parliamentary Assembly as it had called itself) adopted a resolution changing its name to 'European Parliament'. The tactical importance of this move for a body possessing insignificant powers was understandable, but the motive for the change was less convincing: according to the President, M. Poher, the reason for proposing the resolution was the need to provide an identical name for the institution in all the Community languages.[1] Since 1962 only the Council has shown a reluctance to use the new name.[2] However, the name Assembly will disappear from Treaty usage as a consequence of Article 3 of the Single European Act, which describes the institutions of the European Communities '. . . henceforth designated as referred to hereafter . . .' All further references in the Single European Act to the institution describe it as the European Parliament.

1 O.J. 1045, 1962.
2 See: Council Decision 76/787 (ECSC, EEC, Euratom) and annexed Act, O.J. L 278, 8.10.1976 p. 5.

4.4 In 1958 the number of delegates to the Parliament was as follows:

Belgium	14
Germany	36
France	36
Italy	36
Luxembourg	6
The Netherlands	14
Total:	142

The first accession in 1973 added further delegates:

Denmark	10
Ireland	10
United Kingdom	36
Total:	198

As a result of the Act on direct elections and the second and third accessions in 1976, 1981 and 1986 respectively, the allocation of delegates is as follows:

Belgium	24
Denmark	16
Germany	81
Greece	24
Spain	60
France	81
Ireland	15
Italy	81
Luxembourg	6
The Netherlands	25
Portugal	24
United Kingdom	81
Total:	518

The allocation of seats is not in proportion to the population of the States: in Luxembourg one member represents approximately 50,000 persons whereas in Germany a member has over ¾ million constituents.

4.5 Until 1979 the delegates to the Parliament were selected by their national parliaments. However, the third paragraph of Article 138 of the EEC Treaty and its cognates in the other Treaties provided for elections by direct universal suffrage subject to a uniform procedure. The Parliament was to draw up the proposals and the Council was to lay down the appropriate provisions. In 1960 a draft convention, prepared by Fernand Dehousse of the Political Affairs Committee, was adopted by the Parliament. It was ignored by the Council, and it was not until after the first enlargement that the issue resurfaced. In December 1974 the first European Council meeting in Paris indicated its agreement in principle to direct elections and in 1975 the Political Affairs Committee of the Parliament, with the Dutch Socialist Schelto Patijn as rapporteur, presented a new draft convention to the European Parliament.[1] This formed the basis for the Act annexed to the Council Decision of 1976, in which the methods and dates for direct elections were laid out.

The first point to note about the Act is that it does not lay down a uniform method of election; this task remains to be carried out by the Parliament and in the meantime elections will take place in accordance with national procedures (Article 7). Thus, the single transferable vote system applies in Ireland whereas the United Kingdom (excluding Northern Ireland) utilises the 'first past the post' system. The number of representatives from each State is fixed by Article 2. Article 3 fixed the term of office at 5 years. The independence of the members and their privileges and immunities are dealt with in Article 4. Article 6 declares membership of the Parliament incompatible with various other offices including membership of a government of a Member State, and membership of other institutions and committees of the Community. However, according to Article 5, a dual parliamentary mandate is permissible. Elections are held every five years (Article 10) and pending the adoption of a uniform procedure the Member States can lay down rules for filling casual vacancies (Article 12). The first direct election took place between 7–10 June 1979 and the second direct election took place between 14–17 June 1984.

1 O.J. C 32, 11.2.1975 p. 15.

4.6 In Ireland legislation governing elections to the Parliament was enacted in 1977 but was preceded by the publication of the Report of the European Assembly Constituency Commission.[1] The Commission was appointed by the Government to propose constituencies for electoral purposes; its suggestions were adopted by the Oireachtas and are incorporated in the 2nd Schedule of the European Assembly Elections Act, 1977. The constituencies are: Connacht—Ulster (3 seats): Dublin (4 seats); Leinster (3 seats); and Munster (5 seats). The Act provides for election to these constituencies by proportional representation (Section 2), extends the franchise to citizens of Ireland or nationals of other Member States over the age of eighteen (Section 3), disqualifies for election to the Parliament any person not eligible to become a member of the Dail (Section 7), and allows for the registration of political parties for the purposes of contesting a European election. This provision facilitates the larger political parties who are affiliated to groupings in the Parliament and wish to campaign under the European name e.g. the European People's Party (Christian Democrats)—to which Fine Gael is affiliated. The deposit from candidates required by Section 10 is £1,000. Casual vacancies were dealt with in Section 15. This section, which has now been amended, allowed casual vacancies to be filled by the political party to which the outgoing member was attached, or if unaffiliated, by Dail Eireann. Detailed rules for the conduct of elections are contained in the First Schedule to the Act.

The Act was amended by the European Assembly Elections Act, 1984 shortly before the second direct election. The amending Act was necessitated by shortcomings in two particular features of the 1977 Act. The first problem concerned the filling of casual vacancies. The participation of the Labour Party in coalition governments led to a complete substitution of the 4 Labour members elected in 1979. None of the replacements had offered themselves to the electorate, and the Parliament's credentials committee was rumoured to be unhappy with the procedure. Likewise, the Parliament considered the office of Chairman of Dail Eireann to be incompatible with membership of the Parliament. Section 2 of the 1984 Act declares ineligible for election to the Parliament the Chairman and Deputy Chairman of the Dail and Seanad, and Sections

3 and 4 provide for replacement candidates who can be called upon to fill casual vacancies (Section 6).

1 4th October 1977, Prl. 6626.

4.7 Article 137 of the EEC Treaty and Article 107 of the Euratom Treaty describe the powers conferred upon the Parliament as advisory and supervisory. This was an advance on the description in the ECSC Treaty which refers to supervisory powers only. Even so, the 'powers' continued in the 1951 and 1957 Treaties were not those of a typical Western European assembly; there was no power to determine the formation of the 'government'[1] and there was no direct power of legislation or taxation. From this impoverished base the status of the Parliament could only improve, and the implementation of the direct electoral procedure has added impetus to the accretion of real powers—particularly in the budgetary sector. But first, let us examine the powers that were conferred by the original treaties.

The ECSC Treaty entrusted the supervision of the High Authority to the Parliament and the Treaties of Rome continued this function in respect of the Commission. It has been observed that while the High Authority possessed the bulk of executive and legislative functions in the ECSC system the balance shifted in the 1957 Treaties, which gave the greater part of the formal decision making functions to the Council, without making it responsible to the Parliament.[2] The main feature of the supervisory power of the Parliament is the right to question the Commission. The use of the questioning device has developed markedly since the first enlargement. During the existence of ECSC Assembly 57 written questions and 3 oral questions were put to the High Authority,[3] whereas in 1987 members of Parliament tabled 2942 written questions and asked 1109 oral questions.[4] In practice, it is not just the Commission which responds to questions; it is now routine for the Council and the Foreign Ministers to attend part sessions of the Parliament to answer questions. The second supervisory function exercised by the Parliament is its right to discuss in open session the annual general report which the Commission must submit to it (Article 143 of the EEC Treaty).

The third supervisory power is the power of censure, which enables the Parliament to force the Commission to resign from office *en bloc* (EEC Treaty, art. 144). There are procedural restraints on the exercise of this power: a Motion of Censure requires 3 days' notice and must be carried by $\frac{2}{3}$ of the votes cast. But the drastic consequence of the remedy means that it is unlikely to be invoked; in the present institutional framework the Parliament is the natural ally of the Commission and, in any event, there is nothing to prevent the Council from reappointing the same college of Commissioners.

1 Guy Schrans, *loc. cit.*, fn. 1 para. 4.1, at p. 18.
2 Roland Bieber and Michael Palmer, *Power at the top—the EC Council in theory and practice*, (1975) The World Today 310.
3 See: Lional H. Cohen, *The Development of Question Time in the European Parliament*, 16 C.M.L. Rev. (1979) 41.
4 21st Annual General Report 1987, point 9.

4.8 The advisory functions are twofold. Firstly, Parliament may issue resolutions or recommendations on any topic that takes its fancy. Neither of these measures has any legally binding consequence under the terms of EEC Treaty, art. 189. Of greater consequence, however, is the Parliament's right to be consulted by the Council prior to the exercise of decision-making powers by the latter institution. There are 23 instances in the EEC Treaty where the opinion of the Parliament must be procured before the Council can act. An example can be seen in Article 87 which lays down the procedure for the implementation of Articles 85 and 86 of the treaty. Failure to consult the Parliament amounts to infringement of an essential procedural requirement within the meaning of Article 173 of the treaty. A graphic example can be seen in the *Maizena* and *Roquette* cases.[1] The Council was anxious to implement a Regulation for the isoglucose sector and in March 1979 it submitted a proposal to the Parliament for its opinion. In May 1979 the Parliament declined to adopt a resolution on the proposal and referred the matter back for reconsideration to its Agriculture Committee. Without invoking the emergency procedure provided for in the Rules of Procedure of the Parliament the Council adopted the proposal as Regulation 1293/79/EEC.[2] The plaintiffs challenged the validity of the Regulation, mainly because it imposed production quotas. But they also maintained that the measure was void because it infringed essential formalities and in this respect they had the support of the Parliament, which had intervened in the proceedings under Article 37 of the Statute of the Court. The Court agreed with this submission and held that consultation of the Parliament was an essential factor in the equilibrium between the institutions. Disregard of this formality rendered the measure in question void. There is no doubt that the judgment of the Court was a policy decision, in which the Court declared its support for the role and functions of the Parliament. It declared the action by the plaintiffs admissible even though the measure the annulment of which was sought was a regulation; Article 173 of the EEC Treaty does not permit private parties to challenge Regulations. This conclusion is borne out by the decision of the Court in the later case of *Roquette* v *EC Council*[3] in which the plaintiff challenged the validity of the Council Regulation adopted in place of the Regulation invalidated in the earlier case. On this occasion Parliament had been consulted properly and the Court declared the application inadmissible.

The consultative role of the Parliament has been enhanced to a certain extent by the Single European Act, art.s 6 and 7 of which introduce a 'cooperation procedure'. The cooperation procedure takes the form of the insertion of a new paragraph between the existing 2 paragraphs of Article 149 of the EEC Treaty. It involves a five-step procedure which will operate as follows:

(a) In cases where it is obliged to cooperate with the Parliament, the Council, on receipt of a proposal from the Commission, will forward the proposal to the Parliament which will adopt an Opinion on the proposal. The proposal will then return to the Council which, acting by a qualified majority, will adopt a 'common position' and will inform the Parliament of that view and the reasons underlying it.

(b) If the European Parliament approves the common position within 3 months or takes no action with regard to it the Council will adopt the proposal in accordance with its common position.

(c) Within the same 3-month period the Parliament may, by an absolute majority of its 'component members' either reject the common position of the Council or it may propose amendments to it.

(d) If rejected by the European Parliament the act in question can only be adopted by a unanimous vote of the Council. But if the Parliament has proposed amendments then the Commission must re-examine the common position of the Council in the light of the amendments, and forward the proposal to the Council within 1 month indicating at the same time those of the suggested amendments (if any) which it does not accept.

(e) The Council may now do one of three things:
 – acting by a qualified majority, adopt the re-examined proposal;
 – acting unanimously, adopt the proposed amendments of the Parliament which have been rejected by the Commission;
 – acting unanimously, amend the re-examined proposal of the Commission.

In respect of steps (d) and (e) the Council is obliged to act within 3 months. If it has not done so, the original Commission proposal (step (a)) will be deemed not to have been adopted. This complex cooperation system applies only to 10 decision-making provisions of the EEC Treaty: Articles 7; 49; 54(2); 56(2) second sentence; 57, with the exception of the second sentence of paragraph 2 thereof; 100A; 100B; 118A; 130B; and 130Q(2). The latter five provisions have been inserted in the EEC Treaty by the Single European Act.

1 Joined Cases 138 and 139/79 *Roquette Frères SA v EC Council* [1980] E.C.R. 3333, and *Maizena GmbH v EC Council* [1980] E.C.R. 3393.
2 O.J. L 162, 30.6.1979 p. 10.
3 Case 242/81 *Roquette Frères SA v EC Council* [1982] E.C.R. 3213.

4.9 During 1987 the Parliament adopted 520 resolutions and decisions, including 165 resolutions embodying its opinion (13 on first reading under the cooperation procedure). On second reading Parliament approved the Council's common position without amendment in five cases and after amendment in four cases.[1] Nonetheless, there are many areas of Community activity in respect of which Parliament has no consultative role, either because the consultative role has been entrusted to another agency by the Treaty (for example Article 49: the Council must consult the Economic and Social Committee) or because no consultation was envisaged. The conclusion of international agreements by the Community is one such area. But recently there have been a number of developments favourable to the Parliament. In 1975 the Presidents of the Parliament, Council and Commission signed a joint declaration establishing a conciliation procedure designed to give the Parliament effective participation in the preparation and adoption of decisions which give rise to important expenditure or revenue to be charged to the budget of the European Communities.[2] This declaration was adopted shortly after the Communities became fully self-financing on 1 January 1975, and it applies wherever the Council intends to depart from the opinion of the Parliament in respect of Community acts of general application which have appreciable financial implications. The Commission acts as mediator. However, the procedure has not worked well and the Commission proposed an improvement to the system in 1981.[3] The Parliament approved the new procedure in 1983 but the Council has not yet discussed the matter.[4]

A second development concerns the role of the European Parliament in the preparation and conclusion of international agreements and accession treaties. In May 1983 the Commission published a Communication proposing an increase in parliamentary participation in this regard and the European Council accepted the proposal in its Solemn Declaration on European Union signed at Stuttgart on 19 June 1983.[5] In accordance with this undertaking the Parliament was consulted on the accession of Spain and Portugal.[6] In addition, Articles 8 and 9 of the Single European Act require the assent of the European Parliament before any further enlargement of the EEC under Article 237 and before the conclusion of any association agreement under Article 238.[7]

1 21st Annual General Report, 1987, point 9.
2 O.J. C 89, 22.4.1975 p. 1.
3 Commission Communication of 16 December 1981, Bull. E.C. Supp. 3/82.
4 18th Annual General Report, 1984, point 10.
5 Bull. E.C. 6-1983, pp. 26–27.
6 19th Annual General Report, 1985, point 11.
7 In 1987 the new procedure was applied on 20 occasions: 21st Annual General Report, 1987, point 9.

4.10 Perhaps the most significant increase in the powers of the Parliament has taken place in the realm of Community budgetary procedures. Initially, the Parliament had a mere consultative function but the first 'Budgetary Treaty' of 1970 gave the Parliament the last say in respect of expenditure '. . . not necessarily resulting from the Treaty',[1] and the Second Budgetary Treaty of 1975 significantly expanded upon the advances of 1970 by transferring the function of declaring the budget finally adopted to the President of the Parliament and by giving the Parliament, acting by a ⅔ majority, the right to veto the budget as a whole.[2] The Second Budgetary Treaty also transferred to the Parliament the function of giving a discharge to the Commission in respect of the budget (Article 206b). The procedural aspects of the adoption of the budget are considered in the chapter on the Finances of the Community, and we are concerned here only with the ramifications of the increase in the Parliament's power. The first point of note has been the dramatic use of the veto: it has been used twice by the directly-elected Parliament in respect of the draft budget[3] and once in respect of a draft supplementary budget.[4] When the draft annual budget is rejected it invariably brings into play the system of 'provisional twelfths' established by Article 204 of the EEC Treaty (as amended). This means that a sum not exceeding one twelfth of the previous year's budget can be spent for every month during which a new draft budget remains unadopted. It causes great inconvenience and the political feedback to national governments from pressure groups like the farmers is always hostile. The second feature of note has been the lingering feud between the Council and the Parliament as to the meaning of 'expenditure necessarily resulting from the Treaty' and expenditure not necessarily resulting from the Treaty. It was never absolutely clear what was meant by 'necessary' and 'non-necessary' expenditure. The dispute came to a head in 1982 when the President of Parliament declared the adoption of a budget which included items of expenditure fixed by the Parliament but which, in the Council's view, fell under the rubric 'necessary expenditure' and thus outside the jurisdiction of Parliament. The result was a psychological boost for the Parliament: the Council initiated proceedings for the annulment of the budget under Article 173 of the EEC Treaty.[5] The significance of the move was that Article 173 allows the Court of Justice to review the legality of acts of the Council and the Commission; by suing the Parliament the Council was conceding implicitly that the Parliament now possessed the power to adopt legally binding acts. The Court action was not pursued, however, after the Parliament, Council and Commission reached agreement on the classification of expenditure.[6]

1 Treaties establishing the European Communities, 1978 Edition, p. 897.
2 *Loc. cit.* n. 1. See also Article 12, which inserts a new Article 203 into the EEC Treaty, and see in particular paras (7) and (8).
3 14th Annual General Report, 1980, point 44; O.J. C 12, 14.1.1985 p. 89.
4 Bull E.C. 12-1982.
5 Case 72/82. See also: L. Neville Brown, *Judicial Control of Acts of the European Parliament*, LIEI 1983/1, 75.
6 Joint Declaration on various measures to improve the budgetary procedure; O.J. C 194, 28.7.1982 p. 1.

4.11 During the course of 1986, however, actions for the annulment of measures adopted by the European Parliament were successful. In *Partie Ecologiste 'Les Verts' v European Parliament*[1] the successor organisation to the plaintiff—a political party which contested the 1984 direct elections in France—sought the annulment of the decision of the Bureau of the Parliament of 12 October 1982 and the rules governing the use of appropriations for reimbursement of the expenditure incurred by the political groupings for the 1984 direct elections. Not surprisingly, the European Parliament did not contest the admissibility of the action, because it considered that the list of potential defendants to be found in Article 173 (the Council and Commission) is not exhaustive. The Court of Justice agreed, and it held:

'An interpretation of Article 173 of the Treaty which could exclude measures adopted by the European Parliament from those which could be attacked would lead to a result which is contrary both to the spirit of the Treaty as expressed in Article 164 thereof and to its system. Measures adopted by the European Parliament in the context the EEC Treaty could encroach on the powers of the Member States or the other institutions, or exceed the limits which have been set to the Parliament's powers, without its being possible to refer them for review by the Court'[2]

The Court held that an action for annulment will lie against measures adopted by the European Parliament in so far as they are intended to have legal effects *vis-à-vis* third parties, and it declared the contested measures void.

The coming of age of the Parliament as a decision-making institution was confirmed by the Court of Justice in *EC Council v European Parliament*.[3] In this case the Council sought the total or partial annulment of the act of the President of the Parliament of 18 December 1985 by which he declared the final adoption of the budget for 1986. The Council maintained that the rise in non-compulsory expenditure exceeded the maximum rate of increase permitted by Article 203(9) of the Treaty. The Parliament contested the admissibility of an action which sought the annulment of the budget as an act of the European Parliament, but the Court held that the budgetary nature of the contested acts did not have the effect of rendering the application inadmissible. On the substantive issues the Court declared void the act of adoption of the budget by the President of the Parliament but without calling into question the payments made and the commitments entered into for 1986 up to the date of the judgment.

1 Case 294/83 [1987] 2 C.M.L.R. 343.
2 At consideration 25.
3 Case 34/86 [1986] 3 C.M.L.R. 94.

4.12 According to EEC Treaty, art. 139 the Parliament must hold an annual session. In practice it holds 12-part sessions each lasting a week. The Parliament elects the President and 12 Vice-Presidents from among its members[1] and together they constitute the Bureau of the Parliament. The content of the agenda for meetings of the Parliament is determined by the enlarged Bureau that is the Bureau and the leaders of all the political groupings. The Parliament operates through a system of Committees;[2] there are now 18 committees and in terms of their responsibility they correspond roughly to the Directorates-General of the Commission.[3] The committees meet, often in Brussels, in the period between part-sessions and in 1985, for example, the committees met on 403 occasions.[4] When the Parliament refers a question to a committee the committee will usually appoint a rapporteur who becomes responsible for preparing the committee's report and for introducing it in Parliament. The final report of the committee includes a motion for resolution and an explanatory statement.[5] The full Parliament remains free to vote as it wishes on the draft resolution. According to Article 141 of the EEC Treaty the Parliament acts, unless otherwise provided in the Treaty, by an absolute majority of the votes cast. The quorum for a vote exists when ⅓ of the current members of Parliament are present.[6] The Parliament adopts its own rules of procedure and the current rules came into force in 1979 on the occasion of the first sitting of the directly elected Parliament.[7]

Under Rule 36 members may form themselves into groups according to their political affinities. In the present Parliament there are 8 political groupings and the position at 31 December 1987 was as follows.

– Socialists (S)	165
– European People's Party (EPP) (includes Fine Gael)	115

– European Democratic Group (ED) (British Conservatives)	66
– Communists and Allies (Com)	48
– Liberals, Democratic and Reformist Group (LDR)	44
– European Democratic Alliance (EDA) (includes Fianna Fail)	29
– Rainbow Group (Greens)	20
– European Right	17
– Group for Technical Coordination and Defence of Independent Groups of Members	12

There are 2 non-affiliated members.

Generally speaking voting in the Parliament follows party affiliation but it is not uncommon to find members from particular Member States crossing party lines when issues of national importance arise.

Parliament is assisted by a Secretary-General and a Secretariat.[8] The Secretariat is divided into five Directorates-General, staffed by an establishment of 2,946 permanent posts in 1987.[9]

1 EEC Treaty, art. 140; Rules of Procedure, Rule 5, O.J. C 203, 13.8.1979.
2 Rules of Procedure (*loc. cit.*, fn. 1), Rules 37–44.
3 18th Annual General Report 1984, point 13.
4 19th Annual General Report, 1985 point 18.
5 Rules of Procedure, Rule 39.
6 *Idem*, Rule 33.
7 *Loc. cit.* fn. 1.
8 *Idem*, Rule 49.
9 21st Annual General Report, 1987, point 10.

The Council

4.13 Relevant Treaty Provisions:

ECSC Treaty	Articles 26–30
EEC Treaty	Articles 145–154
Euratom Treaty	Articles 115–123
Merger Treaty	Articles 1–8
First Act of Accession	Articles 11–14
Adaptation Decision	Article 4
Second Act of Accession	Articles 11–14
Third Act of Accession	Articles 11–14
Single European Act	Article 10

4.14 The Council is the institution of the Community in which the interests of the Member States, or more correctly the interests of the governments of the Member States, are represented. It is perceived as the body which safeguards national interests against encroachment from the Community, represented by the Commission. Because the scope of the EEC Treaty is significantly greater than the scope of the ECSC Treaty, the retention of control by the Member States over the EEC's activities is correspondingly greater and the bulk of the decision-making powers in the EEC and Euratom Treaties is conferred on the Council.

The Council consists of representatives of the governments of the Member States; each government delegates one of its members to the Council.[1] The membership varies from week to week depending on the subject matter under discussion. For example in the six-month period commencing in July 1986 and ending in December 1986 the following Irish ministers attended Council meetings:

Minister for Agriculture	4 meetings
Minister for Foreign Affairs	3 meetings
Minister of State, Foreign Affairs	6 meetings
Minister for Finance	2 meetings
Minister of State, Finance	3 meetings
Minister for Tourism, Fisheries and Forestry	4 meetings
Minister for Industry and Commerce	3 meetings
Minister of State, Industry and Commerce	4 meetings
Tanaiste and Minister for Energy	1 meeting
Minister for Communications	1 meeting
Minister for the Environment	1 meeting
Minister for Labour	1 meeting
Minister for Education	1 meeting

Thus, ten different Departments were represented at the Council table. In addition, the government was represented by the Permanent Representative, the Deputy Permanent Representative and by the Secretary of the Department of Transport on one occasion each.[2]

In theory, the 'General' Council of Foreign Ministers controls and coordinates the work of the 'specialised' Councils while remaining the forum for the discussion of major new issues. But in practice, as the Report of the Three Wise Men pointed out, the development of specialised Councils has resulted in '. . . a kind of horizontal disintegration' of the Council structure.[3] The Three Wise Men also identified other problems in the Council: inadequately organised and over-crowded agendas; the loss of a sense of collegiality arising from irregular attendance; the loss of authority—upwards to the European Council (which became a court of appeal for unresolved issues)—and downwards over working groups; and a lack of discipline and coherence in the Presidency.

The chairmanship or Presidency of the Council rotates every six months among the Member States according to the alphabetical designation of the State in its official language;[4] thus, Germany, Greece and Spain all precede France in the Presidency. However, as from 1 January 1987 the Presidency will rotate in two different cycles:

(a) for a first cycle of 6 years: Belgium, Denmark, Germany, Greece, Spain, France, Ireland, Italy, Luxembourg, the Netherlands, Portugal, the United Kingdom.

(b) for the following cycle of 6 years: Denmark, Belgium, Greece, Germany, France, Spain, Italy, Ireland, the Netherlands, Luxembourg, the United Kingdom, Portugal.[5]

So, for six months the chairmanship of the Council and of all the specialist committees established by acts of the Council, is the responsibility of one Member State; the level of progress in general, as well as progress on particular proposals, depends to a certain extent on the commitment of the State holding the Presidency. The agenda for Council meetings and the frequency of meetings is fixed by the President-in-Office but the Council can also meet at the request of the Member States or of the Commission.[6] Article 5 of the Merger Treaty provided that the Council was to adopt rules of procedure; the current rules have been in force since 1979 but were amended in 1987 to take account of the new voting procedures under the Single European Act.[7] The Council is assisted by a Secretariat, which had 1,915 established posts in 1987.[8] In that year the Council held 78 meetings at which it adopted 458 Regulations, 40 Directives and 125 Decisions.[9]

1 EEC Treaty, art. 146.
2 27th Report on Developments in the European Communities, Annex IV at p. 101.
3 Report on the European Institutions, Council of the European Communities 1980, Part III, at pp. 28–29.
4 Merger Treaty, art. 2.
5 Third Act of Accession, art. 11.
6 Merger Treaty, art. 3.
7 O.J. L 268, 25.10.1979 p. 1. For amendments see: O.J. L 291, 15.10.1987 p. 27.
8 21st Annual General Report, 1987, point 24.
9 *Idem*, point 12.

4.15 The Council's status as the principal Community legislative authority is conferred by Article 145 of the Treaty which provides that in order to achieve the attainment of treaty objectives the Council shall (a) ensure the coordination of general economic policies, and (b) have the power to take decisions. This extremely general, if not vague, description of the Council's tasks conceals the overall control it maintains within the Community institutional structure. Practically every provision of the treaty which confers a power to act entrusts that power to the Council. But this power cannot be exercised in a vacuum; before the Council can act it must have before it a proposal formulated by the Commission.[1] If the Council decides to depart from a proposal of the Commission its decision must be unanimous.[2] Apart from entrusting the exclusive power of initiative to the Commission, the Treaty also subjects the exercise of power by the Council to the requirement to procure an opinion on the draft measure from one of the consultative organs created by the Treaty. In most instances the Council must consult the European Parliament but in some cases it must consult the Economic and Social Committee[3] and before adopting a Financial Regulation it must consult the Court of Auditors.[4] Failure to consult the relevant institution when required to do so by the treaty renders the purported act of the Council open to review by the Court of Justice under Article 173 of the EEC Treaty on the grounds of infringement of an essential procedural requirement.[5] But it should be stressed that the consultative requirement is a formal requirement only: there is no obligation on the Council to take any account of the opinion of the relevant consultative body. It was this lack of consequence in the consultation procedure that led to the adoption of the Joint Declaration by the Presidents of the Parliament, the Council and the Commission in 1975, the object of which was to set up a conciliation system to be utilised whenever the Council intended to depart from the opinion of the Parliament in matters involving considerable expenditure.[6]

1 See, for example, EEC Treaty, art. 49.
2 EEC treaty, art. 149.
3 See, for example, EEC Treaty, art. 118.
4 EEC Treaty, art. 209 (as amended).
5 See para. 4.8 above.
6 *Loc. cit.* fn. 2, para. 4.9 above.

4.16 Under Article 148 of the EEC Treaty the Council votes by simple majority unless the treaty otherwise provides. This is the most redundant provision in Community Law. First, the Treaty invariably provides that decisions should be taken by unanimity (for matters of great importance such as enlargement and amendment of the Treaty, or on most topics during the original transitional period), or by a qualified majority. The qualified majority system attaches a weighting to each Member State's vote: the four largest States have 10 votes each, Spain has 8 votes, Belgium, Greece, the Netherlands and Portugal have 5 votes each, Denmark and Ireland have 3 votes each, and Luxembourg has 2 votes.[1] Where the Treaty requires a vote by qualified majority there must be a minimum of 54 votes cast in favour of the proposal, or if it is a proposal not originating with the Commission there must be at least 54 votes in favour and at least 8 Member States must approve the proposal. The mathematical permutations of this system are intriguing but have been of little consequence since 1966 when the so called 'Agreement to Disagree',[2] sometimes known as the Luxembourg compromise, put an end to the constitutional crisis of 1965. The effect of the Luxembourg compromise was, and still is, that where a Member State considers that its vital national interests are at stake it can insist that a unanimous vote is required even though the Treaty may specify a qualified majority vote on the proposal in question; in short, there is an unofficial veto in existence.

However, part of the damage to the decision-making process may well be remedied by the Single European Act. New Articles in the EEC Treaty, 8A and 100A, as well as amendments to existing provisions, will permit decision making by way of qualified majority so as to complete by the end of 1992 the establishment of the internal market—which should have been in place by the end of 1969. But the Single European Act makes no mention of the veto so we must assume that it remains 'in force'.

1 Third Act of Accession, art. 14.
2 Bull. E.C. 1-1966.

4.17 The consequences of the Luxembourg compromise have included the creation of a backlog of proposals in Brussels (the 'proposal mountain' as some cynics call it) with progress dependent upon complete agreement on practically every issue. The ramifications of this development have been far reaching. Firstly, it has emphasised the position of COREPER, the Committee of Permanent Representatives. COREPER, whose origins can be traced back to the ECSC, prepares the meetings of the Council and carries out the necessary liaison between the Community institutions and the national bureaucracies. As its name suggests it is a permanent body providing continuity, whereas the Council has a constantly changing and impermanent membership. It was given Treaty status by Article 4 of the Merger Treaty, and it consists of senior national civil servants of ambassadorial rank assisted by a range of state officials drawn from various departments whose activities fall within the ambit of the treaties. Since 1962 COREPER has had a two-tiered structure.[1] COREPER 1, consisting of Deputy Permanent Representatives deals with the business of the specialised Councils, whereas COREPER 2, consisting of the Permanent Representatives, deals with the business of the General Affairs Council. The latter involves foreign, economic and financial policy issues in the main. Since 1975 the work of COREPER 2 meetings is prepared by senior officials designated by the Permanent Representatives, and this collection of officials is known as the Antici Group after the Italian adviser responsible for its establishment. In agricultural matters the functions carried out by COREPER are exercised by a body known as the Special Committee on Agriculture which was set up in 1960.[2] It is made up of spokesmen, usually national officials of very senior standing, and it operates in much the same manner as, but autonomously from, COREPER. It is in COREPER that the compromises and deals on legislative proposals are worked out. If an item is non-contentious (that is agreement has been reached in COREPER) it appears on the Council agenda as an A point and is voted on without debate. Contentious matters are listed as B points—on which Council agreement is required. The question arises whether this procedure was an unauthorised delegation of decision-making power: could an act—agreed to in COREPER and rubber stamped as an A point by the Council—be challenged under Article 173 of the EEC Treaty as an abuse of power? Fears were expressed about the restriction of the independence of the Commission, particularly in the negotiation of international agreements.[3] In article 113 the Treaty provides for the appointment of a committee to supervise the negotiation of trade agreements by the Commission and COREPER is normally delegated by the Council to do this job, but, according to some observers, it takes a much more active role than the Treaty envisaged. Finally, it has been observed that while the Council now attends meetings of the Parliament and answers questions, COREPER is not responsible to Parliamentary control. But despite these fears COREPER has become an indispensable link in the Community decision-making procedure and, in their reports of 1975 and 1979 respectively, Tindemans and the Three Wise Men suggested that more responsibility should be delegated to COREPER. In fact, the Three Wise Men suggested that COREPER was often too high a level for decision making and consensus should emerge more appropriately in working groups. But the Three Wise Men also identified working groups as the cause of much of the stagnation in the legislative process, either because they worked without clear mandates from the Council or COREPER or because national officials in working groups were unwilling to commit themselves without first consulting their superiors.[5]

1 Fiona Hayes, *The Role of COREPER in EEC Decision-making*, Administration, vol. 32, No. 2 p. 177, at pp. 182–183.
2 O.J. 58, 12.9.1960.
3 Emile Noel, *The Commission's power of Initiative*, 10 C.M.L.Rev. (1973) 123.
4 Bieber & Palmer, *op. cit.*, fn. 2, para. 4.7.
5 *Op. cit.*, fn. 2, para. 4.14 at p. 39.

4.18 The second important institutional development has been the emergence of the European Council. In the late 1960s and early 1970s the practice of holding summit meetings of Heads of State and Government became more frequent. In December 1974, at the Paris Summit meeting, it was decided to institutionalise the summit meetings as the European Council, which was to meet three times a year.[1] The President of the Commission attends as an observer. In practice the European Council deals with intractable problems referred to it by the Council properly so-called. In other words it is becoming a 'court of appeal' for cases where agreement has not been reached at ministerial level. The European Council also acts as forum for informal contact between the heads of Government of the twelve Member States from whom guidelines and general directions emerge, and in which new concerns '. . . which do not yet belong to any framework of obligation . . .' can be discussed.[2] In addition the European Council deals with issues concerning European Political Cooperation (*infra* at 4.19). But when it meets is this body acting as the Council of the Communities, albeit at the highest level, or is it simply an unwarranted intrusion into the careful institutional balance set up by the treaties? Part of the difficulty concerns the status of the President of France, who is not a member of a national government and therefore does not qualify as a member of the Council of Ministers as required by Article 146 of the Treaty. There was also an initial fear that decisions would be taken by the European Council and handed to the Commission for execution, by-passing the decision-making procedures of the Treaty.[3] A more pragmatic view of the European Council sees it as an efficient means of breaking the logjam in decision-making procedures, and fears concerning the erosion of the position of the European Parliament have been assuaged by the practice, commenced in 1981, whereby the President-in-Office of the European Council reports to the Parliament on the meetings held during his or her six-month tenure of office.[4] The European Council has now been accorded formal Treaty status by Article 2 of the Single European Act which provides that it will meet at least twice a year. But, by virtue of Article 31 of the Single European Act, its activities will not be subject to review by the Court of Justice.

1 8th Annual General Report 1974, point 12.
2 Report on the European Institutions, Council of the European Communities 1980; Part III.
3 R. Lauwaars, *The European Council*, 14 C.M.L. Rev. (1977) 25.
4 15th Annual General Report 1981, point 15.

4.19 Finally, in a parallel development, the Foreign Ministers of the Member States have been meeting regularly in a formalised framework to coordinate the responses of the Member States to developments in international affairs. The process has become known as European Political

Cooperation (EPC) and originated in a Report adopted by the Foreign Ministers of the Six at Luxembourg in 1970.[1] It involves the harmonisation of foreign policy positions and the framework agreed in 1970 was refined in response to further Reports (Copenhagen 1973, London 1981).[2] In its present format the Foreign Ministers meet four times a year to discuss issues of mutual concern. The agenda for their meetings is prepared by a group of senior officials in the Foreign Ministries known as Political Directors, who meet in a Political Affairs Committee. Under the direction of this committee, a group of correspondents is entrusted with ensuring the implementation of practical cooperation and these officers are in daily contact with one another. In addition, the embassies of the Member States abroad and their representatives in international organisations are included in the political cooperation machinery. The general principles underlying the process are that Europe should endeavour to discharge its international functions with a greater degree of cohesion and unity. The Member States try to proceed by common action wherever possible but, as a general rule, they do not take up final positions on practical problems without prior consultation with their partners within the framework of political cooperation. Agreement is achieved by consensus, and not by coercion.

In its early days EPC gave rise to fears about its effects on decision making in the Community.[3] But, as in the case of the European Council, the European Parliament is kept informed of the results of EPC. The Foreign Minister of the Member State holding the Presidency appears before the Parliament to answer written and oral questions, and four colloquies are held annually with the Parliament's Political Affairs Committee.[4]

Titles I and III of the Single European Act formally associate EPC with the European Communities. According to Article 1, the joint objective of EPC and the Communities is to contribute together to making concrete progress towards European unity. Title III describes the structures and operating principles of EPC and this Title, along with the Luxembourg, Copenhagen and London Reports of 1970, 1973 and 1981 respectively, embody the constitutive documentation for EPC. Two minor structural changes appear in Title III, which is composed of a single Article divided into 12 paragraphs. The Ministers of Foreign Affairs will meet at least four times a year in the company of a member of the Commission (Article 30(3)), and a small secretariat will be established in Brussels to assist the Presidency in carrying out the activities of EPC (Article 30(10)(g)). In Paragraph 6(a) the High Contracting Parties declare themselves willing to coordinate their positions more closely on the political and economic aspects of security, and in paragraph 6(b) they express their determination to maintain the technological and industrial conditions necessary for their security. According to paragraph 6(c), however, closer cooperation in the field of security can be pursued within the framework of the Western European Union or the Atlantic Alliance. Ireland is a member of neither organisation and this clause would appear to have taken into account Professor Dooge's reservation on behalf of Ireland concerning the sections of the Dooge Report on defence and security matters.[5] Finally, although Article 1 of the SEA formally links EPC and the European Communities, their relative spheres of activity are carefully quarantined: Article 31 of the SEA makes it clear that the review powers of the Court of Justice do not apply to Titles I and III of the SEA. But, despite these restrictions and limitations, the Supreme Court—in its majority decision in the *Crotty* case—considered that Title III would bind the State to surrender part of its sovereignty in the conduct of foreign relations (see *infra* at 15.6). Accordingly, a referendum was required to authorise the State to ratify the SEA; on 25 May 1987 the electorate enacted the Tenth Amendment of the Constitution which enabled the government to deposit the instrument of ratification with the Italian Government in June 1987.

1 Bull. E.C. 11-1970, p. 8.
2 7th General Report, 1973, p. 502; *European Political Cooperation*, Press and Information Office of The Federal Republic of Germany, 1982, at point 82.
3 K. Mortelmans, *The Extramural meetings of the Ministers of the Member States of the Community*, 11 C.M.L. Rev. (1974) 62.
4 Bull. E.C. 12-1982, point 2.3.8.
5 *Ad hoc* Committee on Institutional Affairs, *Report to the European Council*, Luxembourg 1985; at p. 23.

The Commission

4.20 Relevant Treaty Provisions:

ECSC Treaty	Articles 8–19
EEC Treaty	Articles 155–163
Euratom Treaty	Articles 124–135
Merger Treaty	Articles 9–19
First Act of Accession	Articles 15–16
Second Act of Accession	Article 15
Third Act of Accession	Article 15
Single European Act	Article 10

4.21 The Commission is the institution charged with the protection of the Community interest; it has often been described as the 'supranational' institution. The Report of the Three Wise Men describes the Commission as the natural executive organ without which the Community could not have been constructed.[1] There are 17 Commissioners[2] chosen on grounds of their general competence and whose independence is beyond doubt although nominated by the governments of the Member States. The larger Member States nominate 2 Commissioners each. But, if the Reports of the Three Wise Men and the Spierenburg Committee are to be believed, there is work enough to justify only ten portfolios. According to Article 11 of the Merger Treaty, the Commissioners are appointed by common accord of the governments of the Member States, but in fact the nominees of Member States are accepted by the other Member States unless there is a particular objection to the appointment.[3] It has now become the practice to appoint the President of the Commission in advance of the other Commissioners so as to allow him the opportunity of participating in the selection of his colleagues for the forthcoming term of office, which is for four years and is renewable.[4] The President and 5 vice-presidents are appointed for a term of 2 years, which may be renewed and invariably is (Merger Treaty, Article 19). The Commissioners may be replaced in accordance with Article 12 of the Merger Treaty which allows for normal replacement, death and compulsory retirement.[5] The Commission is organised into 20 Directorates-General[6] and it also has a number of specialised services such as the Spokesman's Group (for press relations) and the Legal Service. Overall responsibility for these departments is allocated among the Commissioners. It has a full-time establishment of 11,234 posts (including its language services) and there are also 2,647 posts paid for out of the Commission's research appropriation.[7]

1 *Op. cit.* fn. 3, para. 4.14 at p. 49.
2 Third Act of Accession, art. 15.
3 See: K. van Miert, *The Appointment of the Members of the Commission*, 10 C.M.L.Rev. (1973) 257.
4 Merger Treaty, art. 14.
5 See, for example, O.J. L279 2.10.87 p. 26
6 Rules of Procedure, arts. 17 and 18; O.J. (Sp. Ed.) 2nd series VII p. 9.
7 21st Annual General Report, 1987, point 19.

4.22 The Commission acts by a majority of its members.[1] It is a collegiate body; it acts collectively in accordance with its Rules of Procedure.[2] At present eight members constitute a quorum.[3] Under Article 27 of its Rules of Procedure the Commission may delegate to its members clearly defined measures of management or administration. Officials may also be empowered to take such measures if this is indispensable for the proper execution of the Commission's tasks. A good illustration of delegation and sub-delegation at work can be seen in Regulation 17/62.[5] The college of Commissioners retains the decision-making power for most important matters, but the Commissioner for competition affairs was delegated the power to take decisions under art.s 11 and 14 of the Regulation.[6] The Commissioner has, in turn, sub-delegated some functions to the Director-General for Competition or his Directors: the chairmanship of the Advisory Committee on Restrictive Practices and Dominant Position is a case in point.[7] In addition, the President of the Commission may delegate the power of signature to particular members of the Commission.[8]

Decision making by the Commission takes place either at Commission meetings[9] or by way of the 'written' procedure.[10] Proposals for decisions are circulated among the members of the Commission and if no objection is forthcoming the decision is deemed adopted. If there is an objection the proposal comes up for discussion at a meeting of the Commission.

1 Merger Treaty, art. 17.
2 Rules of Procedure art. 1, *loc. cit.* fn. 6. para. 4.21.
3 Rules of Procedure art. 5, as amended. See: O.J. L 127 13.5.81 p. 22.
4 O.J. (Sp. Ed.) 2nd series VII p. 14 as amended. See: O.J. L 199, 30.7.75 p. 43.
5 O.J. (Sp. Ed.) 1959–1962, p. 87.
6 C.J. Kerse, *EEC Anti-Trust Procedure*, (First Edition 1981), at p. 152.
7 *Idem.*
8 Commission Decision 73/2 (ECSC, EEC, Euratom), O.J. L 7, 6.1.1973 p. 2. This power may also be sub-delegated: see C.J. Kerse, *op. cit.* n. 6, at p. 227; and Cases 48, 49, 51–57/69 *ICI and others v EC Commission* [1972] E.C.R. 619, [1972] C.M.L.R. 557 in which the Court of Justice approved the sub-delegation of the power of signature to the Director-General for Competition.

9 Rules of Procedure, art. 12, *loc. cit.* fn. 6, para. 4.21.
10 Rules of Procedure, art. 11 *loc cit.* fn. 6, para. 4.21.

4.23 The responsibilities of the Commission are outlined in Article 155 of the Treaty. Its first task is to ensure that the Treaty provisions are applied. This is its 'watchdog' role, and it is manifested clearly in Article 169 of the Treaty which allows the Commission to instigate proceedings before the Court of Justice to establish infringements of the Treaty or secondary legislation by Member States. Article 213 of the Treaty allows the Commission to collect all the information necessary for the execution of its tasks. The Commission also has the power to ensure that private enterprises do not infringe the Treaty's anti-trust provisions; it has the power to fine enterprises for infringements.[1] Article 155 also provides that the Commission is to have its own power of decision. Various provisions of the treaty confer specific powers on the Commission; for example, Article 93 empowers the Commission to determine whether state aids are compatible with the Treaty. But, as we have noted above, most of the formal decision-making power was entrusted to the Council. However, the Commission may also exercise powers conferred upon it by the Council. This is specifically provided for by the last sentence of Article 155 and it has been utilised extensively, particularly in the agricultural sector, where delegated decision making takes place through management committees.[2] The latter were established originally as an interim measure but they worked so successfully that their existence was continued indefinitely by a Regulation implemented just before the expiry of the transitional period.[3] The procedure and typology of these committees is examined in detail (*infra* at 4.49) but it suffices to note here that the Court of Justice rejected an attack on the validity of decision making by management committee in the *Köster* case.[4]

The Reports of Tindemans (1975) and the Three Wise Men (1979) both recommended further delegation of management powers to the Commission. Such delegation could have been based without difficulty on Article 155 of the Treaty, but when the SEA tackled this issue it did so by way of an amendment to Article 145, which describes the functions of the Council. Article 10 of the SEA reads as follows:

'Article 145 of the EEC Treaty shall be supplemented by the following provision:
"– confer on the Commission, in the acts which the Council adopts, powers for the implementation of the rules which the Council lays down. The Council may impose certain requirements in respect of the exercise of these powers. The Council may also reserve the right, in specific cases, to exercise directly implementing powers itself. The procedures referred to above must be consonant with principles and rules to be laid down in advance by the Council, acting unanimously on a proposal from the Commission and after obtaining the Opinion of the European Parliament."'

This provision is qualified somewhat by the first Declaration annexed by the SEA which reads as follows:

'Declaration on the powers of implementation of the Commission.
   The Conference asks the Community authorities to adopt, before the Act

enters into force, the principles and rules on the basis of which the Commission's powers of implementation will be defined in each case.

In this connection the Conference requests the Council to give the Advisory Committee procedure in particular a predominant place in the interests of speed and efficiency in the decision-making process, for the exercise of the powers of implementation conferred on the Commission within the field of Article 100A of the EEC Treaty.'

Within a fortnight of the entry into force of the SEA the Council adopted Decision 87/373/EEC[5] laying down procedures for the exercise of implementing powers conferred on the Commission. The Decision distinguishes between two different circumstances: where the Council confers implementing powers on the Commission and where the Council confers power on the Commission to decide on safeguard measures. In respect of the former, Article 2 of the Decision sets out three different procedures, any one of which the Council may require the Commission to follow. Procedure I requires the Commission to submit a draft of the measures to be taken to an advisory committee made up of representatives of the Member States, and the Commission must take 'the utmost account' of the views of this committee. Procedure II (which has two variants) requires the Commission to submit a draft to a committee composed of representatives of the Member States which delivers an opinion in accordance with the voting provisions of Article 148(2) of the EEC Treaty. On receipt of this opinion the Commission adopts the proposed measures immediately unless they are not in accordance with the opinion of the committee. In that event, the Commission must communicate the fact immediately to the Council and may defer the implementation of the measures for one month or for three months (variant {a} or {b}); within that latter period the Council may take a different decision, acting by a qualified majority. Procedure III, which also has two variants, is similar to Procedure II but, if the measures envisaged by the Commission are not in accordance with the opinion of the committee or if no opinion is delivered the Commission must, without delay, submit to the Council a proposal relating to the measures to be taken; the Council acts on this proposal by a qualified majority. If within a period not exceeding three months the Council has not acted the Commission may adopt the envisaged measures (variant{a}), unless the Council has decided against the measures by a simple majority (variant {b}).

Article 3 of the Council Decision deals with the procedure to be applied where the Council confers power on the Commission to decide on safeguard measures. The Commission must notify the Council of any decision concerning safeguard measures; any Member State may then refer the decision to the Council within a stipulated time limit. Variant {a} of the procedure allows the Council to take a different decision, by qualified majority, within a time limit to be determined in the act in question. Variant {b} allows the Council to amend, vary or revoke the Commission decision, acting by a qualified majority; and if the Council has not taken a decision within a specified time limit, the Commission decision is deemed to be revoked.

Article 4 of the Decision makes it clear that the Decision does not affect the procedures for the exercise of conferred powers which predated its entry into force; but existing acts may be adapted to conform to the procedures set out in Articles 2 and 3 of the Decision.

It should be remarked that there is nothing particularly novel in any of the procedures set out in Council Decision 87/373/EEC. A close scrutiny of the committee system which predated the SEA (*infra* at 4.47) shows that the 'new' procedures do not differ significantly from the pre-existing management committees and the 'net' and 'safety net' procedures. This lack of novelty also seems to have annoyed the European Parliament, which has initiated an action for the annulment of the Council's Decision.[6]

1 17/62, art. 15.
2 See: Peter Schindler, *The Problems of Decision Making by Way of the Management Committee Procedure*, 7 C.M.L. Rev. (1971) 184.
3 Council Regulation 2602/69 (EEC) O.J. (Sp. Ed.) 1969 (II), p. 588.
4 Case 25/70 *Einfuhr- und Vorratsstelle für Getreide und Futtermittel v Köster* [1972] E.C.R. 1161, [1972] C.M.L.R. 255.
5 O.J. L 197, 18.7.1987 p. 33.
6 Case 302/87, O.J. C 321, 1.12.1987 p. 4.

4.24 The Commission's most significant and most jealously guarded power is the exclusive right of initiative concerning Community legislation.[1] Virtually all the decision-making power of the Council can only be exercised on the basis of a Commission proposal, which will have been worked out in close consultation with national bureaucracies. This right of initiative is protected and emphasised in a number of ways by the Treaty. Article 151 provides that the Council may amend a Commission proposal only by a unanimous decision, and Article 159 permits the Commission to alter a proposal following the opinion of the European Parliament. However, Article 152 provides that the Council may request the Commission to undertake studies and to submit any appropriate proposals. In the aftermath of the Luxembourg compromise it was feared that the Council would use this provision to undermine the Commission's independent right of initiative. Similar fears were expressed with regard to the European Council and European Political Cooperation (see *supra* at 4.18 and 4.19).

1 See: Emile Noel, *The Commission's power of Initiative*, 10 C.M.L. Rev. (1973) 123.

4.25 Finally, although the Commission is not a part of the 'budgetary authority' of the Communities, it has a central role to play in the preparation of budgetary proposals as well as in the collection of Community Revenues and their eventual disbursement in execution of the Budget (EEC Treaty, art.s 203–206b).

Organs of the Community

4.26 Apart from the four main institutions of the Communities the Treaties also provide for four subsidiary organs. These are:

- The Consultative Committee of the ECSC;
- The Economic and Social Committee;
- The European Investment Bank;
- The Court of Auditors

The Economic and Social Committee (ECOSOC)

4.27 Relevant Treaty Provisions:

EEC Treaty	Articles 193–198
Euratom Treaty	Articles 165–170
Convention on Institutions Common to the European Communities	Article 5
First Act of Accession	Article 21
Second Act of Accession	Article 21
Third Act of Accession	Article 21

4.28 The Economic and Social Committee of the EEC and Euratom and the Consultative Committee of the ECSC are designed to permit a vocational and sectorial input to the decision-making process. There are two views of the propriety and suitability of such involvement. First, it is seen as a useful inclusion of interest groups in the legislative process. Institutions of this type can be found in the laws or constitutions of a number of Member States particularly Belgium, France and the Netherlands. In Ireland, the NESC (National Economic and Social Committee), which was established in 1973, is a similar type of body and the phenomenon can also be detected in a less obvious context in Seanad Eireann, a proportion of whose membership is elected from vocational panels. But from two different perspectives, the process is distrusted either because it legitimates the representation of special interests or because it is tainted either by a whiff of syndicalism or by corporatist representation in terms of Catholic social doctrine.[1] These differing perspectives were represented when the 1957 treaties were being negotiated: the favourable view taken by the Benelux countries was met by the hostile attitude of Germany, and this conflict probably explains the limited role given to ECOSOC by the treaties.

1 Gerda Zellentin, *The Economic and Social Committee*, I J.C.M.S. 22.

4.29 According to EEC Treaty, art. 149, as amended, the membership is distributed as follows:

Belgium	12
Denmark	9
Germany	24
Greece	12
Spain	21
France	24
Ireland	9
Italy	24
Luxembourg	6
The Netherlands	12
Portugal	12
United Kingdom	24
Total	189

The Committee is appointed by the Council from a list supplied by the Member States. Each Member State nominates twice as many candidates as there are seats allotted to it. In making appointments the Council consults the Commission and European organisations which are representative of various economic and social activities. According to Article 193 of the EEC Treaty the Committee consists of representatives of producers, farmers, carriers, workers, dealers, craftsmen, professional occupations and representatives of the general public. In practice, the two main groups in ECOSOC consist of employer representatives and trade unionists, but a third group (sometimes described as the 'independents') includes a broad range of interests including those of farmers, consumers and public sector representatives. Under Article 196 the Committee elects its own President; the office rotates among the three groups every two years. According to Article 197 the Committee may form specialised sections on the principal topics covered by the treaty such as agriculture and transport, but such sections operate within the overall structure of the Committee and cannot be consulted separately. The Committee is assisted by a permanent secretariat employing a staff of 471 in 1987.[1]

1 21st Annual General Report 1987, at point 32.

4.30 The Committee must be consulted by the Council where the Treaty so provides. There are ten provisions in the EEC Treaty and seven provisions in the Euratom Treaty which require consultation;[1] failure to consult ECOSOC would amount to an infringement of an essential procedural requirement under Article 173 of the EEC Treaty or Article 146 of the Euratom Treaty, unless the contested decision is purely preparatory or procedural in nature and does not touch on substantive questions which are liable to involve ECOSOC in making an assessment of a socio-economic nature. This latter point was decided in *Germany v EC Commission*[2] in which the Court of Justice held that ECOSOC's function was

'. . . to advise the Council and Commission on the solutions to be adopted with regard to practical problems of an economic and social nature and to deliver opinions based on its specific competence and knowledge.'

Apart from its mandatory consultative role, ECOSOC was not initially in a position to give an opinion unless requested to do so. This limitation was lifted as a result of a decision taken at the Paris Summit of 1972. This new right of initiative as regards opinions was confirmed in the amended rules of procedure adopted by the Council in 1974.[3] The Committee lost no time in using it: a separate and unsolicited opinion on the subject of European Union was submitted to Mr Leo Tindemans in 1975.[4] However, the Committee suffers from a number of operational restraints. First, there is a difficulty in assessing whether the opinions of the Committee have been taken into consideration by the Council, particularly if the European Parliament is also involved in the consultative process.[5] Secondly, the Committee's consultative role is in danger of being undermined by *ad hoc* or semi-official consultative bodies such as the Advisory Committees set up by acts of the Council or the Commission, or by bodies operating in cognate areas such as the Standing Committee on Employment.[6] On the other hand, the Committee's attitude to the European Parliament has changed since the mid-1970s, when the Parliament would have been viewed as a consultative rival; now the Parliament is perceived as a further possible client for advice from ECOSOC.[7]

1 Diarmid McLaughlin, *The Work and Aims of the Economic and Social Committee of the EEC and Euratom*, XV J.C.M.S. 9.
2 Joined cases 281, 283, 284, 285 and 287/85 O.J. C 205 1.8.87 p. 7.
3 Council Decision 74/428 (EEC, Euratom); O.J. L 228, 9.8.1974 p. 1.
4 Bull. E.C. Supp. 9/75.
5 Diarmid McLaughlin, *op. cit.* fn. 1, at p. 15.
6 *Idem*, at pp. 20–21.
7 *Idem*, at p. 23.

4.31 During 1987 the committee held 10 plenary sessions at which it adopted several 'own initiative' opinions including one on the consequences of the Chernobyl nuclear accident.[1]

1 21st Annual General Report 1987, point 30.

The Consultative Committee of the ECSC

4.32 Relevant Treaty Provisions:

ECSC Treaty	Articles 7, 18 and 19
Merger Treaty	Article 19
First Act of Accession	Article 22
Second Act of Accession	Article 22
Third Act of Accession	Article 22

4.33 The Consultative Committee of the ECSC consists of not less than 72 members and not more than 96 members and comprises equal numbers of representatives of producers, workers, consumers and dealers; the members are appointed in a personal capacity for a term of two years by the Council. In the case of producers and workers, organisations designated by the Council nominate twice as many names as there are places allocated to them and appointments are made from this list. For example, in 1985 the Council appointed the leader of the British National Union of Mineworkers, Mr Arthur Scargill.[1]

The Commission is obliged to consult the Consultative Committee whenever the ECSC Treaty so requires, but the consultation procedure is also invoked when it is considered opportune to do so. The Commission may set a time limit of 10 days for the receipt of an opinion. Failure to consult the Committee would constitute breach of an essential procedural requirement under Article 33 of the ECSC Treaty.

In 1987 the Committee met on seven occasions. It examined the Commission's overall plan for the restructuring of the Community steel industry, it was consulted on the market for solid fuels, and it adopted a resolution on the ECSC levy rate.[2]

1 19th Annual General Report 1985, point 41.
2 21st Annual General Report 1987, point 33.

The Court of Auditors

4.34 Relevant Treaty Provisions:

ECSC Treaty	Article 78
EEC Treaty	Article 206
Euratom Treaty	Article 180
Convention on Certain Institutions	
common to the European Communities	Article 6
Merger Treaty	Articles 20–22
First Budgetary Treaty	Articles 3, 6 & 9
Second Act of Accession	Article 20
Third Act of Accession	Article 20

4.35 Before 1977 the auditing functions in the Communities were carried out by an Audit Board for the European Communities and the Auditors for the ECSC. In the early 1970s, however, the European Parliament called for the establishment of a Community Audit Office along the lines of national audit bodies. The existing system permitted part-time appointments and, in the Parliament's view, such a method of auditing would not be tolerated in the Member States.[1] A report prepared by the Parliament's Committee for Finances and Budget identified some of the drawbacks in the practices of Audit Board and the ECSC Auditor as it then operated:

(i) The retroactive nature of control–revenue not yet collected or committed could not be investigated; (ii) the limited circumstances in which spot checks could be carried out; (iii) the limitation on direct contact between the Audit Board and the institutions other than the Commission.[2] Apart from pointing out deficiencies in the auditing system the Parliament was keen to acquire the right to grant a discharge to the Commission in respect of the implementation of the Budget; for this supervisory function the Reports of a strong independent Audit Body would be invaluable.

1 *The Case for a European Audit Office*, European Parliament, 1973.
2 *Idem*, pp. 125–129.

4.36 The Treaty of 22 July 1975 (the Second Budgetary Treaty) repealed Merger Treaty, art. 22 and replaced the Audit Board and the ECSC Auditor with a European Court of Auditors. That this new organ has been elevated from the relative obscurity of the budgetary provisions to secondary institutional status is clear from Article 4 of the EEC Treaty (Article 7d of the ECSC Treaty, and Article 3 of the Euratom Treaty, which declares that the audit shall be carried out by a Court of Auditors acting within the limits of the competence conferred on it by the treaty.

According to Article 206 of the EEC Treaty the Court of Auditors consists of 12 members. They are appointed by the Council, but, unlike the Commission and the Court of Justice, the Parliament must be consulted on the nominees for membership and the Parliament has not always been satisfied that it has been properly consulted.[1] The members must have belonged to external audit bodies in their Member States or must be especially qualified for the job. Thus Mr Michael N. Murphy, first

President of the Court of Auditors had been Secretary of the Department of Finance in Dublin and the present Irish appointee, Mr Richie Ryan, had been Minister for Finance. The term of office is six years and the members of the Court of Auditors must be completely independent in the exercise of their duties: they may not engage in any other occupation during their tenure of office.

Each member is allocated a specific audit function. For example, Mr Murphy was in charge of the audit of the Guarantee Section of the EAGGF which has always accounted for more than 60 per cent of the entire budget. The Court of Auditors is assisted by an administrative secretariat comprised of 310 permanent posts in 1987.[2]

1 European Parliament, Working Documents 1983–1984; Document I—79–/83, 5 October 1983.
2 21st Annual General Report 1987, point 27.

4.37 The functions of the Court of Auditors are listed in Articles 206a and 209 of the EEC Treaty and their cognates in the other basic treaties. Article 206a(1) provides that the Court of Auditors shall examine all revenue and expenditure of the Community and of all bodies set up by the Community where the constitutive instruments do not provide otherwise. Thus, the Court of Auditor's investigatory role extends to non-budgetary expenditure such as the Sixth European Development Fund, which finances the commitments of the Communities under the Third Lomé Convention.[1] The Court of Auditors also investigates the following Community bodies: the European Schools; the European Foundation for the Improvement of Living and Working Conditions (Dublin); the European Centre for the Development of Vocational Training (Berlin); the Euratom Supply Agency; and the JET (the Joint European Torus).

The Court of Auditors is charged with examining '. . . whether all revenue has been received and all expenditure incurred in a lawful and regular manner and whether the financial management has been sound'. The audit is based on records but unlike the old Audit Board the audit may be carried out before the closure of accounts for the year, and on the spot investigations may also be carried out in the institutions or in the Member States (Article 200a(2) and (3)). In carrying out its work in the Member States the Court of Auditors is assisted by the national audit board or other competent authority (in Ireland: the Comptroller and Auditor-General), and this cooperation is reinforced by annual meetings with all the national bodies.[2]

The fruit of the endeavours of the Court of Auditors is published annually along with replies by the institutions to observations made by the Court of Auditors. This practice gave rise to a difference of opinion between the Commission and the Court of Auditors at the outset of the latter's investigatory career.[3] It is on the basis of the annual report of the Court of Auditors that the Parliament gives a discharge of the budget to the Commission (Article 206b). The report is published in the Official Journal, but the annual reports on the bodies like the European schools are not published on grounds of lack of importance and lack of public interest.

When carrying out the audit the Court of Auditors is charged with determining whether all revenue has been received and all expenditure incurred in a lawful and regular manner and whether the financial management has been sound. The first two requirements are commonplace auditing functions but an assessment into whether the 'financial management has been sound' is more problematic and the meaning of the phrase is not exactly clear. However, a past member of the Court of Auditors has suggested that sound financial management can be tested by reference to the three Es—economy, efficiency and effectiveness:

> 'Has a policy been carried out with proper regard to the level of expenditure? Has it been carried out by the employment of the best means? And has it been successful in its aim?'.[4]

The danger with this test is that it sometimes implies an examination of the soundness of the policy in question and that is not an auditorial function. The Court of Auditors can be expected to resist any temptation to trespass in the bailiwick of policy formulators. Consequently, the utility of the 'sound financial management' test can best be described as limited.

1 O.J. L 86, 31.3.1986 p. 210.
2 Sir Norman Price, *The Court of Auditors*, 3 Yearbook of European Law (1983) 239, at p. 245.
3 Daniel Strasser, *The Finances of Europe*, Luxembourg 1981, at p. 97.
4 Sir Norman Price, *op. cit.* fn. 2, at p. 243.

4.38 According to Article 206a(4) the Court of Auditors may, on its own initiative or at the request of one of the institutions, prepare reports or deliver opinions on specific questions, and work of this type forms a not inconsiderable part of the activities of the institution. For example, in 1987 the Court of Auditors produced a report on the system of quotas and additional levies in the milk sector.[1]

1 21st Annual General Report 1987, point 26.

4.39 The Court of Auditors also has a consultative role under Article 209 of the EEC Treaty. It must be consulted on three particular topics concerning budgetary procedure including the preparation of Financial Regulations. Shortly after its establishment in 1977 the Court of Auditors gave an opinion on the Financial Regulation but made its opinion conditional on its right to issue a supplemental opinion on the Regulation.[1]

1 O.J. L 356, 31.12.1977 p. 1, at consideration No. 2 in the preamble.

The European Investment Bank (EIB)

4.40 Relevant Treaty Provisions:

EEC Treaty	Articles 129–130
Statute of the EIB	
(First Protocol Annexed to the EEC Treaty)	Articles 1–29
First Act of Accession	Protocol No. 1
Treaty amending certain provisions of the	
Protocol on the Statute of the EIB (1975)	*Passim*

Second Act of Accession   Protocol No. 1
Third Act of Accession   Protocol No. 1

4.41 The European Investment Bank (the EIB) is the Community's development bank. It is a genuine banking institution and it enjoys real autonomy from other institutions.[1] The EIB was established by Article 129 of the EEC Treaty. This accords the EIB legal personality and constitutes the Member States as its members. The detailed rules for the operation of the EIB are contained in the Statute, which is annexed to the EEC Treaty as its first Protocol. The task of the EIB, as defined in Article 130 of the EEC Treaty, is to contribute to the balanced and steady development of the common market. It does this by having recourse to the capital markets and by utilising its owns resources to grant loans and to give guarantees for three types of projects in all sectors of the economy:

- projects for developing less developed regions; and where the size and nature of a proposal is such that its cost cannot be met by one Member State alone;
- projects for the modernisation or development of new industries;
- projects of common interest to Member States.

In addition, Article 18 of the Statute permits the EIB to grant loans for investment projects to be carried out, in whole or in part, outside the European territory of the Member States.

1 Joseph Licari, *The European Investment Bank*, VIII J.C.M.S. 192, at p. 194.

4.42 According to Article 4(1) of the Statute (as amended) the capital of the EIB is 28,800 million ECU, to which the Member States contribute on a sliding scale. Ireland's share is fixed at 193,288,000 ECU.[1] The subscribed capital is paid in by the Member States at the rate of 9.01367457 per cent (Article 3, Statute). A reserve fund of 10 per cent is required by Article 24 and on 31.12.86, when subscribed capital stood at 28.8 bn. ECU the reserve fund stood at 2.88 bn. ECU.[2]

1 19th Annual Report 1985, p. 106. See also Protocol No. 1, Third Act of Accession.
2 European Investment Bank, Annual Report 1986, p. 94.

4.43 The Member States are the members of the EIB (Article 1, Statute). The EIB is directed and managed by a Board of Governors, a Board of Directors, and a Management Committee. In addition, Article 14 of the Statute provides for the appointment of an audit board, composed of three members, to verify that the operation of the EIB is being conducted and the books kept in a proper way. The Board of Governors (Article 9, Statute) consists of ministers (usually of Finance) designated by the Member States. It appoints the members of the Board of Directors, the Management Committee and the audit board. It lays down directives on the audit policy of the Bank and it approves the annual report and balance sheet. Voting, unless otherwise provided, is by a majority representing at least 40 per cent of the subscribed capital. The Board of Directors (Article

51

11, Statute) consists of 22 members (one nominated by Ireland) and 12 alternates (one nominated by common accord of Denmark, Greece and Ireland). It has the sole power to take decisions in respect of loans and guarantees; it must ensure that the EIB is properly run and managed in accordance with the provisions of the Treaty, the Statute, and the general directives laid down by the Board of Governors. Save as otherwise provided the voting is by simple majority. The Management Committee (Article 13, Statute) consists of a President and six Vice-Presidents. It is responsible for all the current business of the EIB and it prepares the decisions of the Board of Directors in connection with raising loans, granting loans and providing guarantees.

4.44 The EIB enjoys triple A (AAA) Credit rating, even though it is a non-profit making bank (EEC Treaty, art. 130). This is because the EIB operates certain basic rules concerning its operations. Loans are granted only on condition that other financial resources, provided either by the applicant enterprise or by a Member State, are also used (Article 18(2), Statute). Outstanding loans and guarantees cannot exceed the subscribed capital by more than 250 per cent (Article 18(5), Statute). The interest rates charged by the Bank are the commercial rates prevailing on capital markets (Article 19(1), Statute) and it cannot grant reductions in interest rates (Article 19(2), Statute). However, interest subsidies can be provided from other Community resources (the budget) or from the European Development Fund. The EIB cannot speculate on the money markets (Article 23, Statute).

4.45 The bulk of the Bank's lending in 1985 was for projects involving regional development (4.34 bn. ECU), followed by projects in the energy sector (2.22 bn. ECU), environment and cultural heritage (1.57 bn. ECU), modernisation of undertakings (1.28 bn. ECU), and Community infra-structure projects (680 m. ECU).[1] The Bank also grants loans from the New Community Instrument and 447 m. ECU was advanced from this source in 1985.[2]

1 EIB-Information, no. 55, February 1988, Table 2.
2 EIB-Information, no. 55, February 1988, Table 2.

4.46 Article 20 of the Statute provides a type of sanction for Member States failing to comply with their obligations arising out of the Statute: the granting of loans and guarantees may be suspended by the Board of Governors. In addition, EEC Treaty, art. 180 gives the Court of Justice jurisdiction to determine disputes concerning:
  (a) the fulfilment by Member States of obligations under the Statute. The Board of Directors has a function here similar to that of the Commission under EEC Treaty, art. 169.
  (b) measures adopted by the Board of Governors;[1]
  (c) measures adopted by the Board of Directors.

1 See, for example, Case 85/86 *EC Commission v Board of Governors of the European Investment Bank* OJ C77, 24.3.88, p. 6.

Committees

4.47 We have already encountered a number of committees which assist the Council and the Commission in the execution of their tasks: COREPER and the Special Committee on Agriculture prepare the work of the Council while the Consultative Committee of the ECSC and the Economic and Social Committee are general purpose advisory bodies. In addition, the Treaties provide for the establishment of other specialised advisory bodies:

Advisory Committee on Transport	EEC Treaty, art. 83
Monetary Committee	EEC Treaty, art. 105
Negotiation of trade agreements	EEC Treaty, art. 113
Committee of the European Social Fund	EEC Treaty, art. 124
Scientific and Technical Committee	Euratom Treaty, art. 134

These committees are of great importance in the Community system. But there exist more than 200 other committees, constituted in the main by representatives of the Member States (civil servants), scientific experts, or representatives of workers organisations, professional bodies and trade interests. These committees have been established by acts of the Council and the Commission and their work is an indispensable element in the legislative process. Given the minuscule size of the professional corps of *fonctionnaires* in the Commission, the popular image of the faceless Brussels bureaucrat is misleading: the Brussels bureaucracy consists as much of national civil servants and experts as it does of Community employees.

4.48 In 1980 the Commission published a list of these committees[1] and classified them into two general groups: committees which must be consulted in the preparation of Community acts, and committees which need not be consulted. But before examining the various types of committee in existence it might be useful to bear in mind some principles established by the Court of Justice concerning delegation of power because most of the committees which must be consulted have been set up in the context of a delegation of power from the Council to the Commission. The basic principles on the delegation of power were laid down by the Court of Justice in the case of *Meroni v High Authority*.[2] The applicant sought the annulment of a decision of the defendant which confirmed the contribution due by the applicant to the Imported Ferrous Scrap Equalisation Fund, which was administered by the joint Bureau of Ferrous Scrap Consumers. According to the applicant this involved an unlawful delegation of power to the Fund and Bureau. The Court agreed and issued a number of guidelines for the delegation of power: the delegating authority cannot confer on the recipient powers more extensive than those conferred by the treaties; a delegation of power must take place by express decision and cannot be presumed; the exercise of delegated powers must be subject to the same requirements of publicity and review as apply to the delegating authority; only clearly defined executive powers may be delegated—the delegation of discretionary powers, involving a substitution of the choice of the delegator and an actual transfer of authority, is impermissible; any delegation must be entirely subject to the supervision of the delegator. As we have seen above, EEC Treaty, art. 155 permits the delegation of power from the Council to the Commission, and it is clear that when delegation took place in the administration of the CAP the Council had the *Meroni* decision in mind. In the basic Regulations organising the markets for various agricultural products the power delegated to the Commission is specified in detail, and the decision making of the Commission is subject to scrutiny by a management committee. Generally speaking, if the Commission acts contrary to the opinion of a management committee the supervisory role of the Council comes into play. But despite these features the system was challenged in *Einfuhr- und Vorratsstelle für Getreide und Futtermittel v Köster.*[3] The Court held that the system was compatible with the treaty:

'The so-called Management Committee procedure forms part of the detailed rules to which the Council may legitimately subject a delegation of power to the Commission . . . The function of the Management Committee is to ensure permanent consultation to guide the Commission in the exercise of the powers conferred on it by the Council and to enable the latter to substitute its own action for that of the Commission. The Management Committee does not therefore have the power to take a decision in place of the Commission or the Council.'

Other decisions have further established the validity of the management committee system. In *Westzucker v Einfuhr- und Vorratsstelle für Zucker*[4] the Court was faced with an allegation that a Regulation, which withdrew a denaturing premium was vitiated by the fact that in the Management Committee for sugar the Commission had yielded to improper pressure from the French and Italian governments. This argument was rejected on the ground that the very object of the management committee system was to promote cooperation, in the operation of the market sectors concerned, between the Commission and the Member States; within that system it was the Commission's function to arbitrate between conflicting national interests. In *Schouten v Hoofdproduktschap voor Akkerbouwprodukten*[5] the Court, implicitly approved the mechanics of the management committee system. The Commission had submitted a draft Regulation to the management committee for its opinion but no opinion was forthcoming in the alloted time. The plaintiff maintained that the Commission measure should then have been referred for approval to the Council. The Court held, however, that the supervisory role of the Council could only come into play if the Commission adopted a measure not in accordance with an opinion of the Management Committee.

1 Bull. E.C. Supp. 2/80.
2 Case 9/56, [1957–1958] E.C.R. 133.
3 Case 25/70, [1970] E.C.R. 1161.
4 Case 1/73, [1973] E.C.R. 723.
5 Case 35/78, [1978] E.C.R. 2543.

The Classification of Committees

4.49 A *Committees which must be consulted during the preparation of Community acts.*
(1) Committees which must be consulted but whose opinions have no binding consequences.

> *Example*: Advisory Committee on Restrictive Practices and Dominant Positions. Council Regulation 17/62, O.J. (Sp. Ed) 1959–1962, p. 81.

(2) Management Committees.

Procedure: The Commission submits draft measures to the committee:

– if the committee delivers a favourable opinion by a qualified majority, or fails to deliver an opinion (no qualified majority either for or against the draft measure), the Commission adopts measures which are immediately applicable;

– if the Committee delivers an unfavourable opinion, the Commission may likewise adopt measures which are immediately forwarded to the Council. The Council, acting by a qualified majority may decide otherwise within 'x' months (usually within 1 month).

> *Example*: Management Committee for Sheep and Goats. Council Regulation 1837/80 (EEC), O.J. L 183, 16.7.1980, p. 1.

(3) Regulatory Committees.

(a) 'Net' procedure: The committees operate in the same way as the management committees in the case of favourable opinions.

Where the committee delivers an unfavourable opinion or fails to deliver any opinion, the Commission submits a proposal to the Council. If the Council fails to reach a decision within a specified time (usually 3 months), the Commission adopts the proposed measures.

> *Example*: Customs Valuation Committee, Council Regulation 1224/ 80 (EEC), O.J. L 134, 31.5.1980, p. 1.

(b) 'Safety-net' procedure: The procedure applicable to the committees listed below is somewhat different: if the Council fails to approve the measures within three months of the date on which they were submitted to it the Commission adopts the proposed measures and brings them immediately into effect, unless the Council has rejected the said measures by a simple majority.

> *Example*: Standing Committee on Plant Health, Council Decision 76/894 (EEC), O.J. L 340, 9.12.76, p. 25.

B *Committees which need not be consulted during the preparation of Community acts.*
(1) Committees consisting of representatives of the Member States.

(a) Committees intended to help the Member States adopt a common position.

> *Example*: Committee of Governors of the Central Banks, Council Decision 71/142 (EEC), O.J. (Sp. Ed.) 1971 (I), p. 176.

(b) Committees intended to ensure close cooperation between the Member States and the Commission.

Example: Advisory Committee on Common Rules for Imports from the People's Republic of China. Council Regulation 1766/82 (EEC), O.J. L 195, 5.7.1982, p. 21.

(c) Committees intended to assist the Commission in its work.

Example: Technical Committee on The Free Movement of Workers, Council Regulation 1612/68 (EEC), O.J. (Sp. Ed.) 1968 (II), p. 475.

(2) Committees consisting of the Member States and trade unions, professional or economic organisations.

(a) Committees intended to ensure close cooperation between the Member States and the Commission.

Example: Standing Committee on Employment. Council Decision 70/532 (EEC), O.J. (Sp. Ed.) 1970 (III), p. 863.

(b) Committees intended to assist the Commission in its work.

Example: Advisory Committee on The Free Movement of Workers, Council Regulation 1612/68 (EEC), O.J. (Sp. Ed.)1968 (II), p. 475.

(3) Committees consisting of representatives of trade, professional or economic interests.

Example: Advisory Committee on Feedingstuffs. Commission Decision 87/76 (EEC), O.J. L 45 14.2.87, p. 19.

Location of the Institutions of the Communities

4.50 Each of the founding Treaties contains a clause on the seat of the institutions. Article 77 of the ECSC Treaty, Article 216 of the EEC Treaty, and Article 189 of the Euratom Treaty are virtually identical in that they provide that the location of the institutions is a matter for determination by common accord of the Member States. Following the establishment of the ECSC the High Authority and the Court of Justice were located in Luxembourg, as was the Secretariat of the Assembly; the plenary sessions of the latter body, however, were held in Strasbourg. When the 1957 Treaties came into force the Councils and Commissions were located in Brussels while the institutions common to the three Communities, the Assembly and the Court, remained in Luxembourg and Strasbourg. The rules currently in force can be traced back to the rationalisation brought about by the Merger Treaty of 1965. Annexed to the Merger Treaty was a decision of the Representatives of the Member States on the 'provisional' location of certain institutions of the Communities. The principal change brought about by the Decision was the removal of the High Authority, now the Commission, to Brussels; the financial departments of the ECSC, however, were to remain in Luxembourg (see Article 7). Article 1 of the Decision preserves the *status quo ante*: Luxembourg, Brussels and Strasbourg remain as the provisional places of work of the institutions. During April, June and October the Council meets in Luxembourg (Article 2). Article 4 states that the General Secretariat of the Assembly shall remain in Luxembourg and Article 5 provides that the European

Investment Bank shall be located in Luxembourg. Luxembourg and Brussels are specified in Article 6 as the meeting places of the Monetary Committee, while Luxembourg is fixed as the location of the Communities' Official Publications Office (Article 8) and other Commission departments such as the Statistical Office and the Data Processing Department (Article 9). Finally, the economic importance to Luxembourg of the location of Community institutions within its frontiers is recognised in Article 10, which indicates the willingness of the Member States to locate other Community bodies and departments in Luxembourg. This undertaking was honoured in 1977 when the Representatives of the Governments of the Member States decided that Luxembourg should be the 'provisional' location of the Court of Auditors.[1]

1 O.J. L 104, 28.4.1977.

4.51 It will be readily appreciated from the foregoing that the question of institutional location has been the subject of compromise, albeit subject to the need to satisfy the Luxembourg authorities. However, the present arrangements are not entirely satisfactory because of the paucity of air links with both Luxembourg and Strasbourg. In addition there is the anomolous position of the Parliament. Its Secretariat is located in Luxembourg, but the plenary sessions of the Parliament take place in Strasbourg. To complicate matters further meetings of its committees take place in Brussels; this makes good sense because the Council and the Commission are located there. However, between 1967 and 1981 the Parliament, although not obliged to do so, held a limited number of its plenary sessions each year in Luxembourg. This practice had been opposed by France, and in 1981 the Parliament decided that henceforth all its part sessions were to be held in Strasbourg. The Resolution to this effect was challenged in *Luxembourg v European Parliament*,[1] but the Court held that it was clear from Article 1 of the Decision on the provisional location of the institutions that the Member States intended that the Assembly should meet in Strasbourg; any decision by the Parliament, adopted of its own motion, to meet also in Luxembourg could not be regarded as creating a supplementary custom which altered the previous legal position. In the absence of a single place of work the Parliament was free to make the appropriate arrangements to carry out its tasks in its various places of work, but it was not free to transfer the General Secretariat from Luxembourg. In a later case, *Luxembourg v European Parliament*,[2] the Court declared void a Resolution of the Parliament which instructed the Bureau of the Parliament and the Secretary General to arrange for the transfer of the staff of the Secretariat from Luxembourg to Brussels or Strasbourg. The Court declared the resolution void, even though the President of the Parliament had stated that the Resolution was subject to the judgment of the Court in the earlier case (case 230/81) and even though no action had been taken to implement the Resolution, on the grounds that the Parliament's decision was in breach of Article 4 of the Decision on the provisional location of the institutions.

1 Case 230/81 [1983] E.C.R. 255, [1983] 2 C.M.L.R. 726
2 Case 108/83 [1984] ECR 1945.

4.52 Finally, apart from the principal institutions of the Communities a number of minor agencies have been established in various Member States. These include the Euratom research centres at Geel in Belgium, Karlsruhe in Germany, Ispra in Italy and Petten in the Netherlands; the Torus project at Culham in the United Kingdom; the European Centre for the Development of Vocational Training at Berlin; the European Foundation for the Improvement of Living and Working Conditions at Loughlinstown in Co. Dublin; and the European University Institute at Florence.

Privileges and Immunities

4.53 Relevant Treaty Provisions:

ECSC Treaty	Article 76 and Protocol
EEC Treaty	Article 218 and Protocol
Euratom Treaty	Article 191 and Protocol
Merger Treaty	Articles 28 and 30 and Protocol
Second Budgetary Treaty	Articles 7, 15 and 23
76/787 [ECSC, EEC, Euratom]	
and Annexed Act	Articles 4 and 5

4.54 Each of the basic Treaties provided that the relevant Community was to enjoy in the territories of the Member States such privileges and immunities as were necessary for the performance of their respective tasks under the conditions laid down in annexed Protocols. Article 28 of the Merger Treaty repealed those treaty provisions and Protocols and replaced them with a similar, uniform system governing the privileges and immunities of the European Communities. In 1975 the Second Budgetary Treaty provided that the provisions of the Protocol which applied to members of the Court of Justice should also apply to the members of the Court of Auditors. In 1976, the direct elections Act provided, in Article 4(2), that the provisions of the Protocol applicable to members of the Assembly (selected by the National Parliaments) should also apply to the directly elected representatives. However, it is clear that the relevant provisions of the Protocol are unsuited to a directly elected Parliament; accordingly, the Commission has proposed an amendment of the Protocol to take account of the changed circumstances.

In its present form the Protocol deals with immunities and exemptions from taxation, and from search and seizure of the Communities' buildings, property, documents and communications. It also deals with the status and rights of Members of the Parliament (Assembly), officials of the Communities, representatives of the Member States participating in Community activities, and the missions of non-Member States accredited to the Communities. However, Article 18 articulates the underlying rationale: privileges and immunities are accorded solely in the interests of the Communities.[1]

1 See also: case 5/68 *Sayag v Leduc* [1968] E.C.R. 395, [1969] C.M.L.R. 12.

4.55 The issue of privileges and immunities has come before the Court of Justice with surprising regularity, and the bulk of the case-law concerns the immunity of officials from domestic taxation. But an initial difficulty turned around the right of Community officials and other claimants to initiate proceedings before the Court of Justice. In *Humblet v Belgium*[1] the plaintiff contested an assessment to income tax made by the Belgian authorities on his wife's income, which was based on the aggregation of the income of both spouses—even though the plaintiff's income was exempt from national tax by virtue of Article 11(b) of the ECSC Protocol. He sought: (i) a declaration that the assessment was precluded by the Protocol; and (ii) the annulment of the contested assessment. The Court held that it was not at liberty to annul administrative measures of the authorities of the Member States. However, by virtue of Article 16 of the ECSC Protocol, which required all disputes concerning the interpretation of the Protocol to be submitted to the Court of Justice, any person prejudiced by the application or non-application of the Protocol could submit an application, even against a Member State, to the Court of Justice. In the event that the measures of the Member State were contrary to Community law the State was under an obligation to rescind the measures and to make any necessary reparations. This obligation arose from the Treaty and the Protocol, and took precedence over national law.

When the Merger Treaty of 8 April 1965 came into force the provisions of Article 16 of the ECSC Protocol, were not re-enacted. Article 28 of the Merger Treaty, repealed Article 76 of the ECSC Treaty, Article 218 of the EEC Treaty, and Article 191 of the Euratom Treaty, as well as the Protocols annexed to the three parent treaties. They were replaced by Articles 28 and 30 of the Merger Treaty and by a new uniform Protocol on the Privileges of the European Communities. Article 30 provides that the provisions of the EEC and Euratom Treaties concerning the jurisdiction of the Court of Justice are to apply to the provisions of the Merger Treaty and the annexed Protocol. In short, the direct action against Member States permitted under the ECSC Protocol was abolished. This point arose obliquely in *Klomp v Inspektie der Belastingen*,[2] where the plaintiff had been required to pay a contribution under the Dutch General Law on Old Age in respect of the year 1959. Klomp, an ECSC official working in Holland, argued that he was exempt from the charge in question by virtue of the Article 11(b) of the ECSC Protocol. In September 1968 the Gerechtshof at The Hague referred a question on its interpretation to the Court of Justice under Article 41 of the ECSC Treaty. The difficulty about an Article 41 reference, however, is that it can be utilised only in respect of questions relating to the validity of acts of the High Authority (Commission) and the Council, and there was no such question before the national court. A wider jurisdiction had been conferred upon the Court by virtue of Article 16 of the ECSC Protocol and this jurisdiction was similar to the jurisdiction exercised by the Court under Article 177 of the EEC Treaty and Article 150 of the Euratom Treaty: the common objective was the uniform interpretation and application of the Protocols in the six Member States. And although Article 16 of the ECSC Protocol was applicable to facts at issue, the Court held that it was permissible, by reference to a general principle common to the laws of the Member States, to ensure continuity of the legal system where no contrary intention was expressed in amending legislation. Accordingly, the Court had jurisdiction to give a ruling on the request for interpretation.

In *D v Luxembourg*[3] the plaintiff sought to rely on the legal continuity doctrine, outlined in the *Klomp* judgment, to support a direct action against the Grand Duchy. The defendant government had refused to grant the plaintiff's wife a residence permit and D., an official of the Communities residing in Luxembourg, brought an action for a declaration that the defendant's action was contrary to Article 12(b) of the Protocol of the European Communities. His argument was that, notwithstanding the repeal of Article 16 of the ECSC Protocol in the absence of a contrary intention expressed by the legislature the Court had jurisdiction to hear direct actions in all matters relating to the Protocol. However, the Court decided that Article 30 of the Merger Treaty made the EEC and Euratom system of remedies applicable to the Merger Treaty and the Protocol. In this system the Court has no jurisdiction to entertain an action by an individual against a Member State. Therefore, the present action was inadmissible.

1 Case 6/60, [1960] E.C.R. 559.
2 Case 23/68, [1969] E.C.R. 43.
3 Case 1/82, [1982] E.C.R. 3709.

4.56 Article 177 of the EEC Treaty and Article 150 of the Euratom Treaty are the most obvious means of redress in disputes concerning the uniform Protocol. However, other means of action are available. In *EC Commission v Belgium*,[1] an action pursuant to Article 169 of the EEC Treaty, the Court held that Belgium was in breach of Article 5 of the Treaty and Article 12(b) of the Protocol by failing to ensure that municipal bye-laws did not impose fiscal obligations on officials of the Communities. Furthermore, given that certain provisions of the Protocol (Articles 7, 15 and 16) empower the Council to adopt implementing measures, actions for annulment under Article 173 of the EEC Treaty or Article 146 of the Euratom Treaty, are also permissible.

1 Case 85/85 [1987] 1 C.M.L.R. 787.

4.57 The first five Articles of the Protocol (Chapter 1) deal with the property, funds, assets and operations of the European Communities. According to Article 1 the premises and buildings of the Communities shall be inviolable, that is, exempt from search, requisition, confiscation or expropriation. Any administrative or legal measure of constraint against the property or assets of the Communities is permissible only with the authorisation of the Court of Justice. In *Ufficio Imposte di Consumo di Ispra v EC Commission*,[1] the Court held that an investigation by representatives of a tax authority of a Member State, in preparation for an assessment to duty, constituted an administrative measure of restraint requiring the authorisation to submit the request direct to the Court. Article 2 of the Protocol declares the archives of the Community inviolable, and Article 3 concerns the liability to tax of the Communities' assets and revenues. There is no exemption from charges imposed by public utilities; indirect taxes should be refunded where possible; and there is an immunity from direct taxation. Article 4 provides an exemption from customs duties and quantitative restrictions on articles intended for official use and Article 5 permits the ECSC to hold currency of any kind. Articles 6 and 7 of the Protocol (Chapter 2) concern communications and *laissez passer*. Official communications and correspondence enjoy diplomatic status and cannot be subject to censorship, and the Council may issue *laissez passer* to members and servants of the institutions, which must then be recognised as valid travel documents by the Member States.

1 Case 2/68 [1968] E.C.R. 435.

4.58 Articles 8, 9 and 10 (Chapter 3) deal with the position of the Members of the Assembly (Parliament). Article 8 requires the Member States to accord to MEPs favourable customs and exchange control treatment. More importantly, no administrative restrictions can be imposed on MEPs travelling to or from meeting places of the Parliament. In *Lord Bruce of Donington v Aspden*,[1] an MEP (pre-direct elections) was taxed on his subsistence and travel allowances and he argued that this constituted an administrative restriction on his right to travel to and from parliamentary meetings. The Court of Justice, at the request of the Commissioners for the special purposes of the Income Tax Acts, held that while at present there was no rule preventing the Member States from taxing emoluments of Members of the Parliament, EEC Treaty, art. 5 required the Member States to refrain from taking measures likely to interfere with the internal functioning of the European Parliament. The payment of travel expenses constituted a matter of internal organisation of the Parliament and accordingly Member States could only tax such expenses if in reality they constituted disguised remuneration.

Article 9 grants MEPs immunity from legal proceedings or detention in respect of opinions expressed or votes cast by them in the performance of their duties. However, it is Article 10 which has generated the most discussion. In their own Member States MEPs enjoy the immunity accorded to members of the domestic Parliament, and enjoy immunity from detention and legal proceedings in the territory of other Member States. The immunity also applies when Members are in transit to the Parliament but does not apply to offences where the Members are caught *flagrante delictu*. Moreover, the Parliament is entitled to waive the immunity of any of its members. But the immunity provided by Article 10 applies only during 'the sessions of the Assembly'. The interpretation of this phrase has given rise to two rulings by the Court of Justice. In *Wagner v Fohrmann and Krier*,[2] the defendants relied on Article 9 of the three separate Protocols in defamation proceedings in a Luxembourg Court. However, the ECSC Treaty provided for a different annual session from the EEC and Euratom Treaties, and the plaintiff had issued proceedings on a date on which the Assembly provided for in the ECSC Treaty was clearly not in session. The Court of Justice held that these conflicting provisions had to be reconciled, and that the Assembly had to be considered as being in session, even if it was not in fact sitting, until the moment of closure of the annual or extraordinary sessions. This ruling was confirmed recently, in respect of Article 10 of the uniform Protocol, in *Wybot v Faure*,[3] which also involved defamation proceedings in a domestic court. In practice, the sessions of the Parliament extend for a whole year in duration because the formal closure of a session occurs the day before the opening of the new session.

1 Case 208/80 [1981] E.C.R. 2205, [1981] 3 C.M.L.R. 506.
2 Case 101/63 [1964] E.C.R. 195, [1964] C.M.L.R. 245.
3 Case 149/85 [1987] 1 C.M.L.R. 819.

4.59 The uniform Protocol came into force in 1967 but since then there have been significant developments, the most important of which was the direct election of representatives. This has given rise to difficulties, particularly in respect of waivers of immunity. Article 4 of the Direct Elections Act provides that Chapter 3 of the uniform Protocol applies to directly elected Members of the European Parliament, and Article 5 permits Members to hold a dual mandate. Under the present system a minority of MEPs exercise a dual mandate whereas before 1979 all MEPs did so, and applications for waiver of immunity were directed firstly to their national Parliament; only one application for waiver of immunity was lodged with the European Parliament prior to 1979 and this was in respect of *Fohrmann and Krier* (*supra* at 4.58). In respect of post-1979 dual mandate MEPs the European Parliament waits for the decision of the national Parliament before considering requests for waiver of immunity.[1] As regards single mandate MEPs, in the first legislature (July 1979–June 1984) there were eight requests for waivers of which one was granted, and, in the second legislature (July 1984–) approximately 30 requests were received by December 1986 and of the 15 which had been examined at that point in time three were granted.[2]

However, given that most MEPs do not enjoy a dual mandate, Article 10 is now in need of amendment insofar as it stipulates that the immunity accorded to MEPs in the territory of their own States is equivalent to that accorded to domestic parliamentarians. Accordingly, the Commission has proposed an amendment of Article 10 so that the immunity of MEPs will not differ from Member State to Member State. The Commission's proposal, which requires approval in accordance with the Treaty amendment procedure under EEC Treaty, art. 236, also involves changes to Articles 8 and 9 of the Protocol, and has been discussed in the Donnez report[3] drawn up for the Committee on Legal Affairs and Citizens Rights of the European Parliament.

Insofar as Irish MEPs, whether or not they hold a dual mandate, enjoy the same privileges and immunities as national parliamentarians while in Ireland, three particular privileges can be isolated and all three are based on Article 15 of the Constitution: (i) by virtue of Article 15.10 each House of the Oireachtas has the power to ensure freedom of debate, to protect the documents of itself and its members, and to protect itself from any interference with itself or its members. It is not clear how the Dail or Seanad can enforce this power.[4] (ii) According to Article 15.12 the official publications of the Oireachtas and utterances made in either House, wherever published, shall be privileged, and the second part of Article

15.13 provides that members of the Oireachtas shall not be amenable to any court or authority other than the House in question in respect of utterances made in either House. It does seem clear, however, that members can be called upon to explain their actions before tribunals established under the Tribunals of Inquiry (Evidence) Act, 1921 on the grounds that:

'A tribunal set up under the Act to make an inquiry, so far from representing an intrusion into the affairs of Parliament, is the instrument chosen by Parliament itself to make the inquiry.'[5]

(iii) Article 15.13 guarantees members of the Oireachtas freedom from arrest in going to and returning from, and while in the precincts of either House. However, treason, felonies and breaches of the peace are excluded—giving parliamentarians freedom from arrest only in respect of misdemeanours.

It will be observed that these privileges and immunities are quite similar to those listed in the Protocol. However, given the practice of the European Parliament to await the decision of a national parliament on a request for waiver of immunity, a problem might arise in the future because the Irish Constitution is silent on the question of waiver of immunities and privileges. Likewise, the Standing Orders of the Houses do not refer to this possibility.[6]

1 European Parliament, Working Documents, PE 868/fin.
2 Information supplied by European Parliament Office, Dublin. For an illustration of the operation of the waiver procedure, see: The Report drawn up on behalf of the Committee on Legal Affairs and Citizens Rights on the request for the waiver of Mr Lionel Jospin's parliamentary immunity, Working Documents PE 103, 686/fin.
3 *Idem.*
4 David Gwynn Morgan, *Constitutional Law of Ireland*, at p. 164.
5 Report of the Tribunal appointed by The Taoiseach on the 4th day of July, 1975; Prl. 4745.
6 See: Dail Eireann, Standing Orders, 1986, Standing Order 77; Seanad Eirann, Standing Orders 1979, Standing Order 69.

4.60 Articles 11 and 17 of the Protocol extend the usual privileges, immunities and facilities to the representatives and officials of the Member States taking part in Community connected work, and to the Missions of non-Member States accredited to the Communities.

4.61 Articles 12–16 of the Protocol deal with the officials and other servants of the Communities. Article 12(a) provides that officials and other servants enjoy in the territory of the Member States immunity from legal proceedings in respect of acts performed by them in their official capacity. In *Sayag v Leduc*[1] the Court held that the object of the immunity was to protect the official activities of the Community and its servants from scrutiny based on domestic law criteria, thus permitting the Community to accomplish its task in complete independence. However, the Court also ruled that driving a motor vehicle can only exceptionally be considered to be an act performed in an official capacity. The ruling was given in connection with criminal proceedings against a Euratom official for dangerous driving.

Article 12(b) of the Protocol provides that officials and their families shall not be subject to immigration restrictions. This was the basis for the claim in *D v Luxembourg*[2] but, as we have already noted, the court declared the application inadmissible because direct actions against Member States had been abolished under the uniform Protocol. The remaining sub-paragraphs of Article 12 accord favourable exchange control treatment to officials, as well as duty-free facilities in respect of their furniture and personal effects and in respect of a motor car.

Article 13 subjects Community officials to a Community tax on their salaries. More importantly, salaries or wages paid by the Communities are immune from national taxes. The rationale for this exemption was given by the Court in *van Nidek v Inspecteur der Registratie en Successie*:[3] the object is to ensure uniform treatment of wages or salaries for all Community servants so that their respective remuneration does not differ according to their nationality, and to prevent inordinate double taxation. In *EC Commission v Belgium*[4] the Court made it clear that the immunity from domestic taxation applies equally to taxes imposed by local and by central authorities. The immunity provided by Article 11(b) of the ECSC Protocol (identical to Article 13 (second sentence) of the uniform Protocol) prohibited Community remuneration from being taken into account for the purpose of calculating tax on other income. Likewise, such remuneration cannot be considered in assessing taxation on the spouse of an official: *Humblet v Belgium*.[5] However, the immunity only applies to taxation similar to that imposed by the Communities on its servants and officials, that is, periodic taxes on incomes which are intended to provide for the general expenses of public authorities. The immunity does not apply to charges or dues amounting to payment for a given service rendered by a public authority: *van Leeuwen v City of Rotterdam*.[6] Nor does it apply to contributions to social security schemes, even if the contributions are raised in a manner similar to the levying of taxes: *Klomp v Inspektie der Belastingen*.[7] Finally, death duties—which are levied only once on an estate—are not periodic taxes on income to which the immunity applies: *van Nidek v Inspekteur der Registratie en Successie*.[8]

Article 14 of the Protocol provides for the retention of domicile by servants and officials of the Communities when stationed in another Member State, and Article 15 empowered the Council to establish a scheme of social security benefits for officials and servants.

1 Case 5/68 [1968] E.C.R. 395.
2 Case 1/82 [1982] E.C.R. 3709.
3 Case 7/74 [1974] E.C.R. 757, [1975] 1 C.M.L.R. 192.
4 Case 85/85 [1987] 1 C.M.L.R. 787.
5 Case 6/60 [1960] E.C.R. 559.
6 Case 32/67 [1968] E.C.R. 43.
7 Case 23/68 [1969] E.C.R. 43.
8 Case 7/74 [1974] E.C.R. 757.

4.62 In the General Provisions of the Protocol the immunities enjoyed by servants and Officials are extended to the members of the Commission (Article 20), to the Judges, Advocates-General and Registrar of the Court of Justice (Article 21), and to the European Investment Bank, its members and its staff (Article 22). Similarly, the second Budgetary Treaty (Articles 7, 15 and 23) extended the same immunities to the Members of the Court of Auditors. Furthermore, if the Commission's proposal for amendment of the Protocol (*supra* at 4.59) is adopted by the Member States, certain of these immunities (Article 12(b), (c), (d), and (e)) will apply to MEPs taking up residence in one of the places of work of the Parliament.[1] At present MEPs are paid by the authorities of the Member States, and their income is equivalent to that of national deputies or representatives; they are subject to the same tax regime as national representatives and do not benefit from a Community immunity. In Ireland, section 2 of the European Assembly (Irish Representatives) Act, 1979 provides that Irish MEPs are to be paid the same allowance as members of the Dail. An Irish MEP, therefore, would have received £18,887 per annum as of 1 January, 1987.[2]

1 Commission Document COM (84) 666 final.
2 Information supplied by the European Parliament Office, Dublin.

4.63 The Community scheme of privileges and immunities affects Ireland in a number of ways. First, apart from Irish members of the institutions there are hundreds of Irish employees in the service of the Communities at locations in various Member States. Secondly, both the Commission and the European Parliament have offices in Dublin staffed by Community officials. Finally, the European Foundation for the Improvement of Living and Working Conditions is located at Loughlinstown, Co. Dublin. Council Regulation 1365/75 (EEC),[1] which established the Foundation, provides in art. 20 that the Protocol on the privileges and immunities of the European Communities shall apply to the Foundation.

1 O.J. L 139, 30.5.1975, p. 1.

Chapter 5

The Competence and Powers of the Communities

5.1

> 'The conclusion to be drawn from this is that the Community constitutes a new legal order of international law for the benefit of which *the states have limited their sovereign rights, albeit within limited fields*, and the subjects of which comprise not only the Member States but also their nationals.'[1] (Emphasis added.)

This extract from the judgment of the Court of Justice in the *Van Gend en Loos* case is well known; it forms part of the reasoning of the Court in its reply to a question posed by a Dutch tax tribunal as to whether Article 12 of the Treaty had direct application in national law. To arrive at a positive conclusion the court had to look first at the spirit, general scheme and wording of the provisions of the treaty. Thus, the Preamble of the treaty made it clear that the present arrangement was more than a mere exchange of obligations between States, because it referred not only to governments but also to peoples. This was also confirmed by '. . . the establishment of *institutions endowed with sovereign rights*, the exercise of which affects Member States and also their citizens.' (Emphasis added.)

The fact that the establishment of the Community involved the transfer of sovereignty from the original Member States was never in doubt; likewise it was never doubted that Ireland's accession to the European Communities would necessitate a diminution of the state's sovereignty and a limitation of the exclusive right of the Oireachtas, the Government and the Courts to exercise that sovereignty within their respective spheres of responsibility. The Third Amendment of the Constitution was proposed, and adopted, to facilitate a limited transfer of competence.

But what competence, sovereignty or powers have been transferred to the Community and what are the limits, if any, of that transfer?

1 Case 26/62 *Van Gend en Loos v Nederlandse Belastingadministratie* [1963] E.C.R. 1, [1963] C.M.L.R. 105.

5.2 At the outset it should be noted that there is no provision in the EEC Treaty which specifically demarcates all the sovereignty or competence transferred by the States to the Community. The objectives of the Community are stated in very general terms in Article 2 of the Treaty: a harmonious development of economic activities, a continuous and balanced expansion, an increase in stability, an accelerated raising of the standard of living and closer relations between the States belonging to it. These objectives must be achieved by the establishment of a common market and by the progressive approximation of the economic policies of Member States. A clearer view of the extent of the transfer of power can be gleaned from Article 3 of the Treaty, which specifies 11 particular tasks for the Community: the elimination of customs duties and quantitative restrictions; the establishment of a common custom tariff and a common commercial policy; the abolition of obstacles to the free movement of persons, services and capital; the adoption of common policies in the spheres of agriculture and transport; the institution of a competition policy; the creation of short term and medium term economic policy instruments; the approximation of laws of the Member States to the extent required for the proper functioning of the common market; the creation of a European Social Fund; the establishment of a European Investment Bank; and the association of the overseas countries and territories to increase trade and to promote social development.

However, this list is not conclusive concerning the powers of the Community and its institutions because it fails to refer to the tax provisions of the Treaty (art.s 95 to 99). Likewise, although Article 3 refers to the creation of a Social Fund it makes no reference to the principle that men and women should receive equal pay for equal work (art. 119). In other words, an outline of the competence of the Community is given in Articles 2 and 3 of the Treaty but the precise extent of that competence is to be found in specific provisions in the various chapters, titles and parts of the Treaty, and the means by which such competence is to be exercised by the Community's institutions is likewise clearly delineated. For example, Article 87 of the Treaty empowers the Council, acting on proposal from the Commission and after consulting the Assembly, to give effect to the principles set out in Articles 85 and 86 of the Treaty by making Regulations or by issuing Directives. The second paragraph of Article 87 then lists five specific objectives to be addressed by the Council when exercising its powers. It is possible to conclude, therefore, that the Community's powers extend only to what has been expressly conferred by the treaty (in French: *competence d'attribution*). Similarly, the institutions of the Community are subject to an operational limitation of their competence: Article 4(1) of the Treaty provides that each institution shall act within the limits of the powers conferred upon it by the treaty. In the event that Council or Commission exceed the limits of powers conferred on them—or on the Community—the Court of Justice can review the legality of any act, purportedly exercising competence, in an action for annulment under Article 173 of the Treaty.

A further notable feature of the competence of the Community, as conferred by specific provisions of the treaty, is that the conditions for the exercise of power by the institutions vary from sector to sector; in certain chapters of the treaty the details have already been elaborated to a great extent and the Member States are subject to mandatory prohibitions to ensure compliance with the treaty requirements. The need for Community intervention is limited. This is the case with the provisions on the free movement of goods, persons, services and capital, as well as the provisions of tax and, to a lesser extent, the competition rules. These measures are all aimed at the removal of barriers of one sort or another and a simple treaty prohibition usually secures that objective. If there remain any justifiable national restrictions based, for example, on grounds of public security or public health, they can be harmonised according to a common standard. The Directive is the appropriate legislative instrument in this context. But in respect of common policies the treaty provides merely a framework and it is left up to the institutions to formulate the precise rules. This is the case with the Common Agricultural Policy, the Common Transport Policy and the Common Commercial Policy. In view of the wide discretion vested in the institutions, the Regulation, the main normative instrument under Article 189, is widely utilised in these areas.

The greater part of the work needed to remove the restrictions on the free movement of goods, persons and services was carried out by the Community institutions before the expiry of the transitional period for the original six Member States. Likewise, the rules on competition and tax were fully operative and the framework of the Common Agricultural Policy and the Common Commercial Policy were also in position. By contrast, there has been virtually no progress in the coordination of economic policy, and movement towards economic and monetary union has been imperceptible. The explanation for this lies in the fact that the Treaty gives to the Community no more than a power of coordination in matters of economic policy, and decisive power is left in the hands of the Member States (rather than the Council). There are few mandatory requirements and there are no time limits by which power must be exercised. The language of the Treaty is also quite different in respect of economic policy. For example, Article 103(1) says: 'Member States shall regard their conjunctural policies as a matter of common concern.' Article 105(1) reads as follows: 'In order to facilitate attainment of the objectives set out in Article 104, Member States shall coordinate their economic policies. They shall for this purpose provide for cooperation between their appropriate administrative departments and between their central banks.' This is not coercive language. In a similar vein, the Community's goals in respect of Social Policy (Articles 117 to 122) depend to a large extent on cooperation by the Member States.

Progress in these important policy areas depended, therefore, on the goodwill of the Member States, and as one observer noted:

'No new programmes, memoranda, proposals, compromises or speeches were able to conceal the weakness of Community authority which—contrary to the position during the first phase—was unable to fall back on the support of solid Treaty provisions'.[1]

This vacuum in the Community's capacity to act could be filled in a number of ways, and in due course two particular developments began to emerge. One sprang from the case-law of the Court of Justice and the other had its basis in the Treaty.

---

1 Vogelaar, *The Approximation of the Laws of the Member States under the Treaty of Rome*, 12 C.M.L. Rev. (1975) 211.

The implied powers doctrine

5.3 This doctrine first made its appearance in the *Fedechar* case,[1] which was decided by the Court of Justice in November 1956 in the context of the Implementing Convention annexed to the ECSC Treaty. The purpose of this Convention was to set up the institutions of the Community, to provide the measures required to establish the Common Market and to enable production of coal and steel to be adapted to new conditions, while helping to eliminate disequilibria arising out of the existing market conditions. Articles 24 to 28 laid down special safeguard provisions for the coal industry, including an equalisation levy designed to mitigate harmful shifts in price or production levels. This levy could be used, as far as Belgium was concerned, to ensure *inter alia* that all consumers of Belgian coal could be charged prices more in line with the ruling Common Market prices (Article 26(2)). In 1953 the High Authority began to administer a system of aid for Belgian collieries and it published a succession of price lists, applicable to those collieries, so as to calculate the rate of equalisation payments applicable in each case. The plaintiff federation sought the annulment of Decision 22/55 of the High Authority in which such prices were fixed, and more to the point, lowered, on grounds of lack of competence; in its view Article 26(2) of the Convention did not empower the High Authority to *fix* prices—that was a function reserved to the purchasers. The Court dismissed the arguments of the plaintiffs. The equalisation system implied the need to lower Belgian coal prices during the transitional period, although Article 26 provided no indication of how prices were to be reduced. In these circumstances the Court held:

'. . . that without having recourse to a wide interpretation it is possible to apply a rule of interpretation generally accepted in both international and national law, according to which the rules laid down by an international treaty or a law presuppose the rules without which the treaty or law would have no meaning or could not be reasonably and usefully applied'.

The Court added that the High Authority was under an obligation, by virtue of Article 8 of the Treaty, to adopt the measures necessary for the attainment of the objectives of the Treaty. In this case it was necessary to achieve the objective of Article 26 of the Convention and the High Authority had the power, if not the duty, to reduce Belgian coal prices. It should be noted that the Court was careful not to lay down a wide and imprecise rule as to when power could be implied; in subsequent cases the Court rejected claims by the High Authority that it enjoyed implied power to act.[2]

By contrast, the Court's elaboration of the implied powers doctrine in the context of the EEC Treaty has been more dynamic and far reaching, particularly in connection with the Community's competence to conclude international agreements. The *locus classicus* of this approach is the *ERTA* case, *EC Commission v EC Council*.[3] The factual background to this dispute commenced in 1962 with the conclusion, by five of the six Member States, of the European Road Transport Agreement which was concerned with the working conditions of crews of international transport vehicles and was negotiated within the framework of the United Nations' Economic Commission for Europe, located at Geneva. The agreement failed to enter into force because of an insufficient number of ratifications, but steps were taken to resuscitate it in 1967. Meanwhile, the Community was working towards similar objectives and on 25 March 1969 Council Regulation 543/69 (EEC),[4] on the standardisation of driving and rest periods for drivers of road transport vehicles, entered into force. At its meeting of 20 March 1969 the Council discussed the approach to be taken by the EEC Member States at the forthcoming Geneva negotiations on the conclusion of a new European Agreement, and the subsequent negotiations were conducted in accordance with the Council's conclusions of 20 March 1969. On 19 May 1969 the Commission sought the annulment of the Council proceedings. Its main argument was that the negotiation of the *ERTA*, involving a matter arising out of the common transport policy, especially since Regulation 543/69 came into force, could only be carried out by the Community. The Council responded by arguing that the Community only had authority to enter into international agreements where the Treaty expressly conferred power to this effect, as in Articles 113 and 238. Article 75, which in the Commission's view formed the basis for the Community's power to conclude agreements and applied to external relations as well as to domestic transport measures, could not be interpreted as authorising the conclusion of international agreements because, the Council maintained, it related only to measures internal to the Community. At this point it should be noted that, according to Article 74 of the Treaty, the Community's objectives in transport matters were to be pursued within the framework of a common policy, and with this in view Article 75 directed the Council to adopt common rules 'and other appropriate provisions'; these common rules were to be applied to various matters including: . . . 'international transport to or from the territory of a Member State or passing across the territory of one or more such Member States'.

The Court of Justice held for the Council on the merits of the case but decided the matters of principle in favour of the Commission. The fact that Articles 74 and 75 did not expressly authorise the Community to conclude international agreements was not decisive.

'To determine in a particular case the Community's authority to enter into international agreements, regard must be had to the whole scheme of the Treaty no less than to its substantive provisions.

Such authority arises not only from an express conferment by the Treaty—as is the case with Articles 113 and 114 for tariff and trade agreements and with Article 238 for association agreements—but may equally flow from other provisions of the Treaty and from measures adopted, within the framework of those provisions, by the Community institutions.

In particular, each time the Community, with a view to implementing a common policy envisaged by the Treaty, adopts provisions laying down common rules, whatever form these may take, the Member States no longer have the right, acting individually or even collectively, to undertake obligations with third countries which affect those rules.'

From the foregoing it should be clear that according to the Court the Community is *exclusively* competent to conclude international agreements not just where the Treaty expressly conferred such power on the Community; an *implied* power, likewise exclusive in nature, enables the Community to act whenever Treaty provisions or measures taken in implementation thereof require the establishment of relationships with non-Member States. In other words—*in foro interno, in foro externo.*

This radical extension of Community competence was confirmed by the Court in a series of cases in the 1970s, and particularly in opinions given by the Court under Article 228 of the Treaty. This Article lays down the procedure to be followed whenever an international agreement is being concluded by the Community, but the second sentence of paragraph (1) allows the Council, the Commission or the Member States to obtain an opinion from the Court, before the agreement in question enters into force, as to whether the agreement is compatible with the Treaty. If the Court gives a negative opinion the agreement can only enter into force if the Treaty-amending provisions of Article 236 are complied with. This procedure can be compared with the consultative jurisdiction of the Supreme Court under Article 26 of the Constitution.

The parallelism between internal and external competence, first noted in the *ERTA* case, was confirmed in the first opinion given by the Court pursuant to Article 228.[5] The Court was asked by the Commission whether the draft 'Understanding on a Local Cost Standard', being drawn up within the OECD, was compatible with the Treaty, and, if so, did the Community have the exclusive power to conclude the understanding. The Court noted that Article 112 of the Treaty required the Member States to harmonise systems whereby aid was granted for exports to non-Member States, so as to ensure that competition between undertakings of the Community would not be distorted. Thus, the Community already had an internal competence and, in any event, systems of aid for exports necessarily fell within the field of the common commercial policy. In the course of the implementation of measures *necessary* to achieve the principles laid down in Articles 112 and 113 the Community was empowered not only to adopt internal measures but also to conclude agreements with non-Member States pursuant to Articles 113 and 114. The Community's power was necessarily exclusive because any other possibility would risk compromising the effective defence of the common interests of the Community. It was irrelevant, according to the Court, that the obligations and financial burdens inherent in the execution of the agreement would be borne directly by the Member States.

In the case of *Officier van Justitie v Kramer*[6] the Court held that Community law envisaged the transfer of competence in the matter of the protection and conservation of fisheries stocks. This was clear from Article 38 of the Treaty, from secondary legislation—including Council Regulations 2141 and 2142/70,[7] and from Article 102 of the Act of Accession. From this internal competence could be implied the power to conclude international agreements for the conservation of the biological resources of the sea.

The next major development in the implied powers doctrine was Opinion 1/76,[8] which was given by the Court in response to a Commission request as to the compatibility with the Treaty of the draft Agreement establishing a European laying-up fund for inland waterway vessels. The agreement envisaged the establishment of a system to finance the withdrawal of excess carrying capacity on the Rhine–Moselle waterway complex, and was to be concluded by the Community, seven of its Member States and Switzerland. The Court found that the draft agreement was incompatible with the Treaty because, *inter alia*, the Fund Tribunal would have drawn some of its members from the Court of Justice thus compromising the Court's independence in the present institutional structure. But the Court also commented on the Community's exclusive competence to conclude such an agreement. It might be noted, parenthetically, that in earlier cases the Court had pointed to an internal/external parallelism—namely that an internal competence based on Treaty articles and implementing measures could give rise to the power to conclude international agreements. In the present case the Court confirmed this point but went considerably further. It held that implied power to act internationally arose whenever an internal power to act had been used to adopt measures aimed at attaining the objectives of the policy in question, but it was not limited to that eventuality. Even though an internal Community measure would be adopted in this case, *after* the conclusion of the international agreement, the implied power nevertheless flowed from the Treaty provision creating the internal power and from the necessity of participation in an internal agreement in order to achieve one of the objectives of the Community.[9]

The implied powers doctrine was further refined in Opinion 1/78,[10] which was requested by the Commission in order to determine whether the draft International Agreement on Natural Rubber, being drawn up under the auspices of the United Nations Conference on Trade and Development, was compatible with the EEC Treaty and whether the Community was competent to conclude that Agreement. The object of the Agreement was to stabilise trade conditions for natural rubber, to improve the real income of developing countries by increasing export earnings, and to improve competitiveness and marketing conditions. At the core of the proposed Agreement was the creation of a buffer stock of natural rubber which was designed to control the market place by buying in surplus production when prices were low and selling off stocks when prices were rising. The buffer stock was to be financed by the members of the International Rubber Council operating through a Common Fund. During the preparatory stages and the initial negotiations concerning the Agreement a dispute occurred between the Commission, which argued that the Community was exclusively competent to negotiate and conclude the Agreement, and the delegations of the Member States within the framework of the Council, who argued that the negotiations should be viewed in a much wider context. When the matter was referred to the Court for its opinion the Council elaborated on its contention that the agreement should be concluded both by the Community and by the Member States because the proposed Agreement contained provisions which went beyond the scope of the common commercial policy. In particular, account had to be taken of general political considerations and economic policy factors. These are matters which fall to be coordinated by the Member States and not the Community. Joint participation of the Community and the Member States was justified all the more because the

Treaty did not permit the Community to commit the Member States financially in the case of international financial obligations. As regards the Council's argument that the agreement involved considerations of economic policy, and to that extent fell within the competence of the Member States, the Court held that just because international cooperation in the economic field comes, at least in part, under the common commercial policy does not justify the conclusion that such international cooperation could be withdrawn, under the name of general economic policy, from the competence of the Community. However, the Court did rule that the power of the Community to negotiate and conclude agreements might depend on the system of financing. If the financial burdens fall upon the Community budget, the powers will belong to the Community; if the burdens are charged directly to the budgets of the Member States, their participation together with the Community will be necessary. This ruling represents a significant modification of the view, expressed by the Court in Opinion 1/75, that the financial arrangements in international agreements were irrelevant as far as the Community's exclusive competence was concerned.[11]

Thus far, consideration of the Community's implied external competence has arisen mainly in the context of the common commercial policy and the common transport policy. However the *Kramer* case and subsequent fisheries disputes[12] have demonstrated that the Community's internal competence in the field of fisheries conservation is the basis of an implied external competence, and it has also been pointed out that the Community's internal competence as regards harmonisation of law can give rise to a parallel external competence. This is particularly the case with respect to Directives in the environmental protection sector and certain Council Decisions in the field of company law.[13]

1 Case 8/55 *Fédération Charbonnière de Belgique v High Authority* [1954–56] E.C.R. 245.
2 See Case 25/59 *Netherlands v High Authority* [1960] E.C.R. 355.
3 Case 22/70 [1971] E.C.R. 263, [1971] C.M.L.R. 335.
4 O.J. (Sp. Ed.) 1969 (I) p. 170, replaced in part by Council Regulation 3820/85 (EEC) O.J. L 370 31.12.85 p. 1.
5 Opinion 1/75 [1975] E.C.R. 1355.
6 Joined cases 3, 4, 6/76, [1976] E.C.R. 1279, [1976] 2 C.M.L.R. 440.
7 O.J. (Sp. Ed.) 1970 (III) pp. 703, 707, replaced by Council Regulations 101/76 and 3796/81 respectively.
8 Opinion 1/76 [1977] E.C.R. 741, [1977] 2 C.M.L.R. 278.
9 For a discussion of this condition of 'necessity' see A. Barav, 'The Division of external relations power between the European Economic Community and the Member States in the case-law of the Court of Justice' in C.W.A. Timmermans and E.L.M. Volker (eds), *Division of Powers between the European Communities and their Member States in the field of External Relations*, 1981.
10 Opinion 1/78, [1979] E.C.R. 2871, [1979] 3 C.M.L.R. 639.
11 See also Ruling 1/78 [1978] E.C.R. 2151, [1979] 1 C.M.L.R. 131.
12 Case 61/77 *EC Commission v Ireland* [1978] E.C.R. 417, [1978] C.M.L.R. 466. Case 32/79 *EC Commission v United Kingdom* [1980] E.C.R. 2403, [1981] 1 C.M.L.R. 219.
13 See: C.W.A. Timmermans, *Division of External powers between the Community and the Member States in the field of harmonization of Law*; *loc. cit.*, fn. 9. *supra*.

5.4 Apart from the implied powers doctrine the other notable development concerning the distribution of legislative competence between the Community and the Member States has been the increased utilisation of

Article 235 of the Treaty. This measure, which has cognate provisions in ECSC Treaty, art. 95 and Euratom Treaty, art. 203, reads as follows:

'If action by the Community should prove necessary to attain, in the course of the operation of the common market, one of the objectives of the Community and this Treaty has not provided the necessary powers, the Council shall, acting unanimously on a proposal from the Commission and after consulting the Assembly, take the appropriate measures.'

This additional or residual power given to the Community by Article 235 was not heavily utilised during the first decade and a half of the Community's existence. Up to the end of 1972 Article 235 had been used on only 35 occasions.[1] This can be explained by reference to the preoccupation of the Community's institutions with the establishment and consolidation of the common market during the transitional period from 1958 to 1969, a task for which clearly defined powers had been provided by the Treaty. But as soon as the framework for the operation of the common market was in place, attention began to focus on problems having wider economic and political considerations, in respect of which the Community's institutions possessed less concrete decision-making powers. With a view to overcoming this impasse the Summit meeting of October 1972, attended by the Heads of State or Government of the original six Member States and the three new Member States, adopted an ambitious programme for the completion of economic and monetary union and for the creation of a European Union before the end of 1980. With the benefit of hindsight, the declaration issued by the Summit meeting[2] seems remarkably optimistic, particularly in view of the oil crisis and subsequent world economic recession that followed the 'Yom Kippur' war in the Middle East in 1973. However, the Summit authorised the Community's institutions to proceed with the elaboration and implementation of proposals concerning:

(1) the establishment of a European Monetary Co-operation Fund:
(2) the adoption of a Regional Policy and a Regional Development Fund;
(3) the drafting of an action programme on Social Policy;
(4) the introduction of a consumer protection policy;
(5) the drafting of an action programme on industrial, scientific and technological policy;
(6) the establishment of an action programme on environmental policy;
(7) the formulation of an energy policy.

The Summit also approved of initiatives to improve political cooperation and foreign policy harmonisation, as well as proposals to streamline the operation of the Community's institutions. In its penultimate paragraph the summit declaration stated:

'. . . that, for the purpose in particular of carrying out the tasks laid down in the different programmes of action, it was desirable to make the widest possible use of all the dispositions of the Treaties, including Article 235 (EEC) in future'.

74

The wide use to which Article 235 has been put since 1972 is noted below but roughly contemporaneously with the initiatives approved at the Paris Summit was the decision by the Commission to discourage use by the Member States of inter-governmental agreements.[3] These are known as Acts of the Representatives of the Member States taken within the framework of the Council of the European Communities,[4] and have been utilised where the treaties require the Member States to act 'by common accord' without specifying the procedure to be followed or the form of act to be utilised. Examples can be seen in ECSC Treaty, art. 69 and EEC Treaty, art.s 18, 20, 135, 167, 216, 220 and 224. With the exception of Article 220, which has been used as the legal basis for Conventions on the mutual recognition of companies[5] and on the mutual recognition and enforcement of judgments of courts and tribunals in civil and commercial matters,[6] the tendency in the last decade has been to replace 'para-Community' agreements with action based on Articles 100 and 235.[7]

1 I. Schwarz, *Article 235 and Law-making powers in the European Communities*, 27 I.C.L.Q. 614.
2 Sixth General Report on the Activities of the Communities p. 7.
3 *Idem*, p. 614.
4 See G. Bebr, *Acts of the Representatives of the Governments of the Member States Meeting taken within the Council of the European Communities*, [1966] S.E.W. 529.
5 Bull. E.C. Supp. 2/69.
6 O.J. L 304, 30.10.78 p. 1, at p. 36.
7 I. Schwarz, *supra* fn. 1 at p. 614.

5.5 Four conditions must be fulfilled in order to justify the adoption of measures on the basis of Article 235.

(a) *'The attainment of a community objective.'*

It has already been noted above that the objectives of the Community, as outlined in Article 2 of the Treaty, are defined in wide and general terms. Consequently, it is rarely difficult to justify a new initiative. But if the programme adopted by the 1972 Paris Summit is analysed closely it will be seen that most—if not all—of the items listed there can be classified as objectives of the Community in terms of Article 2, but can also be justified by reference to other provisions of the treaty.

For example, Article 39(2)(a), on the implementation of the Common Agricultural Policy, requires account to be taken of natural disparities between various agricultural regions, and Article 92(3)(a) provides that state aids may be compatible with the common market where they are designed to promote economic development in backward regions. Hence, regional policy is a Community concern. Likewise, the protection of consumer interests is mentioned in Articles 39, 85 and 86.

(b) The necessity to attain a Community objective *'in the course of the operation of the common market.'* At first sight this condition would appear to place a very real restriction on the scope of Article 235. It would appear to restrict the use of additional powers to those parts of the Treaty concerned with the establishment of the common market: no reliance could be placed on Article 235 in respect of the coordination of economic policy. However it has been demonstrated that a narrow, mercantilist

interpretation of the phrase 'common market' is not justified by the
contexts in the Treaty in which the phrase occurs:

> 'An examination of these provisions leads to the conclusion that the concept is
> not always used in exactly the same way, but is intended to have a sense (perhaps
> even an indicative rather than normative sense in certain cases), embracing not
> only the structures and principles of the Treaty, but also the activities which take
> place within a normative framework provided by the Treaty or measures
> adopted thereunder.'[1]

(c) *'The necessity to attain that objective by Community action'*.

This condition has been described as leaving a wide margin of discretion
to the Council to determine whether action is necessary.[2] As noted above,
'common Action' by the Member States is discouraged; besides, action
under Article 235 reinforces the institutional framework of the Community
and ensures judicial control of the measures in question by the Court of
Justice. In *EC Commission v Italy*,[3] the defendant argued that the Council
Decision of 1966, based on Article 235, which accelerated the implementation of the customs union, was the result of 'negotiations during which the
contracting parties retained the independence which they enjoyed by
virtue of their sovereignty'. The Decision was therefore a type of
international agreement and the reservations expressed by the Italian
delegation at the time of its negotiation had to be interpreted as a refusal to
accept the Decision as far as Italian lead and zinc products were concerned.
The Court held that

> '. . . a measure which is in the nature of a Community decision on the basis of its
> objective and of the institutional framework within which it has been drawn up
> cannot be described as an international agreement.'

Consequently, the Italian 'reservations' were irrelevant.

(d) *'The absence of the necessary powers.'*

This condition does not require a complete *lacuna* in decision making
power. In *Hauptzollamt Bremerhaven v Massey-Ferguson*[4] the Bundesfinanz-
hof had asked the Court to rule on the validity of Council Regulation
803/68 on the valuation of goods for customs purposes, the preamble of
which stated that it was based on Article 235. According to legal writers,
the Regulation could have been based more appropriately on Articles 27,
28, 100, 110 and 113 of the Treaty, but the Court held that the
requirements of legal certainty justified reliance on Article 235 where the
Treaty had provided partial or incomplete powers.

However, the choice of the basis of a measure cannot be made to depend
solely on an institution's opinion as to the desired aim of a measure but
must be determined by objective factors open to judicial review. This was
decided in *EC Commission v EC Council*[5] in which the plaintiff sought the
annulment of two Council Regulations applying generalised tariff preferences to industrial and textile products originating in developing countries.
The Commission argued that the contested measures constituted an
infringement of an essential procedural requirement, within the sense of
Article 190, by failing to state precisely the legal basis for the Regulations.

In its defence the Council claimed that the recitals of the measures provided a sufficient context from which the legal basis could be determined; although there was no reference to a specific legal basis the Council had intended, at the time of their adoption, to base the contested Regulations on Articles 113 and 235 of the Treaty because the realisation of important development policy objectives exceeded the scope of Article 113 and made it necessary to have recourse to Article 235. The Court held that the dispute as to the correct legal basis was not purely a formal matter since Articles 113 and 235 of the Treaty contained different rules governing the way in which the Council arrived at its decision: Article 113 requires a qualified majority whereas Article 235 requires unanimity. And it followed from the very terms of Article 235 that recourse to that Article as a legal basis for a measure was justified only if no other provision of the Treaty conferred upon the Community institutions the power necessary to adopt that measure. Accordingly, the Regulations were declared void.

Once the conditions for utilising Article 235 have been satisfied the Council, acting unanimously on a proposal from the Commission and after consulting the Assembly, may take the 'appropriate measures'. This gives the Council a free hand as regards the choice of legislative instrument. In the *ERTA* case[6] the Commission argued that if Article 75 of the Treaty was an insufficient basis for the power to conclude international agreements then the Council should have had recourse to Article 235, which was a mandatory provision. The Court rejected that argument:

'For its part, the Council takes the view that, since the means of joint action by Member States was available, there was no need to resort to this provision; moreover the Commission never took the initiative in submitting a proposal to that effect, as is required by the provision in question. Although Article 235 empowers the Council to take any 'appropriate measures' equally in the sphere of external relations, it does not create an obligation but confers on the Council an option, failure to exercise which cannot affect the validity of proceedings.'

1 G. Close, *Harmonization of Laws—use or abuse of the powers under the EEC Treaty?* [1978] 3 E.L. Rev. 461, at p. 474.
2 T. Tizziano, The powers of the Community, in *Thirty Years of Community Law*, p. 54.
3 Case 38/69 [1970] E.C.R. 47, [1970] C.M.L.R. 77.
4 Case 8/73 [1973] E.C.R. 897.
5 Case 45/86 [1988] 2 C.M.L.R. 131.
6 *Supra* fn. 3, para. 5.3.

5.6 Article 235 has frequently been compared and contrasted with Article 100 of the Treaty, which is located in that part of the treaty entitled 'Approximation of Laws', and which states:

'The Council shall, acting unanimously on a proposal from the Commission, issue directives for the approximation of such provisions laid down by law, regulation or administrative action in Member States as directly affect the establishment or functioning of the common market.

The European Parliament and the Economic and Social Committee shall be consulted in the case of directives whose implementation would, in one or more Member States, involve the amendment of legislation'.

The features common to both provisions include the fact that they justify Community action where an absence of power would frustrate the attainment of a Community objective '. . . *in the course of the operation of the common market*' . . . (art. 235) and where national measures would impinge upon '. . . *the establishment or functioning of the common market*' (art. 100). In addition, both articles require that Council measures be adopted unanimously. On the other hand there are notable differences between them. First, Article 100 assumes the existence of inequalities in national law which must be removed because of their distortive effects, or differences in national laws which do not have distortive effects but the harmonisation of which will have immediate beneficial effects on the common market.[1] Article 235 makes no such assumption. Second, the national measures to be approximated must 'directly affect' the establishment or functioning of the common market. The interpretation of this phrase is clearly a matter of degree, but it is a requirement not present in Article 235. Third, Article 100 empowers the Council to act only by way of directives, whereas the Community legislature has a choice of instrument under Article 235. These differences notwithstanding, it is sometimes difficult to distinguish the scope of application of these two provisions. As one commentator has observed:

'The real borders of harmonization lie at the point where national law by reason of its territorial applicability is unfit to provide solution for the Community problems which arise. At that point Article 100 can no longer provide the solution and recourse must be had . . . to Article 235. The borderline is not always easy to draw.[2]

Indeed, it is often unnecessary to demarcate the scope of application of Articles 100 and 235 because the Council Directive in question will refer to *both* Articles as the legal basis on which the Directive was adopted. An example of this is Council Directive 76/403 on the disposal of polychlorinated biphenyl and polychlorinated terphenyls.[3]

1 T. Vogelaar, *supra* fn. 1, para 5.2 at p. 214.
2 T. Vogelaar, *supra* fn. 1, para 5.2 at p. 215.
3 O.J. L 108, 26.4.76 p. 41.

5.7 It is also necessary to compare Article 235 with Article 236, which outlines the procedure for formal amendments of the Treaty. At the outset the dissimilarities should be noted. First, the right of initiative is not confined to the Commission; the governments of the Member States may also submit proposals for the amendment of the Treaty. Second, the amendment procedures require the convening of a conference on the representatives of the Governments of the Member States. Article 235 does not. Third, the amendments require ratification by the Member States in accordance with their respective constitutional requirements. This latter condition does not apply to Article 235, and partly because of it Article 236 has been used sparingly. If the three enlargements of the Community are disregarded (and, in any event, accession is provided for in Article 237), it can be concluded that the treaty has been amended on only five occasions:

(i) the 'Merger Treaty' of 1965; (ii) the first 'Budgetary Treaty' of 1970 (iii) the second 'Budgetary Treaty' of 1975; (iv) the Treaty altering the relationship between Greenland and the Community;[1] *and* (v) the Single European Act.

With the exception of the Greenland Treaty, in each case the amendment has brought about a significant change in the organisational structure of the Community, particularly as regards the balance of power between the institutions. Such an effect is one of three tests suggested by one observer as the means of delimiting the applicability of Articles 235 and 236.[2] But in the final analysis it cannot be denied that Article 235 can be used to extend Community competence; this is the inevitable conclusion to be drawn from a brief examination of the new Community policies, implemented under Article 235 on foot of the mandate given by the Paris Summit of October 1972. In the words of the same commentator:

'It is useless to try to banish the problem by denying that Article 235 itself also constitutes a form of Treaty revision, even if a limited form'.[3]

This is an inference shared by the Court of Justice:

'Under Article 235 the Council acts on a proposal from the Commission and after consulting the Assembly. Although the affect of the measures taken in this manner by the Council is in some respects to supplement the Treaty, they are adopted within the context of the objectives of the Community.'[4]

Finally, it has already been noted that up to the end of 1972 Article 235 has been utilised as the legal basis for acts of the Council on only 35 occasions. By contrast, from 1972 up to the end of 1984 more than 150 measures based on Article 235 were adopted by the Council on matters relating only to regional policy, telematics and information policy, and industrial and scientific research policy.[5] It suffices to say that many hundreds of other Council measures since 1972 have listed Article 235 as their legal basis.

1 O.J. L 29, 1.2.85 p. 1.
2 A. Tizziano, The powers of the Community, in *Thirty Years of Community Law* (1983) p. 58.
3 *Idem.*
4 Case 38/69 *EC Commission v Italy* [1970] E.C.R. 47, [1970] C.M.L.R. 77.
5 See T.M.C. Asser Institute, Guide to EEC Legislation, Supplement 1985, at ch. 42.

5.8 It is now necessary to consider the consequences that flow from the division of competence between the Community and the Member States. A widely accepted formula provides for three distinct categories.

(i) Where the Community is exclusively competent. In these circumstances any unilateral action by a Member State is precluded. In the *ERTA case*[1] the Court held:

'. . . to the extent to which Community rules are promulgated for the attainment of the objectives of the Treaty, the Member States cannot, outside the framework of the Community institutions, assume obligations which might affect these rules or alter their scope'.[2]

The Court also held that where a matter falls within the terms of a common policy the Member States are bound to act jointly in defence of the interests of the Community. As we have noted above, this 'exclusivity' theory was developed by the Court of Justice mainly in the context of the Common Commercial Policy and the Common Fisheries Policy. However, it has been observed that in relation to the Common Agricultural Policy the Court utilised a 'compatibility' theory in the 1970s, according to which the existence of Community competence

'. . . did not in itself exclude national Legislation although national Legislation must not conflict with the express or implied aims or objectives of any Community Legislation on the matter'.[3]

This approach to the question of competence can be seen in the cases of *Galli*[4] and *Van den Hazel*[5] in which national measures had been imposed on products governed by common organisations of the market. A similar approach was taken by the Court in *State v Watson and Belman*[6] which involved restrictions on the free movement of persons. In the 1980s, however, judgments in cases like *Apple and Pear Development Council v Lewis*[7] and *Pluimveeslachterij Midden-Nederland*[8] demonstrate that the Court has reverted to the 'exclusivity' theory in agricultural cases.[9]

(ii) Where the Community is exclusively competent but the competence has not yet been exercised. Under this heading two different situations can be distinguished. (a) Where Community law provides for a transitional period and up to the time of expiry of that period the Community has not yet acted: according to the judgment of the Court in the *Kramer* case,[10] the Member States remain free to act unilaterally. (b) Where a transitional period has expired and the Community has not yet acted: in *EC Commission v United Kingdom*,[11] the Court held that the failure of the institutions to exercise competence did not deprive the Community of its powers nor did it restore to the Member States the freedom to act at will in the field in question. Moreover, by virtue of Article 5 of the Treaty, Member States are under a duty to cooperate so as to ensure fulfilment of the Community's objectives; they are also obliged to abstain from any measures which could jeopardise the attainment of these objectives. In *France v United Kingdom*[12] the Court held that performance of the duties of the Member States under Article 5, which had been made more specific by virtue of a Council Resolution adopted at the Hague in November 1976, was particularly necessary where divergences of national interests had made it impossible to establish a common policy concerning the biological resources of the sea and where worthwhile results could be attained only with the cooperation of all the Member States.

(iii) Where both the Community and the Member States are competent. When examining the doctrine of implied powers (5.3 above) it was noted that the Court ultimately accepted that there may be circumstances in the subject matter of international agreements which justified conclusion of the agreement by both the Community and the Member States. An example of this 'mixed' procedure can be seen in the United Nations Convention on the Law of the Sea. Only part of the subject matter of the Convention affected Community competence, requiring its conclusion by the Member States and the Community.[13] But it has been suggested that the mixed agreement procedure causes difficulties for other contracting parties in as much as it

'. . . casts doubts on the Community's powers to enter into commitments and its capacity to honour them.'[14]

The difficulties surrounding the mixed agreement procedure might be said to be one of the consequences flowing from the *ERTA* judgment. It has also been suggested that as a result of the jurisprudence of the Court

'. . . it is not safe for any Member State to accept any proposed internal Community legislation or external action, however simple, however innocent, however beneficial it may seem for the affairs of the Community, without considering first what effect it will have in the future on external competence'.[15]

The Treaty also provides for the concurrent exercise of competence by the Community and the Member States. The best example is competition policy. Article 87 of the Treaty gave the Council the power to implement Articles 85 and 86 and in so doing it was to determine, *inter alia*, the relationship between national laws and the provisions of Community competition law. This power has not yet been exercised but the Court has had occasion to comment on the relationship between national and Community competition rules. In *Wilhelm v Bundeskartellamt*,[16] where the applicant complained of double jeopardy, the Court ruled as follows:

'. . . (the) parallel application of the national system can only be allowed in so far as it does not prejudice the uniform application throughout the common market of the Community rules on cartels and of the full effect of the measures adopted in implementation of those rules . . . Consequently, conflicts between the rules of the Community and national rules in the matter of law on cartels must be resolved by applying the principle that Community law takes precedence.'

This ruling was endorsed by the Court of Justice in the so-called *Perfume* cases.[17]

1 Case 22/70 [1971] E.C.R. 263, [1971] C.M.L.R. 335.
2 *Idem.*, at p. 275.
3 J.A. Usher, *The Scope of Community Competence—Its Recognition and Enforcement*; XXIV J.C.M.S. 121, 123.
4 Case 31/74 [1975] E.C.R. 47, [1975] 1 C.M.L.R. 211.
5 Case 111/76 [1977] E.C.R. 401, [1980] 3 C.M.L.R. 12.
6 Case 118/75 [1976] E.C.R. 1185, [1976] 2 C.M.L.R. 552.
7 Case 222/82 [1983] E.C.R. 4083, [1984] 3 C.M.L.R. 733.
8 Joined cases 47–48/83 [1984] E.C.R. 1721.
9 Usher, *supra* fn. 3, at p. 126.
10 Case 3, 4, 6/76 [1976] E.C.R. 1279, [1976] 2 C.M.L.R. 440.
11 Case 32/79 [1980] E.C.R. 2403, [1981] 1 C.M.L.R. 219.
12 Case 141/78 [1979] E.C.R. 2923, [1980] 1 C.M.L.R. 6.
13 See Annex IX, United Nations Convention on the Law of the Sea.
14 J.H.J. Bourgeois, Some comments on practice, in Timmermans and Volker (eds), *Division of Powers between the European Communities and their Member States in the Field of External Relations*, *supra* fn. 9, para. 5.3, at p. 106.

15 F. Burrows, The effect of the main cases of the Court of Justice in the field of the External Competences on the conduct of the Member States, in Timmermans and Volker (eds.), *supra* fn. 9, para. 5.3 at p. 108.
16 Case 14/68 [1969] E.C.R. 1, [1969] C.M.L.R. 100.
17 Joined cases 253/78, 1–3/79 *Procureur de la République v Giry* [1980] E.C.R. 2327, [1981] 2 C.M.L.R. 99.

5.9 Apart from the three classifications outlined above there is a further, more basic consequence flowing from the division of competence between the Community and the Member States: any attempt by the Community to exceed the competence transferred to it by the Treaty will be challenged swiftly by the Member States. An example of this can be seen in the joined cases *Germany, France, the Netherlands, Denmark and the United Kingdom v EC Commission*[1] in which the applicants sought the annulment of Commission Decision 85/381[2] which set up a prior communication and consultation procedure on migration policies in relation to non-member countries. The Decision, which was based on Article 118 of the Treaty, required Member States to notify the Commission of their draft measures and draft agreements with regard to workers from non-member States and members of their families concerning such matters as: entry; residence; employment; equal treatment; promotion of integration into the work-force, society and cultural life; and the voluntary return of such persons to their countries of origin (art. 1). Following notification the Commission could arrange for consultation with the relevant Member State (art. 2), and the objectives of that consultation procedure were, *inter alia*, to facilitate the mutual exchange of information to ensure that national measures and agreements are in conformity with the Community's policies and actions, and to examine the desirability of measures to harmonise national legislation on foreigners (art. 3).

The applicants maintained that neither Article 118 nor any other Treaty provision empowered the Commission to adopt a binding decision in a field which fell within their exclusive competence. Article 118 of the Treaty gives to the Commission the task of promoting close cooperation between Member States in the social field; to achieve this end, the Commission is empowered to make studies, deliver opinions and to arrange consultations. The Court of Justice rejected the argument made by the applicants that the Member States were exclusively competent in matters relating to foreign workers. It held that integration of foreign workers into the workforce and into society did fall within the social field within the meaning of Article 118 because these matters were closely linked to employment. But the same could not be said about the cultural integration of immigrant communities, without distinction between migrant workers and other foreigners, and to this extent the decision fell beyond the scope of Article 118. The Court then turned to the question as to whether the Commission was empowered to adopt a binding decision to arrange consultations under Article 118 and, in a passage reminiscent of the judgment in the *Fedechar* case[3] it held that the second paragraph of Article 118 had to be interpreted as conferring on the Commission all the powers which were necessary to arrange the consultations, including the power to require the Member States to notify essential information and to take part in consultations. However, this power was of a procedural nature only, whereas the contested Decision, in

Article 3, sought to assign objectives to the consultations and to determine the outcome of those consultations by debarring national measures considered by the Commission not to be in conformity with Community policies; this exceeded the scope of the Commission's procedural powers under Article 118, and the Decision at issue was void for lack of competence.

1 Joined cases 281, 283, 284, 285, 287/85 *Germany v EC Commission* O.J. C 205 1.8.87 p. 7.
2 O.J. L 217 14.8.85 p. 25.
3 *Supra* fn. 1, para. 5.3.

5.10 We must now consider the likely impact of the Single European Act on the question of Community competence. The first notable feature of the Act is that most of the new areas of competence, mentioned initially at the Paris Summit of 1972 and enacted into Community law on the basis of Article 235, have now been recognised in Treaty form as official subjects of Community competence. This is the case in respect of 'economic and social cohesion' or regional policy (SEA, art. 23), research and development policy (SEA, art, 24), and environment policy (SEA, art. 25).

The provisions on environment are problematical. SEA, art. 25 adds a further title to Part III of the EEC Treaty and it is comprised of three new treaty provisions, Articles 130 R, S and T.

The objectives of, and the limitations on the Community's competence in environment matters are to be found in Article 130R. The general objectives, the preservation and improvement of the quality of the environment and the protection of human health, are listed in paragraph 1. The underlying principles are stated in paragraph 2 and are: (i) preventive action should be taken wherever possible; (ii) environmental damage should be rectified at source; and (iii) the polluter should pay. Paragraph 4 provides that Community action will take place only to the extent that action at Community level will achieve the objectives set out in paragraph 1; national measures and the financing thereof will remain the responsibility of the Member States. Paragraph 5 reads as follows:

> 'Within their respective spheres of competence, the Community and the Member States shall cooperate with third countries and with the relevant international organisations. The arrangements for Community cooperation may be the subject of agreements between the Community and the third parties concerned, which shall be negotiated and concluded in accordance with Article 228.
> The previous paragraph shall be without prejudice to Member States' competence to negotiate in international bodies and to conclude international agreements.'

The Ninth Declaration annexed to the SEA contains a statement to the effect that the Inter Governmental Conference did not consider the principles flowing from the *ERTA* judgment to be affected by the second portion of paragraph 5. However, the status of the Declaration annexed to the SEA is doubtful, but in any event it is clear from the text of paragraphs 4 and 5 of Article 130R that the Member States took some trouble to delineate national and Community competence in environmental matters.

The reference in paragraph 4 to the financial aspects of environmental protection measures indicates that the Member States had carefully considered the case-law of the Court of Justice and the judgment in Opinion 1/78[1] in particular (see above at 5.2), with a view to preserving national freedom of action.

1 [1979] E.C.R. 2871, [1979] 3 C.M.L.R. 639.

5.11 The second important change brought about by the SEA concerns approximation legislation aimed at the completion of the internal market. According to Article 8A (a new provision of the EEC Treaty introduced by SEA, art. 13) the internal market

'shall comprise an area without internal frontiers in which the free movement of goods, persons, services and capital is ensured in accordance with the provisions of this Treaty.'

The first paragraph of Article 100A (introduced by SEA, art. 18) empowers the Council, acting by a qualified majority on a proposal from the Commission and in cooperation with the European Parliament, to adopt measures for the approximation of national laws, regulations or administrative practices, which have as their object the completion of the internal market. This provision, which operates in derogation from Article 100, is a most important new mechanism available to the Community legislature. It permits harmonisation legislation, which would have required unanimity under Article 100, to be adopted by qualified majority; the procedure is also somewhat more democratic in that the European Parliament is involved by way of the cooperation procedure (see above at 4.8); and the range of legislative instruments available to the institutions is not confined to the Directive (as in Article 100) but permits the use of the more flexible and expeditious Regulation.

However, two of the Declarations annexed to the SEA qualify somewhat the scope of Article 100A. As we have already noted (see above at 4.23) the first Declaration invites the Council to give a prominent place to the 'Advisory Committee' procedure in connection with the Commission's powers of implementation under Article 100A, and the fourth Declaration requires the Commission to use Directives if harmonisation proposals would involve the amendment of legislative provisions in one or more Member States. Further qualifications or limitations appear in the other paragraphs of Article 100A. Paragraph 2 excludes from the scope of paragraph 1 fiscal measures as well as provisions concerning the free movement of persons and the rights and interests of employed persons. Paragraph 3 specifies that the Commission will take as a base a high level of protection in its proposals concerning health, safety, environmental protection and consumer protection. Paragraph 5 allows the Community legislative authority to include an exemption procedure in harmonisation proposals; a safeguard clause may authorise the Member States to take '. . . provisional measures subject to a Community control procedure . . .' for one or more of the non-economic reasons referred to in Article 36. Finally, paragraph 4 provides for another exemption procedure but, in contrast to the safeguard clause referred to in paragraph 5, this exemption will operate in an *ex post facto* manner. Where a harmonisation measure has been adopted by a qualified majority and a Member State deems it necessary 'to apply national provisions on grounds of major needs referred to in Article 36, or relating to protection of the environment or the working environment, it should notify the Commission of these provisions'. If satisfied that the national measures do not constitute an arbitrary discrimination or a disguised restriction on trade between Member States, the Commission may confirm the measures. But if the Commission or another Member State considers that improper use is being made of the exception, the offending Member State may be brought directly before the Court of Justice in derogation from the infringement procedure laid down in EEC Treaty, art.s 169 and 170. This abbreviated form of action is similar to the procedure provided for in EEC Treaty, art. 93(2). Finally, it seems clear that the power conferred by Article 100A has a limited duration: Article 8A provides that the Community

'. . . shall adopt measures with the aim of progressively establishing the internal market over a period *expiring* on 31st December 1992 . . .' (emphasis added)

Despite these various qualifications the new power is most significant. If we may hazard a prediction about its use it would be to suggest that a significant rise in the number of disputes between the Member States and the Commission can be expected, in which the issue will be the choice of Article 100A (with qualified majority voting) as the legal basis for Community action rather than some other provision of the treaty which requires unanimity.[1]

1 For an example of this phenomenon, pre-dating the SEA, see Case 68/86 *United Kingdom v EC Council* O.J. C 74 22.3.88 p. 6.

5.12 While there can be no doubt that the new legal order established by the treaties has altered significantly the relationship between the Member States and the Community, it is often difficult to isolate the essential attribute of the new relationship. Indeed, it appears as if the Community perception of this question has changed over the past three decades. In the *Van Gend en Loos* judgment of 1963[1] the Court of Justice referred to a limitation of sovereign rights by the Member States in favour of the Communities. In *EC Commission v France* in 1971 the Court adopted a less concrete formula:

'The Member States agreed to establish a Community of unlimited duration, having permanent institutions invested with real powers, stemming from *a limitation of authority or a transfer of power* from the States to the Community.'[2]

In the early 1980s legislation in the fisheries sector refers to *exclusive Community competence* in waters under the *sovereignty* of the Member States. As a result, in the view of the Court, the Member States were

'. . . no longer entitled to exercise any powers of their own in the matter of conservation measures in waters under their jurisdiction.'[3]

This change in terminology tempted one observer to conclude that

'. . . national sovereignty is the bare legal title retained by the Member States against which the Community may be granted beneficial rights, and it is more accurate, both practically and theoretically, to speak in terms of the exercise of competence rather than in terms of the transfer of sovereignty.'[4]

1 *Supra* fn. 1, para. 5.1.
2 Case 7/71 [1971] E.C.R. 1003, at p. 1018, [1972] C.M.L.R. 453, at p. 480.
3 Case 804/79 *EC Commission v United Kingdom* [1981] E.C.R. 1045, at p. 1073, [1982] 1 C.M.L.R. 543, at p. 570. See also Case 269/80 *R v Tymen* [1981] E.C.R. 3079, at p. 3091, [1982] 2 C.M.L.R. 111, at p. 124, where the Court held that '. . . the Member States are no longer entitled to exercise any power of their own in this matter [fisheries conservation] *and may henceforth only act as trustees of the common interest*, in the absence of appropriate action on the part of the Council.' (Emphasis added.)
4 J.A. Usher, *op. cit.* fn. 3, para. 5.8, at p. 131.

Chapter 6

The Finances of the Communities

6.1 Treaty provisions:

ECSC Treaty	Articles 49–53, 78
EEC Treaty	Articles 199–209
Euratom Treaty	Articles 171–183
Merger Treaty	Articles 20–23
Council Decision (EEC, Euratom) 70/243	*passim*
First Budgetary Treaty	*passim*
First Act of Accession	Articles 127–132
Second Budgetary Treaty	*passim*
Second Act of Accession	Articles
Council Decision (EEC, Euratom) 85/157	*passim*
Third Act of Accession	Articles

Introduction

6.2 The financial provisions of the Treaties have undergone significant amendment and refinement since the ECSC came into operation in 1952. The supranational character of the ECSC was highlighted by its budgetary system which provided it with its own financial resources, to be drawn from levies on producers of coal and steel and from borrowings on the capital market. This provided the new entity with an enviable attribute: it did not have to rely on contributions from its Member States for financial survival. The unseemly squabble concerning personalities and budgetary contributions in UNESCO during the past decade testifies to the importance of financial independence for international organisations. It might seem surprising, therefore, that the EEC and Euratom Treaties provided a system of financing dependent on contributions from the Member States. In fact, both Treaties envisaged the replacement of those contributions by a system of 'own resources' and in 1970 the Council adopted the first own resources Decision which set out to replace national contributions by revenue derived from the Common Customs Tariff, levies imposed under the CAP, and up to 1 per cent of VAT. Delays in harmonisation of VAT legislation meant that this system did not become fully operational until

1980. Within four years this source of revenue proved to be insufficient to meet the needs of the Communities and a further Council measure, the second own resources Decision, was necessary to raise the VAT threshold to 1.4 per cent; present indications are that the Community has already exhausted this increase and a further Council measure will be needed. Agreement in principle to supplement the Community's own resources was reached at the European Council meeting in Brussels in February 1988.

Increased Community expenditure has normally been attributed to uncontrolled agricultural spending. For two decades 60–70 per cent of Community funds have gone to the agricultural sector and these funds were disbursed through the European Agricultural Guidance and Guarantee Fund. However, the EEC Treaty also provided for the establishment of the European Social Fund, and in the 1970s the European Regional Development Fund was established; these two Funds now distribute thousands of millions of pounds annually, and there are other significant heads of Community expenditure not connected with agriculture.

The huge resources now at the disposal of the Communities have to be collected in the Member States and expenditure has to be sanctioned and monitored. Special financial regulations deal with these issues and a special framework also applies to the consolidation of estimates of revenue and expenditure in the draft budget. The budgetary procedure itself has undergone a series of significant changes: the European Parliament now enjoys an enhanced role and has a power of veto over the entire budget.

The budgetary changes were brought about by the First and Second budgetary Treaties of 1970 and 1975. The latter Treaty introduced a new Community institution, The Court of Auditors, which was designed to replace the inadequate Audit Boards of the original Treaties. The Court of Auditors has power to examine and review Community expenditure and to advise the Parliament on the final discharge of each budget.

The budget and most types of Community expenditure are now denominated in ECUs—European Currency Units; however, the method of defining the Community's monetary unit has changed considerably over the past two decades and the present state of affairs, which sees the ECU as a firmly established, proto Euro-currency, can be contrasted with the era of monetary instability in the late 1960s and early 1970s.

In this chapter the Community and domestic measures relating to Community finances, which have been identified above, will be dealt with under the following headings:

> Revenue;
> Expenditure;
> Revenue and Expenditure in Ireland;
> The Budgetary procedure;
> Control and review of expenditure;
> The unit of account.

ECSC Revenue

6.3   Article 49 of the ECSC Treaty empowered the High Authority to raise funds in three ways: by the imposition of levies on coal and steel production; by raising loans; and by receiving gifts. The latter is of no significance. It might be added that another indirect source of revenue is referred to in Article 52 which refers to the transfer to the ECSC '. . . to be used for the purposes intended by this Treaty . . .' of pecuniary sanctions and periodic penalty payments; this includes fines imposed on undertakings for infringement of the rules on prices (Article 64) and on competition (Article 66). The two main sources of revenue, however, are levies and borrowings.

According to Article 50 income from levies was intended to cover administrative expenses, readaptation aid, loans to undertakings and expenditure on technical and economic research. The levies were to be assessed on coal and steel products up to 1 per cent of the annual average value across the Community. Initially, the rate was high, 0.9 per cent, in order to amass, *inter alia*, a sufficient reserve fund to enable the ECSC to borrow on the capital markets.[1] Since the late 1950s the levy has been at a considerably lower rate and has rarely exceeded 0.3 per cent, a fact attributable in part to the depressed conditions in both the coal and steel sectors. Sensitivity to this situation may have accounted for what one observer described as '. . . an element of cross-subsidy . . .' in the financial provisions of the Merger Treaty, Article 20 of which provided for the administrative expenditure of the ECSC to be included in the budget of the European Communities.[2]

The power of the High Authority [Commission] to borrow money is subject to a restriction: Article 54 requires funds raised in this way to be on-lent to undertakings. The first loan was raised in 1954 in the United States for the sum of $100 million;[3] by 1986 the annual borrowing had risen to 1517.4 million ECU.[4]

Mention should be made in passing of the scrap equalisation levy, introduced under Article 53, which gave rise to the leading case in Community law on delegation of powers. The levy was designed to prevent Community prices for scrap metal from being influenced by higher world market prices; this was brought about by subsidising imports and equalising access to imported scrap metal. The scheme was approved by the Court of Justice[5] but the delegation, to a consumers' group and an independent fund, of the power to collect the levy was held to be an unauthorised delegation of power by the High Authority: *Meroni v High Authority*.[6]

1 The basic rules were laid down in High Authority Decisions 2/52 and 3/52 O.J. (Sp. Ed.) 1952–58 pp. 3–8.
2 John A. Usher, The financing of the Community, in *Thirty Years of Community Law* (1983), at p. 196.
3 3rd General Report of the ECSC, at p. 132.
4 20th General Report 1986, point 188.
5 Case 8/57 *Groupement des Hauts Fourneaux et Aciéries Belges v High Authority* [1957–58] E.C.R. 245.
6 Case 9/56 [1957–58] E.C.R. 133.

EEC and Euratom 'Own resources'

6.4 Unlike the ECSC, which was provided with its own budgetary resources from the outset, the EEC and Euratom relied on contributions from Member States. The level of contributions was fixed in Article 200 of the EEC Treaty, and Article 172 of the Euratom Treaty respectively. However, both Treaties provided for the replacement of this system of contributions with an autonomous means of financing the Communities' activities,[1] and as early as 1962 a clear indication of the type of resources that would be utilised was given in Regulation 25 of 1962[2] on the financing of the Common Agricultural Policy (CAP). This regulation was part of the first group of regulations on the CAP and envisaged that import levies on agricultural goods would accrue to the Community at the single market stage. However, the constitutional crises of 1965 meant that the resolution of the problem of financing the CAP was postponed to 1970, when the Member States resolved the issue within the context of an overall budgetary reform package. In that year the Member States first availed of the own resources option, and agreed at the same time (by an amending Treaty) to a change in the budgetary procedure so as to give the Assembly (European Parliament) a greater say in the adoption of the budget. In fact, the own resources decision, Council Decision 70/243 (EEC, Euratom),[3] was adopted one day earlier than the 'first budgetary Treaty,' but its effect was to transfer to the Communities revenue coming from three sources:

   (i) levies derived from the implementation of the common agricultural policy (Article 2(a));
  (ii) customs duties derived from the implementation of the Common Customs Tariff (Article 2(b));
 (iii) resources derived from up to 1 per cent of Value Added Tax collected by the Member States, using a uniform assessment basis (Article 4).

For the original Member States the conversion to the new system took place in accordance with Articles 3 and 4 of the Decision. Under Article 3 agricultural levies became payable immediately, but revenue accruing from the CCT was to be phased in over a five-year period so that from 1 January 1975 all customs duties would be entered in the budget of the Communities. Paragraph 1 of Article 4 required that from 1 January 1975 the Communities should be self-sufficient financially and that its resources should include up to 1 per cent of VAT collected in the Member States according to a common assessment basis. Paragraphs 2 and 3, somewhat prophetically, allowed for the possibility that a uniform basis of VAT assessment might not be in place in the Member States on 1 January 1975, and in this eventuality the shortfall between expenditure and revenue was to be bridged by contributions from the Member States according to a GNP-based scale. As it turned out the GNP-based contributions were utilised until 1980 because the uniform system of assessment was not enacted by the Council—in the form of the 'sixth' Directive on VAT—until May 1977, and was not implemented by all the Member States until 1979.[4]

For Denmark, Ireland and the United Kingdom the implementation of the own resources system was governed by Articles 127–132 of the Act of Accession. Article 127 made the own resources Decision of 1970 applicable to the new Member States, and Article 128 included in the own resources system Accession compensatory amounts and customs duties both of which had to be eliminated by the end of the Accession transitional period. Articles 129 and 130 laid down the rules for the progressive implementation of the own resources system in the new Member States by fixing percentage increases in the rate of transfer of agricultural levies and customs duties and, if necessary, direct financial contributions to the budget. Article 131 provided a corrective mechanism to ensure that none of the new Member States over-contributed to the budgets of 1978 and 1979. The application of this Article gave rise to a lengthy dispute on the contributions of the United Kingdom and, to a lesser extent, Ireland; this was resolved finally to the advantage of the two new Member States.[5]

In 1977 there were two significant events as regards the Communities' budget. First, the 'second budgetary Treaty' of 22 July 1975 entered into force. This Treaty further increased the role of the European Parliament in the establishment of Community expenditure and gave it a veto over the entire budget.[6] Of greater significance, as far as own resources were concerned, was the adoption by the Council of the Sixth Directive on VAT.[7] This Directive set out the uniform system of assessment needed to implement the VAT element in the own resources Decision, and led to the enactment of two Council regulations on 19 December 1977. Regulation 2891/77 (ECSC, EEC, Euratom)[8] laid down general rules for the collection of own resources by the Member States and for their transfer of the Communities. Regulation 2892/77 (ECSC, EEC, Euratom)[9] laid down rules for the calculation of VAT own resources; Member States were given an option as to the method of calculating the amounts to be transferred. Method A was described as the 'return method' and method B was described as the 'revenue method'; Denmark and Ireland chose method A.[10]

The Sixth Directive on VAT was originally scheduled to allow for full application of the own resources system by 1 January 1978 but only Belgium implemented the Directive in time. In June 1978 the Council extended by one year the time limit for the implementation of the Directive but by 1 January 1979 there were still four states, including Ireland, which had not put into force the necessary measures. In Ireland the implementing measures took the form of the Value Added Tax (Amendment) Act, 1978 which came into force on 1 March 1979. The whole saga came to an end on 1 January 1980 when the remaining Member States, Luxembourg and Germany, put the implementing measures into force[11] and the own resources system came into operation definitively for the first time.

In 1980 the VAT own resources were mobilised at the rate of 0.73 per cent which raised 2654 m. EUA,[12] but already the Commission was voicing its concern about exhausting the 1 per cent limit.[13] By 1982 as much as 0.998 per cent of VAT own resources were mobilised by the original and supplementary budgets of that year, and the Commission prepared a Green paper on the future financing of the Community.[14] The problem finally came to a head in 1984 when it became clear that there was insufficient revenue from own resources to cover budgetary expenditure. This necessitated a supplementary budget financed by national contributions from outside the own resources system. Ireland's share of the deficit was fixed at 8,269,400 ECU, and the transfer was facilitated by the European Communities (Supplementary Funding) Act, 1984. The transfer was actually made on 7 December 1984.[15] In the meantime the European Council considered the Commission's proposals at its meeting at Fontainebleau on 25 and 26 June 1984 and reached agreement in principle about increasing the VAT threshold to 1.4 per cent and about providing a corrective mechanism for Member States bearing excessive budgetary burdens in relation to their relative prosperity (the British problem). The Council put these arrangements into legislative form on 7 May 1985 as Decision 85/257 (EEC, Euratom),[16] following conciliation with the European Parliament, and this Decision repealed the first own resources Decision of 1970.

In structure the second own resources Decision does not differ greatly from the first own resources Decision. Article 1 specifies that the Communities should be allocated their own resources in order to ensure that the budget is kept on balance; the budget is to be financed entirely from the Communities' own resources. Article 2 declares that agricultural levies and customs duties form part of the Communities' own resources. Article 3 paragraph 1 states that revenue accruing from VAT, assessed uniformly in the Member States, shall also form part of own resources, and paragraph 2 fixes the maximum rate of 1.4 per cent. It should be noted that the fourth recital of the preamble envisaged an increase to 1.6 per cent in 1988. Paragraphs 3, 4 and 5 provide for a corrective repayment to the United Kingdom. Paragraph 6 requires that the rate at which VAT own resources will be mobilised must be fixed before the start of the new financial year. According to Article 4 own resources revenue must be used without distinction to finance all Community expenditure. Article 5 requires the Community to refund to Member States 10 per cent of agricultural levies and customs duties in order to cover collection expenses. Under Article 6 any surplus of resources over expenditure is to be carried over to the following year. The final substantive Article is Article 7 which requires the Member States to use their existing administrative and legal structures for collection of own resources and to permit inspection and supervision by Community authorities. However, any optimism about the Community's budgetary health in the aftermath of the Fontainebleau agreement was quickly dispelled: by the end of 1986 the Commission had concluded that the additional resources given to the Community by the increase in the VAT limit to 1.4 per cent were already substantially exhausted by the time they became available.[17] The problem was addressed eventually at the Brussels meeting of the European Council in February 1988. But instead of increasing the VAT rate to 1.6 per cent, as envisaged in the preamble to the second own resources Decision, VAT will remain at 1.4 per cent and the shortfall will be made up by supplementary payments based on each Member State's GNP; there will be an upper limit on contributions at a level of 1.2 per cent of GNP on payment credits and 1.3 per cent on payment commitments.[18]

1 EEC Treaty, art. 201 and Euratom Treaty, art. 173.
2 O.J. (Sp. Ed.) 1959–62 p. 126.
3 O.J. (Sp. Ed.) 1970 p. 224.

4 Daniel Strasser, *The Finances of Europe*, Brussels, 1981 (cited hereafter as Strasser), at p. 121 and see also Annex 10.
5 *Idem*, at p. 382.
6 O.J. L 359 31.12.77 p. 1.
7 Council Directive 77/388 (EEC) O.J. L 145, 13.6.1977 p. 1.
8 O.J. L 336 27.12.77 p. 1.
9 O.J. L 336 27.12.77 p. 8.
10 Strasser, at p. 121.
11 *Idem*, p n. 5.
12 14th Annual General Report 1980, at p. 74.
13 *Idem*., p. 77.
14 17th Annual General Report 1983, at pts. 84 and 86.
15 25th Report on Developments in the European Communities, January 1985, (Pl. 3043); points 3.1 to 3.8.
16 O.J. L 128, 14.5.1985 p. 15.
17 20th Annual General Report 1986, at point 82.
18 See: Commission proposal for a Council Decision on the system of the Communities' own resources, COM (88) 137 final.

EEC Revenue

(i) *Agricultural levies*

6.5 All the market organisation regulations have provisions designed to regulate trade with non-Member States. If the basic regulation relates to a product for which an intervention system operates the trading rules will provide for a levy to ensure that intra-Community trade is not harmed by competition from the world market, where prices are normally—but not invariably—lower than in the Community. We have noted above that Regulation 25 of 1962, on the financing of the common agricultural policy, envisaged that revenue from levies would form part of the Community's own resources at the single market stage. This came to pass with the enactment of the first own resources Decision in 1970,[1] Article 2(a) of which transferred to the Community budget revenue derived from the implementation of the common agricultural policy. An example of this can be seen in the milk sector. The basic market organisation measure is Council Regulation 804/68 (EEC)[2] (as amended), which provided for import levies in Article 14(2). In the intervening period since 1968 the milk market has suffered from chronic oversupply and other levies, imposed on Community producers, have been introduced to discourage overproduction. The so-called 'co-responsibility' levy[3] and the 'superlevy'[4] also form part of the Community's own resources, but they are considered as intervention measures within the meaning of Council Regulation 729/70 (EEC)[5] on the financing of the common agricultural policy, and thus form part of the Guarantee Section of the European Agricultural Guidance and Guarantee Fund (*infra* at para. 6.7).

Another difficulty, experienced equally by all product sectors to which a uniform pricing system applied, was brought about by the monetary instability of the late 1960s and 1970s. Instead of allowing the price received by the producer to follow an upward or downward revaluation of his national currency, the Community response was to introduce monetary compensatory amounts[6] (MCAs) which were a sort of tax intended to prevent traders taking advantage of currency fluctuations and thereby causing short-term market instability. But like Topsy, the MCA system growed and growed, and most commentators agreed that the system became a real barrier to trade in agricultural goods in the Community.[7] It is now being dismantled,[8] but during its operation MCAs formed part of the Community's own resources.

(ii) *Customs duties*

Since 1 July 1968 the EEC has operated a uniform tariff for customs purposes: this is known as the Common Customs Tariff (CCT).[9] Article 2(b) of the first own resources Decision provided for the transfer to the Community of customs duties derived from the application of the CCT; this is now subject to a 10 per cent refund to Member States to cover the cost of collecting the duties (Article 5 of the second own resources Decision).

(iii) *VAT*

We have noted (*supra* at para. 6.4) how the objective of the first own resources Decision, that the Communities were to be entirely self-financing from 1975 onwards, was held up by the delay in adopting and implementing the Sixth Directive on Value Added Tax. The system finally came into operation in 1980 when VAT rates were mobilised at the rate of 0.73 per cent, which was already close to the 1 per cent limit set in Article 4 of the first own resources Decision. The 1.4 per cent limit set by Article 3(2) of the second own resources Decision was virtually exhausted in 1987 and it was envisaged that the Council, acting unanimously, would seek to raise the threshold to 1.6 per cent of the revenue accruing from the application of VAT in the Member States; however, the decision of the European Council at its meeting in Brussels in February 1988 left the 1.4 per cent rate intact, and indicated that the shortfall will be made up by GNP-related contributions from the Member States.

(iv) *Taxes on Community civil servants*

Community officials are immune from national taxation on their income but they are subject to a tax for the benefit of the Communities; this is provided for in Article 13 of the Protocol on the Privileges and Immunities of the European Communities (*supra* at para. 4.53). The system of taxation is set out in Council Regulation 260/68 (EEC, Euratom, ECSC),[10] as amended;[11] and this legislation provides in Article 9 that the tax proceeds shall be entered as revenue in the budgets of the Communities.

(v) *Fines*

Regulations adopted by the Council under Article 87 of the Treaty can provide for fines and periodic penalty payments and there are three regulations which empower the Commission to impose fines. These are Council Regulations 11 of 1960,[12] 17 of 1962[13] and 1017/68.[14] In practice only Regulation 17 has been used by the Commission to impose fines, and the policy of the Commission is to use its fining powers under Article 15 of the Regulation primarily for the purpose of ensuring compliance with

Articles 85 and 86 of the Treaty rather than to add to the Community's budgetary resources. Furthermore, the revenue from this source cannot be predicted in advance. In 1985, the latest year for which figures are available, fines contributed over 13 million ECU to the budget.[15]

1 O.J. (Sp. Ed.) 1970 p. 224.
2 O.J. (Sp. Ed.) 1968 p. 176.
3 See Council Regulation 1079/77 (EEC) O.J. L 131, 26.5.1977 p. 6.
4 See Council Regulations 856 and 857/84 (EEC) O.J. L 90 1.4.1984 pp. 10 and 13.
5 O.J. (Sp. Ed.) 1970 p. 218.
6 Council Regulation 974/71 (EEC) O.J. (Sp. Ed.) 1971 (I) p. 257.
7 See, for example, Desmond A.G. Norton, *The Common Organisation of the Market, Smuggling and the Two Percent Levy of 1979*, (1984) J.I.S.E.L. 86.
8 See Council Regulation 855/84 (EEC) on the calculation and dismantlement of monetary compensatory amounts, O.J. L 90 1.4.1984 p. 1.
9 See Council Regulation 950/68 (EEC) O.J. (Sp. Ed.) 1968 p. 275 (I), repealed by Council Regulation 2658/87 (EEC).
10 O.J. (Sp. Ed.) 1968 (I) p. 37.
11 Most recently by Council Regulations 3855 and 3856 O.J. L 359 19.12.1986 pp. 1 and 5.
12 O.J. (Sp. Ed.) 1959–62 p. 60.
13 O.J. (Sp. Ed.) 1959–62 p. 87.
14 O.J. (Sp. Ed.) 1968 (I) p. 302.
15 Final adoption of the general budget of the European Communities for the financial year 1987, European Parliament 87/186 (Euratom, ECSC, EEC) O.J. L 86, 30.3.1987 pp. 68–69.

EEC and Euratom borrowings

6.6 Article 174(2) of the Euratom Treaty expressly permits the Community to contract loans for the purpose of financing research or investment. Two Council Decisions of 1977[1] permitted loans to be raised for the co-financing of nuclear power plants; the Commission is now empowered to borrow up to 3000 million ECU for this purpose.[2]

By contrast, the EEC Treaty contains no specific provisions authorising the Community to raise loans. The Community does, however, borrow money and this takes place through a mechanism known as the New Community Instrument (NCI), which empowers the Commission to lend the proceeds of such loans to investment projects which contribute to greater economic convergence and integration, especially for energy, industry or infrastructure purposes. The NCI was established by Council Decision 78/870 (EEC),[3] and its legal basis is Article 235 of the EEC Treaty. The 1978 Decision empowered the Commission to borrow up to 1000 million ECU but since then further tranches of borrowing have been authorised by the Council;[4] also, the objectives of assistance under the NCI have been altered slightly and action must now be concentrated in favour of small and medium sized enterprises.[5] Loans are raised by the Commission but are deposited with, and administered by, the European Investment Bank (EIB). The procedure for procuring an NCI loan can be illustrated by reference to a recent NCI measure, Council Decision 87/182 (EEC),[6] which authorised the Commission to borrow up to 750 million ECU. According to the Decision, the Commission negotiates the terms of borrowings in the best interests of the Community (Article 6). The EIB is given a mandate to administer loans on behalf of, and at the risk of, the

Community; the Commission decides which projects are eligible whereas the EIB decides the terms on which loans will be granted; loan applications must be transmitted simultaneously to the Commission and the EIB, (Article 7); but loans will normally be granted only through the agency of a financial intermediary (Article 4).

1 Council Decision 77/270(Euratom) and 77/271(Euratom) O.J. L 88, 6.4.1977 pp. 9 and 11.
2 Council Decision 85/537(Euratom) O.J. L 334, 12.12.1985 p. 23.
3 O.J. L 298, 25.10.1978 p. 9.
4 See, for example, Council Decision 84/383 (EEC) O.J. L 208, 3.8.1984 p. 53.
5 Council Decision 83/200 (EEC) O.J. L 112, 23.4.1983 p. 26.
6 O.J. L 71, 14.3.1987 p. 34.

Community expenditure

6.7 Apart from spending connected with the administration of the institutions of the Communities the major expenditure arising out of the Communities' budget is attributable to three funds:

- the European Agricultural Guidance and Guarantee Fund (EAGGF or 'FEOGA');
- the European Social Fund (ESF); and
- the European Regional Development Fund (ERDF).

(i) *The EAGGF*

Article 40(4) of the EEC Treaty provides for the establishment of one or more agricultural guidance and guarantee funds so as to enable the common organisations of agricultural markets to achieve their objectives. Regulation 25 of 1962[1] established a single guidance and guarantee fund which was later divided into two sections—a Guidance Section and a Guarantee Section—by Regulation 17 of 1964.[2] At the end of the transitional period the latter Regulation was replaced by Regulation 729/70 (EEC)[3] which established the definitive arrangements for financing the Common Agricultural Policy.

Article 1 of Regulation 729/70 establishes the EAGGF, which comprises two sections. The Guarantee Section finances: (a) refunds on exports to non-Member States; and (b) intervention intended to stabilise the agricultural markets. The Guidance Section finances measures designed to achieve structural adaptation in the agricultural sector; the farm modernisation and disadvantaged areas schemes fall within this category. Initially, Article 6(5) limited expenditure on the Guidance Section to 285 million units of account per annum; but now the Council establishes expenditure for structural reform programmes over a five-year period.[4] However, it is expenditure on export refunds and intervention that accounts for the greater part of the Communities' budget. Article 2 of the Regulation deals with export refunds and allows the Council to adopt the necessary implementing measures. These can be found in Regulation 2730/79 (EEC),[5] which provides for payment of the merchant or exporter by the authorities of the Member State in which the customs formalities were carried out payment will only be made, however, on production of proof that the commodity has arrived at its destination (and cleared customs there) or has left the customs territory of the Community. Intervention payments are dealt with under Article 3 and implementing legislation adopted by the Council includes Regulation 1883/78 (EEC),[6] which lays down general rules on Community financing of intervention purchases, and Regulation 3247/81(EEC)[7] which specifies the rules applicable to buying-in, storage and sale of agricultural products by intervention agencies.

The administration of EAGGF expenditure is provided for in Article 4 of Regulation 729/70. The Member States were required to designate a national authority to act as 'intervention agent' for the Commission. The Commission makes available to the intervention agency the necessary credits to make export refunds and intervention payments (Article 4(2)), while the Member States are obliged to draw up accounts on an annual basis concerning such expenditure. Regulation 1723/72 (EEC)[8] laid down more detailed requirements on the making up of accounts for the Guarantee Section of the EAGGF. Article 5 of Regulation 729/70 requires the intervention agencies to forward to the Commission annual accounts and statements of cash holdings and estimates of financial needs for the coming year; on the basis of this information the Commission sanctions advance payments. Implementing rules are contained in Commission Regulation (EEC) 3184/83.[9]

The huge sums of money involved in the operation of the Guidance and Guarantee Funds leads inevitably to the question of fraud and other irregularities. Article 8 of Regulation 729/70 requires the Member States to take the necessary legal or administrative action to ensure that activities covered by the Fund are carried out properly, to prevent and deal with irregularities, and to recover sums lost as a result of irregularities or negligence. The cost of fraudulent or negligent losses is borne by the Community unless it can be attributed to the national authorities. There have been a number of implementing measures in this context: Council Regulation (EEC) 283/72[10] concerns the recovery of sums wrongly paid in connection with Fund financing; Council Directive (EEC) 76/308[11] and Commission Directive (EEC) 77/794[12] set up a system of mutual assistance for the recovery of EAGGF claims, agricultural levies and customs duties; and Council Directive (EEC) 77/435[13] provided for the scrutiny by Member States of transactions forming part of the Guarantee Section of the EAGGF.

Finally, the Fund is administered by the Commission (Article 10) which is assisted by the Standing Committee on Agricultural Structure (Article 7) and the Committee for the European Agricultural Guidance and Guarantee Fund (Articles 11–15) which is also known as the 'Fund Committee'.

In the 1987 budget expenditure commitments for 24,130 million ECU were appropriated for the EAGGF.[14]

(ii) *The European Social Fund*

The Social Provisions of the Treaty aim at improving living and working standards in the Community. The European Social Fund (the ESF), established by Article 123 with the object of improving employment opportunities and increasing the geographical and occupational mobility of workers, is a more dynamic instrument of employment policy and complements other Community funds, such as the European Agricultural Guidance and Guarantee Fund, and the European Regional Development Fund, whose objects include the reduction of regional disparities. The purposes for which the Fund could be used, as originally set out in Article 125 of the Treaty, were quite restrictive; on application by a Member State the Fund could meet 50 per cent of the expenditure incurred by public authorities (a) on projects aimed at ensuring the productive re-·employment of workers by means of vocational retraining or resettlement allowances, or (b) on tideover allowances for workers in the event of the conversion of an undertaking to other productive purposes. Payments for vocational retraining and resettlement could only be made if the workers had been in productive employment in their new occupation or place of residence for at least six months, and assistance for workers in the event of the conversion of an undertaking could only be granted, if the workers had been employed in that undertaking for at least six months.

These limitations were largely eliminated by the reform of the Fund, envisaged in Article 126, which enabled the Council, after the expiry of the transitional period, to rule that the forms of assistance referred to in Article 125 should no longer be granted. In February 1971 the Council adopted Decision 71/66 (EEC)[15] in which new tasks for the Fund were outlined. Implementing regulations were adopted in November 1971.[16] The revised categories of intervention were defined in Articles 4 and 5 of the Decision.

The tasks assigned to the ESF were further reformed in 1983 by Council Decision 83/516 (EEC).[17] Article 1 defines the tasks as contributing in particular '. . . to the socio-vocational insertion and integration of young people and disadvantaged workers, to the adaptation of the workforce to labour-market developments and to technological change and to the reduction of regional imbalances in the labour market.' ESF financing is available for operations concerning:

(a) vocational training and guidance;
(b) recruitment and wage subsidies;
(c) resettlement; and
(d) services and technical advice concerned with job creation.

Article 4 requires that priority must be given to the promotion of employment of persons under 25 years of age and this is underlined by Article 7(1) which specifies that not less than 75 per cent of expenditure in any year must be aimed at young people. Article 7(3) also required 40 per cent of available appropriations to be expended in peripheral regions with high unemployment such as Greece, Ireland, the Mezzogiorno and Northern Ireland. Applications for assistance may be made by public authorities or by private institutions (Article 2); as a general rule a project must be supported by public funds in the relevant Member State (Article 5(1)); the Fund pays 50 per cent of the cost of the project but if the scheme concerns an area with especially serious or prolonged unemployment, assistance from the Fund may be increased by 10 per cent (Article 5(2)).

Further rules on the implementation of the tasks of the ESF are contained in Council Regulation (EEC) 2950/83.[18]

The Council Decision also delegated certain functions to the Commission. Article 6 requires the Commission to prepare each year, and for the three following financial years, Fund management guidelines for the purpose of determining operations which reflect Community priorities.[19] Furthermore, the administrative aspects of the Fund are governed by Commission Decision (EEC) 83/673[20] on the management of the European Social Fund. The Commission administers the Fund but is assisted in this task by a 'Fund Committee', (EEC Treaty, art. 124), the rules of which are laid down in Decision 83/517.[21]

In the 1987 budget expenditure commitments for 2,602 million ECU were appropriated for the ESF.[22]

(iii) *The European Regional Development Fund*

The need to eliminate regional disparities is implicit in Article 2 of the EEC Treaty which speaks of '. . . a harmonious development of economic activities' and '. . . a continuous and balanced expansion'. Other provisions of the Treaty also touch upon regional problems of an economic nature.[23] The development of regional infrastructures and the elimination of disparities were initially financed by various Community Funds, including the European Agricultural Guidance and Guarantee Fund, the European Social Fund and the European Investment Bank, but the creation of a co-ordinated regional policy was not seriously considered until the summit meeting held in Paris in October 1972 where it was noted that '. . . priority should be given to the aim of correcting, in the Community, the structural and regional imbalances which might affect the realisation of economic and monetary union'.[24] The institutions were invited to establish a Regional Development Fund before 31 December 1973, but it was not until 1975 that the Council, acting under Article 235 of the Treaty, adopted a Regulation establishing a Regional Development Fund and a Decision setting up a Regional Policy Committee.[25] The Fund had a three-year endowment of 1,300 million units of account, out of which each Member State was assigned a quota which took into account the relative gravity of each Member State's regional problems. The Regulation provided for a review of the operation of the system before 1 January 1978, and on the basis of a Commission communication concerning guidelines for regional policy, which incorporated draft changes in the Regulation,[26] the Council adopted amending Regulations in 1979[27] and 1980.[28]

A further review of the Regulation, which took place over a three-year period, resulted in the enactment of Council Regulation (EEC) 1787/84[29] which reformed the Fund with effect from 1 January 1985. According to the Commission[30] the important innovations in the Regulation were:

(i) the provisions on the coordination of Community policies that impinge on regional development and on the coordination of Community and national regional policies (Title I);
(ii) the amalgamation of the Fund's two sections (quota and non-quota) into a single Fund whose resources will be allocated to Member

States by reference to ranges setting upper and lower limits to the assistance available to each Member State (Title II). According to Article 4, Ireland was to be allocated between 5.64 per cent and 6.83 per cent of the ERDF, but these percentages have been reduced somewhat by the accession of Spain and Portugal to the Communities;

(iii) the gradual changeover from individual project financing to programme financing (Title III);

(iv) provisions designed to exploit the potential for internally generated development of regions (Title III).

Other changes include higher and simplified rates of assistance, a speedier payments procedure through the introduction of a system of advances, and provisions concerning integrated approaches to development.[31]

The Fund is administered by the Commission which is assisted by the ERDF Committee (Article 39); the latter operates in much the same manner as a management committee. In addition, there is a Regional Policy Committee (established by Council Decision 75/185 (EEC);[32] this body consists of senior civil servants and Commission officials, and its principal function is to examine the regional development programmes submitted annually by the Member States but it may also study other regional policy problems either on its own initiative or at the request of the Council or the Commission.

Another major innovation in the area of regional policy was the adoption of Council Regulation 2088/85 (EEC)[33] concerning integrated Mediterranean programmes (IMPs). The Regulation is designed to assist the southern regions of the Community and consists of multi-annual operations covering all spheres of economic activity aimed at stimulating investment in the productive sector and improving infrastructure. Member States which submit integrated programmes are entitled to benefit from substantial financial assistance drawn from existing structural Funds, additional budgetary allocations and loans from the EIB and under the New Community Instrument.[34]

In the 1987 budget expenditure commitments for 3,565 million ECU were appropriated for operations in the regional development and transport sectors.[35]

1 O.J. (Sp. Ed.) 1959–62 p. 126.
2 O.J. (Sp. Ed.) 1963–64 p. 103.
3 O.J. (Sp. Ed.). 1970 p. 218.
4 Council Regulation 870/85 (EEC) O.J. L 95, 2.4.1985 p. 1.
5 O.J. L 317, 12.12.1979 p. 1 repealed by Commission Regulation 3665/87 (EEC) O.J. L 351 14.12.1987 p. 1.
6 O.J. L 216, 5.8.1978 p. 1.
7 O.J. L 327, 14.11.1981 p. 1.
8 O.J. (Sp. Ed.) (Second Series) EAGGF p. 109.
9 O.J. L 320, 17.11.1983 p. 1.
10 O.J. (Sp. Ed.) 1972 (I) p. 90
11 O.J. L 73, 19.3.1976 p. 18.
12 O.J. L 333, 24.12.1977 p. 11.
13 O.J. L 172, 12.7.1977 p. 17.
14 Parliament Decision (Euratom, ECSC, EEC 87/186 O.J. L 86, 30.3.1987 p. 1 (Summary of appropriations pp. 280–285.)

15 O.J. (Sp. Ed.) 1971 (I) p. 52.
16 O.J. (Sp. Ed.) 1971 (III) p. 950 *et seq.*
17 O.J. L 289, 22.10.1983 p. 38.
18 O.J. L 289, 22.10.1983 p. 1.
19 See, for example, Commission Decision (EEC) 86/221 O.J. L 153, 7.6.1986 p. 59, as amended by Commission Decision (EEC) 87/171 O.J. L 68, 12.3.1987 p. 34.
20 O.J. L 377, 31.12.1983 p. 1.
21 *Supra*, n. 18.
22 *Supra*, n. 14. (Summary of appropriations p. 286.)
23 Articles 39(2)(a) and 80(2).
24 6th General Report 1972, point 11.
25 Regulation (EEC) 724/75 O.J. L 73, 21.3.1975 p. 1.
26 O.J. L 161, 9.7.1977.
27 Regulation (EEC) 214/79 O.J. L 35, 9.2.1979 p. 1.
28 Regulation (EEC) 3325/80 O.J. L 349, 23.12.1980 p. 10.
29 O.J. L 169, 28.6.1984 p. 1.
30 18th General Report, 1984, point 346.
31 *Ibid.*, at point 347.
32 O.J. L 73, 21.3.1975 p. 47.
33 O.J. L 197, 27.7.1985 p. 1.
34 19th General Report 1985, point 467.
35 *Supra*, n. 14. (Summary of appropriations p. 285.)

Reform of the structural funds

6.8 Article 23 of the Single European Act added a new Title III to Part III of the EEC Treaty. The new title is called 'Economic and Social Cohesion' and it adds five new articles to the Treaty. The objective of these new provisions is to reduce the disparities between the regions and the backwardness of the least-favoured areas (Article 130A). Article 130D provided for an immediate review of the existing structural Funds as soon as the SEA entered into force, and in September 1987 the Commission published a proposal for a Council Regulation on the tasks of the structural Funds and their effectiveness, and on coordination of their activities *inter se* and with the operations of the European Investment Bank and other financial instruments.[1] The basic feature of the proposal is that Community operations under the Structural Funds should implement the Economic and Social Cohesion provisions of the SEA by contributing to the attainment of five priority objectives:

(1) Promoting the development and structural adjustment of the less-developed regions;
(2) Converting regions affected by economic decline and restructuring declining industries;
(3) Combating long-term unemployment;
(4) facilitating the occupational integration of young people, and
(5) Speeding up the adjustment of agricultural structures and promoting the development of rural areas (Article 1.)

The Funds (The EAGGF Guidance Section, the ERDF and the ESF) would contribute to the achievement of the objectives according to an agreed allocation of responsibilities and would be supported by the EIB and other financial instruments in this regard (Article 2). Agreement in principle was reached at the Brussels meeting of the European Council in

101

February 1988 concerning reform of the structural funds, and a framework Regulation from the Council was promised before the end of May 1988.

1 O.J. C 245 12.9.87 p. 3, enacted in Council Regulation (EEC) 2052/88 O.J. L 185, 15.7.1988 p. 9.

Non-budgetary expenditure

6.9 There are two non-budgetary types of 'expenditure' which should be noted. The first concerns the financing operations of the European Investment Bank (*supra* at para.s 4.40–4.46). The second arises in connection with the trade and aid agreements concluded with the African, Caribbean and Pacific (ACP) States. The origin of these agreements can be found in Articles 131–6 of the EEC Treaty; these provisions envisaged a form of association between the Community and the colonies and overseas territories of the original Member States. The details of this association were laid down in an implementing Convention annexed to the Treaty; this Convention applied for a period of five years and, in Article 1, a Development Fund (known as the First EDF) was established to promote the social and economic development of the non-European countries and territories. The implementing Convention has been replaced roughly every five years (in accordance with EEC Treaty, art. 136) and all the succeeding Conventions—the First and Second Yaounde Conventions of 1960 and 1963, and the First, Second and Third Lomé Conventions of 1975, 1979 and 1984—have made provision for the European Development Fund (EDF). The Sixth EDF made available for distribution to the African, Caribbean and Pacific states 7,400 million ECU. In addition, 1,100 million ECU is available from the resources of the European Investment Bank.[1]

1 18th General Report 1984, point 714.

Community revenue and expenditure in Ireland

(i) *Application of the own resources Decisions*

6.10 How do the own resources Decisions apply in Ireland? Before answering this question it should be noted that the own resources Decisions have a status in Community law somewhat more elevated than a run-of-the-mill Regulation or Directive. One observer has described them as part of the primary constitutional law of the Communities,[1] and they come into existence by virtue of what might be described as an 'internal amendment' of the Treaty. When exercising power under Article 201 of the EEC Treaty the Council must act unanimously, after consulting the Parliament, and must recommend the proposal to the Member State 'for adoption in accordance with their respective constitutional requirements'. With this in mind, Article 8 of the own resources Decision requires the Member States to notify the Secretary General of the Council of the completion of the adoption procedures in accordance with their respective constitutional requirements. But, while an own resources Decision is clearly considered as something special by the Treaty, it does not rank equally with a Treaty amendment properly so-called. It is not a

'Constitutional Treaty' and, therefore, an amendment to section 1(1) of the European Communities Act, 1972 is not necessary.

Nevertheless, in Ireland one would have expected some legislative measure along the lines of the European Communities (Supplementary Funding) Act, 1984, but in fact there was no formal legislative implementation of the second own resources Decision into domestic law. The authorities of the State appear to have taken the view that a sufficient legal basis for compliance with the Directive already existed in the form of the European Communities (State Financial Transactions) Regulations, 1972.[2] Regulation 4 of this Statutory Instrument, adopted under section 3 of the European Communities Act, 1972, provides:

'Any payments *necessitated by the obligations of membership* of the state of the European Communities may be made from the Central Fund or the growing produce thereof.'

(The emphasised passage is clearly a reference to the Third Amendment to the Constitution.)

It is doubtful whether Regulation 4 *does* provide a sufficient legal basis for the application in Ireland of the second own resources Decision or the 1988 reformulation agreed by the European Council (*supra* at para. 6.4). The critical word is 'payments'. When the plain or ordinary meaning of this word is used it would seem to authorise disbursements by the State to recipients in Ireland of Community funds as well as transfers of resources by the State to the Community. Clearly, this would justify transfers to the Community of agricultural levies and customs duties (covered by Article 2 of the second own resources Decision) collected routinely by the Revenue Commissioners. It would also provide the mechanism by which *transfers* of VAT could be made to the Community. However, an altogether more extensive interpretation of 'payments' would be required to justify *raising* the maximum rate at which VAT own resources can be mobilised, and the historical context in which the Regulations were adopted provides an argument against such an interpretation. When Regulation 4 of the statutory instrument entered into force the maximum rate of VAT had been fixed at 1 per cent and the mobilisation of VAT resources was not envisaged before 1975 at the earliest. As we have seen, the system did not enter into force until 1980 so that it is extremely doubtful whether the exhaustion of the VAT resources, and the consequent need to raise the maximum rate, could have been in the contemplation of the Minister for Finance when the Regulations were made. And besides, if Regulation 4 is a sufficient legal basis for the increase in the VAT rate, why was specific legislative authority required for the transfer of Ireland's portion of the supplementary Budget in 1984? Furthermore, it seems strange that a measure having an 'effect equivalent to a Treaty' can enter into force in Ireland without any consultation of, not to mention approval by, the Dail, all the more so when the effect of the measure is to reduce incrementally the exclusive power to raise taxes which the Constitution vests in the Dail.

Similarly, it is doubtful whether reliance can be placed on the protection of the Third Amendment of the Constitution, an echo of which is heard in the text of Regulation 4. If the argument that Regulation 4 does not cover increases in the maximum VAT rate is correct, then the first arm of the second part of the Constitutional amendment cannot apply because it exempts from Constitutional scrutiny, and gives priority to, laws enacted, acts done or measures adopted by the State necessitated by membership of the Communities. To follow the argument to its logical conclusion, no law, act or measure has yet been implemented in Ireland to facilitate VAT transfers up to the rate of 1.4 per cent. Likewise, the second arm of the exemption cannot come into play because, far from setting up a conflict between Community law and domestic law, EEC Treaty, art. 201 and Article 173 of the Euratom Treaty on the one hand, and Article 8 of the own resources Decision, on the other hand, actually envisage national approval of own resources Decisions in accordance with the constitutional requirements of the Member States. The rationale underlying this approval system can be found in the appreciation by the Treaty draftsmen that the creation of an own resources system involved a diminution of national parliamentary sovereignty which should not be disposed of by sleight of hand or without adequate debate.

It is submitted that the necessary measures for compliance with the own resources Decision, in so far as the increase in the maximum VAT rate is concerned, have not yet been adopted by the State. This means that transfers in excess of 1 per cent of VAT collected in Ireland are made in the absence of legislative authority. It follows that the State is in breach of an obligation arising out of its membership of the Communities. Only an act of the Oireachtas or an instrument made under section 3 of the European Communities Act, 1972 can rectify this anomaly.

This leads to a final observation. If the authorities of the State believe that the protective cloak of the Third Amendment, in combination with Regulation 4 of the European Communities (State Financial Transactions) Regulations, 1972, provides an adequate basis for implementation of the VAT element of the second own resources Decision and the GNP element in the reformulation agreed by Council in February 1988,[3] then perhaps the time has come to consider changes in the system of parliamentary supervision of matters relating to the European Communities. This could be done by strengthening the position of the Oireachtas Joint Committee on the Secondary Legislation of the European Communities. The Government should be obliged to refer to the Joint Committee any draft Community or domestic measure which would have the effect of diminishing the powers of any of the organs of State established by the Constitution. The observations of the Committee should then be the subject of a mandatory debate in the Dail and Seanad. Such a supervisory scheme would not in any way undermine the effectiveness of obligations necessitated by membership of the Communities, nor would it impose an undue burden either on the Government to recognise potentially problematic measures or on the Joint Committee to examine and debate them; the number of Community or domestic acts of this type is very limited, but it might ensure that such changes are implemented by Acts of the Oireachtas rather than by obscure formulae in delegated legislation.

(ii) *Collection of Revenue*

Regulation 4 of the European Communities (State Financial Transactions) Regulations, 1972, which the authorities of the State believe justifies the transfer of VAT own resources at the increased rate of 1.4 per cent, constitutes the sole legislative authority for the collection of Community revenue in Ireland. By virtue of this provision an Exchequer account has been established with the Central Bank and customs duties, agricultural levies and VAT own resources, all of which are collected by the Revenue Commissioners, are retained in this account for transmission to the Commission. There is no special enabling legislation empowering the Revenue Commissioners to collect Community revenue; the Customs Act, 1956, applies to the collection of customs duties and agricultural levies, and the Value Added Tax Act 1972 and the Value Added Tax (Amendment) Act, 1978 apply to the collection of VAT own resources. However, there has been a change in the method of collection of VAT. When Regulation (EEC, Euratom, ECSC) 2892/77[4] laid down rules for the calculation of VAT own resources the Member States were given an option: calculation by the 'return method' or by the 'revenue method'. Initially, Ireland and Denmark opted for the return method but in 1986 financial and administrative considerations led the State to adopt the revenue method.

In relation to revenue which may be owing in other Member States the European Communities (Agriculture and Customs) (Mutual Assistance as regards the Recovery of Claims) Regulations of 1980[5] provide a court procedure for recovery in the State of such money. The Regulations, which implement Council Directive (EEC) 76/308[6] and Commission Directive (EEC) 77/794 provide for the Minister of Agriculture or the Minister for Justice, or both, to sue for any amount claimed by an authority of another Member State and such sum will be regarded as a simple contract debt due to the Minister of Finance.

(iii) *Expenditure*

(a) The Common Agricultural Policy If there is a dearth of domestic legislation on the collection of Community revenue in Ireland the same observation can be made of the expenditure of Community funds within the State. It is astonishing to note that the legislative basis for the implementation of the EAGGF, which was responsible for net transfers to Ireland of over £3.7 billion between 1973–1983,[8] consists of no more than three or four clauses in two statutory instruments.

Regulations 6 and 7 of the European Communities (State Financial Transactions) Regulation, 1972[9] permit advances to be made to the Minister for Agriculture from the Central Fund to enable the Minister to discharge CAP obligations and allow for borrowing by the Minister for the same purposes on the strength of guarantees issued by the Minister for Finance.

The European Communities (Common Agricultural Policy) (Market Intervention) Regulations, 1973[10] are somewhat more explicit in the powers they confer on the Minister for Agriculture. Regulation 3 constitutes the Minister as the intervention agent in Ireland within the

105

meaning of Article 4 of Regulation (EEC) 729/70.[11] Whenever arrangements made by the Community require the buying, selling, storing, importation, exportation, grading, processing, disposal or withdrawal from the market of agricultural products, the Minister may carry out those operations, subject in each case to such terms and conditions as he considers appropriate. Regulation 4 permits the Minister, whenever Community arrangements require the storing, grading, processing, disposal or withdrawal from the market of any agricultural product by private parties, to support those persons by making payments to producer organisations, or by paying premiums and subsidies. Regulation 11 empowers the Minister to borrow foreign currency for any of the purposes of his intervention functions. The remaining provisions of the Regulations are administrative in nature: authorised officers may enter premises or vehicles to take samples of any agricultural product which has been or may be the subject of financial assistance under the Regulations (Regulation 7); all purchasers and sellers of goods subject to the Regulations must keep records (Regulation 9); tampering with samples or falsifying records are criminal offences punishable, on summary conviction, with fines of up to £200 (Regulations 8 and 10).

These provisions constitute the sole legislative base for a wide range of activities by the Minister including: intervention purchasing of beef, cereals, butter and skimmed milk; export refunds for beef, butter, whole milk, skimmed milk, pigmeat and processed products; payment of monetary compensatory amounts and accession compensatory amounts; aids for storage of caseins and skimmed milk and for 'social butter'; and research premiums for market development in the ewe and calf sectors.

The European Communities (Common Agricultural Policy) (Scrutiny of Transactions) Regulations, 1980,[12] which implement Council Directive (EEC) 77/435,[13] are designed to control fraud and other irregularities against the EAGGF. Regulation 3 requires any person carrying out transactions connected with the system of financing of the Guarantee sector of the EAGGF to keep records of those transactions for purposes of scrutiny by authorised officers; records must be kept for three years, but the requirement to keep records does not apply to primary producers who are not in receipt of payments or who are not liable for charges connected with the EAGGF. Authorised officers may enter premises to inspect records (Regulation 5). Failure to comply with the Regulations can result in summary prosecution and is punishable by a term of not more than six months imprisonment, a fine of £500 or both (Regulation 6).

(b) The European Social Fund The implementation of ESF expenditure in Ireland is in the hands of the Department of Labour. Apart from the very general authority of the European Communities (State Financial Transactions) Regulations, 1972 (*supra* at para. 6.10), there is no domestic implementing legislation. All applications for assistance from the ESF must be submitted through the Department of Labour, and semi-State agencies have relied heavily on the ESF to alleviate the social problems which have been generated by prolonged recession and high youth unemployment. Consequently, most of the funds from the ESF have been channelled into programmes like the Employment Incentive Scheme and the Youth Employment Agency (both now subsumed into the new entity FAS). In recent years the Irish Management Institute has been the only non-governmental body to receive assistance from the ESF. In fact, recent financial restraints have meant that if a project does not fall within the ESF guidelines it has little chance of procuring matching funds from State resources. This heavy dependence on direct transfers from the Community, to achieve domestic social objectives, has given rise to official disquiet.[14]

By contrast with the early days of the ESF, when there were few applications for assistance, the applications now far exceed the available resources. This means that applications—backed by matching funds from domestic sources—must be submitted by October of the year preceding the projected expenditure.

(c) The European Regional Development Fund Expenditure from the ERDF in Ireland is administered by the Department of Finance and, like the ESF, there is no domestic implementing legislation. It is open to private individuals and corporations to seek assistance from the ERDF but all applications must be channelled through the Department of Finance. This latter requirement also applies to local authorities; and if the publicity placards on the roadsides of Ireland are anything to go by, not a single significant infra-structural project in the State, commenced in the last decade, could have been undertaken without assistance from the ERDF.

1 Rudolf Bernhardt; The sources of Community law, the 'constitution' of the Community; in *Thirty Years of Community Law* (1983), p. 69 at p. 75.
2 S.I. No. 329 of 1972.
3 See Commission proposal for a Council Decision on the system of the Communities' own resources, COM (88) 137 final, enacted in Council Decision (EEC, Euratom) 88/376 O.J. L 185, 15.7.1988, p. 24.
4 O.J. L 336, 27.12.1977 p. 8.
5 S.I. No. 73 of 1980.
6 O.J. L 73, 19.3.1976 p. 18.
7 O.J. L 333, 24.12.1977 p. 11.
8 John Temple Lang, *The Proposal Treaty setting up the European Union:—constitutional implications for Ireland and comments on neutrality*, Irish Studies in International Affairs, Volume 2, No. I, 1985, p. 143, at p. 150.
9 S.I. No. 329 of 1972.
10 S.I. No. 24 of 1973.
11 *Supra*, para. 6.7, n. 3.
12 S.I. No. 301 of 1980.
13 O.J. L 172, 12.7.1977 p. 17.
14 *A Stocktaking of Ireland's membership of the European Communities*, unpublished report of 1986 produced by a working group of Civil Servants.

The budgetary process

6.11 As in the case of national financial arrangements the budgetary procedure in the Communities is a long drawn out and complex affair. Originally, under Article 203 of the Treaty, the process was relatively straightforward: the Commission established the estimates of revenue and expenditure; the Council adopted a draft budget, in respect of which the Assembly (European Parliament) could suggest amendments; and the Council enacted the definitive budget, having accepted or rejected (at its discretion) the suggestions of the Assembly. However, the procedure has become considerably more complicated because of a series of developments which took place in the 1970s.

The first budgetary Treaty of 1970 was the initial step towards democratic legitimacy in the government of the Communities, in so far as the Assembly was given the final decision in respect of expenditure not '. . . necessarily resulting from this Treaty or from Acts, adopted in accordance therewith . . .'.[1] The first budgetary Treaty accompanied the first own resources Decision, and it provided for a transitional period before the new system became fully functional: that period came to an end in 1975, although the VAT element in the own resources system did not begin to operate until 1980 (*supra* at para. 6.5). The first budgetary Treaty provided for another formal but highly significant amendment to the original procedure: on the completion of the budgetary process the declaration that the budget has been adopted is now made by the President of the Parliament rather than the President of the Council (*supra* at para. 4.10). The Parliament was given a marginally greater role in establishing budgetary commitments by the second budgetary Treaty of 1975, and it was also given the power to veto the budget as a whole. But even as the powers of the Parliament were being extended (the decision to hold direct elections was taken at much the same time), there was disagreement about the extent of the Parliament's decision-making power concerning 'non-necessary' expenditure. The problem was not simply one of terminology. In 1974, the year before the system became fully operational, 'non-necessary' expenditure accounted for only 13.9 per cent of expenditure, whereas in 1980 it had nearly doubled to 24.1 per cent.[2] In this regard two developments should be noted. First, at the time of the negotiations of the second budgetary Treaty the Presidents of the Parliament, Council and Commission issued a Joint Declaration on the establishment of a conciliation procedure.[3] According to the second paragraph of the declaration, the procedure can be instituted in respect of '. . . Community acts of general application which have appreciable financial implications, and of which the adoption is not required by virtue of acts in existence.' The object is to ensure the effective participation by the Parliament in the adoption of decisions giving rise to important expenditure or revenue to be charged or credited to the budget of the Communities, and the procedure can be initiated by the Parliament when its opinion has been sought by the Council in respect of decisions concerning 'non-necessary' matters; the Commission acts as facilitator and tries to generate agreement between the Parliament and the Council. However, the Declaration does not state what happens in the event of failure to agree; in such circumstances the Council remains free to ignore the view of the Parliament, which appears to have occurred quite frequently because the Commission proposed an improvement to the system in 1981.[4] The Parliament has accepted the modifications but the Council has not yet responded.

The second occurrence of note was the adoption by the Parliament, the Council and the Commission, on 3 June 1982, of a Joint Declaration on various measures to improve the budgetary procedure.[5] Although the first budgetary Treaty introduced the notion of 'expenditure necessarily resulting from this Treaty', it either deliberately avoided, or failed to define what was meant by 'necessary' and 'non-necessary' expenditure. And because this distinction contained the criterion for the exercise of one of the Parliament's budgetary powers, annual budgetary disputes between the Council and the Parliament became almost inevitable. The 1982 Joint Declaration was intended to encourage harmonious co-operation between the institutions by classifying expenditure in accordance with an Annex attached to the Declaration and by providing principles for classifying new budget items or existing items for which the legal basis has changed. Compulsory expenditure was defined as such expenditure '. . . as the budgetary authority is obliged to enter in the budget to enable the Community to meet its obligations, both internally and externally, under the Treaties and acts adopted in accordance therewith.' It is not entirely clear whether this agreement has resolved the difficulties, because in 1986 the Council succeeded in an action against the Parliament in which it sought the annulment of the act of December 1985 by which the President of the Parliament had declared adopted the budget for 1986: *EC Council v European Parliament*.[6] The case was a landmark decision because the Court of Justice made it clear that the action for annulment, outlined in Article 173 (which mentions only acts of the Council and Commission), also applies to budgetary acts of the European Parliament. On a more mundane level the Court upheld the Council's claim that the Parliament had increased the level of non-necessary expenditure beyond the maximum rate of increase permitted by Article 203(9) of the Treaty.

1 Article 203(4) as amended by Article 4 of the first budgetary Treaty.
2 Strasser, p. 41.
3 O.J. C 89, 22.4.1975 p. 1.
4 Commission Communication of 16 December 1981, Bull.E.C. Supp 3/82.
5 O.J. C 194, 28.7.1982 p. 1.
6 Case 34/86 O.J. C 200, 9.8.1986 p. 200.

6.12 With the exception of the Court of Justice (whose involvement arises *ex post facto*, if at all) the elaboration and implementation of the budget involves all the principal institutions as well as the Court of Auditors. The various stages of the budgetary procedure are set out in Article 203 of the Treaty (as amended). In the Commission one of the college of Commissioners has had specific responsibility for the budget since 1974,[1] and this function is important because Article 203 entrusts to the Commission the task of consolidating into a preliminary draft budget the estimates of expenditure for the next financial year prepared by each of the institutions. The financial year runs from 1 January to 31 December.[2] By 1 September at the latest the Commission must submit the draft budget for the following year to the Council. The Council, assisted by COREPER I,[3] gives the draft budget a first reading, informs the institutions concerned when it intends to depart from the draft budget, and then—acting by qualified majority— establishes the draft budget. The draft budget must be forwarded to the Parliament not later than 5 October. The Parliament has the right to amend the draft budget in matters concerning non-compulsory expenditure, and to propose modifications to compulsory expenditure: concerning the former category of expenditure it acts by a majority of its members but in relation to the latter category it acts by an absolute majority of votes cast.

If the Parliament approves the draft budget within 45 days of receipt from the Council, the budget stands finally adopted; but it should be added that this outcome is most unlikely. Instead, the draft budget returns to the Council, and if within 15 days the Council accepts the Parliament's amendments of non-necessary expenditure and its modifications of necessary expenditure, the budget is deemed finally adopted. The more likely outcome is that the Council will vary the Parliament's amendments and/or modifications, in which case the draft budget must be resubmitted to the Parliament for a second reading. At this stage, the Parliament's room for manœuvre is limited; it has 15 days to act—by a three-fifths majority of the votes cast—on the Council's variations of its amendments to non-necessary expenditure. The final step comes with the declaration by the President of the Parliament that the budget has been finally adopted.

However, the Parliament has a further important power. If it is dissatisfied with the draft budget it may reject it, acting by a majority of its members and by two-thirds of the votes cast, and ask for a new draft to be submitted to it (Articles 203(8)). The veto of the draft budget is likely to occur at a late stage in the process; with this in mind, and also to allow for delays, Articles 204 of the Treaty provides for the system of 'provisional twelfths.' This authorises a sum not exceeding one twelfth of the budget appropriations for the preceding financial year to be spent each month during which the budget has not yet been voted. This means that the Community will not be left without finances, but the combined effect of inflation and increased expenditure commitments is that one twelfth of the previous year's budget is rarely sufficient to meet the Community's needs for any month during which the budget remains unadopted. A graphic illustration of the operation of this system can be seen in the history of the first use of the veto by the Parliament in 1979. This was the year of the first direct elections, so that there were considerably more MEPs—who were paid salaries rather than travelling expenses—and the reference sum for the calculation of provisional twelfths was the 1979 budgetary appropriation for the much smaller, nominated Assembly. Ironically, the people who suffered the greatest discomfort as a result of the rejection of the budget were the MEPs themselves.[4]

By contrast with the system of provisional twelfths, Article 203(9) establishes a system to limit expenditure in the forthcoming year. The Commission is empowered to declare a maximum rate of increase (to which the institutions are required to conform during the budgetary procedure) which is derived from the trend, in volume terms, of the GNP within the Community, the average variation in the budgets of the Member States, and the trend of the cost of living during the previous financial year.

Finally, while the budgetary procedure can now be described as considerably more democratic the potential for inter-institutional disputes, particularly between the Council and the Parliament, has increased greatly and the Joint Declarations of 1975 and 1982 (*supra* at para. 6.11) testify to the lack of consensus between the two arms of the budgetary authority.

1 Strasser, p. 38.

2 EEC Treaty, art. 203(1); Article 5 of the Financial Regulation of 21 December 1977 O.J. L 356, 31.12.1977 p. 1.

3 Article 104 of the Financial Regulation of 21 December 1977, *Supra*, n. 2. See also Strasser p. 43.

4 John A. Usher, The financing of the Community, *Thirty Years of Community Law* (1983), p. 214.

Structure of the budget

6.13 The provisions of the Treaty contain certain basic budgetary principles. Article 199, for instance, specifies that all items of revenue and expenditure must be drawn up in estimates for each financial year, and that budgetary revenue and expenditure must be in balance. Article 202 contains other essential rules relating to the presentation and structure of the budget: expenditure shown in the budget is authorised for one financial year only; unexpended appropriations may be carried forward to the next financial year only; appropriations must be classified under different chapters in a nomenclature; and the expenditure of the Parliament, the Council, the Commission and the Court of Justice must be set out in separate parts of the budget.

Detailed elaboration of these principles can be found in the Financial Regulation applicable to the general budget of the European Communities. The present Regulation,[1] which has been amended on a number of occasions,[2] has been in force since 1977 and was adopted under Article 209 of the Treaty. The latter provision empowers the Council, acting unanimously on a Commission proposal, after consulting the European Parliament and having obtained the opinion of the Court of Auditors: (a) to make Financial Regulations outlining the procedures for presentation and implementation of the budget and the presentation and auditing of accounts; (b) to arrange for the collection of own resources and to meet the Commission's cash requirements; and (c) to determine the rules and responsibilities attaching to authorising and accounting officers.

Titles I and II of the current Financial Regulation deal with matters of form and presentation, and two particular rules can be noted. First, Article 1(3) makes a distinction between commitment appropriations and payment appropriations. The former cover legal obligations for the financial year including activities whose implementation extends beyond the current financial year, whereas the latter applies to expenditure incurred during the current or preceding financial year. The distinction is intended to illustrate to the reader of the budget what must be allocated for immediate payment and what must be kept available for obligations arising under multi-annual programmes. Commitment appropriations and payment appropriations are listed in separate columns in the relevant parts of the budget. Secondly, Articles 15 and 16 of the Financial Regulation specify how the budget is to be laid out: the budget consists of a general statement of the revenue of the Communities, followed by separate sections indicating the revenue and expenditure of the European Parliament, the Council (including the Economic and Social Committee), the Commission, the Court of Justice and the Court of Auditors.[3]

1 *Supra*, para. 6.12, n. 2.

2 See, for example, Council Regulation (Euratom, ECSC, EEC) 1252/79 O.J. L 160, 28.6.1979 p. 1 and, most recently, by Council Regulation (ECSC, EEC, Euratom) 2049/88 O.J. L 185, 15.7.1988 p. 3.

3 See, for example, final adoption of the general budget of the European Communities for the financial year 1987. *Supra*, para. 6.7, n. 14.

Implementation and supervision of expenditure

6.14 In addition to matters concerning presentation and structure, the Financial Regulation of 1977 also lays down detailed rules on financial authorisation and scrutiny. The basic rule concerning expenditure is stated in Article 17: authorising officers and accounting officers must be different individuals. Articles 32–49 lay down the precise rules to be followed concerning commitment, validation, authorisation and payment of expenditure by authorising and accounting officers respectively. Article 19 requires each institution to appoint a financial controller who is responsible for monitoring the commitment and authorisation of all expenditure and for monitoring all revenue; the same Article permits financial controllers to institute proceedings before the Court of Justice. Title V of the Regulation imposes further responsibilities on authorising officers, financial controllers and accounting officers: if they fail to comply with their obligations under the Regulation they render themselves liable to disciplinary action and, where appropriate, to payment of compensation (Articles 68–70).

The next step of the supervision process occurs after expenditure has been incurred. The Commission is obliged to draw up a detailed revenue and expenditure account (Article 75); it must then draw up a balance sheet of the assets and liabilities of the Communities (Article 76) and forward the revenue and expenditure account, the financial analysis and the balance sheet to the European Parliament, the Council and the Court of Auditors by 1 June at the latest (Article 77).

The audit carried out by the Court of Auditors is based on records and, if necessary, on-the-spot inspections (Article 80). The other institutions are obliged to cooperate fully with the Court of Auditors (Article 82); the latter may address comments to any of the institutions in respect of its budgetary expenditure before 15 July at the latest, and the institutions in question may respond by 31 October at the latest (Article 83). Articles 84 and 85 deal with discharge of the budget. The Court of Auditors forwards its report to the Council, Parliament and other institutions before 30 November and its report, together with the replies of the institutions, is published in the Official Journal of the European Communities; on receipt of the report the Council, acting by a qualified majority, recommends to the Parliament that the Commission be given a discharge in respect of the implementation of the budget, but both Article 206b of the Treaty and Article 85 of the Financial Regulation are silent as to what type of majority is required in the European Parliament. The institutions are obliged to take action on the comments appearing in the decisions giving discharge, and must give an account, in the following year's revenue and expenditure account, of the measures taken in the light of those comments.

The unit of account

6.15 Article 207 of the Treaty requires that the budget be drawn up in the unit of account determined in accordance with the financial regulations made pursuant to Article 209. In this regard the Communities followed the ECSC which took as its unit of account the gold value of the United States dollar.[1] The collapse of fixed exchange rates in the late 1960s was followed by a period of profound monetary instability, characterised by attempts to promote a system of floating currencies within certain limits: this was when the 'snake' and the 'snake in the tunnel' made their appearance in the jargon of the economists. Moreover, the confusion extended to the Communities' financial affairs in which a variety of units of account were used for different purposes. In 1975, the Community followed the lead of the International Monetary Fund and created a basket type unit of account made up of specific quantities of the Member States' currencies and with a value, *vis-à-vis* all other currencies, that changed on a daily basis. This was the European Unit of Account (EUA) and its relative success in bringing about a measure of monetary stability was clearly a factor borne in mind by the European Council, meeting at Bremen and Brussels in July and December 1978, when the European Monetary System was being established. A new unit of account, calculated in the same way as the EUA, was introduced for the purposes of the European Monetary Cooperation Fund.[2] This new 'currency' was called the ECU—the European Currency Unit—and it has replaced all other units of account, including the EUA, in all fields of Community activity. By way of illustration, Article 1 of the Financial Regulation of 16 December 1980,[3] which replaced Article 10 of the Financial Regulation of 1977, provides that the budget of the Communities must be established in ECU.

The ECU is also calculated on a 'basket' basis: each Member State's share in the basket is determined by reference to its share of the Community's external trade and its gross domestic product. The Irish pound contributed 1.1 per cent or IR£0.00759 to this 'basket';[4] in 1984 this was altered to 1.2 per cent or IR£0.00871.[5] The ECU operates as a point of reference for exchange rates between participating currencies, as well as a 'divergence indicator'—a means of identifying those currencies which are tending to diverge from those in the system. When a currency manifests a tendency to diverge by more than 2.25 per cent (or 6 per cent for currencies which were floating when the system was introduced) against another currency in the system, intervention is called for, normally by the central banks of the currency or the currencies manifesting the divergence. The ECU is also used as a means of settlement between central banks, and increasing use is made of the ECU by financial and commercial institutions in lending instruments governed by private law.

1 John A. Usher, *Thirty Years of Community Law* (1983), p. 211.
2 Council Regulation (EEC) 3180/78 O.J. L 379 30.12.78 p. 1.
3 Financial Regulation (EEC, Euratom, ECSC) 1176/80 O.J. L 345 20.12.80 p. 23.
4 *Supra*, n. 2.
5 Council Regulation (EEC) 2626/84 O.J. L 247 16.9.84 p. 1.

Part III

Sources of Community Law

Chapter 7

Primary Sources

7.1 The sources of Community law can be divided into two categories: the Primary Sources and the Secondary Sources. The primacy of the first category relates to the superior status and importance of these sources. Primary sources are of greater importance than secondary sources. Secondary sources must at all times conform with primary sources and in the hierarchical order of things if a conflict occurs between primary and secondary law, primary law will prevail. For Irish lawyers this distinction is easily appreciated for it corresponds to a parallel in the Irish legal system where constitutional rules take precedence over ordinary legislation and over delegated legislation.

Because of this hierarchical precedence within the EEC legal system, therefore, it is important to identify the primary sources from the secondary sources.

7.2 The primary sources of Community law are contained in the treaties establishing the European Communities, the annexed protocols and the subsequent amendments thereto. The complete list of these treaties is as follows:

   (1) The Treaty establishing the ECSC 1951;
   (2) The Treaty establishing the EEC 1957;
   (3) The Treaty establishing Euratom 1957;
   (4) The Convention on Certain Institutions Common to the European Communities 1957;
   (5) The Merger Treaty 1965 (Convention establishing a Single Council and a Single Commission of European Communities);
   (6) The First Budgetary Treaty 1970;
   (7) The Treaty of Accession 1972 (Denmark, Ireland and the United Kingdom), together with the Decision of the Council of the same date concerning accession to the ECSC;
   (8) The Second Budgetary Treaty 1975;
   (9) The Treaty of Accession 1979 (Greece);
 (10) The Treaty amending, with respect to Greenland, the Treaties establishing the Communities (1985);

(11) The Treaty relating to the Accession of Spain and Portugal to the EEC and Euratom (1985);
(12) The Decision of the Council relating to the Accession of Spain and Portugal to the ECSC (1985).
(13) The Single European Act 1986.

Since these treaties contain what might be described as the basic constitutional rules it is important to know how these treaties can be amended. Can these treaties be amended, for example, by implication or is a stated and specified procedure always required? One must also examine the status of some other treaties concluded within the Community context to determine whether these too are a primary source and if not what is their status within the Community's legal system.

Amendment to the treaties

7.3 The treaties may be amended only by following a stated procedure. In the case of the EEC the procedure for amendment is provided for in Article 236. It provides that a Member State or the Commission may propose an amendment to the Council. Having consulted the Parliament and, where appropriate, the Commission, the Council can call a conference of the representatives of the Governments to determine by common accord the amendments. The amendments shall enter into force only when they have been ratified by all the Member States in accordance with their respective constitutional requirements.[1] The treaties also provide a special procedure for the admission of new members.[2] Provided these procedures are followed then the amendments will become part of the foundation treaties and of equal status with the rest of the treaties.[3] It would appear that the Member States cannot amend the foundation treaties unless they follow the stated procedure provided for in the treaties.[4] From this one should conclude that the so-called Luxembourg Agreement has no legal significance, whatever its political significance might be.[5]

1 A more simplified amendment procedure is provided for in the case of the ECSC (see ECSC Treaty, art. 96) and Euratom (see Euratom Treaty, art. 204).
2 See EEC Treaty, art. 237 as amended in Single European Act, ECSC Treaty, art. 98, Euratom Treaty, art. 205.
3 Extraordinary amendments are provided for and allowed with the same results in EEC Treaty, art.s 138 and 201. See also ECSC Treaty, art. 95.
4 See R. Bernhardt, 'The Sources of Community Law; the Constitution of the Community', in *Thirty Years of Community Law*, 69, at p. 76. The rule stated in the text would mean that in this matter Community law differs from international law.
5 *Ibid.*

Article 235 of EEC Treaty

7.4 EEC Treaty, art. 235 enables the Community to take fresh powers if it should prove necessary to attain, in the course of the operation of the common market, one of the objectives of the Community. A certain procedure must be followed and is indicated in the Article. Should it be felt necessary to have resort to this Article, then the Community act, to maintain validity, would have to conform to the treaty itself. Such a measure could not be considered as an amendment to the treaty and it could not be classified, as an amendment would be, as a primary source of law.[1]

Other treaties must also be reckoned with. In considering these we must also ask whether these treaties can be regarded (1) as Community law and if so are they to be regarded (2) as primary or secondary Community law. If secondary they are of course subordinate to the foundation treaties in both procedural and substantive matters.

1 See R. Bernhardt, *op. cit.*, 78. For a full discussion on the scope of this article see A. Tizzano, 'The Power of the Community', in *Thirty Years of Community Law* (1983) *op. cit.* para 7.3, fn. 4. esp. p. 50 *et seq.*

Treaties made by Member States *inter se*

7.5 The foundation treaties in certain Articles specifically authorise Member States to conclude agreements between themselves. Examples occur in EEC Treaty, art.s 20, 136 and 220. Article 20 provides that the duties applicable to certain products (List G) shall be determined by negotiation between its Member States. Article 136 provided that certain temporary and transitional measures relating to the overseas territories were for a period of five years to be determined by an Implementing Convention. Article 220 provides as follows:

Article 220
'Member States shall, so far as is necessary, enter into negotiations with each other with a view to securing for the benefit of their nationals:
(a) the protection of persons and the enjoyment and protection of rights under the same conditions as those accorded by each State to its own nationals;
(b) the abolition of double taxation within the Community;
(c) the mutual recognition of companies or firms within the meaning of the second paragraph of Article 48, the retention of legal personality in the event of transfer of their seat from one country to another, and the possibility of mergers between companies or firms governed by the laws of different countries;
(d) the simplification of formalities governing the reciprocal recognition and enforcement of judgments of courts or tribunals and of arbitration awards'.

Already two conventions have been signed under this Article: the Convention on Jurisdiction and Enforcement of Judgments in Civil and Commercial Matters of 27 September 1968, and the Convention on the Mutual Recognition of Companies and Legal Persons, of 29 February 1968, but not yet in force. Opinions vary as to whether such Conventions must be looked on as part of Community law. On the one hand, in favour of treating such conventions as part of Community law, it is pointed out that, not only are they authorised by the treaties, but their objectives are closely related to Community objectives. The Commission takes a leading part in negotiating those agreements and the Court of Justice is given jurisdiction in their interpretation. Moreover, new members are obliged to accede to these treaties.[1] They are, however, even if this view is accepted, merely secondary law in substance and procedure in comparison to the foundation treaties. On the other hand authors such as Louis[2] and Parry and Hardy[3] suggest that because the obligations contained in the conventions derive from Conventions themselves, and not from a Community compulsion, they are strictly speaking not part of Community law.[4]

1 See T.C. Hartley, *The Foundations of European Community Law* (1981), p. 75; D. Lasok and J.W. Bridge, *Law and Institutions of the European Communities*, Fourth Edition (1987), p. 109.
2 J.V. Louis, *The Community Legal Order* (1980), p. 65.
3 Parry and Hardy, *EEC Law*, p. 71.
4 A.G. Toth, *Legal Protection of Individuals in the European Communities* (1978), vol. 1, p. 42.

7.6 Whether treaties between Member States *not* specifically authorised or enjoined by the foundation treaties are part of Community law or not, will depend on facts of each individual case. Assuming that the Member States still retain competence and that the treaty-making power on the topic in question has not been exclusively transferred to the Community[1] the treaty may be part of Community law if its object, the method of negotiation, etc., are closely linked to the Community. The case for regarding it as part of Community law will be strengthened if the Court of Justice is given jurisdiction to interpret the treaty and if new members are obliged to accede to it on joining the Community. The Luxembourg Convention for the European Patent for the Common Market of 1975 provides a good example of such a convention. The object of the agreement was to create a single patent territory for the whole Community with a uniform legal regime operating throughout the common market.

Clearly again this is part of Community law, but it is a secondary, not a primary, source. Lest there be any doubt as to its status *vis-à-vis* the EEC, Article 93 of the Treaty provides, in a manner that might be a model for similar Conventions in the future, that none of its provisions 'may be invoked against the application of any provision of the EEC Treaty'.

1 See *infra*.

Treaties made between Member States and Third Countries

7.7 Agreements between Member States and Third Countries made *prior* to accession are specifically provided for in the EEC Treaty. Article 234 provides:

> The rights and obligations arising from agreements concluded before the entry into force of this Treaty between one or more Member States on the one hand, and one or more third countries on the other, shall not be affected by the provisions of this Treaty.
>
> To the extent that such agreements are not compatible with this Treaty, the Member State or States concerned shall take all appropriate steps to eliminate the incompatibilities established. Member States shall, where necessary, assist each other to this end and shall, where appropriate, adopt a common attitude.

In applying the agreements referred to in the first paragraph, Member States shall take into account the fact that the advantages accorded under this Treaty by each Member State form an integral part of the establishment of the Community and are thereby inseparably linked with the creation of common institutions, the conferring of powers upon them and the granting of the same advantages by all the other Member States'.

Although not part of Community law, these treaties under Article 234 do have an impact in Community law. For example, the Article obliges the institutions to allow the Member States to perform their obligations arising out of these treaties.[1]

Agreements made between Member States and third countries *since* accession, in so far as these are allowed, must conform with the constitutional law of the Community in both substance and procedure.

1 On the full meaning of this article see Hans Smit and Peter E. Herzog, *The Law of the European Community* (1982) Vol. 6, IP 226.4.

Treaties made by the Community with Third Countries or by the Community and Member States (mixed agreements) with Third Countries

7.8 These treaties are authorised by the foundation treaties (EEC Treaty, art. 228) or by principles derived therefrom and consequently, although a source of Community law, must be considered secondary in that in so far as competence and procedure is concerned the enabling provisions must be observed and in so far as substance is concerned they must conform with the foundation treaties.[1]

1 J.V. Louis, *The Community Legal Order* (1980) p. 66; T.C. Hartley, *The Foundations of European Community Law* (1981), p. 179; G. Bernhardt, *op. cit.*, 77. On mixed agreements see J.F.M. Dolmans, *Problems of Mixed Agreements* (The Hague: Asser Institute, 1985). C.W.A. Timmermans and E.L.M. Volker (eds.), *Division of Powers Between the European Communities and their Member States in the Field of External Relations* (The Netherlands: Kluwer, 1984). D. O'Keeffe and H. Schermers (eds.), *Mixed Agreements* (The Netherlands, Kluwer, 1983).

Acts of the Representatives of the Member States[1]

7.9 Separate consideration must be given to agreements and decisions made by the representatives of the Member States meeting in the Council. These kind of agreements are anomalous and are not generally provided for in the foundation treaties. They are, however, and have been for thirty years, a part of the reality of the Community system. Such agreements have been used in particular where the institutions do not possess specific decision-making powers. They are used to bridge a gap in the decision-making process. They have been used in 1960, for example, to speed up the timetable scheduled for the attainment of the customs union.

In one sense this development is difficult to justify since if the subject matter pertains to the objectives of the Community resort to Article 235 should be had to remedy the situation. This has not always been done, however, and these agreements, while their legal status is somewhat obscure and shadowy, remain to be considered and classified.

1 Gerhard Bebr, *Acts of the Representatives of the Governments of the Member States* (1966) S.E.W. 529.

7.10 Hartley suggests[1] that these agreements can be divided into three categories. First, one must consider the position where the decision is enjoined by one of the foundation treaties. For example, where the Merger Treaty, art. 11, provides that members of the Commission are to be appointed 'by common accord of the Governments of the Member States', such appointments being made by the acts of the representatives. Such decisions are of course part of Community law in so far as they are merely executing instructions contained in one of the foundation treaties. The Representatives of the Member States are the indicated instrument for the execution of a Community objective. Other decisions or agreements, however, made by the permanent representatives can find no such authority and must be considered merely as acts of the Member States rather than acts of the Council. This is the second category. As such these are simplified international agreements which have the same status as other treaties made by Member States which have not been specifically authorised.[2] They may in some cases be considered part of Community law, but if they are their status is very much secondary in the Community system. 'Those decisions must, however, remain within the bounds of the Community constitution; they must not be in breach of material constitutional law, nor must the representatives of the Member States undertake the tasks reserved to the Community institutions. The dividing line must be determined in relation to each case'.[3] Thirdly, some agreements made by the permanent representatives are merely of political significance and cannot be considered legally binding in any sense. An example of this type is to be found in the Luxembourg Agreements of 1965.

1 T.C. Hartley, *The Foundations of European Community Law* (1981) p. 78 *et seq.*
2 *Supra.*
3 G. Bernhardt, *op. cit.*, 79. See also H.G. Schermers, *Judicial Protection in the European Communities*, pp. 222–4, 3rd ed.

The Foundation Treaties

7.11 Although the view has some opponents it is helpful if we look upon these treaties as constituting 'the Constitution' of the Community's legal system. For Irish lawyers this is a comforting and familiar comparison: the relationship between these treaties and the Community legal system is analogous to the relationship between Bunreacht na hEireann and the Irish legal system. In both cases the constitution lays down the social objectives and economic targets aimed at,[1] as well as indicating the organs which are to exercise the legislative, the executive and the judicial powers. In both cases the judiciary is entrusted with the power of judicial review which ensures that the organs do not usurp each other's functions and do not act *ultra vires*.

The Irish Constitution also contains an enumeration of fundamental rights which limits the State's activities in its dealings with the individual (and indeed the individuals' dealings with each other) and in so far as this is not an exhaustive list the Irish Courts have been active in discovering additional fundamental rights—the unenumerated fundamental rights—in its more recent case law. The treaties establishing the European Community do not contain an explicit list of citizens' fundamental rights or liberties, but the Court of Justice in a judicial development remarkably reminiscent of the Irish development, has also declared that such rights exist in Community law, and that it is the Court's task to elaborate and articulate these rights in accordance with the general principles common to the legal systems of the Member States. Once more, in a manner not unfamiliar to Irish lawyers, the treaties establish a hierarchy of laws in that the treaties and the principles found therein represent a higher form of law than the normal derived legislation propounded by the institutions established by the treaties. Just as Acts of the Oireachtas and Ministerial Orders must conform with the provisions of the Irish Constitution so also the secondary legislation of Community organs (regulations, directives and decisions) must also comply with the constitutive treaties which establish the European Communities. In this sense the foundation treaties can be resorted to, to invalidate all Community legislation of a secondary character.

1 The statement of objectives and targets mentioned in the Community Treaties are of much more legal significance it would appear than similar objectives in the Irish Constitution. 'Of paramount importance in all three Treaties are those provisions which set out the basic objectives and principles of the Communities. Far from containing merely a general programme devoid of legal effect, these provisions lay down obligatory general principles and objectives which are further elaborated in the special rules of the Treaties and which must always be pursued by the institutions in implementating and interpreting those special rules. The European Court itself interprets individual Treaty provisions in the light of these principles and objectives. . . . The same overall considerations apply to principles and objectives of particular economic matters and sectors brought within Community competence. . . . Some of these principles have such overriding importance for the whole Community (e.g. the principle of non-discrimination) that they can never be departed from even where derogation from the Treaty is otherwise possible under special escape clauses'. (A.G. Toth, *Legal Protection of Individuals in the European Communities* (1978), Vol. 1, p. 40. Footnotes omitted).

Territorial and Temporal Scope of Treaties

7.12 The treaties, just as any national constitution might do, also define the territorial and the temporal scope of the Communities. In so far as the former is concerned the treaties extend to the territories of the twelve Member States including now the continental shelf and the fishery zone.[1] Special provisions apply to Algeria (before it became independent) and to the French overseas departments. The treaties do not apply to the Faroe Islands or the British zones in Cyprus and apply only in part to the Channel Islands and the Isle of Man.[2]

In contrast to the ECSC which was concluded for a period of 50 years[3] the EEC and Euratom were concluded for a period of unlimited duration. This was to signify the irrevocable nature of the commitment although whether a country can withdraw or not because of this commitment is a matter of debate. Greenland on achieving autonomy decided to withdraw and have since renegotiated terms of association with the Community.[4] The United Kingdom in holding its historic referendum in 1975 also presumably felt that if the people had decided to leave the Community, it could legally have extricated itself. The Court of Justice is of the opinion that there has been a permanent limitation of sovereignty by the Member States and 'against which a subsequent unilateral act incompatible with the concept of the Community cannot prevail'.[5] From this it would appear that for a lawful withdrawal the proper procedure for amending the treaties would have to be followed. In other words, the other Member States would have to approve of the withdrawal. A unilateral attempt to withdraw would not have legal effect whatever the practical implications would be.

1 See EEC Treaty, art. 227 and ECSC Treaty, art. 99. Community law applies, for the moment, only to a limited extent to the Canary Islands, Ceuta and Melilla.
2 *Idem.*
3 See ECSC Treaty, art. 97.
4 See Treaty, signed at Brussels, 13 March 1984 O.J. L 29 1.2.85 p. 1.
5 Case 6/64 *Costa v ENEL* [1964] E.C.R. 585, at p. 594, [1964] C.M.L.R. 425, at p. 456.

Basic Constitutional Assumptions

7.13 Arising from the treaties and the kind of community which the treaties establish there are certain assumptions about the nature of the Community which are frequently referred to by the Court of Justice in its jurisprudence. These are not so much principles or rules, in the sense that we will use these words later on, but rather amount to basic assumptions or pre-conditions about the very nature of the European Community itself. They are almost of definitional significance in that it would be difficult to describe the European Community without adverting to them and in this context they are sometimes referred to as fundamental ideas or values.

7.14 Before enumerating some of these assumptions or pre-conditions and to appreciate fully their significance in the present context it is helpful to recall that the EEC Treaty is frequently described as a framework treaty (*traité cadre*) which entrusts to specific institutions legislative powers of implementation and execution. In interpreting the treaty the Court of Justice has adopted various approaches to the text, from the literal to the schematic to the teleological. Generally speaking one may say that the teleological approach—favouring interpretations which promote the basic objectives of the treaty—is the approach most favoured by the Court of Justice.

'Faced with interpreting a framework treaty which necessarily leaves to the institutions considerable powers to enact rules implementing it, the Court has isolated from the technical rules contained in the Treaty the fundamental principles which provide the foundation for building the Community. These principles of the community's 'economic constitution' (*Wirtschaftsverfassung*) serve as the theme or the *leitmotiv* of an extensive case law, concerned both with the achievement of the free movement of goods and persons and with implementing common policies'.[1]

1 J.V. Louis, *The Community Legal Order* (1980), p. 30. Footnote omitted.

7.15 These assumptions or doctrines adverted to can be discussed under the following headings: (i) The Concept of Unity; (ii) The Principle of Freedom (iii) The Concept of Autonomy and (iv) The Idea of Solidarity.[1]

1 Louis includes equality while Lasok and Bridge include Supremacy, Direct Applicability and Direct Effect in such a listing, but we prefer to treat these concepts under the heading of General Principles. (See *infra*.) Other listings include the securing of lasting peace, and economic and social security, as fundamental values.

(i) *The Concept of Unity*

7.16 Principally what is being supported and maintained here is the concept of a *single* market with *common* policies governing the market. However, the concept also seems to embrace the more basic idea of unity in the Community in general: a oneness of approach in all matters relating to the Community. Dagtoglou identifies the various elements in this concept in the following way:

'The "unity" element, which is being emphasized more and more by the Court of Justice, is contained not only in the idea of a common market and common policies but also in the idea of Community in general. The chief signs of this "unity" element are the following:
(a) the principle of the equality of Member States with regard to Community law;
(b) the principle of Community preference;
(c) the principle of Community loyalty or the duty of solidarity;
(d) the principle of indivisibility, balancing benefits and burdens;
(e) the principle of the Community's "external" power to conclude international agreements, to the exclusion of the Member States' power, being parallel and proportionate to its "internal" normative power;
(f) the principle of unity or of the uniform application of Community law, which results in its primacy over national laws and the direct effect of the rules of Community law.'[1]

On another level the Court of Justice has also advanced the functional unity of the three Communities in so far as it declares that the foundation treaty of each Community should be used to assist in the interpretation of the others.[2] '[T]he European Treaties are nothing but a partial implementation of a grand general programme, dominated by the idea of a complete integration of the European States'.[3]

1 D.G. Dagtoglou, 'The legal nature of the European Community', in *Thirty Years of Community Law*, (1983) 33, at 40.
2 D. Lasok and D.W. Bridge, *Law and Institutions of the European Communities*, Fourth Edition (1987), p. 148.
3 Advocate-General Roemer, in Joined cases 27, 39/59 *Campolongo v High Authority* [1960] E.C.R. 391. Cited in Lasok and Bridge, 149.

(ii) *The Principle of Freedom*

7.17 By this principle the idea is accepted that the goal of free movement of goods, persons, services, and capital within a single market is the norm and that in so far as possible it is absolute. Any deviation or restriction is therefore to be considered as abnormal and prohibited. Consequently, in its case-law the Court of Justice imposes the onus of proof on parties who wish to argue for restricted movement, construes all exceptions to the general principle of freedom very narrowly,[1] and has, to take an example, struck down unilateral attempts to restrict free movement of persons.[2] Free movement in this wide sense is one of the foundations of the Community.

1 Case 2/74 *Reyners v Belgium* [1974] E.C.R. 631, [1974] 2 C.M.L.R. 305; Case 36/75 *Rutili v Ministre de l'Intérieur* [1975] E.C.R. 1219, [1976] 1 C.M.L.R. 140.
2 *Reyners* case, *supra*.

(iii) *The Concept of Autonomy*

7.18 The Treaties establishing the European Communities have created a new legal order for the Member States, an order which cannot be explained fully in terms of international law and which is distinct from national systems. It is an autonomous legal order, which although it has close links with national legal systems is independent of them. It rules directly over the territories of the Member States and can be compared with a federal legal system. The principal features of this new and autonomous legal order are that its laws are directly applicable in the territories of the Member States; these laws may give rights to individuals as well as to States; and they are to be given precedence over national laws to the contrary. Procedures for uniform interpretation and application throughout the Community are provided for in the treaties.

It is not helpful in this context to think of the Community legal system as a national development or growth only. It is not merely a national outcrop. It is true that the legal system was created initially by the Member States, but having been created, it now represents a novel creation which has an independent and permanent existence in a different realm irrespective of the wills of the States which created it.

The force and vigour of this view was expressed by the Court of Justice as early as 1963 in the *Van Gend en Loos* case and because it has been confirmed and relied upon in several cases since then, merits quotation.

'The conclusion to be drawn from this is that the Community constitutes a new legal order of international law for the benefit of which the states have limited their sovereign rights, albeit within limited fields, and the subjects of which comprise not only Member States but also their nationals. Independently of the legislation of Member States, Community law therefore not only imposes obligations on individuals but is also intended to confer upon them rights which become part of their legal heritage. These rights arise not only where they are expressly granted by the Treaty, but also by reason of obligations which the Treaty imposes in a clearly defined way upon individuals as well as upon the Member States and upon the institutions of the Community.'[1]

1 Case 26/62 *Van Gend en Loos v Nederlandse Belastingadministratie* [1963] E.C.R. 1 at 12, [1963] C.M.L.R. 105 at 129.

(iv) *The Principle of Solidarity*

7.19 Here the Community is concerned with something approaching the common good. 'Solidarity is the necessary corrective to freedom, for ruthless exercise of freedom is always at the expense of others'.[1] The Community must strive to ensure that within the Community both the advantages and the burdens of the novel experiment are equally and justly shared by the subjects. Moreover, the Member States must also show their acceptance by indicating their willingness to accept the burdens of Community membership as well as its benefits. Unilateral actions contrary to the Community spirit would thus be unacceptable because they strike at the reciprocal loyalty which is at the very heart of Community integration. Accordingly, if a Member State unilaterally attempts to break a Community law or fails to fulfil its obligations or if it attempts to make a unilateral agreement with a third country concerning matters within the common commercial policy it would be in breach of the principle of solidarity.

In one case where a Member State failed to fulfil its obligations the Court put the matter thus:

'In permitting Member States to profit from the advantages of the Community, the Treaty imposes on them also the obligation to respect its rules.

For a State unilaterally to break, according to its own conception of national interest, the equilibrium between advantages and obligations flowing from its adherence to the Community brings into question the equality of Member States before Community law and creates discriminations at the expense of their nationals, and above all of the nationals of the State itself which places itself outside the Community rules.

This failure in the duty of solidarity accepted by Member States by the fact of their adherence to the Community strikes at the fundamental basis of the Community legal order.'[2]

Where a Member State attempted to conclude an agreement with a third country when the Community already possessed competence in this matter the Court declared that the Member State had no right to enter into such agreement.

'To accept that the contrary were true would amount to recognizing that, in relations with third countries, Member States may adopt positions which differ from those which the Community intends to adopt, and would thereby distort the institutional framework, call into question the mutual trust within the Community and prevent the latter from fulfilling its task in the defence of the common interest.'[3]

The obligations undertaken by the Member States are not merely to each other, they are also obligations to the Community. As Judge Donner put it, these obligations are undertaken 'not simply on a reciprocal basis but primarily towards the new collectivity they set up'.[4]

The above list of fundamental values cannot be considered exhaustive and different authors may add or subtract to this list or reclassify values under the heading of general principles. Such differences of approach are not too important. What is important is the fact that the Court of Justice frequently resorts to these values to justify its decisions and invalidate both Community and Member States' actions.

1 The ABC of Community Law, p. 11.
2 Case 39/72 *EC Commission v Italy* [1973] E.C.R. 101, at p. 116, [1973] C.M.L.R. 439, at

p. 457. See also Joined cases 6, 11/69 *EC Commission v France* [1969] E.C.R. 523, [1970] C.M.L.R. 43, at p. 523.
3 Opinion 1/75 [1975] E.C.R. 1355 at 1364, [1976] 1 C.M.L.R. 85 at 93.
4 A.M. Donner, *The Constitutional Powers of the Court of Justice of the European Communities*, 11 C.M.L. Rev. [1974], 128.

The General Principles of Law

7.20 Apart from explicit constitutional rules to be found in the foundation treaties, the Court of Justice has also in its jurisprudence been occupied with the elaboration of Community law derived from 'the general principles of law' and 'the basic principles of the law of the Member States'. In so far as the Court is discharging a constitutional function here such rules and laws might also be considered to be part of the constitutional law of the Community. Certainly for an Irish lawyer, the Irish Courts' decisions as to the unenumerated personal rights would form part of the corpus of Irish Constitutional law. These Community developments must now be considered.

Chapter 8

General Principles Common to the Laws of the Member States

General Principles

8.1 A useful distinction can be made at the outset between what we have already called basic legal values and general principles. The former term as we use it connotes basic doctrines relating to the very nature of the legal system. Such values or doctrines are of definitional significance for the legal system itself. In this sense we might speak of the doctrine of supremacy, which indicates the pre-eminence of Community law over national law, the concept of autonomy, which holds that the Community legal order is one which cannot be fully explained in terms of international law and which is distinct from the national system of the Member States.[1] General principles, however, signify rules which are applied by the institutions to regulate conflicts between the subjects in the system. 'A principle, or a rule of law, on the other hand, can be construed more narrowly as a rule of conduct prescribed in the given circumstances and carrying a sanction for non-compliance. Thus a principle or rule of law consists of a hypothesis, a disposition and a sanction'.[2]

1 See *supra* 3.10 and 7.15.
2 D. Lasok and J.W. Bridge, *Law and Institutions of the European Communities*, Fourth Edition (1987), p. 153. 'By a doctrine, as distinguished from a principle or a rule of law, we understand a general proposition or guidance relating to a fundamental issue such as e.g. the nature of Community law or the conflict between Community and national law'. *Idem.*

8.2 Basic legal values or doctrines have already been referred to (*supra*) and here we are concerned with general principles or rules in Community law. These general principles have been elaborated and developed by the Court of Justice and illustrate well the nature and vigour of judicial law-making within the Community legal system. Judicial law-making seems to be an inevitable feature of most legal systems nowadays, and although it will be more obvious and more candidly acknowledged in some systems than in others, it is present in most, to a greater or lesser extent. The legal system of the EEC is no exception and one may compare the Court of Justice's role in this matter with that of the 13th-century itinerant judges in England who, in the absence of legislation, articulated and elaborated general rules which came to be known as the Common Law. The general principles developed within the EEC now begin to form, in an embryonic fashion, what might be called the Community's *ius commune*. The acceptance of the Court's pronouncements here may undoubtedly be helped by the fact that until recently there was only one court in the Community's legal system and so there was no chance that a judicial pronouncement would be undermined by a simultaneous pronouncement from another court within the system, and also by the fact that the Court of Justice is a collegiate court which issues only one judgment and no dissents are allowed.

8.3 Although there is no general authorisation given to the Court of Justice by the treaties to justify this role of judicial activism, specific articles can be cited which might indicate approval of such activity. EEC Treaty, art. 164, for example, declares that 'The Court of Justice shall ensure that in the interpretation and application of this Treaty the law is observed.' Clearly, 'the law' as used in this article refers to sources other than the treaty and secondary legislation based thereon.[1] Again Article 173 permits the Court of Justice to review the legality of acts of the Council and the Commission on the grounds, *inter alia*, of infringement of this Treaty or of *any rule of law* relating to its application.[2] The Court has accepted that the emphasised phrase covers the general principles of law.[3] Finally, EEC Treaty, art. 215 provides that in the case of non-contractual liability (tortious liability) the Community shall be liable 'in accordance with the general principles common to the laws of the Member States'. This specific reference to the general principles common to the laws of the Member States should be taken as a general indication as to a technique which should be available to the Court generally, and should not be interpreted in a narrow way as indicating that resort to such principles should only be allowed in non-contractual cases.[4] Even in the absence of such specific authorisations, however, it is generally agreed that the Court of Justice would not have hesitated to embrace those general principles common to the laws of the Member States as part of Community law.[5]

1 L. Neville Brown and F.G. Jacobs, *The Court of Justice of the European Communities*, Second Edition (1983), p. 263.
2 Emphasis added.
3 See H.G. Schermers, *Judicial Protection in the European Communities*, Third Edition (1983), pp 39 and 292; A.G. Toth, *Legal Protection of Individuals in the European Communities* (1978), vol. 1, p. 85.
4 H.G. Schermers, op. cit. p. 41; Joined cases 7/56 and 3-7/57 *Algera v Common Assembly* [1957–58] E.C.R. 39.
5 T.C. Hartley, *The Foundations of European Community Law* (1981), p. 121.

8.4 Before examining in further detail some of the general principles adopted by the Court of Justice to date, a few general comments about this source of law might be helpful. First, it might be noted that the development of these general principles at Community level is a development which greatly protects the individual. Many of the rules in question here are rules developed to protect the individual from excesses of the administration. Second, once recognised at Community level these general principles, although not capable of over-ruling express treaty provisions, can invalidate other Community acts of a secondary nature.[1] Third, as well as looking to the legal systems of the Member States to discover these general principles applicable at Community level, the Court of Justice may also extract them from the treaties themselves. For example, it may detect that a specific article of the treaty which expresses a particular rule in a limited context is really a narrow expression of a more general Community principle which can then be recognised and elevated as a general Community principle capable of universal application. For example EEC Treaty, art. 7 which prohibits discrimination on the basis of nationality (e.g. one cannot have one rule for Irish persons and another rule for Germans or citizens of other Member States) has been held by the Court of Justice to be merely an example of the general principle which prohibits discrimination on any unreasonable basis. Moreover, in some instances the Court asserts these general legal principles on its own authority with reference, neither to treaty provisions, nor the laws of the Member States.[2] The wide discretion which the Court possesses in this respect is noteworthy.[3] Fourth, not only can the general principles of law be used to annul acts of the institutions, they are also frequently used to interpret and supplement Community law. Concepts such as *force majeure*, public policy, etc. used, but not defined in the Community context, may have their meanings developed by the Court in the light of national usages and accepted concepts among the Member States.

Fifth, Article 215, in connection with the Community's tortious liability, enjoins the Court to develop rules of liability in accordance 'with the general principles common to the laws of Member States'. This clearly indicates that the Court must look in this instance to the national laws. In other cases too, in looking for general principles the Court will certainly look to the laws of the Member States, but in these other instances their search may not be confined to these laws only. For example, in the case of human rights the Court will look not only to national laws but also to other souces e.g. the European Convention on Human Rights. Moreover, when the court is examining the national laws in its search for general legal principles it must not be thought that this will take the form of a search for the lowest common denominator. Rather will its role be one of creatively synthesising the data before it. This may involve, in the end, a preference for the solution of one Member State over another on the grounds that, when the Community dimension is taken into account, the preferred solution is most suitable for the Community. 'What is required is that a principle should be widely accepted and should provide a solution which is, if measured by the methods of "evaluative comparative law", the most appropriate and most judicious of all comparable solutions, taking into account the particular objectives and nature of Community law.'[4]

Finally, because the original composition of the Communities was comprised of States with a common legal tradition, it is not surprising that civil law concepts should have had a significant impact on the elaboration of general legal principles at Community level in the early years. Since Ireland and England joined the Community in 1973, however, the homogeneity of the Member States is less intense. Not unexpectedly common law concepts are now also beginning to have an impact in this search for general principles.[5]

We now turn to examine those general principles which the Court of Justice has, in its jurisprudence, recognised to date.[6]

1 See A.G. Toth, *Legal Protection of Individuals in the European Communities* (1978), vol. 1, p. 86; L. Neville Brown and F.G. Jacobs, *The Court of Justice of the European Communities*, Second Edition (1983), p. 261; H.G. Schermers, *Judicial Protection in the European Communities*, Third Edition (1983), p. 48; Case 112/77 *Töpfer v EC Commission* [1978] E.C.R. 1019 at p. 1033; P.S.R.F. Mathijsen, *A Guide to European Community Law*, Fifth Edition (1987), pp. 79–80.

2 R.H. Lauwaars, *Lawfulness and Legal Force of Community Decisions* (1973), p. 223.

3 *Idem.*, 242.

4 A.G. Toth, *Legal Protection of Individuals in the European Communities* (1978), vol. 1, p. 86 citing cases 9/69 [1969] E.C.R. 329 *per* A.G.; 5/70 [1971] E.C.R. 1075 *per* A.G.; 63–9/72 [1973] E.C.R. 1229 *per* A.G.

5 See Case 17/74 *Transocean Marine Paint Association v EC Commission* [1974] E.C.R. 1063, [1974] 2 C.M.L.R. 459 and *infra* 8.17.

6 What follows is not an exhaustive listing and attention should be drawn to the fundamental legal values, *supra*, and to basic doctrines, *infra*, which some might classify under the present heading. For an example of an instance where the Court of Justice refused to recognise at Community level the principle of 'objective unfairness' ('sachliche Umbillig-keit' in German law) see Case 299/84 *Neumann v Bundesanstalt für Landwirtschaftliche Marktordnung*, 14 November 1985. Unreported as yet.

1. Fundamental human rights

8.5 Although the EEC Treaty does not contain, for reasons already adverted to, any catalogue of fundamental rights in the sense of Articles 40–44 of the Irish Constitution, several articles in the treaty do contain specific rules which might well be classified as human rights rules. Article 7, for example, contains a prohibition against discrimination on the basis of nationality; Article 40.3 contains a similar prohibition against discrimination in agricultural matters between producers and consumers, and Article 119, as between men and women, guarantees equal pay for equal work. Moreover, Articles 48–58 guarantee free movement of persons within the Community[1] and Articles 85 and 86 outlaw unfair trading agreements and practices as well as the abuse of dominant positions by firms and undertakings. Other examples could also be given. It becomes immediately clear, however, that when one speaks of human rights in the context of the EEC one is speaking primarily of economic and social rights. Because the Community we are speaking of is primarily confined to 'economic' matters, when one speaks of human rights in the Community context one does not imagine cases of incarceration, torture, supression of free speech etc., which might normally spring to mind in such discussions at a national level. This is not to minimise the importance of human rights in the EEC context, however, but rather to emphasise the nature of the context of the discussion.[2]

1 Case 36/75 *Rutili v Ministre de l'Intérieur* [1975] E.C.R. 1219, [1976] 1 C.M.L.R. 140.

2 Explicit, if belated reference is made twice in the preamble to the Single European Act of 1986.

8.6 Apart from these specific instances in the treaty the Court of Justice has been involved in a judicial exercise which should not be unfamiliar to Irish lawyers. Just as the Irish courts have been busy in recent years in elaborating 'the unenumerated rights' guaranteed by the Irish Constitution, so also the Court of Justice has felt obliged to engage in a similar exercise at Community level. The result is that now, because of their judicial activism, we have several human rights, not specifically mentioned in the treaties, recognised in the Court's jurisprudence as basic Community rights. Before adverting further to these, an explanatory word of the pressure which caused the Court of Justice to act in this way is required.

8.7 The development is intrinsically bound up with the doctrine of the supremacy of Community law over national measures to the contrary. The Community position on this, as developed by the Court of Justice,[1] is unequivocal and categorical. Community law prevails over *all* national measures whatever date or status at national level. Thus a Community measure takes precedence over subsequent national measures, over national constitutions and even over the fundamental rights provisions of national constitutions. The Community position on this is clear, and authoritarian. Not wholly unexpectedly, however, some national courts showed some reluctance in swallowing this Community doctrine. Germany, understandably because of its recent history, had some difficulty in accepting that its post-World War II Constitution, and particularly its fundamental rights guarantees, could be undermined by some external judicial development beyond its own control. Faced with the possibility of mutinous revolt within the Community, the Court of Justice felt pressure to sweeten its pill of supremacy which it insisted the Member States must swallow. It did so by elaborating *at Community level* a theory of human rights which uncompromisingly maintained the supremacy doctrine, but which also acknowledged the Court's obligation to develop, at Community level, a theory which protected individual rights in areas and in a manner which was familiar to the legal systems of the Member States. This underwriting of fundamental rights at Community level, it was hoped, would reassure the national courts and enable them to embrace unreservedly the Community's supremacy doctrine.

A brief look at the series of cases which established this position is instructive for many reasons.

1 See *infra*.

8.8 In *Stauder v City of Ulm*[1] the Commission to reduce 'the butter mountain' addressed a decision to the Member States which authorised the Member States to make butter available to low income consumers. In implementing the measure Germany issued coupons attached to stubs which bore the name and address of the beneficiary. Stauder objected to having to disclose his name to benefit from the scheme and contested the legality of the measure before a German Court as being, *inter alia*, an infringement of the Basic Law of Germany. The German Court referred the matter to the Court of Justice under Article 177 of the Treaty and in particular asked whether the German measure of implementing the Commission's decision, by requiring the beneficiary to disclose his name, was compatible with the general principles of Community law. The Court, while ruling against Stauder on the facts, made the statement that the provision at issue contained 'nothing capable of prejudicing the fundamental human rights enshrined in the general principles of Community law and protected by the Court'.[2]

This statement was an open acknowledgement for the first time that there was a theory of human rights at Community level and that it was the function of the Court to protect these rights. It was also clear from this that it would be the Court's function to articulate and elaborate these rights in the future.

1 Case 29/69 [1969] E.C.R. 419, [1970] C.M.L.R. 112. See also for a good general survey, M.A. Dauses, *The Protection of Fundamental Rights in the Community Legal Order* 10. E.L. Rev. 398–419.
2 *Idem* at p. 425.

8.9 Shortly after *Stauder* followed the *Internationale Handelsgesellschaft* Case.[1] The plaintiff company based in Frankfurt-am-Main obtained an export licence which was valid until 31 December 1967 in respect of a quantity of maize. The issuance of the licence was conditional on the lodging of a deposit which would be forfeited by the authorities if the export quota allocated to the licence holder was not taken up by the expiry date of the licence. The purpose of the deposit was to ensure that applicants were genuine and consequently that allocations were accurate estimates of intended transactions. When the deposit was forfeited because the licence holder did not export its allocated quota, the deposit holder claimed that the principles of freedom of action and disposition, of economic liberty and of proportionality guaranteed by the German Basic Law were infringed. A reference under Article 177 was made to the Court of Justice. Having declared that a Community measure 'cannot be affected by allegations that it runs counter to either fundamental rights as formulated by the constitutions of a Member State or the principles of national constitutional structure' the Court was prepared, however, to concede the following:

'However, an examination should be made as to whether or not any analogous guarantee inherent in Community Law has been disregarded. In fact respect for fundamental rights forms an integral part of the general principles of law protected by the Court of Justice. The protection of such rights, whilst inspired by the constitutional traditions common to the Member States, must be ensured within the framework of the structure and objectives of the Community. It must therefore be ascertained, in the light of the doubts expressed by the Verwaltungsgericht, whether the system of deposits has infringed rights of a fundamental nature, respect for which must be ensured in the Community legal system.'[2]

In the event again, however, the Court found that the deposit/forfeiture system did not violate any right of a fundamental nature.

1 Case 11/70 *Internationale Handelsgesellschaft v Einfuhr- und Vorratsstelle für Getreide und Futtermittel* [1970] E.C.R. 1125.
2 Case 36/70 *Getreide-Import v Einfuhr- und Vorratsstelle für Getreide und Futtermittel* [1970] E.C.R. 1107, at p. 1134.

8.10 Since the Court of Justice is, to a degree, at large in its search for Community human rights, where does it look to for instruction? Two sources in particular are used: the constitutions of the Member States and the European Convention for the Protection of Human Rights and Fundamental Freedoms to which all Member States are now parties.[1]

1 See especially Case 4/73 *Nold v EC Commission* [1974] E.C.R. 491, at p. 507; [1974] 2 C.M.L.R. 338, at p. 354. The Court will also look to other international treaties for the protection of human rights on which Member States have collaborated including the European Social Charter as well as to Convention III of the I.L.O.

8.11 In the *Hauer* Case[1] a council regulation provided that Member States could no longer grant authorisations for new vine planting. There was a large surplus of wine in the Community and this measure was designed to limit new production. When refused an authorisation to plant vines Mrs Hauer contended that the measure violated fundamental rights guaranteed by the German Basic Law, in particular, the right to property and the freedom to pursue a trade or profession. The Court recognised the existence of these rights in Community law, but having examined the first protocol to the European Convention for the Protection of Human Rights as well as the provisions of the constitutions of some Member States, it decided that there had been no breach in the present case. It also made the point that none of these rights are ever absolute and that some restrictions in general interest on the *use* of property and the right to pursue an occupation were accepted in all Member States. Moreover, the restrictions in the instant case were not disproportionate to the objectives to be achieved and therefore did not involve any breach of human rights.

As Schermers rightly points out[2] there is no sharp division drawn between basic human rights and other legal principles and some of the matters dealt with below might well be classified as basic human rights by some lawyers. One may assume, therefore, that the rights listed in the European convention and in the constitutions of the Member States are also protected in the Community legal system. This is borne out by the fact that the Court has already recognised as Community protected rights, in addition to those mentioned above, the freedom to practise one's religion,[3] the principle of equality,[4] the right to free movement[5] and the right to associate freely.[6]

1 Case 44/79 *Hauer v Land Rheinland-Pfalz* [1979] E.C.R. 3727.
2 H.G. Schermers, *Judicial Protection in the European Communities*, Third Edition (1983) p. 39.
3 European Convention, art. 9 and Case 130/75 *Prais v EC Council* [1976] E.C.R. 1589, at pp. 1598,9 [1976] 2 C.M.L.R. 708 at pp. 722–4. See also T.C. Hartley, *Religious freedom and equality of opportunity*, 2 E.L. Rev. (1977), pp. 45–57. The Court recognised that it would be wrong if the Commission knowingly fixed written examinations for job applicants on the religious holidays of any of the applicants. The plaintiff in this case was Jewish and the examination was fixed for Saturday—the Jewish sabbath. On the facts, however, there was no violation since the Commission was not aware of the problem when it fixed the examination date.

4 See *infra*.
5 Case 36/75 *Rutili v Ministre de l'Intérieur* [1975] E.C.R. 1219, [1976] 1 C.M.L.R. 140.
6 This included not only the right to form associations with others for legitimate purposes but also that such associations are free to do anything lawful to protect the interests of their members as employees. Case 175/73 *Union Syndicale v EC Council* [1974] E.C.R. 917, at p. 925, [1975] 1 C.M.L.R. 131 at 140 and Case 18/74 *Syndicat Général du Personnel des Organismes Européens v EC Commission* [1974] E.C.R. 933, at p. 944, [1975] 1 C.M.L.R. 144.

8.12 The importance of Community human rights, of course, is that, where they are recognised to exist they may be used to invalidate acts of the Community institutions. No such violation has been proved as yet before the Court of Justice. Whether the Community human rights can be used to invalidate the acts of the Member States seems to be unsettled.[1]

Hartley, however, suggests that 'if Community law grants rights to individuals which must be upheld by the national governments but these rights are subject to a proviso allowing derogations on certain grounds, any derogations thus made by the national governments should not violate the Community concept of human rights'. The reason he suggests for this is that Member State's power to derogate is derived from the Community and is therefore subject to the same restrictions as the powers of the Community itself.[2]

1 H.G. Schermers, *Judicial Protection in the European Communities*, Third Edition (1983), p. 33. See also Case 77/81 *Zuckerfabrik Franken v Germany* [1982] E.C.R. 681; See also Case 152/79 *Lee v Minister for Agriculture* [1980] E.C.R. 1495, [1980] 2 C.M.L.R. 682.
2 T.C. Hartley, *The Foundations of European Community Law*, First Edition (10983), 128 citing Case 36/75 *Rutili v Ministre de l'Intérieur* [1975] E.C.R. 1219, at p. 1232. See also D. Wyatt, (1976) E.L. Rev. 217 at pp. 219–20 and (1978) 3 E.L. Rev. 483 at pp. 486–8.

8.13 From time to time it has been suggested that the European Community should draw up its own catalogue of Human Rights, its own Bill of Rights or at least should adopt the European Convention on Human Rights.[1] To date this has not been favoured and the task of protecting and articulating these rights has been left to the Court of Justice. This is a technique which in view of Irish legal experience is not unfamiliar to Irish lawyers but whether it affords the best protection for the individual within the Community's legal system remains to be seen. The other institutions— the Parliament, the Court and the Commission—in any event have, in a joint declaration, indicated the importance they attach to the protection of these human rights at Community level.[2]

1 See for merits of this suggestion Riedel, 'The Bill of Rights Fallacy' in *In Memoriam J.D.B. Mitchell*, 38, 64. Eds. Bates, Finnie, Usher and Wildberg, London 1983. On position of Convention on Human Rights in the Community legal order see Dauses, *supra* fn. 1, para. 8.8 pp. 410–413.
2 Joint Declaration of 5.4.77 O.J. C 103 27.4.77 p. 1. See also, John Forman, *The Joint Declaration of Fundamental Rights*, 2 E.L. Rev. (1977), 210–15; M.A. Dauses, *supra* fn. 1, para. 8.8 for list of other political declarations, resolutions, etc., at Community level.

8.14 To summarise therefore, one may say that in applying Community law to the subjects before it the Court of Justice is bound by general principles which show respect for the basic human rights of the individual. These basic human rights are not written down or catalogued anywhere in the treaties so the Court is entrusted with the task of articulating and elaborating these rights as they exist in Community law. In this task it has a great deal of discretion and in its search it is inspired and influenced by models and catalogues which exist outside the Community system. In elaborating the Community human rights it takes cognisance of these external influences. In particular, in its search for guidelines, it looks to the constitutional traditions and to the written constitutions of the Member States as well as to international models such as the European Convention on Human Rights. Influenced on occasion by these, it is, as a Court, happy to adopt these provisions and apply them in the *Community*'s legal system. When so approved, however, such provisions or values are accepted as Community measures and in no way are they subordinate to the national fundamental rights provisions. The national provisions may have an historical relevance but they have no legal significance or linkage. If the Court of Justice recognises and adopts such values then their validity at Community level exists because of Community authority and not because of their presence in the constitutions of Member States.

Before leaving this topic, however, it should be noted that this approach by the Court may not be without some theoretical difficulties. For example, what does the Court do when, in its search for principles common to the traditions of the Member States, the principle is to be found in some, or only one, of the Member States? Can it still be elevated to a Community principle? Again, does the Court of Justice, when resorting for inspiration to the European Convention on Human Rights feel bound by its terms or does it merely use it as a non-obligatory guide in its deliberations? The better opinion would seem to suggest that in the latter case the Convention does not bind the Court, but is rather an inspirational signpost. As to the former question it is suggested that to be recognised at Community level a principle does not have to be found in all or in most of the Member States.[1]

1 See address by Advocate General F. Mancini to Irish Society for European Law, *Human Rights in the case-law of the Luxembourg Court*, Dublin, 20 May, 1986.

2. *The principle of equality*

8.15 The principle of equality is fully accepted as a basic principle in Community law. The principle means that equals must be treated equally and unequals must be treated unequally. Arbitrary discrimination is totally outlawed in the Community system. Specific forms of objectionable discrimination are mentioned in the Treaty itself—Article 7 prohibits discrimination on the basis of nationality and Article 119 prohibits discrimination on the basis of sex—but these may be taken to be examples of a general ban on any unreasonable discrimination.[1] EEC Treaty, art. 40(3), for example, prohibits more generally any discrimination 'between producers or consumers within the Community in the matter of the common agricultural policy'[2] and Articles 85 and 86 prohibit agreements and practices which apply 'dissimilar conditions to equivalent transactions with other trading parties'. Moreover, the Court of Justice has clearly stated that the principle is a general one and even in the absence of express prohibition in the treaties must be supported as 'one of the fundamental principles of Community law'.[3]

1 *Hochstrass* Case 147/79, [1980] E.C.R. 3005, 3091.
2 See for recent example *Lion and Loiret* Joined Cases 292–293/81, [1982] E.C.R. 3887.
3 *Frilli* Case 1/72, [1972] E.C.R. 457; *Hochstrass* Case 147/79, [1980] E.C.R. 3005, 3019, consideration 7.

8.16 The concept of equality, however, does not outlaw all kinds of discrimination but only discrimination which cannot be justified on objective and reasonable criteria. 'That principle requires that comparable situations should not be treated differently unless such differentiation is objectively justified'.[1] In other words the discrimination objected to must be 'arbitrary discrimination' and in this connection the court has said that 'Difference in treatment cannot be regarded as constituting discrimination which is prohibited unless it appears arbitrary'.[2] In determining whether discrimination exists, however, the court will look at the reality of the situation rather than at the appearance. When the Irish Government introduced fishing regulations banning vessels whose length exceeded 33 metres or whose engine(s) exceeded 1100 brake horsepower from fishing in Irish waters the Court of Justice held that this amounted to discrimination on the basis of nationality because the factual position was that out of the total Irish fleet of vessels only two boats were of larger dimensions, and those boats in fact never fished in Irish waters. This was disguised, *de facto* discrimination and the Court was not going to be deceived by the surface equality contained in the Irish measures.[3]

Not unexpectedly the highest incidence of unequal treatment within the Community's jurisprudence occurs first, in national measures which favour either the nationals or goods of the Member State itself, and second in the area of sex discrimination.[4]

1 Court of Justice, *Hochstrass supra*, at 3019, see also *Ruckdeschel* Joined Cases 117/76, 16/77, [1977] E.C.R. 1753.
2 *Kendermann* 88/78, consideration 12, [1978] E.C.R. 2477.
3 See *Schönenberg* Case 88/77 [1978] E.C.R. 473.
4 See as example of former *Minister for Fisheries v Schönenberg* [1978] E.C.R. 473, and as example of latter, *Sabbatini* 20/71, consideration 12, [1972] E.C.R. 345. With regard to reverse discrimination see S.D. Kon, *Aspects of Reverse Discrimination in Community Law*, 6 E.C. Rev. (1981) 75–101.

3. *Due process and natural justice*

8.17 Most legal systems in the Western tradition also emphasise the importance of protecting the individual in *procedural matters*. Irish lawyers will of course be familiar in this connection with concepts developed by the Irish Courts relating to the right to a fair hearing, the right to legal representation, *nemo iudex in causa sua*, legal privilege, etc. It is not surprising that these concepts have been (or would be) recognised and protected by the Court of Justice at Community level. In the *Transocean Marine Paint* Case[1] for example, the plaintiffs were held, in a competition case, to be entitled to a hearing, before the Commission could impose unacceptable conditions on an exemption which it (the Commission) intended to give to the Association under Article 85(3) of the Treaty. The Court in giving judgment for the plaintiffs recognised 'the general rule that a person whose interests are perceptibly affected by a decision taken by a public authority must be given the opportunity to make his point of view known'.[2] Brown and Jacobs, suggest that this formulation may be too wide and may have to be refined by the Court in its subsequent case-law.[3] Similarly the Court has held that the right of defence includes a right to be assisted by counsel[4] and the right, in disciplinary proceedings, for the applicant's lawyer to have access to the Commission's file.[5] A worker who was refused recognition that his foreign diploma as a football trainer was equivalent to the national diploma is entitled to have this decision judicially reviewed and is also entitled to ascertain the reasons for the decision.[6] The question of legal professional privilege has also been recognised by the Court.[7] According to the Court communications between the client and his lawyer on the lawyer's file are privileged communications and cannot be used against the client. The privilege, however, only extends to correspondence related to the client's defence with independent lawyers. Internal communications with in-house lawyers are not so privileged.[8]

1 Case 17/74 *Transocean Marine Paint Association v E.C. Commission* [1974] E.C.R. 1063.
2 *Idem* at 1080.
3 L. Neville and F.G. Jacobs, at 268.
4 *Demont Case*, Case 115/80, Consideration 11, [1981] E.C.R. 3147.
5 *Idem*, consideration 12.
6 Case 222/86 *UNECTEF v Heylens*, Unreported as yet, 15 October 1987. Proceedings 20/87.
7 *AM&S v E.C. Commission* Case 155/79, considerations 18, 22, [1982] E.C.R. 1575, [1982] 2 C.M.L.R. 309.
8 *Idem*. Considerations 21, 23, 24, at 1611–12.

4. *Fair application of the law*[1]

8.18 The concern of the Court of Justice with fairness and justice manifests itself in many ways and in a variety of rules. At the bottom of all these instances the Court has shown itself willing to eschew a narrow legal approach and base its decisions on some concept of 'fairness', 'equity' or 'justice'. Careful not to strain the comparison, one might say that the Court of Justice has been prepared to exercise in these cases an equitable approach (in the Common Law sense) to achieve a just result. In the *Luhrs* Case where Luhrs was liable to pay an export tax on potatoes sent to Sweden, the Court held that because of the ambiguity in the regulations 'natural justice demands that for the purpose of converting the tax on exports into national currency the exchange rate which at the material time was less onerous on the taxpayer concerned should be applied.'[2] In the *Walt Wilhelm* Case the Court said there was 'a general requirement of natural justice' which required that in fixing a penalty previous penalties should be taken into account.[3] In the *Costacurta* Case strict adherence to procedural rules under Staff Regulations was dispensed with by the Court because it would in the circumstances be 'contrary to the rules of fairness'.[4] In *Süddeutsche Zucker-AG v Hauptzollamt Mannheim* the Court relied on 'logic and equity' as the basis for its decision.[5]

1 See R. Wainwright, 'Legal Aspects of the Agricultural Policy in the European Community: General Principles of law – recent Developments' pp. 163 *et seq.* in *Memoriam J.D.B. Mitchell* eds. Bates, Finnis, Usher and Wildberg, 1973.

2 Case 78/77 *Lührs v Haupzollampt Hamburg-Jonas* [1978] E.C.R. 169, at 180. Consideration 13.
3 *Walt Wilhelm* Case, 14/68, Consideration 11, [1969] E.C.R. 15.
4 Case 31/75 *Costacurtta v EC Commission* [1975] E.C.R. 1563, at p. 1570; see also Case 34/80 *Authié v EC Commission* [1981] E.C.R. 665, at p. 676. Also fairness was reviewed in Case 127/80 *Grogan v EC Commission* [1982] E.C.R. 869.
5 Case 94/75 [1976] E.C.R. 153, at p. 159; see also Case 64/74 *Reich v Hauptzollamt Landau* [1975] E.C.R. 261, at p. 268, [1975] 1 C.M.L.RR. 396, at p. 405.

8.19 The Court has also adopted the principle of good faith in its case-law. When Mr Meganck, a temporary official, was paid family allowance payments to which he was not entitled he successfully resisted a claim for repayment on the grounds that he did not know of the overpayments from his pay slips and he received them in good faith.[1] Some other paaayments which he ought to have known were not due to him had to be repaid. Again a company was not allowed to rely on the principle that a benefit would not be retroactively withdrawn because it was fully aware that the rule was being vigorously conteested before the Court, and therefore it was not behaving in good faith.[2]

1   Case 36/72 *Meganck v EC Commission* [1973] E.C.R. 527, at p. 534.
2   Case 14/61 First *Hoogovens* Case [1962] E.C.R. 253; see also Case 43/59 *Lachmüller v EEC Commission* [1960] E.C.R. 463, at pp. 474,5.

8.20 The Court has also in several cases adopted what to the Common Law lawyer looks very likke estoppel. Accordingly 'no one may plead a situation created by his own conduct in order to escape an obligation, a sanction, a disciplinary or a judicial proooceeding'.[1] In *GGrogan v EC Commission* the plaintiff, a pension holder, had his pension greatly reduced when the Council addddopted a new rule as to the currencies in which these pensions should be paid. The Court stated in the course of its judgment that

'Whilst theree may be some explanation of the Council's inaction it must none the less not be overlooked that pensioners benefiting from that inaction were entitled to expect the Council to take account of the situation in which they had been placed by the prolonged application of the systtem temporarily used. That is particularly true in the case of pensssions, since they are interested to ensure that officials who have left the service of the Communities enjoy an adequate standard of living.'[2]

In the *Meganck* Case[3] wwe hhave seen that the applicant was able to resist a reclaim of some payments on the grounds that these were received in good faith. Other payments, however, made to the applicant were recoverable because even though not patent to the applicant these overpayments were made bbbecause he had failed to notify, as he ought to have, the Community authorities of a change in his domestic circumstances. 'Thus having placed himself in an irregular situation by his own conduct he cannot rely on his good faith to be released from the obligation to return the sums overpaid during this period'.[4] Similarly in another case the applicant was not allowed to rely on the absence of material out oof a file.[5] It appears, however, that the estoppel principle is less applicable to the actions of the administrative authorities than to individuals in Community law.[6]

1 A.G. Toth, *Legal Protection of Individuals in the European Communities* (1978) Vol. 1, 192. Footnote omitted.
2 Case 127/80 [1982] E.C.R. 869, at p. 885.
3 *Supra.*
4 *Supra.*
5 Case 151/80 *De Hoe v EC Commission* [1981] E.C.R. 3161, at pp. 3175,6; see also Case 67/63 *SOREMA v High AAAuthority* [1964] E.C.R. 151, [1964] C.M.L.R. 350.
6 See H.G. Schermers, *Judicial Protection in the European Communities*, Third Edition (1981), p. 117; A.G. Toth, *supra* fn. 1 Vol. 1, 92; Cases 17 20/61 *Klöckner-Werke and Hoesch v High Authority* [1962] E.C.R. 325, at p. 325.

8.21 The Cooourt has also accepted the principle that money paid without legal basis should be repaid (unjust enrichment).[1]

1 Case 26/67 *Danvin v EC Commission* [1968] E.C.R. 315, at p. 322; Case 71/72 *Kuhl v EC Council* [1973] E.C.R. 705, at pp. 712,3; *Meganck v EC Commission, supra.*

8.22 Similarly the concept of *force majeure* has been embraced by the Court. The concept which is familiar in the legal systems of the Memberrr States relieves a person of his obligation in specified circumsstances where he has not been at fault. It features at Community law in both written form and aas a general principle. As a general principle tthe defence seems to be more broadly formulated at Community level tthan it is in the legal systems of the Member States.[1] In so far as the defence is specified in a regulation, etc. then it must of course be interpreted in accordance with the wwritten form and must be construed in that context. In the *Handelsgggesellschaft* Case where an exporter failed to export the quota allocated to him, by a specified date the Commission purported to forfeit the deposit lodged on the issuance of the licence. The regulation in question excluded forfeiture in cases of *force majeurefl* only and the applicant objected that this was too strict. In the course of its judgment the Court, relying on earlier case-law, made the following statement on the nnaaaature of the defence of force majeure:

> 'The concept of *force majeure* adopted by the agricultural regulations takes into account the particular nature of the relationships in the public law between traders and the national administration, as well as the objectives of those regulations. It follows from those objectives as well as from the positive provisions of the regulations in question that the concept of *force majeure* is not limited to absolute impossibility but must be understood in the sense of unusual circumstances, outside the control of the importer or exporter, the consequences of which, in spite of the exercise of all due care, could not have been avoided except at the cost of excessive sacrifice. This concept implies a sufficient flexibility regarding not only the nature of the occurrence relied upon but also the care which the exporter should have exercised in order to meet it and the extent of the sacrifices which he should have accepted to that end'.[2]

An excessively long delay in postal delivery can constitute a *force majeure* which relieves the individual of an obligation,[3] but, to permit an individual to infringe Community law because of *force majeure*, the Court is more reluctant. In such a case, to relieve the applicant there must be an unavoidable external cause.[4] An attempt by an applicant who had commenced proceedings out of time to claim *force majeure* because the applicant was unable to find a sufficiently well qualified lawyer in Community law during the summer time, did not impress the Court. The Court was not satisfied that the applicant had acted diligently enough in the circumstances.[5]

1 Case 68/77 *Intercontinentale Fleischhandelsgesellschaft v EC Commission* [1978] E.C.R. 353, at p. 370, [1978] 2 C.M.L.R. 733, at p. 753.
2 Case 11/70 *Internationale Handelsgesellschaft v Einfuhr-und Vorratsstelle für Getreide und Futtermittel* [1970] E.C.R. 1125, at pp. 1137,8, [1972] C.M.L.R. 255, at p. 286; see also Case 158/73 *Kampffmeyer v Einfuhr- und Vorratsstelle für Getreide und Futtermittel* [1974] E.C.R. 101, at pp. 110,11; Case 3/74 *Einfuhr- und Vorratsstelle für Getreide und Futtermittel v Pfützenreuter* [1974] E.C.R. 589, at pp. 598–600; Case 70/86 *EC Commission v Greece* O.J. C 274 13.10.87 p. 5: foreseeable bank strike not *force majeure*.
3 Cases 25–26/65 *SIMET and FERAM v High Authority* [1967] E.C.R. 33, at pp. 42,3.
4 Case 154/78 and others *Valsabbia and others v EC Commission* [1980] E.C.R. 907, at p. 1022, [1981] 1 C.M.L.R. 613, at p. 701.
5 Case 209/83 *Valsabbia v EC Commission* [1984] E.C.R. 3089.

5. *The principle of proportionality*

8.23 This principle requires that measures taken by the institutions, at Community or national level, to achieve a Community objective must not be out of proportion to the objective to be achieved. 'The principle requires that the acts of Community institutions must not go beyond the limits of what is appropriate and necessary to attain that objective sought.'[1] The relationship between the means and the end must be reasonable.[2] 'It expresses the general idea that the Community institutions and the national authorities may impose upon Community citizens, for a public interest purpose, only such obligations and restrictions as are strictly necessary for that purpose to be attained. In other words, the individual should not have his freedom of action limited beyond the degree necessary for the general (public) interest.'[3] If the measure adopted is out of proportion to the objectives to be achieved the court may then annul the measure. If the objective sought could be achieved by less onerous means, then the measure adopted will be in breach of the principle. This principle, which is accorded constitutional status in Germany, is designed to protect the individual from legislative and administrative excesses by governmental institutions. It may, however, also apply, in appropriate cases, in favour of the administration.[4]

The principle is especially important in the sphere of economic law where legal instruments are frequently adopted to direct commercial operators in directions which are seen to be desirable to those who manage the economy. The measure adopted, for example, may be designed to eliminate a surplus[5] or to control imports or exports.[6] The principle is also applicable in the case of penalties: penalties imposed by the authorities must bear a reasonable relationship to the offence committed, and if disproportionate, may be annulled.[7]

1 Case 15/83 *Denkavit Nederland BV v Hoofdproduktschap voor Akkerbouwprodukten* [1984] E.C.R. 2171.

2 See Advocate-General in *Handelsgesellschaft* Case, *supra*, para 8.22, fn. 2 at p. 1146.
3 A.G. Toth, *Legal Protection of Individuals in the European Communities* (1978), Vol. 1, 90 footnote omitted. The principle may find a parallel in the Common law rule which suggests that measures must be reasonable and that the 'less restrictive alternative', in the US sense, must be used. See Sandalow and Stein, *Courts and Free Markets*, Vol. 1, 28; L. Neville Brown and F.G. Jacobs, *The Court of Justice of the European Communities*, Second Edition (1983) pp. 263–4; T.C. Hartley, *The Foundations of European Community Law*, First Edition (1981) p. 137.
4 See Case 808/79 *Pardini v EC Commission* [1980] E.C.R. 2103, at pp. 2120,2, [1981] 2 C.M.L.R. 603, at pp. 621–3.
5 Case 114/76 *Bela-Mühle Josef Bergmann v Grows-Farm* [1977] E.C.R. 1211, [1979] 2 C.M.L.R. 83.
6 *Handelsgesellschaft* Case, *supra* fn. 2.
7 Case 8/55 *Fédération Charbonnière de Belgique v High Authority* [1954–56] E.C.R. 245, at p. 299; Case 18/63 *Wollast née Schmitz v EEC* [1964] E.C.R. 85, at p. 97.

8.24 It is clear that the application of this principle leaves a great deal of discretion to the Court, and it will not always be easy to anticipate how the Court will balance the competing interests in any individual case. The Court, however, takes a broad view of the institutions' obligations in this matter, and will strike down the measure only in clear cases. In this regard the Court has said:

'. . ., it does not necessarily follow that the obligation must be measured in relation to the individual situation of any one particular group of operators.

'Given the multiplicity and complexity of economic circumstances, such an evaluation would not only be impossible to achieve, but would also create perpetual uncertainty in the law'.[1]

In the case in question the Court took into account the fact that the immediate and practical measures were required in the area of agriculture because of currency fluctuations.[2] In *Société Laitière de Gacé v FORMA*,[3] the Court held there was no breach of the principle when a measure provided for the loss of the *whole* aid due for processing of skimmed milk into caseins when the applicant failed to conform with maximum water content conditions.[4]

1 Case 9/73 *Schlüter v Hauptzollamt Lörrach* [1973] E.C.R. 1135, at p. 1156.
2 See also *Pardini* Case, *supra* para 8.23 fn. 4. Cases 63–69/72 *Werhahn v EC Council* [1973] E.C.R. 1229, at p. 1250.
3 Case 273/81 [1982] E.C.R. 4193, [1984] 1 C.M.L.R. 542.
4 See also Case 272/81 *RU-MI v FORMA* [1982] E.C.R. 4167.

8.25 It is worth looking at a couple of cases where proportionality was canvassed to illustrate the type of case where the principle might arise. The *Handelsgesellschaft* Case concerned regulations under the CAP. To regulate the volume of corn-flour in the Community, the Commission introduced a licensing system for imports and exports. The Commission estimated in advance the amount of imports and exports that were required and allocated this amount among importers and exporters who applied for licences. An applicant was required to apply for a licence and was also required to make a deposit with the authorities on the issuance of the licence. The purpose of the deposit was to ensure that the allocated quantity was taken up by the licence holder. It was provided that if the licence holder did not import (or export) his allocation within the period of the licence that the deposit would be forfeited. The applicant in the present case did not export the full amount allocated and had his deposit forfeited. He then contested the proportionality of the measure. In balancing the advantages and the disadvantages the Court was not willing to strike down the measure as being out of proportion to the objective to be achieved. In the *Buitoni* Case, however, the Court took a view which favoured the applicant. The context of this case was similar to the *Handelsgesellschaft* Case and involved the licence/deposit mechanism just outlined. In *Buitoni*, however, another regulation extended the forfeiture penalty to traders who had complied with the licence by importing or exporting the allocated quantity, but who failed to furnish the necessary proof of compliance within six months. Since it was in the trader's interest to have his deposit repaid as soon as possible, the Court held that to impose the same penalty for failure to import/export on the one hand, and failure to furnish proof (a much less serious offence) on the other hand, breached the principle of proportionality and the offending article of the regulation in question was declared invalid.[1]

1 Case 122/78 *Buitoni v FORMA* [1979] E.C.R. 677, at pp. 685,6, [1979] 2 C.M.L.R. 665, at p. 676.

6. *Legal certainty*

8.26 Legal certainty is a concept which is assumed by most Western legal systems. By legal certainty we are not, however, insisting that the subject in the legal system should be able to know all the rules relating to his position at any given time. This of course would not be possible. Rather are we suggesting that the subject is entitled to rely on the general continuity of the system and is entitled to expect that the rules of the system will not be changed in an arbitrary fashion without warning. The concept as it applies in Community law embraces three separate, though frequently related, principles:

(1) The Principle which protects Legitimate Expectations.
(2) The Principle which protects Vested (Acquired) Rights.
(3) The Principle which prohibits retroactive laws.

Although these sub-rules represent the main applications of the principle of legal certainty they are not the only examples of the principle.

In the area of trade and commerce the principle has additional relevance because commercial operators invariably make their engagements in reliance on basic assumptions concerning continuity, stability and predictability. Survival and success in commerce and trade is frequently related to the operator's ability to cope with these concepts.

Of course, like all principles of this nature, the principle, while of great importance in Community law, is not an absolute one. In determining its full sphere of application it competes with other principles and in particular with the principles of legality (i.e. that things should be done according to the law) and justice. In the balancing exercise which the Court of Justice must frequently engage in here, the concept of legal certainty may have to yield occasionally to these other values. In this connection Schermers declares that '. . . legal certainty is not a compelling legal principle which must be safeguarded at all costs. The Court rather regards legal certainty as a desirable end but as one which can be outweighed by more momentous legal rules or even by considerations of a more pressing economic or practical character.'[1]

1 H.G. Schermers, *Judicial Protection in the European Communities*, Third Edition (1983) p. 46.

(i) *The principle of legitimate expectations*

8.27 A commercial operator in the legal system of the EEC is entitled to expect that principles, undertakings and rules, whether of a general or specific nature will not be altered to his detriment without notice. So where the Council in the context of wage negotiations made a decision, intended to last for three years with regard to the salaries of Community employees, an attempt by the Council to change the decision after nine months only was struck down by the Court as being in breach of the principle of legitimate expectations.[1] The Court intimated in the same case that the principle was a general one which would prevail over general acts of the institutions as well as over individual decisions. Again in the *CNTA* case the Court held that the system of monetary compensatory amounts (MCAs) introduced to cope with currency fluctuations between the Member States should not be changed without notice or warning to commercial operators. The effect of the MCA system as it operated was such that traders were able to calculate their trading risks without reference to exchange risks. The Court declared:

'The Community is therefore liable if, in the absence of an overriding matter of public interest, the Commission abolished with immediate effect and without warning the application of compensatory amounts in a specific sector without adopting transitional measures which would at least permit traders either to avoid the loss which would have been suffered in the performance of export contracts, the existence and irrevocability of which are established by the advance fixing of the refunds, or to be compensated for by such a loss.'[2]

The principle of legitimate expectations is a general principle of Community law which, in appropriate circumstances, can be used to annul a Community measure adopted in total disregard of the principle. Moreover, it can give the aggrieved party a right to sue for compensation in the proper circumstances.[3] The Court will also use it as a guide to assist it in interpreting Community measures: an interpretation that promotes legitimate expectations will be favoured over one which thwarts such expectations.[4]

In determining whether expectations are legitimate[5] and deserving of protection, the Court of Justice has undoubtedly a good deal of discretion. Much will depend on the individual circumstances of each case. It is not surprising that in exercising its discretion the Court will be moved and influenced, like an equity court in the Common Law tradition, by what is reasonable and what is fair. Accordingly, an unreasonable expectation will not be protected as being legitimate and the Court will not guarantee the continuation of an unintended situation accidently brought about and exploited by speculators. The only reasonable expectation in such circumstances is that the loophole will be plugged by the authorities as soon as possible.[6]

1   Case 81/72 *EC Commission v EC Council* [1973] E.C.R. 575, at p. 584, [1973] C.M.L.R. 639, at p. 657; see, for recent example, Case 344/85 *Ferriere San Carlo v EC Commission* O.J. C 329 8.12.87 p. 3.
2   Case 74/74 *Comptoir National Technique Agricole (CNTA) v EC Commission* [1975] E.C.R. 533, at p. 550, [1977] 1 C.M.L.R. 171, at p. 190; see also Case 78/74 *Deuka v Einfuhr- und Vorratsstelle für Getreide und Futtermittel* [1975] E.C.R. 421, [1975] 2 C.M.L.R. 28.
3   *CNTA Case, supra.*
4   Case 112/77 *Töpfer v EC Commission* [1978] E.C.R. 1019; *Deuka Case, supra.*
5   Case 78/77 *Lührs v Hauptzollamt Hamburg-Jonas* [1978] E.C.R. 169, at pp. 177,8, [1979] 1 C.M.L.R. 657, at pp. 667,8.
6   Case 2/75 *Einfuhr- und Vorratsstelle für Getreide und Futtermittel v Mackprang* [1975] E.C.R. 607, at p. 623, [1977] 1 C.M.L.R. 198, at p. 207. The expectation is 'legitimate' if it is, 'conceived in the mind of a prudent person who acts according to the letter and spirit of the law in confidence that his fidelity to the law will be reciprocated'. D. Lasok and J.W. Bridge, *Law and Institutions of the European Communities*, Fourth Edition (1987) p. 167. See also authorities cited there fn. 18.

(ii) *The principle which protects vested (acquired) rights*

8.28 If legal certainty and the desirability that operators should have confidence in the legal system requires that legitimate expectations (which need not amount to rights) should be protected, then the same concepts should show equal or more concern for rights which have already vested. Community law does indeed take this view, so that if a person is given a licence to import particular goods until 31 March, this right, being vested, cannot be taken from him unless some overriding principle in Community law justifies it.[1]

In the *Algera* Case[2] orders made on 12 December 1955 brought the applicant, a Community employee, within the ambit of Staff Regulations, appointed her to a specific grade and fixed her rank at a specified level of seniority. These orders gave rights to the applicant and an attempt by the authorities to change these conditions and impose new conditions on the applicant was contested as being unlawful. The Court held that the applicant had rights under the earlier measure. The Court then went on to examine whether these rights could be revoked. Since there was no Community law on the matter the Court felt obliged to seek guidance in the administrative law of the Member States and concluded as follows:

'It emerges from a comparative study of this problem of law that in the six Member States an administrative measure conferring individual rights on the person concerned cannot in principle be withdrawn, if it is a lawful measure; in that case, since the individual right is vested, the need to safeguard confidence in stability of the situation thus created prevails over the interests of an administration desirous of reversing its decision. This is true in particular of the appointment of an official.'[3]

The Court went on, however, to accept the principle that administrative measures which were illegal (as where the issuing authority acted *ultra vires*) could be revoked at least within a reasonable length of time. As to whether the revocation should be *ex nunc* or *ex tunc* (retroactive) would depend on the circumstances of each case and would of course be subject to the Court of Justice's review which would have to consider the affected individual's legitimate expectations.

Normally speaking 'therefore' rights which individuals possess by virtue of a legal measure cannot be retroactively withdrawn. Prospective withdrawal is a different matter, however.[4] Here there may well be overriding reasons permitting the change for the future, provided the persons affected are given notice and have time to adapt.

The principle of protecting vested rights is according to some writers no more than one aspect of the principle of non-retroactivity. It is appropriate, therefore, that this latter principle should be examined at this juncture.

1 See D. Lasok and J.W. Bridge, *Law and Institutions of the European Communities*, Fourth Edition, (1987), p. 164 *et seq.*
2 Cases 7/56, 3–7/57 *Algera v Common Assembly* [1957–58] E.C.R. 39.
3 *Idem* at 55.
4 Case 15/60 *Simon v Court of Justice* [1961] E.C.R. 115, at p. 123.

(iii) *The principle of non-retroactivity*

8.29 Legislation can be truly retroactive or quasi-retroactive. A measure is said to be truly retroactive when it applies to completed acts, acts which are over and done with. A measure is said to be quasi-retroactive when it applies to acts which are not completed but are still in progress. An example of a truly retroactive piece of legislation would be a statute which declared that a levy of 20 per cent would now be imposed on all shoes imported during March of last year. An example of a quasi-retroactive piece of legislation would be a statute which imposed a similar levy as from today. This might have the effect of imposing a 20 per cent levy on some importers who have commenced to import shoes yesterday by putting them on-board ship, etc., or indeed who have merely entered into contractual commitments yesterday with a view to importing the shoes next week.

Generally speaking, true retroactivity is not permitted within the Community's legal system on the grounds that it is incompatible with the requirement of legal certainty and the protection of legitimate expectations.[1] The case of *R v Kirk*[2] must also be noted in this context. There the defendant contested the legality of a UK Sea Fisheries Order on the grounds that it was discriminatory. He also claimed that attempts by the Council to validate the measure retroactively were contrary to Community law. In agreeing with Mr Kirk the Court of Justice stated:

'The principle that penal provisions may not have retroactive effect is one which is common to all the legal orders of the Member States and is enshrined in Article 7 of the European Convention for the Protection of Human Rights and Fundamental Freedoms as a fundamental right; it takes its place among the general principles of law whose observance is ensured by the Court of Justice.
   Consequently the retroactivity provided for in Article 6(1) of Regulation No. 170/83 cannot be regarded as validating *ex post facto* national measures which

imposed criminal penalties, at the time of the conduct at issue, if those measures were not valid.'[3]

The Court of Justice, however, in accordance with the rules of the Member States, is not so concerned with the individuals who find themselves at a disadvantage in the quasi-retroactive situation.[4] Retroactivity is admissible in these situations in principle, the individual's only protection being in his ability to convince the Court that because of his legitimate expectations the measure in question should not apply in this particular case retroactively.[5]

1 E. Grabitz, 'The Sources of Community Law: acts of the Community institutions', in *Thirty Years of Community Law*, p. 96; Toth 90; Schermers, 51.
2 Case 63/83 [1984] E.C.R. 2689, [1984] 3 C.M.L.R. 522.
3 *Idem*, at pp. 2718, 538, 462 respectively. Noted by Greenwood, All E.R. Rev. 1985, 147. In this case the Court went against recommendations of the Commission and the Advocate-General.
4 Case 40/79 *Mrs P v EC Commission* [1981] E.C.R. 361, at p. 373.
5 Case 1/73 *Westzucker GmbH v Einfuhr- und Vorratsstelle für Zucker* [1973] E.C.R. 723; Case 143/73 *SOPAD v FORMA* [1973] E.C.R. 1433, [1977] 1 C.M.L.R. 227.

8.30   To the general rule which prohibits true retroactivity, however, there are some well-established exceptions. For example, retroactivity may be permitted if it is for the benefit of affected individuals.[1] Moreover, the law's dislike for retroactivity is more keenly felt in the area of substantive rules than in procedural matters. New procedural rules may apply, for example, in previously initiated cases.[2] In the recent *Tunnel Refineries Ltd v EC Council*[3] case the Court held that while legal certainty prohibits true retroactivity in principle 'it may exceptionally be otherwise where the purpose to be achieved so demands and where the legitimate expectations of those concerned are duly respected'.[4] In these cases the Court had previously struck down certain articles of earlier Council regulations on the grounds that they offended against the general principle of equality (in that case between sugar producers and isoglucose producers). A subsequent 'repairing' regulation was also struck down for failure to observe an essential procedural requirement, namely failing to obtain Parliament's opinion. A third regulation then attempted to apply common provisions for sugar and isoglucose producers and to reinstate with retroactive effect the quota system adopted by earlier regulations. The Court refused to strike down this measure because firstly, the object to be achieved, namely the stabilisation of the Community market in sweetners without arbitrary discrimination between traders, required the provisions to be retroactive and secondly, no legitimate expectation was infringed. Both conditions permitting retroactivity were therefore fulfilled.

There are other instances, too, where retroactivity has been approved. Mention must be made in particular in this context of situations where there is a compelling economic reason. In particular one might think of difficulties caused by currency fluctuations, revaluations and devaluations, etc., which might necessitate retroactive measures[5] and the system of monetary compensatory amounts[6] which by their nature involve a retroactive element.[7] Whether a compelling economic necessity exists in such circumstances is normally a matter for the legislative authority to decide, but its decision is reviewable by the Court.[8]

Two further cases where the rule against non-retroactivity does not apply are noted by Schermers: in the case of (i) interpretations and (ii) amendments.[9] If an ambiguous rule is clarified by a subsequent ruling then the subsequent interpretation can be applied to cases which occurred prior to the interpretation.[10] But just as the Court can, for compelling economic reasons, allow a measure to have retroactive effect, so also can the Court for similar pressing reasons refuse retroactive effect. In *Defrenne v Sabena (No 2)*[11] the Court held that EEC Treaty, art. 119 (enshrining the principle that men and women should get equal pay for equal work) had direct effect from 1 January 1962 for old members of the Community and from 1 January 1973 for new members. This meant that unequal pay after those dates was illegal. Normally this should have entitled affected parties to legal remedies. Because, however, of the huge financial burden this would have imposed on private and public employers, the Court refused in the interests of legal certainty, to apply its ruling retroactively. Legal remedies would only be available for future breaches. 'Therefore, the direct effect of Article 119 cannot be relied on in order to support claims concerning pay periods prior to the date of this judgment, except as regards those workers who have already brought legal proceedings or made an equivalent claim.'[12] This escape was also adopted by the Irish Supreme Court in the *Murphy* Tax Case.[13] Since *Defrenne*, however, the Court has not adopted this 'prospective interpretation' in any other case and it has been quick to point out the exceptional circumstances of the *Defrenne* Case and that interpretations normally apply retroactively as well as prospectively.[14]

1 Case 71/82 *Bundesanstalt für Landwirtschaftliche Marktordnung v Brüggen* [1982] E.C.R. 4647, at p. 4657. Court also considered important here the fact that the application retroactively did not have an appreciable effect on the reliability of the licensing systems in question. Consideration 18.
2 Cases 212–17/80 *Amministrazione delle Finanze dello Stato v Meridionale Industria Salumi* [1981] E.C.R. 2735, at p. 2751.
3 Case 114/81 [1982] E.C.R. 3189, at p. 3198.
4 *Idem*, at p. 3206; see also Case 110/81 *Roquette Frères v EC Council* [1982] E.C.R. 3159.
5 See, for example, Case 37/70 *Rewe Zentral des Lebensmittel-Großhandels GmbH v Hauptzollamt Emmerich* [1971] E.C.R. 23, [1971] C.M.L.R. 238.
6 MCAs—see *infra*.
7 Case 7/76 *IRCA v Amministrazione delle Finanze dello Stato* [1976] E.C.R. 1213, at p. 1229.
8 *Tunnel Refineries Ltd* Case, *supra*.
9 H.G. Schermers, *Judicial Protection in the European Communities*, Third Edition (1983), pp. 56–57.
10 Case 183/73 *Osram GmbH v Oberfinanzdirection Frankfurt-am-Main* [1974] E.C.R. 477, [1974] 2 C.M.L.R. 360.
11 Case 43/75 [1976] E.C.R. 455, [1976] 2 C.M.L.R. 98.
12 *Idem.*, at pp. 481, 128 respectively.
13 The Irish Court cited the *Defrenne* Case in support of its stand. [1982] I.R. 241.
14 Case 69/80 *Worringham v Lloyds Bank Ltd* [1981] E.C.R. 767, at p. 794, [1981] 2 C.M.L.R. 1, at pp. 22,3, [1981] 2 All E.R. 434, at p. 448. See also Case 826/79 *Amministrazione delle Finanze dello Stato v MIRECO* [1980] E.C.R. 2559, at p. 2573.

Chapter 9

Secondary Legislation

Secondary legislation

9.1 Just as the Oireachtas in Ireland has power to make laws under the Constitution so also are the institutions of the EEC empowered by the Treaty of Rome to pass legislation to achieve the objectives of the treaty. Such legislation is frequently described as 'secondary legislation' because it is subordinate to the primary law set out in the foundation treaties. It cannot, therefore, derogate from or contradict the treaties, and it must conform in its procedural aspects to all the rules stipulated in the treaties. For Irish lawyers this distinction should pose no great problems of appreciation.

9.2 Somewhat less familiar to Irish lawyers will be the notion that the legislative acts which the Council of Ministers and the Commission may take are of various kinds and have various legal effects. In distinguishing these acts from each other Community law emphasises the binding and non-binding nature of the acts, the generality or particularity of the act, the nature of the addressees of the act, and whether further action is contemplated by a Member State to implement the Community acts. In particular EEC Treaty, art. 189 contemplates Regulations, Directives, Decisions, Recommendations and Opinions. Because of its importance Article 189 requires to be quoted in full.

> 'In order to carry out their task the Council and the Commission shall, in accordance with the provisions of this Treaty, make regulations, issue directives, take decisions, make recommendations or deliver opinions.
> A regulation shall have general application. It shall be binding in its entirey and directly applicable in all Member States.
> A directive shall be binding, as to the result to be achieved, upon each Member State to which it is addressed, but shall leave to the national authorities the choice of form and methods.
> A decision shall be binding in its entirety upon those to whom it is addressed.
> Recommendations and opinions shall have no binding force.'

9.3 Two points must be made immediately about this Article. First, it confirms the general point that the powers which the institutions of the

Community have, are attributive only. The institutions do not have general and original powers; they merely have what powers are given to them by the Treaties themselves. Second, by specifying that these powers are given to the Council and Commission, the clear implication is that other institutions do not have these powers. The further question then arises as to what extent the Council and Commission may delegate these functions.

9.4 With regard to the first point relating to attribution only, two qualifications must be added. In the first place, the Court of Justice has developed in its jurisprudence a theory which declares that the Community institutions, in addition to their express powers, have also got 'implied powers' where such powers are necessary to achieve the objectives of the treaties.

In the second place the Treaty of Rome itself, in Article 235, gives the Council generous powers of action in residual emergency-type situations where such action is necessary to attain a Community objective. Article 235 reads in full:

> 'If action by the Community should prove necessary to attain, in the course of the operation of the common market, one of the objectives of the Community and this Treaty has not provided the necessary powers, the Council shall, acting unanimously on a proposal from the Commission and after consulting the Assembly, take the appropriate measures.'

An extensive literature exists[1] on the scope of this Article but its terms need not unduly detain us here. Suffice to note that (i) the power is given to the Council; (ii) a stated procedure must be followed; (iii) for the Article to apply action must be necessary to attain a Community objective; and (iv) if the Article applies, the Council is empowered to take *any* '*appropriate measure*' which option includes at least regulations, directives and decisions.

These two qualifications greatly modify the picture that the Community institutions are hobbled by restrictive treaty provisions.

Before going on to examine in more detail the nature of regulations, directives, decisions, recommendations and opinions a few preliminary comments of a general nature require to be made.

1 See *supra* 7.4 and 9.6 fn. 2.

9.5 At the outset it should be stressed that the five acts or measures mentioned in Article 189 are not an exhaustive list of the panoply of instruments available to the institutions of the Community. True, the five mentioned are the most common forms used by the institutions but they are not the only ones. There are other acts or measures of legal significance available to the institutions. This was clearly decided by the Court of Justice in the *ERTA* case.[1] There the Council of Ministers suggested that the six Member States of the EEC should adopt a common stand in relation to the European Road Transport Agreement. Subsequently the Member States acted in concert and the Agreement was declared open for signature as from 1 July 1970. The Commission objected to this procedure claiming that this function had been transferred to the Community and that the Member States no longer possessed powers in this matter and that the Commission should have been the institution to negotiate the agreement. The Commission brought an action against the Council and as a preliminary defence the Council argued that the proceedings at the Council Meeting, which agreed that the Member States should act in concert, was not an act within the meaning of Article 173 and so not capable of judicial review. The Council argued that its action was not a regulation, a directive or a decision and that the coordination of policies created no rights or obligations. The Court rejected this argument in the following language:

> 'Since the only matters excluded from the scope of the action for annulment open to the Member States and the institutions are "recommendations and opinions"—which by the final paragraph of Article 189 are declared to have no binding force—Article 173 treats as acts open to review by the Court all measures adopted by the institutions which are intended to have legal force.
>
> 'The object of this review is to ensure, as required by Article 164, observance of the law in the interpretation and application of the Treaty.
>
> 'It would be inconsistent with this objective to interpret the conditions under which the action is admissible so restrictively as to limit the availability of this procedure merely to the categories of measures referred to by Article 189.
>
> 'An action for annulment must therefore be available in the case of all measures adopted by the institutions, whatever their nature or form, which are intended to have legal effects.'[2]

The *ERTA* Case held that the political consultations held within the framework of the Council of Ministers and leading to concerted action was another type of legal act capable of being judicially reviewed. In *Haegeman v Belgium*[3] the Court came to a similar conclusion in respect of an international agreement concluded with Greece (then a non-member) in so far as it concerned the Community.

It should not, however, be thought that these other acts are very common within the Community legal system. The point must not be over-emphasised. The majority of Community legislation normally takes the form of regulations, directives or decisions. These are the typical forms of legislative action within the Community. That they do not comprise an exhaustive list must, however, be noted.

1 Case 22/70 *EC Commission v EC Council* [1971] E.C.R. 263, [1971] C.M.L.R. 335.
2 *Idem* at pp. 276–7 and p. 357 respectively. See also D.J. Gijlstra *et al.*, *Leading Cases on the Law of the European Communities*, pp. 25–34 (4th ed.).
3 Case 181/73 [1974] E.C.R. 449, [1975] 1 C.M.L.R. 515.

9.6 A further word can be mentioned about the classification of these acts. Simply to call a measure in the Community scheme of things a regulation or a decision, does not make it a regulation or a decision. As the philosophers or linguists might say, the word is different from the thing. To call an object a rose does not make it a rose. To be a rose the object must possess certain features or attributes. Similarly to call a legislative act a regulation or a decision does not make it so. In determining the real nature of the legislative act the Court of Justice will look at the nature, the substance and the quality of the act itself before classifying it. Accordingly, acts which are called regulations by the Commission may in reality be decisions[1] and indeed measures which are termed regulations may be regulations in part and decisions in part.[2]

At all times concern in determining the proper category of the act will be with the substance and not with the title or form.

1 See Case 6/68 *Zuckerfabrik Watenstedt GmbH v EC Council* [1968] E.C.R. 413, [1969] C.M.L.R. 26.
2 Cases 16–17/62 *Confédération Nationale des Producteurs de Fruits et Légumes v EEC Council* [1962] E.C.R. 471, at p. 478, [1963] C.M.L.R. 160, at p. 173. See *infra*, para. 9.18.

9.7 One might at this juncture ask why it is so important to be able to classify into their proper categories various measures, which, in any event, as secondary sources are all subordinate to the Treaties? There are two reasons why proper classification should concern us. Firstly, certain Articles of the Treaty specifically authorise specific legislative acts and where this is the case only this form of action will be permitted. For example, Articles 54 and 56 of the EEC Treaty authorise the institutions to issue directives to promote the right of establishment. The institutions could not issue regulations or decisions under the authority of these Articles. Again Article 87 authorises the institution to issue regulations or directives to give effect to Articles 85 and 86 of the EEC Treaty (Competition rules relating to undertakings). Accordingly, decisions may not be used under this Article. Furthermore, reasons must be given by the Council and Commission in respect of regulations, directives and decisions[1] and Article 191 requires regulations to be published but requires directives and decisions to be notified only to the addressees. Secondly, only acts which are legally binding can be judicially reviewed under the terms of Article 173 as judicially interpreted in the *ERTA* Case.[2] Recommendations and opinions, therefore, cannot be the subject of judicial review proceedings. Furthermore, private individuals have greater standing in seeking judicial review when the measure is a decision as opposed to a regulation.

Important as the classification is, however, too much must not be made of it. In particular one must refer to the fact that the Court of Justice has in its case-law eroded, to a large extent, the formal distinction that exists between Regulations and Directives as defined in Article 189 of the Treaty. Further reference will be made to this below.[3]

It is now necessary to focus a little more sharply on the nature and characteristics of the typical acts enumerted in Article 189 of the Treaty, that is to say, on Regulations, Directives, Decisions, Recommendations and Opinions.

1 EEC Treaty, art. 190.
2 *Supra.*
3 *Infra*, para.s 9.13 and 9.14.

Regulations

9.8 'A regulation shall have general application. It shall be binding in its entirety and directly applicable in all Member States'.[1]

The regulation is the most comprehensive form of Community legislation in its scope, its sphere of application and its legal effect. At national level its closest analogy is to an Act of Parliament. It sets down binding rules applicable generally throughout the whole jurisdiction. It is the legislative act which truly represents the extent to which the Member States have surrendered sovereignty to the Community. Not only is it the most comprehensive in form, it is also the most commonly used, there being an estimated 4,000 adopted annually.

1 EEC Treaty, art. 189.

9.9 'General application' The generality of its application is what distinguishes the regulation from the decision which applies only to particular addressees. The regulation applies generally to objective 'categories of persons viewed abstractly and in their entirety'.[1] 'The general application of a legal act means that it contains general and abstract provisions and that its legal effects extend to an indeterminate group of persons and to a multiplicity of circumstances described in general terms. It is clear from the case-law of the Court that, where the measure has the character of a regulation or of a general decision that character is not called in issue by virtue of the fact that the number and even the identity of the persons to whom it applies may be determined more or less precisely, provided its application depends on an objective legal or factual situation defined by the measure with reference to its purpose.'[2]

A measure addressed to John Smith, or the Ford Motor Co., or to all those importers who have applied for import licences on 30 March last would clearly be a decision since the number of persons to whom it is addressed is defined or identifiable. In contrast, a measure which purports to deal with all doctors or lawyers is general, because, although one could to a greater or lesser extent determine the group, 'the measure is applicable as the result of an objective situation of law or fact which it specifies and which is in harmony with its ultimate objective'.[3]

Moreover, the regulation is of general application in the sense that it applies in full force throughout the whole Community, in all the Member States. Exceptional circumstances may exist, however, where for example the circumstances legislated for exist only in one or some Member States, and in these circumstances the regulation will not lose its general quality simply because of this fact. Provided the measure still retains the other characteristics associated with generality it will still be a regulation.[4]

It may not be so easy in practice, however, to determine always whether a measure is of general or limited application.

1 Cases 16 and 17/62 *supra*, para. 9.6, fn. 2, at p. 478.
2 E. Grabitz, in *Thirty Years of Community Law*, p. 84. Citing in footnote Case 6/68 *supra*, para 9.6, fn.1; Case 64/69 *Compagnie Française Commerciale et Financière v EC Commission* [1970] E.C.R. 221, [1970] C.M.L.R. 369; Case 101/76 *Koninklijke Scholten-Honig v EC Council and Commission* [1977] E.C.R. 797, especially at p. 807.
3 Case 6/68 *supra*, fn. 2, at p. 415. See also Case 64/69 and Case 101/76, *supra*, fn. 2, at p. 808.
4 See, for example, Commission Regulation 834/74 OJ L 99 9.4.74 p. 15, art.s 5 and 6.

9.10 '. . . Binding in its entirety' This is the feature which distinguishes the regulation from the directive. The directive is addressed to Member States and stipulates the objectives which have to be achieved while leaving the means to the Member States. The directive, therefore, binds the Member States only as to the objectives; the regulation binds everyone in its entirety. A Member State cannot pick and choose which parts of the regulation it will accept.[1] No measure of discretion is left to Member States in respect of regulations. They bind, and they bind fully in all their details.

1 Case 128/78 *EC Commission v United Kingdom* [1979] E.C.R. 419 especially at 428–9, [1979] 2 C.M.L.R. 45 at 54–56.

9.11 '. . . directly applicable in all the Member States' The regulation applies directly in the legal systems of the Member States from the commencement date specified therein, or from the twentieth day following publication in the Official Journal.[1] No reception or incorporation process is required. Indeed, it takes effect even if for some internal reason the Member State is delayed or prevented from taking accommodating measures. It also means that any subject of Community law can rely on it as an instrument which confers rights and imposes obligations in the same way as does a national statute. In this sense the regulation may be 'directly effective' in that it can confer rights on individuals which the national courts must protect. In the *Politi* Case the Court has clearly emphasised this:

'By reason of their nature and function in the system of the sources of Community law regulations have direct effect and are, as such, capable of creating individual rights which national courts must protect.'[2]

Because of this feature of direct applicability Member States are not authorised to reproduce Community regulations within their legal system. Such a practice has been condemned by the Court of Justice because it creates an obstacle to the direct effect of the Community measure and endangers their simultaneous and uniform application throughout the Community.[3] Moreover, such a practice would suggest that the rights and obligations contained in these regulations spring from the national measure rather than from the Community act. There is also a danger that such a practice would conceal its origin and create doubt as to the date on which the regulation comes into force.

1 EEC Treaty, art. 191.
2 Case 43/71 *Politi v Ministero delle Finanze* [1971] E.C.R. 1039, at p. 1048, [1973] C.M.L.R. 60, at p. 70; see also Case 84/71 *Marimex v Ministero delle Finanze* [1972] E.C.R. 89, [1972] C.M.L.R. 907; Case 93/71 *Leonesio v Ministero dell'Agricoltura e delle Foreste* [1972] E.C.R. 287, [1973] C.M.L.R. 343; Case 34/73 *Fratelli Variola v Amministrazione Italiana delle Finanze* [1973] E.C.R. 981; Case 65/75 *Tasca* [1976] E.C.R. 291, [1977] 2 C.M.L.R. 183.
3 Case 39/72 *EC Commission v Italy* [1973] E.C.R. 101, at p. 114, [1973] C.M.L.R. 439, at p. 456.

9.12 It would be wrong to think, however, that regulations never contemplate national action. In some cases regulations leave the implementation process to the Member States themselves. Such national action is very usual where common organisations of agricultural markets are established. In such circumstances regulations can be divided into 'basic regulations' and 'implementing regulations'. The former, for example, occur where the Council lays down a structure and principles to govern a situation but does not attempt to set out the details for the situation. The details might then be produced in another regulation implementing the general or basic regulation. Such implementing regulations may be made by the Council itself or by the Commission under authority contained in EEC Treaty, art. 155. These implementing regulations are subordinate to the basic (parent) regulation and cannot derogate from it. Not only[1] must such national measures comply with the parent regulation, but failure by the Member State to take appropriate action cannot deprive the individual of his rights under the regulation. 'In general, all national measures are contrary to Community law which would have the result of obstructing the direct applicability of regulations, of jeopardising their simultaneous and uniform application throughout the whole Community, and of affecting the jurisdiction of the European Court to pronounce on their interpretation or validity.'[2]

1 Case 38/70 *Deutsche Tradax v Einfuhr- und Vorratsstelle für Getreide und Futtermittel* [1971] E.C.R. 145, [1972] C.M.L.R. 213. See also J.-V. Louis, *The Community Legal Order* (1980), 57.
2 A.G. Toth, *Legal Protection of Individuals in the European Communities* (1978), Vol. 1, p. 57.

Directives

9.13 Directives bind Member States only as to the result to be achieved. The means of securing the Community objective as stated in the directive is left to the Member States themselves. The directive is an instrument, therefore, suited to harmonisation programmes where minimum standards might be desirable but where absolute uniformity is not the goal. Where uniformity is thought desirable then the regulation is the more appropriate instrument.[1]

The directive, accordingly, in contrast to the regulation, by its very nature contemplates national action to realise its objectives. The directive contemplates a two-stage process: first, the adoption of the directive at Community level and, second, the implementation by the Member States at national level. The scheme set out in EEC Treaty, art. 189 would suggest a neat, clean, functional difference between regulations and directives. In practice, however, the theoretical difference between the two kinds of legal instrument has become somewhat blurred. Not only do some regulations require national legislation for their full implementation, but some directives are so detailed that the element of discretion left to the Member States in implementing them is very limited.

1 EEC Treaty, art. 100 confirms this.

9.14 Since the directive contemplates national response one might think that the directive cannot be directly applicable in the legal system of the Member States and cannot give individuals rights which the national courts must protect (i.e. cannot be 'directly effective'). This, however, is not the case and the Court has on several occasions held that directives can, in appropriate cases, have direct effect and give individuals rights. This important development will be discussed in greater detail below.[1] The problem frequently arises because most, if not all, directives stipulate a time-limit within which the Member State must make its national response or reaction. When a Member State fails to meet the dead-line the question then arises as to whether an individual may rely on the directive itself as a source of rights. The Court of Justice has on several occasions declared that he can so do in appropriate cases.[2] Failure by the Member State to act in accordance with the stipulated time-table can also result in an action by the Commission for failure to act under EEC Treaty, art. 169.

1 *Infra*, para. 13.19.
2 See Case 9/70 *Franz Grad v Finanzamt Traunstein* [1970] E.C.R. 825, [1971] C.M.L.R. 1; Case 33/70 *SACE v Ministero delle Finanze* [1970] E.C.R. 1213, [1971] C.M.L.R. 123; Case 41/74 *Van Duyn v Home Office* [1974] E.C.R. 1337, [1975] 1 C.M.L.R. 1.

9.15 Directives by their nature are addressed to Member States only. The response which the Member State gives to the directive will vary from state to state depending on the existing state of its own law and the particular problem dealt with in the directive. Normally a Member State will examine the directive against its own law on the matter and it will then make the necessary legal adjustment within its legal system to achieve the results stipulated in the directive. The national response may require an act of parliament, a statutory instrument, a change in administrative practice or, in some cases, where national law already conforms with the directive's objective, no response at all. Whether the national response is adequate in terms of the directive's requirements or not, is of course a matter which can be judicially reviewed at national or Community level.[1]

1 See H.G. Schermers, *Judicial Protection in the European Communities*, Third Edition (1981), p. 125, 3rd ed. See also Case 152/79 *Lee v Minister for Agriculture* [1980] E.C.R. 1495, [1980] 2 C.M.L.R. 682.

Decisions

9.16 A decision differs from a regulation in that it is addressed to a limited and defined number of persons, whereas a regulation is general and applies *erga omnes*. A decision by its nature binds only the addressees. Decisions may be addressed to Member States or to natural or legal persons. A decision differs from a directive in that it is binding in its entirety and not just as to the results to be achieved. Finally, a decision differs from a recommendation or an opinion in that it is a binding instrument which creates legal obligations whereas the latter do not.

9.17 As used in Article 189 the word decision has a technical meaning which must be distinguished from the many other meanings which the word has for the layman. For example decisions can be of an executive nature, of an administrative nature,[1] of a quasi-judicial nature,[2] or of a legislative nature within the Community.[3] These distinctions, however, are not relevant for classification under Article 189. To be a decision for the purpose of this Article, what is required is that the act should be of a kind that it legally affects the rights and obligations of a limited and identifiable group of persons. If the measure does not affect the addressee's legal rights and obligations it cannot be a decision. In the *Cement Convention* Case[4] the Court had to decide whether a letter from the Commission to a group of enterprises indicating that the agreement made between them was contrary to EEC Treaty, art. 85(1), and that an exemption under Article 85(3) was not justified, amounted to a decision. The effect of the communication was to deprive the undertakings of a protection from fines and, from the date of its receipt, to expose the undertakings to the risk of penalties. The Court in commenting on this aspect declared that

'. . . the said measure affected the interests of the undertakings by bringing about a distinct change in their legal position. It is unequivocally a measure which produces legal effects touching the interests of the undertakings concerned and which is binding on them. It thus constitutes not a mere opinion but a decision.'[5]

Earlier in the context of the ECSC Treaty the Court, to distinguish a decision from other non-binding acts declared that 'a decision must appear as an act originating from the competent organisation intended to produce judicial effects, constituting the ultimate end of the internal procedure of this organisation and according to which such organisation makes its final ruling in a form allowing its nature to be identified'.[6] The statement would appear to be equally applicable to EEC decisions.[7]

1 See examples given in D. Lasok and J.W. Bridge, *Law and Institutions of the European Communities*, Fourth Edition (1987), p. 129.
2 E.g. decisions of the Commission in Competition matters.
3 See, for example, Council Decision 64/300 (EEC) O.J. (Sp. Ed.) 1963–64 p. 141. See also D. Lasok and J.W. Bridge, *supra* fn. 1 p. 129; See also Hans Smit and Peter E. Herzog, *The Law of the European Community* (1982), IP 189.15 for other distinctions.
4 Cases 8-11/66 *Cimenteries C.B.R. Cimentsbedrijven v EEC Commission* [1967] E.C.R. 75, [1967] C.M.L.R. 77.
5 *Idem* [1967] E.C.R. 91.
6 Case 54/65 *Compagnie des Forges de Châtillon, Commentry et Neuves-Maisons v High Authority* [1966] E.C.R. 185, at p. 195, [1966] C.M.L.R. 525, at p. 538.
7 See A.G. Toth, *Legal Protection of Individuals in the European Communities* (1978), Vol. 2, pp. 45–7, for measures which have, and have not, been treated as decisions.

9.18 The other feature of the decision which is crucial for its definition, and which distinguishes it from a regulation, is the limited range of persons bound by it.

In this connection, in deciding whether an act is a decision, the Court of Justice appears to emphasise the persons not the number of cases regulated. If the group of persons is fixed, definite and not capable of expansion during the measure's lifetime, then the measure is likely to be a decision.[1] 'This does not mean that those to whom a decision is addressed must be indicated by name. It is sufficient that at the moment at which the decision is made, the number of persons bound by the decision is fixed and cannot change during its period of validity.'[2] Moreover, what has been said already about the substance not the form being the crucial factor in the classification process should be repeated here. This clearly means that a measure which is called a regulation by the issuing authority might still be a decision, or more likely that some provisions of such an act might constitute a decision. If the measure affects the legal interests of a fixed group then it may well be a decision whatever denomination is given to it.[3] Thus the Court has declared in the *Fruit and Vegetable* Case that 'if a measure entitled by its author a regulation contains provisions which are capable of being not only of direct but also of individual concern to certain natural or legal persons, it must be admitted, without prejudice to the question whether that measure considered in its entirety can be correctly called a regulation, that in any case those provisions do not have the character of a regulation and may therefore be impugned by those persons under the terms of the second paragraph of Article 173'.[4]

Finally, it is worth noting that a single provision cannot at one and the same time be a regulation for some persons and a decision for others.[5]

1 *Fuss*, 17 N.J.W. 949 (1964).
2 Hans Smit and Peter E. Herzog, *supra* para. 9.17, fn. 3, IP 189.16.
3 See Cases 41–44/70 *International Fruit Co v EC Commission* [1971] E.C.R. 411, especially at pp. 421,2, [1975] 2 C.M.L.R. 515, at p. 535.
4 Cases 16 and 17/62 *supra*, para. 9.6, fn. 2, at p. 479 and p. 174 respectively. The phrase of 'individual concern' should probably have been 'affects individual rights', or something like this. See Hans Smit and Peter E. Herzog, *supra*, fn. 2, IP 189.15. See also Case 113/77 *NTN Toyo Bearing Co. Ltd v EC Council* [1979] E.C.R. 1185, at p. 1205, [1979] 2 C.M.L.R. 257, at p. 335.
5 Case 18/57 *Nold v High Authority* [1959] E.C.R. 41, at p. 50; Case 45/81 *Moksel Import-Export v EC Commission* [1982] E.C.R. 1129, at p. 1144.

Recommendations and opinions

9.19 Recommendations and opinions have no binding force in law. Although they may be addressed to individuals or undertakings they are most frequently addressed to Member States. The distinction between the two measures is that recommendations are made on the issuing authority's own initiative and usually contain suggested courses of action, whereas opinions are frequently given in response to a request or initiative from elsewhere and give the institution's thinking on a factual or legal situation.

Although, in general, recommendations have no legal significance[1] in the strict sense, they can have a political and psychological significance in the Community context. Sometimes they can, for example, be a prelude to legal acts, and other times they may create 'legitimate expectations' in interested parties. Businessmen, therefore, cannot afford totally to ignore them in arranging their affairs.[2]

1 It might be argued that the general obligation imposed by EEC Treaty, art. 5 does not permit Member States totally to ignore recommendations. This would suggest that recommendations and opinions can have some legal significance. More particularly Articles 102(2) and 169 contain specific legal consequences where a Member State chooses to ignore a Commission recommendation or opinion.
2 Various other non-binding measures are noted by Lasok and Bridge including memoranda, communications, deliberations, programmes, guidelines and resolutions. See *op. cit.*, p. 131.

Binding Acts must be reasoned: Article 190

9.20 EEC Treaty, art. 190 provides that regulations, directives and decisions of the Council or Commission must state the reasons on which they are based and must refer to any proposals or opinions which were required to be obtained before such measures were adopted.

With regard to the reasons to be given, these should include not only an indication of the legal basis on which the measure is based (e.g. 'having regard to the Treaty establishing the EEC and in particular, Articles 48 and 49 thereof') but also a statement of the facts and considerations which motivated the institution to act (e.g. 'whereas the abolition of all discrimination based on nationality between workers of Member States as regards employment . . . should be completed at the latest by the end of the transitional period . . .; whereas . . .').

The Treaty obliges the institutions to indicate clearly their thinking behind such measures in order to protect the individuals and addressees immediately affected by the act, to enable the Court to exercise its control, to enable other interested parties to appreciate legislative policy, and to oblige the law-making bodies to justify to themselves and others the legality and reasonableness of their acts.[1] It is only fair, for example, that individuals should know whether the instrument is considered by the Commission or Council to be one which creates legal obligations for individuals or Member States and whether it is a regulation, a directive or a decision.[2]

The Treaty does not specify how detailed the reasons must be, but the Court has developed sensible standards in this matter. If the measure is a general one (e.g. a regulation or a directive) then the reasons given need only be general too. One cannot expect the Commission or Council to be anything other than general and abstract in such a situation. If the measure is an individual or specific act, however, and deals with a particular situation (e.g. a decision) then the institution will be expected to give more specific and concrete reasons based on the factual situation before it. 'On the other hand, the statement of reasons behind decisions imposing fines in competition cases will only be considered adequate if it indicates clearly and coherently the considerations of fact and of law on the basis of which the fine has been imposed on the parties concerned, in such a way as to acquaint both the latter and the Court with the essential factors of the Commission's reasoning.'[3] The nature of the measure in question, therefore, very much determines the amount of detail which is expected to be provided.[4] Recent case-law indicates that the Court of Justice continues to be indulgent towards the law-making institutions in this matter.[5] Moreover, a more summary form of reasoning will be tolerated where the context in which the measure has to be adopted is one of urgency, technical complexity or administrative difficulty. Pragmatic considerations will justify abbreviated reasons in these cases and will even justify references to reasons given in previous measures without restating them.[6] In such cases, however, it would appear in principle that references to reasons already given should only be acceptable where the previous document is such that persons affected have reasonable access to it.[7] In principle, the reasons should be given at the time the act is issued and not subsequently.[8]

If an act fails to give any, or indeed gives insufficient, reasons, the act may be annulled under Article 173. It may also be declared invalid under Article 177 procedure and form the basis for a plea of illegality under Article 184.

Finally, with regard to proposals and opinions which the institutions are obliged to obtain in making binding acts, the Court is not so demanding. Simple mention of these proposals is sufficient and there is no obligation for the institution to indicate the tenor of these submissions or to refute the arguments contained in such proposals.[9]

1 See Case 24/62 *Germany v EEC Commission* [1963] E.C.R. 63, at, p. 69.
2 The obligation to state reasons probably also extends to decisions *sui generis* which create legal obligations, Hans Smit and Peter E. Herzog, *The Law of the European Community* (1982), IP 190.94. In the *ERTA* Case, *supra* para. 9.5, fn. 1, the Court did not require that the legal act should be reasoned, considering that the Commission's participation in the activities of the Council provided it with sufficient guarantees of the kind specified in Article 190.
3 J.V. Louis, *The Community Legal Order*, 59. Internal quotation taken from Case 41/69 *Chemiefarma v EC Commission* [1970] E.C.R. 661, at p. 690. For an example of detailed reasons in such a case, see Commission Decision 82/896 (EEC) O.J. L 379 31.12.82 p. 1 relating to a proceeding under EEC Treaty, art. 85.
4 See Case 5/67 *Beus v Hauptzollamt München-Landbergerstrasse* [1968] E.C.R. 83, at p. 95, [1968] C.M.L.R. 131, at p. 145, for the extent of reasons required in the making of a regulation; Case 24/62 *supra*, fn. 1, for deficient reasons in the making of a decision; see also Cases 292–293/81 *Lion v Fonds d'Intervention et de Régularisation du Marché du Sucre (FIRS)* [1982] E.C.R. 3887, at p. 3909.
5 See Case 87/78 *Welding & Co. v Hauptzollamt Hamburg-Waltershof* [1978] E.C.R. 2457; Case 166/78 *Italy v EC Council* [1979] E.C.R. 2575, [1981] 3 C.M.L.R. 770.
6 See Case 16/65 *Schwarze v Einfuhr- und Vorratsstelle für Getreide und Futtermittel* [1965] E.C.R. 877, [1966] C.M.L.R. 172. See also R.H. Lauwaars, *Lawfulness and Legal Force of Community Decisions* (1973), 161,2.
7 Hans Smit and Peter E. Herzog, *supra*, fn. 2, IP 190.06; R.H. Lauwaars, *supra*, fn. 6, L 63; T.C. Hartley, *The Foundations of European Community Law*, First Edition (1981) 113.
8 Hans Smit and Peter E. Herzog, *supra*, fn. 2, IP 190.06, 5-632 and authorities cited therein.
9 P.S.F.R. Mathijsen, *A Guide to European Community Law*, Fifth Edition (1987), 103; Case 4/54 *I.S.A. v High Authority* [1954–56] E.C.R. 91, at p. 100.

Publication and entry into force

9.21 Regulations must be published in the Official Journal of the Community, and enter into force on the date specified in them, or, in the absence thereof, on the twentieth day following their publication.[1] Directives and decisions, however, require only notification to the persons to whom they are addressed and they take effect upon such notification.[2] The difference in the publication requirements can be justified in that regulations are normative acts of a general nature which bind the public and accordingly require maximum publicity, whereas directives and decisions are primarily addressed to specific persons only and these persons alone are immediately affected by their provisions. In practice, however, conscious that even directives and decisions may have a significance for persons other than the immediate addressees, the institutions frequently publish these also in the Official Journal.

Failure to observe the publication or notification requirements, however, does not affect the existence of the act in question. In such circumstances only the legal consequences are affected and the act is still a valid one. So where an institution has power to take a measure by a certain date, but not after that date, the legality of an act taken by that date is not affected by the fact that the publication or notification requirements were not met by the date in question.[3]

Provided it is clear that the communication is official, little is required by the Court by way of the formality of notification.[4]

1 EEC Treaty, art. 191.
2 *Idem*.
3 Case 185/73 *Hauptzollamt Bielefeld v König* [1974] E.C.R. 607; R.H. Lauwaars, *Lawfulness and Legal Force of Community Decisions* (1973), 166–7. 'Irregularities in the procedure of notification of a decision are external to the legal act and, therefore cannot vitiate it', Court of Justice in Case 48/69 *ICI v EC Commission* [1972] E.C.R. 619, at p. 652, [1972] C.M.L.R. 557, at p. 620.
4 See Case 8/56 *ALMA v High Authority* [1957–58] E.C.R. 95, Hans Smit and Peter E. Herzog, *The Law of the European Community* (1982), IP 191.05.

Examples of Community Acts

9.22 The following measures may be cited as typical Community acts:

1. Commission Decision relating to the application of Council Directive 72/166/EEC on the approximation of the laws of the Member States relating to insurance against civil liability in respect of the use of motor vehicles, and to the enforcement of the obligation to insure against such liability.
2. Commission Regulation 1836/86 (EEC) O.J. L 158 13.6.86 p. 57 amending Regulation (EEC) No. 685/69 as regards the date of taking over of butter bought in by intervention agencies.
3. Council Directive 82/884 (EEC) O.J. L 378 31.12.82 p. 15 on a limit value for lead in the air.

These are reproduced below at 9.25 for consideration.

Decisions *sui generis*

9.23 Article 189 does not contain an exhaustive list of all the various kinds of acts which the Community institutions may take. Throughout the treaty the institutions are given powers to take action which do not always fit into the categories of act listed in Article 189. For example, one may mention judgments of the Court of Justice, agreements concluded between the Community and third countries, decisions of the representatives of the governments of the Member States in Council, etc.[1]

These atypical acts need not detain us here. Suffice it to make two points about them. First, the legal effects which these acts have must be determined individually in their own context and in this, much depends on the peculiar circumstances of each act. Second, if such a decision creates legal effects then it may be judicially reviewed. The power of the Court of Justice to review the legality of Community legislation is not limited to those acts mentioned in Article 189. Any decision or act which creates for subjects legal rights or obligations is capable of being scrutinised by the Court of Justice.

1 P.S.F.R. Mathijsen, *A Guide to European Community Law*, Fifth Edition (1987), 94–5; J.V. Louis, *The Community Legal Order* (1980), 60–2; R.H. Lauwaars, *Lawfulness and Legal Force of Community Decisions* (1973), 50–4.

Form of Community legal measures

9.24 The form which the binding legislative acts of the Community take can best be appreciated by studying a couple of fairly typical examples. Below are given edited portions of a decision and a regulation from the Commission and a directive of the Council (examples given at para. 9.22). Attention is drawn to the following features of these instruments.

After the title and date of the instrument the issuing authority is identified (Commission or Council). Next the legal basis for the instrument is given as well as an indication that the required opinions of other bodies have been taken into account. There then follows a series of paragraphs introduced by the word 'Whereas . . .' and in this series of recitals are to be found the reasons behind the measure. These will, normally, be more detailed in the case of decisions than in the case of regulations (the examples selected below may not illustrate this point fully). The operative sentence will then follow in which the institution declares that it 'has adopted this Regulation' (Directive or Decision). The substantive text of the measure is produced next in a series of Articles. The final Article in the case of Regulations indicates when the measure is to come into force and in the case of directives or decisions it will indicate the addressee. In the case of Regulations the final sentence is 'This Regulation shall be binding in its entirety and directly applicable in all Member States'. The date and the signature of the appropriate authority is finally appended.

Samples of EEC legislation

9.25 1. Decisions:

COMMISSION DECISION
of 16 May 1986
relating to the application of Council Directive 72/166/EEC on the approximation of the laws of the Member States relating to insurance against civil liability in respect of the use of motor vehicles, and to the enforcement of the obligation to insure against such liability
(86/218/EEC)

The Commission of the European Communities,

Having regard to the treaty establishing the European Economic Community,

Having regard to Council Directive 72/166/EEC of 24 April 1972 on the approximation of the laws of the Member States relating to insurance against civil liability in respect of the use of motor vehicles, and to the enforcement of the obligation to insure against such liability,[1] as last amended by Directive 84/5/EEC,[2] and in particular Article 2(2) thereof,

Whereas on 12 December 1973 the national insurers' bureaux of the nine Member States concluded an agreement (the 'Supplementary Agreement')[3] in conformity with the principles laid down in the first indent of Article 2(2) of Directive 72/166/EEC;

Whereas the Commission subsequently adopted First Commission Decision 74/166/EEC[4] relating to the application of Directive 72/166/EEC, which required each Member State to refrain as from 15 May 1974 from making checks on insurance against civil liability in respect of vehicles which are normally based in the European territory of another Member State and which are the subject of the Supplementary Agreement of 12 December 1973;

Whereas the Greek insurers' bureau has not yet become a party to the Supplementary Agreement of 12 December 1973;

Whereas on 14 March 1986 the insurers' bureaux of Spain and Portugal and of the other Member States, with the exception of Greece, signed an Addendum to the Supplementary Agreement of 12 December 1973 extending that Agreement to include the bureaux of Spain and Portugal;

Whereas, therefore, all the conditions for the removal of checks on insurance against civil liability between Spain and Portugal and the other Member States, with the exception of Greece, are fulfilled,

Has adopted this decision:

Article 1

As from 1 June 1986 checks on insurance against civil liability shall be discontinued in respect of vehicles normally based in Spain and Portugal entering the territory of the other Member States, with the exception of Greece, and in respect of vehicles normally based in the other Member States, with the exception of Greece, and in respect of vehicles normally based in the other Member States, with the exception of Greece, entering the territory of Spain or Portugal.

Article 2

Member States shall forthwith inform the Commission of measures taken to apply this Decision.

Article 3

This Decision is addressed to the Member States.
Done at Brussels, 16 May 1986.

For the Commission
COCKFIELD
Vice-President

1 O.J. No L 103, 2.5.72, p. 1.
2 O.J. No. L 8, 11.1.84, p. 17.
3 O.J. No. L 87, 30.3.74, p. 15.
4 O.J. No. L 87, 30.3.74, p. 13.

2. Regulations:

COMMISSION REGULATION (EEC) No 1836/86
of 12 June 1986
amending Regulation (EEC) No 685/69 as regards the date of taking over
of butter bought in by intervention agencies

The Commission of the European Communities,

Having regard to the Treaty establishing the European Economic Community,

Having regard to Council Regulation (EEC) No. 804/68 of 27 June 1968 on the common organisation of the market in milk and milk products,[1] as last amended by Regulation (EEC) No. 1335/86,[2] and in particular Article 6(7) thereof,

Whereas Article 5(6) of Commission Regulation (EEC) No. 685/69 of 14 April 1969 on detailed rules of application for intervention on the market in butter and cream,[3] as last amended by Regulation (EEC) No. 2576/85,[4] defines the day of taking-over as the day on which the butter enters the refrigerated storage depot designated by the intervention agency;

Whereas experience gained has shown that that provision brings about abnormal situations featuring massive buying-in unwarranted by the actual conditions on the market; whereas the provision in question should be amended accordingly;

Whereas the Management Committee for Milk and Milk products has not delivered an opinion within the time limit set by its chairman,

Has adopted this regulation:

Article 1
Regulation (EEC) No. 685/69 is hereby amended as follows:
1. Article 5(6) is replaced by the following:

'6. For the purposes of this Regulation, the day of taking-over shall be the 60th day following the entry of the butter into the refrigerated storage depot designated by the intervention agency.'

2. In Articles 4 and 6(1), the words 'the day on which the intervention agency takes it over' and 'the day of taking-over' are replaced by the words 'the day on which it enters the refrigerated storage depot designated by the intervention agency.'

Article 2
This Regulation shall enter into force on the day of its publication in the *Official Journal of the European Communities*.

This Regulation shall be binding in its entirety and directly applicable in all Member States.

Done at Brussels, 12 June 1986.

For the Commission
Frans ANDRIESSEN
Vice-President

1 O.J. No. L 148, 28.6.68, p. 13.
2 O.J. No. L 119, 8.5.86, p. 19.
3 O.J. No. L 90, 15.4.69, p. 12.
4 O.J. No. L 246, 13.9.85, p. 19.

3. Directives:

COUNCIL DIRECTIVE
of 3 December 1982
on a limit value for lead in the air
(82/884/EEC)

The council of the European communities

Having regard to the Treaty establishing the European Economic Community, and in particular Article 235 thereof,

Having regard to the proposal from the Commission,[1]

Having regard to the opinion of the European Parliament,[2]

Having regard to the opinion of the Economic and Social Committee,[3]

Whereas one of the essential tasks of the European Economic Community is to promote throughout the Community a harmonious development of economic activities and a continuous and balanced expansion, which cannot be imagined in the absence of a campaign to combat pollution and nuisances or of an improvement in the quality of life and the protection of the environment;

Whereas the use of lead is currently causing lead contamination of many areas of the environment;

Whereas inhaled lead contributes significantly to the total body burden of lead;

Whereas the protection of human health against the hazards of lead requires that the individual's exposure to lead in the air be monitored;

Whereas the first[4] and second[5] programme of action of the European Communities on the environment state that this pollutant should receive priority consideration; whereas the said programmes provide for the coordination of national programmes in this field and for the harmonization of national policies within the Community on the basis of a common long-term plan aiming at improving the quality of life; whereas since the specific powers of action required to this end have not been provided for in the Treaty, it is necessary to invoke Article 235 thereof;

Whereas insufficient technical and scientific information is available to enable the Council to lay down specific standards for the environment generally; whereas the adoption of limit values for the protection of human health will contribute to the protection of the environment as well;

Whereas it is desirable to fix a limit value for lead in the air;

Whereas the measures taken pursuant to this Directive must be economically feasible and compatible with balanced development; whereas in consequence a sufficient time limit should be laid down for its implementation; whereas account should also be taken of the provisions of Council

Directive 78/611/EEC of 29 June 1978 on the approximation of the laws of the Member States concerning the lead content of petrol;[6]

Whereas it is desirable to monitor the quality of the air in places where people may be exposed continuously and for a long period and where there is a risk that the limit value may not be observed;

Whereas it is important that the Commission should obtain information concerning the sites used for sampling, the sampling and analysis procedures . . . as well as the measures taken to avoid a repetition of the occurrence; . . .

Whereas, to implement the Directive, it is desirable to comply with the characteristics adopted in the Annex for choosing the sampling method; . . .

Has adopted this Directive

Article 1

1. This Directive shall fix a limit value for lead in the air specifically in order to help protect human beings against the effects of lead in the environment.
2. This Directive shall not apply to occupational exposure.

Article 2

1. For the purpose of this Directive, 'limit value' means the concentration of lead in the air which, subject to the conditions laid down hereinafter, must not be exceeded.
2. The limit value shall be 2 micrograms Pb/m^3 expressed as an annual mean concentration.
3. Member States may, at any time, fix a value more stringent than that laid down in this Directive.

Article 3

1. Member States shall take the necessary measures to ensure that five years after notification of this Directive, the concentration of lead in the air, measured in accordance with Article 4, is not greaaaateeer than the limit value given in Article 2.
2. Where a Member State considers that the limit value fixed in Article 2(2) may be exceeded in certain places four years after notification of the Directive, it shall inform the Commission thereof.
3. The Member States concerned shall, within two years of the implementation of this Directivvve forward to the Commission plans for the progressive improvement of the quality of the air in such places. These plans, drawn up on the basis of relevant information as to the nature, origin and development of the pollution, shall in particular describe the measures already taken or envisaged and the procedures implemented or plllanned by the Member States concerned. The objective of these measures and procedures must be to bring the concentration of lead in the air in those places below the level of the limit value fixed in Article 2(2) or down to that level, as soon as possible and at the latest seven years after notification of this Directive. These measures and procedures must take

into account the provisions of Directive 78/611/EEC and the results of its application.

Article 4

Member States shall ensure that sampling stations are installed and operated at places where individuals may be exposed continually for a long period and where they consider that Articles 1 and 2 are likely not to be observed.

Article 5

1. For the purpose of applying this Directive, the Member States shall provide the Commission at its request with information on:
— the sites used for sampling,
— the sampling and analysis procedures used to determine the concentration of lead in the air.
2. Member States shall inform the Commission not later than 1 July of each year, beginning in the calendar year following the implementation of this Directive, of the places in which the limit value fixed in Article 2(2) has been exceeded in the previous calendar year and of the concentrations recorded.
3. They shall also notify the Commission, not later than during the calendar year following that in which the limit values were exceeded, of the measures they have taken to avoid recurrence.

Article 6

The Commission shall each year publish a summary report on the application of this Directive, commencing in the second year following its implementation.

Article 7

Application of the measures taken pursuant to this Directive must not bring about a significant deterioration in the quality of the air where the level of pollution by lead, at the time of implementation of this Directive, is low in relation to the limit value fixed in Article 2(2).

Article 8

For the purposes of applying this Directive, Member States shall comply with the characteristics laid down in the Annex for choosing the sampling method; for analysing the samples taken, Member States shall use the reference method mentioned in the Annex or any other method which they prove to the Commission beforehand produces equivalent results.

Article 9

The procedures in Articles 10 and 11 for the adaptation of this Directive to scientific and technical progress shall relate to the characteristics to be complied with for choosing a sampling method and the reference method referred to in the Annex.

This adaptation must not have the effect of directly or indirectly modifying the application of the actual concentration value fixed in Article 2(2).

Article 10

1. A committee on the adaptation of this Directive to scientific and technical progress hereinafter called 'the committee', is hereby set up; it shall consist of representatives of the Member States with a Commission representative as Chairman.
2. The committee shall adopt its own rules of procedure.

Article 11

1. Where the procedure laid down in this Article is to be followed, the matter shall be referred to the committee by its chairman, either on his own initiative or at the request of a representative of a Member State.
2. The Commission representative shall submit to the committee a draft of the measures to be taken. The committee shall give its opinion on that draft within a time limit set by the chairman having regard to the urgency of the matter. Opinions shall be delivered by a majority of 45 votes, the votes of the Member States being weighted as provided in Article 148(2) of the Treaty. The chairman shall not vote.
3. Where the measures envisaged are in accordance with the opinion of the committee, the Commission shall adopt them.

Where the measures envisaged are not in accordance with the opinion of the committee, or if no opinion is delivered, the Commission shall without delay submit to the Council a proposal on the measures to be taken. The Council shall act by a qualified majority.

If within three months of the proposal being submitted to it, the Council has not acted, the proposed measures shall be adopted by the Commission.

Article 12

1. Member States shall bring into force the laws, regulations and administrative provisions necessary to comply with this Directive within 24 months of its notification and shall forthwith inform the Commission thereof.
2. Member States shall forward to the Commission the texts of the provisions of national law which they adopt in the field governed by this Directive.

Article 13

This Directive is addressed to the Member States.
Done at Brussels, 3 December 1982.

For the Council
Ch. CHRISTENSEN
The President

1 O.J. No. C 154, 7.7.75, p. 29.
2 O.J. No. C 28, 9.2.76, p. 31.
3 O.J. No. C 50, 4.3.76, p. 9.
4 O.J. No. C 112, 20.12.73, p. 1.
5 O.J. No. C 139, 13.6.77, p. 1.
6 O.J. No. L 197, 22.7.78, p. 19.

Chapter 10

Court's own jurisprudence, The Community precedent[1]

10.1 In the Common Law tradition judicial precedent constitutes an important source of law. Briefly put, the Common Law doctrine of *stare decisis* provides that in a hierarchy of courts the lower courts are obliged to follow the legal decisions of higher courts in similar matters. In the context of the EEC's legal system it is also legitimate to ask what exactly is the status of the decisions of the Court of Justice. Do they constitute a source of law in the system?

1 'A practice of a Member State which does not conform to Community rules may never give rise to legal situations protected by Community law and this is so even where the Commission has failed to take the necessary action to ensure that the State in question correctly applies Community rules'. Case 5/82 *Hauptzollamt Krefeld v Maizena GmbH* [1982] E.C.R. 4601, at p. 4615. See also T. Koopmans, '*Stare Decisis* in European Law' in O'Keeffe and Schermers, *Essays in European Law and Integration*. 11.

10.2 Before answering this question one must bear in mind one salient fact about the judicial institutions of the EEC; up until recently only one Court existed in the system. There was no hierarchy of courts. Therefore, the question of higher and lower courts did not arise. The only real question, in these circumstances, was whether the Court of Justice was bound by its own previous judgments. The Single European Act has now (since 1987) made provision for the creation of a court of first instance attached to the Court of Justice and from whose decisions an appeal will be on points of law to the Court of Justice. The relationship between the new court and the Court of Justice has yet to be worked out, but it would appear that it will be similar to the relationship that exists at present between the Court and its chambers. In recent times it is also true that with the reorganisation of the Court into chambers, and the increasing tendency for chambers to hear cases, one may get problems if two chambers give different decisions on a matter. To date, however, such questions have not caused serious problems and there are plenty of precedents at national level in the Member States of the Community concerning the relationship between a divisional Chamber and the full court to handle the matter when, and if, it arises. Of course, it scarcely needs mention, let alone elaboration, to state in this context that a decision of the full court will carry more weight than a decision of one of its chambers.

170

Furthermore, it should be remembered that while it is envisaged that the national courts should play an important part in the application and enforcement of Community law, the independence of these institutions is in no way jeopardised within the Community's legal system, and the relationship between the Court of Justice of the EEC and the national courts is not that of superior to inferior in the same hierarchy. The two judicial systems are independent of each other and what interaction takes place between the two systems is principally defined within the context of Article 177 which enables the national courts 'to state a case' (to use an Irish analogy of some familiarity) to the Court of Justice.

Also to be borne in mind in the present discussion is the fact that the doctrine of *stare decisis* has no place within the Civil Law tradition. In the Roman tradition lower courts are *not bound* to follow decisions of higher courts, nor are courts bound by their own previous decisions. It is not surprising, therefore, that the same rule should prevail within the legal system of the EEC, as, for the first twenty-one years, all the Member States were firmly of the Civil Law tradition. *Res judicata*, in the sense that a judgment is binding only where there is an identity of parties, cause and subject-matter, is the extent to which judicial decisions are binding within the Community's system. Once there ceases to be an identity of either the parties, the cause or the subject-matter the binding nature of the judgment ends.[1]

1 See on *Res judicata*, A.G. Toth, *Legal Protection of Individuals in the European Community* (1982), Vol. 1, 79 *et seq.*; D. Lasok and J.W. Bridge, *Law and Institutions of the European Communities*, Fourth Edition (1987), 143.

10.3 It should be clear, therefore, from these comments that the decisions of the Court of Justice do not formally constitute a source of law *strictu sensu* within the Community's legal system. It would, however, be foolish to conclude from this that the Court's pronouncements are not vitally important, and this importance becomes increasingly obvious with the passage of time as the volume of precedents grows. The fact of the matter is that the Court of Justice generally tends to follow its own previous judgments and will depart from these holdings only where there are compelling reasons. Every legal system whether it belongs to the Common Law or the Civil Law tradition, requires a certain amount of certainty and predictability at the judicial level if the confidence of the subjects is to be maintained, and the Community legal system is no exception in this matter. This tendency at Community level for the Court of Justice to follow its previous decisions is very noticeable where the Court, having considered a problem on previous occasions, now arrives at what is called a *jurisprudence constante* (a settled view) on the matter. When such a stage has been arrived at the Court, from that point on, may even adopt and repeat in its decision a settled verbal formula on the issue. This decision then, for practical purposes, assumes enormous importance and as a guide to conduct within the legal system possesses authority not far short of legislative force. Until recently the Court of Justice frequently reproduced these formulae without even referring to earlier cases, but in the more recent case-law a tendency for the Court to refer to its own previous decisions by name[1] has become noticeable.

There are two other reasons why the decisions of the Court of Justice are very important within the Community's legal system. First, the Treaty of Rome is, as has already been pointed out, a framework treaty with many lacunae to be filled in. In the absence of an effective single Community legislative organ, such as we are familiar with at national level, the Court has had to assume a role of judicial activism. Second, the Court not only fills gaps in the normal sense but it also, through imaginative teleological interpretation, advances and promotes various policy views within the system. In particular one can discern from the case-law a tendency to promote interpretations which protect the individual within the system[2] and also a tendency to promote interpretations which are integrationalist in nature. With regard to this last tendency one might cite the case-law of the Court relating to the supremacy doctrine,[3] the concept of direct effect[4] and the expansion of Community external powers,[5] all of which promote a more intense form of integration favouring Community institutions at the expense of the sovereign powers of the Member States.

1 See, for example, Case 107/83 *Ordre des Advocats au Barreau de Paris v Klopp* [1984] E.C.R. 2971, [1985] 1 C.M.L.R. 99 and cases cited by D. Lasok and J.W. Bridge, *Law and Institutions of the European Communities*, Fourth Edition (1987), 144, fn. 6. On the increasing tendency of Advocate-General to cite previous case-law see *Idem* fn. 7. See more generally T. Koopmans, *op. cit.*, 17 *et seq.*
2 See, for example, Court's case-law on Human Rights, *supra*, para. 8.5, and its development of the general principles common to the Member States as a source of Community Law, *supra*, para. 8.1 *et seq.*
3 *Infra*, para. 13.1.
4 *Infra*, para. 13.3.
5 *Supra*, Chapter 5.

10.4 Granted that the Court of Justice is not bound by its own decisions one may next ask what effect do decisions of the Court of Justice have on national courts? As has already been mentioned national legal systems continue to exist outside the Community legal system. Various points of interaction occur, however, between the systems, and the impact of Community judgments on the domestic courts must first of all be discussed within the context of EEC Treaty, art. 177 which is the principal point of contact between the two judicial systems.[1]

Judgments of the Court of Justice handed down in response to a referral from a national court, of course, bind the referring court in the proceedings before it. This is to be implied from Article 177 and is given effect in Ireland by section 2 of the European Communities Act 1972.[2]

What, however, is the effect of such a judgment for other courts and for other proceedings? In the *Da Costa* Case[3] the Court of Justice held that it was not bound by its own previous decisions and the national courts could refer to it questions which the Court had already answered. The national courts' discretion to refer, therefore, is not restricted by previous precedents. In the same case, however, the Court also said that where it had already given an answer to a question, the national court need not refer the matter to the European Court. And this is so, even in the case of courts from whose decision no appeal lies and which are normally obliged to refer the matter to the Court of Justice. In such a case the referral is excused because a clear previous decision exists.[4] Therefore, national courts, it would appear, in such circumstances have a choice of either following the Court of Justice's previous interpretation or referring for a fresh interpretation.

With regard to decisions of the Court of Justice other than those given under Article 177, what is their effect in the national legal systems? In answering this question we must bear in mind that at Community level there is no rule that such decisions of the Court of Justice must bind the national courts. The independence of the national judicial systems would argue against such obligatory effect. Moreover, as we have seen, such decisions do not create an irrevocable obligatory effect even within the Community system for the Court of Justice itself, and in such circumstances it would be difficult to argue that they have such effect in the national legal systems of the Member States. It would appear, therefore, that there is no *Community rule* which obliges the national courts to follow decisions of the Court of Justice. These judgments have no more effect at national level than they have at Community level: they are very persuasive, but no more.

1 See *infra*, Chapter 12. Decisions from the Courts of the other Member States, even on matters relating to Community law, are merely persuasive on Irish Courts. They are no more or no less important than precedents from, say, the USA on Constitutional matters.
2 *Infra*, para. 14.2.
3 Cases 28–30/62 *Da Costa en Schaake NV v Nederlandse Belastingadministratie* [1963] E.C.R. 31, at p. 38, [1963] C.M.L.R. 224, at p. 237.
4 T.C. Hartley, *The Foundations of European Community Law*, First Edition (1981), 269–72; H.G. Schermers, *Judicial Protection in the European Communities*, 591 *et seq.*

10.5 But this is not an end to the matter for national courts. National courts in determining the effect of judgments of the Court of Justice must also consider their own national legislation on the topic. It is possible that national incorporation measures might accord to Community judgments a precedent value which the Community itself does not attach to its own judicial pronouncements. National legislation could, in other words, declare that Community judgments are binding precedents for national courts on matters of Community law. This would appear to be the effect of section 3 of the UK's European Communities Act 1972. This provides as follows:

'3(1) For the purposes of all legal proceedings any question as to the meaning or effect of any of the Treaties, or as to the validity, meaning or effect of any Community instrument, shall be treated as a question of law (and, if not referred to the European Court, be for determination as such in accordance with the principles laid down by any relevant decision of the European Court).

(2) Judicial notice shall be taken of the Treaties, of the Official Journal of the Communities and of any decision of, or expression of opinion by, the European Court on any such question as aforesaid; . . .'[1]

The Irish European Communities Act 1972 does not specifically address this problem. Section 2 of this Act merely provides as follows:

'From the first day of January, 1973, the Treaties governing the European Communities and the existing and future acts adopted by the institutions of those

Communities shall be binding on the State and shall be part of the domestic law thereof under the conditions laid down in those Treaties.'

From this it is clear that decisions of the Court of Justice (i.e. acts of an institution of the Community) are part of Irish domestic law 'under the conditions laid down in those treaties'. Neither the treaties themselves nor Community law generally, however, require the decisions of the Court of Justice to be followed by the national courts, so one can safely assume that there is no rule of Irish law which obliges Irish Courts to treat decisions of the Court of Justice in non-referral cases as binding. The status of these decisions in Ireland is no greater than the status which they enjoy within the Community itself; that is, they are very persuasive, but they do not bind in the strict sense.

Irish Courts are, of course, bound to apply Community law within the Irish legal context, but since decisions of the Court of Justice do not amount to a formal source of Community law, they are merely indicators, albeit powerful indicators, as to what Community law is.

When Irish courts are trying to discover what Community law is on a particular topic it is natural, in the absence of clear legislative measures, for them to look for guidance to the decisions of the Court of Justice. After all, what a treaty provision or a regulation or directive means is best divined from what the Court of Justice says it means. In the end, decisions of the Court of Justice are the most authoritative view as to what Community law is and for this reason, if for no other, one would anticipate that Irish courts would invariably follow decisions of the Court of Justice on matters of Community law.[2] In practice, therefore, the theoretical problem as to whether decisions of the Court of Justice are formally binding or are merely persuasive for Irish courts is not so significant. The truth is that these decisions are extremely important as indicators of what Community law is, and both courts and practitioners in Ireland should treat them as such in giving judgments or advice. From this pragmatic point of view the judgments of the Court of Justice are a very real, if not a strictly legal, source of Community law, for Irish courts.

1 See also L. Neville Brown and F.G. Jacobs, *The Court of Justice of the European Communities*, Second Edition (1983), 283.
2 Cf. Costello J. in Case 177/78 *Pigs and Bacon Commission v McCarren* 30 June 1978, [1978] Journal of the Irish Society of European Law 87.

Opinions of the Advocate-General

10.6 As we have seen the office of Advocate-General is an extremely important one in the European Court of Justice. Although not privy to, or part of, the Court's ultimate decision the Advocate-General does have a constitutional role to play in the judicial process.[1] In every case after the oral proceedings and before the Court proceeds to its private deliberations, the Advocate-General has the right and obligation to address the Court on the problem before it. Normally he will try to take an objective view of the issue, he will analyse the problem and urge a solution on the Court which will take account of the Community dimension to the problem. If the Court accepts his solution it is clear that the opinion, and the thought-process contained therein, will be very important for a clear understanding of the Court's decision which frequently tends to be brief and laconic. If, however, the Court rejects the Advocate-General's suggested solution, the Advocate-General's opinion will naturally be less influential in subsequent cases, even though in this case also it may be of great assistance in providing reasons as to why the Advocate-General's suggestion did not prevail, and, as an aid to interpreting the Court's judgment.[2] In still other cases, the opinion of the Advocate-General may be the only pronounce-ment at Community level on a particular problem. In such cases too, the Advocate-General's *obiter* may be a valuable guide as to what Community law is, and while not as impressive as a decision of the Court, it might nevertheless provide a good indicator as to what the Court is likely to do when, eventually, it is obliged to decide the matter.

1 See EEC Treaty, art. 166.
2 L. Neville Brown and F.G. Jacobs, *supra* para. 10.5, fn. 1, suggest that the Advocate-General's opinion in such a case would be analogous to a dissenting opinion of a Common Law judge in a multiple judge court.

Chapter 11

Public international law[1]

11.1 Unlike the International Court of Justice which sits in the Hague, the European Court of Justice is not specifically enjoined to make international law a source of its law. This of course does not mean that public international law is irrelevant in the Community's legal system. There are some areas where it cannot only be regarded as a guide for the Court but where it must be regarded as a true source of Community law.

The ambivalence of the Court to public international law is caused by the fact that the European Community has some features which liken it to sovereign states, the traditional subjects of international law, and other features which suggest that the Community is a novel experiment establishing a new legal order independent of both national and international systems. To an extent, therefore, we may note that international law is not greatly important in assessing the relationship between the EEC institutions and the Member States or indeed the relationship of the Member States *inter se* within the Community's legal system.[2]

Internally of course one must realise that the EEC is founded on a treaty between the Member States and the *procedural* rules relating to the making of international treaties are relevant in assessing the obligations of the signatory states. Furthermore, the procedural rules of international law are also relevant with regard to other treaties and conventions signed by the Member States within the Community context such as the Patent Convention, the Judgments Convention, etc.[3]

With regard to *substantive* rules, however, of Community law, the rules of international law have less relevance. In matters such as the supremacy of Community law, the existence of a new and separate legal order, direct applicability and the concept of direct effect, the Court of Justice has developed its own rules cognisant more of the novelty of the EEC experiment than the traditional rules of international law.

---

1 Hans Smit and Peter E. Herzog, *The Law of the European Community* (1982), Vol. 4, 5-276[d]; H.G. Schermers, *Judicial Protection in the European Communities*, Third Edition (1983); D. Lasok and J.W. Bridge, *Law and Institutions of the European Communities*, Fourth Edition (1987), 103–4.
2 J.V. Louis, *The Community Legal Order* (1980), p. 62.
3 *Supra*, paras 7.5 and 7.6.

11.2 There have been instances, however, where the Court has adopted and applied general rules of international law when it suited the Community system and other occasions where it has drawn on international law as an inspiration or guide even though not bound to do so. As an instance one may cite the *Van Duyn* Case where the Court declared that 'it is a principle of international law, which the EEC Treaty cannot be assumed to disregard in the relations between Member States, that a state is precluded from refusing its own nationals the right of entry or residence'.[1]

Occasionally, too, the Court of Justice may use the general principles of international law as an interpreting aid in appropriate circumstances but this reliance must be regarded as minor in comparison to the peculiar interpretative techniques adopted by the court and which are considered to be more suited to the unique legal system of the Community. In spite of these references by the court, however, it would seem that Meesen's conclusion is still warranted:[2]

'. . . rules of international law . . . are only applicable insofar as they happen to coincide with principles of Community law, which means that they are hardly of any help in solving legal problems.'[3]

1 Case 41/74 *Van Duyn v Home Office* [1974] E.C.R. 1337, at pp. 1350,1, [1975] 1 C.M.L.R. 1, at p. 18; see also Case 10/61 *EEC Commission v Italy* [1962] E.C.R. 1, at p. 10, [1962] C.M.L.R. 187, at p. 203, where the Court applied the principle of international law that 'by assuming a new obligation which is incompatible with rights held under a prior treaty a State *ipso facto* gives up the exercise of these rights to the extent necessary for the performance of its new obligations'.
2 See, for example, Case 92/71 *Interfood GmbH v Hauptzollamt Hamburg-Ericus* [1972] E.C.R. 231, at p. 242, [1973] C.M.L.R. 562, at pp. 576,7; Cases 69–70/76 *Dittmeyer v Hauptzollamt Hamburg-Waltershof* [1977] E.C.R. 231, at p. 238.
3 *The Application of Rules of Public International Law within Community Law*, 13 C.M.L. Rev. 485.

11.3 One area, however, where the rules of international law are relevant for the Court of Justice, increasingly so with the passage of time, is where the Community as a subject of international law deals with the outside world.

Insofar as the Community has its own legal personality and is a subject of public international law, the rules of that system bind it and the European Court must apply them.[1] This would apply, for example, in its treaty-making functions, in sending and receiving delegations, and, generally in the conduct of its external relations. In this connection it is worth observing that the Community's role is an expanding one. The Community is more and more involved in negotiations with third countries, both in its own right and as successor to the inherited obligations of the Member States.[2]

The position, in Community law, of treaties concluded between Member States (before and after 1957 or accession dates) and treaties with third countries or international organisations concluded or inherited by the Community, has already been adverted to in Chapter 7.

1 'This general international law is binding upon the Community as far as it concerns the legal relations between the Community and third states and to the extent that it pertains to subjects of international law which are not states'. Meesen, *The Application of Rules of*

Public International Law within Community Law, 13 C.M.L. Rev. 485, at 487 (1976). Footnote omitted. See also A.G. Toth, *Legal Protection of Individuals in the European Communities* (1978), Vol. 1, 94. Moreover the rules of international law in such circumstances take precedence over Community secondary law to the contrary. Cases 41–44/70 *International Fruit Co v EC Commission* [1971] E.C.R. 411, [1975] 2 C.M.L.R. 515; Cases 3, 4, 6/76 *Officier van Justitie v Kramer* [1976] E.C.R. 1279, especially at p. 1311, [1976] 2 C.M.L.R. 440, at pp. 470,1. A.G. Toth, *supra*, Vol. 1, 95; H.G. Schermers, *supra*, para. 11.1, fn. 1, 133.

2 The Community has succeeded the Member States in several multilateral agreements: with regard to GATT see *International Fruit Company* Case, *supra*, fn. 1; with regard to Customs Cooperative Council see Case 38/75 *Douaneagent der NV Nederlandse Spoorwegen v Inspecteur der Invoerrechten en Accijnzen* [1975] E.C.R. 1439, at p. 1451, [1976] 1 C.M.L.R. 167, at p. 179; with regard to European Convention on Human Rights see Case 36/75 *Rutili v Ministre de l'Intérieur* [1975] E.C.R. 1219, at p. 1232, [1976] 1 C.M.L.R. 140, at p. 155; Case 4/73 *Nold v EC Commission* [1974] E.C.R. 491, [1974] 2 C.M.L.R. 338; Case 44/79 *Hauer v Land Rheinland-Pfalz* [1979] E.C.R. 3727, at pp. 3745,6, [1980] 3 C.M.L.R. 42, at pp. 64,5; Case 136/79 *National Panasonic (UK) Ltd v EC Commission* [1980] E.C.R. 2033, at p. 2057, [1980] 3 C.M.L.R. 169, at pp. 186,7.

Part IV

Judicial Control

Chapter 12

Judicial Control

Introduction

12.1 The founding Treaties are almost identical in their descriptions of the task of the Court of Justice: it must ensure that in the interpretation and application of the Treaty the law is observed (Article 31 of the ECSC Treaty, Article 164 of the EEC Treaty, and Article 136 of the Euratom Treaty). This may be a satisfactory description in so far as its indicates that the Court is to be the custodian of the judicial function in the Community's system of government, but it gives no real indication of the range of activities within the Court's jurisdiction. Seen from a wider perspective, the Court is the judicial arm of an emerging federal system and, if viewed in that light, three principal areas of control can be identified. First, the Court is empowered, in actions commenced by the Commission or other Member States, to declare that a Member State has failed in its obligations under the Treaty. Secondly, the Commission and the other Community law-making institutions are themselves subject to judicial control at the suit of the Member States, individuals or the other institutions, to ensure that their acts—be they legislative or quasi-administrative in nature—remain within the bounds of legality fixed by the Treaties. The third major competence of the Court, which is its most overtly federal power, is the consultative jurisdiction which enables courts and tribunals of the Member States to seek pre-judicial or preliminary rulings on the interpretation of Community law or the validity of acts of the Community's institutions. Apart from engendering a natural and obvious cooperation between the national and 'federal' judiciaries, this mechanism gives the Court of Justice the pivotal role in determining the uniform application of Community law.

The fact that national courts may seek the assistance of the Court of Justice tells us something more about the law of which the Court is custodian. Community law—in the legislative sense—is proposed, debated and enacted by the political institutions (the Commission, the Council and the Parliament) in Brussels, Luxembourg and Strasbourg; but it falls to be implemented in the territories of the Member States and it forms an integral part of each of the domestic legal orders. For some Member States the style and format of Community law is familiar enough; the Community's legislative techniques are drawn from the civil law tradition and many of the basic rules relating to the Community's administration are drawn from French and German administrative law. The relationship between Community law and the national legal orders is itself an aspect of Community law and the national courts have had an important input in the development of that relationship. Nonetheless, Community law is sufficiently different from the national legal orders, and not just because of its essentially economic preoccupations and objectives, to merit separate consideration.

A noteworthy aspect of the Community legal system is just how central and important a role it plays in the operation and government of the Community. The Commission, which may be described as the policeman of the Treaties, has little or no coercive power and, despite popular misconceptions on this issue, it has a limited administrative infrastructure. Indeed

'. . . there are hardly any custodians of public authority who are, to the same extent as the Community, so dependent on law when carrying out their tasks.'[1]

This feature of the Community's system led Walter Hallstein, former President of the Commission, to describe the emerging federal entity as '. . . a Community based on law' by analogy with the Rechtsstaat (the State based on law) of German political theory. The jurisprudence of the Court has played a major part in the establishment of this Community based on law.

Finally, Community law is the law of integration and, to a greater or lesser extent, the Court of Justice has played its role in the integration process. In the decade following the entry into force of the EEC Treaty the Court issued many of its landmark decisions, such as *Van Gend en Loos*[2] and *Costa v ENEL*,[3] in which the frontiers of the Community legal system were boldly circumscribed; this demarcation was achieved by categorical statements on the autonomous position of Community law in the international legal order and on its pre-eminence over conflicting national rules in areas of competence claimed by the Community. This occurred during a period when the Court was not particularly busy, at least by present standards. By contrast, the next decade in the history of the Community saw a significant increase in the Court's business, particularly in the context of preliminary rulings. This was also the most interventionist phase of the Court's activity. In the 1970s the political and legislative arms of the Community—the obvious sources of integrative momentum—were emasculated by the Luxembourg compromise of 1966 and the so-called 'veto'. The Court found itself having to react to this decision-making inertia and its response included a series of judgments, mostly in answer to requests for preliminary rulings, in which it asserted the direct effectiveness of Treaty rules requiring the abolition of restrictions, notwithstanding the failure of the Community law-making institutions to adopt the necessary harmonising legislation. Cases such as *EC Commission v France*,[4] *Reyners v Belgium*,[5] *Van Binsbergen*[6] and *Dassonville*[7] were decided in this period. The present decade has witnessed a less activist Court,[8] partly because of an increase in workload and partly because the political impasse, inherited from earlier decades, has been painfully overcome and replaced by a new consensus which led ultimately to the adoption of the Single European Act. The Court would now appear to have embarked on a more businesslike, 'minimalist' approach,[9] but the evidence of its earlier activist days will serve to remind the other institutions of the Court's willingness to defend the basic tenets of the Treaties.

1 J.V. Louis, *The Community Legal Order*, Commission of the European Communities, Luxembourg, 1980, p. 25.
2 Case 26/62 [1963] E.C.R. 1, [1963] C.M.L.R. 105.
3 Case 6/64 [1964] E.C.R. 585, [1964] C.M.L.R. 425.
4 Case 167/73 [1974] E.C.R. 359, [1974] 2 C.M.L.R. 216.
5 Case 2/74 [1974] E.C.R. 631, [1974] 2 C.M.L.R. 305.
6 Case 33/74 [1974] E.C.R. 1299, [1975] 1 C.M.L.R. 298.
7 Case 8/74 [1974] E.C.R. 837, [1974] 2 C.M.L.R. 436.
8 Hjalte Rasmussen, *Between Self-restraint and Activism: A Judicial Policy for The European Court*, (1988) 13 E.L. Rev. 28.
9 T. Koopmans, *The Role of Law in the Next Stage of European Integration*, (1986) 35 I.C.L.Q. Q 25.

Structure and composition of the Court

12.2 Relevant Treaty Provisions:

ESCS Treaty	Articles 31 to 45
Protocol on the Statute of the Court of Justice of the European Coal and Steel Community	*passim*
EEC Treaty	Articles 164 to 188
Protocol on the Statute of the Court of Justice of the European Economic Community	*passim*
Euratom Treaty	Articles 136 to 160
Protocol on the Statute of the Court of Justice of the European Atomic Energy Community	*passim*
Convention on certain institutions common to the European Communities	Articles 3 and 4
Protocol on the privileges and immunities of the European Communities	Article 2
First Act of Accession	Articles 17 to 20
Second Act of Accession	Article 16
Third Act of Accession.	Articles 17 to 19
Single European Act	Articles 4, 11, 26

12.3 The European Parliament and the Court of Justice were the first of the institutions of the three Communities to be unified. And although the EEC and the Euratom Treaties contained separate provisions on the Court, including separate protocols incorporating the Statute of the Court, Article 3 of the Convention on certain institutions common to the European Communities provided that the jurisdiction separately conferred by the EEC Treaty and the Euratom Treaty was to be exercised by a single Court of Justice appointed in accordance with the identical *formulae* set out in Article 145 to 167 of the EEC Treaty, and Articles 137 to 139 of the Euratom Treaty. The Convention, which was concluded contemporaneously with the EEC and Euratom Treaties, provided in Article 4 that the Single Court established by Article 3 was to take the place of the Court of Justice established pursuant to the ECSC Treaty. Article 3 also replaced the purely institutional provisions of the ECSC Treaty with those of the EEC and Euratom. This precedent of resolving differences between the Paris Treaty and the Rome Treaties in favour of the latter was followed by the Member States when the Merger Treaty, unifying the Council and Commissions/High Authority of the Communities was concluded in 1965[1] but the Convention on certain institutions common to the European Communities did not alter the substantive jurisdiction conferred on the Court by the different Treaties and, while the framework of remedies available under each of the Treaties is similar, there are significant differences in the manner in which these remedies may be invoked. It is not intended to examine the ECSC and Euratom systems in detail in this work, other than to draw attention to marked differences between the EEC system and those of the other two Communities; in this regard readers are recommended to refer to any of the excellent specialist textbooks on the Court of Justice and the judicial remedies.[2]

1 Gordon Weil, *The merger of the Institutions of the European Communities*, (1967) 61 A.J.I.L. 57.
2 See for example:
   H.A.H. Audretsch, *Supervision in European Community Law*, Second edition 1986.
   G. Beery, *The Development of Judicial Control in the European Communities* 1981.
   A. Bredimas, *Methods of Interpretation and Community Law*, 1978.
   L. Neville Brown and F.G. Jacobs, *The Court of Justice of the European Communities*, Second edition 1983.
   T.C. Hartley, *The Foundations of European Community Law*, 1981.
   K.P.E. Lasok, *The European Court of Justice: Practice and Procedure*, 1984.
   H. Rasmussen, *On Law and Policy in the European Court of Justice*, 1986.
   H.G. Schermers, *Judicial Protection in the European Communities*, Fourth edition 1987.
   A.G. Toth, *The Protection of Individuals in the European Communities*, 1978.
   J.A. Usher, *European Court Practice*, 1983.

12.4 The Court of Justice established under the ECSC Treaty consisted of seven judges assisted by two Advocates-General. Today, the Court has thirteen judges and six Advocates-General.[1] This number of judicial officials allows for the appointment of at least one judge from each of the twelve Member States. The extra judge is rotated between the four larger Member States although Spain has been claiming, in 1988, that it should be considered as a large Member State. By the same unofficial convention four of the Advocates-General are drawn from the larger Member States and the two remaining posts are rotated amongst the smaller States every six years which is the term of office for judges and Advocates-General alike; it may be renewed.

The Court sits either in plenary session or in Chambers of three or five-judges.[2] The Court must sit in plenary session in cases brought before it by the Member States or by one of the institutions of the Communities and in cases of a non-technical nature submitted for a preliminary ruling under Article 177; the presence of a judge of the nationality of one of the parties to an action is not essential. In theory all thirteen judges can sit in such cases but decisions of the full Court are valid if only seven judges are sitting;[3] in *Mary Murphy v An Bord Telecom Eireann*[4] the Court consisted of nine judges including the Irish judge, and in *East v Cuddy*[5] the full Court consisted of eleven judges. The Court now has six Chambers; two of these Chambers are five judge Chambers to which six judges each are allocated and the remaining four Chambers are comprised of three judges.[6] The quorum in any Chamber is three.[7] Originally, Chambers were used only for cases involving disputes under the Staff Regulations, in which the Court acts as an employment tribunal. But amendments to the Rules of Procedure in 1974 and 1979 allowed for the assignment to Chambers of cases involving requests for preliminary rulings of an essentially technical nature and direct actions other than those instituted by Member States or by one of the institutions.[8] The Court is presided over by its President who is elected by the other judges for a three-year term, which is renewable.[9] The current President is the British judge, Lord McKenzie Stewart, who indicated his intention to resign during 1988; accordingly, an election is imminent.[9a] The Presidents of the Chambers of the Court are elected in a similar manner to the President. The President of the Court is in charge of the administration of the Court, both as a Community institution and in terms of the organisation of judicial business.

The Court is a collegiate body: it issues only one judgment, whether it sits in a Chamber or in plenary session, and consequently there must be present an uneven number of judges.[10] The single judgment rule is reinforced by the oath, taken by each of the judges, to preserve the secrecy of the deliberations of the Court.[11] This means that it is impossible to discover whether a decision has been taken unanimously or by a majority of the judges present. Also, the Court has no rule of *stare decisis*; it is free to depart from its earlier judgments. However, the arrival of personnel versed in the common law tradition has modified this aspect of the Court's practice. In the past the Court tended to repeat *verbatim* the *ratio decidendi* of an earlier judgment without making any specific reference to the case in which the judgment was rendered. It required an eye familiar with these 'leitmotifs', as they have been described,[12] to recognise when the Court was relying on an earlier decision. Now, the Court makes direct reference to all its prior case-law but its judgments still utilise the somewhat laconic and detached prose of the civil law tradition; it eschews the individualism which, in the common law system, can give rise to the idiosyncratic but immensely readable prose style of Lord Denning.

The Court is assisted by six Advocates-General.[13] Lawyers from the common law tradition would not recognise this essentially civil law institution. The position of Advocate-General is similar to the *Commissaire du Gouvernement* in the French *Conseil d'Etat* or the *Ministère Public* in the civil courts in France. Article 166 of the EEC Treaty describes the duty of the Advocate-General as

'. . . to make, in open Court, reasoned submissions on cases brought before the Court of Justice, in order to assist the Court in the performance of the task assigned to it in Article 164'.

The Advocate-General does not participate in the deliberations of the Court or any of its Chambers; instead, he/she has a role best described as *amicus curiae.* The Advocate-General's Opinion will review the law and the facts in all cases before the Court, and will suggest to the Court a reasoned and detached view of the conclusion at which the Court should arrive. The Court is, however, free to arrive at its own decision. The Opinion of the Advocate-General normally will be more discursive than the relatively brief judgment of the Court, and from time to time the Court overtly adopts the recommendation of the Advocate-General. For example, in *Hoekstra (née Unger) v Bedrijfsvereniging voor Bestuur der Detailhandel en Ambachten*[14] the Court accepted the proposal of Advocate-General Lagrange on the definition of 'worker' for the purposes of Regulation 3 of 1958 on social security for migrant workers. Indeed, the Advocate-General's definition was adopted in Council Regulation (EEC) 1408/71[15] which replaced Regulation 3 of 1958. The Advocates-General designate, on an annual basis, one of their number to be the First Advocate-General.[16]

The judges and Advocates-General are appointed by the Council for a six-year period[17] and a partial replacement takes place every three years.[18] The qualifications for appointment require that the appointee be a person whose independence is beyond doubt and who is eligible for appointment to the highest judicial office in his/her respective country or who is a jurisconsult of recognised competence. The latter criterion allows for the appointment of university professors, a relatively common phenomenon on the Continent. As far as Ireland is concerned the three appointees to date have fulfilled the former requirement: Judges O'Dalaigh and O'Higgins held the office of Chief Justice of Ireland and Judge O'Keefe was a judge of the Supreme Court and later President of the High Court. The judges and Advocates-General are each assisted by three *référendaires* or legal secretaries. The best analogy to describe the function of the *référendaires* is that of law-clerk in the federal court system in the United States.

The Court has a Registry, presided over by the Registrar, who is appointed by the Court.[19] The Court also has a library and documentation section, translation and interpretation services, and an information office. It produces an official series of law reports, the European Court Reports, but the publication of this series is now scandalously behind schedule. At present there is a two-year delay between the judgments of the Court and their publication in the European Court Reports.

The Court is based at Luxembourg[20] and the judges, the Advocates-General and the Registrar are obliged to reside at the place where the Court has its seat.[21] The Court remains permanently in session,[22] but the judicial vacation is normally taken from mid-July to mid-September of every year. In 1987 the Court had an establishment of six-hundred and six permanent posts.[23]

1 Third Act of Accession, Articles 17 and 18.
2 EEC Treaty, Article 165.
3 Protocol on the Statute of The Court of Justice of the European Economic Community (*hereinafter cited as Statute*), Article 15; Rules of Procedure of The Court of Justice (*hereinafter cited as Rules*) O.J. C 39, 15.2.1982, Article 26.
4 Case 157/86 O.J. C 63 8.3.88 p. 7.
5 Case 143/86 O.J. C 63 8.3.88 p. 7.

6   21st Annual General Report, at point 22.
7   Statute, Article 15; Rules, Article 26.
8   Brown and Jacobs, *op. cit.* para. 12.3, fn. 2, para. 12.3 at pp. 25,6.
9   EEC Treaty, Article 167.
9a Since this chapter was finalised Ole Due of Denmark was elected President.
10 Statute, Article 15.
11 Statute, Article 2.
12 Brown and Jacobs, *op. cit.* fn. 2, para. 12.3 at p. 41.
13 For a recent study see Kirsten Bogsmidt, *The Advocate-General at the European Court of Justice: a comparative study*, (1988) 13 E.L. Rev. 106.
14 Case 75/63 [1964] E.C.R. 177, [1964] C.M.L.R. 319.
15 O.J. (Sp. Ed.) 1971 (II) p. 416, consolidated by 2001/83 O.J. L 230 22.8.1983 p. 6.
16 Brown and Jacobs, *op. cit.* para. 12.3, fn. 2, para. 12.3 at p. 54.
17 EEC Treaty, Article 167.
18 *Idem.*
19 EEC Treaty, Article 168; statute Articles 9 to 11.
20 Article 3, Decision of the Representatives of the Governments of the Member States on the Provisional Location of certain Institutions and Departments of the Communities, Treaties establishing the European Communities, 1978, p. 837.
21 Statute, Article 13.
22 Statute, Article 14.
23 21st Annual Report, at point 24.

12.5 The workload of the Court has increased steadily over the past three decades. The following table gives an indication of the activity of the Court in 1987 in comparison with 1986. There was a significant increase in the number of new cases brought before the Court, with a particularly large increase in the number of requests for preliminary rulings while direct actions remained constant and staff cases increased by about 20 per cent.

Table 1[1]

	1986	*1987*
Judgments delivered	174	208
Interim proceedings (injunctive relief)	25	21
New Cases	328	395
Of which:		
Requests for preliminary rulings	19	144
Direct actions	179	174
Staff cases	58	77

In this chapter our attention will be focused primarily on direct actions and requests for preliminary rulings. Direct actions include the actions against Member States for failure to comply with obligations imposed by Community law, the procedure to review the legality of the acts or inaction of the institutions, and actions involving the unlimited jurisdiction of the Court such as proceedings for damages against Community institutions. The remaining jurisdiction of the Court of Justice will be reviewed briefly and the practice and procedure of the Court will be outlined.

At the outset, however, it is necessary to observe that each of the actions before the Court is subject to certain procedural and jurisdictional obstacles. For example, access to the Court for natural or legal persons under Article 173 depends on whether the decision which they wish to have annulled is addressed to them. If not, they must demonstrate that they have a 'direct and individual concern' in the fate of the decision, and consideration of this issue will be taken as a preliminary point in the action before the Court. If the plaintiff fails to demonstrate direct and individual concern then the Court will declare the action inadmissible and will not go on to consider the merits of the case. In this context the question of admissibility is similar to the relatively novel concept of '*locus standi*' in Irish constitutional law. In proceedings under Article 177, issues of admissibility can also arise: it may be that reference to the Court has been made by a body which is not a court or tribunal; or it may be that there is no genuine dispute before the national court.

1 *Proceedings of the Court of Justice of the European Communities* 1/86 and 1/87. [Hereinafter cited as '*Proceedings*']

Actions against Member States for failure to comply with Community law obligations

12.6 Article 169 of the EEC Treaty lies at the centre of a cluster of remedies designed to ensure that the Member States, the principal subjects of the Community legal system, do not transgress against the Treaty or the secondary legislation of the Community either through acts of commission or acts of omission. The first point to note about Article 169 is that, in the context of a complex international organisation, it depoliticises the role of prosecuting infringements by Member States by entrusting that function to the Commission; as we have already noted (*supra*, para. 4.21) the latter institution is entrusted with protecting the Community interest. Should the Commission fail to exercise this role then any other Member State may assume the prosecutor's mantle in accordance with Article 170, but recourse to the latter remedy has been rare. A second feature of the Article 169 action is that it comprises a number of stages, increasing in formality, which offer the Member States under scrutiny an opportunity to terminate the alleged infringement or risk an action before the Court. There is significant benefit in this arrangement because it secures compliance in the vast majority of cases without the need to resort to litigation. The procedure commences when the Commission sends to the Member State in question a letter of formal notice outlining its complaint and inviting the comments of the Member State. The initiation of this procedure has a dramatic effect either because the Member State terminates the infringement or convinces the Commission that no infringement has taken place. Should this not occur, however, the Commission then proceeds to issue a reasoned opinion in which it states its objections and requires the Member State to comply with its obligations within a specified period, usually two months. If the addressee Member State still fails to satisfy the Commission within the time limit specified in the reasoned opinion, the Commission is free to institute proceedings before the Court of Justice to have the infringement established. But even at the litigation stage there is a possibility for the Member State to comply with its obligation and a reasonable proportion of cases registered with the Court have been removed from the register as a result of late compliance with outstanding obligations. If the case does proceed to a hearing before the Court and if the Commission succeeds in its allegation, Article 171 requires the Member State to take the necessary measures to comply with the judgment of the Court.

Table 2 demonstrates how the procedure achieves a cumulative reduction in the number of outstanding infringement cases.

Table 2[1]

	1986	1987
Letter of formal notice	516	572
Reasoned opinions	164	197
Court actions initiated	71	61
Cases removed from register during		
proceedings	43	41
Judgments	30	41
Of which:		
successful actions	26	36
unsuccessful actions	4	5

However, Table 2 does not illustrate the major disadvantage of the procedure: it often extends over a period exceeding two years.

1 21st Annual General Report 1987, point 929.

12.7 The object of the pre-litigation stage of the Article 169 procedure is to give the Member State concerned an opportunity on the one hand of remedying the position before the matter is brought before the Court and, on the other hand, of putting forward its defence to the Commission's complaints. The Commission's reasoned opinion, which formally states the breach of the Treaty with which the Member State is charged, concludes the pre-litigation stage. This was stated by the Court in *EC Commission v Ireland*[1] in which Ireland had argued that the action was inadmissible because the Commission's reasoned opinion required the abolition within five days of import control measures on poultrymeat and eggs imported from other Member States which permitted vaccination against Newcastle disease. Ireland had pursued a policy of non-vaccination since 1938. The Court deplored the Commission's behaviour but did not declare the action inadmissible because, despite the five-day compliance period, the Commission had waited for Ireland's response to the reasoned opinion before initiating proceedings before the Court. Ireland had also argued, on admissibility grounds, that the Commission had raised a new complaint in its reasoned opinion relating to the form of import licensing system applied in Ireland; Ireland had been deprived of an opportunity to submit observations on that issue before receipt of the reasoned opinion. The

Court rejected this complaint also: although the action brought by the Commission must relate to the same subject matter as the reasoned opinion, which must in turn be preceded by a letter inviting the Member State to submit its observations, there is nothing to prevent the Commission from setting out in detail in the reasoned opinion the complaints which it has already made more generally in its initial letter.

In structure and content the reasoned opinion does not have to follow a precise form. In *EEC Commission v Italy*[2] the Court held that a reasoned opinion must be held to contain legally sufficient grounds when it presents a coherent statement of the reasons that led the Commission to believe that the State in question had failed in one of the obligations incumbent on it by virtue of the Treaty. It should also be stressed that the reasoned opinion is not a decision within the meaning of Article 189 of the EEC Treaty; it is part of the pre-litigation process and cannot be the subject matter for an action for annulment under Article 173: *EC Commission v France*.[3] And, unlike the procedure under Article 173—which specifies a two-month period within which proceedings must be commenced, there is no time limit for the initiation of proceedings by the Commission under Article 169: *EC Commission v France*.[4]

1 Case 74/82 [1984] E.C.R. 317.
2 Case 7/61 [1961] E.C.R. 317, [1962] C.M.L.R. 39.
3 Cases 6, 11/69 [1969] E.C.R. 523, [1970] C.M.L.R. 43.
4 Case 7/71 [1971] E.C.R. 1003, [1972] C.M.L.R. 453.

12.8 The Commission enjoys a complete discretion as to whether and when it will taken an action against a Member State. This was established as early as 1961 in *EEC Commission v Italy*[1] in which the Court held that even if a Member State ultimately respects its Treaty obligations after the expiry of the time limit set out in the reasoned opinion, the Commission cannot be deprived of its right to obtain a judgment at law upon the failure of the Member State in question to respect its Treaty obligations. Conversely, the Commission's discretion also empowers it to terminate proceedings against a Member State which has belatedly complied with its obligations. An example can be seen in *EC Commission v Ireland*,[2] a case which concerned section 20(5) of the Broadcasting Authority Act, 1960 which gave a privileged status to 'Irish Advertisers' and empowered the R.T.E. Authority to fix reduced charges and preferential conditions for advertisements which were 'Irish advertisements'. The case was withdrawn from the Register following the making by the Minister for Posts and Telegraphs of the European Communities (Broadcasting Authority Act, 1960) Regulations, 1983[3] which simply repealed the offending sub-section.

The discretion enjoyed by the Commission means that it may decide not to initiate proceedings against an offending Member State. It has been suggested[4] that there are three circumstances in which the Commission will not act:

(1) When the infringement is trivial and not part of a policy or legislative scheme in the Member State concerned.
(2) Where the infringement involves 'high political issues': in the absence of meaningful sanctions the judgment of the Court would

hardly convince a dissident Member State to comply with its obligations. The position of France during the constitutional crisis of 1965–66 is most frequently cited in this context.

(3) Where the infringement results from the refusal of national courts to apply Community law.

1 *Supra*, fn. 2, para. 12.7.
2 Case 315/82 O.J. C 2, 5.1.1984. p. 7.
3 S.I. No. 187 of 1983.
4 A.C. Evans, *The Enforcement Procedure of Article 169 EEC: Commission Discretion*, [1979] 4 E.L. Rev. 442.

12.9 The refusal of national courts to apply Community law raises a particularly delicate issue and surfaces from time to time when a national supreme court or court from whose decision there is no further remedy refuses to apply Community law or give preference to national law. There have been two notable examples of this in the French Conseil d'Etat: *Semoules*[1] and *Ministre de l'Intérieur v Cohn-Bendit*.[2] In response to questions in the European Parliament[3] the Commission has confirmed that the Article 169 procedure can be utilised in these circumstances; however, it has preferred to make informal approaches to the Member States in question because formal proceedings might be perceived as a threat to judicial independence in that State and might also compromise future cooperation between the national judiciary and the Court of Justice.[4] This 'softly, softly' approach to national judiciaries contrasts sharply with the attitude taken by the Commission and the Court when other constitutionally independent organs of State are involved in an infringement of Community law. In *EC Commission v Belgium*[5] the defendant government had argued that it had used its best endeavours to secure amendments to a discriminatory tax on imports of timber but it had been unable to progress a draft law through the Belgian parliament. The Court dismissed this argument by holding that Treaty obligations devolve upon States as such and

'. . . the liability of a Member State under Article 169 arises whatever the agency of the State whose action or inaction is the cause of the failure to fulfil its obligations, even in the case of a constitutionally independent institution.'

The responsibility for infringements of Community law will be attributed to the State even though the operation of the offending practice may have been entrusted to a private company: *EC Commission v Ireland*.[6] In this case the Irish Government had promoted a 'Buy Irish' campaign which was administered through the agency of the Irish Goods Council. The Commission considered that the campaign was in breach of Article 30 of the EEC Treaty, and was able to demonstrate that the greater part of the expenses of the Irish Goods Council were contributed by the Government, which also defined the broad outlines of the 'Buy Irish' campaign. A more recent example of the general principle at work in these cases can be seen in the case of *EC Commission v Greece*[7] where the defendant government pleaded *force majeure* in an action for failure to pays its financial contributions and subsequent default interest under Council Regulation

191

(EEC) 2891/77;[8] according to the Greek Government a strike by employees of the Bank of Greece amounted to *force majeure* but the Court upheld the Commission's contention that the circumstances were not outside the control of the Greek Government and were in fact foreseeable.

1 [1968] Dalloz Jur. 285, [1970] C.M.L.R. 395.
2 [1979] Dalloz Jur. 155, [1980] 1 C.M.L.R. 543.
3 Responses to: Written Question No. 28/68, O.J. C 71, pp. 1–2; and Written Question No. 349/69, O.J. C 20, p. 4.
4 A.C. Evans, *loc. cit.* fn. 4, para. 12.8 at p. 454.
5 Case 77/69 [1970] E.C.R. 237, [1974] 1 C.M.L.R. 203.
6 Case 249/81 [1982] E.C.R. 4005, [1983] 2 C.M.L.R. 104.
7 Case 70/86 O.J. C 274, 13.10.1987 p. 5.
8 O.J. L 336, 27.12.1977 p. 1.

12.10 The nature of the infringements prosecuted under Article 169 varies considerably but the majority of actions concern the failure of Member States to transform Directives into domestic law. We have already noted that the Court will refuse to absolve an infringement on the grounds that it was the responsibility of a constitutionally independent organ of the State. Similarly, a Member State may not plead provisions, practices or circumstances existing in its internal legal system in order to justify a failure to comply with obligations and time limits resulting from Community Directives: *EC Commission v Ireland*.[1] In this case the State had a failure to implement Council Directive (EEC) 7/91[2] (the Second Directive on company law) within the stipulated time limit. It argued that the complexity of the Directive, being just one of the number of technical and intricate measures on company law adopted at Community level, contributed to the delay and that this fact was borne out by the difficulties encountered by other Member States in implementing the Directive. The Court rejected this argument and added that the governments of the Member States participate in the preparatory work for Directives and must therefore be in a position to prepare, within the period prescribed, the draft legislative provisions necessary for their implementation.

The greater proportion of the cases brought before the Court, which do not involve Directives, concern restrictions on the free movement of goods. Thirty-five of the 61 cases registered with the Court in 1987 concerned Directives, and of the remaining 26 cases 11 were concerned with infringements of Articles 9, 30 and 95 of the Treaty which are the basic provisions concerning the free movement of goods.[3] On occasions, however, the nature of the breach can appear to be minimal, if not esoteric. In *EC Commission v France*[4] the defendant State was held to have infringed Article 48 of the Treaty for failure to amend discriminatory provisions of the Maritime Labour Code, even though the naval agencies responsible for the administration of the code had been instructed verbally not to apply the offending provisions. But the Court held that discrimination, under Article 48 of the Treaty, was prohibited even if it constituted only an obstacle of secondary importance as regards equality of access to employment; the maintenance unamended on the statute book of the offending provision of the Maritime Labour Code constituted such an obstacle.

Just as the Treaty depoliticised actions against Member States by entrusting the prosecution to the Commission, it also provided the Member States with remedies, in the form of Articles 173 and 175, with which to counter unlawful acts or omissions by the institutions of the Community. Accordingly, the Court will not entertain as a defence to an action under Article 169 the claim that an institution has failed to carry out its obligations. In *EEC Commission v Luxembourg and Belgium*[5] the defendants argued, in accordance with the international law doctrine of reciprocity, that they were entitled to maintain discriminatory taxes on dairy products because the Council had failed to introduce a common organisation of the milk market before the expiry of a deadline announced by the Council in a resolution adopted in April, 1962. The Court rejected this argument derived from international law:

'. . . the Treaty is not limited to creating reciprocal obligations between the different natural and legal persons to whom it is applicable, but establishes a new legal order, which governs the powers, rights and obligations of the said persons, as well as the necessary procedures for taking cognizance of and penalising any breach of it. Therefore, except where otherwise expressly provided, the basic concept of the Treaty requires that the Member States shall not take the law into their own hands. Therefore the fact that the Council failed to carry out its obligations cannot relieve the Defendants from carrying out theirs.'

Moreover the fact that other remedies exist does not prevent the Commission from taking action under Article 169. In *EC Commission v Italy*[6] the defendant government had failed to pay export rebates on various agricultural products provided for in a number of Council Regulations and argued, when sued under Article 169, that the correct remedy was for the individuals concerned to rely on the directly applicable rules of Community law before municipal courts. The Court rejected this argument by pointing out that remedies available in national courts and the procedure under Article 169 had different objectives and effects. The logic of this ruling has been extended to discourage Member States from by-passing Treaty mechanisms. In *EC Commission v Ireland*[7] the defendant government sought to justify preferential excise treatment for domestic producers of spirits and beer by pointing to diverging exchange rates between the Irish and British 'Green Pounds'. The Court refused to accept this defence:

'If the Irish authorities consider that the exchange rates in question were not fixed appropriately they should seek the remedy for that situation by the appropriate means. A monetary situation cannot be corrected by means of discriminatory tax provisions.'

1 Case 151/81 [1982] E.C.R. 3573.
2 O.J. L 26, 31.1.1977 p. 1.
3 21st Annual General Report 1987, point 929.
4 *Supra*, fn 4, para. 12.1.
5 Cases 90, 91/63, [1964] E.C.R. 625, [1965] C.M.L.R. 58.
6 Case 31/69, [1970] E.C.R. 25, [1970] C.M.L.R. 175.
7 Case 55/79, [1980] E.C.R. 481, [1980] 1 C.M.L.R. 734.

12.11 It need hardly be stressed that the Commission must prove its infringement allegations and it does not always succeed: in 5 of the 41 judgments delivered by the Court in 1987 the Commission failed to sustain its claims.[1] A pertinent local example can be seen in *EC Commission v Ireland*[2] where the Court dismissed in its entirety the Commission's action for a declaration that the continued application by Ireland of Section 10 of the Value-Added Tax Act, 1972, which reduced the taxable amount of goods sold in conjunction with a trade-in, was in breach of Article 11 of the Sixth Directive on VAT.[3]

1 21st Annual General Report 1987, point 929.
2 Case 17/84, [1984] E.C.R. 2375, [1986] 1 C.M.L.R. 336.
3 Council Directive (EEC) 77/388 O.J. L 145, 13.6.1977 p. 1.

12.12 The Commission initiates proceedings under Article 169 on its own initiative, or on foot of a complaint by individuals or other Member States. The privileged status of the Member States in comparison to other subjects of the Community legal system can be seen in Article 170 which envisages circumstances where, on receipt of a complaint from one of the Member States against another and after offering each of the Member States the opportunity to submit written and oral submissions on the other party's case, the Commission fails to issue a reasoned opinion within 3 months. If this happens the complainant Member State can bring the issue before the Court in place of the Commission.

The procedure has been utilised on only two occasions. In *Ireland v France*[1] the Commission had failed to take action against France for refusing Irish mutton and lamb ('sheepmeat' in Eurospeak) access to the French market. The case was withdrawn when the parties reached a bilateral conclusion to the dispute which permitted Irish (but not British) producers access to the French market; this settlement itself was probably in breach of the Treaty but was merely a minor feature of one of the less savoury episodes in the Court's history (*infra*, para. 12.13). The only instance where an action under Article 170 resulted in a judgment was *France v United Kingdom*[2] which concerned a fisheries dispute. The Commission issued a reasoned opinion in which it held that the UK had infringed its obligations; no time limit for compliance was set in the reasoned opinion and the French government proceeded to raaise the issue before the Court. The Commission then applied, successfully, to the Court to intervene on behalf of France, and the Court upheld the French allegation.

1 Case 58/77, 12th Annual General Report, point 547.
2 Case 141/78 [1979] E.C.R. 2923, [1980] 1 C.M.L.R. 6.

12.13 Article 171 states that a Member State found to have infringed its obligations under Article 169 'shall be required to take the necessary measures to comply with the judgment of the Court of Justice'. There have been a number of instances in which Member States have defaulted on the obligation to comply with the judgment of the Court of Justice under Article 171. In *EC Commission v Italy*[1] the defendant's failure to comply with Article 171 was merely noted by the Court. However, Italy had been placed under immense pressure by the Commission and other Member States to introduce amending legislation before the Court gave judgment because the subject matter at issue, a tax on the exportation of art treasures, had been condemned in a previous Article 169 action[2] and had been referred to critically in a subsequent request for a preliminary ruling under Article 177.[3] A potential constitutional impasse was avoided, after the institution of fresh infringement proceedings, only when the Italian government repealed the offending law. It should be stressed that the circumstances in this case were somewhat unusual, whereas a recent example of an action for infringement of Article 171, *EC Commission v Italy*,[4] has not given rise to any significant comment. In the latter case, which involved national legislation which had been declared by the Court to be incompatible with the common organisation of the market for milk products,[5] the Court observed that several years had elapsed since the judgment and neither the failure of the Italian authorities to rely on the offending provisions nor the mere presentation to Parliament of a draft law for its repeal was sufficient to bring the infringement to an end. The most blatant infringement of Article 171 was committed by France in the so-called 'sheepmeat' case already referred to (*supra*, para. 12.12). On foot of a complaint by the United Kingdom the Commission eventually commenced proceedings in 1978 and the Court delivered judgment more than a year later in September 1979, ruling that the restriction of imports by France was unlawful.[6] France still failed to comply with its obligations so in November 1979 the Commission initiated fresh infringement proceedings for breach of Article 171. The Commission also considered that a modification of the French restrictions, which were equally penal as far as British producers were concerned, constituted a new infringement of the Court's judgment and further proceedings were instituted against France. The two cases were joined in March 1980. The Commission then applied for an interim order under Article 186 of the Treaty to restrain France from imposing restrictions on British imports, but when the matter came on for hearing the Court, with Pilate-like resignation, refused the order on the grounds that it was not 'necessary' in terms of the requirements of Article 186: the purpose of the Commission's application for an interim order was the same in substance as the application which led to the judgment of the Court of September 1979.[7] But the Court did make it clear that political disagreement between the Member States, and the inability of the Community institutions to agree on a common organisation of the market in 'sheepmeat', were factors that had influenced its decision.[8] In fact, the problem was resolved only when a suitable regime for 'sheepmeat', acceptable to France, was agreed by the Council.

It is easy to appreciate the dilemma in which the Court found itself but one wonders whether the same latitude would have been offered to a small Member State, Ireland for example, if it had acted in a similarly cavalier and arbitrary manner.

1 Case 48/71 [1972] E.C.R. 527, [1972] C.M.L.R. 699.
2 Case 7/68 [1968] E.C.R. 423, [1969] C.M.L.R. 1.
3 Case 18/71 *Eunomia v Ministero della Pubblica Istruzione* [1971] E.C.R. 811, [1972] C.M.L.R. 4.
4 Case 225/86 O.J. C 132, 21.5.1988 p. 5.

5 Council Regulation (EEC) 804/68 O.J. (Sp. Ed.) 1968 (I) p. 176.
6 Case 232/78 *EC Commission v France* [1979] E.C.R. 2729, [1980] 1 C.M.L.R. 418.
7 Cases 24, 97/80 R [1980] E.C.R. 1319, [1981] 3 C.M.L.R. 25.
8 For a fuller account see: Hartley, *op. cit.* fn. 2, para. 12.3 at pp. 320–3.

12.14 The nature of the obligations imposed by Articles 169 and 171 was discussed in *Procureur de la République v Waterkeyn*.[1] This was a request for a preliminary ruling under Article 177 and the defendants argued that a judgment of the Court, which declared that France had failed to fulfil its obligations under Article 30 of the Treaty by regulating the advertising of alcoholic beverages in a way discriminatory to products emanating from other Member States,[2] had 'general effect' in as much as the Court had condemned in its entirety the French legislation on the advertising of alcoholic beverages. The Court disputed this interpretation of its judgment and stated that the French legislation had been declared contrary to Article 30 only insofar as it enacted rules which were less favourable to products imported from other Member States when compared with national products which may be regarded as being in competition with them. It went on to emphasise that

'. . . the purpose of judgments delivered under Articles 169 to 171 is primarily to lay down the duties of Member States when they fail to fulfil their obligations. Rights for the benefit of individuals flow from the actual provisions of Community law having direct effect in the Member States' internal legal order, as is the case with Article 30 of the Treaty prohibiting quantitative restrictions and all measures having equivalent effect. Nevertheless, where the Court has found that a Member State has failed to fulfil its obligations under such a provision, it is the duty of the national court, by virtue of the authority attaching to the judgment of the Court, to take account, if need be, of the elements of law established by that judgment in order to determine the scope of the provisions of Community law which it has the task of applying.'

The Court added that the duty of compliance imposed by Article 171 applies not just to the courts of the Member State in question but to all its institutions; for example, if a judgment of the Court declares that certain legislative provisions of a Member State are contrary to the Treaty the authorities exercising legislative power are then under the duty to amend the provision in question so as to conform with the requirements of Community law.

An issue as yet unresolved concerns the payment of restitution and/or damages on foot of a judgment of the Court of Justice under Article 169. The Treaty itself is silent on the issue, but the Court has given some indication of what national courts may or may not do in this context in various judgments. For example, in *EC Commission v Italy*[3] the defendants had failed to pay premiums for the slaughter of dairy cows and for withholding milk and milk products from the market place. The relevant regulations, which entered into force in October 1969 and were revoked in June 1971, had already been the subject matter of a reference for a preliminary ruling under Article 177: *Leonesio v Ministero dell'Agri-coltura e delle Foreste*.[4] When the Article 169 action came on for hearing the Italian government had commenced to pay the slaughtering premiums but argued, in respect of the premiums for non-marketing, that the situation had become irremediable because it would no longer be possible to comply retroactively with the obligations imposed by the regulations. Therefore, the action had lost its purpose on both counts. The Court firmly rejected this argument:

> 'The object holds in the present case since, as regards the premiums for slaughtering, the obligation placed on the Italian Republic is far from being completely performed; the question of the payment to those entitled of interest on the overdue payments, is not settled, and the complaints developed by the Commission in the course of the proceedings relate not only to the delay in carrying out the regulations but also to certain of the methods of application which have in effect weakened their efficacy.
>
> As regards the non-performance of the provisions relating to the premiums for non-marketing, the defendant cannot in any case be allowed to rely upon a *fait accompli* of which it is itself the author so as to escape judicial proceedings.
>
> Moreover, in the face of both a delay in the performance of an obligation and a definite refusal, a judgment by the Court under Articles 169 and 171 of the Treaty may be of substantive interest in establishing the basis of a responsibility that a Member State can incur as a result of its default, as regards other Member States, the Community or private parties.'

More recently, in *EC Commission v Italy*,[5] the Court held that in the absence of Community rules concerning repayment of national taxes collected in breach of Community law, it was the responsibility of Member States to ensure that such taxes were reimbursed, in accordance with the provisions of national law. The Court also held that all methods of proof the effect of which was to make the reimbursement of tax collected in breach of Community law practically impossible or excessively difficult were incompatible with Community law.

National practice on this issue varies considerably. In *Ministre des Affaires Économiques v Fromagerie Franco-Suisse 'Le Ski' SA*[6] the Belgian Cour de Cassation confirmed a decision of the Cour d'Appel which had refused to give effect to a law which had purported to make taxes paid under a royal decree, which had been declared by the Court of Justice to be in breach of Article 12 of the EEC Treaty,[7] irrecoverable. At the other extreme, the Court of Appeal in England has held that the only remedy available in English law to protect rights conferred by Article 30 of the Treaty was judicial review: *Bourgoin v Ministry of Agriculture*.[8] This action followed a judgment by the Court of Justice in which the United Kingdom was held to have infringed Article 30 by imposing restrictions on the importation of turkeys from France in November 1982.[9] The plaintiffs appealed to the House of Lords but the case was settled before a hearing was held for £3.5m.[10] We can only speculate as to why the defendant chose to settle; but the fact that the House of Lords would have been obliged, under Article 177, to refer the issue to Luxembourg may have been a factor. In the meantime the decision of the majority in the Court of Appeal has been strongly criticised[11] but it remains the law in England.[12] In Ireland there has been no case on this point; however, if the Irish courts follow the reasoning of the Supreme Court in *Murphy v A-G*[13] (*supra*, para. 15.5), and the decision of Hamilton P. in *McDermott and Cotter v*

Minister for Social Welfare and A-G[14] (*infra*, para. 24.8) suggests that they will, then the State can expect to escape lightly in respect of infringements of Community law which have the effect of withholding payments from, or inflict measurable economic loss on, individuals or companies.

In conclusion, the problem will not be resolved until the Community's legislative authorities fill the present *lacuna* or until the Court of Justice gives a declaratory ruling on the issue.

1 Cases 314–316/81, 83/82 [1982] E.C.R. 4337, [1983] 2 C.M.L.R. 145.
2 Case 152/78 *EC Commission v France* [1980] E.C.R. 2299, [1981] 2 C.M.L.R. 743.
3 Case 39/72 [1973] E.C.R. 101, [1973] C.M.L.R. 439.
4 Case 93/71 [1972] E.C.R. 287, [1973] C.M.L.R. 343.
5 Case 104/86, O.J. C 105, 21.4.1988 p. 4.
6 [1972] C.M.L.R. 330.
7 *Supra*, fn. 5, para. 12.10.
8 [1985] 3 All E.R. 585.
9 Case 40/82 *EC Commission v United Kingdom* [1982] E.C.R. 2793, [1982] 3 C.M.L.R. 497.
10 Hansard, 23 July 1986, Vol. 102 No. 156 Col. 116.
11 See John Temple Lang, *The Duties of National Courts under the Constitutional Law of the European Community*, The Dominik Lasok Lecture in European Community Law, Exeter 1987, at pp. 9–14.
12 *An Bord Bainne Co-operative Ltd v Milk Marketing Board* [1988] 1 FTLR 145.
13 [1982] I.R. 241.
14 (10 June 1988, unreported) High Court (Hamilton P.).

12.15 There are two variations on the Article 169 remedy in the Treaty. The first of these can be found in Article 93(2) which reads as follows:

> 'If, after giving notice to the parties concerned to submit their comments, the Commission finds that aid granted by a State or through State resources is not compatible with the Common Market having regard to Article 92, or that such aid is being misused, it shall decide that the State concerned shall abolish or alter such aid within a period of time to be determined by the Commission.
>
> If the State concerned does not comply with this decision within the prescribed time, the Commission or any other interested State may, in derogation from the provisions of Articles 169 and 170, refer the matter to the Court of Justice direct.'

It will be observed that the preliminary stages of the Article 169 procedure have been eliminated from Article 93(2); this is logical because the first sub-paragraph of Article 93(2) effectively mirrors the pre-litigation stage of the Article 169 action. In any event, proceedings under Article 93(2) are rare.[1]

Article 100A(4), inserted into the EEC Treaty by Article 18 of the Single European Act, provides for another abbreviated infringement procedure. If the Commission or another Member State considers that a Member State is making improper use of the exemptions under Article 36 or the exemptions concerning protection of the environment or of the working environment, in order to avoid harmonisation legislation adopted by a qualified majority, then the Commission or another Member State may bring the matter directly before the Court in derogation from the infringement procedures laid down in Articles 169 and 170 of the EEC Treaty.

1 For an example, see Case 70/72 *EC Commission v Germany* [1973] E.C.R. 813, [1973] C.M.L.R. 741.

12.16 The Euratom and ECSC Treaties both contain procedures for the establishment of infringements by Member States of obligations arising under the respective Treaties. Articles 141 to 143 of the Euratom Treaty, are identical to Articles 169 to 171 of the EEC Treaty; there has been only one action under these provisions and it was notable for establishing that there is no time limit for the initiation of proceedings under Article 141 of the Euratom Treaty; *EC Commission v France.*[1] This principle is equally applicable to proceedings under Article 169 of the EEC Treaty.

The procedure under Article 88 of the ECSC Treaty is rather different from the EEC/Euratom models. In the pre-litigation stage the Commission follows much the same course as under Article 169 of the EEC Treaty, but instead of issuing a reasoned opinion it records the failure of the Member State in a reasoned decision. Thereafter, the Member State has two months in which to initiate proceedings in the Court of Justice, which is invested with full jurisdiction to investigate the dispute.[2] A further novel feature of the procedure is that it allows for the imposition of sanctions against a Member State which fails in an action under Article 88 and which continues to remain in default of its obligations: the Commission may suspend any payments due to that Member State under the ECSC Treaty or authorise the other Member States to take countervailing action. These sanctions have never been utilised.

1 Case 7/71, [1971] E.C.R. 1003, [1972] C.M.L.R. 453.
2 For examples see Case 3/59 *Germany v High Authority* [1960] E.C.R. 53; Case 25/59 *Netherlands v High Authority* [1960] E.C.R. 355.

Judicial review of acts of the institutions

12.17 The remedies comprised in Articles 173, 175 and 184 of the EEC Treaty are designed to control the unlawful acts or inaction of the Community institutions. The first point to note is that all the remedies are subject to significant procedural restraints and that the barriers to litigation contained in the Treaty have been interpreted restrictively by the Court, particularly in respect of actions initiated by natural or legal persons. The most important remedy is the action for annulment under Article 173. This allows for applications for the annulment of acts of the Council or the Commission; the Court has ruled that acts of the Parliament may also be the subject matter of an application under Article 173 even though the Parliament is not specifically mentioned in the text. Applications must be based on one or more of four grounds: lack of competence; infringement of an essential procedural requirement; infringement of the Treaty or of any rule of law relating to its application; or misuse of powers. The application must be initiated within two months of the publication of the measure or of its notification to the plaintiff. Lastly, there are two separate categories of litigant. The privileged category includes the Member States, the Council and the Commission. Natural or legal persons, the second category, are subject to a *locus standi* requirement; they are permitted to seek the annulment of decisions addressed to themselves, decisions addressed to other persons or decisions which, although in the form of a regulation, are of direct and individual concern to them.

The brief time limit for the initiation of proceedings by both categories of litigant and the narrow scope for action by individuals means that some unlawful acts may go unchallenged. In the case of a Regulation or other act of general application, which cannot be challenged directly by individuals, a different problem may ensue if the Regulation empowers the adoption of a Decision; the Decision itself might be unimpeachable but the underlying measure of general application would be unlawful. Article 184, sometimes known as the plea or exception of illegality, reduces the possibility of injustice in these circumstances by allowing any party in proceedings in which a Regulation of the Council or Commission is in issue to plead the grounds mentioned in Article 173 to invoke the inapplicability of that Regulation, notwithstanding the expiry of the time limit of two months mentioned in Article 173. The remedy provided by Article 184 is a derivative action; it is not a self-contained basis for litigation and, not surprisingly, it has not been invoked frequently.

Likewise, the action for failure to act contained in Article 175 has not been utilised very frequently. In terms of procedural restraints this procedure is very nearly the converse of Article 173. The action is directed against silence or inaction (in infringement of the Treaty) on the part of the Council or Commission; the action to have the infringement established is admissible only if the relevant institution has first been called upon to act. If the institution concerned fails to define its position within two months the action may be brought within a further two-month period. There are two categories of applicant: the Member States and other institutions of the Community, and natural and legal persons. The latter can complain to the Court that an institution has failed to address to them any act other than a recommendation or opinion. By definition, individuals can be the addressees of decisions only.

Finally, certain consequences flow from a successful action: Article 174 provides that an act impugned under Article 173 shall be void but that certain provisions of regulations can be deemed to be definitive. Article 176 imposes an obligation on the institution whose act has been declared void, or whose failure to act has been established, to take the necessary measures to comply with the judgment of the Court.

Article 173: the action for annulment

12.18 What acts of the institutions of the Community are amenable to review by the Court of Justice under Article 173? The wording of Article 173 suggests that the competence of the Court is not limited to the binding legal acts listed in Article 189 of the Treaty, namely: regulations, directives and decisions. Instead the Court is empowered to '. . . review the legality of acts of the Council and Commission other than recommendations or opinions'. Article 189 tells us that recommendations and opinions have no binding legal force, so that it is not really surprising that the Court has refused to limit its competence by reference to purely formal criteria but has preferred to judge an 'act' by assessing whether it has binding legal consequences. The Court will, of course, entertain actions for the annulment of measures formally described as regulations, directives or decisions, but it will also review other forms of conduct which may have legally binding consequences. The first case in which the Court had an opportunity to make such a distinction was *Cimenteries CBR Cementsbed-rijven v EEC Commission*[1] in which the plaintiffs sought the annulment of a communication under Article 15(5) of Regulation 17 which had the effect of removing immunity from fines in respect of the 'Noordwijks Cement Accoord'; this agreement had been notified to the Commission for an exemption under Article 85(3) of the Treaty. The Commission argued that the action was inadmissible because neither the form nor the content of the communication gave rise to any definite legal effects. The Court sustained the plaintiffs' claim by holding that the communication had exposed them to grave financial risk and had brought about a distinct change in their legal position. Moreover, the procedure in question called for a decision within the meaning of Article 189, which would be subject to the legal guarantees which the Treaty provided. In *EC Commission v EC Council*,[2] the 'ERTA' case (*supra*, para. 5.3), the issue was wider in that the Council denied that the Community had any implied competence to conclude international agreements. Furthermore, the Council disputed the admissibility of the action because there was no act within the meaning of Article 173 against which action was possible; it was not given to the Court to review political deliberations which had taken place after a regular Council meeting. The Court rejected this view:

'Since the only matters excluded from the scope of the action for annulment open to the Member States and the institutions are "recommendations or opinions"—which by the final paragraph of Article 189 are declared to have no binding force—Article 173 treats as open to review by the Court all measures adopted by the institutions which are intended to have legal force.

The objective of this review is to ensure, as required by Article 164, observance of the law in the interpretation and application of the Treaty. It would be inconsistent with this objective to interpret the conditions under which the action is admissible so restrictively as to limit the availability of this procedure merely to the categories of measures referred to by Article 189.

An action for annulment must therefore be available in the case of all measures adopted by the institutions, whatever their nature or form, which are intended to have legal effects.'

Therefore, in terms of applications for annulment the list of binding acts in Article 189 is not exhaustive and the action under Article 173 encompasses orthodox measures of a secondary nature described in Article 189, other Community-related measures such as Acts of the Representatives of the Member States meeting within the framework of the Council[3] or the Act by which the Council established the system of direct elections to the European Parliament,[4] and *sui generis* 'acts' such as that at issue in the 'ERTA' case.

A conceptual difficulty of a more theological nature arises in respect of 'non-existent' acts. In the administrative law of some Member States it is possible to attack the validity of a measure by claiming that it is a non-existent act because certain pre-conditions for the enactment of that type of decision have not been met. The measure, therefore, would be void or non-existent. This argument has been raised from time to time before the Court but, apart from one notable exception when the Court actually considered the argument but rejected it,[5] the prevailing theory is that all acts of the institutions enjoy a presumption of validity: in other words, they are voidable rather than void *ab initio*. This appears clearly from a recent decision of the Court: *Consorzio Cooperative d'Abruzzo v EC Commission*.[6] In this case the Commission had made a contribution under the Guidance Section of the EAGGF to a development project submitted by a wine-making cooperative, but its Decision of 7 April 1982 was based on errors on the part of its officers which went undetected for two years; whereupon the Commission adopted a new decision in 1984 which reduced the contribution by nearly Lit.1bn. In response to the applicant's claim to have the 1982 Decision declared valid and irrevocable the Commission argued that the contribution stated in that decision was based on errors and that the decision did not exist. The Court held that under Community law and under the domestic law of various Member States, even if an administrative measure was irregular, there was a presumption that it was valid until it had been duly annulled or withdrawn by the institution by which it was adopted. In this case there was no manifest irregularity on a reading of the decision, and the decision could not be regarded as non-existent. As regards withdrawal of an illegal measure, the Court referred to its judgment in *Alpha Steel v EC Commission*[7] and stated:

'The withdrawal of an unlawful measure is permissible, provided that the withdrawal occurs within a reasonable time and provided that the Commission has had sufficient regard as to how far the applicant might have been led to rely on the lawfulness of the measure.'

In this case the two-year gap between the promulgation and withdrawal of the 1982 Decision was unreasonable and the 1984 Decision was void because it infringed the principles of legal certainty and the protection of legitimate interests.

We have noted that Article 173 permits actions against acts of the Council and Commission. In the light of the constitutional developments of the 1970s which saw the direct election of the European Parliament and the granting of increased budgetary powers to that institution, the Court has held that acts of the Parliament can be the subject matter of actions for annulment under Article 173: *Partie Ecologiste 'Les Verts' v European Parliament*.[8]

Reference must also be made to the distinction between general and individual measures; the differentiation is important for natural and legal persons who cannot seek the annulment of a directive or a regulation (unless the latter is actually a 'disguised decision'). In an early case, *Confédération Nationale des Producteurs de Fruits et Légumes v EEC Council*,[9] the Court laid down the criterion for distinguishing regulations (measures of general application) from decisions:

'Under the terms of Article 189 of the EEC Treaty, a regulation shall have general application and shall be directly applicable in all Member States, whereas a decision shall be binding only upon those to whom it is addressed. The criterion for distinction must be sought in the general "application" or otherwise of the measure in question.

The personal characteristics of a decision arise from the limitation of the persons to whom it is addressed, whereas a regulation, being essentially of a legislative nature, is applicable not to a limited number of persons, defined or identifiable, but to categories of persons viewed abstractly and in their entirety. Consequently, in order to determine in doubtful cases whether one is concerned with a decision or a regulation, it is necessary to ascertain whether the measure in question is of individual concern to specific individuals.

In these circumstances, if a measure entitled by its author a regulation contains provisions which are capable of being not only of direct but also of individual concern to certain natural or legal persons, it must be admitted, without prejudice to the question whether the measure considered in its entirety can be correctly called a regulation, that in any case those provisions do not have the character of a regulation and may therefore be impunged by those persons under the terms of the second paragraph of Article 173.'

In the instant case the plaintiff failed to comply with this test. The distinction between measures of general application and decisions has been steadily refined and was restated most clearly in *Koninklijke Scholten-Honig v EC Council and Commission*,[10] where the Court held that a measure does not lose its character as a regulation simply because it is possible to ascertain with a greater or lesser degree of accuracy the number or even the identity of the persons to which it applies at any given time, as long as there is no doubt that the measure is applicable as the result of an objective situation of law or of fact which it specifies and which is in harmony with its ultimate objective. When the contested regulation was enacted the plaintiff was one of only three producers of isoglucose in the Community.[11]

Lastly, it is not necessary to challenge the entirety of an act in proceedings under Article 173. The Court has annulled parts of a decision and left the remaining parts intact: *Transocean Marine Paint Association v EC Commission*.[12]

1 Joined Cases 8–11/66 [1967] E.C.R. 75, [1967] C.M.L.R. 77.
2 Case 22/70, [1971] E.C.R. 263, [1971] C.M.L.R. 335.
3 See Gerhard Bebr, *Acts of the Representatives of the Governments of the Member States*, (1966) S.E.W. 529.
4 Decision (ECSC, EEC, Euratom) 76/787 O.J. L 278, 8.10.1976 p. 1.
5 Joined Cases 6, 11/69 *EC Commission v France* [1969] E.C.R. 523, [1970] C.M.L.R. 43.
6 Case 15/85 [1988] 1 C.M.L.R. 841.
7 Case 14/81 [1982] E.C.R. 749.
8 Case 294/83 [1986] E.C.R. 1339, [1987] 2 C.M.L.R. 343.
9 Joined Cases 16–17/62 [1962] E.C.R. 471, [1963] C.M.L.R. 160.
10 Case 101/76 [1977] E.C.R. 797, [1980] 2 C.M.L.R. 669.
11 The three producers did, however, succeed in establishing the invalidity of the contested regulation in actions under Article 177. See joined Cases 103, 145/77 *Royal Scholten-Honig (Holdings) and Tunnel Refineries v Intervention Board for Agricultural Produce* [1978] E.C.R. 2037, [1979] 1 C.M.L.R. 675. They did not succeed in their actions for damages under Article 215: Joined Cases 116, 124/77 *G.R. Amylum NV and Tunnel Refineries v EC Council and Commission* [1979] E.C.R. 3497, [1982] 2 C.M.L.R. 590; Case 143/77 *Koninklijke Scholten-Honig NV v EC Council and Commission* [1979] E.C.R. 3583, [1982] 2 C.M.L.R. 590.
12 Case 17/74 [1974] E.C.R. 1063, [1974] 2 C.M.L.R. 459.

12.19 The plaintiffs under Article 173 can be divided into two categories. The privileged category includes the Member States, the Council and the Commission. Actions by the Member States against the Commission are commonplace; for example, recent years have witnessed a significant number of actions by Member States against the Commission in respect of clearance of accounts under the EAGGF. But proceedings against the Council are less common; the first case of this type was *Ireland v EC Council*,[1] a judgment of 1973, in which the State succeeded in its application for the annulment of a regulation fixing accession compensatory amounts on tomatoes. Since the *ERTA* case[2] actions by the Commission against the Council and other institutions are also quite commonplace. A novel departure in recent times can be seen in *EC Commission v Board of Governors of the European Investment Bank*[3] which involved tax erroneously withheld from the salaries and pensions of staff of the European Investment Bank. The novelty of the action springs from the fact that it was the first case under Article 180(b) of the Treaty which allows the Member States, the Commission or the Board of Directors of the Bank to institute proceedings under Article 173 for the annulment of measures adopted by the Board of Governors of the Bank. A problem which has yet to be addressed relates to the status of the European Parliament as plaintiff under Article 173. As we have already seen (*supra*, para. 12.18) the Court held that acts of the European Parliament were capable of review under Article 173: *Partie Ecologiste 'Les Verts' v Parliament*.[4] This judgment characterised the Parliament as the author of legally binding acts for the purposes of Article 173; thus, it would not be straining the logic underlying the judgment of the Court if the right to sue under Article 173 was extended to the Parliament. Indeed, the Parliament has initiated proceedings for the annulment of Council Decision (EEC) 87/373[5] which laid down the procedures for the exercise of implementing powers conferred on the Commission for the purposes of the SEA.[6]

The main advantage enjoyed by the privileged class of litigant is that proceedings can be initiated against any act of the institutions and there is no *locus standi* requirement. This contrasts sharply with the position of natural and legal persons (*infra*, para. 12.22).

1 Case 151/73 [1974] E.C.R. 285, [1974] 1 C.M.L.R. 429.
2 *Supra*, fn. 2, para. 12.18.
3 Case 85/86 O.J. C 77, 24.3.1988 p. 6.
4 *Supra*, fn. 8, para. 12.18.
5 O.J. L 197 18.7.87 p. 33.
6 Case 302/87 O.J. C 321, 1.12.1987, p. 4.

12.20 There are a number of features common to both categories of applicant under Article 173; one is the requirement to initiate proceedings within two months of the publication of the measure or of its notification to the plaintiff, or, in the absence thereof, of the day on which it came to the knowledge of the latter as the case may be. The application of this requirement was discussed in *Misset v EC Council*[1] where the Court held that where the period for bringing an application is expressed in calendar months, that period expires at the end of the day which, in the month determined by that period, bears the same number as the day which caused the period to run, namely, the day of notification. A useful illustration of the operation of this procedural requirement can be seen in the joint action of *Germany v EC Commission*.[2] The application of the Netherlands was submitted one day after the expiry of the two-month time limit and the Court held that its application was inadmissible.

1 Case 152/85 O.J. C 34, 12.2.1987 p. 5.
2 Joined cases 281, 283–285, 187/85 [1988] 1 C.M.L.R. 11.

12.21 The grounds upon which an action may be founded are common to both categories of litigant.

(a) Lack of competence.
None of the institutions of the Community enjoy complete discretionary executive or legislative power; rather, Article 4(1) of the Treaty requires that each institution must act within the limits of the power conferred upon it by the Treaty. In other words, all actions must be capable of being traced back to a legal authority or base in the form of a provision of the Treaty or of secondary legislation. In the absence of such authority the institution lacks competence.

Lack of competence arises mainly in two contexts. The first is where the Community and the Member States are in dispute as to whether the Community possesses the competence to act or whether that competence has been retained by the Member States (*supra*, para. 5.9). A recent example can be seen in *United Kingdom v EC Council*[1] where the plaintiff claimed that a directive on the use of hormones in livestock, which was based on Article 43 of the Treaty, should also have been based on Article 100 which deals with the harmonisation of law. The Court held that Article 43 was a sufficient legal basis even though the Council had departed from its usual practice of basing measures in the field in question on Articles 43 and 100. However, the plaintiff succeeded on other grounds (*infra*, at (b)). The second circumstance in which lack of competence is pleaded is in the context of the delegation of powers (*supra*, para. 4.48). This ground was unsuccessfully relied on in *AKZO v EC Commission*[2] where the plaintiff argued that the delegation by the Commission to the Commissioner responsible for competition matters of the power to order undertakings to submit to investigations under Article 14 of Regulation 17 of 1962 was in breach of the principle of collective responsibility outlined in Article 17 of the Merger Treaty.

(b) Infringement of an essential procedural requirement.
There are two recurring circumstances in which this ground of appeal is pleaded:

(i) Lack of consultation. In *Transocean Marine Paint Association v EC Commission*[3] the plaintiff had applied for an exemption under Article 85(3) of the Treaty in respect of an agreement between its members. The exemption was granted but it included an onerous condition upon which the view of the plaintiff had not been solicited during the exemption procedure. The Court annulled the offending condition. In the *Roquette Frères*[4] and *Maizena*[5] cases the Court annulled a Council regulation because the Council had deliberately failed to procure the opinion of the European Parliament. In *United Kingdom v EC Council*[6] the plaintiff succeeded in its claim for the annulment of a directive on the use of hormones in livestock because in the Council the written procedure was utilised despite the opposition of two Member States. Article 6(1) of the Rules of Procedure of the Council requires the approval of all Member States before recourse can be made to the written procedure.

(ii) Lack of reasoning. Article 190 of the Treaty requires Regulations, Directives and Decisions to state the reasons on which they are based and to refer to any proposals or opinions, which were required to be obtained pursuant to the Treaty. This requirement accounts for the preamble, found in virtually every act of the institutions, which lists the Treaty articles or secondary legislation upon which the acts are based, the institutions which have been consulted, as well as an account of the reasoning underlying the measure ('Whereas . . .'). The importance of the reasoning requirement was given in *Germany v EEC Commission*,[7] a case which involved an application for a tariff quota of 450,000 hectolitres of cheap wine for the production of 'brennwein'. The Commission had approved a quota of only 100,000 hectolitres without indicating clearly why and how it had fixed the lower figure. The Court held that the obligation under Article 190 was not restricted to purely formal considerations. Rather

'. . . (it) seeks to give an opportunity to the parties of defending their rights, to the Court of exercising its supervisory functions and to the Member States and to all interested nationals of ascertaining the circumstance in which the Commission has applied the Treaty. To attain these objectives, it is sufficient for the decision to set out, in a concise but clear and relevant manner, the principal issues of law and of fact upon which it is based and which are necessary in order that the reasoning which has led the Commission to its decision may be understood.'

The Court held that the Commission had not complied with this requirement.

(c) Infringement of the Treaty or of any rule of law laid down for its application.

The first part of this ground of appeal is the most commonly invoked ground of review because its breadth encompasses virtually any vitiating factor in a measure which is being challenged. Accordingly, it tends to be pleaded in addition to other more appropriate grounds of review.[8] The second part of this ground of appeal is nearly as wide. It has been suggested[9] that each of the following can be regarded as sources of rules of law relating to the application of the Treaty:

(1) Community acts (including acts *sui generis*);
(2) Subsidiary conventions;
(3) Acts of the representatives of the Member States;
(4) Treaties with non-Member States binding on the Community;
(5) General principles of Community law.

The final category would also include general principles drawn from the laws of the Member States. An example can be seen in *Consorzio Cooperative d'Abruzzo v EC Commission*[10] where the plaintiff relied successfully on the principles of legal certainty and protection of legitimate expectation in its claim for the annulment of a Commission Decision which withdrew certain financial contributions from it.

(d) Misuse of powers.
This is the least frequently utilised ground of appeal partly because of the difficulty of proof:[11] it is necessary to establish the motive or the intention of the authority exercising the power.[12] In *AKZO v EC Commission*[13] the plaintiff complained that the delegation by the Commission to one of its members of the power to order investigations of undertakings suspected of infringing Articles 85 and 86 of the Treaty was a misuse of power; the 'delicate' circumstances surrounding such investigations should have led the Commissioner responsible for competition to have the decision adopted by the full Commission. The Court rejected this claim.

1 Case 68/86 O.J. C 74, 22.3.1988 p. 6.
2 Case 5/85 [1987] 3 C.M.L.R. 716.
3 *Supra*, fn. 12, para. 12.18.
4 Case 138/79 *Roquette Frères SA v EC Council* [1980] E.C.R. 3333.
5 Case 139/79 *Maizena GmbH v EC Council* [1980] E.C.R. 3393.
6 *Supra*, fn. 1.
7 Case 24/62 [1963] E.C.R. 63, [1963] C.M.L.R. 347.
8 T.C. Hartley, *The Foundations of European Community Law* (1981), at p. 436.
9 *Idem*, at pp. 436–8.
10 Supra, fn. 6, para. 12.18.
11 H.G. Schermers, *Judicial Protection in the European Communities*, (Fourth Edition, 1987) at p. 196.
12 T.C. Hartley, *The Foundations of European Community Law* (1981), at p. 438.
13 *Supra*, fn. 2.

Natural and legal persons

12.22 If the Member States and the institutions are privileged litigants under Article 173 then natural and legal persons are non-privileged or underprivileged because the Treaty places severe restraints on their capacity to bring an action; these restraints have been interpreted most restrictively by the Court of Justice. The rulings of the Court have been a focus for critical comment for over two decades, but one explanation for the restrictiveness of the Treaty in this regard suggests that there was a traditional aversion in the original Member States to empowering the courts to determine the constitutional validity of laws:[1] accordingly, in the Community system, only the privileged litigants would be permitted to seek the annulment of Community acts of a normative nature.

Natural and legal persons can challenge decisions (within the meaning of Article 189) addressed to themselves, acts which, although in the form of a regulation, are actually decisions of direct and individual concern to the applicant, and decisions addressed to other persons which are of direct and individual concern to the applicant.

The least difficulty arises in connection with decisions addressed to the applicant. The majority of cases in this category involve appeals for the annulment of decisions taken by the Commission in application of Articles 85 and 86 of the Treaty. In these circumstances the plaintiff does not have to prove *locus standi*, but does have to convince the Court that the decision is vitiated on one of the grounds of appeal (*supra*, para. 12.21).

Natural and legal persons cannot sue for the annulment of directives. The logic for this exclusion is clear: Article 189 states that directives are addressed to the Member States. Directives require some action, legislative or administrative, to transform them into domestic law, and any resulting rights or duties arise primarily as a matter of domestic law; the main concern of Community law will be whether the directive has been implemented correctly, if at all, by the national transforming measures. Regulations, by contrast, are not addressed to anyone; they are of general application and do not require transformation into domestic law. Thus, there is a much greater possibility that a regulation, or some provisions of it, will affect individual interests in a harmful way, and the second paragraph of Article 173 allows an applicant to allege that a regulation (or a provision thereof) is in fact a 'disguised' decision. It is at this point that the distinction between measures of general and individual application (*supra*, para. 12.18) becomes important. When a claim is lodged for the annulment of a regulation or a provision in a regulation the Court will examine the measure to determine whether it is a normative act of general application; as soon as this is established the Court will declare the action inadmissible. As a general rule, it is only when the Court finds that a regulation or provision thereof is an individual decision[2] or a bundle of decisions[3] or a collective decision[4] relating to named addressees, and is not an integral part of a normative or regulatory scheme, that it will go on to examine whether the contested measure is vitiated on the grounds claimed by the plaintiff.

The tests of 'direct and individual concern' also arise where an applicant is challenging a decision addressed to another person. In *Plaumann v EEC Commission*[5] the Court gave a liberal interpretation to 'person' for the purposes of such an action and held that it included a Member State. But the remainder of the Court's judgment was far more restrictive. The plaintiff, an importer of clementines, had applied to the Court for the annulment of a Commission Decision addressed to the Federal Republic which refused a request by the latter under Article 26(3) of the Treaty to suspend the collection of duties on imported clementines. It need hardly be stressed that a Member State invariably makes such requests on the instigation of private parties engaged in the trade in question and does not make the application on its own behalf.

However, the Court considered that the plaintiff was not individually concerned:

> Persons other than those to whom a decision is addressed may only claim to be individually concerned if that decision affects them by reason of certain attributes which are peculiar to them or by reason of circumstances in which they are differentiated from all other persons and by virtue of these factors distinguishes them individually just as in the case of the person addressed. In the present case the applicant is affected by the disputed decision as an importer of clementines, that is to say, by reason of a commercial activity which may at any time be practised by any person and is not therefore such as to distinguish the applicant in relation to the contested decision as in the case of the addressee.

The Court declared the action inadmissible. It should be noted in passing that the Court reversed the order of the tests set out in Article 173, second paragraph, and considered whether the applicant was 'individually concerned'. It will only consider 'direct concern' if the applicant has satisfied the second limb of the test.[6]

It is virtually impossible to comply with the test of 'individual concern'. However, it would appear that there are two circumstances in which the Court will attribute individual concern to an applicant:

(i) Where the contested decision involves an element of retroactivity affecting the interests of the applicant:[7] *Toepfer v EEC Commission;*[8] *Bock v EC Commission.*[9]

(ii) Where the applicant has been the complainant under a Community scheme which results in a decision addressed to the party whose behaviour is the subject matter of the complaint: *Metro v EC Commission;*[10] *Fediol v EC Commission;*[11] *Cofaz v EC Commission.*[12]

'Direct concern' is less difficult to establish. It is interpreted in a manner similar to the concept of direct effects[13] in the sense that the addressee must have no discretion as regards the implementation of the Decision and that it requires no further implementation.

Having overcome these barriers to the admissibility of an application for annulment of a Decision the plaintiff must go on to prove that the Decision is void on one of the four grounds of appeal (*supra*, para. 12.21).

1 Hjalte Rasmussen in *Thirty Years of Community Law* (1981) at p. 158.
2 Case 100/74 *C.A.M. v EC Commission*, [1975] E.C.R. 1393.
3 Joined Cases 41–44/70 *International Fruit Co v EC Commission*, [1971] E.C.R. 411, [1975] 2 C.M.L.R. 515.
4 See, for example Case 113/77 *NTN Toyo Bearing Co Ltd v EC Council* [1979] E.C.R. 1185, [1979] 2 C.M.L.R. 257.
5 Case 25/62 [1963] E.C.R. 95, [1964] C.M.L.R. 29.
6 Ami Barav, *Direct and Individual Concern: An Almost Insurmountable Barrier to the Admissibility of Individual Appeals to the EEC Court*, (1974) 11 C.M.L. Rev. 191, at p. 192.
7 *Idem*, at p. 196.
8 Joined Cases 106–107/63 [1965] E.C.R. 405, [1966] C.M.L.R. 111.

9 Case 62/70 [1971] E.C.R. 897, [1972] C.M.L.R. 160.
10 Case 26/76 [1977] E.C.R. 1875, [1978] 2 C.M.L.R. 1.
11 Case 191/82 [1983] E.C.R. 2913, [1984] 3 C.M.L.R. 244.
12 Case 169/84 [1986] E.C.R. 391, [1986] 3 C.M.L.R. 385.
13 Barav, *op. cit.* fn. 7 *supra*; at p. 193.

12.23 The restrictiveness of the EEC system for natural and legal persons can be contrasted with the ECSC system. Article 33 of the ECSC Treaty allows for appeals by undertakings against 'general decisions' (the equivalent of EEC regulations) on grounds of misuse of powers. On the other hand, the number of potential applicants under Article 33 is strictly limited because Article 80 of the ECSC Treaty defines undertakings as any undertakings engaged in the production of coal or steel: in *Vloeberghs v High Authority*[1] an enterprise which screened, washed and made briquettes out of imported coal was held not to be an undertaking within the meaning of Article 80.

The effect of the restrictive interpretation of Article 173 of the EEC Treaty can be seen in the number of applications which have been lodged over the years. At the end of 1987 there had been 604 applications under Article 173: 404 had been initiated by Community institutions, 119 by governments of the Member States and only 21 by individuals.[2] Of the individual applications just one has been initiated by an Irish applicant: *Irish Cement v EC Commission*[3] which has not yet been heard by the Court.

However, the restrictiveness of the EEC system may be eased somewhat by the establishment of a tribunal of first instance (*infra*, para. 12.43).

1 Cases 9, 12/60 [1961] E.C.R. 197.
2 21st General Report, 1987; Table 2 of the Annex to Chapter IV.
3 Case 220/86, O.J. C. 252, 9.10.1986. p. 7.

12.24 Article 174 of the EEC Treaty provides that if the Court considers that an action under Article 173 is well-founded it shall declare the act concerned to be void. Requirements of legal certainty demand that in the case of a regulation the Court may state which of the effects of the regulation which it has declared void shall be considered as definitive: a recent example can be seen in the case of *EC Commission v EC Council*[1] where the Court annulled a series of Council regulations on generalised tariff preferences because they failed to disclose the Treaty provisions on which they were based, but held that the requirements of legal certainty made it appropriate to declare definitive the effects of the said regulations.

1 Case 45/86 [1988] 2 C.M.L.R. 131.

The action for failure to act

12.25 Article 175 may be described as the converse procedure to the action for annulment: it provides a remedy against failure by the Council or the Commission to act. The procedure is not heavily utilised: at the end of 1987 only 25 cases had been decided with 4 cases pending. Of the decided cases 19 had been declared inadmissible.[1]

As in the case of Article 173 there are privileged and non-privileged applicants. Article 175 names the privileged applicants as the Member States and the institutions of the Communities. This differs from Article 173 which names the privileged institutions as the Council and Commission. Despite early doctrinal doubt on the matter it is now clear that the European Parliament can commence proceedings under Article 175. In *European Parliament v EC Council*[2] the Court sustained the plaintiff's claim that the defendant had failed to implement the Common Transport Policy insofar as it concerned the freedom to provide services in the international transport sphere. It also decided that the fact that one of the tasks of the European Parliament was to exercise a political review of the activities of the Commission and to a certain extent of the Council, was not capable of restricting its exercise of the same right of action given to all the institutions of the Community under Article 175.

Article 175 states that an action will be admissible only if the institution concerned has been called upon to act; this presupposes a definite demand which alleges that the institution is in default of its obligation to act.[3] The institution then has two months in which to 'define its position'; if it fails to do so the action may be brought within a further two months. The demand for action by the applicant is designed to allow the institution to take action if its transpires that its inaction was the result of an oversight. The definition of position by the institution defines the subject matter of the action and also serves as a marker for the purposes of the two-month time limit for the initiation of actions.[4] One question which has not been fully resolved is whether the definition of position by the institution renders any further action inadmissible.[5] In *Lütticke v EEC Commission*[6] the Court seemed to indicate that no further action could be taken, but the judgment in that case was concerned with a demand by the applicant that the Commission initiate proceedings under Article 169 against the Federal Republic of Germany. As we have already noted (*supra*, para. 12.8) the Commission has an absolute discretion as to whether it will commence proceedings against a Member State. In subsequent cases the Court has not repeated the somewhat peremptory *dictum* from the *Lütticke* case. The better view is that 'definition of position' merely acts as a procedural device to constitute or narrow the issues between the parties for the purposes of later litigation. Seen in this light, it would analogous to the 'implied negative decision' described in the third paragraph of Article 33 of the ECSC Treaty which provides a similar remedy against the inaction of the High Authority (Commission).

The institution which is called upon to act must be under an obligation to act: if the power to act is discretionary no obligation can be imputed to the institution. In *European Parliament v EC Council*[7] the Court rejected the larger claim by the plaintiff that the Council had failed to implement the Common Transport Policy because the Treaty had given the Council a discretion to determine the priorities in the gradual implementation of that Policy. It was only in respect of the freedom to provide services in the international transport sector that the Council lacked that discretion; in the latter context the Council had been obliged to act and had failed to do so.

Natural and legal persons can, under the same conditions applicable to privileged applicants, complain to the Court that an institution has failed to address to that person an act other than a recommendation or an opinion.

In practice, this places the non-privileged applicant in the same position as the non-privileged claimaint under the second paragraph of Article 173 because the only act that can be addressed to an individual is a decision. In *Chevalley v EC Commission*[8] the plaintiff was concerned about Italian draft legislation on agrarian rents which he considered would give rise to differences between the Member States. He called upon the Commission to initiate consultations under Articles 101 and 102 of the Treaty (on the harmonisation of laws) and to instruct him what to do in the event that the Italian proposal became law. The Court held that there was no obligation to act and that the advice sought by the plaintiff would constitute only an opinion in the context of Article 189 of the Treaty. Similarly, in *Lord Bethell v EC Commission*[9] the plaintiff failed in his application to establish that the Commission had failed to act against agreements and concerted practices which he alleged existed between airlines operating scheduled passenger flights in Europe. The Court held that the applicant was not asking the Commission to take a decision in respect of him, but to open an enquiry with regard to third parties and to take decisions applicable to them.

There have been two cases under Article 175 involving Irish litigants. In 1984 in *Ireland v EC Commission*[10] the State commenced proceedings against the Commission for failure to modify data upon which the milk 'super-levy' was to be calculated. The action was withdrawn when agreement was reached between Ireland and the Commission on this issue. The only other action commenced by an Irish applicant is still pending before the Court. In *Irish Cement v EC Commission*[11] the plaintiff initiated proceedings against the Commission for failure to open a procedure under Article 93(2) of the Treaty in respect of an award of a capital grant by the Northern Ireland Development Board to a private enterprise for the construction of a cement factory.

1 21st General Report 1987; Table 2 of the Annex to Chapter IV.
2 Case 13/83 [1985] E.C.R. 1513, [1986] 1 C.M.L.R. 138.
3 Joined Cases 22–23/60 *Elz v High Authority* [1961] E.C.R. 181.
4 H.G. Schermers, *Judicial Protection in the European Communities*, Fourth Edition (1987), at p. 224.
5 A.G. Toth, *The Law as it Stands on the Appeal for Failure to Act*, L.I.E.I. 1975/2, 65; at pp. 82–3.
6 Case 48/65 [1966] E.C.R. 19, [1966] C.M.L.R. 378.
7 *Supra*, fn. 2.
8 Case 15/70 [1970] E.C.R. 975.
9 Case 246/81 [1982] E.C.R. 2277, [1982] 3 C.M.L.R. 300.
10 Case 257/84 O.J. C 256, 8.10.1985 p. 3.
11 Case 166/86 O.J. C 204, 13.8.1986 p. 6.

The plea of illegality

12.26 Article 184 of the EEC Treaty compensates in part for the limited right of access by natural and legal persons to the Court under Article 173. The right of action conferred by Article 184, however, may be utilised by any party to proceedings in which a regulation of the Council or Commission is in issue, and that party may plead the grounds specified in the first paragraph of Article 173 in order to invoke before the Court the inapplicability of that regulation. In one sense it can be said that the procedural restraints imposed by Article 173, in terms of the very brief time limit for the initiation of actions (two months) and the impossibility for private parties to initiate direct actions for the annulment of regulations, militates against the discovery and annulment of invalid regulations. Article 184 recognises these limitations but it provides an ancillary remedy only. A declaration of the inapplicability of a regulation is only contemplated in proceedings brought before the Court under some other provision of the Treaty, and then only incidentally and with limited effect: *Milchwerke Wöhrmann v EEC Commission.*[2] Litigants are not permitted to use Article 184 as an independent means of challenging a regulation: *Etoile Commerciale v EC Commission.*[3] There must be a causal link between the measure at issue in the main proceedings, for example the decision addressed to the applicant (which is being challenged under Article 173) and an earlier regulation the illegality of which is being alleged. In *Italy v EEC Council and Commission*[4] the plaintiff's claim did not succeed because the Court refuted its argument that Council Regulation (EEC) 19/65[5] was based on Regulation 17 of 1962,[6] which Italy claimed was tainted by illegality. In fact, Regulation 19/65 was based on Article 87 of the Treaty. In *EC Commission v Belgium,*[7] an action under the abbreviated infringement procedure contained in Article 93(2) (*supra*, para. 12.15) the Court rejected an attempt by the defendant to have the action declared inadmissible on the grounds that a decision taken by the Commission under Article 93(1) and addressed to Belgium was illegal. The Court criticised the Belgian attempt to avoid the consequences of its own failure to appeal against the decision at issue within the stipulated time limits by relying subsequently on Article 184. In any event, Article 184 was available only when a regulation was at issue and could not be invoked by a Member State to whom an individual decision had been addressed. On one occasion, however, the Court relaxed the requirement that the measure at issue in the main proceedings must be based on a prior (illegal) regulation. In *Simmenthal v EC Commission*[8] the Court annulled a Commission decision allocating import quotas for beef on the grounds that it was based on an invitation to tender which, although not in the form of a regulation, produced similar effects and would not have been amenable to challenge under Article 173 by a natural or legal person.

1 For an analysis, see Ami Barav, *The Exception of Legality in Community Law*, (1974) 11 C.M.L. Rev. 366.
2 Joined Cases 31, 33/62 [1962] E.C.R. 501, [1963] C.M.L.R. 152.
3 Joined Cases 89, 91/86 O.J. C 204 31.7.1987 p. 2.
4 Case 32/65 [1966] E.C.R. 389, [1969] C.M.L.R. 39.
5 O.J. (Sp. Ed.) 1965–66 p. 35.
6 O.J. (Sp. Ed.) 1959–62 p. 87.
7 Case 156/77 [1978] E.C.R. 1881.
8 Case 92/78 [1979] E.C.R. 777, [1980] 1 C.M.L.R. 25.

Staff cases

12.27 Nearly 40 per cent of all the cases initiated before the Court of Justice since 1953 have concerned disputes between civil servants of the Communities and the institutions by which they were employed. Article

179 gives the Court jurisdiction in such disputes, in accordance with the conditions laid down in the Staff Regulations.[1] Articles 91 and 92 of the Staff Regulations determine the conditions under which a dispute can come before the Court. The applicant must submit a complaint to the appointing authority against an act adversely affecting him/her either in terms of a definitive act or a failure to act; this complaint must be made within 3 months; complaints by an official must be submitted through his/her immediate superior; the official then has 3 months within which to appeal to the Court of Justice against the express or implied rejection of his/her complaint to the appointing authority. The procedure that then follows in the Court of Justice is similar to the action for annulment under Article 173 except that in cases involving financial considerations the Court has unlimited jurisidction.

It is an open secret that the members of the Court dislike staff cases;[2] these disputes tend to have a significant factual content but rarely involve legal issues of great moment. It is for this reason that staff cases will be relegated to the court of first instance, when it is established (*infra*, para. 12.43). But from time to time staff disputes have produced judgments establishing important principles. Examples include *Sabbatini (née Bertoni) v European Parliament*,[3] which dealt with the issue of equal pay for equal work; *Prais v EC Council*,[4] which dealt with the issue of religious discrimination; and *Misset v EC Council*,[5] which dealt with the issue of time limits for the purposes of initiating actions against acts of the institutions.

Finally, there have been a number of staff cases involving Irish nationals. In *Oslizlok v EC Commission*[6] the applicant succeeded in his action against a Commission decision which abolished his post 'in the interests of the service', without giving him an opportunity to argue his case for assignment to another post. In *Grogan v EC Commission*[7] the plaintiff succeeded in his claim for annulment of a Commission decision which reduced his pension. An interesting feature of the lattter case was that the applicant was represented before the Court by a Dublin solicitor. The conclusion to be drawn from this fact is that Irish practitioners should be alert to the possibility of claims on behalf of clients employed by the Communities either in Ireland or in other locations (*supra*, para.s 4.50–4.52; 4.63).

---

1 O.J. (Sp. Ed.) 1968 (I) p. 30. The Staff Regulations have been amended on more than 40 occasions.
2 L. Neville Brown and F.G. Jacobs, *The Court of Justice of the European Communities*, Second Edition (1983), Chapter 8.
3 Case 20/71 [1972] E.C.R. 345, [1972] C.M.L.R. 945.
4 Case 130/75 [1976] E.C.R. 1589, [1976] 2 C.M.L.R. 708.
5 *Supra*, fn. 1, para. 12.20.
6 Case 34/77 [1978] E.C.R. 1099.
7 Case 127/80 [1982] E.C.R. 869.

Tortious and contractual liability of the Community

12.28 Article 178 of the Treaty confers jurisdiction on the Court of Justice in cases concerning compensation for damage provided for in the second paragraph of Article 215. If we turn then to Article 215 we see that it concerns more than the 'non-contractual liability' of the Community: the second paragraph states that the Community shall make good any damage caused by its institutions or by its servants in the performance of their duties, in accordance with the general principles common to the laws of the Member States. However, the first and third paragraphs of Article 215 also deal with questions of liability and because these have been utilised relatively infrequently we will examine them before addressing the question of tortious liability of the Community.

12.29 The first paragraph of Article 215 states simply that the liability of the Community in contractual matters shall be governed by the law applicable to the contract in question. Two observations may be made about this provision: it is a standard private international law formula for determining the appropriate forum in which a contractual dispute should be litigated; and its serves to distinguish the Community from other international organisations and sovereign states in that the Treaty has not sought to confer on the Community immunity from suit in commercial matters.[1] It need hardly be emphasised that the Community enters into thousands of contracts annually in the various Member States in which its institutions, organs and representative offices are located; and it suffices to say that no significant disputes have arisen under this provision. Reference should also be made to Article 181 of the Treaty which provides that the Court shall have jurisdiction to give judgment pursuant to any arbitration clause contained in a contract concluded by or on behalf of the Community, whether that contract is governed by public or by private law. It has been suggested[2] that this provision refers to choice of law clauses in contracts rather than arbitration clauses properly so-called, and the judgment of the Court in *Pellegrini v EC Commission*[3] would appear to support that conclusion. This dispute came before the Court under Article 153 of the Euratom Treaty, which is identical to Article 181 of the EEC Treaty, and it concerned the tendering procedure for the award of a cleaning contract for the Joint Nuclear Research Centre at Ispra in Italy. The draft agreement utilised in the tendering process stipulated that Italian law was the governing law of the contract and that the Court of Justice was to have jurisdiction in any dispute between the Commission and the Contractor relating to the Agreement.

1 See, for examples of the application of the doctrine of sovereign immunity in commercial circumstances: *Saorstat and Continental SS Co v De las Morenas* [1945] I.R. 291; and *Zarine v Owners of SS 'Ramava'* [1942] I.R. 148.
2 T.C. Hartley, *The Foundations of European Community Law*, (1981) at p. 477.
3 Case 23/76 [1976] E.C.R. 1807, [1977] 2 C.M.L.R. 77.

12.30 The third paragraph of Article 215 provides that the personal liability of its servants towards the Community shall be governed by the provisions of the Staff Regulations[1] or conditions of employment applicable to them. Article 22 of the Staff Regulations provides that officials may be required to make good, in whole or in part, any damage suffered by the Communities as a result of serious misconduct in the course of, or connected with their duties. The Court has unlimited jurisdiction in such disputes. Moreover, whatever protection officials enjoy under the Protocol on Privileges and Immunities (*supra*, para. 4.61) is accorded solely in the interests of the Communities, and Article 23 of the Staff Regulations makes it clear that officials are not exempt from fulfilling their private law obligations or from complying with the laws and police regulations in force in the Member State in which the Community institution to which they are attached is located.

1 *Supra*, fn. 1, para. 12.27.

12.31 The second paragraph of Article 215 states that the non-contractual (or tortious) liability of the Communities shall be determined in accordance with '. . . the general principles common to the laws of the Member States'. It was to be expected that the phrase 'principles common to the laws of the Member States' would have generated a fertile jurisprudence but, in practice, the similarity of the law of the original Member States meant that this requirement did not give rise to much difficulty and, by the time the common law countries joined the Community, civil law principles were firmly established and no significant alteration of those principles took place. Instead, all the controversy has attached to the restrictive attitude adopted by the Court to the whole notion of the Community's tortious liability; out of 167 cases decided by the end of 1987, 137 were dismissed on the merits, 18 were rejected as inadmissible and only 12 were decided in favour of the applicant.[1] Moreover, the majority of successful litigants, who had secured rulings establishing Community liability in principle, failed to establish measurable loss and, consequently, failed in their claim for damages.

Not surprisingly, the problems surrounding the use of Article 215 as a remedy commenced with the decision of the Court in *Plaumann v EC Commission*.[2] We have already noted (*supra*, para. 12.22) that the decision in this case significantly limited access to the Court by private parties. Apart from seeking the annulment of the decision at issue the plaintiff also sought damages from the Commission but the Court held that:

> '. . . an administrative measure which has not been annulled cannot of itself constitute a wrongful act on the part of the administration inflicting damage upon those whom it affects.'

This meant that before an action for damages could be commenced a successful action for annulment must have been initiated. For natural and legal persons this raised almost an insuperable admissibility barrier.

In the 1970s the Court began to reassess its approach to the application of Article 215. In a series of cases commencing with *Lütticke v EC Commission*[3] and *Schöppenstedt v EC Commission*[4] and culminating with *Merkur v EC Commission*[5] the Court recognised that Article 215 established an independent appeal procedure which had a special function in the system of remedies established by the Treaty and that it was possible to establish the illegality of Community measures in the same proceedings as the application for damages. Nonetheless, this relaxation of the admissibility rules was accompanied by safeguards: the Court would not permit Article 215 to be used as a means of attack against measures which could have been the subject matter of a timely action for annulment under

Article 173. Thus, natural and legal persons could not challenge decisions under Article 215 if the two-month time limit in Article 173 had elapsed.

A second obstacle to successful claims under Article 215 concerned 'the special problem of wrongful legislation'.[6] In the law of most Member States it is not possible to recover damages for loss caused by normative rules (legislation), although some Member States allow for actions in respect of delegated or second legislation.[7] The Treaty is silent on the issue and the Court has taken the view that such actions are not automatically precluded. Predictably, it does not entertain such claims easily. If the regulation at issue concerns a field of activity where the Community legislator is faced with alternative policy options and is vested with the exercise of a wide discretion in terms of implementation (which is especially true of the CAP), then the Court will be extremely reluctant to award compensation to injured parties although it might declare invalid the regulation in question: *Bayerische HNL Vermehrungsbetriebe v EC Council and Commission.*[8]

In such circumstances, individuals have to accept within reasonable limits certain harmful effects on their economic interests as a result of legislative measures, without being able to obtain compensation from public funds, even if that measure has been declared null and void. Damages will be available only in cases where claimants can demonstrate, in actions for compensation in respect of legislative measures involving choices as to economic policy, that there has been a 'sufficiently flagrant violation of a superior rule of law for the protection of individuals': *Schöppenstedt v EC Commission.*[9] In a recent decision, *Zuckerfabrik Bedburg v EEC,*[10] the Court restated this requirement but dismissed the claimant's appeal for damages on each of a number of the grounds which have come to be recognised as 'superior rules of law for the protection of individuals': the right to property; the principle of non-discrimination; the general principle of equality; the principle of proportionality. To this might be added the principle of breach of legitimate expectations.

As if these requirements were not difficult enough to prove, the Court has demonstrated a remarkable alacrity to shift the burden of liability to the Member States. This is particularly the case where the implementation of Community law is in the hands of domestic civil servants; where errors on the part of the latter give rise to a claim for damages the Court has stated categorically the correct course of action is to sue the national authorities in the national courts: *IBC v EC Commission.*[11] But, in the event that the Community and the Member State authorities are jointly or concurrently liable for damage resulting from the implementation of Community law, the claimant must first establish liability on the part of the national authorities in the domestic courts before initiating proceedings before the Court of Justice: *Kampffmeyer v EEC Commission.*[12] Most commentators agree that this feature of the case law of the Court is unsatisfactory and that it has exposed a serious gap in the system of legal protection under Community law.[13]

It must be concluded, as regards the admissibility of actions under Article 215, that the likelihood of being awarded damages is particularly remote. However, one positive aspect should be noted. Natural and legal persons cannot sue directly for the annulment of regulations under Article

173; their remedy lies mainly in the hands of the national courts, which are empowered to seek rulings under Article 177 on the validity of acts of the institutions. The procedure under Article 177 can be very lengthy; accordingly, it is not uncommon for a litigant to commence proceedings in the domestic court, alleging the invalidity of a regulation, and simultaneously to lodge a claim for damages under Article 215. In *Schöppenstedt v EC Commission*[14] the Court held that the non-contractual liability invoked by the litigant presupposes at least the invalidity of the act allegedly causing the damage, so that the claimant has an opportunity to establish the nullity of the regulation much earlier than if the national court alone were to submit the question to the Court of Justice. In other words, the application for compensation inherent in the Article 215 procedure is of less importance than establishing the invalidity of the regulation at issue.

1 21st General Report, 1987; Table 2 of the Annex to Chapter IV.
2 *Supra*, fn. 5, para. 12.22.
3 Case 4/69 [1971] E.C.R. 325.
4 Case 5/71 [1971] E.C.R. 975.
5 Case 43/72 [1973] E.C.R. 1055.
6 Henry G. Schermers, *The Law as it Stands on the Appeal for Damages*, L.I.E.I. 1975/1, pp. 113–45, at p. 119.
7 *Idem*.
8 Joined cases 83, 94/76, 4, 15, 40/77 [1978] E.C.R. 1209, [1978] 3 C.M.L.R. 566.
9 *Supra*, fn. 4.
10 Case 281/84 O.J. C 26, 4.2.1987 p. 3.
11 Case 46/75 [1976] E.C.R. 65.
12 Joined cases 5, 7, 13–24/66 [1967] E.C.R. 245.
13 See, for example, Christopher Harding, *The choice of law problem in cases of non-contractual liability under EEC law*, (1979) 16 C.M.L. Rev. 389; T.C. Hartley, *The Foundations of European Community Law* (1981), Chapter 21, *passim*.
14 *Supra*, fn. 4.

12.32 Assuming that a litigant has overcome all the obstacles placed in the way of his claim for damages, what must he prove? In *Lütticke v EC Commission*[1] the Court held that by virtue of the second paragraph of Article 215 and the general principles to which it refers

> '. . . the liability of the Community presupposes the existence of a set of circumstances comprising actual damage, a causal link between the damage claimed and the conduct alleged against the institution, and the illegality of such conduct.'

The damage must have been caused by one of the institutions or by one of its servants in the course of their duties. In *Sayag v Leduc*[2] an official of the Commission of Euratom (as it then was) attempted to avoid liability for personal injuries sustained by other officials while in an automobile driven by him; his defence failed because he had been employed as a bureaucrat and not as a driver, so that the damage sustained by his colleagues had not occurred in the performance of his duties.

The case of *Adams v EC Commission*[3] illustrates another feature of the action for damages: the liability of the Community may be diminished by the contributory negligence of the plaintiff. In this instance the plaintiff had provided the Commission with incriminating evidence of restrictive practices on the part of his employers, Hoffmann-La Roche. His disclosures led to the imposition of a fine on the latter,[4] but during their investigation of the alleged restrictive practice officials of the Commission let employees of Hoffmann-La Roche see documents which enabled the latter to identify the informant. In the meantime, the plaintiff had resigned from Hoffmann-La Roche but was arrested and charged with economic espionage under Swiss law when entering Switzerland on holiday with his family. He was held *incommunicado* for nearly two weeks during which time his wife committed suicide. He was subsequently tried and convicted in the Swiss criminal courts. In his action for damages under Article 215 the Court held that the Commission had infringed its duty of confidentiality to him but it also concluded that he should have been aware of the risks to which his conduct towards his former employer had exposed him with regard to Swiss legislation, and the he had failed to inform the Commission that his identity could be inferred from the documents he had supplied. The plaintiff's contributory negligence amounted to 50 per cent of the damage suffered by him as a result of the fact that he was identified as the source of the damning information. The Court also held that the amount of the damages was to be agreed between the parties, or failing such agreement, by the Court itself.

1 *Supra*, fn. 3, para. 12.36.
2 Case 5/68 [1968] E.C.R. 395, [1969] C.M.L.R. 12.
3 Case 145/83 [1985] E.C.R. 3539, [1986] 1 C.M.L.R. 506.
4 Decision of 9 June 1976. See Case 85/76 *Hoffmann-La Roche v EC Commission* [1979] E.C.R. 461, [1979] 3 C.M.L.R. 211.

Penalties

12.33 The competence of the Court under Article 215 is often described as plenary or unlimited: this notion marks the distinction between actions such as Article 173, where the grounds of appeal are limited, and other actions where the Court and the parties are not procedurally hindered. Another example of the Court's plenary jurisdiction relates to penalties provided for in regulations made by the Council. The significant regulation in this regard is Council Regulation 17 of 1962.[1] Articles 15 and 16 of this regulation empower the Commission to impose fines and periodic penalty payments so as to control restrictive practices and abuses of dominant position; the level of fines that the Commission may impose is fixed at 10,000,000 ECU or up to 10 per cent of the turnover of the participating enterprises. The power to impose periodic penalty payments allows for daily fines ranging from 50 ECU to 1,000 ECU. In such cases the court has the power to increase the fine or penalty, although in most cases it has confirmed, reduced or annulled the charge. The fact that an enterprise may have been fined under national competition law for the same offence does not provide a defence; but the principle of *non bis in idem* requires the Commission to take national fines into account when fixing Community fines.[2]

1 O.J. (Sp. Ed.) 1959–62 p. 87.
2 Case 45/69 *Boehringer Mannheim v EC Commission* [1970] E.C.R. 769.

Interim Orders

12.34 Article 185 of the Treaty provides that the initiation of an action before the Court does not have the effect of suspending the act or acts under review but, if necessary, the Court can order that the contested act be suspended. Article 186 authorises the court to prescribe any necessary interim measures in cases before it. These two actions resemble national procedures for stays of execution and for injunctive relief. Article 36 of the Statute of the Court empowers the President of the Court, by way of summary procedure, to adjudicate on applications under Articles 185 and 186 and, according to Article 83 of the Rules of Procedure, an action for a stay of execution of an act under Article 185 is admissible only if the plaintiff has challenged the act in proceedings before the Court; a request for interim measures under Article 186 is admissible only if it is made by one of the parties in a case before the Court and refers to that case. The request for a stay of execution or for interim measures must state the subject matter of the dispute, the circumstances giving rise to urgency and the grounds of fact and of law to support a *prima facie* justification for the granting of the interim measure requested.

A survey in 1979[1] suggested that the Court had not developed any consistent principles to govern its awards. The survey concluded that:

- except in cases concerning the competition law of the Communities the applicants' chances of success are not good.
- the Court will not go beyond the protection of the rights at issue in the main claim, nor will it by its award of interim measures pre-judge the main claim or prejudice its effectiveness.
- interim measures will not be allowed where the main action is manifestly not well-founded.
- to succeed the applicant must show that the refusal of interim measures is likely to cause him irreparable harm. The Court will balance this possibility against the possible harm to the defendant and to third parties that would result from an award of interim measures.
- the Court will not interfere with the executive or legislative acts of the Community organs by substituting its own discretion for theirs.

The interim powers granted by the Court under Articles 185 and 186 are not confined to acts of the Community or its institutions: in *EC Commission v Ireland*[2] the Court ordered the State to suspend the operation of the Sea Fisheries (Preservation and Rational Exploitation) Orders (Nos. 1 & 2) of 1977[3] pending the full hearing of the main action under Article 169. An earlier request by the Commission had been refused because it transpired at the hearing that the parties both wished to reach an amicable settlement. When the main action was tried the Court considered that the Irish measures discriminated against fishing vessels from other Member States.

1 Catherine Grey, *Interim measures of protection in the European Court*, (1979) 4 E.L. Rev. 80.
2 Case 61/77R [1977] E.C.R. 1411, [1978] 2 C.M.L.R. 466.
3 S.I. No. 38 of 1977, S.I. No. 39 of 1977.

References for preliminary rulings: Article 177

12.35 As we have already observed the Community legal system is proto-federal in nature. The greater part of the legislation adopted by the Council and Commission applies directly and with general effect throughout the Member States in the form of Regulations, and many provisions of domestic law are based on primary obligations contained in Community Directives. Community law, therefore, forms part of the legal systems of the Member States and the courts of the Member States are obliged to apply and interpret points of Community law which arise in disputes that come before them. Article 177 serves a dual purpose: it enables courts and tribunals to seek the assistance of the Court of Justice when they encounter points of difficulty in cases before them; and it enables the Court of Justice, as the central or 'Supreme' Court in the Community legal order, to achieve a uniformity of interpretation in the application of Community law by national courts and tribunals. Article 177 can be described, therefore, as an instrument of judicial cooperation, and it is not unlike the 'case stated' procedure in the domestic legal system. It is also the means by which the interests of natural and legal persons are protected within the Community legal order; the validity of normative acts of Community law, i.e. regulations, can be questioned in references under Article 177 whereas Article 173—the action for annulment—precludes direct action against regulations by natural and legal persons. Finally, Article 177 has been the vehicle through which the Court has articulated the two central concepts of Community law: the doctrine of supremacy of Community law; and the doctrine of direct effects.

Article 177

The Court of Justice shall have jurisdiction to give preliminary rulings concerning:

(a) the interpretation of this Treaty:
(b) the validity and interpretation of acts of the institutions of the Community;
(c) the interpretation of the statutes of bodies established by an act of the Council, where those statutes so provide.

Where such a question is raised before any court or tribunal of a Member State, that court or tribunal may, if it considers that a decision on the question is necessary to enable it to give judgment, request the Court of Justice to give a ruling thereon.

Where any such question is raised in a case pending before a court or tribunal of a Member State, against whose decisions there is no judicial remedy under national law, that court or tribunal shall bring the matter before the Court of Justice.

The competence of the Court of Justice under Article 177

12.36 According to the first paragraph of Article 177 the jurisdiction of the Court arises under three headings (*supra*, para. 12.35), the third of which has been of little significance. It should be noted that while the Court has the power to give rulings on the interpretation of the Treaty it has no jurisdiction to give rulings on the validity of the Treaty. Nonetheless, requests for rulings on the interpretation of the Treaty, which for the purposes of Article 177 includes amending treaties such as the Acts of Accession, are commonplace; an Irish example can be seen in *Campus Oil Ltd v Minister for Industry and Energy*[1] where, in the context of a dispute over an obligation to purchase petroleum products from the Whitegate Oil Refinery in Cork Harbour, the High Court sought a ruling on the interpretation of Articles 30 and 36 of the Treaty. The second head of competence—rulings on the interpretation or validity of acts of the institutions—is most frequently invoked although there have been considerably fewer cases relating to validity of acts of the institutions than cases on interpretation. Up to the end of 1987 the Court gave rulings on 1,317 requests for preliminary rulings, 1,120 of which related to interpretation and only 197 of which related to validity.[2]

Irish examples of requests for preliminary rulings on the interpretation of acts of the institutions can be seen in *Lee v Minister for Agriculture*,[3] in which the High Court on Circuit sought a ruling as to whether the Farm Modernisation Scheme, introduced by Council Directive (EEC) 72/159[4] encompassed grants for the erection of private dwelling houses; and *Anglo-Irish Meats v Minister for Agriculture*,[5] which involved questionable claims for monetary compensatory amounts under the Common Agricultural Policy, and in which the President of the High Court sought a ruling on the interpretation of Commission Regulation (EEC) 1380/75.[6] Most requests for rulings under this heading of the Court's competence concern Regulations and Directives but the Court will also give rulings on the interpretation of international agreements to which the Community is party. In *Haegeman v Belgium*,[7] the Court held that an association agreement with Greece, concluded under Articles 228 and 238 of the Treaty, was an act of one of the institutions of the Community for the purposes of Article 177.

The restrictive *locus standi* conditions developed by the Court of Justice in respect of applications by natural or legal persons for the annulment of acts of the institutions under Article 173 has meant that such applicants must pursue their remedy through the national courts; this is not an ideal solution because the power to seek a preliminary ruling is vested in the court or tribunal and not in the parties to the litigation, but it does provide the principal mechanism by which natural and legal persons can challenge the validity of Regulations and Directives. An example can be seen in *An Bord Bainne v Minister for Agriculture*[8] in which the High Court sought a ruling *inter alia* on the validity of Commission Regulation (EEC) 2517/74[9] on financial aid for the private storage of butter. The Court concluded that examination of the regulation had disclosed no factor of such a kind as to affect its validity.

It is clear that while the Court is empowered by Article 177 to declare invalid an act of an institution which is the subject matter of a reference by national court, the national courts themselves have no power to declare invalid acts of Community institutions. In a recent judgment, *Foto-Frost v Hauptzollamt Lübeck-Ost*[10] the act at issue in the domestic court was a Commission decision refusing permission to the Federal Minister of Finance to waive post-clearance recovery of duties imposed on binoculars originating in the German Democratic Republic. The Finanzgericht,

Hamburg asked the Court whether it had jurisdiction itself to declare a Commission Decision invalid. It doubted the validity of the decision at issue but considered that the Court of Justice alone was empowered by Article 177 to declare measures taken by the Community institutions invalid. The Court agreed, and held that the Treaty established a comprehensive system of legal remedies and procedures designed to entrust the Court with the task of reviewing the legality of measures taken by the institutions; it was necessary to emphasise that the Court was in the best position to give a ruling on the validity of Community measures. The Court went on to declare invalid the contested decision on post-clearance of import duties.

The powers of the Court under Article 177 relate to Community law; the Court has no competence to rule on the compatibility with Community law of provisions of national legislation: *Costa v ENEL*.[11] Nor is it possible for the Court to apply the provisions of Community law to the fact at issue in the domestic tribunal, but sometimes the reference by the national court is such as to make it extremely difficult for the Court to respond effectively. In *Société Technique Minière v Maschinenbau Ulm GmbH*[12] the Court held that whilst it had no power to take note of the application of the Treaty to specific cases it could extract from the elements of the case referred to it those questions of interpretation or validity which alone fall within its jurisdiction. It went on to suggest that the need to provide a 'serviceable interpretation of the provisions at issue' justified the national court in setting out the legal context in which the requested interpretation was to be placed. In other words, the national court should provide a suitable summary of the principal issues of law and of fact in the proceedings before it; otherwise, the Court will be obliged to give a ruling in the abstract which may be of no assistance to the national court. Although the Court may experience difficulty in extracting the necessary questions from the reference by the national court it will not criticise the judge or judges in question. In *Pigs Marketing Board (Northern Ireland) v Redmond*[13] the United Kingdom Government claimed that it experienced difficulty in identifying the legal problems arising in the context of criminal proceedings pending before the Resident Magistrate, Armagh. The RM had posed a total of 13 questions to the Court and the United Kingdom Government suggested that the Court should indicate before the oral hearing the questions which it regarded as relevant. The Court rejected this suggestion and held that the national court alone had a direct knowledge of the facts of the case and the arguments put forward by the parties and, because the national court would have to give judgment in the case, it was in the best position to appreciate the relevance of the questions of law raised by the dispute before it. But in the event that questions had been improperly formulated or went beyond the scope of the powers conferred on the Court by Article 177, the Court stated that it was free to extract from all the factors provided by the national court the elements of Community law requiring an interpretation.

The rationale for the Court's refusal to insist on a precise formal submission from national courts lies in its perception of the co-operative nature of the procedure under Article 177: in *Schwarze v Einfuhr- und Vorratsstelle für Getreide und Futtermittel*[14] the Court refused to reject a request for a preliminary ruling on the validity of an act of the institutions which had actually been formulated in terms of a question on interpretation. The Court's lack of insistence on formality has been taken to some extreme lengths: in *Wagner v Fohrmann and Krier*[15] the municipal court simply sent the entire file of the case to the Court of Justice which was content to extract from the file the relevant questions of Community law and provide a serviceable interpretation for the domestic court. However, despite this exaggerated lack of formality, the Court does insist that the questions must be submitted by the national court; it is not open to any of the parties to ask further questions or to alter the content of the questions submitted by the national court: *Hessische Knappschaft v Maison Singer*.[16]

In recent years the Court has refused jurisdiction in cases where no genuine dispute exists between the parties to the proceedings in the national court. In *Mattheus v Doego*[17] the Court questioned the legitimacy of a reference from a German court relating to an agreement containing a clause stipulating that its validity was dependent on a decision of the Court of Justice on the practicability in law of the accession of Portugal to the European Communities. The Court considered that such a clause deprived the national court of the independent exercise of the discretion conferred on it by Article 177 but, in the circumstances, responded to the questions submitted by the Court. But in *Foglia v Novello*[18] the Court refused jurisdiction in a reference from an Italian court whereby two private individuals, who were in agreement as to the result to be attained, had inserted a clause in their contract in order to induce the domestic court to give a ruling on that point. The Court will not entertain such an abuse of process.

1 Case 72/83 [1984] E.C.R. 2727, [1984] 3 C.M.L.R. 544.
2 21st General Report, 1987; Table 2 of the Annex to Chapter IV.
3 Case 152/79 [1980] E.C.R. 1495, [1980] 2 C.M.L.R. 682.
4 O.J. (Sp. Ed.) 1972 (II) p. 324.
5 Case 196/80 [1981] E.C.R. 2263.
6 O.J. L 139, 30.5.1975 p. 37.
7 Case 181/73 [1974] E.C.R. 449, [1975] 1 C.M.L.R. 515.
8 Case 92/77 [1978] E.C.R. 497, [1978] 2 C.M.L.R. 567.
9 O.J. L 269, 5.10.1974 p. 24.
10 Case 314/85 [1988] 3 C.M.L.R. 57.
11 Case 6/64 [1964] E.C.R. 585, [1964] C.M.L.R. 425.
12 Case 56/65 [1966] E.C.R. 235, [1966] C.M.L.R. 357.
13 Case 83/78 [1978] E.C.R. 2347, [1979] 1 C.M.L.R. 177.
14 Case 16/65 [1965] E.C.R. 877, [1966] C.M.L.R. 172.
15 Case 101/63 [1964] E.C.R. 195, [1964] C.M.L.R. 245.
16 Case 44/65 [1965] E.C.R. 965, [1966] C.M.L.R. 82.
17 Case 93/78 [1978] E.C.R. 2203, [1979] 1 C.M.L.R. 551.
18 Case 104/79 [1980] E.C.R. 745, [1981] 1 C.M.L.R. 45.

Courts and tribunals for the purposes of Article 177

12.37 What courts and tribunals may submit references to the Court of Justice for a preliminary ruling? Difficulties rarely arise in connection with courts properly so-called because the constitutions of the various Member States normally make provision for the exercise of judicial power. Difficulties do occur, however, in respect of tribunals and the Court has given some surprising decisions in this context.

In Ireland the courts entitled to refer to the Court of Justice under Article 177 are the courts established under Article 34 of the Constitution: the Supreme Court, the High Court and the other courts established by law, namely the courts of local and limited jurisidiction—the Circuit Court and the District Court—and the Court of Criminal Appeal.[1] The Special Criminal Court is also a court for the purposes of Article 177.[2] Community law has been pleaded in all but the Court of Criminal Appeal (*infra*, para. 13.1) and references have been made by all courts except the Special Criminal Court and Court of Criminal Appeal; a clear majority of the preliminary rulings requested by Irish courts have been submitted by the High Court.

It is reasonably easy to identify national courts but a much more difficult problem concerns the identification of a tribunal for the purposes of Article 177. The Court first encountered the issue in the case of *Vaassen-Göbbels v Beambtenfonds voor het Mijnbedrijf*.[3] That case concerned a request for an interpretation of the first Community regulation on social security matters and it was submitted by the arbitral tribunal of a Dutch social security fund. The fund itself contested the validity of the reference by the tribunal and argued that the tribunal was not a judicial institution for the purposes of Dutch law. However, the Court of Justice noted that the tribunal was set up under public law, its rules and any subsequent amendments of them had to be approved by a Dutch Minister of State, the members of the tribunal were appointed by the responsible Minister, the tribunal followed adversary rules of procedure similar to those used by ordinary courts of law, and the tribunal was bound to apply rules of law in disputes coming before it. It followed from these considerations that the arbitral tribunal was a tribunal for the purposes of Article 177. The Court utilised similar reasoning in *Broekmeulen v Huisarts Registratie Commissie*[4] which was a reference from the Appeals Committee of the General Practitioners Registration Committee in the Netherlands, which had to consider the recognition of the medical qualifications of a Dutch national which had been procured in a Belgian university. The court applied the criteria of the *Vaassen-Göbbels* Case and added that if, under the legal system of a Member State, the task of implementing provisions of Community law is assigned to a professional body acting under a degree of governmental supervision, and if that body creates appeal procedures which may effect the exercise of rights granted by Community law, it is imperative that the Court should have an opportunity of ruling on issues of interpretation and validity arising out of such proceedings. Needless to say, not every professional organisation will be recognised as a tribunal for the purposes of Article 177: in *Re Jules Borker*[5] the Court refused to respond to a request for a preliminary ruling submitted by the Conseil de l'Ordre des Avocats of Paris, which did not have a case before it which it was under a legal duty to try, but rather a request for a declaration relating to a dispute between a member of the Bar and the courts or tribunals of another Member State.

In the *Vaassen-Göbbels* and *Broekmeulen* cases the national entities in question can best be described as administrative/judicial bodies. There has been only one case in which a genuine arbitral tribunal sought a reference under Article 177 and in that case, *Nordsee Deutsche Hochseefischerei v*

Reederei Mond,[6] the Court held that it had no jurisdiction to entertain the reference, despite the fact that the arbitrator was obliged to decide the dispute according to law and that this award had the force of *res judicata*, because the arbitration was not mandatory on the parties—they could choose to have their dispute settled either by a court or by arbitration— and because the link between the arbitration procedure and the organisation of legal remedies through the courts in Germany was not sufficiently close. This decision has been criticised[7] but it raises the question whether an arbitrator operating pursuant to the Arbitration Act, 1954 could submit a reference to the Court under Article 177. It is submitted that because the conduct of an arbitration can be so closely supervised by the High Court under the terms of the Arbitration Act, 1954, an arbitrator would be permitted to submit a reference to the Court of Justice under Article 177 and that the Court of Justice would recognise such a reference. A reference from an arbitrator would be most likely to occur in the context of the application of Articles 85 and 86 of the Treaty to commercial contracts.

When we come to examine Irish administrative and quasi-judicial tribunals in the light of the case-law of the Court of Justice it is perhaps worth nothing that the Irish courts have been faced with a similar difficulty when considering whether quasi-judicial tribunals exercise judicial power or administer justice within the meaning of Articles 34 and 37 of the Constitution;[8] the tests established by Irish courts in this context are not completely dissimilar to the criteria used by the Court of Justice.[9] For ease of identification, however, it is best to distinguish between those tribunals to which specific duties, derived from Community law, have been attributed and those tribunals before which questions of Community law may be raised incidentally. Into the former category would fall the Labour Court and the Employment Appeals Tribunal which have been given specific responsibilities by the Anti-Discrimination (Equal Pay) Act, 1974, the Employment Equality Act, 1977, and the Protection of Employees (Employers' Insolvency) Act, 1984; these Statutes implemented obligations imposed by Community Directives (*infra*, Chapter 24). In the United Kingdom references have been made on a frequent basis by the National Insurance Commissioner[10] and by the Commissioners for the special purposes of the Income Tax Acts.[11] Following these British precedents, it seems logical to assume that the Irish equivalents, the Special Commissioners under the Income Tax Act, 1967 and Appeals Officers under the Social Welfare (Consolidation) Act, 1981[12] would be empowered to submit references. Other tribunals before which points of Community law are likely to arise, and which could qualify as tribunals under Article 177, include: the Censorship of Films Board;[13] the Censorship of Publications Board;[14] An Bord Uchtala;[15] and An Bord Pleanala.[16] In addition, Article 177 may be available to professional tribunals established pursuant to Statute.[17]

1 Courts of Justice Act, 1924; Courts (Establishment and Constitution) Act, 1961.
2 Article 38 of the Constitution; Offences Against the State Act, 1939.
3 Case 61/65 [1966] E.C.R. 261, [1966] C.M.L.R. 508.
4 Case 246/80 [1981] E.C.R. 2311, [1982] 1 C.M.L.R. 91.
5 Case 138/80 [1980] E.C.R. 1975, [1980] 3 C.M.L.R. 638.
6 Case 102/81 [1982] E.C.R. 1095.

7 Gerhard Bebr, *Arbitration Tribunals and Article 177 of the EEC Treaty*, (1985) 2 C.M.L. Rev. 489.
8 See, for example, *Lynham v Butler (No 2)* [1933] I.R. 74; *Foley v Irish Land Commission* [1952] I.R. 118; *re Solicitors' Act, 1954* [1960] I.R. 239.
9 See, for example, the tests laid down by Kenny J. *in McDonald v Bord na gCon (No 2)*, [1965] I.R. 217.
10 See, for example, Case 17/76 *Brack v Insurance Officer* [1976] E.C.R. 1429, [1976] 2 C.M.L.R. 592.
11 See Case 44/84 *Hurd v Jones* [1986] E.C.R. 29, [1986] 2 C.M.L.R. 1.
12 See Robert Clark, *Social Welfare Insurance Appeals*, (1978) XVII Ir. Jur. (ns) 265.
13 Censorship of Films Act, 1923.
14 Censorship of Publications Act, 1946.
15 Adoption Act, 1952.
16 Local Government (Planning & Development) Act, 1976.
17 See, for example, Veterinary Practitioners Act, 1931; Solicitors (Amendment) Act, 1960; Medical Practitioners Act, 1978; Nurses Act, 1984; Dentists Act, 1985.

Discretion to refer to obligation to refer?

12.38 The third paragraph of Article 177 makes it clear that courts or tribunals from whose decision there is no remedy within the national legal system must refer to the Court of Justice when a question of Community law arises before them. Consequently, it is necessary to distinguish between courts obliged to refer and courts under no such obligation. A simplistic reading of Article 177 would suggest that it is only national supreme courts (the Supreme Court in Ireland, for example) that would be obliged to make a reference. However, at a very early stage the Court of Justice made it clear that any court or tribunal, from whose decision there was no appeal, was under an obligation to submit a reference to the Court of Justice: *Costa v ENEL*.[1] In Ireland this means that the Circuit Court and the High Court when hearing appeals from the District Court and the Circuit Court respectively would be obliged to refer to the Court of Justice. It goes without saying that where a question of law arises, before the Supreme Court on appeal from the High Court, a decision on which it is necessary to give judgment in the instant case, the Supreme Court is obliged to refer to Luxembourg.

Apart from supreme courts and courts obliged to make a reference, other national courts enjoy the widest possible discretion under Article 177; national rules of procedure or rulings on point of law by superior courts cannot deprive a lower court of its power to refer to the Court of Justice: *Rheinmühlen-Düsseldorf v Einfuhr- und Vorratsstelle für Getreide und Futtermittel (No 2)*.[2] But what about an appeal to a superior court against a reference order made by an inferior court? This issue came up for consideration in *Campus Oil v Minister for Industry and Energy*[3] where the defendants appealed to the Supreme Court against a reference by Murphy J. who sought an interpretation of Articles 30 and 36 of the Treaty. The appeal was rejected. In the Supreme Court, Walsh J. held that the request under Article 177 was not an appeal to a higher court but rather the exercise of a right which was by its very nature non-contentious.

'The national judge has an untrammelled discretion as to whether he will or will not refer questions for a preliminary ruling under Article 177 and in doing so he is not in any way subject to the parties or to any other judicial authority.'

Even if a reference was a decision within the meaning of Article 34 of the Constitution (and therefore amenable to appeal) it would have to yield to the primacy of Article 177. Finally, the fact that provision had been made in other Member States for appeals against references was irrelevant because the question before the Court had to be decided on the grounds of Irish law only. This decision has been criticised[4] but it remains the law in Ireland: no appeals are possible against reference orders.

Courts from whose decision there is no further judicial remedy in the national legal order are obliged to make references to the European Court. The logic underlying this obligation is simple: it is designed to enable a citizen, who feels sufficiently aggrieved to pursue an appeal to the highest tribunal, to ensure that the point of Community law at issue is considered by the Court of Justice. However, it is now clear that there are three circumstances in which a court of last resort is not obliged to submit a reference for a preliminary ruling: (i) where there has been a previous preliminary ruling: *Da Costa en Schaake NV v Nederlandse Belastingadministratie*;[5] (ii) where the question of Community law arises during interlocutory proceedings: *Hoffmann-La Roche v Centrafarm*;[6] and (iii) where the domestic court is faced with an *acte clair*, that is, where the correct application of Community law is so obvious as to leave no scope for any reasonable doubt: *C.I.L.F.I.T. v Ministro della Sanità.*[7]

1 *Supra*, fn. 11, para. 12.36.
2 Case 166/73 [1974] E.C.R. 33, [1974] 1 C.M.L.R. 523.
3 [1982–1983] J.I.S.E.L. 43.
4 See, for example, David O'Keeffe, *Appeals against an Order to Refer under Article 177 of the EEC Treaty*, (1984) E.L. Rev. 87; Finbarr Murphy, *Case Note*, (1984) 21 C.M.L. Rev. 741.
5 Joined cases 28–30/62 [1963] E.C.R. 31, [1963] C.M.L.R. 224.
6 Case 107/76 [1977] E.C.R. 957, [1977] 2 C.M.L.R. 334.
7 Case 283/81 [1982] E.C.R. 3415, [1983] 1 C.M.L.R. 472.

12.39 It now remains to consider the effect of preliminary rulings on national courts. The court which has made the reference is bound by the ruling of the Court of Justice. As regards other courts, they are free to treat the judgment of the Court as a useful precedent and the judgments of Irish courts, when considering whether to make references under Article 177, contain frequent references to judgments of the Court on various issues. A particular problem arises concerning judgments of the Court which have declared invalid an act of an institution. Article 177 makes no reference to the consequences of a declaration of invalidity but the Court has been constructing the juridical effects by analogy to Articles 174 and 176.[1] In *International Chemical Corpn v Amministrazione delle Finanze dello Stato*[2] the Court held that while a declaration of invalidity of a Council regulation is directly addressed only to the national court which brought the matter before the Court of Justice, it is sufficient reason for any other national court to regard the act as void for the purposes of this judgment which it has to give.

1 Hjalte Rasmussen in *Thirty Years of Community Law* (1983), at p. 179.
2 Case 66/80 [1981] E.C.R. 1191, [1983] 2 C.M.L.R. 593.

Other types of preliminary rulings

12.40 Article 41 of the ECSC Treaty provides for a limited form of reference by national courts concerning the validity of acts of the institutions of the ECSC. This procedure has been utilised rarely. Of much greater importance is the reference system established under the Protocol annexed to the Convention of 27 September 1968 on Jurisdiction and Enforcement of Judgments in Civil and Commercial Matters;[1] this Convention was concluded under Article 220 of the Treaty, and provides for preliminary rulings at the instance of superior courts (in Ireland the Supreme Court), but also by certain national authorities such as Procurators-General of the Courts of Cassation. In Ireland the Attorney-General is likely to be designated as the competent authority for this purpose. The Convention has now been ratified by Ireland following the enactment of the Jurisdiction of Courts and Enforcement of Judgments Act, 1988.[2]

1 O.J. L 304, 30.10.1978 p. 1.
2 See A.V. Gill, The EEC Convention on Jurisdiction and the Enforcement of Judgments in Civil and Commercial Matters, in *The Legal Implications of 1992*, Irish Centre for European Law, 1988.

Consultative jurisdiction of the Court

12.41 The Court is empowered to give opinions under Article 228 of the EEC Treaty and Article 103 of the Euratom Treaty. Under these provisions the Court may be asked to rule on the compatibility with the Treaty of international obligations being contemplated by the Communities. The jurisdiction of the Court is similar to the consultative jurisdiction of the Irish Supreme Court under Article 26 of the Constitution. The procedure has been utilised on a number of occasions, although the first opinion was only requested in 1975.[1] The significance of the procedure is that if the Court gives a negative opinion the international agreement in question can only be ratified by the Community if the procedure under Article 236, for the amendment of the Treaty, is utilised.

Article 95 of the ECSC Treaty, by contrast, provides for a *petite révision* of the ECSC Treaty: the procedure has been utilised on only three occasions.[2]

1 Opinion 1/75 [1975] E.C.R. 1355, [1976] 1 C.M.L.R. 85. See also Chapter 5.
2 Hjalte Rasmussen, in *Thirty Years of Community Law* (1983), at p. 189.

Procedure before the Court

12.42 Article 188 of the Treaty provides that the Court shall adopt its Rules of Procedure which require the unanimous approval of the Council. The present Rules of Procedure were adopted in 1974[1] and have been amended on a number of occasions since then, particularly to take account of the enlargement of the Communities. The procedural aspects of the Rules are, to a large extent, elaborations of the principles contained in Title 3 of the Statute of the Court.

Title 1 of the Rules deals with the organisation of the Court. The provisions are institutional in the main, although Articles 29 to 31 deal with the language to be used in cases. The basic rule is that the language of a case is chosen by the applicant from among: Danish, Dutch, English, French, German, Greek, Irish, Italian, Portuguese and Spanish. Irish is somewhat exceptional in that the official publications of the Communities, including publications of the Court, are not published in that language and the Court does not possess the translation facilities necessary to deal with an application in Irish. It is understood that the Irish Government has undertaken to bear the cost of providing translation and interpretation services should they be required.

Title 2 deals with procedure proper and a basic rule (Article 58) is that the parties to proceedings may address the Court only through an agent, adviser or lawyer. This is an echo of Article 17 of the Statute which requires that natural or legal persons must be represented by a lawyer entitled to practise before the Court of a Member State; a certificate to this effect must be lodged with the Registry. The lawyer also states an address for service in Luxembourg, usually at the offices of a Luxembourg advocate. The institutions and Member States must be represented by agents, who may be assisted by an adviser or a lawyer. Significant emphasis is placed on the development of the case by way of written procedure, if only because of the linguistic restrictions in which the Court operates. The original of each pleading must be signed by the agent or lawyer and must state the name and address of the parties, the subject matter of the dispute and the grounds on which the application is based, the form of the order sought by the applicant and the nature of any evidence relied on by him. Within one month of service, the defendant must lodge a defence, and both the application and defence may be supplemented by a reply and rejoinder respectively. Any supporting material should be annexed to the application or defence. The case is normally allocated to a judge of the Court or of the Chamber to which the case has been assigned. That judge, known as the *Juge-Rapporteur*, makes a written summary of the issues of law and fact and the arguments of the parties for the benefit of his colleagues. Once the written procedure has closed the Court may open preparatory enquiries if it wishes, and it may make arrangements to hear witnesses although this is not very common. In comparison to the common law system the oral procedure before the Court is extremely brief and the Court has issued guidelines, which are also issued to counsel before the oral hearing, in which it stresses the limited time available and emphasises that the members of the Court will have read the papers already submitted by the parties. The available time should not be spent on a rehearsal of the arguments developed during the written procedure. It is impossible to understate the difference between Luxembourg procedure and domestic advocacy[2] but a brief illustration may be of some assistance. In the so-called *Sugar* cases[3] the applicants sought the annulment of a Commission Decision which has imposed large fines on a number of undertakings for breach of Articles 85 and 86. The Commission Decision was 31 pages in length, the summary of the facts and of the arguments of the parties (prepared by the Juge-Rapporteur) came to 241 pages, the Advocate General's opinion was 78 pages in length and the judgment of the court was 115 pages long. There was one intervener, four witnesses, and last, but not least, there were 16 applicants. The oral hearing before the Court lasted only 5 days.

Some time after the Court has heard the opinion of the Advocate-General, which is normally delivered a few weeks after the oral hearing, it delivers its judgment in open court; certified copies are made available to the parties. Clerical errors may be adjusted within two weeks of delivery of the judgment. As regards costs, the basic principle is that the unsuccessful party must pay, but the costs of a reference for a preliminary ruling will be a matter for the referring court.

It is open to the parties to discontinue proceedings, whereupon the Court will order the case to be removed from the Register. Procedural time limits are subject to extension to account for official holidays and for distance; apart from Luxembourg, the allowance for distance ranges from two days for Belgium to ten days for the more distant Member States, including Ireland.

Finally, Title 3 of the Rules of Procedure deals with special forms of procedure including preliminary rulings, intervention of persons claiming an interest in the result of a case before the Court, applications to set aside judgments procured by default, third party proceedings and applications for rescission of judgments.

1 For a codified version of the Rules of Procedure see O.J. C 39, 15.2.1982. p. 1.
2 For a useful account of advocacy before the Court of Justice see: John Temple Lang, *Advocacy at the Court of Justice, with special reference to the role of the Commission*, Bar European News, 1987 No. 17.
3 Joined cases 40–48, 50, 54–56, 111, 113–114/73 [1975] E.C.R. 1663, [1976] 1 C.M.L.R. 295.

Court of First Instance

12.43 Articles 4 and 5, 11 and 12, and 26 and 27 of the Single European Act provided for the establishment of a Court of First Instance to hear certain classes of actions initiated by natural and legal persons, subject to a right of repeal to the Court of Justice on points of law only. The new Court of First Instance would not be competent to hear actions brought by Member States nor would it be empowered to give preliminary rulings. In mid-1988 the Court of Justice produced its proposal for a Decision of the Council on the establishment of a Court of First Instance of the European Communities. Briefly, the Court proposed that the new Court of First Instance should have its seat in Luxembourg, that the Court should consist of seven judges and no Advocates General, and that the Court should sit in Chambers of three judges. In Article 3 the Court proposed that the jurisdiction of the Court of First Instance should extend to staff cases and to actions under Articles 173 and 175 instituted by natural and legal persons relating to:

- the implementation of the competition rules applicable to undertakings; and
- measures to protect trade within the meaning of Article 113 (dumping or subsidies); and
- certain cases under the ECSC Treaty.

The remaining draft provisions of the Court's proposal relate to changes in the Statute and the Rules of Procedure to accommodate the new Court of First Instance. The Commission, in responses published in May and July 1988[1] took issue with certain of the proposals of the court. It doubted that seven judges would be sufficient to take on the workload likely to flow from the jurisdiction of the new Court; instead, it proposed twelve judges and questioned the wisdom of omitting Advocates General. In particular, the Commission had reservations about delegating cases of an economic nature to the new Court of First Instance.[2]

1 COM SEC (88) 366 final; COM SEC (88) 1121 final.
2 In Council Decision 88/591 (ECSC, EEC, Euratom) the Council established a Court of First Instance staffed by 12 Judges—from whom Advocates General could be chosen. The scope of jurisdiction of the new court is more limited than the proposal of the Court of Justice, although Article 3(3) envisages the extension of jurisdiction '. . . in the light of experience'.

Part V

Community Law and National Law

Chapter 13

General Problems: Direct Applicability, Direct Effect, and Supremacy

Introduction

13.1 In this chapter we are concerned with the complex relationship that exists between Community law and the national law. Prior to accession to the EEC the Irish legal system, like other national legal systems, had to concern itself only with international law as an outside legal order impacting on its legal system. Since 1973, however, the impact of Community law on the Irish legal system has also to be evaluated and analysed and since the Community system is a much more sophisticated and integrative system the series of problems caused by the interface of the national and the Community legal systems is more complicated and more acute. Moreover, because of the uniqueness of the Community's experiment, the relationship between international and domestic law could not provide guidelines or precedents very helpful for the analysis of the Community–domestic law relationship.[1]

1 Pierre Pescatore, *The Law of Integration* (1974), at p. 69; Gerhard Bebr *The Development of Judicial Control of the European Communities* (1981), at pp. 550, 615.

13.2 Before examining in detail the relationship between Community law and national law, however, it is essential to bear in mind that there are two viewpoints from which this problem can be seen: the Community point of view and the national point of view. It is natural when contemplating the position initially for lawyers to approach the problem from the national point of view. After all, the national legal system preceded the Community and the Community came into existence only because the Member States willed it. Further, in the Irish and British traditions since international law was seen as inferior to national law, there was a tendency for lawyers to approach the Community law–national law relationship in the same way, and to view the Community legal system through the glass of the national system and to define Community law in national terms.[1] Sometimes the inability to appreciate the two viewpoints has led to confusion. In tackling the problems for the first time it is helpful to keep the two approaches separate. In this chapter we will view the problems from the Community stance. The national view will be dealt with later.

1 See, for example, Lawrence Collins, *European Community Law in the United Kingdom,* First Edition (1975), at p. 455.

13.3 In dealing with the relationship between Community law and national law one is immediately faced with two problems. Firstly, in the event of a conflict between Community law and national law which law is to prevail? This is referred to as the *supremacy* question. Secondly, can a citizen within the national system rely on Community law as a source of rights which will be respected by the national courts? This question is referred to as the question of '*direct effects*'. In particular, it asks whether a Community measure has a direct effect in the national legal system in the sense that it gives the individual citizen rights which the national courts must uphold. Closely related to this is a third question, the question of '*direct applicability*' which raises the problem of whether an international commitment entered into by a state comes into the national legal system or whether its legal implications are confined to the international legal order. Normally one would, from a national point of view, examine these latter two problems in the inverse order to that in which they have been raised here. One would first of all ask whether the international commitment was directly applicable in the national legal system (had it become part of the national legal order?) and only if it had, would one ask whether within the legal system the measure was of such a kind as to give an individual within the system legal rights.[1] For the purpose of exposition, therefore, the two questions raised by Community law became three and they will be treated here in the following sequence:

(1) Is Community law *directly applicable* in the Member States?
(2) Is Community law *directly effective* in the Member States?
(3) In the event of a conflict between Community law and the law of a Member State which prevails? (Supremacy Issue).

Before examining these questions from the Community viewpoint in greater detail it might be helpful to orientate the reader by answering the questions in a very general way. Fortunately, at this stage in the development of Community jurisprudence one can now with a degree of confidence not possible some years ago provide to these questions brief answers which are not wholly distortive.

(1) Community law is directly applicable in the Member States. It does not have to be received or incorporated into the national legal system by separate legal act to have an impact therein. Unlike international law, Community law by its nature enters the Irish legal system and is part of Irish law without separate acts of reception.
(2) Provided certain well defined conditions are fulfilled Community laws can have direct effect in the Irish legal system and bestow on individuals rights which the national courts must protect. In other words, the impact which the directly applicable provision can have in the national legal system is particularly intense: it gives rights to individuals which the national courts must uphold.

(3) In the event of a conflict between Community law and national law, Community law will prevail in all circumstances.

This then is the stance of the Community on these issues but before one examines in greater detail the Community's attitude one must first of all advert to the concept developed by the Court of Justice which is fundamentally important to a proper understanding of the Community's position in this area, namely, the idea that the Community's legal system is an autonomous and independent legal order.

1 J.W. Winter, *Applicability and Direct Effect—Two Distinct and Different Concepts of Community Law*, 9 C.M.L. Rev., 425 (1972). Most writers accept the distinction and the present authors adopt it unreservedly. It should be pointed out, however, that some writers (e.g. Toth, Vol. 1, p. 119, fn. 1) do not favour it. The Court of Justice (although its decisions appear to be consistent with the distinction) is not consistent in its terminology and earlier case law and comment use different language.

Autonomous legal system

13.4 To appreciate what is at issue here it is helpful to realise that legal orders are not always independent and autonomous. For example, one might contemplate for a moment the legal order encompassed by a local authority. Here the local authority might have power to legislate in a range of specified matters within a given geographical area. In exercising its powers, however, the authority cannot afford to be oblivious to the national legal system. For one thing its powers are defined by a national statute which limits the local authority and which can be altered by the national Parliament at any time. Furthermore, an affected individual might claim that his constitutional rights are being infringed by the local authority, and the actions of the authority may be reviewable for various reasons by the courts of the national legal system. One can see from this simple example that a legal system may not always be autonomous of other legal systems, but may have to operate within the constraints imposed by its relationship to other, and sometimes superior, legal orders. The national legal order too may not be autonomous. It may, for example, be limited by the international legal order. Some states do indeed ascribe to the international legal order a status higher than the national legal system.

For various historical reasons, however, the national legal order tends in our legal culture to be the most important order and other legal orders tend to be explained or justified by reference to it rather than the reverse.

With the establishment of the European Community it was not unnatural that there should be a tendency to examine and define the nature of the new Community legal order, first and foremost, in terms of the national legal systems. By adopting this approach some were of the opinion that the new legal monster could, if contained within the traditional relationships, be more or less tamed and rendered amenable to national legal systems. This of course was something which the European Court did not wish to happen and from an early date it raised the theory that the Community legal system was an independent and autonomous legal system in its own right. Freed from the limitations and restrictions which a dependent relationship with national, or indeed international, orders might impose on it, the Court of Justice was in a position to make its own rules, oblivious to the external impact which its theories might have for other legal orders. Liberated from these theoretical relational justifications and limitations the Court could develop its own theories in an independent and uninhibited fashion. Provided the solutions offered were more or less reasonable, the only question then, and this was not a doctrinal one, was whether the national courts would accept the new Community doctrines. As already mentioned this was not a theoretical jurisprudential problem now, however, but rather one which called for a shrewd, pragmatic sense of political judgment. Once it was appreciated that the Community's legal system was an independent legal order the Court had a *tabula rasa* on which to write Community rules on such issues as the 'direct effects' issue and the supremacy issue. If the Court did not have such a liberating hypothesis, but had to justify its position to other legal orders, then it would have been intellectually very difficult to maintain the stand it wished to take on these very fundamental questions such as direct effects, direct applicability and supremacy.

13.5 The *locus classicus* of the Court of Justice's attitude is to be found in the *Van Gend en Loos* case[1] and has been confirmed so consistently since then that it merits further attention. The facts of the case related to the Customs classification of a product known as ureaformaldehyde. In 1960 the Dutch Government introduced a new classification to that which prevailed on 1 January 1958, the date of entry into the EEC. The effect of this was that ureaformaldehyde was switched into a different category where it attracted an *ad valorem* import duty of 8 per cent in contrast to the 3 per cent it attracted under the old classification. The import duty for the product in question, therefore, was effectively increased after 1 January 1958 and this according to Van Gend en Loos was in breach of EEC Treaty, art. 12 which prohibits Member States from introducing new or increasing old import duties after that date. The Tariefcommissie, before whom the matter was being argued, referred to the Court of Justice, under Article 177 procedure, the question whether Article 12 gave rise to an individual right which the courts must protect. Before holding that Article 12 did indeed have such effect the Court felt obliged to deliver itself of some pertinent observations on the nature of the new legal order created by the EEC Treaty.

In looking to see whether provisions of international treaties give rights to individuals it held that it is necessary first of all to consider the spirit, 'the general scheme and the wording of those provisions'. The objective of the EEC Treaty was the establishment of a Common Market which was of direct concern not only to the Member States but also to the citizens of Member States. The preamble of the Treaty speaks not only of governments but also of the peoples; the exercise of the powers by the institutions affect not only the Member States but also the citizens; and the nationals of the Member States are institutionally represented in the European Parliament and the Economic and Social Committee. These factors together with the referral procedure set out in Article 177 acknowledge that Community law can be invoked by nationals before national courts.

'The conclusion to be drawn from this is that the Community constitutes a new legal order of international law for the benefit of which the states have limited their sovereign rights, albeit within limited fields, and the subjects of which comprise not only Member States but also their nationals. Independently of the legislation of Member States, Community law therefore not only imposes obligations on individuals but is also intended to confer upon them rights which become part of their legal heritage. These rights arise not only where they are expressly granted by the Treaty, but also by reasons of obligations which the Treaty imposes in a clearly defined way upon individuals as well as upon Member States and upon the institutions of the Community.'[2]

The Court returned to this notion with even greater vigour in *Costa v ENEL*[3] a little over a year later. In this case Mr Costa contested that an Italian law which nationalised the electricity industry and established the ENEL Company (the equivalent of the ESB) was contrary to EEC law. He refused to pay his electricity bill and when sued in the Italian court pleaded the Community law point. Once more the matter was referred under Article 177 to the Court of Justice. The Court's words on the nature of the new legal order were of seminal significance and because of their importance ought not to be paraphrased. To the submission of the Italian Government that the national court could apply national law the Court replied:

'By contrast with ordinary international treaties, the EEC Treaty has created its own legal system, which, on the entry into force of the Treaty, became an integral part of the legal systems of the Member States which their courts are bound to apply.

'By creating a Community of unlimited duration, having its own institutions, its own personality, its own legal capacity and capacity of representation on the international plane and, more particularly, real powers stemming from a limitation of sovereignty or a transfer of powers from the States to the Community, the Member States have limited their sovereign rights, albeit within limited fields, and have thus created a body of law which binds both their nationals and themselves.

'The integration into the laws of each Member State of provisions which derive from the Community, and more generally the terms and the spirit of the Treaty, make it impossible for the States, as a corollary, to accord precedence to a unilateral and subsequent measure over a legal system accepted by them on the basis of reciprocity. Such a measure cannot therefore be inconsistent with that legal system. The executive force of Community law cannot vary from one state to another in deference to subsequent domestic laws without jeopardising the attainment of the objectives of the Treaty . . . .

'It follows from all these observations that the law stemming from the Treaty, an independent source of law, could not because of its special and original nature, be overridden by domestic legal provisions, however framed, without being deprived of its character as Community law and without the legal basis of the Community itself being called into question.'[4]

From this we can see that the Community legal order is separate from the national legal systems. Its jurisdiction extends and its laws run throughout the territories of all the Member States. Not only is the Community system independent of the national legal systems, it is also separate from the international legal order. The implications of these propositions from the Community's point of view are as follows:

(1) Community laws extend throughout all the Community territory. Their scope cannot be stopped by national measures. In strictness the question of direct applicability should not arise in Community law. Community law runs throughout Community territory and Member States cannot prevent this, no more than a local authority (e.g. Kerry County Council) could prevent a national act from having effect within its jurisdiction. The unity of the legal system would insist on this.[5]

(2) In so far as a national measure conflicts with a Community measure the Community measure prevails. When the Community has jurisdiction then the Member State can no longer legislate and any attempt to do so would be void as being an unlawful usurpation of function.

(3) Since the Community protects individuals also a Community measure may be relied on by an individual within the Community system and on Community terms. This clearly means that an individual may plead it before the Community court in proper cases. It also means, however, that the individual can rely on it whenever national courts are charged with applying Community laws.

1 Case 26/62 *Van Gend en Loos v Nederlandse Belastingadministratie* [1963] E.C.R. 1, [1963] C.M.L.R. 105.
2 *Supra*, n. 1, at pp. 12 and 129 respectively. The phrase 'of international law' in the early part of the quotation is unfortunate and has been dropped by the Court in subsequent cases.
3 Case 6/64 [1964] E.C.R. 585, [1964] C.M.L.R. 425.
4 *Supra*, n. 3.
5 Schermers puts the matter this way: 'The Court of Justice has repeatedly ruled that it considers the relationship between national law and Community law to be monist. There can be no transformation of Community law into national law. It must be of direct use to Community citizens within their national legal orders, and in the case of a conflict arising Community law muຈt take priority over national law irrespective of the date when the latter legislation was adopted.' H.G. Schermers *Judicial Protection in the European Communities*, Fourth Edition (1987) pp. 86–87. Footnote citing, *inter alia*, Case 83/78 *Pigs Marketing Board v Redmond* [1978] E.C.R. 2347, at p. 2373, [1979] 1 C.M.L.R. 177, at p. 204, omitted.

13.6 While it is right and proper to emphasise the independence and autonomy of the Community legal system in a forceful way, it would not be accurate to leave the discussion without adding some qualifications. The independence of the Community's legal system is not absolute or total. For its effectiveness the Community sometimes relies quite heavily on the cooperation of the national authorities. For example, the Court of Justice in some cases draws on national law, as in Article 58 to define the beneficiaries of the right of establishment, and in Article 215 to establish the conditions of the Community's civil liability. Again when articulating the general principles of Community law, including Community human rights the Court has resort to national laws for inspiration. Moreover, various Community tasks (e.g. the collection of customs duties, the operation of the intervention system in CAP) have to be executed by national authorities and the question of enforcing Community law is, in the absence of a Community enforcement agency, left to national enforcement agencies. Again when the Community issues a directive it relies on the Member States to adopt suitable measures to attain the Community objectives set out therein. Finally, while national courts cannot test the validity of Community measures against national law, they certainly do have an important role in interpreting, applying and enforcing Community law within national legal contexts. The whole Article 177 procedure testifies to this.[1]

In spite of this close interaction between the national and the Community legal orders the final line must stress the autonomous nature of the Community's legal system and the fact that 'Community law, as a whole, constitutes a new, independent (autonomous), supra-national, self-contained, uniform and unitary legal order of a *sui generis* type, with a limited field of application'.[2] It is only if this is kept to the forefront of one's mind that one is able to appreciate fully the consistent, if authoritarian, position adopted by the Court of Justice in the elaboration of rules relating to direct applicability, direct effects and supremacy.

1 The division of competences between the Court of Justice and national courts means that the national courts, even at the risk of multiple applications throughout the Community. are given a measure of discretion in procedural matters even where a matter is held by the Court of Justice to be directly effective. Different limitation periods, for example, are tolerated on this basis. See also A.G, Toth, *Legal Protection of Individuals in the European Communities* (1978), Vol. 1, p. 12 and p. 24; Gerhard Bebr, *The Development of Judicial Control of the European Communities* (1981), p. 602.

2 A.G. Toth, *Legal Protection of Individuals in the European Communities* (1978), Vol. 1, p. 8.

Direct Applicability

13.7 To appreciate the concept of direct applicability of Community law in the legal systems of the Member States, one must once more advert to traditional theories concerning the relationship between public international law and national legal systems. Traditionally, there are two[1] approaches as to the effect which an international convention has on the legal system of a signatory state. Firstly, one can subscribe to the viewpoint that international obligations undertaken in this way immediately enter the domestic legal system on the signature of the State involved. No separate legal act is required to bring the international legal measure 'home' to the national legal system. No separate act of incorporation is required for the international commitment to make an impact in the signatory state's own system. The treaty in question therefore at one and the same time will create obligations in the international order and in the national order. This approach is known as the monist approach. The second approach envisages that before such an international commitment can make an impact in the national legal system a separate legal act is required. According to this theory a state which signs a treaty certainly undertakes an obligation in the international legal order, a breach of which will expose it to remedies appropriate to the international sphere, but such a commitment has no impact internally in its domestic legal system until the international measure is incorporated ('received', 'brought home') by a separate legal act. It does not enter the domestic legal system automatically. This approach is known as the dualist approach because before the international commitment makes an impact at domestic level two separate steps are required: the signing of the treaty and the passing of the incorporating act. The dualist approach views the international and the national orders as separate and distinct legal systems, whereas the monist approach tends to view the national system as part of the greater system which operates at the international level.

When jurists first began to examine the relationship between the Community legal system and the national systems of the Member States it was not unnatural at the outset that the question should be phrased, in traditional terminology, namely: Is Community law directly applicable in the legal systems of the Member States? In other words does a Community law require a separate incorporating act before it becomes part of the law of the Member States? Formulating the problem in this fashion was understandable and made sense from a national point of view.[2] Indeed this approach was to some extent encouraged by the wording of EEC Treaty, art. 189, which provides that regulations are 'directly applicable' in all Member States. If one, however, appreciates the point already made that the Treaty of Rome establishes a new autonomous legal order then one will readily realise that, from the Community point of view, the traditional question of the direct applicability of Community law has little or no significance. The Community makes its own laws which extend uniformly throughout its own jurisdiction, (i.e. throughout the territories of the twelve member States). In other words, after accession, where the Community's writ runs is not dependent in any way on the acts of the Member States. Once the Member States joined the Community they accept this limitation of their sovereign rights. And this is true even where the Community measure contemplates further actions by a Member State as in the case of a directive.[3] Such a measure penetrates the national legal system in question not because it is 'directly applicable' in traditional terminology but rather because the Community's writ runs that far.[4] Kapteyn and Verloren van Themaat anticipating the eventual Court of Justice's stand put the matter in these words: 'Rules of Community law, therefore, have internal effect without reference to the national legal order, viz. in the area that has been created in consequence of the limitation of national sovereignty. In other words, the national constitutional law with regard to the internal effect and the internal order of priority to be given to rules of international law does not apply with reference to rules of Community law, because it can apply only within the limits of sovereignty. Beyond these limits, i.e. within the Community legal order, the municipal court without being hampered by constitutional restrictions, may give to the rules of Community law the effect desired by the European Court. If the municipal court comes across legal measures conflicting with Community law, it must refrain from applying them, not because they are of a lower order than Community law, but because in such a case the national legislator has acted *ultra vires*.'[5]

The effect the Community measure creates within the Community system, i.e. whether it gives individuals rights within the Community system, is another question the answer to which depends very much on the nature of the measure itself. In some cases it creates obligations for individuals while in other cases it only obliges Member States themselves. Timmermans puts the matter this way:

'One can only derive from these [i.e. *Van Gend en Loos* and *ENEL* cases] and subsequent rulings of the Court of Justice that the whole body of Community law, written or unwritten, is as such incorporated within the national legal systems, at least in so far as the rules of Community law can be of any relevance in these national systems.'

In other words, if regulations do not require any incorporation in view of the explicit text of Article 189, directives do not need it either, according to the case law of the Court of Justice. This is not to say of course that directives as a whole need always be directly applied. Normally they cannot be, for they require further implementation by national authorities. But that is quite a different matter.

'The distinction between "to be incorporated", which a directive does not require, and "to be implemented", which a directive normally does need, is not an academic one. Without having been implemented directives might nevertheless produce effects of various kinds in the national legal systems. Precisely because the hurdle of incorporation has already been jumped, directives can in principle be invoked before the national courts, and for different purposes.'[6]

The notion of direct applicability therefore ought to have no significance in examining the relationship between Community law and national law *from a Community viewpoint*. It may be more relevant when one has to consider the relationship between the two legal systems *from a national point of view*[7] and also when considering the relationship between international law and Community law.[8] Unfortunately, the Court of Justice does use the incorporation concept in its analyses and one cannot afford to ignore this approach in examining the problem even from the Community point of view.

1 H.G. Schermers, *Judicial Protection in the European Communities*, Fourth Edition (1987), for a third approach which he calls 'Mitigated Dualism', at pp. 82–3.
2 The traditional terminology here used the term 'self-executing treaties'. This term has not found favour in Community law and has never been used by the Court of Justice. On the meaning of 'self-executing' and its unsuitability in Community law analysis see Gerhard Bebr, *The Development of Judicial Control of the European Communities* (1981), p. 549 *et seq.*
3 See R. Kovar, The Relationship between Community Law and National Law, in *Thirty Years of Community Law* (1983), 132; Timmermans, *Directives: their effect within the National Legal Systems*, [1979] C.M.L. Rev. 533, especially at 534; T.C. Hartley, *The Foundations of European Community Law* (1981) at p. 118: '. . . there can be little doubt that in principle all Community law is valid within the national legal order'. Footnote omitted.
4 See P.J.G. Kapteyn and P. Verloren van Themaat, *Introduction to the Law of the European Communities* (1973), p. 25.
5 *Idem*, 30.
6 C.W.A. Timmermans, *Directives: their effect within the National Legal Systems*, 16 C.M.L. Rev. 533, at 534–535. Footnotes omitted. What is said here about directives can be equally applied, with modifications justified by their different legal nature, to decisions also, and of course to the treaties themselves.

7 *Infra*, Chapter 14.
8 *Supra*, para. 3.2.

13.8 Although the EEC Treaty specifically provides for direct applicability only in the case of regulations there can be little doubt in theory and especially in view of the jurisprudence of the Court of Justice[1] that the Treaty provisions themselves are also directly applicable in the Member States in the sense that they are an integral part of their legal systems.[2]

Directives, as already mentioned, and decisions must also, insofar as their nature as Community law permits, penetrate into the Member States independently of any national measure.[3]

1 *Van Gend en Loos* and *Costa v ENEL supra* para. 13.5, n. 1 and n. 3.
2 See Kovar, The Relationship between Community Law and National Law in *Thirty Years of Community Law* (1983), p. 109, at pp. 131–132; H.G. Schermers, *Judicial Protection in the European Communities*, Fourth Edition (1987), pp. 76–7, C.-A. Morand, *La Legislation dans les Communautés Européennes* (1968), p. 58; P.J.G. Kapteyn and P. Verloren van Themaat, *supra* 29.
3 See also H.G. Schermers, *Judicial Protection in the European Communities*, Fourth Edition (1987), at paras. 159 and 162; T.C. Hartley, *The Foundations of European Community Law* (1981), at p. 118.

13.9 The consequences of this 'bold and ambitious'[1] stance taken by the European Court are interesting. Clearly Community laws cannot be kept out of the Member States because they have not been incorporated or received into the national system by a separate national legal act. The Court of Justice is not content, however, with this minimalist position. The court also prohibits measures designed to transpose Community regulations into national law as being unnecessary and confusing. Such transposition and reception measures might have the effect of concealing the Community nature of the legal rule and the consequences flowing from it.[2] National laws which conflict with directly applicable provisions of Community law are automatically inapplicable and no new national measures may be validly adopted if in conflict with directly applicable Community law. Moreover, the obligation imposed in this regard on Member States is not merely a negative one—to refrain from actions preventing Community laws from coming into the Member States—the Court of Justice also imposes an obligation on the Member States to take positive action to ensure that Community law has full effect within the national legal systems, for example, by obliging the Member State to make whatever legislative adjustments are necessary to remove confusion and to establish certainty.[3] This applies to the proper execution of directives also. It also means

'. . . that a national court which is called upon, within the limits of its jurisdiction, to apply provisions of Community law is under a duty to give full effect to those provisions, if necessary refusing of its own motion to apply any conflicting provision of national legislation, even if adopted subsequently, and it is not necessary for the court to request or await the prior setting aside of such provision by legislative or other constitutional means.'[4]

By way of summary, therefore, one may declare that all Community law, and not only regulations, apply throughout the Community's area of jurisdiction. Community law is law in the Member States irrespective of incorporating measures.[5] Member States cannot take unilateral action which would impede Community law from coming into the national legal systems. Indeed Member States, and the national courts in particular, must make every effort to ensure the full efficacy of Community law within their own legal systems.

1 T.C. Hartley, *The Foundations of European Community Law* (1981), at p. 190.
2 Case 94/77 *Fratelli Zerbone v Amministrazione delle Finanze dello Stato* [1978] E.C.R. 99, at p. 116; D. Wyatt, (1978) E. L. Rev. 303.
3 Case 167/73 *EC Commission v France* [1974] E.C.R. 359, [1974] 2 C.M.L.R. 216.
4 Case 106/77 *Amministrazione delle Finanze dello Stato v Simmenthal* [1978] E.C.R. 629, at p. 644, [1978] 3 C.M.L.R. 263 at p. 284.
5 *Supra*, para 13.7, and fn 5.

Direct Effect

13.10 Equally important to the question of direct applicability just discussed is the question of 'direct effect' by which we mean to ask whether a Community measure gives individuals rights which they may maintain before the national courts.[1] In this sense the question of 'direct effects' is merely a question of interpretation: is the nature of the Community measure such that it bestows rights on individuals?

The question should not frighten Irish lawyers since although not dressed in familiar terminology the concept is hardly a strange one even in the Irish legal system. One may thus look at any Irish statute and ask the same question: does this act give the individual rights which the courts must protect? In relation to Irish statutes one may say that some do and some do not. To find out whether the act does give such rights one must look at the act itself and interpret it. So, for example, an act such as the Electricity (Supply) Act 1927 makes provision for the setting up of the Electricity Supply Board and makes general provision for the attainment of that objective. It imposes on specified bodies certain tasks in this connection. But it does not bestow rights on individuals if the Board does not act. Other acts, such as the Hotel Proprietors Act 1963, for example, clearly do intend to give rights to individuals, where, in the example given, for instance, the hotel guest suffers personal or property injury while in a hotel.

Similarly the question of the direct effect of a Community provision within the Community legal order can arise and this should cause no problem of comprehension. If the measure is determined to have direct effect within the Community legal order the Court of Justice will enforce the individual's rights in Community law. No problem arises since there is only one legal system involved, and there is no possibility of conflict with any rule from another legal order. The difficulties arise principally when one asks the question whether a *Community* provision has direct effect in the *national* legal order for here one is faced with two different systems and the possibility of conflict between them.[2]

The doctrine of direct effects in Community law, therefore may, at the risk of simplification, be merely a quest for criteria as to when a

Community law gives an individual rights in the Community system which the national courts must enforce. Fortunately, after a great deal of controversy and debate, the Community's general position on the matter has now clarified: provided certain specified conditions are fulfilled Community measures, whether treaty rules, regulations, directives or decisions, are capable of bestowing rights on individuals which the national courts must uphold. Moreover, it should be noted that the doctrine may impose *obligations* on individuals also, and where applicable, may be enforced by Member States as well as by individuals. We will now turn to an elaboration of those conditions and to an examination of the Court of Justice's steady progress to its present position.

1 The jurisprudence of the Court on this has been described as 'the cornerstone of the whole edifice for the effectiveness of Community law'. Pierre Pescatore, *Address on the Application of Community Law in each of the Member States*, Court of Justice, Judicial and Academic Conference VI at p. 16 (Luxembourg, 27–28 September, 1976). Clearly the phrase 'which national courts must protect' must be interpreted liberally, if a measure is directly effective the individual must be protected by any national authority and not only by the courts. See Gerhard Bebr, *The Development of Judicial Control of the European Communities* (1981), pp. 564–5.

2 See *Deuxième colloque international de droit européen* 146 (1963); Berb, 564–565.

13.11 Before one does so, however, it is worth pausing a moment to emphasise the separate nature of the three problems of direct applicability, direct effects and supremacy of Community law. In practice the three concepts are very closely linked and indeed many writers suggest that they are all facets of the same problem. Whatever the view one takes of this, it is not necessary to elaborate further on this matter other than to provide a concrete example so as to show how these issues can arise for the individual in practice. Suppose an individual in Ireland is of the opinion that he is entitled to some benefit or some protection under Community law, but that the Irish legislation does not reflect the Community position. The individual may, in these circumstances, claim that the conflict between his Community rights and those afforded to him by national law should be determined in favour of the former. The individual's opportunity to assert his Community right in the Community Court is limited and normally he will have to assert it in the national courts. This he may do by taking positive action (e.g. suing the Irish Government for non-payment of the Community benefit) or by resisting a prosecution made by the national authorities. In both cases he will be asserting that national law is in conflict with Community law and the latter must be allowed to prevail (Supremacy of Community law). In hearing the case the Court will initially be concerned with the other two issues: is the Community law on which the individual relies part of the national legal system (directly applicable) and is it of such a kind that it gives the individual rights which the national courts must uphold (direct effect). This close relationship between the three concepts[1] also explains why the seminal precedents (*van Gend en Loos* case and *Costa v ENEL* case) reappear as relevant authorities on all three issues. In such a case, because the questions raised are matters of Community law the national court is likely to avail of the referral procedure contained in Article 177 under which it can 'state a case' to the Court of Justice in Luxembourg.

1 See R. Kovar in *Thirty Years of Community Law* (1983), at p. 138; Gerhard Bebr, *The Development of Judicial Control of the European Communities* (1981), at pp. 548, 556; P.S.R.F. Mathijsen, *A Guide to European Community Law*, Fourth Edition (1985), p. 228, fn. 5.

13.12 Finally, before one investigates the criteria required before a Community measure is considered directly effective it is worth examining the reasons why the Court of Justice insists on providing individuals with rights in this matter. Firstly, since the treaties apply to individuals and oblige them in many respects it is only proper that they should also give them rights which are judicially enforceable. Second, to confine individuals who feel that their rights have been infringed by Member States, to the enforcement procedures provided for in EEC Treaty, art.s 169 and 170 would be to deny these individuals real and effective remedies. The enforcement procedures provided for in Articles 169 and 170 can be availed of only by the Commission and, as well as being cumbersome and slow, may be subject to wider political considerations. For the individual at most they may be said to provide only indirect protection. Moreover, by providing individuals with rights which national courts must enforce the Court of Justice is in fact making available additional means of supervising Member States and ensuring that they fulfil their obligations. It promotes the process of integration. Third, it is important that the concept of 'direct effect' should be centrally and uniformly developed. If the concept were left to the national courts a variety of interpretations would emerge with the result that the individual would have his rights defined and protected differently throughout the Community. This would undermine the Community rules which '. . . must be fully and uniformly applied in all Member States . . .'.[1] It would also undermine the supremacy doctrine for by 'refusing to recognize a Treaty provision to produce a direct effect, a national court could prevent a Community provision from penetrating into the national legal order and so preclude its supremacy'.[2]

1 *Simmenthal* Case *supra*, para. 13.9, n. 4, at p. 643; See also Case 13/68 *Salgoil v Italian Ministry for Foreign Trade* [1968] E.C.R. 453, [1969] C.M.L.R. 181 and Case 14/68 *Wilhelm v Bundeskartellamt* [1969] E.C.R. 1, [1969] C.M.L.R. 100.
2 Gerhard Bebr, *The Development of Judicial Control of the European Communities* (1981), at p. 55. Procedural variations, however, are tolerated to some extent. See R. Kovar, The Relationship between Community law and national law, in *Thirty Years of Community Law* (1983), at p. 109, especially pp. 146–149, on tension which direct effects rule involves for national courts. See also on this Gerhard Bebr, *The Development of Judicial Control of the European Communities* (1981), at p. 602.

Community Criteria before a Measure is deemed to have Direct Effect

Treaty Provisions

13.13 As already intimated the question of direct effect is really one of interpretation. In approaching this question the Court of Justice has moved away from the traditional approach of seeking 'the intention of the parties', which is unsuited to the new autonomous legal order established in the EEC, to a search based on an examination of 'the spirit, the general scheme and the wording of the Treaty'.[1] It is sometimes said that before a treaty provision will be declared to be directly effective it must be 'complete and legally perfect'.[2] The Court of Justice has stated that a treaty provision will meet this requirement when the provision is

(a) clear and precise
(b) unconditional
(c) of such a kind that it requires no further action on the part of the Community institutions or the Member States or, if the measure requires execution, that it leaves no discretion to the Member State in the execution of the measure.[3]

Of course the content of the provision must also be such that it can cause direct effect.[4]

A further word on each of these requirements would not be inappropriate.

1 *Van Gend en Loos* Case, *supra.* para. 13.5, n. 1; Case 28/67 *Molkerei-Zentrale Westfalen/Lippe v Hauptzollamt Paderborn* [1968] E.C.R. 143, [1968] C.M.L.R. 187; Case 9/70 *Grad v Finanzamt Traunstein* [1970] E.C.R. 825, [1971] C.M.L.R. 1. It is important to bear this in mind here, since whether provision has direct effect or not, is primarily a question of interpretation and construction, and the Courts teleological and schematic approaches in these matters are of some significance. Accordingly, the identity of the addressee is not determinative: provisions addressed to Member States may, for instance, create rights for individuals within the national legal systems. (*Van Gend en Loos, supra*; Case 2/74 *Reyners v Belgium* [1974] E.C.R. 631, [1974] 2 C.M.L.R. 305.)
2 Case 57/65 *Lütticke v Hauptzollamt Saarlouis* [1966] E.C.R. 205, at p. 210, [1971] C.M.L.R. 674, at p. 684.
3 See *Van Gend en Loos* Case, *supra*, n. 1; *Costa v ENEL, supra*, para. 13.5, n. 3; *Lütticke* Case, *supra*, n. 2; *Molkerei-Zentrale* Case, *supra*, n. 1; *Salgoil* Case, *supra*, para. 13.12, n. 1.
4 For list see H.G. Schermers, *Judicial Protection in the European Communities*, Fourth Edition (1987), p. 104.

(a) Clear and Precise

13.14 Some provisions in the Treaty are of such a kind that they are too vague and general to give individuals rights. For example Article 5(1) provides as follows

'Member States shall take all appropriate measures, whether general or particular, to ensure fulfilment of the obligations arising out of the Treaty or resulting from action taken by the institutions of the Community. They shall facilitate the achievement of the Community's tasks.'

There is little doubt that it would be difficult to maintain that this is the kind of provision which is precise or specific enough to give rights to the individual.[1] By way of contrast negative prohibitions addressed to Member States obliging them to refrain from doing something are especially suited to be considered sufficiently clear and precise. In the first case where the matter arose—*Van Gend en Loos* once more—the Court had no hesitation in declaring Article 12 to be directly effective. The Article reads as follows:

'Member States shall refrain from introducing between themselves any new customs duties on imports or exports or any charges having equivalent effect, and from increasing those which they already apply in their trade with each other.'

The suggestion in the wake of this case, that direct effect would be confined to those articles of the treaties which were expressed as negative commands, was not followed by the Court in it subsequent jurisprudence so that now many treaty articles imposing *positive* obligations have also been held to have direct effect.[2] Article 52 was the article in question in *Reyners v Belgium*.[3] The case is interesting and merits further attention.

Reyners, a Dutch national, was born in Brussels of Dutch parents. All his schooling was received in Belgium and he took his University law degree and his professional bar exams in that country. When he applied for admission to the Belgian Bar, however, he was refused because he did not fulfil another condition, namely the condition that he should be a Belgian national. Reyners contended that the Belgian law was contrary to Community law and the matter came before the Court of Justice on a referral under EEC Treaty, art. 177. Reyners relied on Article 52 of the Treaty which reads, in part, as follows:

'Within the framework of the provisions set out below, restrictions on the freedom of establishment of nationals of a Member State in the territory of another Member State shall be abolished by progressive stages in the course of the transitional period.'

In spite of the fact that it was envisaged by the Treaty (Articles 54–57) that the full realisation of the right of establishment would be achieved only through the adoption of a general programme which would be implemented by directives in due course, only some of which had been adopted when the case was being heard, the Court nevertheless held the article to be directly effective. According to the Court Article 52 expressed in a specific instance the general rule contained in Article 7 of the Treaty prohibiting discrimination on the basis of nationality.[4] It further declared:

'In laying down that freedom of establishment shall be attained at the end of the transitional period, Article 52 thus imposes an obligation to attain a precise result, the fulfilment of which had to be made easier by, but not made dependent on, the implementation of a programme of progressive measures, . . .

'After the expiry of the transitional period the directives provided for by the Chapter on the right of establishment have become superfluous with regard to implementing the rule on nationality, since this is henceforth sanctioned by the Treaty itself with direct effect. . . .

'It is right therefore to reply to the question raised that, since the end of the transitional period, Article 52 of the Treaty is a directly applicable provision despite the absence in a particular sphere, of directives prescribed by Articles 54(2) and 57(1) of the Treaty.'[5]

At the end of the transitional period the suspensive condition no longer applied, and Article 52, at least in relation to non-discrimination on the basis of nationality, flowed into the legal systems of the Member States and became directly effective. Reyners could insist on having the offending national measure struck down and on being registered with the Belgian bar.

Moreover, that the Treaty contemplates an exception or a derogation to the main provision in question, does not detract from the clarity or preciseness of the obligation itself. So where free movement of workers is guaranteed, subject to public policy, public health and public security, the latter limitation does not make the treaty obligation any less precise.[6]

1 Case 9/73 *Schlüter v Hauptzollamt Lörrach* [1973] E.C.R. 1135; Case 10/73 *Rewe-Zentral v Hauptzollamt Kehl* [1973] E.C.R. 1175. See art.s 6(1) and 50 for a similar provision. Case 149/77 *Defrenne v Sabena (No 3)* [1978] E.C.R. 1365, [1978] 3 C.M.L.R. 312 concerning EEC Treaty, art.s 117 and 118. T.C. Hartley, *The Foundations of European Community Law* (1981), pp. 191,2.
2 For list see H.G. Schermers, *Judicial Protection in the European Communities*, Fourth Edition (1987), p. 105 and authorities cited there.
3 Case 2/74 [1974] E.C.R. 631, [1974] 2 C.M.L.R. 305.
4 *Supra*, n. 3, at p. 650.
5 *Supra*, n. 3, at pp. 651–2. For 'directly applicable' read 'directly effective' in terminology adopted by present authors.
6 Case 41/74 *Van Duyn v Home Office* [1974] E.C.R. 1337, [1975] 1 C.M.L.R. 1.

(b) Unconditional

13.15 To be directly effective the treaty provision must not be dependent on any condition. What is meant here, it would appear, is that the provision is conditional if its operation depends on the action of the Community institutions or on the discretion of a Member State.[1] Article 33(4) of the Treaty, for example, provides that, *if the Commission finds that imports are below a certain level* for any product this shall not be taken into account in calculating the total value of the global quotas. 'In such case, the Member State shall abolish quota restrictions on the product concerned.' Clearly, the Member State's obligation here is conditional on a prior finding by the Commission, and so cannot have direct effect.

In truth this requirement is closely connected with the third requirement below.

1 See *Salgoil* Case, *supra*, para. 13.12, n. 1, at pp. 464–8; See also T.C. Hartley, *The Foundations of European Community Law* (1981), at p. 193; Gerhard Bebr, *The Development of Judicial Control of the European Communities* (1981), at p. 570.

(c) No Further Action Required

13.16 If the provision contemplates further action on the part of the institutions of the Community or the Member States then the measure is not legally complete or self-sufficient and therefore not of a kind which gives individuals rights. But even in this case where an intervening act is called for, such an act will only prevent a direct effect where the authority in question is exercising a discretionary power.[1] If the authority does not have any choice then the measure can have direct effect.[2] On the other hand, if a Community institution or a Member State is given real discretion in implementing or executing the obligation imposed by the Treaty there can be no direct effect. In fact the treaty obligation is held back by the contemplated wedge interposed between the treaty provision and the individual seeking to rely on it. Similarly, a provision may be denied direct effect because a certain time limit has not passed. For example, a Member State may be obliged to do something by the end of the transitional period.

No direct effect can then be given to this provision until the time stipulated has passed. When, however, the time limit has passed the measure can become directly effective from that moment on. The time limit in such a case merely suspends the obligation, and provided the treaty provision is in other respects clear and unconditional, when the time limit expires the treaty obligation flows into the national legal system and may be relied on by individuals therein. The *Reyners* Case above clearly illustrates this and the Court of Justice has reaffirmed it several times in its later jurisprudence.[3]

The erosion of conditions (b) and (c) above by the Court of Justice has led one commentator to suggest that the real test nowadays of whether a Community measure is directly effective or not 'is really one of feasibility: if the provision lends itself to judicial application it will almost certainly be declared directly effective; only where direct effect would create serious practical problems is it likely that the provision will be held not to be directly effective'.[4]

1 Case 27/67 *Fink-Frucht v Hauptzollamt München-Landsbergerstrasse* [1968] E.C.R. 223.
2 *Costa v ENEL*, *supra*, para. 13.5, n. 3.
3 See Case 33/70 *SACE v Ministero delle Finanze* [1970] E.C.R. 1213, [1971] C.M.L.R. 123; *Lütticke* Case, *supra*, para. 13.13, n. 2; Case 77/72 *Capolongo v Azienda Agricola Maya* [1973] E.C.R. 611, [1974] 1 C.M.L.R. 230; Case 43/75 *Defrenne v Sabena (No 2)* [1976] E.C.R. 455, [1976] 2 C.M.L.R. 98.
4 T.C. Hartley, *The Foundation of European Community Law* (1981), at p. 197; A measure will have direct effect 'if the Court of Justice feels able and sufficiently equipped to apply the provision without any further act by the authorities of the Community or its Member States'. W. van Gerven, cited by H.G. Schermers, *Judicial Protection in the European Communities*, Fourth Edition (1987), at para. 99, fn. 317.

13.17 Normally speaking when an individual raises in the national courts the possibility of a Community measure having 'direct effect' he does so to establish a failure of a Member State in respect of its obligations, either to claim that the Member State has passed, or failed to repeal, legislation contrary to Community law. This is known as the vertical effect, because the measure attacked is 'coming down' to the individual from the State. The question can also be posed in relation to 'direct effect', as to whether the doctrine has horizontal effects in the sense that it can be maintained by an individual *against another individual* or undertaking in the national courts. After some hesitation, the Court of Justice has now unequivocally declared that it can. In the *Walrave and Koch* Case,[1] for example, the plaintiffs, pacemakers in the world of professional cycling, were able to have struck down a rule adopted by an International Cyclists' Association to the effect that in the world championships the pacemaker had to be of the same nationality as the stayer. The Court of Justice held that this discriminated on the grounds of nationality and that 'Prohibition of such discrimination does not apply only to the action of public authorities but extends likewise to rules of any other nature aimed at regulating in a collective manner gainful employment and the provision of services'.[2] Regulations must also be capable of creating 'horizontal' direct effects[3] but the Court of Justice has recently decided that no 'horizontal' effect can be claimed in respect of directives.[4]

1 Case 36/74 *Walrave and Koch v Association Union Cycliste Internationale* [1974] E.C.R. 1405, [1975] 1 C.M.L.R. 320.
2 *Supra*, n. 1, at p. 1418. See also Second *Defrenne* Case, *supra*, para. 13.16, n. 3. Equal pay for equal work provision in EEC Treaty, art. 119 enforceable against employers.
3 J.V. Louis, *The Community Legal Order* (1980), at p. 85.
4 See *Marshall* Case, *infra*, 13.19, n. 14 and accompanying text. See also R. Kovar, The Relationship between Community Law and National Law in *Thirty Years of Community Law* (1983), p. 109, at p. 145. See also Gerdhard Bebr, *The Development of Judicial Control of the European Communities* (1981), at p. 601; A.J. Easson, *Can Directives Impose Obligations on Individuals?* (1979), 4 E. L. Rev. pp. 67–79.

Secondary Legislation
1. Regulations

13.18 The question of 'direct effect' first arose in connection with treaty provisions but the Court of Justice has now declared in several cases that secondary legislation can also create 'direct effects'. Once the distinction between the concepts of direct applicability and direct effect is accepted it is not difficult to embrace this proposition in respect of regulations at least. Regulations, by virtue of EEC Treaty, art. 189, clearly penetrate into the national legal systems, and just as one may ask in connection with a treaty provision, one may also enquire of such a measure whether it gives rights to individuals. The Court has unequivocally answered yes to this on several occasions applying the same criteria already developed in connection with the treaty provisions to determine whether a particular regulation has direct effect or not.

One example will be sufficient to illustrate the court's attitude. *The Slaughtered Cow* Case[1] concerned Regulations 1975/69 and 2195/69 which introduced a system of premiums to encourage the slaughter of dairy cows and to dissuade farmers from marketing milk products. The Italian government had failed to implement the appropriate measures when Mrs Leonesio slaughtered five dairy cows and claimed a premium of 625,000 lire. The matter was referred to the Court of Justice as to whether the regulations were directly effective and whether national legislation could postpone payment of the claim. The court held:

'The second paragraph of Article 189 of the Treaty provides that regulations shall have "general application" and "shall be directly applicable in all Member States". Therefore, because of its nature and its purpose within the system of sources of Community law it has direct effect and is, as such, capable of creating individual rights which national courts must protect.'[2]

Although it is not entirely consistent in the terminology it uses, it is submitted that the Court of Justice, in its holding now implicitly accepts the distinction made between 'direct applicability' and 'direct effect'.[3] Regulations are by their nature of such a kind that they do not require incorporation measures and in many cases may give the individual rights. In later cases the Court makes this clearer when it says: 'Regulations are directly applicable and therefore by virtue of their nature capable of producing direct effects.' Whether they do in fact give individual rights in any given case requires an examination of the instrument itself in the light of the criteria elaborated above.[4]

1 Case 93/71 *Leonesio v Ministero dell'Agricoltura e delle Foreste* [1972] E.C.R. 287, [1973] C.M.L.R. 343.
2 *Idem* at p. 293.
3 *Grad* Case, *supra*, para. 13.13, n. 1, at pp. 837 and 23 respectively; see also Case 148/78 *Pubblico Ministero v Ratti* [1979] E.C.R. 1629, at p. 1641, [1980] 1 C.M.L.R. 96, at pp. 109,10, and T.C. Hartley, *The Foundations of European Community Law* (1981), p. 199.
4 See also Case 43/71 *Politi v Ministero delle Finanze* [1971] E.C.R. 1039, [1973] C.M.L.R. 60; Case 84/71 *Marimex v Ministero delle Finanze* [1972] E.C.R. 89, [1972] C.M.L.R. 907; Case 34/73 *Fratelli Variola v Amministrazione Italiana delle Finanze* [1973] E.C.R. 981.

2. Directives

13.19 Because directives and decisions are of a less penetrating form of Community legislation—directives especially contemplating further action by the Member States—there was some hesitation on the issue as to whether these instruments could create direct effects. It was argued that by specifically stating that regulations were directly applicable and binding in their entirety, Article 189 implied that directives and decisions could not possess these qualities. Further state action in the case of directives also suggested that the third condition elaborated by the Court in connection with the Treaty provisions could never be fulfilled in relation to directives. These arguments were, however, rejected by the Court of Justice and in a series of unequivocal judgments the Court has held that individuals may derive rights from directives also.

In the *Grad* Case the Court ruled that:

'. . . although it is true that by virtue of Article 189, regulations are directly applicable and therefore by virtue of their nature capable of producing direct effects, it does not follow from this that other categories of legal measure mentioned in that article can never produce similar effects.'[1]

The Court emphasised that Article 189 was concerned in its definitions in Article 189 with the manner in which its legislative powers are to be exercised, but no reference is made therein to the effects of the respective legislative measures, in the legal systems.[2]

Whether an individual derives rights from Community legislation therefore is not dependent on the form of the legislation but rather on whether there has been an infringement of a Community obligation and whether the measure meets the other criteria—that it is clear, unconditional and requires no further action. This is not to say that the form of the legislation is irrelevant in this connection. Bearing in mind the difference between regulations and directives it has been well said that in the case of directives there is a presumption which may be rebutted, against direct effect.[3] In this matter, Bebr concludes:

'firstly, only a specific provision of a directive, not however the entire act, may produce a direct effect; secondly, such a provision must, in each instance, meet the criteria required for a provision directly effective; and finally, a direct effect of a directive is an exception rather than a rule'.[4]

The clearest case of the Court's position on the direct effect of directives is the *Van Duyn* Case.[5] The earlier cases[6] contained clear dicta of the Court's position, but their precedent value was weakened because the Court linked the direct effect of the directives in question to treaty provisions already held to be directly effective in the Court's jurisprudence. In *Van Duyn*, however, the substantive effect of a directive itself was held to be directly effective, without support from other treaty provisions. The facts were as follows.

Ms Van Duyn, a Dutch national, was offered employment by the Church of Scientology in Great Britain. Under the Treaty free movement of workers is guaranteed subject to the host state's right to exclude entry on the grounds of 'public policy, public security or public health'. In an effort to harmonise the scope of this exception and to minimise the abuse of it by Member States the Community issued a directive[7] which attempted to define more specifically these concepts. When Ms Van Duyn was refused entry to Britain on the ground that, although not illegal, the activities of the Church of Scientology were socially harmful and contrary to public policy, she contested the exclusion order on the basis that it violated her Community rights as expressed in Directive 64/220.

In particular she drew attention to the fact that the directive stipulated that national measures taken on the grounds of public policy had to be based exclusively on the personal conduct of the individual concerned,[8] and that her membership of the Church of Scientology did not constitute such personal conduct. On this matter the Court declared that

'By providing that measures taken on the grounds of public policy shall be based exclusively on the personal conduct of the individual concerned, Article 3(1) of Directive 64/221 is intended to limit the discretionary power which national laws generally confer on the authorities responsible for the entry and expulsion of foreign nationals. First, the provision lays down an obligation which is not subject to any exception or condition and which, by its very nature, does not require the intervention of any act on the part either of the institutions of the Community or of Member States. Secondly, because Member States are thereby obliged, in implementing a clause which derogates from one of the fundamental principles of the Treaty in favour of individuals, not to take account of factors extraneous to personal conduct, legal certainty for the persons concerned requires that they should be able to rely on this obligation even though it has been laid down in a legislative act which has no automatic direct effect in its entirety.'[9]

Moreover, that provisions may be ambiguous and require interpretation, is not, because of the Article 177 procedure available in the Treaty, sufficient to render it unclear and imprecise.

Although Ms Van Duyn won the legal argument on this point, her victory was a Pyrrhic one because her conduct in relation to the Church of Scientology was indeed held to be personal conduct and so her exclusion could be justified even in terms of the directive.[10]

In *Becker v Finanzamt Münster-Innenstadt*[11] the Court of Justice confirmed its approach in the *Grad* Case and the *Ratti* Case[12] that a taxpayer may rely on the provisions of a directive if they are unconditional and sufficiently precise. In that case a German taxpayer claimed exemption from VAT in respect of credit negotiation transactions based on Directive 77/388 concerning the harmonisation of turnover taxes which at that time had not been implemented in Germany. The failure by the national authorities to implement the directive could not prevent the individual from relying on the directive in appropriate cases.[13]

Finally, in the present context the question arises as to whether a directive as well as giving rights to individuals against recalcitrant Member States, might also give rights to individuals against other individuals (i.e. could it also have 'horizontal' effects?) In *Marshall v Southampton and South West Hampshire Area Health Authority (Teaching)*[14] the Court of Justice answered no to this question. However, it appears that a Member State will be bound by the direct effects principle even where it is was acting in its capacity as an employer and not exercising its government powers in the case in question and to this extent there may be limited 'horizontal' effects. Conceivably, therefore, a public employee might have more rights in this matter than an employee in private employment.[15] The Court held, in effect, that a lower compulsory retirement age for women than for men was discrimination on the grounds of sex and was contrary to Directive 76/207.

1 *Supra*, para. 13.13, fn. 1, at pp. 837 and 23 respectively. See also *SACE* Case, *supra*, par. 13.16, n. 3. The arguments for and against direct effect in these cases were outlined by the Commission in the *Grad* Case [1970] E.C.R. 825, at 831–832.
2 *Idem*. See also Gerhard Bebr, *The Development of Judicial Control of the European Communities* (1981), at p. 558.
3 See A. Dashwood, *The Principle of Direct Effect in European Community Law*, XVI J.C.M.S. 229 (1978), at p. 241; Gerhard Bebr, *The Development of Judicial Control of the European Communities* (1981), at p. 585.
4 Bebr, 585–6.
5 Case 41/74 [1974] E.C.R. 1337, [1975] 1 C.M.L.R. 1.
6 *Grad* Case, *supra*, para. 13.13, n. 1 and *SACE* case, *supra*, para. 13.16, n. 3.
7 Council Directive 64/221 (EEC) O.J. (Sp. Ed.) 1963–64 p. 117.
8 Art. 3(1) and (2).
9 *Idem* at p. 1348.
10 *Idem* at p. 1351.
11 Case 8/81 [1982] E.C.R. 53, [1982] 1 C.M.L.R. 499. See also Case 286/85 *McDermott and Cotter v Minister for Social Welfare and A-G* [1987] I.L.R.M. 324 *Infra*, 24.8.
12 *Supra*, para. 13.18, n. 3.
13 This holding clarified the law since both the German Federal Court and the French Conseil d'Etat had denied direct effect of Directive 77/388 because it had not been implemented by a national statute.
14 Case 152/84 [1986] 1 C.M.L.R. 688.
15 See 11 Eur. L. Rev. 117–118. Editorial. This could be important in the Irish scene where there are so many State-sponsored commercial bodies.

3. Decisions

13.20 Decisions addressed to individuals bind the persons to whom they are addressed by virtue of EEC Treaty, art. 189 and so have direct effect on them. The question remains whether individuals can rely on decisions addressed to other persons, whether these be other private individuals or Member States. Again the Court of Justice has answered this, in principle at least, in the affirmative declaring first, that to deny individuals the possibility of rights in such cases would be contrary to the binding force given to decisions in Article 189 and second that the useful effect ('effet utile') of such acts would be greatly weakened if individuals could not, in principle, enforce them in national courts.[1]

Whether a particular decision bestows rights on individuals to whom it is not addressed, however, depends very much on the nature and content of the decision itself. Moreover, to be directly effective such a measure must also meet the usual criteria required for other Community acts.[2]

One other difference between regulations on the one hand, and directives and decisions on the other, is that the former require to be published in the Official Journal of the Community while the latter do not. Is it possible that the non-publication could cause difficulties in directly applying such measures? Too much must not be made of this argument, since in practice nearly all decisions and directives are in fact published by the Communities. Moreover, the worst effect non-publication can have here, since the addressees will be notified in any event, is that an individual may go in ignorance of his rights. There is no question in this case of the individual being saddled with obligations without his knowledge. The worst is that vigilant and informed individuals may have an advantage over those who are not so alert. In these circumstances there is no question of denying direct effect to provisions in directives or decisions on the ground of non-publication. To hold otherwise would mean that a Community institution could, by not publishing an act, deny it direct effect. In Bebr's view this would be a 'preposterous result'.[3]

1 *Grad* Case *supra.*
2 *Grad* Case *supra.*
3 Gerhard Bebr, *The Development of Judicial Control of the European Communities* (1981) at p. 589.

Supremacy of Community law

13.21 Community law applies not only in the Community legal order, it also applies in the legal systems of the Member States. Consistently the Court of Justice declares that Community law has become an integral part of the national legal systems[1] and must be enforced by the national courts as part of their own law. It contemplates, therefore, the existence of two legal systems and the continued existence of laws from two sources: the Community source and the national source. From this stand it must, therefore, contemplate the possibility of a conflict between the two sources of law and must give an answer to the question: in the event of a conflict between the systems which is to prevail?

The treaties do not expressly refer to the principle of Community supremacy although some provisions implicitly suggest it.[2] Essentially, however, in spite of the treaty provisions, one must in the end consider the doctrine to be a product of judicial activism, and it is in the Court of Justice's jurisprudence that the history of the doctrine is to be found.

The Community's approach to this problem has been a consistently authoritarian one. Firstly, the Court of Justice has declared that it has the exclusive jurisdiction to determine the supremacy issue and that the national courts do not have any say in the matter. Secondly, it declares that in the event of any conflict between Community law in any form and national law in any form, Community law must *always* prevail.[3] A further word about each of these is necessary.

With regard to the jurisdiction question—which court has the right to determine the supremacy issue—when two jurisdictions are competing, as in the present case, neither system would appear to have an inherent exclusive right to determine the matter in the absence of agreement. To allow each Member State, however, to have a right to determine this issue would be to invite a chaos which would strike at the very foundation of the Community itself. 'Although national courts have from time to time attempted to solve conflicts by applying the rules of their own legal (i.e. constitutional) systems, it is clear that such attempts are in principle not correct . . . and that only Community law can provide a solution which then must have uniform validity for the Community as a whole.'[4]

With regard to the substantive issue as to which system should prevail in the event of a conflict the court has from the earliest date taken a strong uncompromising stance. To appreciate fully the force of its position it might be helpful for an Irish lawyer to recall how conflicts between laws *within* the national system are resolved by the Irish courts. What happens, for example, in the Irish legal system, if two laws conflict with each other? Which prevails? Two principles are used to resolve such conflicts. Firstly, there exists in the Irish system, and in most systems, a hierarchy of laws, the more important laws being superior to the less important. In Ireland the constitution ranks above statutory law and statutory law ranks above Ministerial regulations derived therefrom. In a conflict situation Ministerial orders yield to statutes, and statutes yield to the constitution. With regard to a conflict situation between measures of *equal* rank the later prevails over the earlier: *lex posterior derogat lege priori*. In relation to a conflict between Community law and national law, however, Community law will not permit either of these principles to be used to undermine Community supremacy. From the Community's point of view it could be said that Community law comes in at the apex of the national system and is supreme in the hierarchy and, therefore, it cannot be challenged from any other law in the system. Its supremacy is guaranteed as such. Neither a national constitutional provision nor a later statute can successfully challenge it. The supremacy is absolute.

In *Costa v ENEL*,[5] the facts of which are already given, the conflict was between the EEC Treaty provision and a subsequent Italian statute setting up ENEL. The Court of Justice, to whom the case was referred under Article 177, made the following strong statement on this matter:

'The integration into the laws of each Member State of provisions which derive from the Community, and more generally the terms and the spirit of the Treaty, make it impossible for the States, as a corollary to accord precedence to a unilateral and subsequent measure over a legal system accepted by them on a basis of reciprocity. Such a measure cannot vary from one State to another in deference to subsequent domestic law, without jeopardizing the attainment of the objectives of the Treaty set out in Article 5(2) and giving rise to the discrimination prohibited by Article 7.

'The obligations undertaken under the Treaty establishing the Community would not be unconditional, but merely contingent, if they could be called in question by subsequent legislative acts of the signatories. Wherever the Treaty grants the States the right to act unilaterally, it does this by clear and precise provisions (for example Articles 15, 93(3), 223, 224 and 226) which would lose their purpose if the Member States could renounce their obligations by means of an ordinary law.

'The precedence of Community law is confirmed by Article 189, whereby a regulation "shall be binding" and "directly applicable in all Member States". This provision, which is subject to no reservation, would be quite meaningless if a State could unilaterally nullify its effects by means of a legislative measure which could prevail over Community law.

'It follows from all these observations that the law stemming from the Treaty, an independent source of law, could not, because of its special and original nature, be overriden by domestic legal provisions, however framed, without being deprived of its character as Community law and without the legal basis of the Community itself being called in question.

'The transfer by the States from their domestic legal system to the Community legal system of the rights and obligations arising under the Treaty carries with it a permanent limitation of their sovereign rights, against which a subsequent unilateral act incompatible with the concept of the Community cannot prevail.'[6]

Later in the *Internationale Handelsgesellschaft* Case,[7] where the conflict was between a Community regulation and the fundamental rights provisions of the German constitution, the Court was equally uncompromising. Here the plaintiff company obtained an export licence for corn-flour under a Community regulation. The company was obliged to lodge a deposit as a guarantee that it would effect the export in accordance with the licence. When it failed to fulfil the terms of the licence, notice of intention to forfeit the deposit was served on it. The company contested that the proposed forfeiture was contrary to its fundamental rights, in particular to its freedom of action and disposition, to its economic liberty and to the principle of proportionality protected by Articles 2(1) and 14 of the German Basic Law. In referral proceedings under Article 177 the Court of Justice declared:

'Recourse to the legal rules or concepts of national law in order to judge the validity of measures adopted by the institution of the Community would have an adverse effect on the uniformity and efficiency of Community law. The validity of such measures can only be judged in the light of Community law. In fact, the law stemming from the Treaty, an independent source of law, cannot because of its very nature be overriden by rules of national law, however framed, without being deprived of its character as Community law and without the legal basis of the Community itself being called in question. Therefore the validity of a Community measure or its effect within a Member State cannot be affected by allegations that it runs counter to either fundamental rights as formulated by the constitution of that State or the principles of a national constitutional structure.'[8]

The Court did, however, to soften the blow and to make its uncompromising stand more acceptable to national courts, go on to say that it had a duty to examine whether any analogous guarantee in Community law had been disregarded by the forfeiture measure. In other words it felt obliged to elaborate on the concept of Community human rights. While Community legislation could not be reviewed in the light of national standards it could be reviewed in the light of the Community's own standards. This important development has been examined elsewhere.[9]

1 *Simmenthal* Case *supra*, para. 13.9, n. 4, at pp. 643 and 283 respectively.
2 See, for example, art.s 5, 7, 15, 17(4), 25, 26, 73, 93, 169, 170, 171, 177, 223, 226.
3 'The whole of Community law prevails over the whole of national law. This axiom sums up exactly the principles on which the Court of Justice has operated.' R. Kovar, The Relationship between Community Law National Law in *Thirty Years of Community Law* (1983), 109, at 113.
4 A.G. Toth, *Legal Protection of Individuals in the European Communities* (1978), Vol. 1, 21; See also Gerhard Bebr, *The Development of Judicial Control of the European Communities* (1981), at p. 634.
5 *Supra*, para. 13.5, n. 3.
6 *Idem*, at pp. 593–4.
7 Case 11/70 *Internationale Handelsgesellschaft v Einfuhr- und Vorratsstelle für Getreide und Futtermittel* [1970] E.C.R. 1125, [1972] C.M.L.R. 225.
8 *Idem* at p. 1134.
9 *Supra*, para. 8.5, n. 1. See also Case 14/68 *Wilhelm v Bundeskastellamt* [1969] E.C.R. 1, [1969] C.M.L.R. 100; Case 48/71 *EC Commission v Italy* [1972] E.C.R. 527, [1972] C.M.L.R. 699; Case 118/75 *Watson and Belmann* [1976] E.C.R. 1185, [1976] 2 C.M.L.R. 552; Case 88/77 *Ministry for Fisheries v Schönenberg* [1978] E.C.R. 473, [1978] 2 C.M.L.R. 519. On supremacy of Community regulations over subsequent national legislation, see *Politi* Case and *Marimex* Case, *supra*, para. 13.18, n. 3.

13.22 The clearest and most vigorous expression of the supremacy of Community law by the Court of Justice is now to be found in the Second *Simmenthal* Case.[1] In this case the Simmenthal company claimed that certain veterinary and health fees levied by the Italian Government on beef and veal imports were unlawful in Community law. It sought repayment and the local Italian Court referred to the Court of Justice which held in favour of Simmenthal.[2] The Italian Finance Administration was ordered to repay by the national court, but it appealed the order to the appropriate Italian tribunal as being contrary to an Italian law of 1970. Italian jurisprudence at the time held that in the event of a conflict between a Community law and a national measure, Italian courts were not entitled to set the national law aside but had first of all to refer the matter to the Italian Constitutional Court. In the present proceedings, however, the Italian Court decided to avail of Article 177 procedure and refer to the Court of Justice for a preliminary ruling without going to the Italian Constitutional Court. Essentially what it sought was advice and guidance on the consequences of a conflict between a Community law and a subsequent national measure and whether it was obliged to refer to the Italian Constitutional Court before it could apply Community law.

The Court of Justice held that the rule of Community precedence meant that contrary national measures were 'automatically inapplicable' once the Community measure was in force, and that the adoption of any *new* national legislative measures incompatible with Community law was precluded. Moreover, any rule in the national system which prevented this from taking effect immediately—such as the rule obliging national courts to consult first with the national Constitutional Court before giving Community law effect—was contrary to Community law. The Court of Justice concluded:

'The first question should therefore be answered to the effect that a national court which is called upon within the limits of its jurisdiction, to apply provisions of Community law is under a duty to give full effect to those provisions, if necessary refusing of its own motion to apply any conflicting provision of national legislation, even if adopted subsequently, and it is not necessary for the court to request or await the prior setting aside of such provision by legislative or other constitutional means.'[3]

Apart from unequivocally asserting the supremacy of Community law here, the Court of Justice also made clear that the introduction of new legislation by the Member States which conflicted with Community law is precluded and that national courts must do everything in their power, disregarding where necessary national rules which might inhibit it, to effect the full realisation of Community law in the national legal system. Apart from this it is worth noting that the Court of Justice did not say that the national measure was void and did not attempt to set the measure aside. It merely declared that it was 'inapplicable' and that it was for the national court to set the national provision aside.[4] The exact effect which the Community law has on existing national laws to the contrary is a matter for each national system to determine for itself. All the Community requires is a declaration that they are inapplicable. Whether they are totally 'void' or not is a matter for the national courts to determine in accordance with its own national rules.

1 Case 106/77 *Amministrazione delle Finanze dello Stato v Simmenthal* [1978] E.C.R. 629, [1978] 3 C.M.L.R. 263.
2 Case 70/77 *Simmenthal v Amministrazione delle Finanze dello Stato* [1978] E.C.R. 1453, [1978] 3 C.M.L.R. 670.
3 Second *Simmenthal* Case, *supra*, n. 1, at pp. 644 and 284 respectively.
4 *Idem*, at pp. 840,1 and 283 respectively.

13.23 The reasons which the Court of Justice gives for the strong position it takes on the supremacy question are the familiar ones already used in connection with the doctrine of direct effects. Firstly, the fact that Member States have transferred sovereignty to the Community would make little sense if supremacy was not given to the Community laws at the same time. Further, the unique autonomous nature of the EEC together with the need for unity and uniformity of application also requires a rule favouring Community law's supremacy. Moreover, supremacy is a necessary corollary to the concept of direct effect. Direct effect has only real meaning where it is suggested that the rights given by the Community measure must take precedence over national measures to the contrary. Finally, any other rule would threaten the very basis of the legal community and would deny the effective operation of the Community's legal system.[1]

In sum, therefore, it may be concluded that Community law insists on the supremacy of Community law in all cases, and insists on national courts accepting this position for *proper Community reasons*.[2]

1 On the underlying reasons, see *Costa v ENEL*, *supra*, para. 13.5, n. 1; *EC Commission v Italy*, *supra*, para. 13.21, n. 9; Second *Simmenthal* Case, para. 13.22, n. 1.
2 On this, see *infra*, para. 14.15.

Part VI

Reception of Community Law in Ireland

Chapter 14

Constitutional and Legislative Adjustments Required by Accession to the European Communities

Introduction

14.1 The Irish legal system had to adapt in several respects to enable Ireland to accede to the European Communities. Apart from amending the Constitution it was necessary to enact some legislative measures of an enabling nature and to make administrative adjustments in various areas. Since January 1973 several other statutes and numerous ministerial orders were required to fulfil Ireland's continuing obligations within the Communities. Community law also has had a significant impact on the Irish Courts and has continued to affect administrative practices in many ways. The purpose of this chapter is to examine and explain the legal adjustments required to enable Ireland to join the European Communities and to assess the continuing impact which Community law has on the Irish legal system since accession in 1973.[1]

---

1 For related material see B. McMahon *'Constitutional Adjustments necessitated by Community Membership'*, (1976) 1 E.L. Rev., pp. 86–90 and *'The Oireachtas and Community Legislation'*, (1977) 2 E.L. Rev., pp. 150–54. See also F. Murphy, The European Community and the Irish Legal System in D. Coombes, (ed.) *Ireland and the European Communities—Ten Years of Membership*, (Dublin 1983) pp. 29–42.

Bunreacht na hEireann (The Constitution of Ireland) 1937

14.2 The Constitution of Ireland is a formal document which indicates the 'general pattern of political and legal organisation and relationships' that exist in Ireland.[1] Many of the concepts in the Constitution—the sovereign authority of the people (not the State), the separation of powers (between the executive, the legislative and the judiciary), judicial review, the fundamental rights provisions, and the directive principles of social policy, etc.—represent what has been termed 'a not unhappy blend of liberal democracy and Catholic social doctrine'.[2] The document, therefore, as well as controlling Government, also gives a fairly accurate, if formal, picture of Governmental structures and legal organisation as it exists in Ireland today. Like any Constitution, however, the principles enshrined therein must continue to respond to social developments and needs and, as a result, a correspondingly heavy task falls on the Courts to develop, by dynamic interpretation, the principles of the Constitution. Recently, the Courts in Ireland have been responding well to this need.

Three Constitutional features which distinguish the Irish from the British context must be mentioned. First, the Irish Parliament, unlike its British counterpart, is subject to a written Constitution. The doctrine of absolute Parliamentary Sovereignty does not operate in the Irish legal system. In Ireland sovereignty vests in the people. Secondly, Bunreacht na hEireann entrusts the judiciary with the function of ensuring that legislation is compatible with the Constitution. Legislation which is not compatible can be struck down by the Courts. Third, Articles 40–44 of the Constitution contain guarantees relating to fundamental human rights and, in recent years, the evolving pattern of the Supreme Court's attitude to such rights has been characterised by an awareness of the individual's needs and a willingness to uphold his interests against State interference. Such an approach may be illustrated by the expanding interpretation given by the Supreme Court to 'personal rights' when it held that the citizen's personal rights are not exhausted by the enumeration of 'life, person, good name and property rights' contained in Article 40 of the Constitution,[3] but are capable of expansion, and in recent years the Courts have in fact recognised many additional rights not specifically mentioned in the Constitution.[4]

Because the 1937 document (influenced as it was by the 1922 Constitution of the Irish Free State) not unnaturally reflected the more nationalistic mood of the time it is not surprising that several articles in it were incompatible with the supra-national legal system which the European Communities purports to be. Some examples will illustrate this point.

First, Article 6 of Bunreacht na hEireann provides that legislative, executive and judicial powers are to be exercised only by the organs established by the Constitution. The establishing treaties of the European Communities, however, contemplate these powers being exercised by Community bodies. Secondly, Article 15(2) of the Constitution declared that the only body to make laws for the country shall be the Oireachtas (Parliament, i.e., the Dail, the Seanad and the President). This article was, of course, incompatible with membership of the European Communities, the establishing treaties of which also give legislative functions to the Council of Ministers and the Commission. Accession to the EEC therefore required that this article of the Constitution should be amended. Thirdly, Articles 34 to 38 of Bunreacht na hEireann dealing with the Courts of Justice declared that only the Courts established in accordance with the Constitution have power to administer justice and that the final court of appeal shall be the Supreme Court. On joining the European Communities, however, the Coonstitution would have to recognise the jurisdiction of the Court of Justice of the European Communities. Finally, and in a more vague fashion, the question of sovereignty was raised in the discussion that preceded accession: Was Article 5 of Bunreacht na hEireann—'Ireland is a sovereign, independent, democratic State'— compatible with full membership of the European Communities? Although many felt that this article was not incompatible with such accession there was by no means unanimity on this matter.[5]

The above is sufficient to show that some amendment to the Constitution was necessary if the political decision to join the Common Market was to be legally realised in Ireland. An amendment was accordingly drafted and, as the only method of altering the Constitution is by referendum (Article 46 of Bunreacht na hEireann), was put to the people of Ireland on 10 May 1972. It was approved by 83 per cent of those who voted. The Amendment ('The Third Amendment'), which was inserted as Article 29.4 of the Constitution, reads as follows:

> The State may become a Member of the European Coal and Steel Community (established by Treaty signed at Paris on the 18th day of April, 1951), the European Economic Community (established by Treaty signed at Rome on the 25th day of March, 1957) and the European Atomic Energy Community (established by Treaty signed at Rome on the 25th day of March 1957). No provision of this Constitution invalidates laws enacted acts done or measures adopted by the State necessitated by the obligations of membership of the Communities or prevents laws enacted acts done or measures adopted by the Communities, or institutions thereof, from having the force of law in the State.

The Amendment may be said to do three things:

(1) The first sentence enables the State to join the three European Communities. As a purely enabling provision its legal interest is limited. The only point worth mentioning is that the wording of the provision permits accession by the State to the existing (named) Communities. It does not give the State a *carte blanche* to join different Communities. Consequently, if the European Economic Community becomes the European *Political* Community, a further amendment to the Constitution may be required. The provision permits membership of the existing Communities and obviously the State will continue to be a member as long as the Communities in question evolve in the way envisaged by the Treaties. But if the Communities change their nature a new referendum will, it seems, be necessary in Ireland. At what exact point of evolution the Community may be said no longer to be the European Economic Community to which Ireland acceded in 1973, could obviously be a difficult legal question which Irish lawyers will ultimately have to face.[6] The amendments to the Treaties agreed by the Member States in 1986,[7] and which the Danes felt required a referendum, did not constitute, in Irish eyes, a sufficiently new departure to require another referendum in Ireland.

(2) The first part of the second sentence—'No provision of this Constitution invalidates laws enacted acts done or measures adopted by the State necessitated by the obligations of membership of the Communities . . .'—protects from Constitutional challenge Governmental acts 'necessitated by' membership of the European Communities. Normally in Ireland a statutory provision can be challenged on the grounds that it is inconsistent with the Constitution or some section of it. This power of the Courts to review statutes in the light of their compatibility with the constitution (and especially in the light of the fundamental rights provisions, Articles

40–44) is excluded, therefore, in the case of acts 'necessitated by' membership of the EEC. The only possibility of challenging Governmental action on constitutional grounds in this context, therefore, would seem to be the possibility of testing the fact that the action was 'necessitated by' the obligations of membership.[8]

(3) The second part of the second sentence of the amendment—'No provision of this Constitution . . . prevents laws enacted acts done or measures adopted by the Communities, or institutions thereof, from having the force of law in the State'—similarly protects from Constitutional challenge lawful Community acts. The only limitation on this would seem to be the requirement that the Communities (or the institutions) act within their own terms of reference and, in particular, within the establishing Community Treaties. Provided the Communities (or the institutions) do so, however, their actions cannot be declared unconstitutional in an Irish Court.

The Third Amendment of the Constitution thus enables the State to join the named European Communities and generally protects from attack on constitutional grounds both Community acts and governmental acts necessitated by membership.

1 F.B. Chubb, *The Government and Politics of Ireland* (London, 1970), p. 43.
2 See generally Chubb, *op. cit.*, pp. 61–69.
3 *Ryan v A-G* [1965], I.R. 294.
4 See John Kelly, *The Irish Constitution* (Dublin, 1980) pp. 335 *et seq.*, 362 *et seq.*; Mary Redmond, Fundamental Rights in Irish Constitutional Law, in *Morality and the Law*, ed. D. Clarke, p. 97; R.V.F. Heuston, *Personal Rights Under the Irish Constitution*, (1976) XI The Irish Jurist 205.
5 See John Temple Lang, '*Legal and Constitutional Implications for Ireland of Adhesion to the EEC Treaty*', 9 C.M.L. Rev., 1972, pp. 167 and 168.
6 *Infra* 14.3. The amendment is discussed in the *Crotty* case *infra*. The Falklands crisis in 1982 emphasised this point. Ireland refused to support the EEC economic sanctions against Argentina on the grounds that Ireland's neutrality might be compromised by such action. Nothing in the Treaty of Rome obliged it to act otherwise.
7 See Single European Act 1986, Supplement 2/86—Bull. E.C.
8 It might be helpful to note that the original version of the Third Amendment used the phrase 'consequent on' membership of the Communities but, being too vague, it was dropped in favour of the present phrase 'necessitated by the obligations of membership'.

The Single European Act

14.3 In February 1986 the Governments of the Member States signed the Single European Act. The Act had to be ratified in accordance with the constitutional requirements of each of the Member States and could not come into force unless and until it was ratified by all the Member States. The question arose in Ireland as to whether the original amendment (the 'Third' Amendment) covered the SEA or whether a new amendment was required to validate this new development or extension. The matter came before the Courts in *Crotty v An Taoiseach*.[1] Before examining these decisions a further word must be said as to the nature and scope of the SEA.

1 [1987] I.L.R.M. 400, Barrington, J; [1987] I.L.R.M. 443 Sup. Ct., Finlay C.J., Walsh, Henchy, Griffin and Hederman, JJ.

The Scope of the SEA[1]

14.4 The SEA may be said to introduce changes in the following respects. First, certain institutional changes are proposed: Parliament's role in the decision making process is strengthened; a shift from unanimous to qualified majority voting is accepted in some cases; a new court of first instance is proposed; and the existing European Council (an anomalous and pragmatic institutional development) is formally recognised and provided for. Second, the act adopts 1992 as the latest date for the attainment of the free internal market in goods, persons, services and capital. Third, new provisions are introduced in respect of Monetary Policy and Social Policy, and new titles are introduced in respect of Economic and Social Policy (Regional Policy), in respect of Research and Technological Development and in respect of the Environment. Fourth, there is provision for European Cooperation in the sphere of Foreign Policy.

1 For full description of the scope and effect of the Single European Act see F. Murphy, *The Single European Act* XX, The Irish Jurist (n.s.), pp. 17–42 and pp. 240–263.

'New' Community which requires 'new' approval?

14.5 In considering whether these proposals change the nature of the European Community, membership of which has already been approved by the Irish people in 1972, one need have little reservation in respect of the first three of these. These changes appear to be merely incremental in nature and do not radically change the nature of the Community to which the Irish people adhered in 1973. In joining the EEC it was clear that the Irish people were joining a dynamic and vibrant Community. It was not a commitment to a static organisation. It was a commitment to a moving train. The Irish people might not have known where exactly the journey would terminate, but they committed themselves to a forward movement. Since 1972, membership of the Community has grown from 9 to 12 and the market has grown dramatically. These developments have necessitated consequential changes and amendments even if only to accommodate the new scale of things. Indeed, in many cases the proposed changes in the SEA merely recognise pragmatic developments and solutions already in operation for many years. These developments can be termed normal evolutionary corollaries and as such are clearly developments envisaged by the original commitment. In these matters the evolution of the Community has been broadly as anticipated, and the fact that the changes involve an amendment to the Treaty of Rome should not alter this view. After all there have been extensions of Community Powers before now (under Article 235) and the Treaty of Rome itself (in Article 236) contemplates that amendments to the Treaty may be required from time to time.

14.6 This view was substantially upheld in the Supreme Court in a decision handed down on 9 April 1987.[1] In this case the plaintiff contested the constitutionality of the European Communities Act 1986 which purported to introduce into Irish law Article 3(1); Title II; Article II; Article 31; Article 32 and in part Articles 33 and 34 of the Single European Act

('SEA'). It was suggested that the amendments to the original Treaties establishing the European Communities and brought in by the referred to sections of the SEA required new approval by the people of Ireland. The original amendment ('The Third Amendment') passed by the people in 1972, it was maintained, and the first sentence in particular, which permitted Ireland to join the European Communities as named, did not permit accession to this new Community. In other words it was contended by the Plaintiff that the consent of the people given in 1972 did not extend to this new Community which because of these new changes had changed dramatically since that date and therefore required a new approval from the people.

The Court held for the defendants on this matter. In this the Supreme Court upheld Barrington J's position in the High Court where he concluded: 'It seems clear that what the founders had in mind was a growing dynamic Community gradually achieving its objectives over a period of time'.[2] 'It is the opinion of the Court that the first sentence in Article 29:4:3 of the Constitution must be construed as an authorisation given to the State not only to join the Communities as they stood in 1973, but also to join in amendments of the Treaties so long as such amendments do not alter the essential scope or objectives of the Communities.'[3]

Having examined the amendments proposed by the SEA the Supreme Court also came to the conclusion that the changes were incremental and were within the terms of the original amendment to the Constitution.

> 'Having regard to these considerations, it is the opinion of the Court that neither the proposed changes from unanimity to qualified majority, nor the identification of topics which while now separately stated are within the original aims and objectives of the EEC, bring these proposed amendments outside the scope of the authorisation contained in Article 29:4:3 of the Constitution [i.e. the Third Amendment].'[4]

This case did not dispose of the problem, however, as there still remained the matter of co-operation in the sphere of foreign policy. This matter is dealt with in Title III of the SEA and, worthy of note, this development is not inserted as an amendment to the Treaty of Rome. It is a separate commitment by the Member States.

It is certainly true that for many years now within the EEC there have been developments and processes of co-ordination in foreign policy matters. These, however, have not been formally institutionalised in a treaty form and have not extended to military and defence matters. The SEA attempted to give more formal recognition to these matters now. The provisions in Article 30 of the SEA which might be considered to be new extensions involving new commitments are set out hereunder.

> Article 30 of SEA (excerpts).
> '30.1 The High Contracting Parties . . . shall endeavour jointly to formulate and implement a European foreign policy . . .
> 2(c)   . . . the High Contracting Parties shall ensure that common principles and objectives are gradually developed and defined . . ,
> 3(b)   The Commission shall be fully associated with the proceedings of Political Cooperation.

(c) . . . the High Contracting Parties shall, as far as possible, refrain from impeding the formulation of a consensus and the joint action which this could produce.

4. The High Contracting Parties shall ensure that the European Parliament is closely associated with European Political Cooperation.

5. The external policies of the European Community and the policies agreed in European Political Cooperation must be consistent.

6(a) . . . [The High Contracting Parties] are ready to coordinate their positions more closely on the political and economic aspects of security . . .

(c) Nothing in this Title shall impede closer cooperation in the field of security between certain of the High Contracting Parties within the framework of the Western European Union or the Atlantic Alliance . . .

10(g) A Secretariat based in Brussels shall assist the Presidency in preparing and implementing the activities of the European Political Cooperation.'

1 *Crotty v An Taoiseach*, Sup. Ct., *supra*. This action was commenced in accordance with the provisions of Article 34.4.5 of the Constitution. See for comment on this case Casey, J., *Constitutional Law in Ireland* (London, 1987) pp. 179–185.
2 [1987] I.L.R.M. 417. Divisional H.Ct.
3 [1987] I.L.R.M. 444, Sup. Ct.
4 [1987] I.L.R.M. 446–447. But see Henchy J's statement that the inclusion of the foreign policy commitments would change the nature of the Community from being a purely economic community to being a political community also. 'As a Treaty, Title III is not designed in static terms. It not alone envisages changes in inter-state relations, but also postulates and requires those changes. And the purpose of those changes is to erode national independence in the conduct of external relations in the interests of European political cohesion in foreign relations. As I have pointed out, the treaty marks the transformation of the European communities from an organisation which has so far been essentially economic to one that is to be political also.' *Idem*, pp. 463–464.

14.7 In the second decision of the Supreme Court delivered on the same day and brought by the same plaintiff the Supreme Court held that the Irish Government had not the authority to bind itself in the envisaged way under the SEA. According to the majority of the Court, the Supreme Court had power to review the acts of the Executive in discharging its functions in international relations, in certain respects at least.[1] Moreover, the Constitution as *at present written* does not authorise the Government to commit itself irrevocably to the political foreign policy commitments envisaged in SEA.

Walsh J., in the majority, put the matter in these words:

'In enacting the Constitution the People conferred full freedom of action upon the Government to decide matters of foreign policy and to act as it thinks fit on any particular issue or issues so far as policy is concerned and as, in the opinion of the Government, the occasion requires. In my view, this freedom does not carry with it the power to abdicate that freedom or to enter into binding agreements with other States to exercise that power in a particular way or to refrain from exercising it save by particular procedures, and so to bind the State in its freedom of action in its foreign policy. The freedom to formulate foreign policy is just as much a mark of sovereignty as the freedom to form economic policy and the freedom to legislate. The latter two have now been curtailed by the consent of the People to the amendment of the Constitution which is contained in Article 29, s.4, subs. 3 of the Constitution [i.e. the "Third" amendment, 1972]. If it is now desired to qualify, curtail or inhibit the existing sovereign power to formulate and to pursue such foreign policies as from time to time to the Government may seem proper, it is not within the power of the Government itself to do so. The foreign policy organ of the State cannot, within the terms of the Constitution, agree to impose upon itself, the State or upon the People the contemplated restrictions upon freedom of action. To acquire the power to do so would, in my opinion, require a recourse to the People "whose right it is" in the words of Article 6, . . . "in final appeal, to decide all questions of national policy, according to the requirements of the common good". In the last analysis it is the People themselves who are the guardians of the Constitution. In my view, the assent of the People is a necessary prerequisite to the ratification of so much of the Single European Act as consists of Title III thereof.'[2]

Henchy J., also in the majority, expressed his view in these words:

'In testing the constitutional validity of the proposed ratification of the SEA (insofar as it contains Title III) it is important to note that the Constitution at the very outset declares as follows in Art. 1:
   "The Irish Nation hereby affirms its inalienable, indefeasible and sovereign right . . . to determine its relations with other nations . . . in accordance with its own genius and traditions."
It appears to me that this affirmation means that the State's right to conduct its external relations is part of what is inalienable and indefeasible in what is described in Art. 5 as "a sovereign, independent, democratic state". It follows, in my view, that any attempt by the Government to make a binding commitment to alienate in whole or in part to other States the conduct of foreign relations would be inconsistent with the Government's duty to conduct those relations in accordance with the Constitution.'[3]

Moreover, Henchy J. continues that Article 6.1 of the Constitution provides that the Government's powers in the conduct of foreign relations are to be discharged according to the requirements of the common good of the Irish people. Under Title III the point of reference is required to be the common position determined by the Member States, and Ireland would not be able to escape its obligations under Title III by referring to its obligations under the Irish Constitution. 'In this and in other respects Title III amounts to a diminution of Ireland's sovereignty which is declared in unqualified terms in the Irish Constitution.'[4] In a short judgment Hederman J. (who agreed with Walsh and Henchy JJ.) stated: 'The State's organs cannot contract to exercise in a particular way or by a particular procedure, their policy making roles in any way to fetter powers bestowed unfettered by the Constitution. They are guardians of these powers—not the disposers of them.'[5]

1 Walsh J. had no difficulty in this matter—*Idem*, pp. 454–455. Griffin J., who was in a minority with Finlay C.J. also appears to agree with the majority on the right of the Court to review the Government's acts in this matter. He, however, said that the plaintiff in the present case had not established any invasion or breach of constitutional rights as a result of the State being a party to Title III of the SEA (*Idem*, p. 469) Government's acts.
2 *Idem*, p. 459.
3 *Idem*, p. 462.
4 *Idem*, p. 463.
5 *Idem*, p. 469.

14.8 Finlay, C.J., dissented on the basis that in his view Title III did 'not impose any obligations to cede any national interest in the sphere of foreign policy. They do not give to other High Contracting Parties any right to override or veto the ultimate decision of the State or any issue of foreign policy.'[1] Moreover, the plaintiff had not established any actual or threatened invasion of any constitutional right enjoyed by him as an individual arising from the terms of Article 30 of the SEA. Finally, he did not think that the Courts had the power in the present case to intervene with the Executive's formation of policy in external relations. Griffin J., in a separate judgment substantially agreed with the Chief Justice.

The net result of this was that the Government was obliged to hold a referendum on the matter. On 6 May 1987 the following question was put to the people:

'The State may ratify the Single European Act (signed on behalf of the Member States of the Communities of Luxembourg on the 17th day of February, 1986, and at the Hague on the 28th day of February 1986).'

The result of the referendum was: For—70%; Against—30%. Only 45% of the electorate turned out to vote.

1 *Idem*, p. 448.

The Reception of Community Law into the National System

14.9 There remained, however, the additional problem of how Community laws should be incorporated into Irish domestic law. This problem arises because international obligations assumed by States do not always automatically create obligations in the internal legal systems of signatory States. Two competing theories exist on this matter. On the one hand there is the theory (based on the idea that international law is a superior source of law) that once international obligations are assumed by States they automatically become part of the domestic legal systems of such States. No separate legal act is required to make these obligations part of the domestic legal system. The other theory states that international law and national law are two separate systems and before international obligations become part of the domestic scene a separate legal instrument is required. In other words, the national door must be opened by a separate legal act to admit international commitments to the domestic scene. This theory maintains that State law is superior to international law which exists only because States will it.[1] Within the EEC some Member States favour the monist approach to this problem while others favour the dualist approach.[2] Obviously the response which a legal system gives to its international obligations will depend on which theory it supports in this matter.

In Ireland the starting point to a discussion on this problem is Article 29.6 of Bunreacht na hEireann which reads as follows:

No international agreement shall be part of the domestic law of the State save as may be determined by the Oireachtas.

271

The effect of this article is, briefly, as follows: international treaties are not part of domestic Irish law until they are received, or 'brought home', by an act of the Oireachtas. A separate reception process is necessary before treaties create national, as opposed to international, obligations. Thus Ireland, like England, subscribed to the 'dualist' view in relation to this matter. It could be argued that the Third Amendment to the Constitution, mentioned above, might have overridden this requirement in relation to Community matters, but it was felt that a statute clearly complying with the requirements of Article 29.6 would be a more desirable method of dealing with the problem in order to dispel any doubts on the matter.

1 These two theories are known as the 'monist theory' and the 'dualist theory'. In the latter, two separate steps are created: first, the signing of the Treaty which creates the international obligation and second, the Act of Parliament which brings the international obligations into the national legal system. Under the dualist theory until the Act of Parliament is passed, although international obligations will arise, no domestic obligations are created.
2 Contrast the position in the Netherlands and France with German and Belgian constitutions. See D.J. Gilstra *et al.* 139 *et seq*.

14.10 The European Communities Act, 1972 is very short (only four sections apart from the definition section and a title section) and was designed to deal with three problems. First, there was the problem of bringing into Irish law the corpus of EEC law which had already been adopted by the institutions of the Communities and the future acts of the institutions of the Communities which purported to be directly applicable. Secondly, there was the problem of making adequate provision to enable Community matters which were not directly applicable to have effect in Ireland without undue delay, and in particular without the need of a statute on each occasion. Thirdly, there was the problem, not to be under-estimated in the Irish context, of retaining for the Irish Parliament (the Oireachtas) some real control and power in the enactment process of a great number of legislative measures which would ultimately be required by membership of the Communities. The European Communities Act, 1972 set out to solve these problems in the following way.

(1) Section 2, the general incorporating provision declared:

'From the first day of January, 1973, the Treaties governing the European Communities and the existing and future acts adopted by the Institutions of those Communities shall be binding on the State and shall be part of the domestic law thereof under the conditions laid down in those Treaties.'[1]

(2) The second problem, which recognised the need to give full and, sometimes, immediate effect to the EEC measures (especially non-directly applicable provisions, such as directives) without having, on every occasion, to submit to the full legislative process was solved by enabling Ministers to make Ministerial orders to this effect. Section 3(1)) reads:

A Minister of State may make regulations for enabling section 2 of this Act to have full effect.

The only limit on the Minister's power here is that such orders shall not create indictable offences (Section 3(3)).

(3) Although such orders were to have full statutory effect once issued, they were to lapse within six months unless confirmed by a separate Act of Parliament (Section 4(1)). This provision, addressing the third problem, purported to recognise the legitimate interest of Parliament in this whole process, by according to it what was felt to be an adequate supervisory role. Moreover, this supervisory role was underlined, firstly by Section 4(2), which enabled one-third of the members of the Dail (the lower house of Parliament), by notice in writing, to summon a meeting of Dail Eireann if the House stood adjourned, and secondly, by section 5 which obliged the Government to report developments in the European Communities twice yearly to Parliament.

The system of parliamentary control envisaged in Section 4, however, proved to be unsatisfactory, and when the first and only Confirmation Act (the European Communities (Confirmation of Regulations) Act, 1973 was passed, on 1 June 1973), not even the texts of the 22 regulations to be confirmed were readily available for Members of Parliament. Strong criticism was voiced in Parliament of the sham parliamentary control which was provided by Section 4 of the European Communities Act, 1972, and as a result of this criticism, the new Coalition Government introduced the European Communities (Amendment) Act, 1973. This was principally aimed at repealing Section 4 and replacing it with a new and more realistic form of parliamentary supervision.[2]

The 1973 Act abandons the idea of a parliamentary control which gives Ministerial orders in this matter only temporary statutory effect, requiring confirmation by Parliament within six months. Instead, it accords full and permanent statutory effect to the Ministerial orders in this matter with the proviso that they may be annulled by Parliament on a recommendation of the new Joint Committee on the Secondary Legislation of the European Communities, established by the Act. The Joint Committee is comprised of 25 Members of Parliament chosen both from the Dail and the Seanad and which originally included all 10 Irish Members of the European Parliament.[3] Power to recall Parliament, if it stands adjourned, is still retained but, under the new Act, one-third of the members of either House (Dail or Seanad) will suffice to effect this emergency recall. The new section reads in part as follows:

(1) (a) Regulations under this Act shall have statutory effect.
(b) If the Joint Committee on the Secondary Legislation of the European Communities recommends to the Houses of the Oireachtas that any regulations under this Act be annulled and a resolution annulling the regulations is passed by both such Houses within one year after the regulations are made, the regulations shall be annulled accordingly and shall cease to have statutory effect, but without prejudice to the validity of anything previously done thereunder.

1 For judicial interpretation of the effect of this section, see Costello J., in *Pigs and Bacon Commission v McCarren*, High Court, 30 June 1978 [1978] *JISEL* 87, 126.

2 See for comment Mary T.W. Robinson, 10 C.M.L. Rev. 1973 pp. 352–354 and pp. 467–470.
3 Since 1978 Members of the European Parliament while still retaining the right to attend and participate no longer have a vote when attending sessions of the Joint Committee. See Orders of Reference, 21 June 1983 (Dail Eireann) and 29 June 1983 (Seanad Eireann).

The Oireachtas and Community Legislation

14.11 In order to ensure that the Oireachtas (Irish Parliament) would retain some relevancy, and would be in a position to discharge its new function in the enlarged Community, political leaders in Ireland agreed, first, that it should have available to it regular information on Community developments, and, second, that Community measures and Irish measures necessitated by membership should be monitored by Parliament.

Government Reports

14.12 The need for a regular flow of adequate information was merely a recognition of the fact that much of the formulation and drafting of Community measures is carried out at committee level by administrators rather than by elected politicians. Irish civil servants would, of course, be represented at these meetings, but to ensure that this information, and the progress of these meetings, would percolate through to Parliament, Section 5 of the Irish European Communities Act, 1972 requires the Government to submit twice yearly to each House of the Oireachtas reports on developments within the European Communities. This information is considered to be essential if the Oireachtas is to influence Community measures while still at the drafting stage. This influence can be exerted within the Oireachtas by bringing to the notice of Government Ministers, and to Members of the Oireachtas who are also Members of the European Parliament, criticisms and comments on on-going drafts, thereby indirectly influencing the two institutions which have an opportunity of considering such measures: the Council of Ministers and the European Parliament.

Since accession, twenty-five such reports, as of March 1986, have been submitted by the Irish Government to the Oireachtas. These reports describe major developments in all areas of the European Communities for the six-month period which they cover, and list the various Irish regulations fulfilling Community commitments which have been adopted in the relevant period. Because of the wide area which they purport to cover, the reports are long[1] and tend to be general (perhaps of necessity) in the information they provide. Consequently, a Member of the Oireachtas who wishes to make a contribution to the debates on a Community draft document would normally require some additional source of information. Nevertheless, the reports do supply, in an incidental fashion, members of the public with relatively up-to-date information on the Community—a fact which is not without significance in view of the obligatory nature of the decision of the European Court in *EC Commission v France*.[2] It is hard to resist the conclusion, however, that these reports 'serve a more useful purpose as reference works than as the basis for stimulating political debates and securing accountability to Parliament'.[3]

1 Reports 4 and 5, for example, run to 162 and 231 pages respectively.
2 Case 167/73 [1974] E.C.R. 359, [1974] 2 C.M.L.R. 216. In this case the Court of Justice emphasises the duty of Member States to keep their nationals informed on Community law.
3 M.T.W. Robinson, *Irish Parliamentary Scrutiny of European Community Legislation*, 16 C.M.L. Rev. no. 1, 1979, p. 9.

The Joint Committee on the Secondary Legislation of the European Communities[1]

14.13 The watchdog role of the Oireachtas is at present discharged by the Joint Committee on the Secondary Legislation of the European Communities. Being a sub-committee of the Oireachtas (Parliament) the Joint Committee's life is co-extensive with the life of the Parliament itself. Because Parliament has been dissolved three times since 1973 there have in fact been four joint Committees since accession. During that period certain changes in composition and in procedures have taken place although the general function and objective of the Committee has remained unaltered. The original orders of reference of the Committee provided that it was to be composed of the 10 Irish Members of the European Parliament and 16 other Members of Parliament—10 from the Dail (lower chamber) and 6 from the Seanad. During the life of the First Joint Committee it became evident that Members of the European Parliament found it difficult to attend regularly. Accordingly since 1978, Members of the European Parliament, while still entitled to attend and participate, are no longer accorded the right to vote in the Committee's proceedings. Overall membership is now twenty-five—eighteen from the Dail and seven from the Seanad. As is appropriate in the case of such a watchdog Committee (and an established principle of Irish Parliamentary procedure), the Chairman of the Committee is selected from the Opposition party in Parliament. Its proceedings are open to the press, and verbatim reports of its meetings are published; the Committee does, however, have the right to go into private session, in which event there is no record of the proceedings. The Joint Committee before issuing a report must lay such report before both Houses of the Oireachtas. (Over two hundred such reports have been adopted by the successive Joint Committees to date). The proceedings and the periodic reports of the Joint Committee, therefore, provide the public with a further source of information, keep Parliament informed about EEC matters that concern it, and also provide a discussion forum and a briefing centre for the Irish representatives in the European Parliament.

In order to appreciate fully the functions of the Joint Committee, it may be useful to quote part of the present terms of reference of the Committee.

'The Committee's function is now
(a) to examine
(i) such programmes and guidelines prepared by the Commission of the European Communities as a basis for possible legislative action and such drafts of regulations, directives, decisions, recommendations and opinions of the Council of Ministers proposed by the Commission,
(ii) such acts of the institutions of those Communities,

(iii) such regulations under the European Communities Act, 1972 (No. 27 of 1972), and

(iv) such other instruments made under statute and necessitated by the obligations of membership of those Communities

as the Joint Committee may select and to report thereon to both Houses of the Oireachtas; and

(b) to examine the question of dual membership of Dail Eireann or Seanad Eireann and the European Assembly and to consider the relations between the Irish representatives in the European Assembly and Dail Eireann and Seanad Eireann and to report thereon to both Houses of the Oireachtas; . . .'[2]

1 For an extensive examination of the workings of this Committee see M.T.W. Robinson, *supra* n. 1, para. 14.7. See also *infra* Chapter 16.14.
2 Orders of Reference, Dail Eireann, 21 June 1983; Seanad Eireann, 29 June 1983.

Direct applicability and the implementation of Community measures which are not directly applicable

14.14 Provisions of the Treaties establishing the European Communities and acts of the Community institutions which are considered to be directly applicable by the European Court have full legal effect in Ireland by virtue of the European Communities Act, 1972, and require no specific legislative response to achieve this effect. In addition to this positive attitude towards direct applicability, Ireland also, it seems, fully embraces the doctrine of the 'supremacy of Community law'. This last statement, however, may pose some theoretical difficulties, especially in relation to the fundamental rights provisions of the Constitution, which, according to the Constitution, are in some cases 'antecedent to positive law'. It is suggested that a fundamental right 'antecedent to positive law' in Irish Constitutional theory cannot implicitly be overriden by a Constitutional amendment (e.g., the Third Amendment), by specific legislation (e.g., the European Communities Acts, 1972 and 1973), or by Community measures 'necessitated by' membership.[1] Theoretical problems apart, however, the distinct attitude, insofar as it can be perceived, favours a clear-cut option for Community supremacy.[2]

It is ironic, then, that the unequivocal acceptance to the extent described in Irish legal theory of the twin pillars of Community law—direct applicability and supremacy—should cause another problem in this respect: the problem of legal uncertainty. This arises because, if a provision is directly applicable, it may be felt that not only is domestic legislative response unnecessary, but that it is even undesirable. Consequently, members of the Irish public do not necessarily receive from the Irish Government a specific indication of what Irish provisions are over-ruled by the directly applicable provisions of the EEC. For example, the combination of the European Communities Act, 1972 and the direct applicability of Articles 52 and 59 of the EEC Treaty, as interpreted by the European Court in *Reyners v Belgian State*[3] and *Van Binsbergen v Bestuur van de Bedrijfsvereniging voor de Metaalnijverheid*,[4] have effectively repealed (with respect to EEC nationals) various Irish legislative provisions which discriminate on the basis of nationality. These provisions, however, have not been identified or publicised by the Irish Government, and so the Irish citizen (and his lawyer) must not only apply for himself the legal provisions of the EEC, but must also continue to guess at, without any guidance from the Government itself, the Irish Government's attitudes to particular pieces of legislation.[5]

The Joint Committee in its *Eleventh Report*[6] drew attention to the particular problem of the direct applicability of directives. The Report states:

'The Joint Committee's concern is to see that the power of the Oireachtas (that is, Parliament), as the sole legislative body in the State, is curtailed only to the minimum extent necessary to meet the Treaty obligations. It would prefer a simple rule that all directives should be implemented by statute or statutory instrument, except where existing Irish legislation already provided the necessary authority. It is not entirely convinced that the direct applicability of some directive provisions does more than add another dimension to the accepted supremacy of Community law over national legislation in the areas covered by the Treaty. If, however, the Government considers that it would be inadvisable to seek to incorporate a provision in Irish law because it is advised that it is directly applicable by virtue of the Community instrument, the Joint Committee believes that the Houses of the Oireachtas have no grounds for objection. It considers, however, that it is the duty of the Executive to ensure that, where a Community directive is implemented without the intervention of domestic legislation, its provisions are either directly applicable or are already covered by existing legislation.'

The problem is heightened even further where the Irish Government decides to fulfil its obligations in relation to the Community directive by merely implementing a Departmental Scheme not embodied either in a statute or a statutory instrument. This has been done, for example, in the agricultural sphere, by the Disadvantaged Areas Scheme of 28 April 1975 of the Department of Agriculture.[7] One of the dangers of this form of implementation is that the Scheme 'may well be held to be completely within the discretion of the Minister, so that a person aggrieved by his treatment under the Scheme may find it impossible to challenge the adverse decision in the national courts'.[8]

As a partial solution to this problem, the Joint Committee has proposed the following:

'To enable it to discharge its functions, the Joint Committee considers that it should be formally notified by the Government Department concerned within a month of the publication of a directive whether it is (a) to be implemented by statute, (b) to be implemented by statutory instrument, (c) covered by existing legislation, or (d) considered to be directly applicable.'[9]

It is not known, as yet, what response the Executive will make to this request. However, it is submitted that such notification would indeed assist the public and the legal profession in its task of familiarising itself with Community law. Moreover, since the decision in *EC Commission v France*[10] it would seem that the Irish Government ought not, on the strength of the direct applicability argument, to permit legal uncertainty to continue in such a matter. In the present instance the Committee's recommendation was not, however, accepted by the Department of Agriculture.[11]

Finally, the Joint Committee has recently drawn attention to the practice of Irish authorities, whenever a legislative response to a Community measure is necessary, of invariably resorting to a statutory instrument (Ministerial Order). The Joint Committee suggests that, while this practice is undoubtedly permitted by the European Communities Act, 1972, in some cases a separate statute might be more appropriate and might be warranted by the Community measure in question.[12]

In this connection, too, the Joint Committee has recently drawn attention to the method of implementing Community measures (directives or regulations) in Irish law especially by ministerial regulation. The Committee has criticised some of those implementing measures because sometimes they do not refer to the Community measure which inspired the national response[13] while at other times the national measure is not self-explanatory in that while it may refer to the EEC measure as the reason for the national regulation it does not 'set out in terms normally used in Irish legislation what obligations are being imposed or what rights are being conferred on individual citizens'.[14] A greater effort should be made to ensure that national implementing measures should spell out clearly in Irish legal terms, and not by way of reference to other legislation only, what rights and obligations are being conferred or imposed on the citizen by this legislation. This matter is being pursued with various Government Departments so that the implementing measures 'would better reflect the legislative supremacy of the Oireachtas in the domestic sphere and make it easier for persons affected to be aware of their obligations under Irish implementing legislation'.[15]

In drawing attention to these general problems the Joint Committee is certainly doing a service to Parliament, the legal profession and to the public, generally. There remains, however, a lingering reservation as to whether the Joint Committee is satisfactorily fulfilling the role which Parliament cast for it in the European Communities Act, 1973.

1 See also Walsh, J. in *McGee v A-G* [1974] I.R. 284. On constitutional problems on these matters in Germany and Italy see Gilstra, *et al.*, 147 and 153 (4th ed.).
2 See *infra*.
3 Case 2/74 [1974] E.C.R. 631, [1974] 2 C.M.L.R. 305.
4 Case 33/74 [1974] E.C.R. 1299, [1975] 1 C.M.L.R. 298.
5 For example, Section 45 of the Land Act 1965, which discriminated against nationals of Member States of the EEC in land purchase, and was clearly contrary to EEC law since the *Reyners* Case in 1974, was not expressly repealed by Irish legislation until 1983. See S.I. No. 144 of 1983.
6 Prl. 4669. See also *Thirtieth Report*, Prl. 5419, para. 2, *Sixty-Sixth Report*, paras. 3–6, *Eighty-Ninth Report*, Prl. 9681.
7 Implementing Council Directive (EEC) 75/268 O.J. L 128, 19.5.1975 p. 1. See *Eighty-ninth Report of Joint Committee*, Prl. 9681, p. 7.
8 See also *Latchford & Sons Ltd v Minister for Industry and Commerce* [1950] I.R. 33.
9 *Eleventh Report of Joint Committee*, Prl. 4669, p. 11.
10 *Supra*, fn. 2, para. 14.12.
11 *Eighty-ninth Report of Joint Committee* Prl. 9681, p. 7.
12 *Thirtieth Report of Joint Committee*, Prl. 5419. On possible unconstitutionality of this see *infra* fn. 1, para. 14.16.
13 See *Twentieth Report* (Prl. 7279) and *Twenty-Ninth Report* (Prl. 7530) of *Joint Committee*. Also *Sixty-sixth Report* (Prl. 8620) where an improvement is noted.

14 Report No. 23 of Fourth Joint Committee on Secondary Legislation of the European
   Communities, 18 December 1985, p. 2.
15 *Idem* p. 4.

European law in the Irish Courts[1]

14.15 Since the law of the EEC is an integral part of Irish domestic law the
Courts in Ireland must now take full cognisance of EEC principles, rules
and regulations. Accordingly, a party to a dispute before an Irish Court
may raise, in appropriate circumstances, EEC law to over-ride an Irish
legal rule to the contrary. More frequently, however, if a question of EEC
law is raised by an Irish litigant the Irish Court, if unsure of the EEC legal
rule on the matter, will suspend the Irish proceedings and will refer the
case to the Court of Justice in Luxembourg for advice. This referral
system, provided for by Article 177 of the EEC Treaty, enables the Irish
Court to get a ruling on the law of the EEC from the authoritative source
of the Court of Justice. Armed with this the Irish Court can then resume
the proceedings and apply EEC law to the facts before it. Between 1973
and 1985 of the thirty cases which involved EEC law in Irish Courts a
decision to refer under Article 177 was taken in fifteen. There have been
references from the District Court, from the Circuit Court, from the High
Court and most recently from the Supreme Court.[2]

Moreover, there is little evidence of any reluctance on the part of the
Irish Courts to embrace fully Community jurisprudence and doctrine in
these matters. Costello J.'s comment in *Pigs and Bacon Commission v
McCarren*,[3] although an early judicial pronouncement on the matter, may
confidently be taken as an indicator of the Community spirit that pervades
the Courts in Ireland on this issue.

'The effect of [Section 2 of the European Communities Act, 1972] is that
Community law takes legal effect in the Irish legal system in the manner in which
Community law itself provides. Thus, if according to Community law a provision
of the Treaty is directly applicable so that rights are conferred on individuals
which national courts must enforce, an Irish court must give effect to such a rule.
And if, according to Community law, the provisions of Community law take
precedence over a provision of national law in conflict with it an Irish court must
give effect to this rule.'[4]

In *Campus Oil Ltd v Minister for Industry and Energy, Ireland, A-G and
Irish National Petroleum Corp Ltd*,[5] where an appeal was made to the
Supreme Court against a High Court order to refer an issue under Article
177 to the Court of Justice of the European Communities, the Supreme
Court held that

'It is a matter of Irish law that Article 177 confers upon an Irish judge an
unfettered discretion to make a preliminary reference to the Court of Justice . . .
To fetter that right by making it subject to review on appeal would be contrary
both to the spirit and letter of Article 177 . . .'[6]

There is every reason to believe that this co-operative attitude will
˄rsist. Indeed there is even evidence that EEC judicial precedents will be

relied on as supportive authorities by Irish courts in their own deliberations, where although not bound, Irish Courts find it helpful to do so. In *Murphy v The Revenue Coms*,[7] for example, where an Irish tax provision was held to be unconstitutional, the Supreme Court being reluctant for pragmatic reasons to order a repayment of all taxes collected under the void provision, found support for a non-retroactive approach in the EEC Court of Justice's decision of *Defrenne v Sabena (No 2)*.[8] Henchy J. declared that the *Defrenne* judgment stands as

> 'a cogent example of the principle that what has been done or left undone under a constitutionally invalid law may, in certain events, such as the evaluation of a set of circumstances which it would be impossible, or unjust, or contrary to the common good, to attempt to reverse or undo, have to be left beyond the reach of full redressive legal proceedings and to be treated as an exemplification of the maxim *communis error facit ius*.'

With regard to the subject matter it is not surprising, considering the nature of the Irish economy, that twenty-three of the thirty-one cases which involved a discussion of EEC law before the Irish Courts involved agriculture and fishery matters, and three related to the right of establishment and the supply of services. In a recent survey of these cases the following general comment was deemed appropriate.

> 'In 1982, at the conclusion of the survey of Community law in Irish Courts from 1973 to 1981, it was suggested that Irish case law was contributing to the development of Community rules in the fisheries sector and in the prevention of fraud in the CAP. By way of conclusion to the present review of the case-law from 1982 to 1985, it is suggested that the most notable aspect of these cases is the effect that Community law has had on domestic procedural law. The period under review has seen a considerable development of the law relating to preliminary rulings, and in the *Campus Oil* case the domestic rules on the requirements for the award of interlocutory relief were refined. Finally, the administration of the CAP has provoked the discussion of the right to set off on four different occasions in a two-year period'.[9]

1 *Infra* Chapter 15. See generally F. Murphy, *Community Law in Irish Courts 1973–1981*, (1982) 7 E.L. Rev. 331, August 1982, and *Community Law in Irish Courts 1982–1985*, (1986) 11 E.L. Rev. 99, February 1986.
2 *Idem*. The Supreme Court referred in the case of *Robert Fearon & Co Ltd v Irish Land Commission* [1982–3] J.I.S.E.L. 115.
3 [1978] J.I.S.E.L. 87, High Court, Costello J., 30 June 1978.
4 [1978] J.I.S.E.L. Law 87, p. 126.
5 [1982–1983] J.I.S.E.L. 56.
6 *Idem*, at 58 per R. Walsh J., for criticism of rationale see F. Murphy, (1984) 21 C.M.L. Rev. 741 and D. O'Keeffe (1984), 9 E.L. Rev. 87.
7 (25 April 1980, unreported), Supreme Court, 27 January 1980.
8 Case 43/75 [1976] E.C.R. 455, [1976] 2 C.M.L.R. 98.
9 F. Murphy, *supra*, fn. 1, at p. 112.

Legislation and statutory instruments required by membership

14.16 As an indication of the impact which the European Communiti have had on the Irish legal system since accession it is worth n that since January 1973 more than twenty Acts of Parliament and four hundred Ministerial Orders have come into force because of membership obligations. From these figures it is apparent that the usual legal response in Ireland to Community legal obligations is made by way of Ministerial Order. Indeed the Joint Committee on Secondary Legislation has commented on this, suggesting that a statutory response might be more appropriate in certain circumstances.[1] Other criticisms made by the Joint Committee on the implementation process at national level have been noted above in para. 14.9.

The range of matters covered by this legislation is of course confined by the Treaty of Rome itself and accordingly is primarily related to trade and commerce matters generally. The range of activity covered can be sensed from the following random selection of recent statutory instruments adopted in Ireland:

(1) European Communities (Stock Exchange) Regulations, 1984 (S.I. No. 282 of 1984).
(2) European Communities (Dangerous Substances and Preparations) (Marketing and Use) Regulations, 1985 (S.I. No. 244 of 1985).
(3) European Communities (Antioxidant in Food) (Purity Criteria) Regulations 1985 (S.I. No. 187 of 1985).
(4) European Communities (Surveillance of Certain Motor Car Tyre Imports) Regulations, 1985 (S.I. No. 262 of 1985).
(5) European Communities (Recognition of General Nursing Qualifications) Regulations, 1980 (S.I. No. 237 of 1980).
(6) European Communities (Retirement of Farmers) Regulations, 1980 (S.I. No. 238 of 1980).
(7) European Communities (Conservation of Wild Birds) Regulations, 1985 (S.I. No. 291 of 1985).
(8) European Communities (International Carriage of Foods by Road) Regulations, 1985 (S.I. No. 283 of 1985).

Apart from implementing Community policies many of these statutory instruments are attempts to harmonise the laws of Member States so as to equalise trading conditions throughout the Communities. Their impact is much more extensive than normal business people seem to realise and there is little doubt that the volume of such legislation will continue unabated.

1 See comment in G. Hogan and D. Morgan *Administrative Law* (London, 1986) pp. 16–18, where it is suggested that implementing directives by ministerial regulation might be constitutionally suspect in light of Article 15.2 of Bunreacht na hEireann.

Conclusion

14.17 Accession to the European Communities required, and continues to require, a variety of responses from a variety of people in the legal system. Administrators and civil servants are involved daily in the Dublin–Brussels shuttle formulating various draft instruments at Community level. Our legislators have become involved in a similar exercise in the Oireachtas in

Dublin and in the European Assembly in Strasbourg. Government Ministers, as well as issuing many statutory instruments to comply with continuing obligations, are also participating in decision-making at the highest level in the Council of Ministers. The Irish Judiciary too have had to absorb new legal influences and have had to dovetail the native legal system with the EEC order. Finally, the people themselves in amending the Constitution have been called on to approve of the whole political and legal commitment which accession involved.

In general, even this brief survey of events in the decade and a half since accession clearly indicates that the response within the Irish legal system has, by and large, been enthusiastic and generous. Indeed, the chord struck by the people when they voted overwhelmingly for entry in 1972 (83 per cent of those voting, in favour) seems to have been taken up by others involved in the legal process. The approach in general has been very 'communautaire', and where some dragging-of-heels has occurred one feels that it has been due more to a manpower shortage than to any reluctance to embrace the doctrines of the new system. Perhaps this unambiguous acceptance of the legal obligations associated with membership of the European Communities reflects a desire by Irish lawyers to move out from the shadow cast for so long by our dominant neighbour. In recent years, especially in some areas, Irish lawyers, both bench and bar, have begun to look for inspiration from, and precedents in, the legal system of the United States of America. The confidence gained from this experience has perhaps conditioned Irish lawyers also to approach the Continental and Civil Law system, which underlies EEC law, in a positive and courageous way. In any event, one may surmise that the combined forces woven from the desire to minimise old historic authorities and the desire to embrace new influences has resulted in Irish lawyers responding very positively to the challenge which accession to the European Communities presented in 1973.

Although the less than spectacular success of the European Monetary System, the divisions revealed by the Falklands crisis and the recent strain placed on the Luxembourg Accords might suggest otherwise, in an exercise like the current one, the continued survival of the European Communities must be assumed. On this assumption, it is clear that, as integration intensifies, legal regulation in the areas of trade, commerce and economics will increase, and more and more legal instruments will continue to emerge from Brussels. From the evidence we have to date, there is no reason to believe that Irish lawyers will lack the wit, the skills or the enthusiasm, or that the legal system will be found wanting, in adapting or responding to this continuing challenge.

Chapter 15

Community Law in Irish Courts

15.1 Community law is applied in Ireland mainly by the courts established by virtue of Article 34 of the Constitution, that is the High Court and the Supreme Court and the courts of local and limited jurisdiction, the Circuit Court and the District Court. Cases have arisen in all these courts in which Community law has been a factor, if not the decisive element, but there has not yet been a case in the court of Criminal Appeal (which is also a court established under Article 34 of the Constitution). The Special Criminal Court, for which Article 38 of the Constitution made provision, was created by the Offences Against the State Act, 1939, and although its remit mainly concerns offences of a subversive nature there is no reason in principle why Community law should not be pleaded before it. In the '*Marita Ann*' gun-running case[1] the defendants claimed that the criminal proceedings against them were vitiated by infringement of Schedule 4 of the European Communities (Units of Measurement) Regulations, 1983,[2] because the charges against them referred to distances in terms of nautical miles rather than in metric measurements. However, this plea was rejected.

1 *D.P.P. v Gavin Mortimer*, Bill 27 of 1984, Sentence passed on 11 December 1984.
2 S.I. No. 235 of 1983.

15.2 None of the provisions of the EEC Treaty create criminal offences, but Community law is frequently pleaded in criminal proceedings in domestic courts in a variety of circumstances, and both the defence and prosecution may utilise provisions of Community law. For example, in cases where nationals of one Member State are deported from another Member State for criminal behaviour, such as possession of drugs,[1] the Treaty clauses permitting the restriction of the free movement of persons on grounds of public policy, public security and public health are often raised. In the case of *Griffith v Fitzpatrick*[2] the applicant sought to prevent his extradition to the United Kingdom to face a charge of obtaining money by false pretences from the Intervention Board for Agricultural Produce, the British agency responsible for collecting levies and making payments in connection with the Common Agricultural Policy. He pleaded unsuccessfully that this was a revenue offence for which he could not be extradited.

Criminal proceedings are more commonly used in Ireland to enforce obligations laid down in Regulations or Directives. Prosecutions are initiated regularly against fishermen from Ireland, from other Member States and from non-Member States for fishing in contravention of Community conservation measures. The cases of *Minister for Fisheries v C.A. Schönenberg*[3] and *A-G v Burgoa*[4] are early examples of such prosecutions. It should be noted, however, that in view of the diplomatic ramifications of initiating criminal proceedings against vessels from other states the function of prosecuting fisheries offences has been reserved to the Attorney-General rather than the Minister for Fisheries or the Director of Public Prosecutions.[5]

Another example of a Community measure imposing an obligation on Member States to initiate criminal proceedings can be seen in Council Regulation (EEC) 729/70.[6] Article 8 of the Regulation requires Member States to ensure that activities financed by the European Agricultural Guidance and Guarantee Fund are carried out and executed properly, and to prevent and deal with irregularities. This provision came up for consideration in *Irish Grain Board (in liquidation) v Minister for Agriculture*.[7] The plaintiff had sued, successfully, in the High Court for payment of monetary compensatory amounts in connection with the export of grain to Northern Ireland. Neither the customs authorities of the State nor those of Northern Ireland were satisfied that the grain had been placed on the market by the importers, at least some of whom were considered by D'Arcy J. to have been guilty of fraudulent carousel trading and other irregularities. But D'Arcy J. also held that the plaintiff was not privy to those irregularities and did not forfeit its entitlement to payment of the MCAs by reason of the misconduct of the purchasers in Northern Ireland. In the Supreme Court the defendant/appellant argued that he was entitled to refuse payment because of the irregularities that came to light and particular reliance was placed on Article 8 of Regulation 729/70. The Supreme Court referred a number of questions to the Court of Justice for a ruling on the interpretation of the MCA regulations, and the Luxembourg court gave a ruling favourable to the defendant.[8]

Finally, section 3(3) of the European Communities Act, 1972 empowers any Minister of State to create offences in any implementing orders adopted under section 3(1) of the Act. Such offences, however, can only be of a summary nature. An example of the implementation of this power can be seen in the case of *Minister for Agriculture v Norgro Ltd*[9] in which the defendant was prosecuted in the District Court for displaying for sale 26 two-stone bags of carrots in contravention of Regulation 3 of the European Communities (Fruit and Vegetable) Regulations, 1973.[10]

---

1 See, for example: Case 30/77 *R. v Bouchereau* [1977] E.C.R. 1999, [1977] 2 C.M.L.R. 800; *R v Marlborough Street Stipendiary Magistrate, ex p Bouchereau* [1977] 3 All E.R. 365.
2 [1979] J.I.S.E.L. 35.
3 [1977] J.I.S.E.L. 22, [1978] E.C.R. 473, [1978] 2 C.M.L.R. 519.
4 [1979] J.I.S.E.L. 73.
5 Section 5, Prosecution of Offences Act, 1974.
6 O.J. (Sp. Ed.) 1970 p. 218.
7 High Court: [1981] I.L.R.M. 11; Supreme Court: 25 June 1985, *Unreported*.

8 Case 254/85 *Irish Grain Board (Trading) Ltd (in liquidation) v The Minister for Agriculture*
   O.J. C 308, 2.12.1986 p. 3.
9 [1980] I.R. 155.
10 S.I. No. 20 of 1973.

15.3 Apart from the courts provided for in the Constitution and established by law, Community law also arises for consideration in quasi-judicial tribunals. This might happen in a number of ways. First, a provision of the Treaty or secondary legislation might be relied upon directly by one of the parties. This occurred in the case of *Robert Fearon and Co Ltd v Irish Land Commission*[1] where the appellant argued that the initiation of a compulsory purchase procedure under section 35(1) of the Land Act, 1965 was in breach of various provisions of the EEC Treaty and in particular the right of establishment under Article 52. The Judicial Commissioner rejected the argument and refused to make a reference under Article 177. On appeal, the Supreme Court sought a preliminary ruling on the interpretation of Article 58 of the Treaty but the outcome was unfavourable to the appellant.[2] Secondly, Community law is regularly implemented and applied in a derivative form by entities such as the Employment Appeals Tribunal. This body was established by an Act of the Oireachtas and it adjudicates on disputes arising out of rights and duties imposed by Irish legislation. Some of this legislation was adopted specifically to comply with obligations contained in Council Directives. In the United Kingdom the Employment Appeal Tribunal has held that it has no jurisdiction to enforce Article 119 of the EEC Treaty (which requires Member States to apply the principle of equal pay for equal work) because its jurisdiction derived only from the Sex Discrimination Act, 1975; the appropriate forum in which to invoke Article 119 was the High Court.[3] Lord Denning has disagreed with this restrictive view of the ability of tribunals to apply Community law[4] and it seems likely that an Irish court would similarly reject it, particularly in the light of the acceptance here of the doctrines of direct effect and supremacy of Community law (*infra* at paras 15.6 to 15.9), if the Community law provision was cognate to the matters within the jurisdiction of the tribunal. Other tribunals that might be called upon to apply Community law, either directly or in derived or implemented form, include the Appeal Commissioners of Income Tax, the Labour Court, Appeals Officers under the Social Welfare Acts, an Bord Pleanála, an Bord Uchtála, the General Medical Council, and an Bord Altranais. In most cases the legislation establishing the tribunal provides for an appeal on a point of law to one of the courts established by Article 34 of the Constitution; and it is in the courts that one can expect to find significant disputes involving Community law. This sequence of events occurred in the case of *Murphy v An Bord Telecom*.[5] The female plaintiffs claimed that the work they did was equal in value to that of a better paid male employee. The equality officer concluded that the plaintiffs' work was superior in value to that of their male colleague, and consequently, because they were not employed in 'like work', their claim for equal pay under section 3(C) of the Anti-discrimination (Equal Pay) Act, 1974 was unsuccessful. Their appeal to the Labour Court was also unsuccessful and they further appealed to the High Court on a point of law. It should not be concluded, however, that tribunals cannot apply Community law in cases pending before them, nor does it mean that they are precluded from making a reference under Article 177 of the Treaty.

It is also possible for Community law to be pleaded before an arbitrator appointed pursuant to a clause in a contract and subject to the provisions of the Arbitration Act, 1954, but no such case has come to light.

1 [1982–3] J.I.S.E.L. 115.
2 [1984] E.C.R. 3677.
3 *Snoxell v Vauxhall Motors Ltd* [1978] Q.B. 11, [1977] 3 All E.R. 770.
4 *Shields v E Coomes (Holdings) Ltd* [1979] 1 All E.R. 456.
5 High Court (Keane J.) (4 March 1986, not yet reported). This was ultimately referred to the Court of Justice where the plaintiff's claim was successful.

15.4 There are no special procedural considerations applicable to pleas based on Community law. The European Communities (Rules of Court) Regulations, 1972,[1] empowered the rules committees for the various courts to adopt special rules of court for the purposes of the Communities. No such rules have been promulgated. In *Campus Oil v Minister for Industry and Energy*[2] Walsh J. in the Supreme Court, in the context of an appeal against a reference order under Article 177, said:

> 'There are no rules of court and there is no statutory provision in Irish law which purports to permit this appeal to this court. The decision not to make any such rules of court was based upon the opinion that such rules would be in breach of the Treaty rights conferred upon the national judge.'[3]

In the absence of specific rules the ordinary rules of procedure apply, and a plurality of cases in Ireland have been commenced by plenary summons in the High Court. But there have also been instances of proceedings commenced by summary summons[4] or by requests for interlocutory relief.[5]

In *Lee v Minister for Agriculture*[6] the plaintiff was dissatisfied with the refusal of the defendant to meet expenses allegedly incurred under the Farm Modernisation scheme. Instead of seeking a declaration or relief by way of a State Side order the plaintiff, who drafted his own pleadings, sued for a liquidated debt in the Circuit Court. Neither the Circuit Court nor the High Court, on appeal, seemed to find anything peculiar in this form of review of administrative discretion. A further novel feature of the *Lee* case was the plaintiff's successful request for legal aid in the proceedings before the Court of Justice in Luxembourg. As regards legal aid in Irish courts, no special provisions have been adopted to assist litigants whose claims rest on Community law, but the problem is not likely to occur in cases other than those in which a request for a preliminary ruling has been made. Such a ruling forms an integral part of the proceedings before the domestic court and, as the Court of Justice always emphasises in Article 177 cases, the costs are a matter for the national judge to decide. With this in mind there seems to be no reason why a certificate given under the Criminal Justice (Legal Aid) Act, 1962 should not extend to the costs of making a reference for a preliminary ruling.

In proceedings before the Court of Justice either in cases involving direct actions, for example under Article 173 of the Treaty, or in requests for preliminary rulings,[7] *the Court may grant legal aid.*[8]

There are no special time limits for the initiation of actions involving Community law but an action will not be maintainable if the facts giving rise to the dispute occurred before the entry into force of the Act of Accession. In *Dreher v Irish Land Commission*[9] the plaintiff, a German national, commenced proceedings by plenary summons in 1974 in which he alleged that the compulsory purchase of lands by the Land Commission was in breach of the EEC Treaty. The compulsory purchase procedure was initiated in 1964 and Hamilton J. held that the arguments based on the Treaty could be of no assistance to the plaintiff because the compulsory purchase procedure had been initiated and completed before 1 January 1973.

Judgments of the Court of Justice and decisions of the Council and Commission imposing pecuniary obligations on persons other than Member States may be enforced in Ireland under the terms of the European Communities (Enforcement of Community Judgments) Regulations, 1972.[10] Application must be made to the Master of the High Court, by the person entitled to enforce the Community judgment, for an enforcement order; such an order confers on a Community judgment the same status as a judgment or order made by the High Court and may be executed accordingly.

Under the terms of the European Communities (Judicial Notice and Documentary Evidence) Regulations, 1972[11] judicial notice shall be taken of the Treaties, the Official Journal and of any decision of the Court of Justice, and *prima facie* evidence of the Treaties and acts of the institutions may be given in all legal proceedings by the production of a copy printed under official supervision or by a copy certified by an official of the relevant institution.[12]

1 S.I. No. 320 of 1972.
2 [1983] IR 82.
3 *Idem* at p. 58.
4 *North Kerry Milk Products v Minister for Agriculture and Fisheries* [1977] J.I.S.E.L. 18; *Portion Foods and Coolock Trading Co Ltd v Minister for Agriculture* [1981] J.I.S.E.L. 38.
5 *Campus Oil v Minister for Industry and Energy* [1983] IR 82.
6 [1979] J.I.S.E.L. 31, [1980] E.C.R. 1495, [1980] C.M.L.R. 682.
7 Case 152/79 *Lee v Minister for Agriculture* [1980] E.C.R. 1495, [1980] 2 C.M.L.R. 682.
8 Rules of Procedure of the Court of Justice, art. 76; O.J. L 350, 28.12.1974 p. 1.
9 [1980] J.I.S.E.L. 72.
10 S.I. No. 331 of 1972.
11 S.I. No. 341 of 1972.
12 For a discussion of this issue see: Colin P. Stevenson, *Proof of Legislation in Litigation*, XVIII Irish. Jurist. (N.S.) 95.

15.5 As can be seen from the preceding paragraph judicial notice must be taken of the case law of the Court of Justice, and judgments of the Court have been discussed routinely in various decisions of Irish courts.[1] But Irish courts seem willing to consider judgments of the Luxembourg court as persuasive precedents in matters unconnected with Community law. In *Murphy v A-G*[2] the plaintiffs successfully challenged the validity of sections 192–197 of the Income Tax Act, 1967. It goes without saying that many married couples were affected by the provisions requiring cumulation of income for the purposes of the Income Tax Act but although the Supreme Court held that the provisions were void *ab initio*, it also decided that only the plaintiffs could recover overpayments of tax for the years 1978–79 and 1979–80 (i.e. the period commencing after the initiation of proceedings to impugn the provisions of the Income Tax Act). The administrative difficulties of repayment figured highly in the Court's decision and it sought support for its conclusions in the case-law of other jurisdictions. The strongest supportive authority came from Community law:

'A good example, from a different judicial metier of the subjugation of abstract principle and the symmetry of logic to the compulsion of economic and practical demands is to be found in the judgment of the EEC Court in *Defrenne v Sabena (No 2)* [1976] 2 C.M.L.R. 98 . . . it stands as a cogent example of the principle that what has been done or left undone under a constitutionally invalid law may, in certain events, such as the evolution of a set of circumstances which it would be impossible, or unjust or contrary to the common good, to attempt to reverse or undo, have to be left beyond the reach of full redressive legal proceedings and to be treated as an exemplification of the maxim *communis error facit ius*' (per Henchy J.)[3]

The willingness of Irish courts to apply Community law is not without its limits. In *Doyle v An Taoiseach*[4] the defendants/appellants appealed against an order of Barrington J. which invalidated a 2 per cent levy imposed on the sale of bovine animals. They had three main arguments, two of which were based on Community law. Henchy J. (*nem. diss.*) dismissed the appeal and said:

'In my judgment the dispute between the parties is susceptible of a conclusive determination under the domestic law of the State. I consider that a decision on a question of Community law as envisaged by Article 177 of the Treaty of Rome is not necessary to enable this Court to give judgment in this case. Just as it is generally undesirable to decide a case by bringing provisions of the Constitution into play for the purpose of invalidating an impugned law when the case may be decided without their invoking constitutional provisions, so also, in my opinion, should Community law, which also has the paramount force and effect of constitutional provisions, not be applied save where necessary for the decision in the case.'

This statement seems to accord with orthodox dogma but it could give rise to problems. No difficulty would arise if the result was identical under domestic law and Community law; but if the result was to differ the principle of supremacy of Community law would require the determination of the issue according to Community law. It might also be added that the appeal in the *Doyle* case was against a judgment of Barrington J. in which, *inter alia*, he applied a ruling of the Court of Justice given in response to a request under Article 177. Thus, it is somewhat surprising that the Supreme Court would not even discuss an issue considered by the High Court to be sufficiently important to merit a reference—a procedure which involves considerable expense and delay for the parties. Finally, there is also the possibility that the High Court judge may have applied the ruling of the Court of Justice incorrectly: this occurred in *Pigs and Bacon Commission v McCarren Ltd.*[5]

A further discordant note was sounded in the judgment of Keane J. in *Murphy v An Bord Telecom* (*supra* at para. 15.3). The judge considered that the phrase 'equal in value' in section 3(C) of the Anti-discrimination (Equal Pay) Act, 1974 was clear and unambiguous. Although the plaintiffs were performing work of superior value for less pay, it would do impermissible violence to the language used by the Legislature to read the words 'equal in value' as being applicable to cases where the work was unequal in value. The words used in the statute had to be construed in their ordinary and natural meaning. The use of the teleological or schematic approach, utilised by the Supreme Court in *Nestor v Murphy*[6] was not appropriate in a case such as the present

'. . . where the Legislature could by the use of apt language have provided for a particular situation but has failed to do so, whether intentionally or by an oversight. For the same reason, it is not possible to pray in aid the provisions of the EEC Treaty or the Council Directive on equal pay in the absence of any ambiguity, patent or latent, in the language used by the legislature.'

This *dictum* must be treated with circumspection. It subjects the interpretation of obligations imposed on the State by Community law, and transformed by the State into domestic law, to purely domestic rules of statutory construction. Whether the State has correctly transformed those obligations into domestic law can only be judged by reference to the antecedent and superior provisions of Community law. In the final part of his judgment, Keane J. did, however, express reservations as to whether the consequences of the domestic legislation were reconcilable with Article 119 of the EEC Treaty, and the ruling of the Court of Justice in the case of *Defrenne v Sabena (No 3).*[7] and he submitted three questions to the Court of Justice for a preliminary ruling under Article 177.

The Court of Justice gave its ruling in February 1988.[8] In a remarkably brief judgment for Court adopted an interpretation favourable to the plaintiffs:

'. . . if the principle [of equal pay] forbids workers of one sex engaged in work of equal value to that of workers of the opposite sex to be paid a lower wage than the latter on grounds of sex, it *a fortiori* prohibits such a difference in pay where the lower-paid category of workers is engaged in work of high value.

To adopt a contrary interpretation would be tantamount to rendering the principle of equal pay ineffective and nugatory . . .

It is for the national court, within the limits of its discretion under national law, to give it [Article 119], where possible, an interpretation which accords with the requirements of the applicable Community law and, to the extent that this is not possible, to hold such domestic law inapplicable.'

When the ruling of the Court of Justice came to be applied by Keane J. he gallantly conceded that he should apply the teleological or purposive approach originally suggested by counsel for the plaintiffs, and that the passage from his earlier judgment (quoted above) was misleading.[9]

The restrictive approach to the interpretation of Community statutory law initially taken by Keane J. in *Murphy v An Bord Telecom* can be contrasted with the much more *communautaire* attitude to statutory interpretation taken by Murphy J. in *Lalor v Minister for Agriculture*.[10] In this case the plaintiff challenged the national arrangements for the implementation of the milk superlevy scheme and in particular, the provisions of a statutory instrument which required the transfer of milk quotas on the sale or sub-division of farm holdings. In construing the Community provisions at issue, Murphy J. utilised the teleological or schematic approach and referred for support to a paper read at a judicial and academic conference held in Luxembourg in 1976 by Judge Hans Kutscher, former President of the Court of Justice.

1 See, for example: *Pigs and Bacon Commission v McCarren* [1978] J.I.S.E.L. 87.
2 [1982] I.R. 241.
3 *Idem.* at p. 324.
4 (29 March 1985, unreported), Supreme Court.
5 [1981] J.I.S.E.L. 31.
6 [1979] I.R. 321.
7 Case 149/77 [1978] E.C.R. 1365, [1978] 3 C.M.L.R. 312.
8 *Supra*, para. 15.3, fn. 5.
9 *Mary Murphy v An Bord Telecom Eireann*, (11 April 1988, unreported), High Court (Keane J.).
10 (20 October 1987, unreported, High Court (Murphy J.).

15.6 The relationship between Community law and national law is characterised by the operation of certain concepts developed by the Court of Justice. The most important of these is the doctrine of supremacy of Community law. Prior to the decisions of the High Court and the Supreme Court in the *Crotty* case (*infra* at para. 15.7) Irish courts accepted this doctrine without difficulty. Costello J. in *Pigs and Bacon Commission v McCarren*[1] summarised the position as follows:

> 'The effect of (section 2 of the European Communities Act, 1972) is that Community law takes legal effect in the Irish legal system in the manner in which Community law itself provides. Thus, if according to Community law a provision of the Treaty is directly applicable so that rights are conferred on individuals which national courts must enforce, an Irish court must give effect to such a rule. And, if according to Community law, the provisions of Community law take precedence over a provision of national law in conflict with it an Irish court must give effect to this rule. That Community law enjoys precedence over a conflicting national law has been made clear in a number of recent decisions of the European Court and most recently in Case 106/77 *Amministrazione delle Finanze dello Stato v Simmenthal*.'[2]

This view was reiterated in the Supreme Court in *Campus Oil Ltd v Minister for Industry and Energy*.[3] The Court held that an order of the High Court referring questions to the Court of Justice in Luxembourg for a preliminary ruling was not a decision of the High Court within the meaning of Article 34 of the Constitution, and was not subject to the right of appeal to the Supreme Court. But, in the view of Walsh J.:

> '. . . even if the reference of questions to the Court of Justice was a decision within the meaning of Article 34 I would hold that by virtue of the provisions of

Article 29 section 4 subsection 3 of the Constitution the right of appeal to this Court from such a decision must yield to the primacy of Article 177 of the Treaty. This Article, as a part of Irish law qualifies Article 34 of the Constitution in the matter in question.'[4]

A further consequence of the Third Amendment of the Constitution was suggested by McCarthy J. in *Pesca Valentia v Minister for Fisheries and Forestry*.[5] In that case a fishing vessel belonging to the plaintiff company was arrested for fishing otherwise than in accordance with a licence issued under Section 222(b) of The Fisheries (Consolidation) Act, 1959. The licence required at least 75 per cent of the crew to be Irish citizens or nationals of other Member States (Spain had not yet acceded to the Communities). The plaintiffs claimed that the licence requirement, inserted into the 1959 Act by the Fisheries (Amendment) Act, 1983, was inconsistent with the Constitution and with Community law. They sought an interlocutory injunction to prevent the enforcement of the licence pending the hearing of the action. This was granted by Lardner J. On appeal to the Supreme Court it was contended on behalf of the appellants that the Court should never grant an injunction the effect of which would be to suspend the exercise of statutory powers conferred by acts enjoying the presumption of consistency with the Constitution. The Supreme Court rejected this contention: there were no grounds for departing from the ordinary principles governing interlocutory applications. McCarthy J., in a separate concurring judgment, doubted that the constitutional presumption would operate when a conflict was alleged between domestic law and Community law:

'. . . the Constitution itself envisages at least some freedom from constitutional scrutiny of "laws enacted, acts done or measures adopted by the Communities, or institutions thereof", as to having the force of law in the State. (Art. 29.4.3.) Such a shield from constitutional scrutiny can scarcely carry the presumption of constitutional validity attaching to the Legislation of the Oireachtas.'

A more practical example of the principle of supremacy in operation can be seen in the case of *Minister for Fisheries v Schonenberg*.[6] A number of Dutch registered fishing boats had been arrested for contravening the Sea Fisheries (Conservational and Rational Exploitation) Orders 1977,[7] which imposed a 50-mile limit within which only boats below a certain size could fish. Lawyers for the defendants requested a preliminary ruling on the compatibility of these orders with Community law and Carroll D.J. agreed to this request. Pending the ruling of the Court of Justice he adjourned any decision on the prosecutions. But under existing fisheries law the fishing vessels and masters thereof had to remain in port. This would have had disastrous economic consequences for the boats in question because of the length of time required to procure a preliminary ruling (it took one year and nine months in the instant case). Consequently, the District Justice ordered the masters of the boats in question to pay a bond into court and allowed them to return to sea, even though no power to make such an order was conferred by law.

An example of the non-judicial acceptance of the supremacy of Community law can be found in the case of *EC Commission v Ireland*.[8] In this case, initiated by the Commission under Article 169 of the EEC Treaty, the Irish Government was alleged to have infringed its obligations under Community law by implementing the orders at issue in the *Schonenberg* case. The Court of Justice ordered the interim suspension of the measures in question on 13 July 1977, but there was no formal suspension of the orders by the Irish Government because, according to the Government, the suspension order of the Court of Justice had the force of law in Ireland and had the effect of suspending the Sea Fisheries order on the date laid down therein. This followed from the provisions of the Constitution and the European Communities Act, 1972.[9] Neither the Commission nor the Court of Justice objected seriously to this view but, if only on the grounds of legal certainty, an Irish court would be unlikely to accept that measures of domestic law would cease to be of legal force in the State because of conflict with a superior rule of Community law without some formal revocation of the domestic measure by a court of law or by the relevant legislative authority.

1 *Loc. cit.*, fn. 11, para. 15.5.
2 *Idem*, at p. 109.
3 *Supra, Loc. cit.*, fn. 3, para. 15.4.
4 *Idem*, at p. 58.
5 [1985] I.R. 193, [1986] I.L.R.M. 68.
6 [1979] J.I.S.E.L. 35.
7 S.I. No. 38 of 1977, S.I. No. 39 of 1977.
8 Case 61/77 [1978] E.C.R. 417, [1978] 2 C.M.L.R. 466.
9 *Idem*, at p. 442.

15.7 The adoption of The Single European Act and its implementation in Ireland by The European Communities (Amendment) Act, 1986, provoked the action commenced by Mr Raymond Crotty against the Government and required the High Court and the Supreme Court to subject the Third Amendment of the Constitution to a much more rigorous examination than it had received heretofore.

In June 1985, the European Council, meeting at Milan, convoked the first Inter-Governmental Conference since the signing of the Treaties of Rome in March 1957. The objective of the Conference was twofold:

– to formulate various amendments to the EEC Treaty; and
– to prepare a draft treaty on co-operation in political and security matters.

The conclusions of the conference were approved by the European Council at its meeting of 2 and 3 December at Luxembourg. The texts prepared by the Conference were consolidated and formally adopted as the Single European Act on 17 and 28 February 1986. The European Council indicated that it wished the process of ratification of the Single European Act by the various Member States to be concluded before the end of 1986 in order to facilitate its entry into force on 1 January 1987.

The Single European Act (SEA) brought about a series of amendments to the Treaties. On the institutional plane, it provided for the establishment of a court of first instance with a right of appeal to the Court of Justice, the extension of the legislative role of the European Parliament (whose name was officially changed from 'Assembly'), and the delegation of further powers from the Council to the Commission. The substantive changes include the streamlining of the decision-making process insofar as it concerns the completion of the internal market and the formal inclusion in the EEC Treaty of 'new competences' in the field of social policy, economic and social cohesion (regional policy), research and development and the environment. These provisions are contained in Title II of the SEA, and have been referred to generally throughout this work.[1] For the purposes of discussing the decisions in the *Crotty* case it is necessary to refer only to Article 30(6) of Title III concerning European Political Cooperation. The text reads:

'6(a) The High Contracting Parties consider that closer cooperation on questions of European security would contribute in an essential way to the development of a European identity in external policy matters. They are ready to coordinate their positions more closely on the political and economic aspects of security.
 (b) The High Contracting Parties are determined to maintain the technological and industrial conditions necessary for their security. They shall work to that end both at national level and, where appropriate, within the framework of the competent institutions and bodies.
 (c) Nothing in this Title shall impede closer cooperation in the field of security between certain of the High Contracting Parties within the framework of the Western European Union or the Atlantic Alliance.'

It should also be observed that Articles 31 and 32 of the SEA provide that the judicial review powers of the Court of Justice of the European Communities do not extend to Title III of the SEA and that, amongst other provisions, Title III does not affect the Treaties establishing the European Communities or any subsequent Treaties and Acts modifying or supplementing them.

In Ireland the debate on SEA started in the press in mid-1986 and two questions appeared to dominate the debate: the constitutionality of the SEA and the consequences on the policy of neutrality pursued by successive governments since the Second World War. This should have alerted the Government to the public disquiet concerning the SEA. But the Government's reaction was hesitant and half-hearted; the European Communities (Amendment) Bill was presented to the Dail on 23 September 1986 and in response to considerable public pressure, an 'Explanatory Guide to the Single European Act' was issued by the Government on 18 November 1986. On 3 December 1986 the Oireachtas Joint Committee on the Secondary Legislation of the European Communities published its report on the Single European Act: the Committee called for an informed debate on the European Communities (Amendment) Bill of 1986 in order to calm public fears on various points.[2] In particular, the Committee felt it incumbent on the Government '. . . to convince the members of the Oireachtas that there existed no threat real or potential to our neutrality . . .'. In the opinion of the Committee, this could be achieved by appending to the act of ratification a formal reiteration of Ireland's position of neutrality outside military alliances.

The European Communities (Amendment) Bill of 1986 comprised only three sections, of which the first was the most important. Section 1 provided for the amendment of Section 1(1) of the European Communities Act, 1972 by the addition of the following clause:

'(o) The following provisions of the Single European Act signed at Luxembourg on the 17th February 1986 and at the Hague on the 28th February 1986, namely Article 3, paragraph 1, Title 2, Articles 31 and 32, and, in so far as they refer to the said Article 3, paragraph 1, the said Title 2 and the said Articles 31 and 32, 33 and 34.'

The object of this provision was to incorporate into Irish law the elements of the SEA which amend the basic treaties establishing the European Communities. In short, only Article 3(1) of Title I (which changes the name of the European Parliament from 'Assembly'), Title II (which contains all of the essential amendments), and Articles 31 and 32 of Title IV (which delimit the powers of control of the Court of Justice as well as the effects of the SEA on the basic treaties establishing the European Communities), form part of domestic law. In other words, the provisions of the Single European Act on European political cooperation (Title III) do not form part of domestic law.

The Bill was accompanied by a number of motions, one of which was designed to dispel any public fear that Ireland's traditional policy of neutrality outside military alliances was being undermined by participation in European political cooperation (EPC). Despite a stormy debate in both Houses of the Oireachtas, the Government succeeded in passing the European Communities (Amendment) Bill of 1986—and the accompanying motions—by a comfortable majority. The Bill was signed by the President and all that remained was for the instrument of ratification to be lodged with the Italian Government in accordance with Article 34 of the SEA.

On Christmas Eve 1986, Barrington, J., in the High Court, granted an interlocutory injunction to Mr Raymond Crotty, an agricultural economist, to prevent the Government from depositing Ireland's instrument of ratification of the SEA with the Italian Government. Mr Crotty alleged that, if ratified, the SEA could not be challenged because it would benefit from the protection of the Third Amendment of the Constitution; he was being deprived of his right as a citizen to vote in a referendum on proposals which involved a further diminution of the legislative, judicial and executive powers of the State. In view of the fact that the SEA was not yet binding on the State, Barrington J. decided that the *status quo* should be preserved pending the resolution of this constitutional issue.[3]

The case came on for plenary hearing in January 1987 before a Divisional Court of the High Court (Hamilton P., Barrington and Carrol J.J.) and the plaintiff claimed:

(i) A declaration that the State could not become bound by the SEA except by virtue of a Referendum to amend the Constitution;
(ii) A perpetual injunction to restrain the Government from depositing with the Italian Government any purported instrument of ratification of the SEA; and

(iii) A declaration that the European Communities (Amendment) Act, 1986 was invalid having regard to the provisions of the Constitution. The Plaintiff claimed that the SEA extended the objectives of the EEC Treaty and diminished the sovereignty of the organs of government established by the Irish Constitution; procedures were currently in train to amend the Constitution without holding a Referendum in which, as a citizen he was entitled to vote; by virtue of his right to vote in a Referendum he had the necessary *locus standi* to voice his complaint; but that if the instrument of ratification of the SEA was lodged with the Italian Government it would be too late for him to seek relief because the European Communities (Amendment) Act, 1986 would be immune from constitutional attack by virtue of the Third Amendment of the Constitution.

In a unanimous decision the Court rejected these arguments. It held that the European Communities (Amendment) Act, 1986 (or the Order bringing it into force) was immune from constitutional challenge

'. . . but only if it does not go outside the licence granted by the first sentence of [the Third Amendment]. That is a licence to join a living dynamic Community . . .'

The Court was not satisfied that the mere deposit of the instrument of ratification would confer any immunity from challenge on the Act of 1986 and, having failed on this point, the plaintiff had no *locus standi* to make the other points which were advanced on his behalf. Consequently, the plaintiff's applications were dismissed.[4]

From this judgment the plaintiff appealed to the Supreme Court, which delivered two sets of judgments. The first judgment was delivered in accordance with the requirements of Article 34.4.5 of the Constitution, which requires that where the constitutionality of any act is challenged in proceedings before the Supreme Court, only one judgment may be delivered and that judgment cannot indicate whether there were assenting or dissenting judgments. The first judgment, therefore, dealt with the constitutional validity of the European Communities (Amendment) Act, 1986. The Court held, without providing reasons, that the plaintiff had sufficient *locus standi* to challenge the Act. The net issue in that challenge was whether the Act was protected by the Third Amendment of the Constitution. It was clear to the Court that ratification of the SEA was not '. . . necessitated by the obligations of membership of the Communities . . .' within the meaning of the second sentence of Article 29.4.3. But the Court agreed with the contention of the defendants that the first sentence of Article 29.4.3 authorised the State to join Communities which were '. . . dynamic and developing entities . . .' and this authority extended to amendments to the Treaties which were within the original scope and objectives of those Treaties:

'To hold that the first sentence of Article 29.4.3 does not authorise any form of amendment to the Treaties after 1973 without a further amendment of the

Constitution would be too narrow a construction; to construe it as an open-ended authority to agree, without further amendment of the Constitution, to any amendment of the Treaties would be too broad'.

The Court then examined the substantive changes to the EEC Treaty and concluded, that in the light of the presumption of constitutionality (which imposed a burden of proof on the plaintiff) that none of the provisions of the Act of 1986 had been shown to be unconstitutional.[5]

The second set of judgments[6] dealt with the Plaintiff's claim for an injunction to prevent the State ratifying the SEA on the grounds that Title III of the SEA was inconsistent with the Constitution. By a 3–2 majority the Court held that, without the appropriate constitutional amendment, the ratification of the SEA (insofar as it contained Title III) would be impermissible under the Constitution. Walsh J. and Henchy J. (with both of whom Mr Justice Hederman agreed) considered that Title III was intended to bind the State in its conduct of its foreign policy in accordance with the procedures of European Political Cooperation as stated in Article 30. This meant that:

'. . . if Ireland were to ratify the Treaty [the SEA] it would be bound in International Law to engage actively in a programme which would trench progressively on Ireland's independence and sovereignty in the conduct of foreign relations'. (*Per* Henchy J.)

But the Constitution did not entitle the Government to alienate in whole or in part the conduct of foreign policy; Title III of the SEA would bind the State to surrender part of its sovereignty in the conduct of foreign relations, and the ratification of Title III would therefore require a constitutional amendment.

The Chief Justice (Mr Justice Finlay) and Griffin J. disagreed with the majority. Mr Justice Finlay noted that Title III does not give to the other Member States any right to override or veto the ultimate decision of the State on any issue of foreign policy, and Griffin J. noted that the language used by the High Contracting Parties in Title III had been carefully chosen to permit the utmost freedom of action in the sphere of foreign policy. The permissive terminology of Title III was in stark contrast to the mandatory terms used in other parts of the SEA.

The decisions of the Supreme Court and, to a lesser extent, the decisions of the High Court are open to criticism from three separate perspectives. From the domestic law perspective, the first criticism concerns the decisions of the High Court and Supreme Court to admit Mr Crotty's action in the first place. Article 29 of the Constitution is a dualist provision: it empowers the Government to enter into international agreements but provides in paragraph 6, that no such agreement can form part of domestic law unless it has been approved by the Oireachtas. We have already noted that Articles 31 and 32 of the Single European Act provide that the review powers of the Court of Justice do not extend to Title III of the Single European Act and we have also seen that the European Communities (Amendment) Act of 1986 incorporated into domestic law only Article 3(1), Title II and Articles 31 and 32 of Title IV. It follows that Title III of the SEA does not form part of domestic law and, therefore, cannot create rights or obligations for citizens before domestic tribunals. Accordingly, Mr Crotty had no *locus standi* to challenge Title III and neither the High Court nor the Supreme Court had competence to entertain his action.

A second criticism from the point of view of domestic law is that the judgments of the Supreme Court represents an intrusion into an area of government reserved by the Constitution to the executive and legislative organs of state. As we have already observed, Article 29 of the Constitution grants to the executive organ of State, namely the Government, exclusive power to conclude international agreements; there are two limitations on this exclusive right. Firstly, paragraph 5 of Article 29 requires every international agreement to which the State becomes a Party to be submitted to the Dail and, further, no international agreement will be binding on the State if it involves a charge on public funds unless the terms of the agreement have been proved by the Dail. The second limitation, which is contained in paragraph 6 of article 29, embodies the dualist approach of the State to international contractual arrangements: no international agreement can be part of the domestic law of the State unless it has been approved by the Oireachtas. It should be clear from the foregoing review of Article 29 that the authors of the Constitution did not envisage a role for the judiciary in the conduct of international affairs, and this assessment is borne out by reference to previous decisions of the Supreme Court.[7]

The most serious criticism of the majority judgments in the *Crotty* case concerns the implications for other international agreements entered into by the State. If the *Crotty* decision is taken at face value it means that, in every case where the State has entered into an arrangement at international level which involves the application of a procedure of consultation or discussion, the restrictions on the exercise of foreign policy inherent in that arrangement are incompatible with the Constitution. The most obvious example of an international arrangement which accords with this description is the General Agreement on Tariffs and Trade (GATT). However, the international agreement most endangered by the *Crotty* doctrine was the Anglo-Irish Agreement of 1985. This Agreement established structures designed to deal in a regular manner with the political insecurity problems of Northern Ireland, as well as legal issues and border cooperation. Article 1 of the Agreement stipulates that 'a determined effort shall be made . . . to overcome any disagreement . . .' in all of these areas. These efforts have to be carried out through the medium of the Inter-Governmental Conference established by the Agreement. It need hardly be added that neither the GATT nor the Anglo-Irish Agreement were submitted to the People for their approval in a Referendum. And while the State remains obliged to observe the terms of these agreements in international law their status in domestic law remains most unclear. Not long after the delivery of the judgment in the *Crotty* case an action was commenced in the High Court in which the validity of the Anglo-Irish agreement was contested, and the plaintiffs relied on the reasoning of the majority in the *Crotty* case to establish their *locus standi*.

Note:

If we turn now to the Community law aspects of the judgments of the

Supreme Court it will be recalled that the majority considered that the effect of Title III was to bind the State in its conduct of foreign policy in accordance with the procedures of European Political Cooperation outlined in Article 30. The minority (Mr Justice Finlay and Mr Justice Griffin) observed that Title III did not give to the other Member States any right to out-vote or veto the final decision of the State in matters of foreign policy, and that the language utilised by the High Contracting Parties in Title III had been chosen with care so as to permit the greatest degree of liberty of action in the field of foreign policy; the liberal terminology of Title III contrasted sharply with the imperative terms utilised in other parts of the SEA. It is submitted that this line of reasoning is unimpeachable. It is difficult to comprehend how a process whose terms were laid down in verbal formulae in the Luxembourg (1970), Copenhagen (1973), and London (1981) Reports, as well as in the Stuttgart declaration (1983), and which was '. . . informal, aspirational or, at most declarational . . .' (in the words of Mr Justice Henchy) could be transformed into a series of binding obligations when precisely the same verbal formulae were utilised in Title III of the SEA. According to Mr Justice Henchy, the encapsulation of European Political Cooperation into a 'solemnly covenanted' treaty format was the critical transforming element. However, this attaches excessive importance to purely formal considerations and neglects the content and effect of the disputed provisions. As we have noted above, Article 32 of the SEA specifically excludes European Political Cooperation from the judicial review powers of the Court of Justice. In short, it is absurd to attribute the status of a binding legal obligation to an international arrangement in respect of which the participating parties have excluded all means of judicial adjudication. And, as one distinguished Irish critic has observed, '. . . Few people in Europe would consider this judgment as a balanced description of the present effects of Title III, or of its correct legal interpretation'.[8]

All of the preceding observations have been critical of negative aspects of the decisions in the *Crotty* case. However, the significance of the first judgment of the Court should not be underestimated. In this judgment the Court upheld the validity of the European Communities (Amendment) Act, 1986, which had the effect of incorporating into domestic law the proposed modifications of the basic Treaties establishing the European Communities. The Court held that the authorisation given to the State by the Third Amendment of the Constitution was not simply to accede to the Communities in the state in which they existed in 1973, but to participate in amendments of those Treaties which did not exceed the objectives of the Communities. This dynamic interpretation of the Third Amendment recognises the expanding nature of the Communities and allows for organic change. It also disposed of any doubts on the validity in Irish law of the two enlargements of the Communities in 1981 and 1986 as well as the amending treaties of 1975 and 1985. In particular, the Budgetary Treaty of 1975, which established the Court of Auditors and which gave a significant budgetary role to the European Parliament, would have been particularly imperiled by a restrictive interpretation of the Third Amendment and while the Court held that the SEA was not an Act '. . . necessitated by the obligations of membership of the Communities' it also rejected the argument that no amendment to the Treaties establishing the Communities was possible after 1973 without a supplementary amendment of the Constitution. Conversely, the Court refused to interpret the second paragraph of the Third Amendment as an open authority to agree without further amendment to the Constitution to any amendment of the basic treaties.

In terms of international law, the majority judgments of the Supreme Court are more notable for what they do not say than for what they actually establish. There is no reference whatsoever in the judgments of the Court to the policy of military neutrality; this is not surprising because the formulation of policy is a matter reserved exclusively to the Government under Article 28 of the Constitution. But the casual observer is left with the suspicion that the Supreme Court's intervention in the field of foreign policy formulation, which involved a radical departure from its previous jurisprudence, was motivated by the desire to ensure that the People had the opportunity to vote on a proposal which might, in the long term, involve a departure from the policy of neutrality espoused by successive governments and supported by a very large majority of the population.

1 For a detailed analysis of the SEA see: Murphy, F. *The Single European Act*, XX Irish Jurist (n.s.) pp. 17–42, 239–263.
2 Report No. 34, *The Single European Act*, 3 December 1986.
3 [1987] I.L.R.M. 400, at p. 405.
4 *Idem*, at p. 415.
5 *Idem*, at p. 443.
6 *Idem*, at pp. 447, 452, 460, 464 and 469.
7 See, for example: *Boland v An Taoiseach* [1974] I.R. 338.
8 John Temple Lang, *The Irish court case which delayed the Single European Act: Crotty v An Taoiseach and others*, 24 C.M.L. Rev. [1987] 709.

15.8 The decisions of the Supreme Court gave rise to unprecedented criticism, particularly in the Dail, where some deputies felt that the Court had crossed the Rubicon of the separation of powers and had accorded to itself a power of review of international agreements which had not been provided by the Constitution.[1] But the result meant that a Referendum had to be held before the Government could ratify the SEA. In the meantime a general election had resulted in a change of administration; the Fianna Fail Party, led by Mr Charles Haughey TD, took power as a minority government. The new administration was faced with an ironic dilemma: it was obliged to formulate a proposal for a Referendum to amend the Constitution in respect of a measure—the SEA—that it had opposed vociferously while in opposition. The eventual proposal, to be placed before the people for their approval, was contained in the Tenth Amendment of the Constitution Act, 1987 and it proposed to insert between the first and second sentences of the Third Amendment (Article 29.4.3) the following clause:

'The State may ratify the Single European Act (signed on behalf of the Member States of the Communities at Luxembourg on the 17th day of February, 1986 and at The Hague on the 28th day of February 1986).'

The text of the Referendum was subject to some criticism in the Dail.[2] As has been pointed out above, the majority decisions in the *Crotty* case raised serious doubts about the validity of international agreements entered into by the State which involved participation in a formal procedure of consultation. Opposition deputies argued that the opportunity should be taken to amend the Constitution so as to protect the validity of international agreements entered into by the State prior to the decision in the *Crotty* case.[3] However, the Government was satisfied to proceed with the Referendum on the basis of the reasonably narrow wording produced above.

The Referendum was held on 25 May 1987 and, with an extremely low turnout of voters (only 44.1 per cent of the electorate voted), the proposal was approved by a margin of approximately 70–30 per cent. The number of votes cast in favour was 755,423 and the number of votes cast against was 324,977. The result of the Referendum permitted the State to ratify the SEA. The instrument of ratification, along with a declaration on neutrality outside military alliances, was deposited in Rome by Brian Lenihan TD, Minister for Foreign Affairs, on 24 June 1987. Thus, in accordance with Article 33(2), the SEA entered into force on 1 July 1987, the first day of the month following that in which the last instrument of ratification was lodged with the Italian Government.

1 See, for example: Dail Debates, vol. 371 at cols. 2224–2230.
2 *Ibid.* at cols 2442–2444.
3 *Ibid.* at col 2457.

15.9 In the period since the *Crotty* decision the High Court and the Supreme Court have both had the opportunity to consider a potential clash between provisions of the Constitution and the EEC Treaty.

In *A-G (at the relation of the Society for the Protection of Unborn Children) v Open Door Counselling Ltd and the Dublin Wellwoman Centre Ltd*[1] the plaintiff sought declarations: (i) that the non-directive counselling by the defendants of pregnant women, and the provision by the defendants of assistance to such women to travel abroad to procure an abortion, was unlawful having regard to the provisions of Article 40.3.30 of the Constitution; and (ii) that such counselling and provision of assistance amounted to a conspiracy to corrupt public morals. The plaintiff also sought an order restraining the defendants from counselling and assisting pregnant women to travel abroad to obtain an abortion or to obtain further advice on abortion outside the jurisdiction. Article 40.3.30 of the Constitution (the Eighth Amendment) reads as follows:

'The State acknowledges the right to life of the unborn and, with due regard to the equal right to life of the mother, guarantees in its laws to respect, and, as far as practicable, by its laws to defend and vindicate that right.'

The defendants argued, *inter alia*, that by virtue of Articles 59 and 60 of the Treaty, in conjunction with the Third Amendment of the Constitution, a pregnant woman has a right to travel to another Member State to be the recipient of the service of abortion and the 'corollary right' to receive information relating to that service. In the High Court, Hamilton P. dismissed this claim because:

'. . . the issues and facts relevant to the issue in these proceedings relate to the activities of the Defendants, their servants or agents within this State and that, consequently, the provisions of the law of the European Communities are not applicable.'

This reasoning can be criticised in so far as it suggests that in order to benefit from the EEC Treaty right to provide services the activities of the beneficiary must take place in another Member State.

In any event, the plaintiff succeeded in the High Court on the other grounds and the defendants appealed, unsuccessfully, to the Supreme Court, where their Community law arguments received somewhat lengthier consideration, but no more sympathy, than in the High Court. The Supreme Court held that no question of the interpretation of the Treaty fell to be decided in the case. According to the Court (Finlay C.J., *nem. diss.*) the appellants had argued that a pregnant woman had a right to travel abroad to be the recipient of the service of abortion—although it was not suggested by them that the Order of the High Court prevented women from following this course of action; a necessary corollary to that right was the right to receive information relating to the service of abortion in another Member State. But counsel for the appellants had expressly conceded that the corollary right for which they contended was confined to obtaining information about the service of abortion and could not be extended to the obtaining of assistance to avail of or receive the service. However, in the opinion of the Court:

'What is sought to be restrained in this case is in no way confined to the question of information nor does the Order of the High Court in any way prevent a pregnant woman from becoming aware of the existence of abortion outside the jurisdiction. In fact what is here sought to be restrained is assistance to a pregnant woman to travel abroad and obtain the service of abortion.'

And, because the appellants had already conceded that 'obtaining of assistance' was not a corollary right to the right to receive services, the issue of European law raised in the pleadings did not arise in the case. Accordingly, there was no need to refer to the Court of Justice for a ruling under Article 177, nor was there any need to consider wider the general issues of abortion and the right to receive services under Community law.

Two observations can be made: firstly, it is debatable whether the concession made by the appellants—to the effect that 'obtaining assistance' to avail of an abortion was not a corollary right to the right to receive services—was correct in Community law. Secondly, the reasoning cannot be described as compelling because it turns on the niceties of pleading rather than on points of principle.

By way of conclusion, the judgment in this case, taken in tandem with the *Crotty* decision, suggests that the doctrine of supremacy of Community law will not give rise to domestic controversy where the subject matter is of a routine economic or legal nature, such as disputes concerning the common agricultural policy. The reaction of the courts will be far less predictable, however, where questions of high policy are at issue.

1 High Court, (Hamilton P.) [1987] I.L.R.M. 477. Supreme Court, Unreported, 16 March 1988.

15.10 The doctrine of direct effects, which so often operates in tandem with the doctrine of supremacy of Community law, has been considered by Irish courts on a number of occasions. As can be seen from the extract from the judgment of Costello J. in *Pigs and Bacon Commission v McCarren* (at para. 15.6 *supra*) the courts will give effect to directly applicable provisions of Community law. Following an initial lack of familiarity with Community secondary legislation, the High Court now interprets and applies regulations, particularly in agriculture cases, without any allusion to their origin or juridical effects.[1]

The direct effectiveness of Directives has arisen in two different contexts. In *The State (Cotter) v Minister for Social Welfare and A-G*[2] the issue was whether Article 4 of Council Directive (EEC) 79/7[3] was directly effective after the expiry of the time allowed to the State to implement the Directive. The Court of Justice, in response to the reference under Article 177, ruled that it was. But in *East v Cuddy*[4] and *Murphy v An Bord Telecom*[5] the issues did not concern the failure of the State to implement the Directives in question within the specified time limits. Instead, the issues turned on the compatibility of national measures with a Directive (*East v Cuddy*) and the proper implementation of a Directive (*Murphy v An Board Telecom*). In both cases the judge requested a ruling under Article 177 on the direct effectiveness of the relevant provision of the Directives. In *East v Cuddy* the Court of Justice held that a direct effect of the provision of the Directive at issue did not arise and in *Murphy v An Bord Telecom* the Court held that the provision of the Directive at issue was directly effective.

The direct effectiveness of Directives arose in an oblique way in the case of *Lee v Minister for Agriculture*.[6] Council Directive (EEC) 72/159[7] was implemented in Ireland in a non-statutory form by the publication of Department of Agriculture's Farm Modernisation Scheme, the last clause of which provided that the decision of the Minister on any matter relating to the scheme was final. This did not appear to prevent Mr Lee from pursuing his claim through the Circuit Court, the High Court and the Court of Justice in Luxembourg. The latter court (in which the plaintiff was legally aided) gave a ruling on two questions concerning the interpretation of the Directive on which the scheme was based.[8]

The issue of the direct effectiveness of provisions of the EEC Treaty in the context of other international agreements was considered by Gleeson J. in *A-G v Burgoa*.[9] The defendant was the master of a Spanish fishing boat which had been arrested for fishing within the exclusive fisheries limits of the State. The defendant argued that he had been arrested outside the limits fixed by the London Fisheries Convention of 1964 to which both Ireland and Spain were parties and that the antecedent rights created by that treaty were maintained and upheld by Article 234 of the EEC Treaty. This prompted Gleeson J. to adjourn proceedings before the Circuit Court in Cork and seek a preliminary ruling on four questions dealing with the direct effectiveness of Article 234.[10]

1 See, for example: *Incorporated Food Products Ltd (in liquidation) v Minister for Agriculture* (6 June 1984, unreported), High Court (Lynch J.).
2 (13 May 1985, unreported) High Court (Hamilton P.).
3 O.J. L 6, 10.7.1979 p. 24.
4 (11 November 1985, unreported) Circuit Court (Sheehy J.).
5 *Loc. cit.*, fn. 5, para. 15.3.
6 *Loc. cit.*, fn. 6, para. 15.4.
7 O.J. (Sp. Ed.) (1972) p. 324.
8 [1980] E.C.R. 1495, [1980] 2 C.M.L.R. 682.
9 [1979] J.I.S.E.L. 73.
10 Case 812/79 *A-G v Burgoa* [1980] E.C.R. 2787, [1981] 2 C.M.L.R. 193.

Chapter 16

The Community and the Apparatus of the State

16.1 In an earlier chapter we noted that the legislative authorities of the Communities enact approximately 5,000 legally binding measures annually. Most of this legislation is adopted by the Commission using powers delegated to it by the Council; in doing so the Commission will consult with an advisory committee or a management committee, and these committees are composed either of national civil servants or of representatives of trade or professional interests. And when the Council exercises power itself it is made up of Ministers or Junior Ministers who are assisted by teams of national civil servants. Furthermore, the immense paper flow generated by the legislative system of the Communities has necessitated a permanent liaison between the national civil service and the institutions in Brussels. In this chapter we consider the structures for national policy formulation on Community issues, as well as the participation of the domestic civil service in the legislative system in Europe and the subsequent mechanisms of supervision and control operated by other constitutional organs. But first, we must trace the origins of the present national structures back to Ireland's first application for membership of the EEC in 1961.

16.2 'The Department of Finance can be said, as far as Ireland is concerned to have discovered the European Communities.'[1]

The Department of Finance enjoyed a period of unchallenged pre-eminence amongst the Departments of State at the end of the 1950s and this continued into the new decade as a radical reformulation of economic policy was instigated under the leadership of Kenneth Whitaker. Not surprisingly, it was the Department of Finance, rather than the more obvious Departments of Industry and Commerce or External Affairs, that carried out the negotiation of the Anglo-Irish Free Trade Agreement and of the Protocol of accession to the General Agreement on Tariffs and Trade.[2] Similarly, the Committee of Secretaries (of Departments) which the Government established to prepare for negotiations for entry to the EEC, was under the chairmanship of the Department of Finance, and it was this Department which prepared the first White paper on the EEC in 1961.[3]

The dominance of Finance in foreign economic policy-making came to an end in the late 1960s partly because of changes of personnel in Government, and partly to bring Irish practice into line with the Member States of the Community. Ireland established diplomatic relations with the EEC in December 1959,[4] and the Irish ambassador to Belgium and Luxembourg was appointed Head of the new Irish mission. In October 1966 a separate Irish mission to the three Communities was established, and this mission was under the control of External Affairs; officials of other Departments were seconded to External Affairs for the duration of their stay in Brussels. The retirement of Sean Lemass as Taoiseach in 1966, and the withdrawal of Frank Aiken from Iveagh House in 1969, brought about major changes in foreign policy-making. Lemass had enjoyed a virtual monopoly over trade and economic issues, while Aiken's perspective of the role of External Affairs concentrated—at a bilateral level—on relations with Britain, and—at the international level—on participation in the United Nations. When the final bout of negotiations commenced in 1970, Foreign Affairs (as it had become) assumed control of the Committee of Secretaries and also took over the coordination of the negotiations, a function exercised in the other applicant States and in the Six by the Foreign Ministers. This assumption of power was confirmed after accession when the permanent mission in Brussels became the *Irish Permanent Representation* (under the control of Foreign Affairs and headed by a Permanent Representative with ambassadorial status) while, in Dublin, the Committee of Secretaries became the *European Communities Committee*—under the chairmanship of Foreign Affairs.

The predominance of Foreign Affairs on Community issues has come under challenge recently, but this time from the Department of the Taoiseach. At the commencement of Irish membership of the Communities the Department of the Taoiseach had a minuscule staff, but a number of factors combined to bring about a rapid increase in its personnel. One of these factors was the emergence of the European Council in 1974 (see above at 4.18). The first meeting of the European Council was held in Dublin Castle under the Presidency of Mr Liam Cosgrave, and thereafter the schedule of three meetings per annum necessitated a high level of preparation and briefing for the Taoiseach. Staffing levels were increased accordingly, and a further accretion of officials exposed to European Affairs came with the disbandment of the Department of Economic Development. The latter Department had come into existence after Fianna Fail's landslide victory in the 1977 election, a success based to a large extent on an election manifesto drafted by Dr Martin O'Donoghue. O'Donoghue was appointed to the new portfolio and during its short existence his Department had an input to many Community-related issues; the Department was represented on the European Communities Committee, and the Minister was a regular visitor to Brussels where he participated in meetings of the Council on economic and financial and budgetary matters. On the accession to power of Mr Charles Haughey in 1979 the Department was disbanded and its personnel were allocated to other civil service responsibilities; many were transferred to the Department of the Taoiseach. During Haughey's first administration the latter Department expanded rapidly, a reaction in part to the demands of the Presidency and of European Council meetings. Dermot Scott has suggested that the expansion may also have sprung from

'. . . Haughey's view of the role of the Taoiseach, and possibly from his view of the relative capabilities of himself and his ministers, or from a wish to keep them on a tight rein.'[5]

Moreover, Haughey was said to have enjoyed less than cordial relations with the senior bureaucracy in Foreign Affairs, particularly on the issue of Northern Ireland; high level intervention by Irish-American politicians was rumoured to have prevented Haughey from replacing the then Irish Ambassador to the United States. During Dr Garret Fitzgerald's tenure of office the Department kept its structure, but Fitzgerald seemed content to leave the overall coordination of Community affairs to Foreign Affairs, probably because of his familiarity with that Department, whose major expansion took place under his stewardship as Minister from 1973 to 1977.

The differences in style between Haughey and Fitzgerald as Taoiseach, and the ensuing domestic structural consequences, can be seen clearly in the changes instigated by Haughey on his return to power in March 1987. Shortly after his election as Taoiseach it was announced that a greater involvement in Northern Ireland affairs would be undertaken by the Taoiseach's Department and that a special cabinet sub-committee on Northern Ireland would be serviced by staff from the Department of the Taoiseach. Furthermore, the chairmanship of the European Communities Committee would now be taken by the Minister of State at the Department of the Taoiseach with responsibility for European Affairs. This function had been exercised previously by officials from the Department of Foreign Affairs. The general consensus about these changes was that they signified Haughey's preference for '. . . maintaining a close personal interest in all aspects of government . . .' but that they also represented a downgrading of the Department of Foreign Affairs.[6]

Thus, at the outset of Irish contact with the European Communities the principal foreign policy functions were fragmented between several government departments. At the time of accession to the Communities the control of policy towards the Communities had been centralised to a great extent in the Department of Foreign Affairs, but in recent years Foreign Affair's hegemony has been challenged by the Department of the Taoiseach. And, as a more coherent system of policy management emerged in the years after the State's first application for membership of the EEC, the range of foreign policy preoccupations became more sophisticated. At the end of the 1950s, Ireland's foreign policy had two main elements: Anglo-Irish relations and participation in the United Nations and its specialised agencies. Two decades later, Irish foreign policy was said to have four main pillars: Anglo-Irish bilateral relations; economic foreign policy (operating mainly through the Communities); European Political Cooperation (EPC); and Development Cooperation.[7] On closer examination, it can be seen that the latter two concerns are directly connected with Community membership: EPC is directly related to the Communities, and Ireland's bilateral aid programme was put on a formal footing with membership of the Communities in view.

1 Dermot Scott, *EEC Membership and the Irish Administrative System*, 31 Administration 147. See also by the same author: Adapting the Machinery of Central Government, in David Coombes (Ed), *Ireland and the European Communities—Ten Years of Membership*, (Dublin 1983).
2 Dermot Scott, *op. cit.* fn. 1 at p. 151.
3 'European Economic Community', laid before both Houses, 30 June 1961.
4 White Paper entitled 'European Communities' laid before both Houses, April 1967, at p. 181.
5 Dermot Scott, *op. cit.* fn. 1 at p. 173.
6 John Cooney, *Irish Times*, 23 March 1987.
7 Patrick Keatinge, Ireland: Neutrality inside EPC, in Christopher J. Hill (Ed.) *National Foreign Policies and European Political Cooperation* (London 1983).

16.3 *The Irish Permanent Representation* in Brussels plays a pivotal role in the relationship between the Communities' institutions and the administration of the State. It is the conduit for all Community legislative proposals to the national bureaucracy. It maintains essential contacts with the Permanent Representations of the other Member States and it keeps in touch with officials at all levels in the institutions, particularly the Commission. Most significantly, the Permanent Representative and his colleagues from other Member States collectively constitute COREPER—the Committee of Permanent Representatives (see above para. 4.17).

In 1986 the Permanent Representation had a staff of 24; the officials were drawn from a variety of Departments of State with the greatest number coming from Foreign Affairs. During their stay in Brussels, usually three or four months in duration, the non-Foreign Affairs officials are seconded to Foreign Affairs and are accorded diplomatic rank by reference to their civil service grade equivalents. Although the Permanent Representation in Brussels probably ranks lower than Washington or London in importance as a diplomatic posting, it is certainly the most arduous assignment on the diplomatic circuit. The Permanent Representative and his Deputy are always officials from the Department of Foreign Affairs.

The staff of the Permanent Representation provide the State presence at many of the working groups established by the Council (and supervised by COREPER) to resolve differences between the Member States on proposals emanating from the Commission; they are in direct contact, often on a daily basis, with officials based in parent Departments in Dublin. The allocation of responsibilities generally follows Departmental competences, but the overall control is in the hands of the Permanent Representative and his Deputy; nonetheless, the officials play an important part in the formulation of the State's position on any issue before the Council. Although the written briefs for Ministerial attendance at Council meetings will have been prepared in Dublin; much of the input will have originated in the Permanent Representation and the responsible official, who may have attended the relevant working group, will be present at the oral briefing of the Minister when he or she arrives in Brussels or Luxembourg for the Council meeting.[1]

The Deputy Permanent Representative participates in the work of COREPER I which deals with the work of specialised Councils, while the Permanent Representative assumes responsibility for COREPER II, the General Affairs Council made up of the Ministers of Foreign Affairs. The personal assistant of the Permanent Representative participates in the

'Antici' group: this body prepares the agenda for COREPER II and acts also as the coordinating agency for EPC.[2]

In the agricultural sector the functions of COREPER are carried out by the Special Committee on Agriculture. The Irish spokesman on this committee has equivalent rank to the Deputy Permanent Representative, and usually retains the position for three or four years; if unavailable, the spokesman's place is taken by one of the agricultural counsellors from the Permanent Representation. The Special Committee on Agriculture operates in much the same manner as COREPER; there is an 'A' point and 'B' point procedure and the voting practices are similar. Although the Luxembourg compromise of 1966 affected agricultural and other Community issues equally, a practice has grown up in recent years whereby the chairman (from the Member State holding the Presidency) notes that a qualified majority exists for the particular proposal and this device has frequently brought the minority Member States into line. At Council working groups on agricultural matters the State is represented occasionally by counsellors from the Permanent Representation but more often by officials from Dublin, and the Department now sends relatively junior officers, at administrative officer or higher executive officer level, to participate in working groups.

By contrast, neither COREPER nor the Special Committee on Agriculture are involved in the work of consultative committees designed to assist the commission (*supra* paras 4.48–49). The personnel for these Committees is provided by the relevant Departments in Dublin; for example, the Irish representatives on management committees are selected by the Department of Agriculture, usually at Head of Division or Principal officer level.

1 Marian O'Leary, The Presidency of the Council of Ministers of the European Communities: Ireland and its EC Membership; in Colm O Nuallain (Ed.), *The Presidency of the European Council of Ministers* (London 1985).
2 *Idem*, at p. 152.

16.4 Back in Ireland, the day-to-day management of Ireland's relations with the Communities is in the hands of the Department of Foreign Affairs, and this Department has been affected by membership of the Communities more than any other Department or Office of State. Dermot Scott has demonstrated how Community membership was the main factor behind the dramatic three-fold increase in staffing levels, with the Economic and Political Divisions as principal beneficiaries; a new Division, dealing with Development Cooperation came into existence primarily because of Community commitments in the development cooperation sector. In fact, Ireland's bilateral aid programme did not officially commence until after accession.[1] Also, Ireland's diplomatic and consular representation abroad increased significantly between 1971 and 1986: in 1971 the State had 26 resident missions abroad but by 1986 this number had risen to 39.[2] Scott considers that the establishment of embassies in Luxembourg and Athens was directly connected with accession, while the opening of embassies in Vienna, Moscow and Beijing, probably inevitable in the long run, was also dictated by Community-linked considerations.[3]

The routine administration of Community business is handled mainly by the Economic Division, and the Department has been described as a sort of letter-box between the Permanent Representation in Brussels and the 'line' Departments in Dublin.[4] The Economic Division is the clearing house for all communications between Brussels and Dublin, although there is a tendency for line Departments to deal directly with their representatives in the Permanent Representation with copies or acknowledgments to Iveagh House.

The increasing burden borne by the Minister for Foreign Affairs has been recognised in recent times by the appointment of a *Minister of State* at the Department. Up to 1986 the Minister of State had been responsible first for Development Cooperation and latterly for Anglo-Irish Affairs, but in the ministerial reshuffle of 1986 the junior minister was allocated the portfolios of Development Aid and European Community Affairs. Junior ministerial responsibility for European Affairs has been continued by the Fianna Fail administration that took office in March 1987; significantly, however, the Minister of State in question is attached to the Department of the Taoiseach and not the Department of Foreign Affairs.

There is no requirement under the Ministers and Secretaries Acts that junior ministers be allocated to specific departments or to particular portfolios. Similarly, there is no statutory basis for the *European Communities Committee*, the successor to the pre-accession Committee of Secretaries. This committee meets once a month and is composed of representatives—at Deputy Secretary or Assistant Secretary level—from the principal Departments concerned with Community affairs. It does not concern itself with the everyday detail of Community business; rather, its brief is to maintain an overview of policy developments and it is responsible ultimately to the Government. Until 1987 the European Communities Committee was chaired by an official from the Department of Foreign Affairs. However, when the new administration took office in 1987 it was announced that the Committee would operate henceforth under the chairmanship of the Minister of State at the Department of the Taoiseach with responsibility for European Affairs.

From time to time the European Communities Committee establishes working groups to examine particular problems. An example can be seen in a report produced in 1986 by a group of officials drawn from the Departments of the Taoiseach, Finance, Foreign Affairs, Industry and Commerce, and Agriculture. Entitled 'A stocktaking of Ireland's membership of the European Communities', the report carried out an analysis of the positive and negative results of membership in terms of the expectations of membership at the time of accession. In the agricultural sector the State had received more than £4.5 bn. from the European Agricultural Guidance and Guarantee Fund and there had been a consequential reduction in Exchequer subsidisation of farmers. Ireland received more from the other Community Funds, relatively speaking, than any other Member State. Industrial output had increased significantly, but job losses in traditional industries had not been compensated for by jobs in the new technological industries; and there had been significant trade diversification, with the UK accounting for only 26 per cent of exports in 1985 compared with 60 per cent in 1972. Less tangible benefits included a noticeable boost to national morale and a diminution in the Anglo-centricity of Irish attitudes. The report also pinpointed certain negative aspects of membership. The convergence aspirations listed in Protocol 30 of the Act of Accession (on the economic development of Ireland) had not been realised. In the agricultural sector further development would be hindered by coresponsibility and super levies which were designed to deal with chronic structural surpluses. Enlargement of the Community would put further strains on the CAP and would reduce Ireland's share of other Structural Funds. Ominously, the report concluded that Ireland had the highest rate of dependence on direct transfers from the Community Budget and was ill equipped to deal with a serious deterioration in the level of benefits emanating from Brussels. Among the policy objectives, which the working group saw on placing a limit on negative developments while protecting Irish interests, were the following: raising budgetary expenditure to the ceiling of VAT 'own resources'; securing a customised aid programme for Ireland along the lines of the Integrated Mediterranean Programmes; the preparation of a special case for presentation when the review of the structural funds takes place (provided for in Article 130D of the SEA); and, in the agricultural sector, encouraging the development of quality products with value-added in Ireland so as to counter overdependence on intervention.

At the level below the European Communities Committee ten *inter-departmental working groups* were established shortly after accession,[5] and by the mid-1970s the number had risen to eleven.[6] These bodies do not appear to have survived for long on a formally structured basis; instead, working groups—such as that which produced the 'stocktaking' report—have been established from time to time on an *ad hoc* basis. However, the failure of the formal working group system should not be viewed in a totally negative light: it has often been pointed out that the relatively small size of the Irish Civil Service allows for a much greater degree of direct personal contact between officials of different Departments.[7] When policy disagreements occur they are usually resolved by informal consultation, but if difficulties persist they will be considered at a coordination meeting—normally arranged by the Department of Foreign Affairs.[8] Should a problem prove to be intractable it might be referred to the European Communities Committee or, ultimately, to the Government. In a sense, the European Communities Committee occupies the middle ground between inter-departmental working groups (*ad hoc* or otherwise) which are answerable to it, and the final policy-making authority, the Government, to which it is in turn answerable.

---

1 Dermot Scott, *op. cit.* fn. 1, para. 16.2, at p. 162–163.
2 State Directory, 1971 and 1986.
3 Dermot Scott, *op. cit.* fn. 1, para. 16.2, at p. 165.
4 Marian O'Leary, *op. cit.* fn. 1, para. 16.3, at p. 144.
5 Patrick Keatinge, *A Place Among the Nations*, (Dublin 1978); at p 214.
6 Brigid Burns and Trevor C. Salmon, *Policy-making coordination in Ireland on European Community issues*, XV J.C.M.S. 272, at p. 278.
7 Marian O'Leary, *op. cit.* fn. 1, para. 16.3, at p. 147.
8 *Idem*, at p. 147.

16.5 *Cabinet control* over European Community policy matters has undergone a number of changes since accession in 1973. The Coalition Government of 1973 to 1977 established a Cabinet committee on Community affairs which comprised the Ministers of Agriculture and Fisheries, Industry and Commerce, Foreign Affairs, and Finance, as well as the Taoiseach and Tanaiste. But the committee met infrequently and its effect on policy-making was reported to be limited.[1] The Fianna Fail government of 1977 to 1981 did not retain the committee but when the Coalition of Fine Gael and Labour took office in 1982 the committee was re-established and it was convened on a reasonably regular basis. Its membership was similar to its predecessor and it considered the most pressing Community issues of the day, including the milk superlevy negotiations of 1984 and the preparation of the Single European Act in 1985 and 1986. Predictably, Fianna Fail took a different approach to the Coalition government, and in March 1987 Mr Haughey announced that a special Cabinet committee made up of himself, the Minister for Finance and the Minister for Agriculture would oversee the forthcoming negotiations on the EEC budget and on reform of the CAP. As we have already noted, Mr Haughey appointed a Minister of State attached to his own Department to chair the European Communities Committee. The senior civil servant—as regards Community issues—was now reputed to be the Deputy Secretary in the Department of the Taoiseach, rather than the Deputy Secretary in charge of the Economic Division of the Department of Foreign Affairs.

It remains to be seen whether these changes will have any major effect on policy formulation. It has been suggested that in the Irish administrative system the initial work on a file is carried out by relatively junior officials in the responsible department but that serious policy questions are determined, in the main, by middle-level and senior-level bureaucrats.[2] The Irish system of government is such that Ministers do not, as yet, possess *cabinets* of politically-appointed advisers to assist them in policy formulation; as a consequence Ministers are obliged to rely on civil servants for advice. When issues do reach the Cabinet, via the European Communities Committee, it is usually at a very late stage of the policy-making process and, as Patrick Keatinge has described it, the Cabinet's function is to

'. . . act as a court of appeal, in order to reconcile departmental differences in which the policy options have already been drastically reduced.'[3]

1 Brigid Burns and Trevor C. Salmon, *op. cit.* fn. 6, para. 16.4, at p. 275.
2 Marian O'Leary, *op. cit.* fn. 1, para. 16.3, at p. 147.
3 *Loc. cit.* fn. 5, para. 16.4, at p. 219.

16.6 We have already noted that the European Council, which has acted as a 'court of appeal' for Community decision-making problems, was a major stimulus to the growth of the Department of the Taoiseach (*supra* at para. 16.2). The Taoiseach represents Ireland at European Council meetings, the preparation for which is coordinated by his Department, with briefs coming from other Departments; the European Communities

Committee and the Permanent Representative will also have been consulted.

16.7 The assumption by Ireland of the *Presidency of the Council* puts great pressure on the administrative structures of the State. This function, which rotates among the Member States every six months, devolved upon Ireland every four and a half years in the period after accession. However, the Presidency will now be assumed by Ireland every five or six years as a result of the modified rotation system introduced by Article 11 of the Third Act of Accession.

Most of the burden of the Presidency falls on the Permanent Representation in Brussels, which starts making preparations up to a year in advance and which prepares the initial assessment for the Government of the issues and problems likely to arise during Ireland's period of office. Some issues will be inherited from previous Presidencies whereas others will arise (unannounced) during the course of the term of office. The Chernobyl disaster is an example from the latter category: although its health and security ramifications were immediate it also had a less obvious trade dimension.

The Permanent Representation becomes the focus of most presidency-related activity, and members of the delegation assume the chairmanship of the working groups in which they had been involved prior to the Presidency; other Irish officials, flown out from Dublin, carry out the task hitherto exercised by the delegation. Back-up for the delegation comes from the Secretariat of the Council but, surprisingly, the staff of the Permanent Representation is not increased significantly during this period.[1] Where members of the delegation are not in the chair officials from Dublin, selected well in advance, carry out this function, and the Administration Division of the Department of Foreign Affairs has provided training courses for such officials, originally at the Institute of Public Administration but now at the Civil Service Training Centre in Landsdowne House, Dublin. Apart from language instruction, the courses provide information on the structure and policies of the Community institutions, and on chairmanship skills. The Economic Division of the Department of Foreign Affairs is, as one would expect, heavily involved in the administration of the Presidency, as is the Administration Division, which coordinates accommodation and related problems for meetings held in Dublin. At present Dublin Castle is undergoing a substantial refurbishment to facilitate its use as the national centre for European Council meetings.

There is also a foreign dimension to the Presidency. During the six-month term of office Irish embassies and delegations abroad assume a major, albeit temporary, importance and this is particularly true of the United Nations delegation; the Irish delegation speaks on behalf of the Twelve during this period. Likewise, Irish embassies in other Member States become

'. . . the channel for official communications between the Presidency and the host country.'[2]

Finally, it should be recalled that the Minister for Foreign Affairs becomes President-in-Office of the Council and immediately assumes a very high profile internationally. He is obliged to carry out a variety of tasks on behalf of the Community such as visiting non-Member State capitals and signing Council legislation. A notable feature of the three Irish presidencies has been the conclusion of the 1st, 2nd, and 3rd Lomé Conventions, with the Minister for Foreign Affairs of the day signing on behalf of the Communities.

1 Marian O'Leary, *loc. cit.* fn. 1, at para. 16.3, at p. 152.
2 *Idem*, p. 155.

16.8 The structures and operating procedures of *European Political Cooperation* (EPC) have been discussed elsewhere (*supra* at para. 4.19) but certain pertinent features can be restated. First, foreign policy coordination does not form part of the competence transferred by the State to the Communities on accession in 1973. But it is clear that EPC, which had commenced in 1970, was intended to constitute a 'second dimension' of European integration.[1] This was made clear in 1970 by the President-in-Office of the Council, Pierre Harmel, when outlining the negotiating conditions for the applicant States: they would have to accept '. . . the Treaties and their political aims, the decisions of all kinds taken since their entry into force.'[2] That membership of the Community would also involve participation in EPC was evident from the White Paper produced by the Government in 1972: four pages were devoted to a discussion of the emerging EPC process. Thus, 'Irish involvement in EPC was at once a consequence and corollary of entry into the EEC.'[3] Secondly, EPC operates by consensus. There is no voting system, no mandatory clause requiring the Member States to adopt a particular point of view.

In Ireland EPC is handled by the Political Division of the Department of Foreign Affairs. This division has undergone a radical change since 1967 when it had a staff of four officials who were responsible for 'all political questions'.[4] Two decades later, it has a staff of 24 officials and it deals with United Nations and Council of Europe business as well as EPC. It does not, however, deal with Anglo-Irish matters. The Political Director, for EPC purposes, is an official with Assistant Secretary status. The Correspondent is usually an official at the level of Counsellor or First Secretary. The effects of participation in EPC are hard to gauge but two features can be noted. First, the amount of information available to the Irish diplomatic bureaucracy has increased dramatically; this flow of information emanates from the COREU telex network, which connects the Group of Correspondents, and from the Foreign diplomatic missions of the Member States:

'Now in purely practical terms, instead of having to depend entirely on our own foreign service and on a small network of perhaps 25 or 30 embassies for information on what is happening with regard to issues which are discussed in EPC, we are able to take advantage of the continued resources of the Twelve which cover practically the whole globe.'[5]

Second, it has been suggested that Ireland is no longer at liberty

'. . . to choose the issues with which it wishes to become involved.'[6]

However, one important issue excluded from EPC is the Northern Ireland problem; both the British and Irish Governments have been content to deal with it on a bilateral basis.

Particular pressure is placed on the Political Division during Ireland's tenure of the Presidency. As we have already noted, the Permanent Representative organises the Presidency business in Brussels, while in Dublin the Political Division coordinates the meetings of the Group of Correspondents, the Political Directors and the Foreign Ministers which, cumulatively, amount to between sixty and eighty meetings per Presidency. As in the case of the Permanent Representation, the staff of the Political Division does not increase significantly during the Presidency but on each occasion there has been an increase in the secretarial and linguistic assistance available to the Division.[7]

Until recently EPC did not attract much attention in Ireland, even though there is a section on EPC in the bi-annual Report on Developments in the Communities presented to the Oireachtas. But expressions of concern began to be heard when questions of security and defence were raised, in slightly different contexts, in the Tindemans Report in 1975, the Genscher-Colombo proposal of 1983, the Solemn Declaration on European Union of 1983, the Spinelli initiative of 1984 and the Dooge Report of 1985. Questions about the viability and integrity of Ireland's policy of neutrality came to the fore during the debates on the Single European Act. SEA, art 30 formalises the practices of EPC and links it, albeit at arm's length, with the European Communities. However, paragraph (6) of Article 30 introduced a novel concern:

'(a) The High Contracing Parties consider that closer cooperation on questions of European security would contribute in an essential way to the development of a European identity in external policy matters. They are ready to coordinate their positions more closely on the political and economic aspects of security.

(b) The High Contracting Parties are determined to maintain the technological and industrial conditions necessary for their security. They shall work to that end both at national level and, where appropriate, within the framework of the competent institutions and bodies.

(c) Nothing in this Title shall impede closer cooperation in the field of security between certain of the High Contracting Parties within the framework of the Western European Union or the Atlantic Alliance.'

The general criticism levelled at this paragraph was that it compromised Irish neutrality. So, in order to assess the arguments, it is necessary to attempt a definition of Irish neutrality.

---

1 Desmond Dinan, Irish Involvement in European Political Cooperation, in Bill McSweeney (Ed.), *Ireland and the Threat of Nuclear War* (Dublin 1985), at p. 147.
2 Government White Paper, *Accession to the European Communities*, 1972, at p. 7.

3 Padraic MacKernan, *Ireland and European Political Cooperation*, Irish Studies in International Affairs vol. 1, no. 4, 1984, at p. 24.
4 Patrick Keatinge, Ireland: neutrality inside EPC, in Christopher J. Hill, (Ed.), *National Foreign Policies and European Political Cooperation* (London 1983), at p. 147.
5 Deputy Maurice Manning, Vol. 370 Dail Debates, at col. 2078.
6 Marian O'Leary, *op. cit.* fn. 1, para. 16.3, at p. 155.
7 *Idem*, p. 154.

16.9 There is nothing in the Constitution of 1937 which requires Ireland to espouse a policy of neutrality, although certain sentiments expressed in Article 29 could provide justification for such a posture: devotion to the principle of the pacific settlement of international disputes is an example. There is no legislation dealing with the matter and there has never been a coherent Government statement on the principles underlying Ireland's 'traditional' policy of neutrality. In fact

'Irish neutrality defies precise definition. It is, apparently, neither political nor ideological, but theological.'[1]

The core element of Irish neutrality, which can be traced back to the Second World War, is non-participation in military alliances. This contrasts with the behaviour of the so-called Permanent Neutrals (Austria, Finland, Sweden and Switzerland). According to Hanspeter Neuhold,[2] Permanent Neutrality pre-empts membership of military alliances—even those of a purely defensive character—but it also assumes the ability of the state in question to defend itself in a meaningful manner. There have been grave reservations for some time concerning Ireland's defence capabilities.[3] Neuhold also argues that Permanent Neutrality excludes participation in supranational movements of an economic nature. According to Patrick Keatinge, the European neutrals regard Ireland's position as the only non-NATO member of the EEC as '. . . equivalent to squaring the circle'.[4]

Prior to the debates in the Oireachtas on the ratification of the SEA the Joint Committee on the Secondary Legislation of the European Communities had expressed concern on the question of neutrality. In its report on the Draft Treaty on European Union the Joint Committee drew attention to the security ramifications of the European Parliament's proposal, and it warned of the effects on Irish neutrality:

'. . . neutrality is a principle of Irish foreign policy and should not be bargained against material advantage.'[5]

And, in its penultimate report before the dissolution of the Dail, the Joint Committee examined the Single European Act and called on the Government to append

'. . . formal reiteration of our position of military neutrality to the act of ratification.'[6]

In the debate in the Dail on the SEA the Government's position was stated by Peter Barry, the Minister for Foreign Affairs:

'. . . the Single Act poses no threat to our neutrality. Our neutral position outside military alliances has been fully accommodated by our partners.'[7]

But, in response to Fianna Fail pressure, the Government introduced a motion by which the Dail and Seanad 'reaffirmed Ireland's position of neutrality outside military alliances',[8] and Mr Barry indicated that it was his intention to submit this resolution alongside the instrument of ratification of the SEA. Fianna Fail emphasised Ireland's 'long established policy of neutrality';[9] in fact Mr Haughey considered that

'. . . (w)e have reached, perhaps gone beyond, what is strictly compatible with Irish neutrality.'[10]

The left wing view of the matter was put by the Worker's Party. According to Mr Prionsias de Rossa, neutrality meant being non-aligned

'. . . in the sense that we will not take sides in disputes between east and west.'[11]

In a separate motion, which was defeated, the Worker's Party called for the renegotiation of the SEA to protect Irish neutrality.[12] At the other end of the political spectrum, Professor John Kelly of Fine Gael suggested that the formulators of the policy of neutrality during the Second World War would have regarded with amazement and contempt the modern interpretation of their actions which committed the State

'. . . to a miserable form of neutrality which 50 years later would be taken as forbidding us to enter a purely defensive alliance with other European democracies, democracies which not only share our values but contribute through the European Communities very substantially to our material welfare.'[13]

Given this wide range of views, it is hard not to concur with Deputy David Molony's claim that there was no such thing as a 'long established' policy of neutrality.[14]

At the conclusion of the debate the Dail and the Seanad passed the European Communities (Amendment) Bill, 1986, and the Dail also agreed to a Government motion approving the terms of the SEA.

It was in the foregoing context that the Supreme Court was called upon to rule on the compatibility of Title III of the SEA in *Crotty v An Taoiseach*[15] (*supra* at para. 15.7).

---

1 Desmond Dinan, *op. cit.* fn. 1, para. 16.8, at p. 142.
2 *Permanent neutrality in contemporary international relations: a comparative perspective*, Irish Studies in International Affairs, vol. 1 no. 3, 1982; at p. 19.
3 Deputy Gay Mitchell, Vol. 370 Dail Debates, at col. 2651.
4 Patrick Keatinge, *op. cit.* fn. 4, para. 16.8, at p. 137.
5 Report No. 14, Pl. 3063, at point 69.
6 Report no. 34, at point 115.
7 Vol. 370 Dail Debates, col. 1910.

8 Vol. 370 Dail Debates, at col. 1888; Vol. 115. Seanad Debates, at col. 1251.
9 Vol. 370 Dail Debates, at col. 2625.
10 Vol. 370 Dail Debates, at col. 1925.
11 Vol. 370 Dail Debates, at col. 2644.
12 Vol. 370 Dail Debates, at col. 2666.
13 Vol. 370 Dail Debates, at cols. 1944–1945.
14 Vol. 370 Dail Debates, at col. 2641.
15 [1987] I.L.R.M. 400.

16.10 This far we have considered the various departments and structures by which and through which Irish policy towards the Community is formulated. But what happens when a question of law arises? The Department of Foreign Affairs has a Legal Division (which employed five officials in 1986) and the Department of the Environment also has a Legal Adviser. These two exceptions apart, all other Departments of State consult the Office of the Attorney-General when a legal difficulty is encountered, particularly if connected with the Communities. According to Article 30.1 of the Constitution, the Attorney-General is the adviser to the Government on matters of law and legal opinion; Article 30.3 nominates the Attorney-General as the principal prosecutor of crimes and offences—other than those tried in courts of summary jurisdiction. Although nominated by the Taoiseach, the Attorney-General is an independent constitutional officer;[1] he or she is not subject to direction from the Government. The Attorney-General may not be a member of the Government but in practice the Attorney attends Cabinet meetings and is often called upon by the Taoiseach to give legal advice. The Attorney is not answerable to Dail Eireann, even if the holder of the Office is also a member of the Dail:[2] questions concerning the Attorney-General's functions are normally answered by the Taoiseach or by a Minister of State attached to his Department.[3]

The Office of the Attorney-General has been affected by membership of the Communities more than most Departments of State. Traditionally, the Attorney-General prosecuted all indictable offences, albeit by utilising the services of members of the Bar, and in civil matters his brief extended to advising the Government on constitutional issues and on general legal problems; he was also expected to tender advice to those Government Departments which did not have independent legal advisers. In addition, his Office included amongst its personnel the Parliamentary Draftsman and his staff, as well as the Statute Law Reform Office. Finally, The Attorney-General, in association with the Chief State Solicitor (whose office and staff also fall within the responsibilities of the Attorney-General), dealt with all litigation involving the State. In 1971 the Office of the Attorney-General had a complement of 52 officials—80 per cent of whom were employed in the Chief State Solicitor's office.[4]

By 1986 the Attorney-General's office had a complement of 76 public servants, but only half of these were in the Chief State Solicitor's Office. Furthermore, the bulk of the Attorney-General's prosecuting functions had been transferred to the Director of Public Prosecutions, a new office created by the Prosecution of Offences Act, 1974. A major factor in this development was the increase in the volume of advice being sought by

Government Departments on European Communities issues.[5] The resumption by the Attorney-General of prosecuting functions in sea fisheries' cases in 1978 can also be seen as a consequence of membership. As a result of the extension of the State's exclusive fishing zone to 200 miles, fisheries prosecutions are now commenced regularly against vessels from Member States and non-Member States alike. The diplomatic ramifications of these proceedings were considered sufficient grounds for involving the Attorney-General in the prosecution process.[6] An early example of this practice can be seen in the case of *A-G v Burgoa*.[7]

The Attorney-General advises the Government on any constitutional issues involving the Communities, and it need hardly be emphasised that the Attorney was closely involved in the negotiations leading to the conclusion of the SEA. For example, during the Dail debate on the ratification of the SEA the Minister for Foreign Affairs went so far as to read into the record the Attorney-General's opinion as to why it was not possible to attach a unilateral declaration on neutrality and cohesion (as proposed by Fianna Fail) to Ireland's instrument of ratification of the SEA.[8] The Attorney-General also deals on a regular basis with routine legal problems, connected with the Communities, submitted by the Government or by one of the Departments of State. An example of the latter can be seen in Report No. 32 of the Fourth Joint Committee on the Secondary Legislation of the European Communities. The Committee criticised the Department of Labour for effecting a blanket amendment of a number of statutory instruments rather than amending the instruments separately.[9] When questioned by the Joint Committee, the Department of Labour solicited the advice of the Attorney-General and this advice confirmed the view of the Committee. There is, however, one issue on which the Attorney-General does not give advice: it appears that any legal problem concerning European Political Cooperation is dealt with by the Legal Division of the Department of Foreign Affairs.

The Attorney-General also handles any domestic litigation involving Community issues in which a Minister of State is the Defendant. In such circumstances the Chief State Solicitor instructs counsel briefed by the Attorney-General; it is not uncommon for disputes of this type to be referred to Luxembourg under Article 177 of the EEC Treaty. The Attorney-General also briefs counsel in direct actions before the Court of Justice, particularly in proceedings against Ireland under Article 169 of the EEC Treaty.

1 *McLoughlin v Minister for Social Welfare* [1958] I.R. 1.
2 As was the case from 1973 to 1977 when Declan Costello T.D. was Attorney-General.
3 J.P. Casey, *The Office of the Attorney-General in Ireland* (Dublin 1980); at p. 70.
4 State Directory, 1971.
5 J.P. Casey, *op. cit.* fn. 3, at p. 115.
6 See Minister for Fisheries (Mr Brian Lenihan), 305 Dail Debates, Cols. 1792–3; see also J.P. Casey, *op. cit.* fn. 3, at p. 117.
7 [1979] J.I.S.E.L. 73.
8 Vol. 370, Dail Debates, Cols. 2356–8.
9 The offending statutory instrument was the European Communities (Employment Equality) Regulations, 1985, [S.I. No. 331 of 1985]. See also Appendix 2 of Report No. 32 in which correspondence between the Committee and the Department of Labour is reproduced.

16.11 The office of the Attorney-General is often consulted, through the Parliamentary Draftsman, after policy has been formulated and converted into Community legislation. The need for domestic legislation rarely arises in respect of Regulations, which are described in Article 189 of the EEC Treaty as directly applicable; however, it is sometimes necessary to provide for the imposition of fines for non-compliance with Community Regulations.[1] Domestic implementing legislation is more frequently required for Directives although the choice of means of implementation is left to the State; under Community law the State has full discretion in this regard,[2] so that the choice of legislation (either primary or delegated) or administrative action as the implementing technique becomes a matter of domestic constitutional law. As regards legislation, the State may choose to execute its obligations either by enacting a Bill in the Oireachtas or by means of powers delegated to Ministers under Section 3 of the European Communities Act, 1972 or to Ministers or other entities under other Acts of the Oireachtas. Implementation by administrative action occurs far less frequently and is much more problematic. For instance, who decides whether implementation of a Directive should be by administrative action? This issue has been raised on a number of occasions by the Joint Committee on the Secondary Legislation of the European Communities. The 4th Joint Committee considered that no implementing legislation was required if a legislative framework sanctioned by the Oireachtas was already in existence. But if the measures necessitated by the Directive require legislation then the obligation on the State can only be discharged by the Oireachtas or by persons or entities delegated by it; the 'choice of form and methods' under Article 189 belongs only to the Oireachtas.[3] Although this problem has arisen from time to time in the reports of the Joint Committee it has not yet given rise to litigation in the Courts.

If a Directive is likely to affect major domestic legislation, such as the Companies Acts, the preferred method of converting it into domestic law is by means of a Bill initiated either in the Dail or the Seanad. In such a case the promoting Department, which will have been involved in the negotiations in Brussels on the terms of the Directive and, at an earlier stage, in the formulation of Irish policy towards the Commission's proposal for a Directive, will prepare a general scheme of the proposed Bill as well as a memorandum outlining the need for the Bill, its relationship to other legislation, and the estimated cost to the Exchequer of the operation of the Bill. These are circulated to other interested Departments (including the Department of Finance) for comments or reservations, after which it is sent to the Government for its approval. If the Government approves the scheme and accompanying memorandum it is then forwarded to the parliamentary draftsmen in the Attorney-General's office who put the scheme into Bill form in cooperation with officials from the promoting Department. The draft Bill now goes to the Attorney-General for his consideration, then back to the sponsoring Department and other interested Departments for comment before being printed on white paper and submitted to the Government for approval. Following Government approval the Minister in charge is authorised to initiate the Bill either in the Dail or in the Seanad. The Bill (printed on green paper if initiated in the Dail or on yellow paper if initiated in the Seanad) must now pass the five stages of legislation.[4]

Implementation of Directives by Statutory Instruments is much more common, particularly if the subject matter is technical in nature. There are two noteworthy features concerning this form of compliance with Community law obligations. First, section 3 of the European Communities Act, 1972, delegates to any Minister wide powers to make 'regulations' to enable full effect to be given to Community law obligations. Although the vast majority of Directives are implemented by use of section 3 of the 1972 Act, powers delegated to specific Ministers in other Acts are sometimes used to give effect to Directives. For example, the Medical Preparations (Licensing of Manufacture) (Amendment) Regulations, 1975,[5] were adopted pursuant to section 5 of the Health Act, 1947, in order to give effect to Council Directive (EEC) 75/319,[6] the object of which was to approximate the administrative or legal provisions in the Member States concerning the manufacture of medical and toilet preparation. Secondly, we have already noted that the Department of Foreign Affairs and the Department of the Environment have their own legal personnel. The Legal Adviser in the Department of the Environment enjoys a further distinction in that he drafts all the statutory instruments for the Departments of the Environment, Health and Social Welfare; the latter two Departments were hived off from the old Department of Local Government in 1947. All other statutory instruments are drafted by the parliamentary draftsmen, but the procedure is similar in both instances. A preliminary draft is forwarded by the sponsoring Department to the draftsman who prepared a formal draft in consultation with officers from the relevant Department. A final version is then submitted to the responsible Minister who initials and seals the instrument, which is then given a number by the Stationery Office, and notice of its adoption is published in Irish Oifigiuil. The instrument will then be transmitted to the Dail or Seanad, or both, to comply with the confirmatory procedures specified in the parent Act. In the 24th Oireachtas copies of instruments were sent to the Joint Committee on Legislation or the Joint Committee on the Secondary Legislation of the European Communities, as appropriate. The mechanics of these confirmatory and regulatory procedures are considered below.

1 See, for example, *Minister for Agriculture v Norgro Ltd* [1980] I.R. 155, where the defendant was prosecuted for contravention of Article 3 of the European Communities (Fruit and Vegetables) Regulations, 1973.

2 Case 152/79 *Lee v Minister for Agriculture* [1980] E.C.R. 1495, [1980] 2 C.M.L.R. 682.

3 Fourth Joint Committee on the Secondary Legislation of the European Communities, report no. 32.

4 David Gwynn Morgan, *Constitutional Law of Ireland* (Dublin 1985), at p. 97.

5 S.I. No. 302 of 1975.

6 O.J. L 147, 9.6.1975 p. 13.

16.12 It now remains to consider the various means of supervision and control of executive and legislative action connected with the European Communities.

The main supervisory body is the *Oireachtas Joint Committee on the Secondary Legislation of the European Communities (The Joint Commit-*

tee). It was the first of the new brand of Oireachtas Joint Committees but, unlike the other Joint Committees, it exercises a statutory function which is outlined in the European Communities (Amendment) Act, 1973. This Act was passed because of dissatisfaction with the original procedure for confirming statutory instruments (or 'regulations') made under section 3 of the European Communities Act, 1972.[1] Instead of being confirmed by an Act of the Oireachtas within six months of their adoption, statutory instruments are now presumed to be valid unless, acting on the recommendation of the Joint Committee, either the Dail or the Seanad passes a resolution revoking the instrument within one year of its making.[2] Apart from this regulatory function, the terms of reference[3] of the Joint Committee permit it to examine and report on:

(i) draft Community legislation, including programmes and guidelines for possible legislative action;
(ii) acts of the institutions;
(iii) regulations made under the European Communities Act, 1972;
(iv) other instruments made under Statute and necessitated by the obligations of membership of the Communities.

The Joint Committee was also empowered to examine the question of dual membership of either the Dail or Seanad and the European Parliament and to consider the relationship between the Irish representatives in the European Parliament and the Dail and Seanad, and to report thereon.

However, there are a number of serious *lacunae* in the Joint Committee's terms of reference. First, the Joint Committee is not empowered to investigate non-statutory implementation of Community schemes.[4] Second, the Joint Committee is not permitted to review European Political Cooperation.

There have been four Joint Committees since the first was constituted in July 1973. No members of the 22nd Oireachtas, which had an unusually short duration of only 7 months, were appointed to the Joint Committee; in the 23rd Oireachtas, which lasted for only 8 months before dissolution of the Dail, members of the Committee had been selected but no reports had been published. Thus, only the First, Second and Fourth Committees were really effective and they produced 59, 94 and 36 reports respectively (see Table 1). Nonetheless, it is clear that a serious difficulty faced by the Joint Committee concerns continuity; it has a duration which is coterminous with the Dail. And because the Seanad elections take place well after a new Dail holds its inaugural meeting the Committee invariably suffers a hiatus of about 6 months in its work. Thus, no Joint Committee was appointed during the brief existence of the 22nd Oireachtas (June 1981 to January 1982) and although the Third Joint Committee had been appointed it produced no final reports in its four and a half months of existence. As a consequence, the Fourth Joint Committee (1983 to 1987) spent much of its initial period in office catching up on the two-year gap between the last report of the Second Joint Committee and its own first meeting.

Table 1

Joint Committee	Duration	Number of Reports
1st	26.7.73–25.5.77	59
2nd	14.12.77–21.5.81	94
3rd	16.6.82–4.11.82	–
4th	29.6.83–21.1.87	36

The fact that the Fourth Joint Committee produced only 36 reports would tend to suggest that it was less productive than its predecessors. This is misleading because the 24th Oireachtas established an unprecedented number of Joint Committees which placed heavy demands on the time of members, most of whom served on at least two committees.[5] It must also be said that the range and quality of the work of the Fourth Joint Committee was impressive. The Joint Committee operated through four sub-committees dealing with the following topics:

(i) economic, commercial and financial affairs;
(ii) social, environmental and miscellaneous issues;
(iii) agriculture and fisheries; and
(iv) statutory instruments and legal affairs.

The subject matter covered in the 36 reports was varied covering for example acid rain,[6] proposals concerning the insurance industry in Ireland,[7] Community employment policy[8] and Company law and worker participation.[9] The two most productive sub-committees were those on Agriculture and Fisheries (under the chairmanship of Joe Walsh T.D.) and on statutory instruments and legal affairs (under the chairmanship of Maurice Manning T.D.). In preparing its reports the Joint Committee was assisted by a variety of civil servants, although on one occasion the Department of Energy declined to send officials to a hearing on acid rain.[10] The Joint Committee also heard the views of the Ministers for Agriculture and for Labour, Commissioner Sutherland,[11] as well as senior officials in the Commission.

The sub-committee on statutory instruments carried out the all important supervisory function in respect of the exercise by Ministers of delegated powers under section 3 of the European Communities Act, 1972, and the European Communities (Amendment) Act, 1973.[12] As we have already noted, the Joint Committee may recommend to the Dail and the Seanad the annulment of 'regulations' made under section 3 and either House may pass a resolution to that effect within one year of the making of the regulations in question. The First Joint Committee recommended the annulment of the European Communities (Fresh Poultry Meat) Regulations, 1976,[13] on the grounds that they created unnecessary offences. Although the appropriate resolutions were tabled in the Dail and Seanad the Dail was dissolved shortly afterwards, and by the time the Second Joint

Committee had been appointed the one year challenge period had virtually elapsed. The Second Joint Committee also recommended the amendment of two sets of Regulations on the mutual recognition of dental and general nursing qualifications—unless a Ministerial undertaking to amend the Regulations was forthcoming; it was, and the threat of annulment was not carried out.[14] The Fourth Joint Committee did not call for the annulment of any regulations, but it indicated that it would have recommended the annulment of the European Communities Motor Vehicles (Registration of Importers) Act, 1968 (Repeal) Regulations, 1984.[15] The Joint Committee deplored the fact that the Regulations neglected to make any reference to the secondary legislation of the Communities on which the exercise of power to make the Regulations depended. But for the fact that the instrument implemented important Treaty obligations, resolutions for annulment would have been tabled. The Joint Committee also recommended the repeal of two statutory instruments and the incorporation of their effects into amending primary legislation.[16] Notwithstanding its use of, or threats to use, the draconian power to recommend annulment, the Joint Committee has kept a watchful eye on the form and content of statutory instruments. All three Joint Committees have criticised Ministers for failure to cite in the body of the instrument the Community measure which the instrument seeks to implement.[17] Another recurring theme has been the disapproval of Regulations that impose fees for services rendered in carrying out obligations imposed by Directives. According to the Joint Committee, section 3 of the 1972 Act does not authorise a Minister to delegate to himself power to fix fees administratively: such a power would require specific authority of the Oireachtas delegated in unequivocal terms.[18] Likewise, successive Committees have frowned on the amendment, by Ministerial Regulations under the 1972 Act, of codes of legislation of major public importance such as the Companies Acts or the Road Traffic Acts; any amendments to these codes necessitated by Community law should be brought about by primary legislation. On occasion the Joint Committee has questioned whether the Community possessed the initial competence to adopt Directives.[19] All these criticisms have not gone unnoticed and the Joint Committee has been able to record significant improvements in drafting. But the need for vigilance remains. In its penultimate report the Fourth Joint Committee felt obliged to draw the attention of the Minister for Health to Regulations made by the Minister for Communications and to commend the Regulations as a model to be followed when prescribing fees.[20]

The vast majority of statutory instruments giving effect to Community law obligations are made under the power given to Ministers under section 3 of the European Communities Act, 1972. However, it is quite lawful for Ministers to use powers delegated by the Oireachtas under other Acts. The use of this option gives rise to two possible difficulties. First, we have already referred to the Medical Preparations (Licensing of Manufacturers) (Amendment) Regulations, 1975[21] as an example of alternative powers available to Ministers. The scrutiny and supervision of this instrument falls within the terms of reference of the Joint Committee, but the annulment procedure applicable to this instrument differs considerably from the procedure laid down in the 1972 Act. The parent Act of the instrument in question (the Health Act, 1947) specifies that Regulations made under the Act may be annulled by a resolution of either House within 21 days of the laying of the instrument before the Houses. The time constraints inherent in this system could cause difficulties for the Joint Committee which, as we have observed, suffers from a problem of continuity. A second possible difficulty arose during the term of office of the Fourth Joint Committee and it concerned the terms of reference of the Oireachtas Joint Committee on Legislation. The latter Joint Committee was empowered to examine all statutory instruments other than those made under the European Communities Act, 1972, and to recommend, if necessary, that instruments should be annulled. Although the Joint Committee on Legislation produced only one report on statutory instruments[22] two of the instruments under scrutiny implemented Community obligations and could have been examined by the Joint Committee on the Secondary Legislation of the European Communities. There would not appear to have been a working arrangement between the two Joint Committees so that a potential duplication of effort was always a possibility.

In passing, it might be noted that the Joint Committee on Legislation had completed a major report on statutory instruments in general, but publication of the report did not occur because of the dissolution of the Dail. Consequently, we can only speculate as to the observations of that Joint Committee on Circular 4/59 of the Department of Finance entitled 'Printing and Publication of Statutory Instruments'. This document gave rise to comment, not all of it favourable, in the 32nd and 35th reports of the Fourth Joint Committee in the context of an enquiry of the Joint Committee into the inadequate explanatory notes attached to the European Communities (Employment Equality) Regulations, 1985.[23] In its initial response the Department of Labour had simply referred to paragraph 13 of Circular 4/59 which states that each statutory instrument should be accompanied by a brief explanatory note describing the general purport of the instrument and should be headed as follows:

'*Explanatory Note*

This note is not part of the instrument and does not purport to be a legal interpretation.'

The Joint Committee had objected to the explanatory notes in question because they failed to state that the instrument was intended to meet the objections of the Commission in Brussels. But the Department of Labour refused to change its view and, when replying to the Joint Committee, again referred to Circular 4/59 and also cited advice from the Attorney-General's Office to the effect that

'. . . it is never the practice in regulations to refer to any matter other than legally binding instruments which confer the power or create the obligation to make the Regulations'[24]

On closer examination Circular 4/59 is merely an explanatory guide to the obligations incumbent on rule-making authorities by virtue of the Statutory Instruments Act, 1947. But given the subject matter of the Circular it would seem that the appropriate agency for issuing such guidance is the Attorney-General's office rather than the Department of Finance.

1 Mary T.W. Robinson, *Recent Legal Developments in Ireland in Relation to the European Communities*, 10 C.M.L. Rev. (1973) 467. *Supra* 14.13.
2 Section 4(1) of the European Communities Act, 1972 as amended by the European Communities (Amendment) Act, 1973.
3 See 1st Report of the Fourth Joint Committee Pl. 2296. February 1984.
4 30th Report of the First Joint Committee, 28.4.76, Prl. 5419.
5 There were no less than ten committees in operation in the 24th Oireachtas.
6 Report no. 25, 18.12.85.
7 Report no. 24, 18.12.85.
8 Report no. 4, 27.6.84.
9 Report no. 20, 3.9.85.
10 Report no. 25, 18.12.85.
11 Report nos. 2 and 6, 7.3.84 and 17.10.84 respectively.
12 Report no. 29, 4.6.86.
13 S.I. no. 317 of 1976; see Report 58 of the First Joint Committee, Prl. 6266.
14 Report no. 88 of the Second Joint Committee, Prl. 9680.
15 S.I. no. 367 of 1984: see Report no. 16 of the Fourth Joint Committee, 31.7.85.
16 European Communities (Recognition of Midwifery Nursing Qualifications) Regulations, 1983, S.I. no. 20 of 1983; European Communities (Life Insurance) Regulations, 1984, S.I. no. 57 of 1984. See report no. 10 of the Fourth Joint Committee, 7.11.84.
17 See for example: First Joint Committee, report no. 22; Second Joint Committee, report no. 20; Fourth Joint Committee, report no. 13.
18 See, for example: First Joint Committee, report nos. 8 and 49; Second Joint Committee, report no. 20; Fourth Joint Committee, report no. 35.
19 Second Joint Committee, report no. 16, regarding proposals on unfair and misleading advertising; Fourth Joint Committee, report no. 31, on Council Directive (EEC) 79/409 O.J. L 103, 25.4.1979 p. 1 on the conservation of wild birds.
20 European Communities (International Carriage of Passengers) Regulations, 1985 (S.I. no. 369 of 1985). See also Fourth Joint Committee report no. 35 at point 13.
21 S.I. No. 302 of 1975.
22 Report of 30 April 1986 on 18 Statutory Instruments, Pl. 4006.
23 S.I. no. 331 of 1985.
24 Fourth Joint Committee, Report no. 35 at point 4.

16.13 Instruments made under section 3(1) of the European Communities Act, 1972 are, of course, subject to judicial review. The constitutional immunity for

'. . . measures adopted by the State necessitated by the obligations of membership of the Communities . . .' (see Article 29.4.30)

applies only in cases of conflict between implementing measures and provisions of the Constitution. No instance of such a conflict has yet occurred, but this is not to say that the power possessed by Ministers under Section 3(1) is restricted. On the contrary, section 3(2) of the 1972 Act provides:

'Regulations made under this section may contain such incidental, supplementary and consequential provisions as appear to the Minister making the regulations to be necessary for the purposes of the regulations (including provisions repealing, amending or applying with or without modification, other law, exclusive of this Act).'

But this extraordinarily wide power is subject to certain limitations and the principal limitation can be found in the combined effect of sections 2 and 3(1) of the 1972 Act itself. Section 2 provides that

'. . . the treaties governing the European Communities and the existing and future acts of the institutions thereof shall be binding on the State and shall be part of the domestic law thereof under the conditions laid down in those treaties.'

Section 3(1) empowers Ministers to make regulations

'. . . for enabling section 2 of this Act to *have full effect*.' (Emphasis added)

In short, anything which goes beyond what is necessary to enable a Community measure to have full effect is *ultra vires* the Minister in question, and is open to review by a domestic court. Likewise, there would appear to be no reason in principle why an arbitrary, capricious or unreasonable exercise of the power delegated by section 3(1) of the 1972 Act should not be capable of review by the Courts.[1]

1 See, for example: *Cassidy v Minister for Industry and Commerce*, [1978] I.R. 297.

16.14 Apart from legislative and judicial control of delegated powers there are two other means of supervision and scrutiny of State activities connected with the Communities.

First, *the Dail and Senead may hold debates* on European issues and the opportunity for doing so arises frequently. For example, the Government is obliged by section 5 of the European Communities Act, 1972 to report twice annually to both Houses on developments in the European Communities. These reports are prepared by the Department of Foreign Affairs, and while the Seanad has endeavoured to debate the reports on a regular basis[1] the same cannot be said of the Dail. Furthermore, both Houses have been called upon regularly by the Joint Committee to debate particular topics. The Fourth Joint Committee called for debates in ten of its reports, but on two occasions it complained bitterly that its call for debates as well as its reports were being ignored completely. Three of its reports did receive a wide welcome: report no. 14 on the European Parliament's Draft Treaty on European Union, report no. 29 on Completion of the Internal Market, and report no. 34 on the Single European Act. It need hardly be added that subject matter of these closely-related reports had become a politically divisive issue before the reports received the attention they merited.

It seems that the cause for complaint—the absence of debates—has now been remedied in part. On 20 November 1986 the Dail agreed to a motion whereby two hours every Tuesday evening would be set aside to take note of reports laid before the Dail.[2] Whether this practice will be continued in the 25th Dail remains to be seen.

Finally, there remains the device of the *parliamentary question*. The Indexes to the Dail Debates show that the number of questions listed under the heading of 'European Communities' fluctuates between 50 and 150 per annum. However, as many questions dealing with Community issues are classified under other headings such as 'beef', 'farm modernisation' and 'fisheries', the volume of Community-related questions is probably significantly higher.

1 Fourth Joint Committee, report no. 34 on The Single European Act, at point 117.
2 Vol. 370, Dail Debates, col. 7.

Part VII

The Substantive Rules of the EEC

Chapter 17

The Free Movement of Goods[1]

17.1 The establishment of a common market involves the creation of a customs union in the first place. This in turn means that goods must be permitted to move freely within the market and that a common customs tariff and a common commercial policy should be established for dealing with third countries (See Articles 2 and 3 of the EEC Treaty). The EEC is much more than a mere customs union, however, since it envisages also the free movement of persons, services and capital as well as the adoption of common policies in agriculture, transport, environment, etc. In this chapter we will, however, confine ourselves to the provisions relating to the attainment of the free movement of goods within the market.

The main provisions are contained in Articles 9 to 37 of the EEC Treaty.[2] These sections apply to products or goods orginating in Member States and to products coming from third countries which are in free circulation in the Member States. Once goods coming from third countries clear the hurdle of the Community's Customs Tariff they are considered to be in free circulation within the Community and are treated as goods which originate within the Community. The establishment of the Common Customs Tariff is dealt with in Articles 18 to 29.

1 See generally, L. Gormley, *Prohibiting Restrictions on Trade Within the EEC*; P. Oliver, *Free Movement of Goods in the EEC*; D. Lasok and W. Cairns, *The Customs Law of the European Community*; Commission of European Communities, *Thirty Years of Community Law*, The Free Movement of Goods by C.W.A. Timmermans, in *Thirty Years of Community Law* (1983) p. 237.
2 Other articles of relevance to this topic would include Articles 2, 3, 85, 86, 95.

17.2 The principal obstacles to the free movement of goods are identified as *customs duties* on imports and exports and *quantitative restrictions* between Member States. Traditionally, Member States controlled imports and exports by these two means. A country might typically in a protectionist climate declare that the importation of bicycles shall be subject to a customs duty of 20%. Or it might say that only 20,000 bicycles shall be imported in any given year. Clearly in a market where total free movement was an objective these methods of regulating imports and exports within the market area had to be outlawed. But there were other less obvious measures which might equally inhibit the free movement of goods and which, although not charges or quantitative restrictions *strictu sensu*, had the same effect. These too, had to be prohibited by the Treaty. Consequently, Articles 12 to 17 prohibit not only customs duties but also *any charges having an equivalent effect* while Articles 30 to 37 prohibit not only quantitative restrictions but *all measures having an equivalent effect*. The Court of Justice has been busy in recent years in determining and defining the scope and ambit of those emphasised phrases. In recent years, especially in the wake of the oil crisis, and because of high unemployment figures, and the general economic recession, Member States have been slipping back into protectionist habits, and ever conscious of the electorate, national Governments have been resorting to measures which are anti-Community in nature. These measures are looked at suspiciously by other Member States and by the Commission and are frequently challenged by individuals before the Court of Justice as being incompatible with Community obligations. Further attention will be given to this body of case law below.

17.3 Before addressing these problems in greater detail, however, a few general points can be made. First, much of the law in this area is judge-made law. In particular phrases such as 'charges which have equivalent effect to customs duties' and 'measures which have equivalent effect to quantitative restrictions' have been subjected to active interpretation by the Court of Justice. Similarly it has fallen to the Court to define the exceptions that are to apply to this whole area. Second, the critical Articles in this area have all been held to be directly effective which means that individuals derive rights from these Articles. This in turn means that individuals are also watchdogs (in addition to the Commission) in respect of the Treaty. Furthermore, the negative formulation of the principal rules in this area ('Member States shall not . . .') makes the task of the Court easier in enforcing its policy in this matter. Finally, the basic principle established in this whole area is that freedom of movement is the normal situation. Anything that restricts or interferes with this freedom, particularly within the Market, is suspect and must be justified by the party supporting the restriction.

Goods and Products covered by Articles 9 to 37

17.4 Article 9(2) provides that the relevant provisions of the Treaty shall apply to 'products originating in Member States and to products coming from third countries which are in free circulation in Member States'. Goods coming from third countries shall be considered to be in free circulation in a Member State if the import formalities have been complied with and any customs duties, etc., which are payable have been levied in that Member State provided they have not benefited from a total or partial drawback.[1] The basic idea is that when goods have jumped the Community barrier at one point they are then assimilated to goods which have originated within the Community itself and thereafter such goods can move freely within the Community without being subjected to further restrictions. The entry fee is payable only once and then it entitles the payer to full club privileges.

In determining where goods originate Council Regulation (EEC) 802/68[2] provides that products are to be regarded as originating in the country in which the last substantial process or operation that is economically justified was performed.[3]

Since the Treaty does not distinguish between 'goods' and 'products' it is felt that these words can be used indiscriminately in the present context.[4] No definition is given to either word in the Treaty but in *EC Commission v Italy*[5] where certain national treasures and artefacts were in question the Court held that goods included products[6] which can be valued in money and which are capable as such, of forming the subject of commercial transactions'.[6] This wide definition seems to be subject only to the exceptions contained in the Treaty itself (e.g. arms in Article 223) and the mere fact that a product or good is of particular and peculiar importance to a Member State does not remove it from the ambit of the Treaty.

'Goods', however, does not include money or other methods of payment: unless the money has ceased to be legal tender and is now considered to be of value merely as collectors' items.[7] The classification by the Court of Justice[8] of the broadcasting of television signals and their transmission by cable as services rather than treating them as goods has caused some criticism.[9]

1 Article 10(1). Exceptions are allowed in some cases, e.g., EEC Treaty, art. 115.
2 O.J. (Sp. Ed.) 1968 p. 168, last amended by Commission Regulation (EEC) 3860/87 O.J. L 363 23.12.87 p. 30.
3 See for example Case 34/78 *Yoshida Nederland B.V. v Kamer van Koopkandel* [1979] E.C.R. 115, [1979] 2 C.M.L.R. 747.
4 See L. Gormely, *op. cit.*, fn. 1, para. 17.1
5 Case 7/68 [1968] E.C.R. 423, [1969] C.M.L.R. 1. First Art Treasures Case.
6 *Idem*, at p. 428.
7 See Case 7/78 *R v Thompson, Johnson and Woodiwiss* [1978] E.C.R. 2247, [1979] 1 C.M.L.R. 47.
8 Case 155/73 *Italian State v Sacchi* [1974] E.C.R. 409, [1974] 2 C.M.L.R. 177; Case 52/79 *Procureur du Roi v Debauve* [1980] E.C.R. 833, [1981] 2 C.M.L.R. 362.
9 See N.M. Hunnings (1980) 17 C.M.L. Rev. 564; L. Gormley, *op. cit.* fn. 1, para. 17.1.

Common Customs Tariff: Articles 18–27[1]

17.5 As already mentioned an essential element in the establishment of a customs union is the establishment of a common customs tariff around the community in place of the national tariffs. This problem is addressed in Articles 18–27. The essential idea is that national tariffs vis-à-vis third countries are to be replaced by a Community tariff. Two problems had to be addressed. Firstly, on what basis was the Community tariff to be fixed, and secondly, from what date would the Community tariff take effect. With regard to the first problem Articles Community tariff was fixed by taking the arithmetical average of the tariffs that prevailed for a particular product on 1 January 1957.

If, for example, the tariffs operating in the four areas (Benelux was treated as a single entity) for bicycles were 8%, 10%, 12% and 14%, the Community tariff was fixed at 11%, i.e. 44−4.[2] Provision was made for the most 'sensitive' products (products in list G) where the arithmetical average method was not a suitable method for setting the Community tariff. The applicable duty in these cases was arrived at by negotiation between the Member States on 2 March 1960 in accordance with Article 20 of the Treaty.[3]

The second problem was solved by adopting a progressive timetable to which Member States had to adhere until the transition from national levels to Community level was achieved.[4] In respect of the original Member States the transition was completed by 1 January 1968 some eighteen months ahead of schedule.[5] For Ireland, the UK and Denmark who joined on 1 January 1973, the period of transition was completed on 1 July 1977. Similar abbreviated arrangements were made for Greece (completed 1 January 1986) and for Spain and Portugal (see Articles 30 *et seq* and 189 *et seq* of their Accession Treaty) to align their tariffs with the Community level.

The CCT is published annually by the Commission and consists of lists of goods grouped under various headings and sub-headings. Appropriate customs duties and quotas are applied to the various groups. An importer wishing to find what duty applies to his product looks up the list and reads the appropriate rate applicable to the product in question. The nomenclature adopted consists of approximately 3,700 headings and the descriptive sections are based on an international convention, the Brussels Convention, signed in 1950. The duties payable are, of course, fixed by the Community now. This means that Member States can no longer take unilateral decisions in these matters.[6] Alterations or suspension of duties may be allowed in special circumstances under Article 28 (as amended in the SEA) but only as a temporary measure and to a limited extent.[7] (See also Article 115 for other crisis provisions). Where there are special difficulties or insufficient supplies derogations (generally of a temporary and limited nature) may also be allowed under Articles 25 and 26.

The CCT is directly applicable since it is incorporated into a Community Regulation and gives rights to individuals which the Courts must protect.[8] To encourage uniformity in interpretation the Court of Justice[9] has indicated that in the absence of relevant Community provisions, the CCT nomenclature and the explanatory notes and the tariff notices prepared in accordance with the procedure under the Brussels Convention, should be regarded as authoritative. Any national attempts to clarify matters arising from the operation of the CCT must be subject to Community law.[10] Where the Commission has issued an Explanatory Note to the CCT this can be used as an important aid in the interpretation of the CCT although it cannot modify the text of the CCT nor the introductory notes to the chapters which are an integral part of the CCT.[11]

In Ireland at present information in relation to allowable and prohibited imports and exports are contained in the Customs and Excise Tariff of Ireland published by the Revenue Commissioners. Nowadays it very much complies with Community rules on these matters. The Tariff sets out the customs duties chargeable on imported goods and indicates where other charges of a customs nature are payable. It also sets out the Excise duties chargeable. A new Council Regulation from 1 January 1988 establishes a Combined Nomenclature ('CN') based on the harmonised system to replace both the present CTT and NIMEXE nomenclatures.[12] It also requires the E.C. Commission to establish an integrated tariff of the Communities, the 'Taric', based on the 'CN' and for whose management

334

the Commission is to be responsible. The 'CN' together with the rates of duty, etc., and the tariff measures included in the 'Taric' are to constitute the CCT to be applied to the import of goods into the Community.[13]

The tariff incorporates the Official Statistical Classification for External Trade (NIMEXE) used for both imports and exports of goods. The tariff also gives particulars of preferences, exemptions, drawbacks and other provisions relating to customs duties and enumerates the prohibitions and restrictions on the importation and exportation of goods.

Recently, the procedures and paperwork with regard to imports and exports have been greatly simplified in Ireland and details of these can be had from the Secretary, Revenue Commissioners, Dublin Castle, Dublin 2, or from any Custom House.

1 On CCT generally see D. Lasok and W. Cairns *op. cit.* fn. 1, para. 17.1, pp. 143–198.
2 Certain exceptions to this method were provided for in Article 19(2).
3 See O.J. C 80, 20.12.1960 p. 1825.
4 EEC Treaty, art. 23.
5 See Reg. 950/68, O.J. 1968, L 172, updated version Reg. 1/74 O.J. 1974, L. 1; amended by Reg. 2723/76 O.J. 1976, L 314. Acceleration is permitted under Article 24.
6 Case 74/69 *Hauptzollamt Bremen-Freihafen v Waren-Import Gesellschaft Krohn & Co* [1970] E.C.R. 451, [1970] C.M.L.R. 466; D. Lasok, *The Law of the Economy in the European Communities* 82.
7 See also Article 115 for other 'crisis provisions'.
8 Case 9/73 *Carl Schlüter v Hauptzollamt Lörrach* [1973] E.C.R. 1135.
9 Case 14/70 *Deutsche Bakels GmbH v Oberfinanzdirektion München* [1970] E.C.R. 1001, [1971] C.M.L.R. 188.
10 Case 38/75 *Douaneagent der NV Nederlandse Spoorwegen v Inspecteur der Invoerrechten en Accijnzen* [1975] E.C.R. 1439, [1976] 1 C.M.L.R. 167.
11 Case 54/79 *Hako-Schuh Dietrich Bahner v Hauptzollamt Frankfurt-am-Main-Ost* [1980] E.C.R. 311.
12 Council Regulation 2658/87, O.J. L 256, 7.9.1987, p. 1 repealing regulations 950/68 and 97/68.
13 The new coding and description system was introduced by EC Council Decision 87/369 (O.J. L 198, 20.7.1987, p. 1). Transitional measures are provided for in Commission Regulation 2289/87. See *Halsbury's Laws of England*, 1988 Cumulative Supp., Pt. 2, Vol. 52, p. 1.

17.6 The case law that has arisen at Community level in connection with the CCT has generally been concerned with two issues: the classification and the valuation of goods.[1] These issues are worth litigating for an importer because if he can get a good or product reclassified to a different category he might be able to benefit from a lower tariff, and secondly, if he can get a lower value put on the product he will have to pay less on importing it. For example, caribou meat, not having a classification of its own could be classified either as domestic meat (as it is in Scandinavia) or as game (as it is in Greenland) under the CCT. Since domestic meat and game attracted different tariffs the matter was of some importance for the importer involved in importing such meat.[2] Once more it is easy to appreciate that since the CCT tariff is an *ad valorem* duty based on the value of the goods in question it is a matter of some importance to the importer to know how the value of the product is arrived at. If the customs authorities fix the value at 100 u.a. whereas the importer contests that the goods are worth only 80 u.a., on a 10% tariff the difference to the importer would be 2 u.a. per item.

If no specific heading exists for a particular product then the Court has held that it should be placed in a category which contains products most analogous to it. In deciding whether goods are 'like' other goods, consideration is given not only to their physical properties but also to their end use and their commercial value.[3] If, however, a product can be classified under a specific heading on the basis of its composition then there can be no resort to analogy to re-classify it.[4] In classifying goods for the purposes of the CCT the proper criterion is the characteristics and the objective properties of the product in question.[5] A few examples will illustrate the kind of classification problem that has faced the Court from time to time. Is caribou meat, for instance, to be classified as 'domestic meat' or 'game'? The Court held that caribou is game if they live in a wild state and are hunted.[6] Are 'laughing devices' (plastic battery operated gadgets which, when a button is pressed, emit a human-like laughing noise) which are principally designed for incorporation into dolls to be classified as 'parts and accessories of dolls' (Classification 97.02 B) or as 'other toys' (Classification 97.03 B)? The Court held the former category to be the more appropriate one.[7] In another case the Court held that 'ice cream' refers to products whose essential characteristic is that they melt at a temperature of approximately 0°C. Products therefore having a milkfat content in excess of 15% cannot be classified as ice-cream.[8] Of particular interest to Ireland is the case concerning the classification of 'fresh or chilled separated forequarters of beef or veal from which the atlas bone has been removed'. The Court held that such a piece of meat could not be classified under sub-heading 02.01 A II(a) 2 sub-paras aa) and bb) since this category from the Notes, etc., meant a half carcase 'comprising all the bones, etc.'. Classification under sub-heading 02.01 A II(a) 4aa) was more appropriate since it covered products other than carcases, half-carcases, forequarters and hindquarters and unboned or boned cuts.[9]

1 On classification and CCT Nomenclature and Valuation of goods see D. Lasok and W. Cairns, *The Customs Law of the European Economic Community*, pp. 149 *et seq.* and 182 *et seq.*
2 Case 149/73 *Witt v Hauptzollamt Hamburg-Ericus* [1973] E.C.R. 1587.
3 Case 40/69 *Hauptzollamt Hamburg-Oberelbe v Paul G Bollmann* [1970] E.C.R. 69, [1970] C.M.L.R. 141
4 Case 38/76 *Industriemetall LUMA GmbH v Hauptzollamt Duisburg* [1976] E.C.R. 2027.
5 *Ibid.*
6 *Supra*, at fn. 2.
7 Case 22/76 *Import Gadgets Sàrl v LAMP SpA* [1976] E.C.R. 1371.
8 Case 53/75 *Belgian State v Vandertaelen and Maes* [1975] E.C.R. 1647.
9 Case 196/80 *Anglo-Irish Meat's v Minister for Agriculture* [1981] E.C.R. 2263.

Customs Duties and Charges having equivalent effect: Articles 9 to 17[1]

17.7 Article 9 states clearly that the Community shall be based upon a customs union which shall cover all trade in goods and which shall involve 'the prohibition between Member States of customs duties on imports and exports and of all charges having equivalent effect, and the adoption of a common customs tariff in their relations with third countries'. Articles 12 to 17 then go on to deal with these matters in a more specific way. Article

12 is the familiar standstill provision which prohibits Member States from introducing between themselves any *new* customs duties on imports or exports or any charges having equivalent effect, and from increasing those which they already apply in their trade with each other. By freezing the situation and preventing it from deteriorating from its present position, it was felt that one could then address the problem of dismantling the existing charges. This task would have been more difficult if Member States could continue to change their position after the Community was established. Once a standstill is achieved Article 13 and Article 16 enjoin the Member States to abolish as between themselves (i) customs duties on imports and charges having equivalent effect and (ii) customs duties on exports and charges having equivalent effect, according to a timetable indicated in the Treaty.

In the celebrated case of *Van Gend en Loos*[2] Article 12 was held to be directly effective and of such a nature that it could be relied on by an individual before national courts. The facts are worth reciting. For the purposes of customs, goods coming into Holland were placed into various classifications. Goods in the highest category were charged the highest duty and goods in the next category were charged a lower duty and goods in the third category were charged the lowest rate. Duties during the transitional period were to be reduced according to a certain timetable until they were eventually eliminated completely. The Dutch Government by switching goods from the lower categories to the higher categories effectively *increased* the duty payable on imported ureaformaldehyde. The plaintiff complained that this was in breach of Article 12 of the Treaty. On this issue the Court had this to say:

> 'Further, with regard to the prohibition in Article 12 of the Treaty, such an illegal increase may arise from a re-arrangement of the tariff resulting in the classification of the product under a more highly taxed heading and from an actual increase in the rate of customs duty.
>
> It is of little importance how the increase in customs duties occurred when, after the Treaty entered into force, the same product in the same Member State was subject to a higher rate of duty.'[3]

what was the out come of Van Genden loos Case ??

Customs duties have been defined as '[a] tax on the importation and, rarely, on the exportation of particular goods, levied by a national government and payable to it when the item crosses the nation's boundary',[4] and cause no real problem of identification. Moreover, since the obligation to abolish them is absolute any exception must be clear and unambiguous and if it exists must be narrowly construed.[5]

More difficult is the concept of 'charges having equivalent effect to customs duties' and a good deal of case law has been generated by this phrase. Loosely speaking, any monetary payment demanded from an importer or exporter can amount to a charge having equivalent effect.[6]

In some of the early case law the Court of Justice in attempting to determine the critical criterion which determines whether a charge has an equivalent effect to a customs duty seems to have emphasised *the effect* which such a charge has. If the effect was similar to the effect which a customs duty has then it would be treated as equivalent to a customs duty. So in the *Gingerbread* Case the Court stated:

'The concept of a "charge having equivalent effect" to that of a customs duty, far from being an exception to the general rule of prohibition against customs duties, is, on the contrary, a necessary complement to it, giving it its effectiveness.

This expression, constantly used in conjunction with that of 'customs duties', indicates an intent to prohibit not only those measures which openly take on the classic customs form, but also all those which, presented under other names, or introduced through other routes, would have the same discriminatory or protectionist effect as customs duties.

In order to recognise that a charge has an effect equivalent to that of a customs duty, it is important to consider this effect in the light of the objectives proposed by the Treaty, particularly in that part, title and chapter where Articles 9 and 12 were placed, i.e. in relation to the free movement of goods and, even more generally, in the light of the objectives of Article 3, which seeks to prevent the distortion of competition. It is therefore of little importance to determine whether all the effects of customs duties are present, or only one of them, or even whether, together with such effects, other principal or accessory purposes were involved, as long as the charge adversely affects the above-mentioned objectives of the Treaty and originates not from a Community procedure but from a unilateral decision.

The result of all these factors is that, within the meaning of Articles 9 and 12, a charge having an effect equivalent to a customs duty, regardless of what it may be called or the manner in which it may be levied, may be considered as a duty unilaterally imposed either at the time of entry or later, and which, since it is applied specifically on a product imported from a Member State and not on a similar domestic product, has, in altering its price, the same effect on the free movement of goods as a customs duty.'[7]

In later years, however, the Court has taken a wider formulation. In *Denkavit Loire v French State*,[8] for example, the Court stated the criterion to be less linked to the 'effects' of the charge when it held as follows:

'As the Court has acknowledged several times, and in particular in its judgment of January 25, 1977, in Case 46/76 *WJG Bauhuis v Netherlands State* [1977] E.C.R. 5 . . . any pecuniary charge, whatever its designation and method of application, which is imposed unilaterally on goods by reason of the fact that they cross a frontier and which is not a customs duty in the strict sense, is a charge having an equivalent effect, within the meaning of Articles 9, 12, 13 and 16 of the Treaty. Such a charge, however, escapes that classification if it is the consideration for a benefit provided in fact for the importer or exporter representing an amount proportionate to the said benefit. It also escapes that classification if it relates to a general system of internal charges applied systematically and in accordance with the same criteria to domestic products and imported products alike, in which case it does not come within the scope of Articles 9, 12, 13 and 16 but within that of Article 95 of the Treaty.'[9]

1 D. Lasok and W. Cairns, *op. cit. supra* fn. 1, para. 17.1 35–44; C.W.A. Timmermans in *Thirty Years of Community Law*, (1983) p. 237.
2 Case 26/62 [1963] E.C.R. 1, [1963] C.M.L.R. 105. See also Cases 2–3/69 *Sociaal Fonds voor de Diamantarbeiders v Chougol Diamond Co* [1969] E.C.R. 211, [1969] C.M.L.R. 335.
3 *Supra*, fn. 2, at pp. 14,5 and 131 respectively.
4 *McGraw-Hill Dictionary of Modern Economics*, 2nd ed., 578.
5 Cases 52 and 55/65 *Germany v EEC Commission* [1966] E.C.R. 159, [1967] C.M.L.R. 22, at pp. 170 and 43 respectively; Cases 2–3/62 *EEC Commission v Luxembourg and Belgium* [1962] E.C.R. 425, [1963] C.M.L.R. 199.

6 It should be noted that the corresponding phrase used in connection with Article 30 which outlaws quantitative restrictions is wider. In this Article quantitative restrictions and measures having equivalent effect are outlawed. 'Measure' is a much wider word than 'charge', the latter involving some form of pecuniary payment. See *infra*. 17.11.

7 *Supra*, n. 5, at pp. 432 and 216 respectively.

8 Case 132/78 [1979] E.C.R. 1923, [1979] 3 C.M.L.R. 605.

9 *Idem*, at pp. 1934 and 613 respectively. See also Case 132/80 *United Foods NV v Belgium* [1981] E.C.R. 995, [1982] 1 C.M.L.R. 273; Case 158/82 *EC Commission v Denmark* [1983] E.C.R. 3573, [1984] 2 C.M.L.R. 658.

17.8 Some examples will show that this last interpretation is almost settled nowadays. Inspection charges levied on imports of fresh, dried, salted and smoked poultry meat from other Member States,[1] a postal charge imposed by a Postal Authority in respect of customs clearance of a parcel sent from another Member State,[2] a charge for the protection of public health and for the organisation of markets on meat and lard imports, which is not levied on domestic products or is levied on different criteria,[3] a statistical levy on imported and exported goods,[4] a *% add valorem* duty for 'administrative services' on imports from other Member States,[5] and a tax imposed on an egg importer in respect of the egg containers,[6] have all been held to be charges equivalent to customs duties and prohibited by the Treaties. Moreover, it is no defence to argue that the charge is small[7] or that it is collected or fixed by an authorised national agency other than the Government[8] or that it is for the benefit of the economy or the industry in general.[9]

Reference must also be made to *Martin Doyle v Government, A-G and Revenue Comrs*.[10] This judgment dealt with the application by the domestic Court of a preliminary ruling of the European Court. The High Court had sought a ruling on the compatibility with Community Law of a 2 per cent Excise duty on cattle, milk, cereals and sugar beet delivered for export from the State or for processing within the State. The levy was intended to make the farming Community bear an equitable share of the general tax burden in the State, but the plaintiffs, amongst others, argued that it interfered with the price formation mechanisms of the CAP and constituted a measure of effect equivalent to a customs duty. The European Court ruled that the levy was not in principle incompatible with Community law but it would be incompatible if it had the effect of impeding the common organisation of the markets in question especially in terms of price formation and the regulation of supply. It was left to the national court to determine whether in fact the duty had such effects.

1 Case 314/82 *EC Commission v Belgium* [1984] E.C.R. 1543, [1985] 3 C.M.L.R. 134.

2 Case 39/82 *Donner v Netherlands* [1983] E.C.R. 19, [1983] 1 C.M.L.R. 711.

3 *Supra*, fn. 8, para. 17.7.

4 Case 24/68 *EC Commission v Italy* [1969] E.C.R. 193, [1971] C.M.L.R. 611.

5 Case 8/70 *EC Commission v Italy* [1970] E.C.R. 961.

6 Case 77/72 *Capolongo v Azienda Agricola Maya* [1973] E.C.R. 611, [1974] 1 C.M.L.R. 230.

7 Case 132/82 *EC Commission v Belgium* [1983] E.C.R. 1649, [1983] 3 C.M.L.R. 600.

8 Case 158/82 *Supra* fn. 9, para. 17.7.

9 *Ibid*.

10 [1982–1983] J.I.S.E.L. 83, 26 April 1983, Barrington J; [1981] E.C.R. 735. For earlier history see (1982) 7 E.L. Rev. 33, 337–8; Revised on other grounds Sup. Ct. 29 March 1985.

17.9 Even in the case of more plausible charges, for example, for public health inspections of meat,[1] or phyto-sanitary inspection of fruit,[2] these have also been struck down and are prohibited unless properly authorised by the Community and applied accordingly.

Such charges are acceptable only if (i) they can be justified on the grounds that the pecuniary charge imposed represents the consideration for a service actually rendered to the importer and is of an amount commensurate with that service,[3] or (ii) they constitute internal taxation within the meaning of Article 95.

With regard to (i) the Court of Justice in the *Bauhuis* Case,[4] in condemning a charge equivalent to a customs duty, explained that 'the position would be different only if the charge in question is in consideration for a benefit provided in fact for the exporter representing an amount proportionate to the said benefit . . .'.[5] From this it would appear that to be justified the charge must benefit the importer in an individual way and must result in a personal advantage; it is not sufficient that through a general scheme (e.g. through collecting statistics or carrying out general health surveys) the importer may benefit in some indirect or general way from the national exercise which is the subject of the charge.

The other exception which may save such charges from being considered as 'charges having equivalent effect' is when such charges constitute internal taxation within the meaning of Article 95 of the EEC Treaty. Since the Court of Justice has held[6] that a charge cannot simultaneously belong to the realm of taxation and the realm of customs duties the distinction between the two is important. Articles 9 to 17 provide for the *abolition* of customs duties and charges having equivalent effect, whereas Article 95 merely provides that internal taxation must be *non-discriminatory*. The Court's statement as to what constitutes internal taxation is important. 'In order to come within the scope of a general system of internal taxation and thereby escape classification as a charge having an effect equivalent to a customs duty, a pecuniary charge must be applied systematically to the imported products and domestic products concerned in accordance with identical criteria, that is to say, as the Court has held in the past, the charge must be imposed in accordance with the same basis of assessment, at the same production or marketing stage, in accordance with the same basis of calculation and in consequence of the same chargeable event.'[7] Accordingly, health inspection levies collected by Belgium and not charged systematically on landed and imported fish but charged on imported fish only, and then at a different rate and on different criteria, etc., cannot constitute internal taxation within the meaning of Article 95.[8]

An Irish case of interest in this area arose when under the Imposition of Duties (No. 221) (Excise Duties) Order 1975 Irish producers of spirits, beer and wine were allowed between four and six weeks deferment of payment of the duty whereas in the case of the same products from other Member States the duty became payable either on the date of importation or of delivery from the customs warehouse. This was held to be a discriminatory tax and as such not permitted under Article 95.[9]

---

1 Case 29/72 *Marimex SpA v Ministero delle Finanze* [1972] E.C.R. 1309, [1973] C.M.L.R. 486; Case 35/76 *Simmenthal SpA v Ministero delle Finanze* [1976] E.C.R. 1871, [1977] 2 C.M.L.R. 1; Case 106/77 *Amministrazione delle Finanze dello Stato v Simmenthal*

SpA [1978] E.C.R. 629, [1978] 3 C.M.L.R. 263; Case 70/77 *Simmenthal SpA v Amministrazione delle Finanze dello Stato* [1978] E.C.R. 1453, [1978] 3 C.M.L.R. 670; Case 46/76 *Bauhuis v Netherlands* [1977] E.C.R. 5.

2 Case 39/73 *Rewe Zentralfinanze GmbH v Direktor der Landwirtschaftskammer Westfalen-Lippe* [1973] E.C.R. 1039, [1977] 1 C.M.L.R. 630.

3 Case 132/82 *supra*, fn. 7. The exceptions mentioned in Article 36 and which relate to quantitative restrictions and measures having equivalent effect, cannot be invoked to exempt charges prohibited under Article 13. Case 3/69 *supra*, n.31; Case 24/68 *supra*, n.42.

4 Case 46/76 *supra*, n. 49.

5 *Idem*, at p. 15.

6 Case 77/76 *Cucchi v Avez SpA* [1977] E.C.R. 987; Case 105/76 *Interzuccheri v Rezzano* [1977] E.C.R. 1029.

7 Case 132/80 *supra*, n. 38, at pp. 1010 and 286 respectively. See also Case 193/85 *Cooperativa Co-Frutta Srl. v Amministrazione delle Finanze dello Stato* O.J. C 152, 10.6.1987 p. 6.

8 *Idem.* For case whose levy was upheld under Article 95, see Case 90/79 *EC Commission v France* [1981] E.C.R. 283, [1981] 3 C.M.L.R. 1 'The essential feature of a charge having an effect equivalent to a customs duty which distinguishes it from an internal tax therefore resides in the fact that the former is borne solely by an imported product as such while the latter is borne by both imported and domestic products'. On Article 95, see also Case 140/79 *Chemical Farmaceutici SpA v DAF SpA* [1981] E.C.R. 1, [1981] 3 C.M.L.R. 350; Case 57/65 *Lütticke v Hauptzollamt Saarlouis* [1966] E.C.R. 205, [1971] C.M.L.R. 674; Case 27/67 *Fink-Frucht v Hauptzollamt München-Landsbergerstrasse* [1968] E.C.R. 223, [1968] C.M.L.R. 187; Case 74/76 *Iannelli and Volpi v Meroni* [1977] E.C.R. 557, [1977] 2 C.M.L.R. 688; Case 171/78 *EC Commission v Denmark* [1980] E.C.R. 447, [1981] 2 C.M.L.R. 688. D. Lasok and W. Cairns, *op. cit. supra* fn. 1, 133 *et seq.*; C.W.A. Timmermans in *Thirty Years of Community Law* (1983), p. 246 and p. 254 *et seq.*

9 Case 55/79 *EC Commission v Ireland* [1980] E.C.R. 481, [1980] 1 C.M.L.R. 734.

Quantitative Restrictions and Measures having Equivalent Effect: Articles 30–36

17.10 Articles 30 to 36 tackle the problem of quantitative restrictions and measures having equivalent effects. Such restrictions are prohibited in Articles 30 (imports) and 34 (exports) while Article 31 (the standstill provision) prohibits Member States from introducing between themselves any new restrictions of this kind. The original treaty provided for the dismantling of existing quotas, etc., according to a given timetable so that all such restrictions would be abolished by the end of the transitional period at the latest (i.e. by 1 January 1970) (Article 32). In the event, the original Member States were able to achieve their objectives in this regard earlier than projected[1]

With regard to the new Member States similar arrangements were provided for in the various Treaties of Accession, except that in these cases the transitional periods were much shorter.[2]

In construing Articles 30 to 36 the Court of Justice had to consider first of all what kinds of activities were covered by the phrase 'measures having equivalent effect to quantitative restrictions'. Second, it had to decide whether the measures had to be discriminatory before being struck down or whether it was sufficient that they interfered with intra-Community trade. Finally, consideration had to be given to the exceptions to the general prohibition contained in Articles 30 to 36. In particular attention here must focus on Article 36 and on the 'rule of reason' judicially developed by the Court of Justice.

1 Abolition achieved by July 1968. In Article 35 the Member States had declared their readiness to achieve the abolition of these quotas more rapidly if possible than the timetable provided for in the Treaty.
2 See Article 42 of Treaty of Accession for Ireland, UK and Denmark—five years from January 1973; Article 35 of Treaty of Accession for Greece and Articles 30 *et seq.* and 189 *et seq.* of Treaty of Accession for Spain and Portugal.

17.11 'Measures having equivalent effect to quantitative restrictions' in particular was a phrase that invited judicial interpretation. Apart from the wide range of activities that could be encompassed by the word 'measure',[1] a basic question arose in connection with Article 30 since from the beginning the Article was susceptible to various interpretations.

Some suggested that the prohibition should apply only when the national measure in question discriminated between imports and domestically produced goods. If the national measure insisted on standards more difficult for imported goods than for domestic goods then it was prohibited by Article 30, but not otherwise. Others took a wider approach and contended that Article 30 should apply whenever the national measure could affect trade between the Member States. The Commission's interpretation fell somewhere in between these two positions.[4] The debate was somewhat stilled by the Court of Justice in the *Dassonville* Case[5] where the wider formulation which protected the Community's interest was clearly adopted. In that case the Court declared that measures having an equivalent effect meant '[a]ll trading rules enacted by Member States which are capable of hindering, directly or indirectly, actually or potentially, intra-Community trade . . .'[6] As can be seen from this, the Court did not insist on different treatment between national and imported goods for the prohibition in Article 30 to apply.

This wide formulation has been confirmed and repeated by the Court of Justice on many occasions since it was pronounced in 1974, and because it prohibits such a wide range of activities it has yielded a particularly rich jurisprudence. A few examples of measures which are caught by the provision will illustrate the variety of the measures now prohibited. The examples taken will use Irish illustrations in so far as possible.

A Government order obliging oil importers to purchase a certain percentage of their requirements from the national oil refinery at Whitegate was a measure having an equivalent effect to a quantitative restriction and had to be justified in terms of Article 36 if it were to survive.[7] In *Pigs and Bacon Commission v McCarren*[8] the plaintiff, a body established under the Pigs and Bacon Act, 1935 (as amended), had extensive powers of marketing control in the pigmeat sector including the power to impose a levy on pig carcasses intended for the manufacture of bacon. This levy was intended to finance the plaintiff's operating costs, to underwrite a rationalisation plan for production, and to provide export bonuses for certain grades of bacon. Following the accession of the State to the European Communities in 1973 the Irish Bacon Curers Society Limited (on behalf of the producers) had a meeting with the plaintiff and the Minister for Agriculture and agreed, on a voluntary basis, to use the plaintiff as a central export marketing agency. The production levy was retained. In 1975 the defendant withdrew from the scheme and set up its own export arrangements. The plaintiff then instituted proceedings for the payment of IR£28,594; this represented the production levy for the period from 1 January 1975. The defendant counterclaimed for IR£52,787.10 representing the levies paid since 1 February 1973, on the grounds that the levy distorted the common organisation of the market in pigmeat. Costello J. referred the matter to the Court of Justice under Article 177. The Court of Justice ruled that: (i) having regard to the provisions of the Treaty relating to the free movement of goods, Regulation (EEC) 2759/75 on the common organisation of the market in pigmeat must be interpreted as meaning that a national system involving a levy on all production is incompatible with the common organisation of the market, (a) if the levy is used to finance export bonuses for certain products, (b) if the levy inflicts a financial disadvantage on producers who decline to use the services of the central export marketing agency (ii) the levy was not due from producers in so far as the purposes to which the levy was devoted were incompatible with Community law. It is clear from this case that if a common organisation of the market is established then the measure in question must comply first with the Community market regulations and then it must be examined to ensure compatibility with the Treaty provisions on free movement of goods.[9] In the *Redmond Case*,[10] a referral from Northern Ireland, a similar marketing system incompatible with the common organisation of the pig market established by Regulation (EEC) 2759/75 was held to be a measure having equivalent to a quantitative restriction because it impeded the free movement of pigs. In *EC Commission v Ireland*[11] a Government sponsored 'Buy Irish' campaign was struck down as being a measure having equivalent effect to a quantitative restriction. Such a campaign could obviously influence imports and in any event was clearly discriminatory.

Other examples of measures which have been held to be equivalent to quantitative restrictions are price controls,[12] import licencing requirements,[13] as well as inspection fees demanded on imports for statistical reasons,[14] or for veterinary and public health inspection of meat,[15] or for the phytosanitary examination of imported fruit.[16]

---

1 The word 'measure' is much wider than the word 'charge' used in Articles 9 and 12. 'Charge' involves pecuniary payment, but 'measure' while including 'charges' also encompasses many other forms of action. On this topic generally, see D. Lasok and W. Cairns, *op. cit. supra* fn. 1, para. 17.1 pp. 45–120; C.W.A. Timmermans in *Thirty Years of Community Law* (1983), p. 247 and pp. 261–272.

2 See for survey of this viewpoint L. Gormley, *op. cit. supra* fn.1, para. 17.1, 13 *et seq.*

3 *Idem*, 14 *et seq.*

4 L. Gormley, *supra op. cit.* fn. 1, para 17.1, at p. 12. See Commission Directive (EEC) 70/50 O.J. (Sp. Ed.) 1970 (I) p. 17.

5 Case 8/74 *Procureur du Roi v Dassonville* [1974] E.C.R. 837, [1974] 2 C.M.L.R. 436.

6 *Idem*, at pp. 851 and 453,4 respectively.

7 Case 72/83 *Campus Oil Ltd v Minister for Industry and Energy* [1984] E.C.R. 2727, [1984] 3 C.M.L.R. 544.

8 Case 177/78 [1979] E.C.R. 2161, [1979] 3 C.M.L.R. 389.

9 L. Gormley, *op. cit.* fn. 1, para. 17.1, at p. 73; P. Oliver, *The Free Movement of Goods* (1982), at p. 213.

10 Case 83/78 *Pigs Marketing Board (Northern Ireland) v Redmond* [1978] E.C.R. 2347, [1979] 1 C.M.L.R. 177.

11 Case 249/81 *EC Commission v Ireland* [1982] E.C.R. 4005, [1983] 2 C.M.L.R. 104.

12 See Case 82/77 *Openbaar Ministerie v Van Tiggele* [1978] E.C.R. 25, [1978] 2 C.M.L.R. 528; Cases 80, 159/85 *Nederlandse Bakkerij Stichting v Edah BV* [1988] 2 C.M.L.R. 113.

13 Case 13/68 *Salgoil SpA v Italian Ministry for Foreign Trade* [1968] E.C.R. 453, [1969] C.M.L.R. 181.
14 Case 84/71 *Marinex SpA v Ministero delle Finanze* [1972] E.C.R. 89, [1972] C.M.L.R. 907.
15 Case 21/75 *Schroeder v Oberstadtdirector der Stadt Köln* [1975] E.C.R. 905, [1975] 2 C.M.L.R. 312.
16 *Marinex* Case, *supra*, fn. 14; *Simmenthal* Cases 35/76, 106/77, 70/77, *supra*, fn. 1, para. 17.9.

Article 34

17.12 Article 34 parallels Article 30 in that it prohibits quantitative restrictions and measures having equivalent effects on all *exports*. It was initially thought that the general *Dassonville* formula relating to Article 30 would also apply to Article 34 and that any measure would be struck down which directly or indirectly, actually or potentially affected intra-Community trade. In other words such measures, to be prohibited, would not have to be discriminatory also and it would not be necessary to show that different regulations applied to goods bound for export and those destined for the home market. This is not the way the case law developed, however, and it seems now fairly well established that at least in those cases where no common Community organisation of the market exists the measure in question, if it applies without distinction as to the destination of the goods concerned, must be discriminatory if it is to be struck down.[1]

Restrictions imposed only on goods destined for exports (e.g. a requirement of an export licence) are of course contrary to Article 34 and the *Dassonville* principle applies here with full force.[2] Similarly, if a common organisation of the market exists for the product in question the Court has been consistent with its position on Article 30 as expressed in *Dassonville*. In other words, in such circumstances restrictions do not have to be discriminatory to run foul of Article 34. Indeed, national measures in such a case must both conform to the rules of the common organisation in question and also comply with the Treaty Articles in question, and in this context 'the better view is to think of the rules of systems of common organisation and Treaty provisions on the free movement of goods as being a coherent whole or at least complementary sets of rules . . .'[3]

Finally, although not of great practical importance, it would appear that the rule of reason as expressed in *Dassonville* and *Cassis de Dijon* should also apply to Article 34 in appropriate circumstances.[4]

1 Case 155/80 *Oebel* [1981] E.C.R. 1993, [1983] 1 C.M.L.R. 390; Cases 141–143/81 *Holdijk* [1982] E.C.R. 1299, [1983] 2 C.M.L.R. 635; Case 286/81 *Oosthoek's Uitgevermaatschappij BV* [1982] E.C.R. 4575, [1983] 3 C.M.L.R. 428. See also L. Gormley, *op. cit.* fn. 1, para. 17.1, pp. 96 *et seq*.
2 L. Gormley, *op. cit.* fn. 1, para. 17.1, p. 96. Case 53/76 *Procureur de la République, Besançon v Bouhelier* [1977] E.C.R. 197, [1977] 1 C.M.L.R. 436; Case 237/82 *Jongeneel Kass BV v Netherlands* [1984] E.C.R. 483, [1985] 2 C.M.L.R. 53.
3 L. Gormley, *op. cit.* fn. 1, para. 17.1, p. 122. See also Case 51/74 *Van der Hulst's Zonen v Produktschap voor Siergewassen* [1975] E.C.R. 79, [1975] 1 C.M.L.R. 236; Case 111/76 *Officier van Justitie v Van den Hazel* [1977] E.C.R. 901, [1980] 3 C.M.L.R. 12; *Redmond* Case, *supra*, fn. 10, para. 17.11; *McCarren* Case, *supra*, fn. 8, para. 17.11.
4 See L. Gormley, *op. cit.* fn. 1, para. 17.1, p. 110; P. Oliver *The Free Movement of Goods* (1982), at p. 83.

17.13 Normally within the EEC the general rule is that goods must be allowed to move freely. Free movement is the norm. Restrictions on or prohibitions of this movement are at least suspect and at the most illegal. The principal exceptions which allow restrictions are contained in Article 36 of the Treaty. In construing the scope of these exceptions the normal rule of interpretation applies, exceptions to a general rule must be construed narrowly and strictly so as to derogate as little as possible from the principal rule. The Court of Justice has been particularly keen to preserve this approach.[1] Moreover, the onus is on the party who is relying on the restriction to justify it.[2]

Apart from Article 36, however, the Court has also recognised that there may be valid reasons why Member States could, in other circumstances, with justification also restrict the free movement of goods. If a *recognised interest* requires protection and the Community has not as yet acted to protect it the Member States may have a margin of discretion to prevent the movement of goods when such an interest is threatened. Such a restriction would in the circumstances be reasonable and should be allowed. The interest to be protected, however, would have to be generally recognised as worthy of Community protection, and furthermore, once the Community has recognised it in legislative form at Community level by adopting, for example, a regulation or a directive, etc., the Member States' unilateral powers to act cease.[3] This last exception is, in contrast to Article 36, an important example of judicial activism. It is sometimes referred to as the 'rule of reason'.

The possibility of the existence of such a judicial exception to the prohibition contained in Article 30 was first mooted in the *Cassis de Dijon* case.[4] In that case Rewe-Zentral AG wished to import into Germany certain potable spirits including the liqueur 'Cassis de Dijon'. To do so it applied for permission from the German licensing authority which refused the application on the grounds that such liqueur could not be sold in Germany because of a law which provided that only potable spirits having a wine–spirit content of at least 32 per cent may be sold in that country. The matter was referred to the Court of Justice pursuant to Article 177 of the EEC Treaty. In its judgment the Court of Justice held that Member States could maintain national measures which restricted free movement of goods in certain circumstances other than those provided for in Article 36. The Court in effect created a judicial exception to Article 30.

'In the absence of common rules relating to the production and marketing of alcohol . . . it is for Member States to regulate all matters relating to the production and marketing of alcohol and alcoholic beverages on their own territory.

Obstacles to movement within the Community resulting from disparities between the national laws relating to the marketing of the products in question must be accepted in so far as those provisions may be recognised as being necessary in order to satisfy mandatory requirements relating in particular to the effectiveness of fiscal supervision, the protection of public health, the fairness of commercial transactions and the defence of the consumer.'[5]

Although the German authorities failed, on the facts before it, to convince the Court of Justice that its minimum alcohol content law either protected public health or the consumer, the principle was obviously conceded: if a recognised interest worthy of Community protection exists, and the Community has not yet acted to protect it, then Member States have a reasonable margin of discretion to protect such an interest when it is threatened. In determining what interests are legitimate and worthy of Community recognition, and whether the protective action taken by the Member States is necessary and warranted in terms of proportionality, the Court of Justice has itself a margin of discretion which is very wide.[6]

1 Case 7/68 *EC Commission v Italy* [1968] E.C.R. 423, [1969] C.M.L.R. 1, at pp. 431 and 11 respectively.
2 Case 251/78 *Denkavit Futtermittel GmbH v Minister für Ernährung* [1979] E.C.R. 3369, [1980] 3 C.M.L.R. 513, at pp. 3392 and 539 respectively.
3 L. Gormley, fn. 1, para. 17.1, p. 174. See generally on 'rule of reason' L. Gormley, 51 *et seq.*, and p. 3 fn. 25, and pp. 4–5 fns. 48 and 49.
4 Case 120/78 *Rewe-Zentral AG v Bundesmonopolverwaltung für Branntwein* [1979] E.C.R. 649, [1979] 3 C.M.L.R. 494.
5 *Supra*, fn. 4, at pp. 662 and 508–9 respectively. On the fairness of commercial transactions, see Case 58/80 *Dansk Supermarked v Imerco* [1981] E.C.R. 181, [1981] 3 C.M.L.R. 590.
6 '. . . a Member State must be able to prove that the measure before the Court is intended for the "protection of a legitimate interest" and that the obstacle to trade among Member States is no more than is necessary for the adequate protection of that interest. There must therefore be a proper balance between the means and the end in view'. C.W.A. Timmermans, in *Thirty Years of Community Law* (1983), p. 268.

Article 36

17.14 The principal exception to the prohibition of quantitative restrictions, etc., is contained in Article 36 of the Treaty which reads as follows:

'The provisions of Articles 30 to 34 shall not preclude prohibitions or restrictions on imports, exports or goods in transit justified on grounds of public morality, public policy or public security; the protection of health and life of humans, animals or plants; the protection of national treasures possessing artistic, historic or archaeological value; or the protection of industrial and commercial property. Such prohibitions or restrictions shall not, however, constitute a means of arbitrary discrimination or a disguised restriction on trade between Member States.'[1]

At the outset it should be noted that Article 36 does not apply to products specifically excluded from the ambit of the Treaty (e.g. arms and war materials, see Article 223) or to products specifically dealt with in the Treaty (e.g. agricultural products in Articles 38, *et seq.*). When it applies, however, Article 36 must be applied strictly to derogate as little as possible from the general prohibition contained in Article 30 *et seq.*[2] Moreover, any derogation permitted by Article 36 first sentence, must not be 'a means of arbitrary discrimination or a disguised restriction on trade between Member States'.[3]

The proper sequence of questions to be posed in examining measures alleged to be quantitative restrictions or measures having equivalent effect within the Treaty has been said to be as follows:

'(a)   does the contested measure in fact fall within the set of measures basically prohibited? If so, then:

(b)   does it qualify for exemption under the first sentence of Article 36? If so, then:

(c)   does it nevertheless fail because of the second sentence of Article 36?'[4]

A brief word on each of these exceptions is now called for.

1   SEA, art. 18 in supplementing EEC Treaty, art. 100 contains provisions, in a new Article 100A, which have a bearing on Article 36. In general, if after a Community harmonisation programme has been adopted a Member State deems it necessary to apply national provisions on grounds of major needs referred to in Article 36, *or relating to protection of the environment or the working environment*, it must notify the Commission of these provisions. The Commission confirms these provisions having first verified that they are not a means of arbitrary discrimination or a disguised restriction on trade between Member States. The SEA also provides that harmonisation measures shall, in appropriate cases, include a safeguard clause authorising Member States to take, for a non-economic reason referred to in Article 36, provisional measures subject to a Community control procedure. See *infra*, Chapter 20.

2   The principle of proportionality applies to such unilateral measures: *Campus Oil* Case, *supra*, fn. 7, para. 17.11; See also Case 124/83 *EC Commission v United Kingdom* [1983] E.C.R. 203, [1983] 2 C.M.L.R. 1, at pp. 206 of E.C.R.

3   Article 36, sentence two.

4   L. Gormley, *op. cit*. fn. 1, para. 17.1, pp. 123–4. Footnotes omitted. D. Lasok and W. Cairns, *op. cit*. fn. 1, para. 17.1, 63, contend, however, that the second sentence in Article 36 'does not add a further condition for invoking Article 36', since any measure which constitutes a 'means of arbitrary discrimination' or a 'disguised restriction on trade between Member States' will never be 'justified' within the meaning of the first sentence.

Public Morality, Public Policy and Public Security

17.15 Just as in the case of free movement of persons where a State may refuse entry on the grounds of public policy, public security and public health, a similar margin of discretion is given to Member States in respect of free movement of goods. Whereas in the case of the free movement of persons, however, the Commission saw fit to issue a directive on the meaning of the phrase public policy, public security and public health, to minimise the possibility of Member States abusing the exceptions, it was left to the Court to define the corresponding phrase used in connection with the movement of goods, i.e. public morality, public policy and public security.

Using the basis of public morality a Member State might in appropriate circumstances, therefore, under the protection of this clause, prohibit the importation of obscene books or films, for example. In doing so the Member State in question would, because no Community standard exists, be given a certain margin of discretion in determining what is contrary to its public morality. In *R v Henn and Darby*[1] an importer who tried to import inflatable sex dolls into the UK was prohibited from doing so by the British Government on the grounds of public morality. There was little doubt that the British Government was entitled to exercise such discretion in a *bona fide* way if it so desired, but because such objects could be manufactured and sold by home manufacturers in England the Court held that the plea by the British Government was unconvincing. How could the British Government maintain that it was contrary to public morality to

347

import and sell such objects in England when home producers were openly doing so and were legally entitled to do so? In these circumstances, the plea of public morality rang particularly hollow in the mouth of the British Government.

1 Case 34/79 [1979] E.C.R. 3795, [1980] 1 C.M.L.R. 246.

17.16 Public policy is a somewhat vaguer term and as such is capable of being easily abused by Member States. The Court of Justice has been vigilant in this respect, however, and allows Member States to restrict the flow of goods *only* when important interests of the State are involved. For example, it has become clear that merely because a measure is reinforced by penal sanctions is not sufficient reason to make it justified on the grounds of public policy.[1] Gormley having surveyed the case law on this topic made the following pronouncements which are hard to resist.

'The conclusion must be, then, that the concept of public policy relates purely to the fundamental interests of the State and that the interpretation of the concept is consistent with that adopted in relation to persons and services.'[2]

1 Case 16/83 *Prantl* [1984] E.C.R. 1299, [1985] 2 C.M.L.R. 238.
2 *Op. cit.* fn. 1, para 17.1, at pp. 132–3.

17.17 The defence of public policy was raised by the Irish Government in the *Campus Oil* Case[1] but the Court held that it was irrelevant to the issue before it. In the Court's opinion the 'public security' issue was more relevant in that case. The facts were as follows. The Irish Government, in an effort to keep the State-owned oil refinery at Whitegate viable, introduced an Order requiring all importers of oil to purchase a percentage of their requirements from Whitegate.[2] The Court had little difficulty in holding the order to be a measure having equivalent effect to a quantitative restriction on imports. It went on to hold, however, that the Irish Government's action could be justified on the 'public security' exception. Where a Member State is totally or almost totally dependent on imported oil the Court felt that 'in the light of the seriousness of the consequences that an interruption in supplies of petroleum products may have for a country's existence, the aim of ensuring a minimum supply of petroleum products at all times is to be regarded as transcending purely economic considerations and thus as capable of constituting an objective covered by the concept of public security'.[3] Moreover, the fact that the justified measure taken by the Member State also promotes other economic objectives will not rob the measure of its exempted status under Article 36.[4]

1 *Campus Oil* Case, *supra*, fn. 7, para. 17.11.
2 Fuels (Control of Supplies) Order, 1982, S.I. No. 280 of 1982, slightly amended by Fuels (Petroleum Oils) Order 1983, S.I. No. 2 of 1983.
3 *Supra*, fn. 7, para. 17.11, at pp. 2752 and 570 respectively.
4 *Ibid*. See for discussion L. Gormley, fn. 1, para 17.1, esp. pp. 134–9.

The Protection of Health and Life of Humans, Animals and Plants

17.18 The Court of Justice has been keen to ensure that national measures brought in under this heading do not 'drive a coach and four' through the general prohibition laid down in Article 30. In particular the Court has maintained that the exception must be construed narrowly, must be used only to the minimum extent necessary to achieve the health and life objectives (i.e. the principle of proportionality must be observed) and will not be allowed if it constitutes a means of arbitrary discrimination or a disguised restriction on trade between Member States. Moreover, if a Community system has been established then, in principle, the Member States cannot resort to the cover of Article 36 for protection since the interest in question (life and health) has then been adopted for Community protection at central level.

The case law in relation to straightforward bans on imports, distribution or advertising does not disclose many instances where an attempt to justify these measures was made under Article 36. Furthermore, in such cases the Court has, even where a national measure might conceivably find justification under Article 36, frequently struck down a measure as being disproportionate. To this extent in these cases the Court has been heard to say: Even if the measure can be considered justified within the terms of Article 36, it is nevertheless not allowed because it contravenes the principle of proportionality.[1]

1 Cf. L. Gormley, *supra* fn. 1, para 17.1, p. 140.

17.19 Much of the case law in relation to this aspect of Article 36 concerns inspections and authorisations required by Member States in respect of imported goods. While it is clear that Member States may have a right to insist on such inspections and authorisations, where *no Community system* applies to particular sectors, the Court of Justice has, once more construed the right narrowly and has insisted that the measures be proportionate to the objectives to be achieved. It goes without saying that if it is not made for *bona fide* reasons concerning health and life the provisions will not get the protection of Article 36.

Even where an *incomplete Community system* exists the Member States may still have rights to regulate the movement of goods because of health and life considerations. In this case, however, it is clear that the Member States' acts will be subjected to even closer scrutiny by the Court of Justice and in any event they will have to conform to whatever limits are laid down by Community Directives which may partially occupy the ground.

Where the *Community has adopted harmonisation directives* or has established a common organisation of particular agricultural markets the ability of the Member States to resort to the protection of Article 36 is even more limited. In this matter the Court's approach here is parallel to its 'rule of reason' jurisprudence.[1] The same is true where the area in question is covered by international conventions to which the Member States are parties.[2]

A few cases will help to illustrate the above rules.

In the *de Peijper* Case[3] the accused was prosecuted for being in breach of Dutch law for supplying pharmacies in Holland with medical preparations imported from the UK without the consent of the Netherlands Government and also for not having in his possession certain documents connected with these medical preparations, namely the 'file' and the 'records' prescribed by Dutch legislation. These documents were designed to protect the public and the law declared that the importer had to have documentation (i) which contained detailed particulars with regard to the composition, the method of preparation and the packaging of pharmaceutical products in general ('the file') and (ii) which recorded that each particular product put on the market had been manufactured and certified in accordance with the standards set out in 'the file' ('the records'). The accused defended himself by stating that he had bought the products in question from a British wholesaler and imported them ('in parallel') into the Netherlands and that the manufacturer or his representative in the Netherlands would not cooperate in supplying him with the help which was absolutely essential to obtain the relevant documentation. The Court held that the requirements in question were measures having an equivalent effect to a quantitative restriction and so were contrary to Article 30. With regard to the defence that these measures were justified in the terms of Article 36, on the grounds that they protected the health and life of humans, the Court held that the exception would not save the measures where the interest in question could be protected by less drastic measures. In particular, the Court held that where national authorities already had 'files' on a product it was not justified in requiring importers to produce once more this information to the authorities. It was otherwise with 'the records', however, because in this case the authorities had a legitimate interest in being able to check that a particular batch of the product complied with the particulars on 'the file'. In doing so, however, the national authorities must ensure that the least obstructive means have been chosen. Rules which make it possible for the manufacturer or his representative simply by refusing to produce 'the file' or 'the records' to a parallel importer thereby giving them a monopoly must be considered as unduly restrictive and not entitled to the protection of Article 36. For these rules to enjoy this protection the authorities would have to show that any other rules or practices would be beyond that which could be reasonably expected of the administration.

In *EC Commission v Germany*[4] the Commission contended that German laws which prohibited the marketing of beer lawfully produced and marketed in another Member State on the ground that such beer did not comply with German legal requirements which provided, *inter alia*, (i) that only fermented drinks which comply with Paragraph 9 of the Biersteuergesetz may be marketed under the designation 'beer' and (ii) that foodstuffs and consumer goods which contain any additives could not be marketed unless specifically authorised (thereby effectively restricting imports containing these additives).

It was not disputed that a law which reserved the use of the word 'beer' to drink manufactured from malted barley only (and excluding the term when rice and maize, for example, were the raw materials used) presented an obstacle to the importation of beer using other raw materials in their manufacture. The German Government argued, however, that its laws could be justified by overriding considerations of consumer protection. First the Court refused to believe that when German consumers drank 'beer' they were consciously influenced by the fact that German beer contained no additives. Consumer attitudes, according to the Court, changed from one Member State to another, and also from time to time. Second, the designation 'beer' in other Member States (and in the Community's Common Customs Tariff) is generic in nature and is not so narrowly defined. The German law for this reason was in breach of Article 30 of the EEC Treaty.

The Court was also unimpressed by the argument that the absolute prohibition on the marketing of beer containing additives could be justified on the grounds of public health. (It was not contested that such a rule was contrary to Article 30). It held that restrictions passed in the name of public health must be construed narrowly. It stated that

> . . . the use of a given additive, permitted in another Member State, must be authorised for a product imported from another Member State where, having regard to the results of international scientific research, in particular the work of the FAO and WHO, and the eating habits in the Member State of importation, that additive does not constitute a danger for public health and it marks a real need, in particular a technological need.

In addition the Court declared that the principle of proportionality also required that businessmen should be able, by means of an easy and reasonably rapid procedure, to request that the use of specific additives be authorised by a measure of general application. Moreover, the German Government's argument that certain additives might be harmful to health and should not be allowed in the manufacture of 'beer' was unconvincing since some of these additives were permitted in German law for almost all other drinks.

1 See *Supra*, para. 17.13. See also SEA, art. 18 amending EEC Treaty, art. 100.
2 D. Lasok and W. Cairns, *supra* fn. 1, para. 17.1, p. 61.
3 Case 104/75 *Officier van Justitie v de Peijper* [1976] E.C.R. 613, [1976] 2 C.M.L.R. 271.
4 Case 178/84 [1988] 1 C.M.L.R. 780.

The Protection of National Treasures Possessing Artistic, Historic or Archaeological Value

17.20 The Court of Justice has not had occasion to address this excusing provision as yet. One can easily appreciate, however, how Member States might claim justification in relation to an export ban on works and treasures of national importance. One merely has to think for example of the high feeling that might arise if there was a suggestion that the Derrynaflan Chalice was to be sold and exported from Ireland. Short of nothing the exception, however, we will refrain from speculating on the exact scope of a Member State's right in this matter.[1] It might nevertheless be worth commenting that a Member State in these circumstances might also attempt to justify an export ban in such circumstances, for example, on the grounds of public policy.

1 L. Gormley, *op. cit.* fn. 1, para. 17.1, pp. 182–4; P. Oliver, *The Free Movement of Goods* (1982), fn. 1, para. 17.1.

The Protection of Industrial and Commercial Property

17.21 It should be clear that the owner of a copyright or a trademark could by insisting on his legal rights under national law affect the free movement of goods within the Community. In the absence of Community protection for such interests it was never the intention that national laws on these matters should be abolished. Article 36, therefore, by way of derogation to the general prohibition on restrictions to the free movement of goods, allows restrictions which can be justified for the protection of industrial and commercial property. The problem here for the Court of Justice is how to reconcile these legitimate national interests with the Community's interest in the free movement of goods. Space does not permit a full exposure of the law on this topic and the reader is referred to other sources for more detailed treatment of the topic. A useful survey of the law is provided by Mathijsen and is sufficient for our purposes.

> 'The various rules elaborated with regard to property rights and free movement of goods over the years were restated by the Court as follows: (1) the Treaty does not affect the existence of property rights recognised by the law of a Member State; (2) the exercise of those rights may nevertheless, depending on the circumstances, be restricted by the prohibitions of the Treaty; (3) in as much as an exception to the fundamental principles of the Treaty is provided, it applies only to the extent necessary to safeguard rights which constitute the specific subject-matter of that property; (4) the owner of a right cannot rely on national law to prevent the importation of a product which has been marketed in another Member State by the owner or with his consent; (5) it is the same when the right relied on is the result of a subdivision, either voluntary or publicly imposed, of a trade-mark which originally belonged to a single owner; (6) even when the rights belong to different proprietors, national law may not be relied on when the exercise of these rights is the purpose, means or result of a prohibited agreement; (7) it is compatible with the Treaty provisions concerning free trade for the owner of a trade-mark to prevent the importation of a products from another Member State and legally bearing a name giving rise to confusion with the trade-mark, provided there is no agreement or link between the owner and the producer in the other Member State and that their respective rights have arisen independently. A specific case is that of the owner of two different trade-marks one in each of two Member States, for the same product: he may oppose the importation of those products in the other Member State by a third party. It follows from the decisions of the Court that the general principles set out above, will in the present state of Community law answer most if not all cases regarding the extent to which industrial and commercial property rights may be exercised with regard to the Treaty rules concerning free movement of goods and competition.'[1]

1 P.S.R.F. Mathijsen, *A Guide to European Community Law* Fourth Edition (1985), pp. 228–9. Footnotes omitted.

Chapter 18

Free Movement of Persons[1]

18.1 In this chapter we are concerned with the free movement of persons which term we take to include the free movement of workers, the right of establishment and the free supply of services. Each of these topics finds separate treatment in the Treaty. Free movement of workers is dealt with in Articles 48 to 51 of the Treaty, the right of establishment in Articles 52 to 58 and the free supply of services in Articles 59 to 66. The aspiration in all three sections is for full freedom of movement in a single market. Workers should be able to take up employment anywhere within the Community; the self-employed and business companies should be able to set themselves up and establish secondary enterprises throughout the Community; and the providers and recipients of services should be able to function on a Community-wide basis.

The right to free movement also involves the right to national treatment. If a person in exercise of his Community rights enters another Member State then he must be given the same treatment as that which the host state accords its own nationals. He cannot be discriminated against on the grounds of nationality.

Although the three areas covered are dealt with separately in the Treaty, and must be distinguished from each other, they share common features and in some respects common rules govern them.[2] For this reason we may deal with the common rules together before examining the three topics separately and in more detail.

---

1 See generally Burrows; D. Lasok, *Professions and Services in the EEC*; 52 *Halsbury's Laws of England*, 423 *et seq.*, P. Watson, *Social Security Law of the European Communities*; *Thirty Years of Community Law*, 285–321.
2 Commenting on Articles 48, 52 and 59 the Court of Justice in *Procureur du Roi v Royer* said:

> '. . . comparison of these different provisions shows that they are based on the same principles both insofar as they concern the entry into and residence in the territory of Member States of persons covered by Community law and the prohibition of all discrimination between them on grounds of nationality' Case 48/75 [1976] E.C.R. 497 at 509, [1976] 2 C.M.L.R. 619.

> The Treaty provisions concerning workers, establishment and services are all 'based on the same principles both insofar as they concern the entry into and residence in the

territory of the Member States of persons covered by Community law and the prohibition of all discrimination between them on grounds of nationality'. Case 118/75 *State v Watson and Belmann* [1976] E.C.R. 1185, [1976] 2 C.M.L.R. 552.

The three concepts: Workers, Establishment and Services

18.2 Essentially a 'worker' is a wage or salary earner and he is normally engaged under a contract of employment. The supply of services is usually a sporadic exercise of temporary duration and payment is by fee or fixed sum. An Irish lawyer, for example, might fly to England to advise a client or the client might go to Ireland for the same service. Alternatively, the supply of service might involve no movement of persons as where the advice is given by letter or by telephone. The right of establishment is concerned with mobility of a more permanent nature and covers the rights of non-wage-earners in industrial, commercial and professional activities. Each of these will be dealt with in turn.

An examination of this topic will involve an examination of the Treaty provisions, the secondary legislation (principally regulations and directives) implementing the Treaty[1] and the jurisprudence of the Court of Justice. Reference will also have to be made to the co-ordinating measures which attempt to harmonise national laws on these matters.

It is proposed, therefore, to examine first matters common to all three areas including (1) The Right of Entry and Residence (2) the Right to National Treatment and (3) the Exceptions to the right of free movement, before outlining in more detail the right of free movement of workers, the right of establishment and the rights relating to the supply of services.

---

1 The principal Community legislation on these matters is as follows: **Workers**: Council Directive (EEC) 64/221 O.J. (Sp. Ed.) 1963–64 p. 117 on the co-ordination of measures on grounds of public policy, public security or public health; Council Directive (EEC) 68/360 O.J. (Sp. Ed.) 1968 (II) p. 485 on the abolition of restrictions on movement and residence within the Community for workers of Member States and their families; Council Regulation (EEC) 1612/68 O.J. (Sp. Ed.) 1968 (II) p. 475 on freedom of movement for workers within the Community—amended by Regulation (EEC) 312/76 O.J. L 39, 14.2.1976 p. 2; Commission Regulation (EEC) 1251/70 O.J. (Sp. Ed.) 1970 (II) p. 402 on the right of workers to remain in the territory of a Member State after having been employed in that state. **Right of Establishment and Freedom to Provide Services**: Programme général pour la suppression des restrictions à la libre prestation des services (English version not available) O.J. 2, 15.1.1962 p. 32; Programme général pour la suppression des restrictions à la liberté d'établissement (English version not available) O.J. 2, 15.1.1962 p. 36; Council Directive 64/221, *supra*; Council Directive (EEC) 73/148 O.J. L 172, 28.6.1973 p. 14 on the abolition of restrictions on the movement and residence within the Community for nationals of Member States with regard to establishment and the provision of services; Council Directive (EEC) 75/34 O.J. L 14, 20.1.1975 p. 10 on right to remain after having pursued an activity in a self-employed capacity; Council Decision (EEC) 85/368 O.J. L 199, 31.7.1985 p. 56 on comparability of vocational training qualifications between the Member States; Council Directive (EEC) 75/368 O.J. L 167, 30.6.1975 p. 22 on measures to facilitate the effective exercise of freedom of establishment and freedom to provide services in respect of various activities (ex ISIC Division 01 to 85) and, in particular, transitional measures in respect of those activities. On secondary legislation relating to specific sectors see text accompanying fn. 3, para. 18.39, *infra*. For full list see O.J. of European Communities, *Directory of the Community Legislation in Force and Other Acts of the Community Institutions* (updated every six months).

Entry and Residence

18.3 A person who is entitled to the benefit of free movement under the Treaty must be facilitated by his own country and by the host country in respect of exit and entry. Documentation or regulations must not be such as to prevent or inhibit entry and residence in the country where he proposes to pursue his economic activity. The principal pieces of Community legislation on this are Council Directives (EEC) 68/360 and 73/148[1] and these have been implemented in Ireland by the European Communities (Aliens) Regulations—1977.[2] Under these Regulations a national of a Member State who (a) is established or wishes to become established, in Ireland, (b) is coming to provide or receive a service in Ireland, (c) is coming to take up or pursue an activity as an employed person, or (d) is a dependant of a person referred to in (a), (b) or (c) cannot be refused leave to land unless he is suffering from a disease or disability specified in the Second Schedule or his personal conduct has been such that it would be contrary to public policy, or would endanger public security. Member States must grant this facility to nationals merely on the production of a valid identity card or passport. They cannot demand a visa or any equivalent document.[3]

Member States must grant to a national of another Member State the right of residence on production of the document of entry and proof of his employment in the host state. Moreover, the right of residence must also be granted to members of a worker's family who produce the document of entry and proof of the relationship and, in the case of dependency, proof of the dependency from a competent authority of the state of origin.

Although the right of residence is a Community right and is rooted in the Treaty and in secondary legislation Member States must provide, on production of appropriate documentation, a residence permit as *proof* of residence.[4] Because the right of residence is Community based, a qualified person not in possession of a national resident permit does not lose his right to residence in these circumstances.

The residence permit must be valid for at least five years, and be valid throughout the territory of the Member State and be automatically renewable. Temporary residence permits must also be available in appropriate circumstances. A residence permit which is valid shall not be withdrawn from a person who has been employed solely on the grounds that he is no longer in employment if this unemployment is caused by his being temporarily incapable of work as a result of illness or accident or is otherwise involuntary. A person who has been involuntarily unemployed for a continuous period of more than twelve months may have the first renewal of his permit limited to twelve months, and if at the expiration of that period the person is still unemployed, a further renewal may be refused.

Provision is also made for workers, and certain members of the family, to remain on in the host state when his employment has terminated.[5]

1 *Supra*, fn. 1, para. 18.2.
2 S.I. No. 393 of 1977 and amended by S.I. No. 39 of 1985.
3 Case 157/79 *R v Pieck* [1980] E.C.R. 2171, [1980] 3 C.M.L.R. 220. See also Directive 68/360, art. 3(2).

4 See *Royer* Case, *supra*, fn. 2, para. 18.1.
5 EEC Treaty, art. 48(3)(d) and Regulation 1271/70.

Right to be treated equally: National Treatment

18.4 In the present context equal treatment means the right not to be discriminated against on the basis of nationality or on the basis of residence. Rules which say that persons cannot practise law in Belgium unless they are citizens of Belgium[1] or which provide that 75 per cent of a ship's crew should be French[2] or which insist that, in professional cycling, the pacemaker and the cyclist must be of the same nationality, are clear examples of discrimination on the basis of nationality.[3] Similarly, a law which imposes greater financial burdens on foreigners, for example, by insisting that they lodge a security deposit or pay a higher tax, or which makes access to vocational training more difficult for foreigners would also be discriminatory.[4] Clear examples, in the Irish context, were to be found in Section 45 of Land Act 1965 (now remedied by S.I. No. 144 of 1983).

1 Case 2/74 *Reyners v Belgian State* [1974] E.C.R. 631, [1974] 2 C.M.L.R. 305.
2 Case 167/73 *EC Commission v France* [1974] E.C.R. 359, [1974] 2 C.M.L.R. 216.
3 Case 36/74 *Walgrave and Koch v Association Union Cycliste Internationale* [1974] E.C.R. 1405, [1975] 1 C.M.L.R. 320.
4 See General Programmes on the Abolition of Restrictions on Freedom of Establishment and Freedom to Provide Services, *supra*, fn. 1, para. 18.2. For recent example, see Case 270/83 *EC Commission v France* [1986] E.C.R. 273, [1987] 1 C.M.L.R. 401. See also Case 96/85 *EC Commission v France* [1986] E.C.R. 1475, [1986] 3 C.M.L.R. 57.

18.5 Equal treatment prohibits not only overt discrimination but also covert[1] or disguised discrimination. Accordingly, a law which insists on residency or a language proficiency may also constitute a prohibited discrimination in appropriate circumstances.[2] If, however, residency or linguistic proficiency is essential in the nature of the job then it may justifiably be required. For example, no objection could reasonably be taken to an Irish language requirement for a newscaster in Radio na Gaeltact or for a dispensary doctor in an all-Irish speaking community. Such requirements should be individually assessed in each case, however, and should probably be considered suspect at the outset. Similarly, in *Choquet*[3] the Court held that a national who resided in another Member State for a year could be obliged to acquire the host State's driving licence. And in *Coditel*[4] Belgium was permitted to maintain a ban on the retransmission of broadcast T.V. advertisements from other Member States (where they were lawfully made) while such advertisements were banned in Belgium. National licence requirements, however, cannot be insisted on where the national from another Member State possesses a licence or permit issued on *comparable conditions* in another Member State. The interest in the subject of concern (e.g. public safety, financial stability, etc.) in such circumstances may be protected adequately by the foreign licensing arrangements.[5] In the *Thieffry* Case,[6] French rules required that persons who wished to practise as a French advocate had to have both a professional certificate and a French diploma in law. Thieffry, a Belgian advocate, had the professional certificate and the Belgian diploma in law. The Sorbonne University had recognised that the Belgian diploma was equivalent to the French diploma for University purposes. Thieffry was entitled to be admitted to practise in such circumstances, and the Court of Justice held that national authorities should accept foreign *equivalents* in such circumstances.

In this connection it is also important to remember that these prohibitions apply not only to public authorities but also to private individuals and organisations. In the *Walgrave and Koch* Case, in striking down the rules of an international cycling organisation, the Court declared that the prohibitions contained in Articles 48 and 59 (and by analogy in Article 52) do 'not only apply to the action of public authorities but extends likewise to rules of any other nature aimed at regulating in a collective manner gainful employment and the provision of services'.[7]

1 Case 41/84 *Pinna v Caisse d'Allocations Familiales de la Savoie* [1986] E.C.R. 1, [1988] 1 C.M.L.R. 350.
2 Case 33/74 *Van Binsbergen v Bestuur van de Bedrijfsvereniging voor de Metaalnijverheid* [1974] E.C.R. 1299, [1975] 1 C.M.L.R. 298; Case 152/73 *Sotgiu v Deutsche Bundespost* [1974] E.C.R. 153. See also Commission of the EEC, Freedom of Movement for Persons in the European Community, Periodical 3/1982 pp. 25–26.
3 Case 16/78 [1978] E.C.R. 2293, [1979] 1 C.M.L.R. 535.
4 Case 62/79 *Coditel v Ciné Vog Films* [1980] E.C.R. 881, [1981] 2 C.M.L.R. 362; (Case 262/81 No 2) [1982] E.C.R. 331, [1983] 1 C.M.L.R. 49.
5 Cases 110–111/78 *Ministère Public and Chambre Syndicate des Agents Artistiques et Impresarii de Belgique Asbl v Van Wesemael and Follachio* [1979] E.C.R. 35, [1979] 3 C.M.L.R. 87. See also Case 205/84 *EC Commission v Germany* [1987] 2 C.M.L.R. 69.
6 Case 71/76 *Thieffry v Conseil de l'Ordre des Avocats à la Cour de Paris* [1977] E.C.R. 765, [1977] 2 C.M.L.R. 373.
7 *Supra* fn. 3, para. 18.4 at 1418 and 332 respectively. See also Case 13/76 *Donà v Mantero* [1976] E.C.R. 1333, [1976] 2 C.M.L.R. 578.

18.6 Equality of treatment is not confined to the equalisation of conditions in relation to the conditions of employment and work or connected with the self-employed's business. Certainly Article 48 in prohibiting any discrimination 'as regards employment, remuneration and other conditions of work and employment' might suggest a narrow scope of application. Likewise, Regulation 1612/68 on the freedom of movement of workers concentrates heavily on equality in relation to working conditions. But Article 51 of the Treaty and Article 7(2) of Regulation 1612/68 clearly indicate that such equality must also be extended to workers in tax and social measures. And this is clearly supported by Article 7 of the EEC Treaty which clearly prohibits in a more general fashion any discrimination on the basis of nationality.

Qualified beneficiaries exercising their right to free movement can also claim equal treatment in respect of housing[1] (specifically recognised for workers in Regulation 1612/68) admission to vocational training,[2] and financial assistance in respect of educational programmes.[3] In one case the Court of Justice held that reduced-fare passes for large families which were introduced in France to counter the decline in the birth rate should also apply (by virtue of Article 7 of Regulation 1612/68) to the families of migrant workers.[4]

1 Specifically recognised for workers in Regulation 1612/68.
2 Case 76/72 *Michel S v Fonds National de Reclassement Social des Handicapés* [1973] E.C.R. 457.

3 Case 9/74 *Casagrande v Landeshaupt München* [1974] E.C.R. 773, [1974] 2 C.M.L.R. 423.
See also on education rights: Case 293/85; Case 293/86 (Humbel); Case 42/87 (Belgium).
On education of children of migrant workers see Council Directive (EEC) 77/486 O.J. L
199, 6.8.1977. p. 32.
4 Case 32/75 *Fiorini v SNCF* [1975] E.C.R. 1085, [1976] 1 C.M.L.R. 573.

18.7 More specifically equality in social security benefits which arise for migrant workers is dealt with in Regulation 1408/71.[1] Three principles underlie these Regulations:[2]

(1) The principle of aggregation whereby a worker is entitled to aggregate years worked in different Member States to calculate allowances.
(2) The principle of exportability which allows social security benefits to be paid in any Member State irrespective of the Member States where the entitlement has been acquired.
(3) The *pro rata temporis* principle whereby certain benefits are paid by the authorities in proportion to the time the worker has spent in each State.

The Regulation applies to the following branches of social security:

(i) Sickness and maternity benefits;
(ii) invalidity benefits,[3] including those intended for the maintenance or improvement of earning capacity;
(iii) old age benefits;
(iv) survivors' benefits;
(v) benefits in respect of accidents at work and occupational diseases;
(vi) death grants;
(i) unemployment benefits;
(viii) family benefits.

In practice, however, the principle of equality is applied by Member States to other social benefits as well and the social security benefits mentioned in Regulation 1408/71 have now been extended by Council Regulation (EEC) 1390/81[4] to beneficiaries under the right of establishment and the supply of services. Moreover, the general principle of equality in Community law (Article 7 of the Treaty) is not confined in its application by Regulation 1408/71. The general principle applies across the board and to all nationals of Member States availing of Community rights including, but not limited to, workers. The advantage of benefiting under a Regulation, of course, is that it gives greater concrete expression and application to the vague principle and, where applicable, it makes life a lot easier for the worker and his lawyer.

1 O.J. (Sp. Ed.) 1971 (II) p. 416, and implementing Council Regulation (EEC) 574/72 O.J.
(Sp. Ed.) 1972 (I) p. 159—both consolidated by Council Regulation (EEC) 2001/83 O.J.
L 230, 22.8.1983 p. 6. For useful summaries of these provisions see Commission of EEC,
Freedom of Movement for Persons in the European Communities, Periodical 3/1982,
pp. 41–43; Gijlstra, Schermers, Volker, Winter, *Leading Cases on the Law of the
European Communities*, 4th ed., 333–7.
2 'Worker' for the purposes of social security has been given an extended meaning and

covers, not just workers in the strict sense, but also 'everyone, who by way of his social insurance, has to be regarded as a wage-earner, independently from the fact how he has to be qualified from the point of view of labour law . . .' Gilstra, *et al.*, *supra*, pp. 333–4. Similarly, 'migrant' worker is not confined to workers who change their residence. It also extends to workers who move to another Member State for whatever reason—a family visit, a holiday, etc. *Idem*, 334.

3 See Case 300/84 *Van Roosmalen v Béstuur van de Bedrijsvereniging voor de Gezondheid* O.J. C 288, 15.11.1986 p. 3. Unreported as yet.

4 O.J. L 143, 29.5.1981 p. 1.

Exceptions to Free Movement:
Public Service and Exercise of Public Authority

18.8 The free movement of persons guaranteed by the Treaty does not extend to employment in the public service or to activities which are connected, even occasionally, with the exercise of official authority. (Articles 48(4), 55, 66). This means that Member States can legitimately prevent nationals from other Member States from becoming judges, or from applying for such jobs as Revenue Commissioners or for positions in the army or in the Garda Siochana. Similarly, certain positions in the local authorities could be reserved for nationals.[1]

The concepts of public service and public authority are Community concepts and it is principally for the Court of Justice to define them. As usual the Court tends to construe these exceptions narrowly and its jurisprudence on this matter is characterised by a clear intention to promote the basic objectives of the Chapter within which they occur, i.e., full free movement of persons within the Community.[2] In *EC Commission v Belgium*[3] the Court declared that the concept of public service was confined to jobs involving direct and indirect exercise of public authority and functions whose objects were to safeguard the general interest of the State, particularly those connected with internal and external security.[4]

In relation to establishment and services the Treaty provides: 'The provisions of this Chapter shall not apply, so far as any given Member State is concerned, to activities which in that State are connected, even occasionally, with the exercise of official authority'.[5] Some initial doubt about the extent of this exception has now been resolved. The doubt arose because of the phrase 'even occasionally'. Did the phrase preclude non-nationals from practising medicine or law because doctors or solicitors may occasionally be called on to exercise official authority, e.g. in the signing of a death certificate or notarising a public document respectively? In the *Reyners* Case[6] the Court of Justice held that the exception must be construed narrowly and that it must be interpreted as excluding foreigners only from that function which involves the exercise of official authority and not from the general activity in its entirety. In other words, in our example, under the exception, non-nationals might be excluded from signing a death certificate or notarising a document but not from practising medicine or law generally.

1 Case 149/79 *EC Commission v Belgium* [1982] E.C.R. 1845, [1981] 2 C.M.L.R. 413, at pp. 1851 and 436 respectively; 52 *Halsbury, European Communities*, 449.

2 Case 152/73, *supra*, fn. 2, para, 18.5.

3 Case 149/79, *supra*, n. 1.

4 See also Case 307/84 *EC Commission v France* [1987] 3 C.M.L.R. 555; see Case 66/85
  Lawrie-Blum v Land Baden-Württemberg [1987] 3 C.M.L.R. 389.
5 Article 55.
6 *Supra*, fn. 1, para. 18.4.

Public Policy, Public Security and Public Health

18.9 According to Article 48 Member States are entitled to derogate from
the free movement obligations in respect of workers on grounds of public
policy, public security or public health. A similar derogation applies in
respect of the right of establishment and the supply of services.[1]
  In an attempt to reduce the possibility of national abuse in this matter
the Council issued Directive 64/221 in 1964. The directive is concerned
with establishing in particular what conduct Member States will *not* be
allowed to plead under this heading.[2] In particular, Member States cannot
invoke economic reasons for refusing entry or residence to a national of
another Member State.[3] This essentially means that a Member State could
not refuse entry simply on the grounds of high unemployment figures, for
example, in the host state.[4] More positively Article 3 provides that
'[m]easures taken on grounds of public policy or of public security shall be
based exclusively on the personal conduct of the individual concerned'.
Previous criminal convictions shall not in themselves constitute grounds for
refusal or expulsion.[5] Neither shall the expiry of a national's identity card
or passport justify expulsion.[6]

1 Articles 56 and 66.
2 It is also concerned with setting down procedural guarantees—due process—for
  application in relation to entry and residence permits: Cases 115–116/81 *Adoui and
  Cornuaille v Belgium* [1982] E.C.R. 1665, [1982] 3 C.M.L.R. 631; Case 98/79 *Pecastaing v
  Belgium* [1980] E.C.R. 691, [1980] 3 C.M.L.R. 685.
3 Article 2(2).
4 In the Accession Treaties, however, the Member States recognised that new Member
  States might be exposed to serious social disturbances and that should such difficulties
  arise the matter might be brought before the institutions of the Communities. Joint
  Declaration on the Free Movement of Workers in Accession Treaties.
5 Article 3(2).
6 Article 3(3). Reasonable penalties may, however, be allowed for such administrative
  breaches, if they are not discriminatory or disproportionate to the offence: Case 8/77
  Sagulo [1977] E.C.R. 1495, [1977] 2 C.M.L.R. 585.

Public Health

18.10 Only diseases and disabilities listed in the Annex to Directive 64/221
can be used to justify refusal of entry or refusal to issue a first residence
permit. Diseases which endanger public health include diseases subject to
quarantine under World Health Organisations No. 2 of 25 May 1951;
tuberculosis; syphilis; other infectious diseases if they are subject of
provisions for protection of nationals of the host country. Drug addiction
and profound mental disturbance are also permitted grounds on the basis
that they threaten public policy or public security.

Public Policy

18.11 As already mentioned previous criminal convictions shall not in themselves constitute grounds for refusal or expulsion. Such convictions may, however, amount to evidence which could be taken into account in assessing whether the national in question is *at present* a threat to public policy or public security.[1] Moreover, breaches of the criminal law of the host state by the national of another Member State do not automatically justify expulsion. It is only where the criminal conduct in question contains 'a genuine and sufficiently serious threat to public policy' that it may be used to curtail the right to free movement.[2]

1 52 *Halsbury* 445; Case 30/77 *R v Bouchereau* [1977] E.C.R. 1999, [1977] 2 C.M.L.R. 800.
2 *Thirty Years of Community Law*, 298 and fn. 55.

18.12 Some cases can be cited to illustrate the above points. In the *Bonsignore* Case[1] an Italian national was convicted of unlawfully possessing a firearm. In handling the firearm he accidentally killed his brother. Following the criminal conviction a fine was imposed by the Court, and the German Aliens Authority ordered, in subsequent proceedings that Bonsignore be deported. This order could only be justified on grounds that it would act as a deterrent to other aliens. The Court of Justice on a referral held that Directive 64/221, in providing that national measures should be based exclusively on the *personal* conduct of the individual, meant that an expulsion order based on other grounds, extraneous to the individual case, could not be justified. Any national order which was intended to give an example to others or to act as a deterrent was not authorised by the directive. In *Rutili*,[2] an Italian national, who was born and lived all his life in France, was married to a Frenchwoman. A trade union official, who was involved in politics, he was made the subject of a deportation order in 1968 and later he was obliged by order to reside in particular districts of France only. The Court of Justice held that Member States could curtail free movement only 'if [a person's] . . . conduct constitutes a genuine and sufficiently serious threat to public policy'[3] and that restraints could not be imposed when the movement was linked with the exercise of trade-union rights. Moreover, free movement within the Community refers to the whole territory of the Member States and not just parts of it. This decision restricted somewhat the apparently wide discretion allowed to Member States in the *Van Duyn* Case.[4] In that case the Government of the UK was held to be entitled to refuse a Dutch national entry because it considered that the Church of Scientology which proposed to employ the Dutch national, although not illegal, was contrary to public policy. The Court of Justice did not upset this decision accepting that a certain margin of appreciation in these matters must be allowed to Member States. In the *Boucherau* Case[5] a French national was found guilty on two separate occasions of unlawful possession of drugs. The Magistrates' Court in the UK was minded to make a recommendation to the Secretary of State to have the Frenchman deported but before doing so referred certain questions to the Court of Justice for interpretation. The Court held that 'The terms of Article 3(2) of the directive, which states that 'previous criminal convictions shall not in themselves constitute grounds for the taking of such measures' must be understood as requiring the national authorities to carry out a specific appraisal from the point of view of the interests inherent in protecting the requirements of public policy, which does not necessarily coincide with the appraisals which formed the basis of the criminal conviction'.[6]

1 Case 67/74 *Bonsignore v Stadt Köln* [1975] E.C.R. 297, [1975] 1 C.M.L.R. 472.
2 Case 36/75 *Rutili v Ministre de l'Intérieur* (1975) E.C.R. 1219, [1976] 1 C.M.L.R. 140.
3 *Idem*, at pp. 1231 and 155 respectively.
4 Case 41/74 [1974] E.C.R. 1337, [1975] 1 C.M.L.R. 1. Discussed above at para. 13.19.
5 *Supra*, fn. 1, para. 18.11.
6 *Idem*, at pp. 2012 and 823 respectively.

Public Security

18.13 Public security must be considered on an individual basis and will be construed narrowly. The onus of establishing the exception is firmly on the shoulders of the Member State who asserts it.[1]

1 *Cf.* Case 72/83 *Campus Oil Ltd v Minister for Industry and Energy* [1984] E.C.R. 2727, [1984] 3 C.M.L.R. 544.

Free Movement of Persons: Workers[1]

18.14 Articles 48 to 51 of the EEC Treaty apply to workers and guarantees in particular the right of workers to accept offers of employment, to move within the territory of Member States for this purpose, to stay in a Member State for employment purposes on the same conditions as nationals,[2] and to remain on, subject to conditions, in the Member State after having been employed in that State.[3] Equality of treatment with regard to conditions of work and employment is also guaranteed in Article 48(2).

1 See for useful summary of law Gilstra, *et al. supra*, fn. 1, para. 18.7, at pp. 304–7.
2 See generally Council Directive (EEC) 68/360 O.J. (Sp. Ed.) 1968 (II) p. 485 on abolition of restrictions on movement and residence within the Community for workers of Member States and their families; Council Regulation (EEC) 1612/68, *supra*, fn. 1, para. 18.2.
3 EEC Treaty, art. 48(3); Commission Regulation (EEC) 1251/70 O.J. (Sp. Ed.) 1970 (II) p. 402; Council Directive (EEC) 72/194 O.J. (Sp. Ed.) 1972 (II) p. 474. Same rights extended to self-employed persons and their families by Council Directive (EEC) 75/35 O.J. L 14, 20.1.1975 p. 14.

18.15 'Worker' is not defined in the Treaty but must be taken to cover any person employed for payment on a contract of employment. The term is to be given a Community meaning[1] and although the laws of the Member States may provide an inspiration the Court of Justice has held that the word must not be interpreted restrictively.[2] It must, however, genuinely relate to an economic activity.[3] To benefit under Articles 48 to 51 a person must also be a 'national' of a Member State. In this area no attempt is made to provide a Community definition of this concept, it being left to each Member State to define who its nationals are.

The extended definition of worker given by the Community would include persons looking for employment;[4] persons who are unemployed either involuntarily or in some cases voluntarily, incapacitated workers, and retired workers. Such persons may enjoy some, but perhaps not all, of the rights accorded to workers in the strict sense. In the recent case of *Kempf v Staatssecretaris van Justitie*[5] the Court held that 'a person pursuing effective and genuine activities on a part-time basis could not be excluded from the scope of the rules governing the free movement of workers (which must be interpreted broadly) merely because he endeavoured to supplement his remuneration, which was below the minimum for subsistence, by other lawful means'.[6]

1 Case 75/63 *Hoekstra (née Unger) v Bedrijfsvereniging voor Bestuur der Detailhandel en Ambachten* [1964] E.C.R. 177, [1964] C.M.L.R. 319.
2 Wyatt and Dashwood, *The Substantive Law of the EEC*, 157 *et seq.* and 132.
3 *Walrave & Koch* Case, *supra*, n. 3, para. 18.4.
4 *Royer* Case, *supra* fn. 2, para. 18.1.
5 Case 139/85 [1987] 1 C.M.L.R. 764.
6 Twentieth General Report on the Activities of the European Communities 1986, 385.

18.16 Dependants of workers[1] (or of beneficiaries under the right of establishment) are also entitled to take up any economic activity as an employed person in the state where the worker is employed. Dependants include the worker's spouse and children under the age of 21 or older children dependent on him. The rights of dependants do not require that they be nationals of any Member State.[2] Accordingly, the American wife of a Frenchman working in Ireland would qualify as a dependant in this context. Dependent children are entitled to avail of the educational facilities of the host state on the same terms as nationals of that state.[3]

1 See generally Council Regulation (EEC) 1612/68, *supra*, fn. 1, para. 18.2.
2 See Case 131/85 *Gül v Regierungspräsident Düsseldorf* [1986] E.C.R. 1573, [1987] 1 C.M.L.R. 501.
3 Case 9/74 *Casagrande v Landeshauptstadt München* [1974] E.C.R. 773, [1974] 2 C.M.L.R. 423; Case 68/74 *Alaimo v Préfet du Rhône* [1975] E.C.R. 109, [1975] 1 C.M.L.R. 262; Case 293/85 *EC Commission v Belgium* O.J. C 60, 4.3.1988 p. 5.

The Right of Establishment[1]

18.17 Basically, the right of establishment consists of the right of nationals and companies of Member States to set themselves up (for example, to set up a factory, to commence farming or to commence any business activity) and/or to set up branches, agencies and subsidiaries (in any such activity) in the territory of any Member State without discrimination on the grounds of nationality.

In this section we will attempt to answer the following questions:

(a) What exact *benefits* are contemplated in Articles 52 to 58?
(b) *Who* will benefit from the provisions set out in these Articles of the Treaty of Rome?
(c) How are the benefits *implemented* by the EEC and by the Member States?

1 See generally 52 *Halsbury's Laws of England*, 463; McMahon, Ireland and the Right of Establishment in the Treaty of Rome, VI Irish Jurist (n.s.) (Winter 1971) 271–92.

(a) *Nature and Scope of Right of Establishment*

18.18 'Freedom of establishment shall include the right to take up and pursue activities as self employed persons and to set up and manage undertakings, in particular companies or firms within the meaning of Article 58, under the conditions laid down for its own nationals by the law of the country where such establishment is effected, subject to the provisions of the Chapter relating to capital.'[1] Freedom to pursue activities as self-employed persons must be distinguished, on the one hand, from free movement of workers and, on the other, from free supply of services. The latter are usually supplied across state lines and, even if rendered within the other state, are not part of a continuous activity; they are a residual class of activity and include giving expert advice, giving entertainment, providing insurance cover and the transmission of television programmes by cable.[2] The former cover activities for which a regular wage or salary is paid. Freedom in both these types of activity was considered to be a necessary corollary to the right of establishment, but as we have seen, each is governed by its own provisions and does not come within the Articles concerning establishment.

By way of contrast, 'self employed persons' include proprietors of businesses and partners and the phrase extends to commercial, industrial and professional activities. The idea of 'establishment' also conveys a certain element of permanence as opposed to the supply of services which may entail only one act. This would seem to indicate that individuals who set themselves up in another country do not have to engage in non-wage-earning activities continuously. Too much must not be read into this last statement, however, especially since the Treaty (Article 52) speaks of the right to take up and pursue *activities* as self-employed persons and Audinet argues: 'that if an individual settles in a Member State to exercise even quite accessorily or occasionally, a lucrative activity, he would be able to avail himself of the provisions of Articles 52 to 58'.[3] This, however, would only be true where an individual *sets himself up* in another country. With regard to the beneficiary who sets up secondary enterprises, Article 52, sentence two, requires him to comply with the further condition of being 'established', if not in that Member State, at least somewhere within the Community. And in this matter establishment implies material installation.

Generally speaking, the beneficiaries are allowed to set themselves up and to set up agencies, branches or subsidiaries in the territory of any other Member State. These rights are self-explanatory and generally need no comment as far as individuals are concerned.

1 EEC Treaty art. 52.
2 *Infra*. 18.33.
3 Audinet, 'Le droit d'etablissement dans la Communaute economique europeenne' *86 Journal du Droit International*, 982 at 1001 (1959).

18.19 In the case of companies, however, something more must be said. What does the right to 'set itself up in a Member State's territory' mean in respect of a company? Clearly it cannot signify the complete transfer of a company from one country to another within the Community. The company law of each Member State recognises that to effect this there must be a dissolution followed by a new incorporation in the host country and the Treaty also at Article 220 acknowledges this position. Nor can it mean the setting up of branches, agencies or subsidiaries, for this right is granted separately under Title I(d) of the General Programme. It is submitted that the right of a company 'to set itself up' refers 'to less tangible involvements—e.g., advertising, distributing and selling goods from outside without employing personnel inside the Member State—based on foreign legal personality'.[1]

As has just been pointed out, a company cannot transfer itself completely from one country to another with the same facility as an individual. This is true both in the Common Law and the Civil Law countries. Such a transfer of the company's registered office entails dissolution and, if the company wishes to carry on business as a company, in the host country, it must re-register and start again as a new company.

The inconvenience and the expense involved in such a procedure prohibits companies within the Community from enjoying to the fullest extent the rights of establishment. The legal disadvantages involved might be sufficient, in many cases, to dissuade a company within the Community from transferring its registered office to a locality which offers greater economic attractions for the conduct of its business. This problem, however, was considered to relate to private international law and was not an economic question and consequently it was deemed to be outside the scope of the Treaty. It is for this reason that we find no mandate either to the Member States or to the Community institutions to provide a solution. The Member States, however, are requested, in Article 220, to engage in negotiations to ensure for the benefit of their nationals '. . . the maintenance of their legal personality in cases where the registered office is transferred from one country to another, and the possibility for companies subject to municipal law of different Member States to form mergers'. To comply with this it will be sufficient for the Member States to sign an international treaty (which need not be confined to Member States only) providing for the continuance of existence in the event of such a transfer. Various attempts to have such a Convention ratified have failed.[2]

1 Harding, 'Freedom of Establishment and the Rights of Companies' in *English Law and the Common Market* (Keeton and Schwarzenberger, eds.) (London, 1963) 169.
2 D. Lasok and D. Stone, *Conflict of Law in the European Communities*, 89–91.

18.20 It must be remembered at this stage that the Treaty, even in its most demanding provisions, requires of Member States nothing more than that foreigners be assimilated to nationals in exercising non-wage-earning activities. There is no unvarying, objective criterion which would produce uniformity of conduct if complied with in all the Member States: that foreigners be treated as nationals is as far as the Treaty goes. It is clear since *Reyners* Case[1] that the obligation not to discriminate on the basis of nationality is directly effective since the end of the transitional stage and does not depend on whether directives have been issued or not.

Since the application of this requirement will vary from country to country within the Community, depending on whether a liberal or a restrictive trade-participation policy predominates in the particular country, one will, as a result, find that there is no uniformity throughout the Community. For example, assume that entry into the retail trade in Ireland is difficult, but the conditions are the same for nationals and foreigners, i.e., a licence is required for all; and in France, it is easy for nationals to be admitted, but a permit is required for all foreigners to participate. When the EEC rule that foreigners are to be assimilated to nationals is applied to this example the permit requirement in France will have to be abolished as it is discriminatory, whereas no change will have to be made in Ireland (although the general policy is much stricter) because nationals and foreigners are treated equally. The result will be that the requirements for entry into the retail trade need not and, indeed, will not, be uniform throughout the Community, but may vary from one country to the next. Co-ordination is provided for in the Treaty itself (see *infra*) to level out such differences should they create distortion and, if these provisions prove inadequate, Article 235, which gives the Council a general power to act where the Treaty 'has not provided for the requisite powers of action', could provide the solution to this problem.

1 *Supra*, fn. 1, para. 18.4.

18.21 In view of this last point, one might expect that Member States would adopt strict policies in regulating entry to trades (like Ireland in our example) so that they could favour their own nationals in the administrative procedure that is inherent in such a restrictive policy. If everyone in Ireland had to apply to the Minister for Industry and Commerce for a licence to operate in the retail trade in Ireland the administration would naturally be inclined to show favour towards its own nationals. Predictably, however, such insidious discrimination will not be tolerated, and the General Programme (expanding Article 54(3)(c)) makes it clear that:

'Conditions which a legislative or administrative provision or an administrative practice place on admission to or the exercise of a non-wage-earning activity and which, even though applicable irrespective of nationality, result exclusively or mainly in restricting admission to or exercise of such activity by foreigners'[1]

must be lifted. This broad mandate would seem to extend to the abolition of a language sufficiency test which, although required for all, might, in some circumstances, be primarily discriminatory against foreigners.

1 General Programme, Title III B.

Exceptions to the Right of Establishment

18.22 The Treaty does, however, contain some exceptions to the general ordinance that all restrictions on the right of establishment are to be abolished. These exceptions recognise that there are areas of activity where integration is undesirable as yet. Generally, these exceptions only reserve for nationals those offices and trades which are fundamental to the safety of the state. In view of Article 7 of the Treaty, which prohibits any discrimination on the grounds of nationality, and because free movement is a basic principle of the Community system, all these exceptions must be given a narrow interpretation by the Court and other institutions of the Community.

The first exception occurs in Article 55 and relates to the exercise of official authority. This has been dealt with at para. 18.8 above and requires little discussion here. One further point is all that requires emphasis. The exception contemplated in Article 55 does not apply to nationalised industries or State monopolies since these industries are excluded to nationals as well as foreigners and there is no question of discrimination. It would also seem that Government participation in the many 'Semi-State Bodies' that play such an important role in the Irish economy do not come within the exception.

'The fact that a particular activity is carried on by a nationalised undertaking does not mean that an exercise of an official authority is involved; the activity must involve the performance of functions which fall within the prerogatives of the state and not, for example, commercial operations which may be carried on by any body but which are, in the case of the activity in question, assigned to a body controlled by or identified with the state'.[1]

The second exception occurs in Article 56: special administrative or legislative provisions for foreigners may be allowed on grounds of public policy, public security and public health. The extent of this exception has already been dealt with.[2]

The third exception occurs in Article 223 and it permits Member States to exclude foreigners from 'the production of or trade in arms, munitions and war material'. These industries are considered essential for the security of the State and it might be expected that in these areas the State is slow to surrender their rights.

As a precautionary measure, the Council has also retained to itself[3] the power (on a qualified majority vote) to exclude at a later stage any activity from the application of the provisions on establishment. This power was probably reserved by the Council to deal with any unforeseen difficulties that might arise in this area and will be used only in exceptional cases. No action has been taken under this provision to date nor is any such action contemplated in the near future.

1 52 *Halsbury, European Communities*, 478.
2 *Supra*, para.s 18.9–13.
3 Article 55(2).

(b) *The Beneficiaries of the Right of Establishment*

18.23 According to the EEC Treaty the beneficiaries of the provisions guaranteeing the right of establishment under Articles 52 to 58 are:
  (i) natural persons who are nationals of any Member State; and
  (ii) 'companies or firms formed in accordance with the law of a Member State and having their registered office, central administration or principal place of business within the Community'.[1]

1 EEC Treaty, art. 58.

18.24 (i) With regard to natural persons the only qualification required of them is that they be 'nationals' of a Member State. In this respect it is important to note that each State can, subject to some international law principles, determine who are its nationals. The Treaty in no way alters this prerogative of the Members. Thus a business man from France would be free to set himself up in business in Ireland, if he was a national of France, according to French law.

This requirement of nationality will mean that residence alone will not be sufficient to enable an individual to benefit from these Articles. Nor will residence outside the Community be always detrimental to a national of one of the Member States who wishes to avail of the rights guaranteed under this part. Illustratively, a Swiss businessman residing in France will not be able to take advantage of the Treaty provisions to establish a business in Ireland. But a French national residing in the USA would not be barred from setting himself up in Ireland merely because of his residence. In this area it is his nationality that qualifies or disqualifies him.

In one case, however, residence within the Community may be required even for a national of a Member State. Under Article 52, paragraph 1, a national can set up a secondary enterprise (branch, agency or subsidiary) only if he is already 'established' in the territory of a Member State. Accordingly, in this latter case the individual will also probably have to reside within the Community, if he is to gain the benefit of the provision. But the test of 'residency' here is not so much where the individual has his home, but where he has his main place of business. So that, to give another example, the Frenchman whose home is in Paris, but whose main business is in Switzerland, will not be able to avail himself of these provisions, to establish a secondary enterprise in Ireland. As his main place of business is outside the Community he does not satisfy the test. In the context of Article 52, paragraph 1, it is worth noting that the requirements are: nationality of any Member State and establishment anywhere within the Community. In short, to set up a secondary 'off-spring' enterprise within the Community, the national must also have a parent *business* (but not necessarily his home) within the Community. Moreover, it should be noted that, to benefit, the individual does not have to be a national of the country where his main business concern is located; as long as his nationality and his establishment pertain to countries within the Community—though different—he is covered.

As 'nationality' is the magic word in this area it is clear that refugees and stateless persons can never benefit from the provisions on establishment. The fact that some host countries do, on occasions, afford national treatment to such refugees, to enable such persons to make a living, does not oblige other Member States to treat them as 'nationals of a Member State'.[1] One country's charity cannot create obligations for other Member States.

---

1 Everling, *The Right of Establishment in the Common Market*, para. 303 (Chicago, 1964); 52 *Halsbury, European Communities*, 472. Non-nationals may benefit indirectly and may be granted privileges by Community legislation: D. Lasok and D. Stone, *Conflicts of Laws in the European Communities*, p. 33.

18.25 (ii) 'Companies' are the second class of beneficiaries contemplated under the provisions dealing with the right of establishment and, under Article 58, they are to 'be treated in the same way as natural persons who are nationals of Member States'. The drafters of the Treaty met some difficulty when they sought to limit the application of these provisions to companies that were really within the sphere of the Treaty. In the case of individuals, the concept of 'nationality' provided a ready-made yardstick which could be applied without difficulty. But as regards companies there was no such convenient test. Accordingly, the drafters, instead of relying on the 'nationality of a company' as the norm, declared that companies must comply with two conditions before they could benefit from the provisions on establishment. First, the company had to be 'formed in accordance with the law of a Member State'.[1] Second, such a company had to have its 'registered office, central administration or principal place of business within the Community'.[2] If these conditions were fulfilled, then the company would be assimilated to the nationals of Member States in the matter of establishment. Such a company, however, in order to establish *secondary* enterprises must show 'a continuous and effective link with the economy of a Member State . . .'.[3] Thus, a mere registered office within the Community will not be sufficient if such a company is to establish a *secondary* enterprise elsewhere within the Common Market.

From the above discussion it can be seen that the EEC Treaty is not concerned at all with the nationality of the members of the company in determining whether or not it is to have freedom of establishment. If the two conditions above mentioned are complied with, it necessarily means that the company is a constituent part of the Community's economy deserving of favourable treatment, and the fact that all the shareholders are nationals of non-Member States will not alter this position.

'"Companies or firms" as used in Article 58 means companies or firms constituted under civil or commercial law, including cooperative societies, and other legal persons governed by public or private law, save for those which are non-profit-making.'[4]

The broad terms used in this definition (which includes partnerships) indicate the wide range intended to be covered, and the unambiguous phraseology calls for little comment. Two points, however, are worth mentioning. The Irish lawyer should remember the significance of the phrase 'other legal persons' among civil lawyers. In the Civil Law system legal personality is not confined, as it is in the Common Law, to natural persons and companies; it also extends to economic associations (*wirtschaftliche Vereine*) and to foundations (*Stiftungen*) which would not be considered legal entities in the jurisprudence of the Common Law.[5] The second point concerns the only exception contemplated in the definition: legal persons which are non-profit-making. This provision succeeds in excluding from the ambit of the definition trade unions, clubs and charitable or other non-profit-making organisations. Nor must such exclusion be wondered at since, after all, the Treaty is, basically, an economic one and only those business associations which participate in economic activity should benefit from the right of establishment.

1 EEC Treaty, art. 58(1).
2 *Ibid.*
3 General Programme, Title 1(d).
4 Article 52, para. 2.
5 W.G. Salmond, *Jurisprudence*, p. 336 (8th ed. London).

18.26 To sum up then, a national from another Member State can only avail of the right of establishment in Ireland if he is a national of a Member State according to the law of one of the Member States. For a 'company or a firm' to benefit it must (i) be formed in accordance with the law of a Member State and have (ii) its registered office, central administration or principal place of business within the Community. Further, if such a company or firm has only its registered office within the Community, and it wishes to establish a *secondary* enterprise in Ireland, it must show 'a continuous and effective link with the economy of a Member State'.

(c) *The Implementation of the Rights*

18.27 In implementing these rights on freedom of establishment a familiar procedure was adopted: under Article 53 a wide prohibition against all *new* restrictions is proclaimed and to deal with *existing* restrictions the dismantling procedure of a general programme supplemented by Council directives is adopted.[1]

Article 53 declares categorically that 'Member States shall not, subject to the provisions of the Treaty, introduce any new restrictions on the establishment in their territories of nationals of other Member States'. The direct and forceful language used leaves little doubt as to the meaning and effect of this Article. In *Costa v ENEL* the Court of Justice declared: 'Article 53 constitutes a Community rule capable of creating individual rights which the national courts must protect'.[2]

1 'The objectives of the treaty provisions [on establishment and supply of services] are attained in part through the prohibition of restrictions . . . directly or pursuant to secondary legislation, and in part through secondary legislation setting out common rules to be applied in all the member states . . . and the mutual recognition of diplomas, certificates and other evidence cf. formal qualifications' 52 Halsbury, *op. cit.*, 464. In the area of free movement of workers the Community makes greater use of regulations (*supra* fn. 1, para. 18.2). The probable reason for this is that in the worker area it is desirable to have one uniform Community law, whereas in the right of establishment (a much more complex area) co-ordination is all that is desirable.
2 Case 6/64 [1964] E.C.R. 585, [1964] C.M.L.R. 425, at pp. 599 and 460 respectively.

18.28 To remove all *existing* restrictions on the right of establishment the Treaty relies on a General Programme[1] which is to be implemented by subsequent directives. The exact legal effect of the General Programme is somewhat uncertain and it finds no mention in Article 189 which defines the various legislative acts of the institutions of the Community. At the very least, however, it must constitute an international treaty between the Member States which enunciates, in a more detailed fashion, the principles found in Articles 52 to 58. Everling goes further and declares that the General Programme 'is an act of a special kind by which the Council binds itself and the other institutions for future acts'.[2] The General Programme promulgated a timetable for the progressive removal of restrictions in specific areas and by the end of the transitional period it was hoped that all restrictions would have been abolished. The more detailed liberalisation was to be achieved by the issuance of directives[3] which bind Member States as to the goal to be attained while leaving the exact means to the States' discretion.

1 *Supra* fn. 1, para. 18.2.
2 Everling, *supra* fn. 1, para. 18.24 at p. 58. See also, J. Temple Lang, *The Common Market and the Common Law*, 155–6; Van Gerven, *The Right of Establishment and the Free Supply of Services*, 3 C.M.L. Rev. 344, at 345–50.
3 EEC Treaty, art. 54(2), as amended by SEA, art. 6.

18.29 Apart from the General Programme and the directives, the Treaty also provides for some co-ordinating measures to implement the right of free establishment, and the effect of such co-ordinating measures must not be underestimated. The diversity of laws among the several Member States made some sort of co-ordination imperative for a full realisation of the establishment provisions. Complete uniformity was not aimed at, much less desired,[1] and the successful operation of the Community was in no way dependent on such uniformity as could be proved from the experience in the United States of America. Nevertheless, it was obvious that some minimal co-ordinating measures were essential within the EEC and it has been well said in this connection that: 'However fascinating their solution may be to a lawyer, conflicts of laws do not create a climate favourable to business, and it is far better to abolish rather than solve them'[2]

Recognising the problem, the authors of the Treaty have provided generally for the approximation of the laws of the Member States in Articles 100, 101 and 102. These provisions have a widespread and general application and extend to all 'provisions of the Member States as have a direct incidence on the establishment of functioning of the Common Market'[3] or when such national laws 'distort' conditions of competition.[4] More specifically in the area of establishment co-ordination is authorised within Articles 52 to 58: in respect of company law (Article 54(3)(g)), the mutual recognition of diplomas, certificates and other evidence of formal qualifications (Article 57(i)), the co-ordination of national provisions concerning the taking up and pursuit of activities as self employed persons (Article 57(2)) and the meaning of the exception permitted on the grounds of public policy, public security or public health (Article 56(2)).

1 See E. Stein, *An Emergent Legal Community: The Common Market Countries' Plans for Harmonization of Law*. 9 Am. J. Comp. L. 353 (1960). See also P. Leleux, 'The Right of Establishment within the EEC' in *Doing Business in the Common Market* (European Common Market Conference at George Washington Univ., 1963) at 33.
2 Audinet, 86 Journal du Droit International 1041 (1959).
3 EEC Treaty, art. 100, amended now by SEA, art. 18 introducing into EEC Treaty new Articles 100A and 100B.
4 EEC Treaty, art. 101. See *supra*, fn. 3.

Direct Effects and the Directives

18.30 At the outset there were two obstacles to the full realisation of the right of establishment and the freedom to provide services which had to be addressed under such a programme. First, there was the problem of discrimination on the basis of nationality where Member States had one set of regulations for their own nationals and another more difficult set for foreigners. Second, there was the problem of some Member States having higher and more demanding standards for certain activities than other states. For example, a regulated trade in one state might require six years' apprenticeship while in another country only four years' apprenticeship might be required. Insofar as these latter regulations were applicable to nationals and foreigners alike they were not discriminatory but they impeded free movement of persons nonetheless. After the *Reyners*[1] and *Van Binsbergen*[2] Cases the first problem was solved insofar as the Court of Justice held in these cases that Articles 52 and 59 were directly effective since the end of the transitional period (i.e. 31 December 1969). Directives passed to achieve this objective were, since that date, superfluous. Complaining parties who claimed discrimination could henceforth rely on the Treaty itself. The second problem remained, however, also the need for directives to coordinate entry requirements to the various activities throughout the Community.

1 *Supra* fn. 1, para. 18.4.
2 *Supra* fn. 2, para. 18.5.

18.31 Two types of directives were adopted to tackle this latter problem. Some directives, relating principally to the craft trades, now indicate that proof of actual practice of that activity or trade in one Member State for a certain number of years will have to be accepted as proof of competence and will entitle the individual to enter this activity in any other Member State. Further, whenever a Member State requires an individual to show good repute or solvency those directives also provide that certificates from designated authorities in the home State must be accepted by the host State. Other directives, principally in the liberal professions and particularly in the area of medicine, etc., list the diplomas and degrees of the Member States which other Member States must recognise while at the same time they set out general definitions of certain minimum requirements regarding the duration and content of the courses. This compromise is designed to guarantee minimum Community standards, on the one hand, while leaving a certain amount of autonomy to the Member States, on the other. Apart from the medical professions, however, progress in the other liberal professions has been less than spectacular.

18.32 Apart from craft trades and the professions many directives also exist in relation to the harmonisation of company law and banking, insurance, stock-exchange transactions, etc. It is not within the scope of this work to discuss these. Readers are referred to the appropriate sources for further information on these topics.[1]

1 On harmonisation of company law in Ireland see (1984) J.I.S.E.L. (Vol. 7) pp. 1–85. On other matters, especially directives on specific sectors see 52 *Halsbury*, *op. cit.*, 499 *et seq.*

Supply of Services[1]

18.33 The supply of services involves the cross-frontier provision of non-wage-earning activities on a temporary or occasional basis. It can involve the provider coming to the client on a once-off visit, for example, a tax consultant or a surgeon, *or* the client coming to the provider *or* indeed no movement of persons, where the service is provided by correspondence or telephone.[2]

1 See generally 52 *Halsbury's Laws of England*, 463.
2 Transport, banking and insurance services are regulated separately. See EEC Treaty, art. 61.

18.34 The Treaty provisions governing Services[1] adopt a similar approach as that adopted in the Freedom of Establishment provisions.[2] New restrictions are prohibited in Article 62, and Article 59 provides for the progressive dismantling of existing restrictions. The dismantling process is to be achieved by the adoption of a General Programme[3] and the subsequent issuance of directives. Pending the abolition of all restrictions Member States are obliged to apply the restrictions without discrimination on the basis of nationality or residence.[4]

1 EEC Treaty, art.s 59 to 66, as amended by SEA art.s 6 and 13 to 19.
2 Articles 52 to 59.
3 *Supra*, fn. 1, para. 18.2.
4 Article 65.

18.35 Since Article 66 declares that the provisions of Articles 55 to 58 (on Establishment) also apply to the Supply of Services much of what has already been said in relation to Entry and Residence, Discrimination, Derogations and Exceptions does not have to be repeated here.

18.36 Article 59 providing for the abolition of restrictions on the provision of services clearly applies to discriminatory restrictions i.e. restrictions which make the provision more difficult for non-nationals. There is some authority now, however, that non-discriminatory restrictions are also covered. In *Van Wesemael*[1] a licensing requirement in respect of the provision of services as an employment agency, and which applied to nationals and foreigners alike, was considered to be a restriction if the cross-frontier service was subject to *comparable* supervision in the home state. In other words, equivalent or comparable regulations in the home state had to be accepted in the host state.[2] The matter is the subject of some controversy.

1 *Supra*, fn. 5, para. 18.5.
2 See also Case 279/80 *Webb* [1981] E.C.R. 3305, [1982] 1 C.M.L.R. 719, especially at pp. 3333 and 729 respectively. See also N. Forewood and M. Clough, *The Single European Act and Free Movement*, 11 E.L. Rev. 383, at 387–91 and 401 *et seq.*

18.37 Apart from the 'public authority' exception and the 'public policy, public security and public health' provision which also apply to the provision of services the Court of Justice has also established a judicial exception analogous to the 'rule of reason' exception created by the Court in respect of Article 30 in *Dassonville*[1] and *Cassis de Dijon*.[2] According to Forewood and Clough 'the judicial exception regards requirements imposed on cross-frontier suppliers of services as compatible with the Treaty if they have as their purpose the application of rules regulating certain types of activity, and provided certain conditions are fulfilled.

(1) The rules must be justified by the general interest, e.g. rules of

conduct connected with the administration of justice and with respect for professional ethics (*Van Binsbergen*); . . .

(2) The rules are binding on persons established in the host Member State, i.e. non-discriminatory (see *Van Binsbergen, Debauve*, and *Van Wesemael*).

(3) The supplier of services is not, in the Member State of his establishment, subject to comparable rules and to proper supervision covering his activities whatever the Member State in which the services are provided (see *Van Wesemael* and *Webb*—'the doctrine of equivalence').

(4) It is not possible to apply other, less restrictive, measures to ensure respect for these rules—the principle of proportionality.'[3]

1 Case 8/74 *Procureur du Roi v Dassonville* [1974] E.C.R. 837, [1974] 2 C.M.L.R. 436.
2 Case 120/78 *Rewe-Zentral AG v Bundesmonopolverwaltung für Branntwein* [1979] E.C.R. 649, [1979] 3 C.M.L.R. 494.
3 *Op. cit. supra*, fn. 2, para. 18.36 at p. 389. Footnote omitted.

18.38 Article 59 was held to be directly effective in *Van Binsbergen*[1] and if, as *Van Wesemael* suggests, Article 59 applies to non-discriminatory as well as to discriminatory measures then its impact is quite extensive. It would appear that this position will not be dramatically affected by the new amending provisions introduced as new Articles 100A and 100B of the EEC Treaty by the Single European Act.[2]

1 *Supra*, n. 2, para. 18.5.
2 See, SEA art.s 8A, 18 and 19. See also Forewood and Clough, *supra*, fn. 2, para. 18.36 at pp. 401 *et seq*.

18.39 The degree of co-ordination which has taken place in the area of Services has not been dramatic to date. It has principally been in the areas of medicine, architecture and hairdressing.[1] In this connection it should be noted that Article 100B, introduced by the SEA, enables the Council, during 1992, to decide that the provisions in force in a Member State must be recognised as being equivalent to those applied by another Member State. This recognition of the value of the judicial doctrine of equivalence could have a very significant accelerating effect on liberalising this whole area in due course.

1 See for further details 52 *Halsbury, Laws of England, European Communities*, 499 *et seq*.

Completing the Internal Market by 1992

18.40 The Community considers that the obstacles that remain to free movement should be removed by 1992, and in the SEA it introduces a new Article 8A to the EEC Treaty which declares in part: 'The Community shall adopt measures with the aim of progressively establishing the internal market over a period expiring on 31st December 1992 . . .'. The internal market is defined in this article as 'an area without internal frontiers in which the free movement of goods, persons, services and capital is ensured in accordance with the provisions of this Treaty'. Although a Declaration to the SEA states that the fixing of 'the date 31 December 1992 does not create an automatic legal effect', there is little doubt of the Commission's commitment to this deadline. In particular the Commission has issued new proposals to facilitate the free movement of workers and professionals in the Community. A Council framework directive should greatly facilitate recognition of higher educational qualifications. 'This new system is based on the principle of mutual trust between the Member States and the comparability of university studies: this should permit the mutual recognition of degrees and diplomas without prior harmonisation of the conditions for access to and the exercise of the activities concerned.'[1] Essentially, the proposal is that a Member State would have to accept a person as a carpenter, an insurance broker, an auctioneer, etc., if that person was qualified as such in another Member State. In other words, the host State would have to trust and accept the standards of other Member States in these matters. In its White Paper on Completing the Internal Market the Commission declares its policy on this matter as follows:

'For this reason, with the aim of removing obstacles to the right of establishment, the Commission—which approved the conclusions of the Adonnino report—will submit to the Council a draft framework Directive on a general system of recognition in the course of this year. The main elements in this system will be: the principle of mutual trust between the Member States; the principle of the comparability of university studies between the Member States; the mutual recognition of degrees and diplomas without prior harmonisation of the conditions for access to and the exercise of professions; and the extension of the general system to salary earners. Lastly, any difference, notably as regards training, between the Member States would be compensated by professional experience.'[2]

Hopes that progress in this area would be more spectacular in the immediate future as a result of the Commission's White Paper and the ratification of the SEA have not materialised and a measure of the Commission's frustration on this can be seen from its report to the Council and Parliament in May 1987. Commenting on its lack of progress in relation to the Council's failure to act on proposals for a general system of mutual recognition of higher education diplomas and on the right of residence for nationals not yet or no longer employed in another Member State it expressed its impatience in unusually strong terms:

'This sorry state of affairs cannot, indeed must not, be allowed to continue. The Council must come to terms with the fact that it can no longer prevaricate as it did for 17 years for example before it got around to adopting the Commission's proposal on the right of establishment of architects.'[3]

1 European Parliament (Directorate General for Research En III/J p. 1. (PE 100.200).
2 Commission of the European Communities, Document, Completing the Internal Market (White Paper from the Commission to the European Council) June 1985, para. 93.
3 Commission of the European Communities, Second Report from the Commission to the Council and the European Parliament on the Implementation of the Commission's White Paper on Completing the Internal Market, para. 36 (11 May 1987). C.O.M. (87) 203 final.

Chapter 19

The Free Movement of Capital and the Free Movement of Payments

19.1 The provisions dealing with capital in the EEC Treaty, Articles 67 to 73, are to be found in Title III of Part II, along with the provisions on the free movement of workers, the right of establishment, and the freedom to provide services: indeed, these four matters are grouped together in paragraph (c) of Article 3 of the Treaty which outlines the activities to be pursued by the Community in order to achieve the objectives set out in Article 2. The link between the free movement of capital and these other freedoms is logical:

> '. . . the freedom to move certain types of capital is, in practice, a precondition for the effective exercise of other freedoms guaranteed by the Treaty, in particular the right of establishment.'[1]

When the Treaty entered into force one of the most serious obstacles to the exercise of these other fundamental freedoms was to be found in the exchange control systems operated by the Member States and, to a surprising extent, this remains true today.

But, despite the close relationship of capital movements to the full exercise of the other freedoms, there are significant points of difference between the Treaty rules on persons and services on the one hand and on capital on the other hand. For a start, capital movements '. . . are closely connected with the economic and monetary policy of the Member States',[2] and the control of capital movements is an important economic policy instrument. The provisions of the Treaty dealing with economic policy are to be found in Title II of Part III of the Treaty and Articles 104 to 109 in particular. These provisions differ from those dealing with the establishment of the Common Market in that the ultimate decision-making power rests, as a general rule, with the Member States: there are few deadlines for the achievement of legislative programmes and thus few of the provisions are likely to be of direct effect. But the Treaty does impose certain responsibilities on the Member States: Article 104 requires the Member States to pursue the economic policies necessary to ensure equilibrium in their balance of payments, maintain confidence in their currency, and to ensure high levels of employment and a stable level of prices; to this end the Member States undertook, in Article 105, to

376

co-ordinate their economic policies; and Article 107 requires the Member States to treat their exchange rate policies as matters of common concern. These responsibilities echo certain of the objectives in Article 2 of the Treaty in which the Member States pledged themselves to achieve: '. . . a continuous and balanced expansion . . .' and '. . . an increase in stability . . .'. Nonetheless, Articles 104 to 109 are concerned '. . . with the overall balance of payments and . . . for this reason relate to all monetary movements.'[3] When viewed from this perspective, there is always a danger that unrestricted capital movements could '. . . undermine the economic policy of one of the Member States or create an imbalance in its balace of payments . . .'[4] and Article 67 would thus be brought into conflict with Articles 104 to 109. In such a conflict the provisions of Articles 104 to 109 prevail over Article 67. As Advocate General Capotorti pointed out in the *Casati* case, it would be inconsistent to entrust the Member States with responsibility for their respective monetary policies and to impose on them an unconditional and unlimited obligation to liberalise transfers of currency not made for a consideration of equal value.[5] In this regard, a further conclusion can be drawn: completely unrestricted capital movements will depend ultimately on a much more systematic co-ordination of the economic policies of the Member States.[6]

The fact that freedom of capital movements is subordinated to the requirements of the economic policy (of the Member States) is partly reflected in the language of Articles 67 and 71; the former requires the abolition of discriminatory restrictions on the movement of capital between the Member States '. . . to the extent necessary to ensure the proper functioning of the Common Market . . .' and according to the latter, which is a standstill clause, '. . . the Member States will endeavour to avoid introducing within the Community any new exchange restrictions on the movement of capital.' This is not the mandatory or compulsive language which the Court of Justice has held to be directly effective in the equivalent provisions of the chapters on the free movement of goods, persons and services such as, for example, Article 12[7] or Article 48.[8] In *Casati* the Court of Justice ruled that Article 67(1) was not directly effective, because the restriction on the liberalisation of capital movements '. . . to the extent necessary to ensure the proper functioning of the Common Market . . .' varies in time and depends on an assessment of the requirements of the Common Market and on an appraisal of both the advantages and risks which liberalisation might entail for the Common Market.[9] That assessment is a matter for the Council, utilising the power to adopt directives conferred by Article 69; and this assessment, involving as it does a discretionary power, means that Article 67 paragraph 1 on its own does not comply with the criteria for direct effects. Likewise, Article 71 does not create direct effects. Although it has the character of a standstill clause it is more flexible and less exacting.[10] The Court concluded from its wording that Article 71 does not impose on the Member States an unconditional obligation capable of being relied upon by individuals.[11]

Another difference between the capital rules and those on the free movement of persons and services is that the meaning of capital (and therefore the extent of the liberalisation requirement) was not defined in the Treaty. It seems that the authors of the Treaty were unable to agree on a definition;[12] instead a flexible and pragmatic mechanism was put at the disposal of the Council. A Nomenclature of Capital Movements was drawn up in the first and second Directives on capital movements[13] and different degrees of liberalisation were attached to specific categories of those capital movements (Lists A, B, C and D).

In once sense, however, the scope of the prohibition of restrictions on capital movements is broader than the equivalent prohibitions in the chapters on workers, establishment and services. In the latter provisions the determining element of the prohibition is discrimination on grounds of nationality, whereas Article 67(1) speaks of abolishing restrictions based on the residence or nationality of the parties involved or on the place where the capital is invested. In practice the residence criterion has been adopted because it is often difficult to ascribe 'nationality' to capital and because a narrow interpretation would not contribute to the optimum allocation of capital throughout the Common Market.[14]

Finally, the capital provisions differ from the other freedoms in that they contain an 'escape clause' properly so-called, while the provisions on workers, establishment and services are subject only to *exceptions* based, for example, on public policy, public security or public health.[15] Article 73 allows the Member States to take protective measures if movements of capital lead to disturbances in the functioning of the capital market. Articles 108 and 109, on the balance of payments, allow for much wider protective measures which would include restrictions on capital movements.

1 Case 203/80 *Casati* [1981] E.C.R. 2595, [1982] 1 C.M.L.R. 365, at pp. 2614 and 392 respectively.
2 *Idem.*
3 Case 7/78 *R v Thompson* [1978] E.C.R. 2247, [1979] 1 C.M.L.R. 47.
4 *Supra*, n. 1.
5 *Idem*, pp. 2626 and 377 respectively.
6 C.W.M. van Ballegooijen, *Free Movement of Capital in the European Economic Community*, Legal Issues of European Integration; 1976/2, at p. 7.
7 Case 26/62 *Van Gend en Loos v Nederlandse Belastingadministratie* [1963] E.C.R. 1, [1963] C.M.L.R. 105.
8 Case 167/73 *EC Commission v France* [1974] E.C.R. 359, [1974] 2 C.M.L.R. 216.
9 *Supra*, n. 1.
10 Christopher Prout, 'Free Movement of Capital; Part 17' in: David Vaughan (Ed.), *Law of European Communities*, (2 Vols.), (London 1986); at para. 17.19. Hereinafter cited as 'Prout'.
11 *Supra*, n. 1, at pp. 2616 and 394 respectively.
12 van Ballegooijen, *op. cit.* n. 6, at p. 4.
13 Council Directive (EEC) of 11 May 1960 O.J. (Sp. Ed.) 1959–62 Council Directive p. 49, 63/21 O.J. (Sp. Ed.) (EEC) 196 3–64 p. 5.
14 van Ballegooijen, *op. cit.* n. 6, at p. 8.
15 See, for example, EEC Treaty, art. 48(3) and (4).

19.2 There are other provisions in the Treaty which deal with transactions that are comparable with, but not identical to, capital movements. For example, Article 221 required the Member States, within three years of the entry into force of the Treaty, to accord to nationals of the other Member States the same treatment as their own nationals as regards participation in the capital of companies or firms within the meaning of Article 58, without prejudice to the application of the other provisions of the Treaty. It has been suggested that this provision applies to transactions that do not involve movements of capital between Member States, for example, where a Belgian resident in the United Kingdom buys shares in a United Kingdom registered company. But if the transaction involved a capital movement across frontiers then the provisions of Articles 67 to 73 would take precedence.[1] Article 221 has not yet given rise to any litigation.

Of much greater importance, however, is Article 106 of the Treaty which deals with current payments and invisible transactions. In Article 106(1) the Member States undertook to authorise, in the currency of the Member State in which the creditor or beneficiary resides, any payment connected with the movement of goods, services or capital, and any transfer of capital and earnings, to the extent that the movement of goods, services, capital and persons between Member States has been liberalised pursuant to the Treaty. They also agreed to speed up the liberalisation of payments if their general economic situations (and balance of payments in particular) so permitted. Thus, payments for goods and services were to be liberalised in tandem with the timetable for the abolition of restrictions on the free movement of goods, persons and services. Article 106(2) required the Member States to abolish progressively restrictions on payments for goods, services or capital in cases where the restriction on payments constituted the only obstacle, i.e. where the underlying transaction was no longer subject to a restriction. In Article 106(3) the Member States undertook not to introduce between themselves new restrictions on transfers connected with invisible transactions; existing restrictions on invisible transactions were to be removed in accordance with the provisions of Articles 63 to 65 of the Treaty (on services) insofar as their abolition was not covered by other provisions of the Treaty. Thus, Article 106(3) operates with residual effect. Annex III to the Treaty provides a four and a half page list of invisible transactions including items such as freight and service charges for all types of transport, warehousing and customs charges, commissions and brokerage, business travel, tourism, travel for health, education or family reasons, salaries and wages, emigrants' remittances, rent, authors' royalties, inheritances and dowries.

The 'free movement of payments' has been described as an essential complement to the free movement of goods, persons, services and capital.[2] These other basic freedoms would be rendered nugatory if the essential monetary remuneration involved was subject to restrictions; for example, if a migrant worker was prevented from remitting his savings to his home Member State, or if a subsidiary was prevented from repatriating profits to its parent company. Moreover, the importance to world trade of the liberalisation of current payments had been recognised before the creation of the EEC. Section 2(a) of Article VIII of the Articles of Agreement of the International Monetary Fund (signed at Bretton Woods, New Hampshire in July 1944) provided that no member of the Fund was to impose restrictions on the making of payments and transfers for current international transactions.[3]

The question now arises: how can capital movements be distinguished from current payments? This is of great importance because the liberalisation requirements are much wider in respect of current payments and because '. . . capital movements account for only a part of the transactions

379

involving transfers of currency.'[4] In practice the distinction can be difficult to draw. Many of the transactions listed in Annex III to the Treaty as invisible transactions were also listed in the Nomenclature of Capital Movements annexed to the First and Second Directives; for example, dowries and inheritances. But it is clear that the listing of a transaction, either in Annex III or in the Nomenclature of Capital Movements, is not conclusive. In *Luisi and Carbone* the Court had to decide *inter alia* whether the physical transfer of bank notes constituted a current payment or a capital movement. The Court held that

> '. . . in the annexes to the two above directives a list is given of the various movements of capital together with the nomenclature. Although the physical transfer of financial assets, in particular bank notes, is included in that list, it does not mean that any such transfer must in all circumstances be regarded as a movement of capital.'[5]

The Court has had the opportunity to discuss the relationship between current payments and capital movements in two cases. In *Casati* the defendant in the main proceedings had been charged with exporting DM24,000 from Italy in breach of Italian exchange control regulations. Under list D (as it then was) of the capital Directives the Member States were under no obligation to liberalise the physical export of bank notes. Casati maintained that he had imported the money into Italy, without declaring it, with a view to purchasing equipment which he needed for his business in Germany and was obliged to re-export the currency because the factory at which he intended to buy the equipment was closed for the holidays. One of the questions asked by the national court referred to the standstill obligation contained in Article 106(3) according to which the Member State had agreed not to introduce any new restrictions on invisible transactions. But the Court ruled that the re-exportation of funds imported with a view to making purchases of a commercial nature could not be classified as an Annex III type transaction if the purchases had not in fact been effected. The Court went on to interpret Article 106(1) and (2) even though the national court had not sought guidance as to their meaning. Having stressed the importance of the liberalisation of payments for the free movement of goods, the Court added that

> . . . those provisions do not require the Member States to authorise the importation and exportation of bank notes for the performance of commercial transactions, if such transfers are not necessary for the free movement of goods. In connection with commercial transactions, that method of transfer, which, moreover, is not in conformity with standard practice, cannot be regarded as necessary to ensure such free movement.'[6]

In other words, the payment of approximately £7,000 in cash by Mr Casati would have been a distinctly irregular means of payment. The decision of the Court is noteworthy for two reasons. First, the Court seems to have discarded the requirement, specified in Article 106(1) and (2), that the payment be tendered in the currency of the Member State in which the creditor or beneficiary resides. In the particular circumstances of the case the alleged payment would have been transacted in the currency of the

380

Member State in which the purchaser resided. Secondly, the Court would appear to have added a condition to Article 106(1) and (2) which now authorises the Member States to verify the 'conformity with standard practice' or the genuineness of the commercial transactions involved.

In *Luisi and Carbone* the plaintiffs had been fined by the Italian Minister for the Treasury for purchasing various foreign currencies (including US dollars, Swiss francs, German marks and French francs) for use abroad to a value exceeding the maximum permitted by Italian law per annum namely, Lire 500,000 (approx £250). In the national court Mrs Luisi stated that she had used the money for the purpose of visits to France and Germany as a tourist and to Germany for medical purposes. Mr Carbone spent his foreign currency during a three month visit to Germany. Both argued that the Italian restrictions were in breach of the Treaty requirements concerning current payments and the movement of capital. The national court referred a series of questions to Luxembourg asking whether the exportation of foreign currency for the purposes of tourism, business, education or medical treatment constituted an invisible transaction within the meaning of Article 106(3), a current payment in respect of the receipt of services (for example tourism), or a transfer of cash within the meaning of the capital Directives. In order to answer the question the Court had to interpret the meaning of the freedom to provide services. According to the Court tourists, persons receiving medical treatment and persons travelling for the purposes of education or business are to be regarded as recipients of services because the freedom to provide services includes the right, for the recipients of services, to go to another Member State in order to receive services there, without being obstructed by restrictions even in relation to payments. The Court then examined the general scheme of the Treaty and compared Articles 67 and 106, and this examination produced a helpful but not exhaustive formula for distinguishing between current payments and capital movements. It held that current payments covered by Article 106 are transfers of foreign exchange which constitute the consideration within the context of an underlying transaction, while the movement of capital covered by Article 67 are financial operations essentially concerned with the investment of the funds in question rather than remuneration for a service. The physical transfer of bank notes may not therefore be classified as a movement of capital where the transfer in question corresponds to an obligation to pay arising from a transaction involving the movement of goods or services. The Court further held that because tourism and travel connected with medical treatment were to be classified as services for the purposes of the Treaty, currency transactions connected with them were current payments and not invisible transactions, even though such transfers were listed in Annex III of the Treaty. Article 106(3) is subsidiary to Articles 106(1) and 106(2) and thus applies in a residual fashion, i.e. when the provisions on services or capital are inapplicable. Finally, Article 106 compels Member States to authorise the payments referred to in that provision in the currency of the Member State in which the creditor or beneficiary resides; payments in the currency of a third country (US dollars or Swiss francs, for example) are not therefore covered by that provision.

Article 106 is directly effective and may be relied on in national courts, but only to the extent that the movement of goods, persons, services and capital have been liberalised. All restrictions on the free movement of goods, persons and services were abolished at the end of the transitional period so that restrictions on payments relating to goods, services or persons should also have been abolished at the end of the transitional period.[7] Insofar as current payments connected with capital movements are concerned (interest or rent, for example) it would appear that Article 106 has been directly effective since the end of the first stage of the transitional period (see Article 67(2)).

The judgment in *Luisi and Carbone* was delivered in 1984 but ten years earlier reliance had been placed on Article 106 in the English Courts in *Schorsch Meier v Hennin*.[8] In that case the defendant owed DM 3765.03 for motor car parts which had been supplied by the plaintiff. In the County Court the judge offered a judgment in sterling but the plaintiff refused because sterling had depreciated significantly between the date of the contract and the date of the judgment. When the matter came before the Court of Appeal Lord Denning had no hesitation in relying on Article 106 to justify making an order in Deutschmarks in favour of the plaintiff. Unfortunately, Lord Denning also used the occasion to declare redundant the sterling judgments rule formulated in the House of Lords' decision in *Re United Railways of Havana and Regla Warehouses Ltd*.[9] As a direct consequence of the decision in the *Schorsch Meier* case the House of Lords had to consider the abolition of the sterling judgments rule in *Miliangos v George Frank (Textiles) Ltd*.[10] They concurred in the result proposed by Lord Denning but rebuked him severely for his use of Article 106 of the EEC Treaty as the means by which the result was achieved.

1 Peter Oliver, *Free Movement of Capital Between Member States: Article 67(1) EEC and the Implementing Directives*; (1984) 9 E.L. Rev. 401, at p. 416.
2 Georg Ress, 'Free Movement of Persons, Services and Capital'; in *Thirty Years of Community Law*, (1983), at p. 318. Hereinafter cited as 'Ress'.
3 For text see Bretton Woods Agreements Act, 1957; Schedule, part I.
4 *Supra*, fn. 1, para. 19.1, at pp. 2616 and 394 respectively.
5 Joined Cases 286/82, 26/83 *Luisi and Carbone v Ministero del Tesoro* [1984] E.C.R. 377, [1985] 3 C.M.L.R. 52, at pp. 403 and 78 respectively.
6 *Supra*, fn. 1, para 19.1, at pp. 2617 and 395 respectively.
7 *Supra*, n. 5.
8 [1975] Q.B. 416.
9 [1961] A.C. 1007.
10 [1975] 2 C.M.L.R. 585.

19.3 Although the Court did not rule on the issue in the *Casati* and *Luisi and Carbone* cases, it seems unlikely that the provisions of Articles 67 to 73 on capital movements and Article 106 on current payments could be applied cumulatively to the same transaction.[1] This conclusion can be justified by reference to the decisions of the Court which have ruled out the cumulative application of different basic Treaty rules. For example, in *Iannelli and Volpi v Meroni*[2] the Court held that Articles 9, 12, 16 and 95 were inapplicable to measures falling within the remit of Articles 30 to 34 of the Treaty, and in *Statens Kontrol v Larsen*[3] the Court held that Articles 16 and 95 could not be applied cumulatively to the same national measures. Although not directly relevant to the question of the cumulative application of Articles 67 to 73 and 106, it should be noted that the Court has implicitly ruled out cumulative application of Articles 30 to 37 and Article 67. In the case of *R v Thompson*[4] the Court held that Articles 30 to 37 of the Treaty were inapplicable to means of payment such as alloy coins which are legal tender in a Member State or to gold coins such as Krugerrands which circulate freely in a Member State. At the time when the Court's judgment was delivered 'means of payment' was a transaction which appeared in List D of the capital Directives. Thus, the implication to be drawn from the judgment is that Articles 30 to 37 cannot be applied cumulatively to a transaction covered by Articles 67 to 73.

1 Oliver, *op. cit.* fn. 1, para. 19.2, at p. 416.
2 Case 74/76 [1977] E.C.R. 557, [1977] 2 C.M.L.R. 688.
3 Case 142/77 [1978] E.C.R. 1543, [1979] 2 C.M.L.R. 680.
4 *Supra*, fn. 3, para. 19.1.

19.4 We have already observed (at 19.1) that Articles 67 to 73 do not contain a definition of capital. It might also be noted that the decisions of the Court of Justice have not added much by way of clarification. In *R v Thompson*[1] the national court asked the Court of Justice whether three types of coins were 'capital' for the purposes of the Treaty. The three types were (i) gold coins in circulation in a Member State—Krugerrands in this case; (ii) silver alloy coins which are legal tender in a Member State; and (iii) silver alloy coins which are no longer legal tender in that Member State. The Court responded by reformulating the questions and went on to hold that the third category of coins fell within the provisions of Articles 30 to 37 of the Treaty, but that the other two categories of coins were means of payment which could not be considered as goods falling within Articles 30 to 37. The Court did not specify whether these 'means of payment' were to be considered as capital. In *Casati*[2] the Court did not discuss the notion of capital but instead outlined the effects of Article 106 on current payments and invisible transactions. In any event, the exportation of bank notes was a List D transaction to which no liberalisation requirement applied. In *Luisi and Carbone*[3] the Court did provide a limited definition of capital movements and current payments. It described the former as '. . . financial operations essentially concerned with the investment of the funds in question rather than remuneration for a service . . .' whereas the latter '. . . are transfers of foreign exchange which constitute consideration within the context of an underlying transaction.' This is helpful in distinguishing between capital movements and current payments but as a definition of capital it presents certain problems. Does it mean that the movement of capital cannot involve the movement of non-financial assets?[4] This would pose particular difficulties for 'immaterial' capital movements (for example: patents, designs and trade marks) and 'real' capital movements (for example: gold and real estate) which are not financial assets but which were to be found in the lists of capital movements annexed to the First and Second Directives.[5]

1 *Idem.*
2 *Supra*, fn. 3, para. 19.1.
3 *Supra*, fn. 5, para. 19.2.
4 Prout, at para. 17.15.
5 van Ballegooijen, *op. cit.* fn. 6, para. 19.1, at p. 5.

19.5 We must turn, therefore, to the Council Directives for a clearer idea as to what constitutes a capital movement for the purposes of Articles 67 to 73. In the chapter on capital the decision making provision is Article 69 and it confers on the Council, acting on a proposal of the Commission, after consulting the Monetary Committee (provided for in Article 105), the power to issue Directives for the progressive implementation of Article 67. The Council was obliged to act unanimously during the first two stages but by qualified majority thereafter. This decision making power has been used sparingly since 1958 and the explanation can be found in the restrictive terms of Article 67(1):

'1. During the transitional period and to the extent necessary to ensure the proper functioning of the Common Market, Member States shall progressively abolish between themselves all restrictions on the movement of capital belonging to persons resident in Member States and any discrimination based on the nationality or on the place of residence of the parties or on the place where such capital is invested.'

We have already noted that in *Casati* the Court of Justice decided that the expiry of the transitional period did not automatically result in the abolition of restrictions on capital movements because the obligation to abolish restrictions outlined in Article 67(1) depended on the assessment by the Council of the requirements of the Common Market and the advantages and the risks which liberalisation of capital movements would entail. The Council had decided, in the First and Second Directives, that the exportation of bank notes need not be liberalised and, according to the Court, there was '. . . no reason to suppose that, by adopting that position, it has overstepped the limits of its discretionary power.'[1] This last phrase has given rise to suggestions that the Court could decide that the Council was abusing its discretionary power by failing to liberalise certain categories of capital movements when such liberalisation became necessary for the proper functioning of the Common Market.[2] To this extent, Article 67(1) would have direct effect. But, in any event, there is no reason why provisions of the Directives could not be held to be directly effective provided that they comply with the relevant criteria.

The enactment of the First and Second Council Directives of 1960 and 1963 respectively[3] did not in fact result in any significant reduction of barriers to capital flows; as the preamble to the Second Directive acknowledged, the Member States were already committed to a programme of liberalisation within the context of the OECD (the Organisation for Economic Co-operation and Development) and the principal value of the Directives was that they constituted, in effect, a Community codification.[4] In this regard, too, the Directives were less than original: they were based on the Code of Liberalisation of Capital Movements prepared by the OEEC (the predecessor of the OECD) in 1955.[5] The First Directive had two annexes: the second of these annexes was entitled 'Nomenclature of Capital Movements' and it divided capital transactions into fourteen different categories. In Annex I these categories, or sub-sections of them, were rearranged into Lists. Originally there were four lists—Lists A, B, C and D—to which a different level of liberalisation applied.

Although they have now been completely abolished by Council Directive (EEC) 88/361[6] the Lists require some explanation. *List A* included direct investments, investments in real estate, transfers of capital and savings by emigrants and migrant workers and transfers of monies required for the provision of services; all of these transactions are closely connected with the free movement of goods, persons and services. Article 1(1) of the First Directive required the Member States to grant all foreign exchange authorisations to enable such capital transfers between residents of Member States. *List B* included stock exchange operations in domestic securities by non-residents and operations in foreign securities by residents, excluding bonds and unit trusts; Member States were required by Article 2(1) of the First Directive to grant general permission for the conclusion or performance of such transfers between residents of Member States. *List C* included the issue and placing of foreign and domestic securities on capital markets, dealings in bonds and unit trusts, medium and long-term credits, loans and credits (whether or not related to commercial transactions), and sureties and guarantees. Member States were required by Article 3(1) of the First Directive to grant all foreign exchange requirements necessary for the performance of transactions between residents of Member States. However, this requirement operated in a differential manner because those Member States which maintained exchange control restrictions in respect of dealings in securities when the Directive entered into force were permitted to maintain or re-introduce them. *List D* covered a number of essentially speculative transactions such as short-term investments in Treasury Bills, the opening of current and deposit accounts, loans and personal capital movements; it also covered the physical importation and exportation of financial assets, which were defined in the Nomenclature as including gold and all means of payment. According to Articles 4 and 7 of the First Directive there was no obligation on the Member States to liberalise the capital movement set out in List D.

The Second Directive repealed Article 2(3) of the First Directive and effected a number of amendments to both Annexes; the amended texts were reproduced in full as an appendix to the Second Directive and thereafter the two Directives were always cited and construed as a whole. No further changes occurred until 1985 although there had been a proposal for a Third Directive in the 1960s which was rejected by the Council.[7] Then, in Council Directive (EEC) 85/583,[8] a further amendment to the Annexes took place so as to take account of Council Directive (EEC) 85/611[9] which harmonised the laws and practices of Member States concerning certain undertakings for collective investment in transferable securities (UCITS, or unit trusts). Apart from its effect in liberalising an important type of capital transaction, Directive 85/583 demonstrated the close connection between the right to provide financial services and the free movement of capital: as soon as the Council had agreed on the approximation of national rules on the marketing of unit trusts it became necessary to remove exchange control restrictions on the transfer of such unit trusts. In this regard, attention should also be drawn to Article 61(2) of the Treaty which expresses the same sentiment with regard to banking and insurance services connected with the movement of capital; the liberalisation of such services is to be effected in step with the progressive liberalisation of movements of capital.

The next development was the enactment of Council Directive (EEC) 86/566.[10] The connection between greater financial integration and the general economic and monetary policies of the Member States was emphasised in the preamble to the Directive: the liberalisation of capital movements should take place jointly with progress towards increased convergence of the economic policies of the Member States, great monetary stability and the development of the EMS. The 1986 Directive introduced a number of important alterations to the system that had operated almost unchanged since 1963. The nomenclature of Capital Movements in Annex II of the First Directive was amended to refine and extend the meaning of certain capital transactions, and the Explanatory Notes attached to the Nomenclature were also subject to a number of minor variations. But the major changes took place in Annex I, where List B was abolished and the capital transactions listed therein were transferred to List A, and where the former Lists C and D became lists B and C respectively. Finally, further liberalisation took place in respect of the admission of bonds and securities to stock exchanges, which were transferred from the old List C to List A.

1 *Supra*, fn. 1, para. 19.1, at pp. 2615 and 393 respectively.
2 Michael Petersen, *Capital Movements and Payments under the EEC Treaty after Casati*, (1982) 7 E.L. Rev, at p. 172.
3 *Supra*, fn. 13, para. 19.1.
4 van Ballegooijen, *op. cit.* fn. 6 para. 19.2, at p. 3.
5 Prout, at para. 17.07.
6 O.J. L 178, 8.7.1988 p. 5.
7 Oliver, *op. cit.* fn. 1, para. 19.2, at pp. 406–7.
8 O.J. L 372, 31.12.1985 p. 39.
9 O.J. L 375, 31.12.1985 p. 3, as amended by Council Directive (EEC) 88/220 O.J. L 100, 19.4.1988. p. 31.
10 O.J. L 332 26.11.86 p. 22.

Council Directive (EEC) 88/361[1]

19.6 The definitive stage in the liberalisation of capital movements came with the adoption of Council Directive 88/361. This Directive supersedes all the earlier Directives on capital movements and is based on Articles 69 and 70(1) of the Treaty. In addition, the preamble refers to Article 8A of the Treaty—inserted by Article 13 of the Single European Act—which obliges the Community to adopt measures for the completion of the internal market before the end of 1992, and which defines the internal market as comprising:

'. . . an area without internal frontiers in which the free movement of goods, persons, services and capital are ensured in accordance with the provisions of this Treaty.'

Unlike the earlier Directives, which carefully qualified the liberalisation of capital movement by reference to Lists A, B, C and D, Article 1(1) of the

Directive requires the Member States to abolish all restrictions on movements of capital taking place between residents of Member States; Article 6(1) obliges the Member States—subject to specific transitional arrangements for Spain, Portugal, Greece and Ireland (*infra*, para. 19.9)—to comply with the Directive by 1 July 1990. For the purposes of the Directive capital movements are classified in accordance with the Nomenclature set out in Annex I; the categorisation of the Nomenclature into lists has been dispensed with because the obligation to abolish restrictions on capital movements is not qualified in any way (see Appendix 1 of this chapter). Paragraph (2) of Article 1 complements the obligation to remove all obstacles to the movement of capital by stipulating that the exchange rate conditions applicable to current transactions shall also apply to capital movements.

When compared with the original Nomenclature of capital movements (contained in the Second Directive), Annex I of Directive 88/361 follows roughly the same structure but there are some notable differences. First, there are 13 classifications in the current Nomenclature whereas the original had 14, and the order of classification differs between the present and the original texts. Headings II, III and IV of the original version, dealing with the liquidation of direct investments, the admission of securities to capital markets and investment in short-term Treasury Bills, have been eliminated from the current Nomenclature; instead, they have been integrated into classifications more representative of modern financial realities. Classifications III, IV and V in the current Nomenclature deal with operations in securities dealt with on the capital markets, unit trusts, and operations in securities and other instruments dealt with on the money markets. The single most noticeable alteration has taken place in classification XII (formerly XIII) entitled 'Physical import and export of financial assets', where the reference to gold has been eliminated. This means that gold now falls to be classified either under 'Means of payment of every kind' (classification XII), or under 'Miscellaneous' (classification XIII entitled 'Other capital movements'). Finally, the Explanatory Notes have been expanded to account for the reformulation of the Nomenclature, particularly in relation to securities.

The liberalisation requirement of Article 1 applies to capital transfers or movements between *residents* of Member States, and in this respect the present Directive is merely re-enacting the equivalent provisions of the First Directive. The residence test is considerably wider than the nationality criterion which is utilised in the chapters on the free movement of goods, persons and services, and it is clear that citizens of, or companies with their principal place of business in, non-Member States may also benefit from the liberalisation rules. However, in the Explanatory Notes attached to the Nomenclature of Capital Movements in Annex I 'Residents and non-residents' are described as,

'Natural and legal persons according to the definitions laid down in the Exchange Control Regulations in force in each Member State'.

Accordingly, there is no Community definition of residents and the issue falls to be determined under the different national frameworks of exchange control rules.

1 *Supra*, fn. 6, para. 19.5.

19.7 Article 4 of the Directive permits Member States to take all requisite measures to prevent infringement of their laws and regulations particularly in respect of taxation and the prudent supervision of financial institutions; they are also permitted to lay down procedures for the declaration of capital movements for administrative or statistical purposes. This provision should be contrasted with Article 5 of the First Directive which empowered the Member States to verify the nature and genuineness of capital transfers; in an environment in which only some capital transactions had been liberalised Article 5 permitted the Member States to use the verification power to detect, and then to prevent, capital movements which had not been liberalised. This interpretation was upheld by the Court in *Luisi and Carbone*.[1] Article 4 of the current Directive gives considerably less scope to the authorities of the Member States because the liberalisation of capital movements is now undifferentiated: Article 1 of the Directive requires the abolition of *all* restrictions. And, in any event, the second paragraph of Article 4 makes it clear that measures designed to deal with tax evasion, to ensure the prudent supervision of financial institutions, and to collect statistical information may not have the effect of impeding capital movements.

In *Brugnoni and Ruffinengo*[2] the Court was called upon to rule on the effect of Article 5(1) of the First Directive, in the context of Commission Decision (EEC) 85/16[3] authorising Italy to take special protective measures under Article 108 of the Treaty in respect of the purchase by residents of foreign securities or domestic securities issued on a foreign market. Italy was authorised to insist upon the lodging by the purchaser, in a non-interest earning bank account, of a sum equivalent to 50% (later reduced to 30%) of the sum invested; the securities in question also had to be held by the purchaser for a period of at least one year. In addition to these conditions, the Italian decree of 1981 concerning the purchase of foreign securities required the securities to be placed in the custody of an agreed bank. The first named plaintiff, acting through the agency of the second named plaintiff, purchased securities issued in Deutschmarks by the ECSC to the value of DM5000. Apart from having to deposit 30% of the value of the securities in a non-interest earning account, the plaintiff never actually saw the securities in question because the defendant bank had an arrangement with other Italian banks to maintain a collective depository at the premises of correspondent banks in Germany. The plaintiffs claimed that the transaction was a completely liberalised transaction to which List B (in its original form) applied, and that the additional Italian condition on the custody of the securities was a discrimination based on the place where the capital was invested. The Court held that the Commission Decision was valid and that Member States retained the right to verify the nature and genuineness of transactions; this right extended to measures designed to ensure respect for the safeguard measures authorised by the Commission. But it was for the national court to decide whether the additional Italian requirement, to deposit the securities with an agreed bank, was 'indispensable' to prevent infringements of Italian laws and regulations. The strong implication in the judgment of the Court was that the additional condition was an unnecessary administrative obstacle to 'the fullest liberalisation' of capital movements.

In the *Casati* case[4] the Court raised an issue relating to the question of verification, namely the power of Member States to adopt control measures and to enforce compliance by means of criminal penalties. The Court held that administrative measures or penalties must not go beyond what is strictly necessary and the control procedures must not be accompanied by a penalty which is so disproportionate to the gravity of the offence that it becomes an obstacle to the exercise of freedoms granted by the Treaty. The rule of proportionality could be applicable to control measures taken within the context of Article 5 of the First Directive, but in the instant case the transaction in question had not been liberalised, with the result that the Member States' power to impose penalties for breach of control measures was not restricted.

1 *Supra*, fn. 5, para. 19.2.
2 Case 157/85 *Brugnoni and Ruffinengo v Cassa di Risparmio di Genova e Imperia* [1988] 1 C.M.L.R. 440.
3 O.J. L 8, 10.1.1985 p. 34.
4 *Supra*, fn. 1, para. 19.1.

19.8 Articles 1 and 4 of the present Directive were obviously based on Article 69 of the Treaty which is the decision-making provision for the purposes of the elimination of restrictions on capital movements. Articles 2 and 3 of the Directive, by contrast, are based on Article 70 of the Treaty, which empowers the Council to issue directives for the co-ordination of the exchange policies of Member States in respect of the movement of capital between those States and third countries. Article 2 requires the Member States to notify the Committee of Governors of the Central Banks, the Monetary Committee and the Commission of measures to regulate bank liquidity which have a specific impact on capital transactions carried out by credit institutions with non-residents. Such measures must be confined to what is necessary for the purposes of domestic monetary regulation. Article 3 of the Directive empowers the Commission to authorise the Member States to take protective measures in respect of the capital movements listed in Annex II of the Directive, where short-term capital movements of exceptional magnitude impose severe restraints on foreign exchange markets and lead to serious disturbance in the conduct of a Member State's monetary and exchange rate policies. Annex II lists categories of capital transactions and operations of an essentially speculative nature: operations in securities, in current and deposit accounts, and in unit trusts; short-term loans and credits; and the physical importation and exportation of financial assets. Member States may themselves take the protective measures described above, on grounds of urgency, and the Commission may, after their entry into force, confirm or refuse to confirm the measures in question; Commission decisions under Article 3 can be revoked or amended by the Council acting by a qualified majority; but protective measures taken pursuant to this provision cannot exceed 6 months in duration.

Articles 2 and 3 of Directive 88/361 replace Council Directive (EEC) 72/156[1] on the regulation of international capital flows and neutralising their undesirable effects on domestic liquidity. The latter Directive was based on Articles 70(1) and 103 of the Treaty, and was adopted at the height of the turbulence in European capital markets in the early 1970s when exceptionally large speculative capital movements played havoc with the exchange markets of the Member States. The Directive obliged the Member States to have available monetary instruments to deal swiftly with:

(i) investment on the money market and payment of interest on deposits by non-residents, and the regulation of loans and credits not related to commercial transactions; and

(ii) the regulation of the net external position of credit institutions, and the fixing of minimum reserve ratios for holdings of non-residents.

It will be noted that the current Directive gives the Commission a much stronger role, although its new decision-making power may be overriden by the Council; likewise, where the Member States retain freedom of action, the scope of their discretion has been reduced considerably.

Article 70 of the Treaty is also the legal basis for Article 7 of the present Directive. Paragraph (1) of Article 7 introduces a novel concept in that the Member States have agreed to endeavour to attain the same liberalisation, in the treatment of capital transfers to or from third countries, as applies to capital movements between residents within the Community. Although it is aspirational in tone it is clear that the degree of liberalisation of capital movements aspired to by the present Directive is considerably wider than under the First and Second Directives.

However, if large-scale short-term capital movements seriously disturb the domestic or external financial situation of one or more Member States or cause strain in the exchange relationships in the Community or with third countries, the Member States may consult with one another, in the context of the Committee of Governors of Central Banks and the Monetary Committee, as to what measures should be taken to counteract the difficulties. By contrast with the powers its possesses concerning intra-Community speculative capital movements under Article 3 of the Directive, Article 7(2) gives the Commission only a consultative role where disturbances in capital markets involve third countries.

1 O.J. (Sp. Ed.) 1972 (I) p. 296.

19.9   Article 1 of the Directive requires the abolition of all restrictions on capital movements between residents of Member States, and the Member States are obliged to comply with this obligation by 1 July, 1990 at the latest. There are no exceptions to this requirement, but the full application of the Directive is subject to a transitional regime for some of the Member States with weaker economies. The Directive does not affect the provisions of the third Act of Accession, which dealt with the application to Spain and

Portugal of the provisions on the free movement of capital: Article 5. Moreover, the Iberian countries, along with Greece and Ireland, are permitted to continue to apply or to re-introduce certain restrictions on capital movements, and to defer liberalisation of others which are set out in Lists III and IV respectively of Annex IV of the Directive. In both cases the deferment of the application of the Directive applies until 31 December, 1992; however, in the event that Portugal and Greece experience balance of payments difficulties, Article 6(2) envisages an extension for up to 3 years. Lists III and IV of Annex IV refer to capital movements often associated with speculative transactions: List III concerns operations in securities dealt in on the capital market, operations in unit trusts, and medium and long-term financial loans and credits; List IV refers to operations in securities and other instruments normally dealt with on the money markets, operations in current and deposit accounts, short-term financial loans and credits, personal loans and the physical importation and exportation of financial assets.

Article 6 contains two other provisions of note: national restrictions on the purchase of a second residence may be maintained until the Council adopts the necessary rules (paragraph (4)); and the Council and Commission are obliged by paragraph (5) to introduce measures designed to reduce distortion and tax evasion arising from the diversity of national systems for the taxation of savings.

19.10 The requirement in Article 67(1) of the Treaty to abolish restrictions on the movement of capital is the principal provision in the chapter on capital, but there are other subsidiary rules which will now be examined briefly.

Article 67(2) required current payment connected with the movement of capital to be freed from all restrictions by the end of the First Stage at the latest. Examples of current payments connected with capital movements would include banking commissions and charges, interest charges, and rent. In *Luisi and Carbone*[1] the Court confirmed what is stated clearly enough in Articles 67(2) and 106(1), namely that such current payments are not to be considered as capital transactions. By analogy with the decision in *Luisi and Carbone*, Article 67(2) is almost certainly directly effective, although there has been no specific statement to this effect. Article 68(1) requires the Member States to be as liberal as possible in granting such exchange control authorisations as are still necessary after the entry into force of the Treaty. As in the case of Article 71 (the 'standstill provision') the language of this clause is aspirational only and does not impose a directly effective obligation on the Member States. On the other hand, Article 68(2) is directly effective:[2] the Member States are obliged to act in a non-discriminatory manner when applying domestic rules governing the capital market and the credit system to movements of capital which have been liberalised. Article 68(3) restricts the granting of loans to local or regional authorities or to the central government of a Member State; such loans can only be issued or placed in another Member State with the agreement of both Member States concerned.

1 *Supra*, fn. 5, para. 19.2.
2 Ress, *op. cit.* fn. 2, para 19.2, at p. 321.

19.11 In the *Casati* case the Court of Justice observed that capital movements were closely connected with the economic and monetary policy of the Member States.[1] It is not surprising, therefore, that the Treaty contains a number of 'escape clauses' which permit the Member States to derogate from the liberalisation requirements in certain concrete cases in order to overcome economic difficulties.[2] In respect of capital movements there are two sets of escape clauses which can be utilised. Article 73(1) permits the Commission, having consulted the Monetary Committee, to authorise a Member State to take preventive measures in the field of capital movements where such movements lead to disturbances in the capital market of that Member State. The Council can revoke or amend the authorisation given by the Commission. Article 73(2) permits a Member State in difficulties, on grounds of secrecy or urgency, to act on its own initiative but the Commission may decide that the State concerned shall amend or abolish the measures. It will be noted that the protective measures under Article 73 apply only in respect of disturbances caused by capital movements. By contrast, Article 108 applies where a Member State is in difficulties as regards its balance of payments, either because of an overall disequilibrium in its balance of payments or because of the currency at its disposal; the Commission may then state what measures the Member State can take. If the measures taken do not have the appropriate effect the Commission can recommend to the Council the granting of mutual assistance to overcome the difficulties. If the measures of mutual assistance are not granted by the Council acting under Article 108(2), or are insufficient to deal with the problem, the Commission may, acting under Article 108(3), authorise the State in difficulties to take protective measures the terms of which the Commission shall determine.

Article 109 authorises the Member States to take protective measures where a sudden crisis in the balance of payments occurs, and where mutual assistance measures are not immediately forthcoming; the Commission and other Member States must be informed not later than the time of entry into force of the protective measures, and the Council may, at a later stage, decide that the Member State concerned shall amend, suspend or abolish the crisis protective measures.

The escape clause in Article 73 has been utilised far less frequently than Article 108; in fact it was first used only in 1979, when Denmark introduced protective measures prohibiting the sale of Government bonds to non-residents.[3] The alternative—Article 108—has been resorted to much more frequently[4] because it has proved to be 'an equally effective and more attractive option'; it can be used to deal with balance of payments problems *and* capital disturbances.[5] Ireland has utilised the procedure set out in Article 108(3) on at least four occasions to restrict the purchase by Irish residents of foreign securities,[6] and the validity of one of the Commission Decisions was the subject matter of legal proceedings in Court of Justice following a reference under Article 177 from the Circuit Court.[7] The issue was not novel. In *Brugnoni and Ruffinengo*[8] the plaintiffs in the domestic proceedings argued that national measures taken pursuant to a Commission Decision under Article 108(3), which authorised Italy to maintain restrictive measures in respect of purchases of foreign securities, were contrary to Articles 67 and 68 of the Treaty because the transactions in question fell into a category which had been completely liberalised. The Court did not answer this allegation directly. It considered it sufficient to demonstrate that the disputed Commission Decision applied in point of time to the Italian protective measures. The plaintiffs also complained that the consultation procedure in Article 73 had not been followed but the Court held that that procedure did not apply to decisions and measures adopted by the Member States or by the Commission pursuant to Article 108. From this we may conclude that protective measures taken under Article 108 are capable of suspending movements of capital which fall under Articles 67 to 73, including transactions which have been completely liberalised.

A final observation on the escape clauses concerns a dictum in the *Luisi and Carbone* case: the Court stated that Articles 108 and 109, which remain operative even after the free movement of capital has been fully achieved, relate only to periods of crisis.[9] It would appear that the phrase 'periods of crisis' is given a wide interpretation: Italian measures restricting the purchase by residents of foreign securities were in force pursuant to a succession of Commission Decisions from 1974 to 1987, and Ireland has maintained similar restrictions since 1978. The Commission would now appear to accept the need to apply the safeguard clauses in a more discriminating manner. In its White Paper on the Completion of the Internal Market the Commission argued that Articles 70(1) and 108(3) should be used in future for limited periods only, should be subject to continual review and should not be used in respect of speculative short term movements of capital.[10]

1 *Supra*, fn. 1, para. 19.1.
2 Martin Seidel, *Escape clauses in European Community law with special reference to capital movements*, 15 C.M.L. Rev. (1978) 283.
3 Prout, at para. 17.21.
4 Seidel, *op. cit.* fn. 2, para. 19.7, at p. 286.
5 Prout, at 17.21.
6 Commission Decision (EEC) 78/153 O.J. L 45, 16.2.1978 p. 29; Unpublished Commission Decision of 3 December 1980; Commission Decision (EEC) 85/15 O.J. L 8, 10.1.1985 p. 32; Commission Decision (EEC) 87/150 O.J. L 63, 6.3.1987 p. 34; Commission Decision (EEC) 88/12 O.J. L 5, 8.1.1988 p. 39.
7 *East v Cuddy and Cuddy* (11 November 1985, unreported), Circuit Court, Sheehy J.
8 *Supra*, fn. 2, para. 19.7.
9 *Supra*, fn. 5, para. 19.2, at pp. 406 and 80 respectively.
10 Luxembourg, June 1985, at para. 128.

Capital movements, current payments and Accession

19.12 Title V of Part Four of the First Act of Accession contains the transitional measures which applied to capital movements involving Denmark, Ireland and the United Kingdom. Articles 120 to 126 laid down the conditions under which the New Member States were permitted to depart from the pre-Accession Community rules on the liberalisation of capital movements. Article 122, in particular, enabled Ireland to defer for up to two years the liberalisation of direct investment in other Member States by Irish residents; to defer for two and a half years liberalisation of restrictions on (i) exportation of capital by emigrants and (ii) dowries, gifts and succession duties; and to defer for up to five years liberalisation of the operations set out in List B of the Directives.[1]

Similar postponements of capital liberalisation requirements were negotiated for Greece, Spain and Portugal in the second and third enlargements of the Community. In *EC Commission v Greece*[2] the effect of Article 52 of the Second Act of Accession was considered by the Court of Justice. Article 52 required blocked funds owned by residents of other Member States to be progressively abolished by 1 January, 1986. The Greek government argued that Article 52 required the release of funds blocked in Greece belonging to residents of other Member States solely so that they could be used in Greece and not transferred out of the country. The Court dismissed this argument: it held that Article 52 was contained in a section of the Act of Accession entitled 'Capital Movements'. The Article had to be interpreted as referring to the release of the funds at issue not merely in order to permit their use in Greece but also their transfer out of the country since the mere fact of being able to use them freely within the country did not imply any capital movement between the Member States.

In the Third Act of Accession the deferments applicable to Spain were contained in Articles 61 to 66; Articles 222 to 232 laid down a more extensive body of derogations in favour of Portugal in respect of both capital movements and invisible transactions. Articles 5 and 6 of Directive 88/361 preserve these derogations in favour of Spain and Portugal.

1 See J.P. Puissochet, *The Enlargement of the European Communities*, Leiden 1975, at pp. 307–14.
2 Case 194/84 O.J. C 352, 30.12.1987 p. 4.

Capital movements and current payments in Irish law

19.13 In Ireland capital movements and current payments are regulated to a great extent by the Exchange Control Acts, 1954 to 1986, and the regulatory powers conferred by that legislation are exercised by the Central Bank. Exchange Control, as an aspect of economic law, became a feature of the Irish legal landscape at the outbreak of the Second World War. The Emergency Powers Act, 1939 enabled the Government to exercise extraordinary powers for the purposes of the state of emergency as defined in Article 28.3 of the Constitution, and a series of Emergency Powers Orders over the following two years set up the first system of exchange control. The functions exercised by the Department of Finance under these Orders included the power to restrict payments abroad, to control the acquisition of securities, to compel residents to sell their dollar balances to the Minister for Finance, and to oblige exporters to demonstrate that they would receive effective payment that would serve to increase Irish foreign exchange resources.[1] At the end of the War the Emergency Powers Act was superseded by the Supplies and Services (Temporary Provisions) Act, 1946. The Exchange Control Order of 1947,[2] adopted under the 1946 Act, consolidated the various Emergency Powers Orders into a coherent body of rules on exchange control.[3] The Supply and Services (Temporary Provisions) Act, 1946, had to be continued in force on an annual or biannual basis and this legislative feature has been retained in the present legislation. Section 2(2) of the Exchange Control (Continuance) Act, 1986 provides that the Act shall continue in force until 31 December 1990, when it will expire. In other words, the basic legislation of 1954 and 1978 (when a number of important amendments took place) must be confirmed in force every four years.

Unders section 28 of the 1954 Act the Minister for Finance was permitted to delegate any of his powers under the Act (other than the power to make any order or regulations); this power of delegation was exercised in an unpublished letter dated 26 April 1965 in which the Minister's functions under the Act were transferred to the Central Bank. The 1954 Act imposed restrictions on dealings in gold and foreign currencies (section 4), on payments to persons resident outside the 'scheduled territories' (sections 5, 6 and 7), on transactions in securities involving non-residents and on the importation and exportation of other financial assets (sections 8 to 16). Also the exportation of goods from the State was prohibited unless the Revenue Commissioners were satisfied that payment had been or would be made, and that the payment represented an adequate return for the goods (section 17). Most of the prohibitions or restrictions in the Act may be waived or made subject to conditions (section 25); in virtually all of the substantive provisions the restriction is phrased so as to prohibit transactions '. . . except with the permission of the Minister'. Because most of the restricted transactions take place through the agency of banks their cooperation is required; thus, they are permitted to engage in many of the restricted transactions as 'authorised dealers', subject to directions from the Minister—now the Central Bank (section 26). Until 1978 may of the restrictions imposed by the 1954 Act applied in a modified form to 'the scheduled territories'. This was an oblique reference to the 'sterling area' which was the name applicable to the group of countries which cooperated in financial and monetary policies, held their foreign balances in London, and (in some cases) directly linked their currencies with sterling.[4] When the European Monetary System (EMS) was being established in 1978, the Minister for Finance was empowered by section 3(1) of the Exchange Control (Continuance and Amendment) Act, 1978 to amend the definition of 'the scheduled territories' in the 1954 Act. When it became clear that the United Kingdom would not participate in the EMS the definition was changed so that 'the scheduled territories' means the State only. In this way the link with sterling was broken.

The day to day administration of exchange control is carried out by the Central Bank; the rules are summarised in Exchange Control Notices issued periodically by the Central Bank and consolidated in an Exchange Control Manual. The Exchange Control Notices, particularly EX 15 on capital movements between Ireland and other EEC countries, are examined *infra* at 19.17 and 19.18.

1 G.P.S. Hogan, 'The Administration of Exchange Control in Ireland'; in F.C. King (Ed.), *Public Administration in Ireland*, Vol. III, Dublin, 195. At p. 117.
2 S.R. & O. No. 349 of 1947.
3 G.P.S. Hogan, *op. cit*. fn. 1, at p. 117.
4 *Idem*, at p. 115.

19.14 Another important statute affecting capital movements and current payments is the Bretton Woods Agreements Act, 1957—as amended.[1] The purpose of the Act was to authorise the acceptance of the Agreements establishing the International Monetary Fund and the World Bank. Approval of acceptance was necessary because the agreements involved charges upon public funds within the meaning of Article 29.5.3 of the Constitution. Section 2 of Article VIII of the Fund Agreement reads as follows:

'Avoidance of restrictions on Current Payments.

(a) Subject to the provisions of Article VIII, Section 3(b) and Article XIV, Section 2, no member shall, without the approval of the Fund, impose restrictions on the making of payments and transfers for current international transactions.

(b) Exchange contracts which involve the currency of any member and which are contrary to the exchange control regulations of that member maintained or imposed consistently with this agreement shall be unenforceable in the territories of any member. In addition, members may, by mutual accord, cooperate in measures for the purpose of making the exchange control regulations of either member more effective, provided that such measures and regulations are consistent with this agreement.'

Article XIX(i) of the Fund Agreement defines 'payments for current transactions' as:

'. . . payments which are not for the purposes of transferring capital, and includes, without limitation:

(1) All payments due in connection with foreign trade, other current business, including services, and normal short-term banking and credit facilities;

(2) Payment due on interest on loans and on net income from other investments;

(3) Payments of moderate amount for amortisation of loans or for depreciation of direct investments;

(4) Moderate remittances for family living expenses.'

A number of important consequences in Irish law flow from paragraphs (a) and (b) above: the first noteworthy feature concerns current payments and the second concerns the enforceability of contracts that contravene exchange control laws.

As regards current payments, the State accepted the obligations arising out of paragraph (a) of section 2 of Article VIII in February, 1961.[2] Up to this point in time, the State had operated restrictions on payments and transfers under the transitional provisions of Article XIV, Section 2 of the Fund Agreement. Article VIII, therefore, governs transactions concluded with residents of non-Member States. Article 106 of the EEC Treaty (and in limited circumstances, Article 67(2)) applies to current transfers within the Community. Attention might also be drawn to Article XIX(i) of the Fund Agreement which defines 'payments for current transactions'. It is not at all dissimilar to the formula employed by the Court of Justice to distinguish between capital and current payments in the *Luisi and Carbone* case (*supra*, fn. 5, para. 19.2).

As regards the enforceability of contracts in breach of exchange control requirements (paragraph (b) of Section 2 of Article VIII), section 3(8)(c) of the Bretton Woods Agreements Act, 1957 provides that the first sentence of paragraph (b) has the force of law in the State. This is most important because although section 20 of the Exchange Control Act, 1954 provided that contraventions of the Act are criminal offences, no civil consequences were expressed. That omission was remedied by the incorporation into domestic law of the IMF obligation. There have been no cases in Ireland on the effect of Article VIII, Section 2(b) of the Fund Agreement, but in England a 'blue pencil' rule has been applied. In *United City Merchants (Investments) Ltd v Royal Bank of Canada*[3] the Court of Appeal severed that portion of a contract tainted by Exchange Control infringements from the valid commercial transaction. However, there are conflicting decisions of the Court of Appeal as to the meaning of 'exchange contracts' for the purposes of Article VIII(2)(b).[4]

1 Bretton Woods Agreements (Amendment) Act, 1969.
2 Press release issued by the International Monetary Fund, February 1961.
3 [1982] Q.B. 208.
4 *Sharif v Azad* [1969] 1 Q.B. 605; *Wilson, Smithett and Cope Ltd v Terruzzi* [1976] Q.B. 683. For a critical discussion of these cases see Michael Forde, *Contracts that contravene Exchange Control*, G.I.L.S.I. March 1986, pp. 52–8.

19.15 In the 1950s the purposes of exchange control were described as follows:

– it can either alone, or in conjunction with physical controls over the movement of goods, be used to regulate the country's balance of payments, either generally, or in relation to particular countries or monetary areas;
– it can ensure that foreign currencies or securities payable in such currencies which are in private ownership will be mobilised and controlled for State purposes;
– it can enable the State to choose the objects on which foreign exchange, and, particularly, hard currencies, will be spent;
– it can prevent a flight of capital from a country in economic distress and provide a weapon whereby forces threatening the value and stability of a country's currency as a means of exchange abroad can be opposed.[1]

In the present day some or all of these objectives are pursued by the State in the Exchange Control rules administered by the Central Bank. These rules are contained in nineteen Exchange Control Notices, a list of which is annexed to this Chapter as Appendix 2. The Notices are updated periodically and are collected in an Exchange Control Manual published by the Central Bank. The most recent changes took place on 1 January 1988. Apart from raising the general level of Exchange Control allowances, new Notices were issued for travel (EX 9) and emigration (EX 10) and an entirely new Notice (EX 19) was issued entitled 'Purchase of foreign securities, individual private investor's allowance—1988'.

An examination of the Notices shows that their principal concerns are to safeguard the national external reserves and to regulate the effects of capital movements on exchange rates. As regards the former concern, limits are placed on the amounts of foreign exchange held outside the national reserves;[3] accordingly, current payments are supervised while capital movements are restricted;[4] residents are required not to withhold funds accruing from external sources from the external reserves;[5] and external investment is permitted provided it will benefit the economy by increased foreign currency earnings.[6] The effects of capital movements on the exchange rate are regulated by ensuring that no unauthorised exportations of capital take place;[7] in respect of trade, residents are obliged to repatriate foreign currency receipts and to convert them to Irish pounds as soon as possible;[8] while unauthorised movements of capital are restricted, genuine personal movements are liberalised;[9] at the same time, limits are placed on non-essential outflows of capital.[10]

In respect of many of the controlled transactions specific permission is required from the Central Bank.[11] But a variety of permitted exchange transactions can be carried out by licensed banks, who are described for this purpose as Authorised Dealers.[12] A limited number of transactions can take place through the medium of approved Agents,[13] defined as licensed banks, members of the Stock Exchange-Irish, or solicitors. Travel agents and building societies, licensed by the Central Bank, may provide foreign exchange facilities for travel purposes;[14] likewise, limited types of insurance business involving foreign currency payments can be transacted by Authorised Insurers.[15]

The general criterion for the application of the Exchange Control Notices is residence and not nationality. It has been noted above (at 19.6) that, for the purposes of Community law, residence is defined in accordance with the rules and regulations in force in the Member States. In Ireland residential status for exchange control purposes may differ from that applicable for tax purposes; persons are considered to be resident if they have been living in the State for at least three years. Recent arrivals intending to live in the State indefinitely are also considered to be residents.[16] Dual residence for exchange control purposes is not permitted.[17] Any firm operating in the State—whether as a registered company, branch or partnership—is regarded as resident in Ireland even if it is not controlled by persons resident in the State.[8] Cases of doubt must be referred to the Central Bank for decision.[19]

The Exchange Control Notices are often described incorrectly as 'regulations'—even by the Central Bank itself.[20] Only the Minister for Finance is empowered by the Exchange Control Act, 1954 to make regulations and section 24 of the Act expressly states that this power cannot be delegated by him. His ministerial functions can, and have been delegated but the legality and scope of that delegation can be reviewed by the Courts.[21] Similarly, the exercise by the Central Bank of delegated functions is subject to review, for instance to determine whether the duty to act fairly and judicially in accordance with the principles of natural justice is being observed.[22]

Finally, it is clear that the entire corpus of Exchange Control Notices will have to be reviewed to take account of Directive 88/361. This review should also permit the Central Bank to eliminate a number of glaring inconsistencies between the domestic requirements, as set out in the Notices, and the original Directives.

1 G.P.S. Hogan, *op. cit.* fn. 1, para. 19.13, at p. 112.
2 These changes were summarised in a press release issued by the Exchange Control Department of The Central Bank on 16 November 1987.
3 Notice EX 3, at point 2.
4 Notice EX 5, at point 1.
5 Notice EX 7, at point 1.
6 Notice EX 14, at point 1.
7 Notice EX 4, at point 3.
8 Notice EX 4, at point 2.
9 Notice EX 8, at point 2.
10 Notice EX 12, at point 2.
11 For example, dealings in gold. Notice EX 4, at points 65–70.
12 Notice EX 2, at point 2.
13 Notice EX 2, at point 3; Notices EX 5 and EX 6.
14 Notice EX 9, at points 26–29.
15 Notice EX 18, at points 28–30.
16 Notice EX 7, at point 9.
17 Notice EX 7, at point 12.
18 Notice EX 7, at point 8.
19 Notice EX 7, at point 11.
20 See, for example, Notice EX 8, at point 5.
21 *Cityview Press v An Chomhairle Oiliuna* [1980] I.R. 381.
22 *East Donegal Co-operative Livestock Mart v A-G* [1970] I.R. 317.

19.16 Exchange Control Notice EX 15, which deals with Capital movements between Ireland and other EEC Member States, was the means by which the State claimed compliance with the obligations imposed by the original Directives:

'The liberalisations introduced to date are set out in this Notice. Although prior reference must still be made to the Central Bank of Ireland in relation to liberalised transactions, the regulations [*sic*] are now supervisory rather than restrictive'[1]

This was quite misleading: the liberalised payments and transactions described in the Notice concern inward and outward direct investment, securities issued by 'EEC' Institutions (including ECSC and Euratom securities), payments by residents taking up permanent or temporary residence elsewhere in the European Communities, purchase of property for personal use in the EEC, Gifts, Endowments and Dowries, and Succession duties. A quick comparison with List A of the original Directives shows that there were other fully liberalised capital movements which were not mentioned. For example: transfers in performance of insurance contracts; sureties; and authors' royalties. Operations in securities, also in List A, were the subject matter of a Commission Decision under Article 108(3) and are discussed below (at 19.17).

The liberalised capital movements mentioned in the Notice were stated to be subject to an application '. . . which the Central Bank will approve . . .'. This formula was compatible with Article 1(1) of the First Directive (*supra*, para. 19.7), and it allowed the State to verify the genuineness of transactions. But compatibility with the Directive did not extend to the condition imposed on residents who own or acquire firms in other EEC Member States to repatriate a substantial proportion of such firms' profits in order to benefit the national reserves. No such condition is authorised by Community law.

This was not the only irregularity in the Exchange Control Notices. As noted above, notice EX 15 lists only some of the completely liberalised transactions referred to in List A of the capital Directives. Certain omitted transactions are dealt with in other Notices but only in the overall context of exchange control. Where reference was made in these Notices to EEC liberalisation requirements it was frequently misleading, and there were a number of instances where restrictions were applied that were in breach of Community law.

A clear and unambiguous infringement of Article 1(1) of the First Directive appeared in Notice EX 13 concerning royalty, licensing and other similar agreements: *prior* permission to enter such agreements with non-residents was required; permission would be granted if the terms of the agreement were *acceptable* to the Central Bank.[2] Royalty agreements appeared as a List A capital movement, in respect of which the State was obliged to grant authorisation.

The examples cited above concern capital movements. Although reference is made in Notice EX 1 to the acceptance by the State in February, 1961 of the obligations of article VIII of the IMF Agreement in respect of current payments,[3] no reference is made to the current payment obligations arising out the EEC Treaty and Article 106 in particular. It will be recalled that in *Luisi and Carbone* the Court of Justice held that restrictions on payments for services had been abolished as from the end of the transitional period (*supra*, para. 19.2). Although Member States may verify whether transfers are genuinely connected with liberalised payments, controls introduced for that purpose may not limit such payments to a specific amount for each transaction or for a given period; but flat-rate limits, below which no verification is carried out, are permissible.[4] In this connection two Notices are of dubious legality in that they fail to distinguish between current payments connected with the Community and current payments to residents of non-Member States. Even in its recently amended form, Notice EX 9 imposes limits upon specific amounts and for given periods in respect of travel for tourism, business, health and educational purposes.[5] Notice EX 11 imposes similar restraints on miscellaneous payments including trade fair expenses, machinery hiring charges, and salary allowances to residents or non-residents.[6]

1 Notice EX 15, at point 2.
2 At points 28–30.
3 At point 11.
4 *Supra*, fn. 5, para. 19.2, at pp. 407 and 81 respectively.
5 At point 16.
6 At points 9, 10, 18 and 19.

19.17 From 1978 onwards Ireland was authorised by the Commission under Article 108(3) of the Treaty, to impose restrictions by way of derogation from the Directives. The latest in a series of such authorisations was Commission Decision (EEC) 85/15[1] (as amended by Commission Decisions (EEC) 87/150 and 88/12).[2] In respect of operations in securities (a List A transaction) it permitted the State to prohibit or to make subject to authorisation the acquisition by residents of foreign securities, *or of domestic securities issued on a foreign market* (emphasis added).

In *East v Cuddy and Cuddy*[3] the validity of an earlier unpublished decision of 3 December 1980 was called into question and the Court of Justice was also asked to rule on direct effectiveness of Article 2(1) of the First Directive. Article 2(1) has now been repealed, but it obliged Member States to give general permission for transactions appearing on the 'old' List B. These questions arose in proceedings for non-payment by the defendants of their account with the plaintiffs, a firm of London stockbrokers. The latter had bought and sold, on behalf of the defendants, shares in companies registered in Ireland and quoted on the Stock Exchange in London. The defendants pleaded that the transactions were unenforceable because they were in breach of exchange control rules. The Commission Decision of 1980 empowered Ireland to prohibit dealings in foreign securities dealt with on a Stock Exchange. The issue, as formulated in the questions referred to Luxembourg, turned on whether the transactions in question fell under the 1980 Decision. If they did, and if the Decision was valid, did the Decision suspend the liberalisation requirement in Article 2(1) of the First Directive? Was Article 2(1) directly effective?

The Court, however, looked at the issue from a different perspective. It noted that the liberalisation requirements of Article 2(1) of the Council Directive of 1960 applied to 'acquisitions by residents of foreign securities' whereas the contested transaction involved the purchase of domestic securities on a foreign stock exchange; such transactions were not covered by the Directives at the time when the events giving rise to the main proceedings took place and, accordingly, the Irish Government continued to have the power to regulate them.[4] It might be added that even if the Court had looked at the question of the validity of the decision addressed to Ireland under Article 108, the plaintiffs were unlikely to benefit from such an examination; the Commission Decision of 1980 was virtually identical to the Decision at issue in *Brugnoni and Ruffinengo*, in respect of which the Court found no invalidating factor (*supra* 19.12).

Finally, it should be noted that a significant liberalisation of the existing restrictions on the purchase of foreign and domestic securities by Irish residents took place on 1 January 1988 when the new Scheme of allowances announced by the Central Bank came into effect. As regards foreign securities, individual private investors may invest up to £5,000 in foreign securities during 1988 but the outflows under the Scheme are subject to an overall national limit of £30m in 1988. In addition, the Scheme does not apply to the acquisition by residents of domestic securities issued outside the State or to American Depository Receipts of resident companies; such securities may now be freely acquired by conversion from Irish Pounds.[5]

1 *Supra*, n. 6, para. 19.11.
2 *Idem*.
3 (11 November 1985, unreported) Circuit Court, Sheehy J.
4 Case 143/86, *East v Cuddy and Cuddy*, O.J. C 63, 8.3.1988 p. 6.
5 Notice EX 19, issued 1 January 1988.

Appendix 1

Nomenclture of the Capital Movements referred to in Article 1 of the Directive

I — Direct Investments
II — Investments in real estate
III — Operations in securities normally dealt in on the capital market
IV — Operations in units of collective investment undertakings
V — Operations in securities and other instruments normally dealt in on the money market
VI — Operations in current and deposit accounts with financial institutions
VII — Credits related to commercial transactions or to the provision of services in which a resident is participating
VIII — Financial loans and credits
IX — Sureties, other guarantees and rights of pledge
X — Transfers in performance of insurance contracts
XI — Personal capital movements
XII — Physical import and export of financial assets
XIII — Other capital movements

Appendix 2

Exchange Control Notices

EX 1   Introduction to Exchange Control
EX 2   Definitions
EX 3   Dealings in Foreign Currency
EX 4   Imports, Exports, Trade Financing, Dealings in Gold
EX 5   Irish quoted securities
EX 6   Foreign currency securities
EX 7   Accounts of non-residents
EX 8   Estates, intestacies, Settlements Inter Vivos and Gifts
EX 9   Travel
EX 10   Emigration
EX 11   Miscellaneous payments
EX 12   Purchase of property for personal use outside the State
EX 13   Direct investment in Ireland
EX 14   Outward direct investment
EX 15   Capital Movements between Ireland and EEC Member States
EX 16   Rhodesia
EX 17   Persons taking up permanent residence in Ireland
EX 18   Insurance
EX 19   Purchase of foreign securities. Individual private investors allowance—1988

Chapter 20

Approximation or Harmonisation of Laws[1]

Introduction

20.1 It is worth repeating that the creation of the common market involves the establishment of a market where goods, persons, services and capital can move freely. Restrictions which inhibit the movement of these factors must be abolished. Principally this means that laws which Member States use directly to check the flow of these factors must be abandoned. Tariff and quantitative restrictions as well as entry and residence laws, for example, must be scrutinised and amended or abandoned in so far as they prevent the attainment of the common market.

There are other national laws, however, which less obviously prevent the full realisation of the common market and these too may have to be amended by the Member States if the common market is to be fully achieved. Consider the following examples. Manufacturer A in Germany in putting his jam product on the market is obliged to comply with strict German legislation designed to protect the consumer. The standards which he must comply with and the information which he must print on the label on the container may be very detailed. Manufacturer B in Ireland, in contrast, does not have to comply with any such legislation and consequently, he can put up his product more cheaply than his German competitor but he cannot sell his product in Germany because it does not comply with German legislation. Again, it may be that the company law requirements (designed to protect the worker, the creditor and the shareholder) in France are much more demanding (and consequently more troublesome and more expensive to comply with) than the company law requirements in the UK. Or it may be that because the liability of the manufacturer for damage caused by his product is much stricter in France (where strict liability rules prevail) than in Ireland (where negligence must be shown) the French manufacturer has an extra cost to bear over his Irish counterpart. In all these cases we can see that the laws of a country might distort competition and might influence a manufacturer in deciding where he should locate his business. They might also affect free movement in so far as jam manufactured in Ireland may not be allowed onto the German market since it does not comply with German health and safety legislation. In so far as these *legal* requirements may influence *economic* decisions they may distort competition and artificially affect the establishment of a full and free market.

Similar objection could be taken against laws which regulate, in the Member States, entry to trades and professions. Illustratively, one Member State may require a student to complete six years third level education before becoming a doctor whereas other Member States may require only four years' study. If a person who qualifies in one of the latter states wishes to practise medicine in the former state he will be faced immediately with the objection that he does not meet the local standards.

The above examples, simple though they are, should illustrate that the attainment of the common market and the establishment of a fair competition arena may be affected or impeded by national laws of many kinds. If a full and real free movement is to be achieved these differences in the various legal systems must be addressed and must be eliminated at least to the extent that they seriously distort competition and prevent the establishment of the common market. This is essentially what the Community's Harmonisation of Laws Programme attempts to do.[2]

With regard to technical barriers to trade the problems arise in the following way. Articles 30 *et seq.* outlaw quantitative restrictions and measures which have equivalent effect. This of course means that as far as this prohibition is concerned the Community rule applies and no question of harmonisation arises. Article 36, however, as we have seen creates exceptions and allows Member States to derogate from the general rule especially where issues relating to public health and consumer and environmental interests are at stake. In these cases therefore Member States may still have different laws. These laws then provide the focus for the Community's harmonisation programme.

This point is clearly seen from the Commission's statement in the White Paper on Completing the Internal Market at paragraph 77.

'Following the rulings of the Court of Justice, both the European Parliament and the Dooge Committee have stressed the principle that goods lawfully manufactured and marketed in one Member State must be allowed free entry into other Member States. In cases where harmonisation of regulations and standards is not considered essential from either a health/safety or an industrial point of view, immediate and full recognition of differing quality standards, food composition rules, etc. must be the rule. In particular, sales bans cannot be based on the sole argument that an imported product has been manufactured according to specifications which differ from those used in the importing country. There is no obligation on the buyer to prove the equivalence of a product produced according to the rules of the exporting State. Similarly, he must not be required to submit such a product to additional technical tests nor to certification procedures in the importing State. Any purchaser, be he wholesaler, retailer or the final consumer, should have the right to choose his supplier in any part of the Community without restriction. The Commission will use all the powers available under the Treaty, particularly Articles 30–36, to reinforce this principle of mutual recognition.'

1 See generally G. Close, *Harmonization of Laws: Use or Abuse of Powers under the EEC Treaty*, 3 E.L.R. 461 (1978); Editorial Comment, *New Roads for Harmonisation of Legislation*, 17 C.M.L. Rev. 463 (1980); L. Gormley, *Article 100 EEC: New and Proposed Legislation*, 5 E.L.R. 400 (1980); G. Morse, *Harmonisation of Laws, Some Recent Developments*, 2 E.L.R. 373 (1977).

2 It is doubtful if Articles 100 to 102 can be used to influence the *general economic policies* of the Member States such as budgetary policy, monetary policy or the general medium-term plans or programmes adopted by some Governments. See Hans Smit and Peter E. Herzog, *The Law of the European Community* (1982); 3–476.

20.2 It should be immediately pointed out that what is required here is not total unification of the laws of the Member States. It is not necessary that the laws on such matters be identical in all the Member States. All that is required, even in the federalisation process, as we can see from the experience of the USA, is that the gross disparities be eliminated. And this is the principal aim of the Community's programme. This is not to say, however, that in some instances harmonisation may not lead to partial and even almost complete uniformity. But it is not essentially so. All that is required is that the gross legal distortions which would prevent the attainment of the objectives of the Community (i.e. principally the creation of common policies and the achievement of the 'four freedoms' and the attainment of fair competition) should be removed. Apart from promoting the main objectives of the Community, the Harmonisation Programme will also be concerned with advancing other subsidiary objectives such as the promotion of public health (e.g. in regulating pharmaceutical products) public safety (e.g. in insisting on compulsory seat-belt fittings) consumer protection (e.g. in adopting the directive on Products' Liability) and the protection of the environment.

20.3 It is also worth mentioning at this juncture that harmonisation is unnecessary if a directly applicable provision of Community law applies. For example, since the end of the transitional period, Article 52 of the EEC Treaty has been held to be directly applicable and since that date discrimination on the basis of nationality in relation to establishment is prohibited by the Treaty itself. No harmonisation measure, therefore, is required to achieve this. Indeed a directive which purported to do this now would be superfluous.[1] Similarly, if a common policy has been adopted by the Community the national rules are replaced by the Community rules and the question of harmonisation does not arise. Some consequences follow from this. First, harmonisation is a residual remedy which arises only where the Treaty does not make adequate provision for the object to be achieved. Harmonisation, therefore, is not an end in itself but a means of achieving general Community objectives. In this sense it is merely an extension of the Treaty. Second, like many other policies, the powers of the institutions in the area of harmonisation are attributive: before they act in this area the institutions must be able to show a legal basis for their actions.

1 'This means that it is only to the extent that the realization of these goals is hampered directly by differences between the Member States' provisions, whether legislative, regulatory, or administrative, that these differences must be removed or minimized through approximation. The requirement of direct effect thus narrows down somewhat the scope of application of Article 100, and the broad terms used to formulate the approximation requirement cannot imply that the Council has a broad discretionary margin for the issuance of the directives, but must instead be construed as expressing the intent to restrict approximation measures to situations where the conditions of a single market cannot be brought about without them.' CCH, Common Market Reporter, paras. 3302–7.

Legal Bases
General Basis: Article 100

20.4 In part three of the EEC Treaty, Title I Chapter 3 deals with Approximation of Laws. It contains three articles—Articles 100 to 102 and Article 100 in particular provides the Council with the legal authority for most of its harmonisation programme. This Article has been extended now by the SEA through the insertion of new Articles 100A and 100B into the EEC Treaty. The scope of these provisions will be dealt with below.

Specific Bases

20.5 Besides this general authority, however, harmonisation is also permitted more specifically in other articles of the Treaty. For example, Article 54(3)(g) authorises the Council and Commission to coordinate the company laws of the Member States. Other examples of specific authorisations occur, for instance, in Articles 43(2) (Common Agricultural Policy), 49 (free movement of workers), 56 (right of establishment), 57 (mutual recognition of diplomas, certificates), etc. Where such specific authorisation occurs then the institutions may not have to resort to the general provisions contained in Article 100. The better opinion, however, seems to be that the specific authorisation does not preclude resort to the general provision in Article 100 also if the institution feels this is necessary.[1] Indeed in many cases the institutions will cite as the basis for their legal measure both the specific article where appropriate and the general authority contained in Article 100.

1 Hans Smit and Peter E. Herzog, *The Law of the European Community* (1982), 3–471.

Article 220: Related Conventions

20.6 Before examining Article 100 in greater detail reference must also be made to two other articles which can provide a legislative basis for Community action in this area: Articles 220 and 235. Article 220 authorises Member States to enter into negotiations with each other with a view to securing for the benefit of their nationals, (i) national treatment in other Member States, (ii) the abolition of double taxation, (iii) the mutual recognition of companies, the retention of legal personality in the event of a transfer from one country to another and the possibility of mergers between companies in different countries and (iv) the reciprocal recognition and enforcement of judgments.[1] Under this authority the following Conventions have been adopted by the Member States: Convention on the Grant of European Patents; Convention for the European Patent for the Common Market; Convention on Jurisdiction and Enforcement of Judgments in Civil and Commercial Matters; Convention Relating to the Mutual Recognition of Companies and Legal Persons; and Convention on the Law Applicable to Contractual Obligations.

1 The specific authority contained in Article 220 does not, it appears, preclude action under any other provision of the Treaty. See Commission of the European Communities, Bulletin of the European Communities, Supplement 3/85, p. 6, para. 6.

Article 235: Residual Powers

20.7 Article 235 is a residual power given to the Council to cater for the situation where Community progress would be thwarted because, through oversight, no power of action was given to the institutions. The Article provides as follows:

> 'If action by the Community should prove necessary to attain, in the course of the operation of the common market, one of the objectives of the Community and this Treaty has not provided the necessary powers, the Council shall, acting unanimously on a proposal from the Commission and after consulting the Assembly, take the appropriate measures.'

Two points should be noted about this article. First, to bring the Article into operation Community action must be necessary to attain one of the objectives of the Community[1] and the necessary powers must be absent under the Treaty. Second, once these conditions are fulfilled the Council, acting unanimously, is authorised in such circumstances, having observed the stipulated procedure, to take 'the appropriate measures'. This last phrase enables the Council to adopt not only directives but also regulations or other appropriate legislative acts. In this sense Article 235 is wider than Article 100 which, when it operates, only permits the institutions to use directives. Some controversy has arisen as to the relationship between Article 100 and Article 235, in particular as to when resort may be had to Article 235 instead of Article 100. It would appear that if Article 100 is insufficient to achieve the objectives of the Community because, for example, uniformity rather than similarity is required then resort to Article 235 may be justified.[2] In the customs area, for example, Article 235 has been used to justify Regulations which make common provision for (i) the definition of the origin of goods,[3] (ii) the valuation of goods,[4] (iii) the Community export declaration form,[5] (iv) the repayment or remission of import or export duties[6] and (v) the Community transit system.[7] In all these cases it could be conceded that it was necessary to give the rules the character of common provisions which would replace the former national rules.[8] The Court of Justice has more than once recognised the legitimacy of the wide interpretation of Article 235.[9]

---

1 See Commission's answer to Question No. 172/77, O.J. C 180, 28.7.1977 p. 19; Sasse and Yourow, *The Growth of Legislative Power of the European Communities* pp. 95–7.
2 Hans Smit and Peter E. Herzog, *The Law of the European Community* (1982), Vol. 3 at p. 471.
3 Council Regulation (EEC) 802/68 O.J. (Sp. Ed.) 1968 (I) p. 165; last amended by Commission Regulation (EEC) 3860/87 O.J. L 363, 23.12.1987 p. 30.
4 Council Regulation (EEC) 803/68 O.J. (Sp. Ed.) 1968 (I) p. 170; replaced by Regulation (EEC) 1224/80 O.J. L 134, 31.5.1980 p. 1.
5 Council Regulation (EEC) 2102/77 O.J. L 246, 27.9.1977 p. 1; replaced by Regulation (EEC) 1900/85 O.J. L 179, 11.7.1985 p. 4.
6 Council Regulation (EEC) 1430/79 O.J. L 175, 12.7.1979 p. 1; last amended by Regulation (EEC) 3069/86 O.J. L 286, 9.10.1986 p. 1.
7 Council Regulation (EEC) 222/77 O.J. L 38, 9.2.1977 p. 1; last amended by Regulation (EEC) 1674/87 O.J. L 157, 17.6.1987 p. 1.
8 See J. Amphoux, 'Customs Legislation in the EEC', 6 *Journal of World Trade Law* (1972) at 144.
9 See Case 8/73 *Hauptzollamt Bremerhaven v Massey-Ferguson GmbH* [1973] E.C.R. 897.

See also Sasse and Yourow, *op. cit.* 95–7; J. Amphoux, *supra*, 144; A. Tizzano, 'The Powers of the Community' in *Thirty Years of Community Law*, *50 et seq*. See also *supra* Chapter 5.4 for fuller treatment of Article 235.

Articles 100 to 102

20.8 Article 100 is the best known and the most frequently relied on basis for Community action in this area. The Article provides as follows:

'The Council shall, acting unanimously on a proposal from the Commission, issue directives for the approximation of such provisions laid down by law, regulation or administrative action in Member States as directly affect the establishment or functioning of the common market.

The Assembly and the Economic and Social Committee shall be consulted in the case of directives whose implementation would, in one or more Member States, involve the amendment of legislation.'

The Article provides the Community with power to harmonise where measures in the Member States 'directly affect the establishment or functioning of the common market'. The phrase 'common market' is not defined in the Treaty, but in the present context and against the background of the general principles contained in Articles 2 and 3 of the Treaty, the phrase must include (i) the attainment of the four freedoms— free movement of goods, services, persons and capital (ii) the guarantee of free and fair competition conditions and (iii) the attainment of common policies in agriculture, foreign trade and transport. Moreover, the provision that the Article comes into play not only if the establishment of the common market is at issue, but also if the *functioning* of the market is at stake, gives a very wide area of application to the Article. And this wide interpretation is not greatly restricted by the requirement that the market must be 'directly affected' as this phrase must be interpreted flexibly in a way which admits of differences of opinion and which gives the parties a margin of appreciation.

Articles 101 and 102

20.9 Articles 101 and 102 are not much used and only require a brief comment. Article 101 provides that where provisions in the Member States interfere and *distort competition* in the Common Market so that they need to be eliminated the Commission shall consult the Member States. If such consultation does not produce agreement to eliminate the distortions then the Council on a proposal from the Commission may by qualified majority issue the necessary directives. But if necessary the Commission and Council may also take other measures provided for in the Treaty. The vagueness of the word 'distortion' and the difficulty of establishing all the required conditions have meant that Article 101 has been little used to date.[1]

Where there is apprehension that one Member State is about to introduce a measure which will cause a distortion within the meaning of Article 101 then Article 102 provides that such Member State must consult with the Commission. The Commission may issue a recommendation on the matter and if the Member State chooses to ignore it then other Member States will not be subject to the obligation of Article 101 which might otherwise require them to change their laws. If the Member State complies with the recommendation, however, then the other Member States can be subjected to Article 101 and may be obliged to change their laws to eliminate the distortion.

1 See Commission's Answer to Written Question No. 2226/80. O.J. C 257, 29.9.1983 p. 1. Hans Smit and Peter E. Herzog, *The Law of the European Community* (1982), 3–481, 3–482. See also P. Collins and M. Hutchings, *Articles 101 and 102 of the EEC Treaty: Completing the Internal Market.* 11 E.L.R. 191.

20.10 When Article 100 applies, it enables the Council to act only by issuing directives. Until recently the directive was seen to be the most appropriate instrument to achieve harmonisation. It fixed the targets to be achieved, as well as a deadline, and it left to each Member State the choice of the means by which the targets could best be attained within its own legal context and tradition.[1] It was sometimes felt that the Regulation might be a more effective instrument for harmonisation, but it was not available under Article 100 as it stood in 1986. The SEA in 1987 introduced some important changes in this respect. These are dealt with below.

1 For examples of implementing measures in Ireland see Ireland: *Digest of Legislation* (1978), 3 E.L. Rev. 416–441; (1980) E.L. Rev. 74–79; (1982) 7 E.L. Rev. 422–435; (1987) 12 E.L. Rev. 284–307.

Principal Areas of Harmonisation Efforts

20.11 The principal areas where harmonisation efforts have been most obvious have been in the areas of customs legislation, fiscal legislation, public contracts and in connection with non-tariff obstacles to inter-state trade.[1] In the former several measures have issued dealing with such matters as the definition of the common customs territory,[2] definition of the origin of goods,[3] definition of value of goods for customs purposes.[4] and deferred payment of import duties or export duties.[5]

1 In the Directory of Community Legislation in Force as at 1 June 1988 (11th Edition), the measures adopted are grouped under the following headings and these give a good indication as to the range of topics being harmonised in the EEC: motor vehicles, agricultural and forestry tractors, metrology, electrical material, foodstuffs, colouring matters, preservatives, other provisions, proprietary medicinal products, cosmetics, textiles, dangerous substances, other sectors (miscellaneous).
2 Council Regulation (EEC) 2151/84 O.J. L 197, 27.7.1984 p. 1; amended by Regulation (EEC) 319/85 O.J. L 34, 7.2.1985 p. 32.
3 Council Regulation (EEC) 570/86 O.J. L 56, 1.3.1986 p. 1; replaced by Regulation (EEC) 1135/88 O.J. L 114, 2.5.1988 p. 1.
4 Council Regulation (EEC) 1224/80 O.J. L 134, 31.5.1980 p. 1; last amended by Regulation (EEC) 1055/85 O.J. L 112, 25.4.1985 p. 50.
5 Council Directive (EEC) 78/453 O.J. L 146 2.6.78 p. 19.

20.12 In the matter of non-tariff barriers to state trade, directives have been aimed at eliminating the technical obstacles to trade and the establishment of Community minimum standards.[1] Many of the directives adopted up to 1985 established technical standards (sometimes in great detail) which had to be complied with by the Member States. Once goods complied with these standards—which tended to be the least common standard prevailing in the Member States—the goods were entitled to free circulation within the Community. The directives in the area of technical barriers were of two kinds depending on whether optional or compulsory harmonisation was envisaged. In the former the Member States were not obliged to adopt Community standards. It would have to accept goods coming in from other Member States which complied with the Community standard but it did not have to introduce Community standards for its own manufacturers. If such an approach were adopted by a Member State then it would mean that manufacturers from that State might not be able to avail of the full possibilities of the common market. In the case of compulsory harmonisation the Member States were not given a choice: they had to introduce as law the Community standard as expressed in the directive. Compulsory harmonisation was orginally favoured but it gave way to optional harmonisation in more recent years because experience showed that total harmonisation was not necessary and that Member States should be allowed a margin of discretion to retain national and regional characteristics.

1 As already noted, however, the SEA indicates that such Community standards must now be at a high level of protection where the interest to be protected relates to health, safety, the environment or the consumer and the lowest common denominator approach will no longer suffice.

20.13 With regard to these technical barriers the Commission has recently adopted a new major initiative which has been approved by the Council. This development has been described by the Commission in the following language:

'Technical barriers are technical barriers whether they apply to goods or services and all should be treated on an equal footing. The general thrust of the Commission's approach in this area will be to move away from the concept of harmonisation towards that of mutual recognition and equivalence. But there will be a continuing role for the approximation of Member States' laws and regulations, as laid down in Article 100 of the Treaty. Clearly, action under this Article would be quicker and more effective if the Council were to agree not to allow the unanimity requirement to obstruct progress where it could otherwise be made.'[1]

1 Commission of European Communities, *Completing the Internal Market* (White Paper June 1985) pp. 6–7.

SEA Changes

20.14 With regard to the unanimous requirement in the Council the SEA introduces important changes which must now be addressed.[1] Articles 18 and 19 of the SEA add two new provisions to Article 100 of the EEC Treaty. Arguably, the two new measures, Articles 100A and 100B, are the two most important provisions in the SEA. It should be noted at the outset that both provisions constitute derogations from Article 100. Article 100 empowers the Council to issue directives for the approximation of national legislation or administrative measures which directly affect the establishment and functioning of the common market. In so doing the Council must act unanimously. The new Article 100A(1) will empower the Council, acting by a qualified majority, on a proposal from the Commission and '. . . in cooperation with the European Parliament and the Economic and Social Committee (*sic*) . . .' to adopt 'measures' for the approximation of national rules, regulations, or practices which have as their object the establishment and functioning of the internal market. Initially, this appears to be a significant advance on Article 100 in that unanimity is no longer required in the Council, the European Parliament is more directly involved through the cooperation procedure, and the range of legislative instruments available to the Council is extended beyond the Directive: the more effective and expeditious Regulation can now be utilised. However, two of the Declarations annexed to the SEA qualify somewhat the scope of Article 100A(1). The first Declaration invites the Council to give a prominent place to the 'Advisory Committee' procedure in connection with the Commission's powers of implementation under Article 100A, and the fourth Declaration requires the Commission to use Directives if harmonisation proposals would involve the amendment of legislative provisions in one or more Member States. Further qualifications or limitations appear in the other paragraphs of Article 100A. Paragraph (2) excludes from the scope of paragraph (1) fiscal measures as well as provisions concerning the free movement of persons and the rights and interests of employed persons. Paragraph (3) specifies that the Commission will take as a base a high level of protection in its proposals concerning health, safety, environmental protection and consumer protection. Paragraph (5) allows the Community legislative authority to include an exemption procedure in harmonisation proposals; a safeguard clause may authorise the Member States to take '. . . provisional measures subject to a Community control procedure . . .' for one or more of the non-economic reasons referred to in Article 36. Finally, paragraph (4) provides for another exemption procedure but, in contrast to the safeguard clause referred to in paragraph (5), this exemption will operate in *ex post facto* manner. Where a harmonisation measure has been adopted by a qualified majority and a Member State deems it necessary '. . . to apply national provisions on grounds of major needs referred to in Article 36, or relating to protection of the environment or the working environment, it should notify the Commission of these provisions'. If satisfied that the national measures do not constitute an arbitrary discrimination or a disguised restriction on trade between Member States, the Commission may confirm the measures. But if the Commission or another Member State considers that improper use is being made of the exception, the offending Member State may be brought directly before the Court of Justice in derogation of the infringement procedure laid down in Articles 169 and 170 of the EEC Treaty. This abbreviated form of action against the Member States is similar to the procedure provided for in Article 93(2) of the EEC Treaty.

Article 19 of the SEA introduces the last element of the blueprint for the achievement of the internal market: Article 100B. Under this new clause the Commission must draw up, during 1992, an inventory of measures not yet harmonised and this list must be prepared in sufficient time to permit the Council to take action. The Council, in accordance with the decision making procedure laid down in Article 100A, may decide that the provisions in force in a Member State must be recognised as being equivalent to those applied by another Member State. Article 100B is thus an incentive to the Member States to adopt harmonisation legislation under Article 100A or run the risk of having as many as 12 different systems of technical or administrative requirements validated by default. In such circumstances the lowest standards would prevail. But the usefulness of this threat is diluted by the fifth Declaration annexed to the SEA which notes that Article 8C is of general application and will apply also to proposals under Article 100B. Thus, temporary derogation may be made for Member States experiencing special difficulties.

1 The following text was originally produced in F. Murphy, 'The Single European Act', XX, *The Irish Jurist* (n.s.) 1985 at 246–8.

20.15 In its Second Report to the Council and Parliament on the implementation of the Commission's White Paper on Completing the Internal Market,[1] the Commission notes in exasperation that although the Council has unambiguously expressed its approval and support for the programme, progress is still difficult and it blames the Heads of Government for not ensuring that their administrations translate their own political will into positive tangible results.[2]

1 Commission of European Community, Second Report to the Council and Parliament COM (87) 203 final, paras. 81–88.
2 On the most recent developments and proposals in this area see Twentieth General Report on Activities of the European Communities 1986 p. 91 *et seq*.

Chapter 21

Competition Law

21.1 The two provisions in the EEC Treaty which are most likely to be familiar to Irish lawyers and businessmen are Articles 85 and 86.

Article 85

'(1) The following shall be prohibited as incompatible with the Common Market: all agreements between undertakings, decisions by associations of undertakings and concerted practices which may affect trade between Member States and which have as their object or affect, the prevention, restriction or distortion of competition within the Common Market, and in particular those which:

(a) directly or indirectly fix purchase or selling prices or any other trading conditions;

(b) limit or control production, markets, technical development, or investment;

(c) share markets or sources of supply;

(d) apply dissimilar conditions to equivalent transactions with other trading parties, thereby placing them at a competitive disadvantage;

(e) make the conclusion of contracts subject to acceptance by the other parties of supplementary obligations which, by their nature or according to commercial usage, have no connection with the subject of such contracts.

(2) Any agreements or decisions prohibited pursuant to this Article shall be automatically void.

(3) The provisions of paragraph 1 may, however, be declared inapplicable in the case of

— any agreement or category of agreements between undertakings;
— any decision or category of decisions by associations of undertakings;
— any concerted practice or category of concerted practices;

which contributes to improving the production or distribution of goods or to promoting technical or economic progress, while allowing consumers a fair share of the resulting benefit, and which does not:

(a) impose on the undertakings concerned restrictions which are not indispensable to the attainment of these objectives;

(b) afford such undertakings the possibility of eliminating competition in respect of a substantial part of the products in question.'

413

Article 86

'Any abuse by one or more undertakings of a dominant position within the Common Market or in a substantial part of it shall be prohibited as incompatible with the Common Market insofar as it may affect trade between Member States. Such abuse may, in particular, consist in:

(a) directly or indirectly imposing unfair purchase or selling prices or other unfair trading conditions;
(b) limiting production, markets or technical development to the prejudice of consumers;
(c) applying dissimilar conditions to equivalent transactions with other trading parties thereby placing them at a competitive disadvantage;
(d) making the conclusion of contracts subject to acceptance by other parties of supplementary obligations which, by their nature or according to commercial usage, have no connection with the subject of such contracts.'

21.2 In simple terms Article 85 can be said to apply to restrictive agreements or restrictive practices while Article 86 is concerned with monopolies or, to be precise, firms in a dominant position in the Common Market or a substantial part of it. There are certain clear differences between Articles 85 and 86. Article 85 prohibits restrictive agreements which conflict with the terms of paragraph (1). Any such agreement is automatically void and this introduces to Irish law a new category of void contracts. However, paragraph (3) of Article 85 permits certain agreements, or categories of agreements, to be exempted from the prohibition in paragraph (1) if certain conditions are met. By contrast, Article 86 does not prohibit a dominant position *per se*; it is only the abuse of a dominant position that is prohibited. Secondly, Article 86 makes no provision for contractual nullity or invalidity, largely because the abuse of a dominant position rarely takes the form of contractual restraints. A third distinction between Articles 85 and 86 can be found in the fact that there is no provision for exemption from the prohibition in Article 86.

Despite these differences there are a number of features common to Articles 85 and 86. Both provisions utilise certain common concepts: for example, both measures refer to 'undertakings' and both provisions prohibit behaviour that '. . . may affect trade between Member States.' Secondly, Articles 85 and 86 provide almost identical, but non-conclusive, lists of examples of restrictive practices and abuses of dominant position. Thirdly, the Court of Justice has declared, in *Belgische Radio en Televisie v Sabam and Fonior*,[1] that Articles 85 and 86 produce direct effects in relations between individuals and create rights directly in respect of the individuals concerned which national courts and tribunals must safeguard.

The commercial importance of these two provisions was recognised in the United Kingdom by Lord Denning: in *Application des Gaz v Falks Veritas*,[2] he described Articles 85 and 86 as '. . . part of our law. They create new torts or wrongs . . .'. While it was completely in keeping for Lord Denning to recognise a new remedy and to make it available quickly to litigants, it is open to question whether Articles 85 and 86 actually do create new torts or whether they should be considered as causes of action *sui generis* arising out of the EEC Treaty.

1 Case 127/73 [1974] E.C.R. 51.
2 [1974] Ch 381.

21.3 There is now in existence a large *corpus* of law relating to Articles 85 and 86. Apart from the primary Treaty obligations themselves, there is a significant number of regulations of an implementing nature. Article 87 of the Treaty is the decision-making provision which empowers the Council, acting on a proposal of the Commission, having consulted the Parliament, to adopt Regulations or Directives to give effect to the principles set out in Articles 85 and 86. Paragraph (2) of Article 87 sets out the objectives that implementing Regulations (or Directives) should achieve:

— compliance with the prohibitions in Articles 85(1) and 86 by making provision for fines and periodic penalty payments;
— the elaboration of rules for the application of the exemption provided for in Article 85(3);
— definition of the scope of Articles 85 and 86 in the various branches of the economy; and
— determination of the relationship between national and Community competition rules.

A list of the legislative measures adopted pursuant to Article 87 is contained in Appendix 1.

It would be a mistake, however, to view the development of Community competition rules solely in terms of the Regulations adopted pursuant to Article 87. Since 1962 the Commission has adopted more than 200 Decisions in individual cases and these are considered as persuasive precedents unless, of course, they have been overturned on appeal by the Court of Justice. The judgments of the Court must also be taken into account, and there have been more than 100 rulings on competition law since the first case came before the Court in 1961; another interesting and welcome development is the increasing importance of the judgments of national courts and tribunals on EEC competition law issues. Furthermore, the Commission has from time to time issued Notices and Announcements in which it has outlined certain policy attitudes. By and large these Notices have stated that the Commission did not consider that certain types of contracts or relationships, such as that between a principal and a commercial agent, fell under the prohibition of Article 85(1). None of the Notices or Announcements are legislative instruments and most of them have been issued without prejudice to any interpretation that might be given to them by the Court of Justice. Nevertheless, they constitute an important indication of Commission policy on competition matters. A list of these Notices and Announcements is contained in Appendix 2.

A useful summary of the application of the Community competition rules can be found in the Annual Report on Competition Policy which is produced in conjunction with the Annual General Report on the activities of the Communities presented by the Commission to the Parliament. This series commenced in 1971 and there have been 17 reports since that date.

Finally, European competition law has been the subject of many articles and commentaries in the periodical literature, and a significant number of learned monographs and treatises have been written on the subject.[1]

---

1 D. Barounas, D.F. Hall and James, *EEC Anti-Trust Law* (1975); C. Bellamy and D.G. Child, *Common Market Law of Competition* Third Edition (1987); B.T. Cawthra,

Industrial Property Rights in the EEC Second Edition (1986); T.D.J. Gijlstra and I.D.F. Murphy, *Leading Cases and Materials on the Competition Law of the EEC* Third Edition (1984); V. Korah, *An Introductory Guide to EEC Competition Law* Third Edition (1986); C.J. Kerse, *EEC Anti-Trust Procedure* Second Edition (1987).

Development of competition policy

21.4 The various sources of law discussed above are frequently referred to as 'competition policy'. Three distinct phases can be identified in the development of this policy.

The first phase commenced with the enactment of Regulation 17 of 1962[1] which remains the single most important legislative instrument in the field of competition law. The principal feature of the Regulation is the delegation by the Council to the Commission of significant administrative and quasi-judicial powers. For example, the Regulation empowers the Commission to terminate restrictive practices or abuses of dominant position, to investigate restrictive practices, and to impose fines and periodic penalty payments for infringements of Articles 85 and 86. The Regulation also empowers the Commission to give negative clearances ('a clean bill of health') to agreements and to exempt restrictive practices from the prohibition in Article 85(1) in accordance with the criteria set down in Article 85(3), on application by individual enterprises. The investigative and exemption powers of the Commission gave rise to two further Regulations: Commission Regulation 27 of 1962,[2] on the form and content of applications for exemptions; and Commission Regulation (EEC) 99/63[3] on the procedure to be followed at hearings of investigations into infringements or applications for exemptions.

The implementation of Regulation 17 resulted in a huge number of applications for exemptions and negative clearances; by early 1964 nearly 40,000 agreements had been notified to the Commission. Certain frequently recurring varieties of agreement became apparent: the most common were exclusive distribution agreements, patent licence agreements and specialisation agreements, and a preliminary examination of these agreements showed that while most contained restrictions incompatible with Article 85(1) there were also positive features which complied with the exemption requirements of Article 85(3). Accordingly, the Council adopted two framework or enabling Regulations which empowered the Commission to declare, by means of a Regulation, group or block exemptions for certain types of agreement. Council Regulation 19/65[4] empowered the Commission to create group exemptions for exclusive distribution agreements and patent licence agreements; this led to the adoption of Commission Regulation 67/67[5] on exclusive distribution and purchasing agreements. This Regulation enabled the Commission to dispose of the vast majority of notifications pending before it. A further significant reduction in the backlog of notifications occurred as a result of the implementation of Council Regulation 2821/71[6] which empowered the Commission to adopt group exemption Regulations for specialisation agreements and for research and development cooperation agreements. Commission Regulation 2779/72[7] on specialisation agreements was enacted on this basis.

During this first phase special Regulations were adopted to apply Articles 85 and 86 to the agricultural and transport sectors: Regulation 26 of 1962[8] concerns agriculture and Regulations 1017/68,[9] 1629/69[10] and 1630/69[11] applied the competition rules to transport by road, rail and inland waterway. The final legislative measure passed in the first phase was Regulation 2988/74[12] which subjected the Commission's fining and investigative powers to a limitation period.

The second phase of the development of the Community's competition policy extended from the mid-1970s to the mid-1980s, and this period saw the gradual extension of group or block exemptions under Article 85(3) to more specialised or complex types of restrictive agreement. If we take the Council enabling regulations as our point of departure it can be noted that Regulations 1983/83[13] and 1984/83,[14] on exclusive distribution agreements and exclusive purchasing agreements respectively, replaced Commission Regulation 67/67. Also based on Council Regulation 19/65 were Commission Regulation 2349/84[15] which provides for group exemptions for patent licence agreements, and Regulation 123/85[16] which gives the benefit of a group exemption to motor distribution agreements. Council Regulation 2821/71 now forms the basis for two Commission group exemption Regulations: Regulation 417/85[17] is the specialisation group exemption Regulation (replacing Regulation 2779/72). Regulation 418/85[18] gives the benefit of a group exemption to research and development cooperation agreements.

The third and present phase of the development of competition policy commenced in 1985 and coincided with the presentation of the new Commission's plans for the completion of the internal market by the end of 1992. This period saw the aggressive extension of Commission interest in the services sector, including insurance, banking and commodity trading, as well as the adoption of basic Regulations for the application of the Treaty Rules on competition to the sea transport[19] and air transport[20] sectors.

1 O.J. (Sp. Ed.) 1959–1962, p. 87.
2 O.J. (Sp. Ed.) 1959–1962, p. 132.
3 O.J. (Sp. Ed.) 1963–1964, p. 47.
4 O.J. (Sp. Ed.) 1965–1966, p. 35.
5 O.J. (Sp. Ed.) 1967, p. 70.
6 O.J. (Sp. Ed.) 1971, III, p. 1022.
7 O.J. (Sp. Ed.) 1972 28 Dec – 30 Dec, p. 80.
8 O.J. (Sp. Ed.) 1959–1962, p. 129.
9 O.J. (Sp. Ed.) 1968, O, p. 302.
10 O.J. (Sp. Ed.) 1969, II, p. 371.
11 O.J. (Sp. Ed.) 1969, II, p. 381.
12 O.J. L 319, 29.11.1974.
13 O.J. L 173, 30.6.1983.
14 O.J. L 173, 30.6.1983.
15 O.J. L 219, 26.8.1984.
16 O.J. L 15, 18.1.1985.
17 O.J. L 53, 22.2.1985.
18 O.J. L 53, 22.2.1985.
19 Regulation (EEC) 4056/86, O.J. L. 378, 31.12.1986.
20 Regulation (EEC) 3975/87, O.J. L 374, 31.12.1986; Regulation (EEC) 3976/87, O.J. L 374, 31.12.1987.

Features common to Articles 85 and 86

21.5 Articles 85 and 86 of the Treaty are, in one sense, merely a further elaboration of the objective set out in Article 3 of the Treaty; this provision includes in the activities of the Community

'. . .(f) the institution of a system ensuring that competition in the Common Market is not distorted . . .'

This is not merely a shibboleth devoid of legal effect: in *Europemballage and Continental Can v EC Commission*[1] the Court held that Articles 85 to 90 laid down general rules applicable to undertakings with a view to safeguarding the objectives set out in Articles 2 and 3 of the Treaty which are indispensable for the achievement of the Community's tasks. The competition rules provided for in Article 3(f) and Articles 85 to 90 of the Treaty are concerned mainly, but not exclusively, with undertakings. In *Association des Centres Edouard Leclerc v Au Blé Vert*,[2] which concerned French retail price fixing legislation, the Court held that while Articles 85 and 86 were directly concerned only with the conduct of undertakings and not with the legislative activity of the Member States, the latter were, nonetheless, obliged under the second paragraph of Article 5 not to detract, by means of national legislation, from the full and uniform application of Community competition law or its implementing measures. Articles 2 and 3 of the EEC Treaty set out to establish a market characterised by the free movement of goods where the terms of competition were not distorted; Member States should not jeopardise the attainment of that objective.

Articles 85 and 86 have been declared directly effective by the Court of Justice in *Belgische Radio en Televisie v Sabam and Fonior*.[3] This poses no difficulties as far as Article 85(1) and (2) and Article 86 are concerned. The direct effectiveness of Article 85(3) is more problematical; firstly, it does not comply with the traditional characteristics of a directly effective provision in that while it is clear and precise it is definitely not unconditional and it leaves a considerable margin of discretion to the Commission. Secondly, Article 9(1) of Regulation 17 makes it clear that the Commission has sole power to declare Article 85(1) inapplicable pursuant to Article 85(3) of the Treaty. The logic underlying this particular provision is that the Commission is much better placed than any national court or tribunal to assess, on the basis of the criteria set out in Article 85(3), the pertinent economic and legal factors of agreements which have been notified for exemption. But this does not prevent national courts or tribunals from applying any of the six *group* or *category* Regulations which confer automatic exemptions under Article 85(3) to any agreement complying with their requirements. Whatever about the direct applicability of the entirety of Article 85, it is clear that in the absence of implementing measures for a particular sector, (such as the air and sea transport sectors until very recently), Articles 85 and 86 cannot be considered to be directly effective. In such circumstances, the transitional provisions of Articles 88 and 89 of the Treaty continue to apply, and these permit the national authorities and the Commission to investigate cases of infringements of

Articles 85 and 86. In *Ministère Public v Asjes*[4] the Court held that this system is too fragmentary to ensure a complete application of Article 85 because it distributed the task of applying the Treaty Rules between national authorities and the Commission.

The scope of application of the competition rules in the EEC Treaty is determined partly by Article 227 of the Treaty and partly by the 'effects' doctrine elaborated by the Court of Justice. Article 227 (as amended) defines the scope of application of the Treaty and applies, in general terms, to the territories of the Member States. However, in the so called Dyestuffs decision of 1969[5] the Commission fined a number of enterprises located both inside and outside the Community for participation in a concerted practice the object of which was to share the market in aniline dyestuffs. A number of Swiss and British firms appealed to the Court of Justice for the annulment of this decision on the grounds that it constituted an extra-territorial exercise of jurisdiction; in *ICI v EEC Commission*[6] the plaintiff argued that because its registered office was outside the EEC the Commission was not empowered to impose fines on it in respect of action which was alleged to have taken place outside the Community, but the Court held that the Community did have jurisdiction to penalise the plaintiff because its behaviour had produced effects within the Common Market. This doctrine gave rise to some controversy at the time[7] but neither the Commission nor the Court have departed from it. In fact the Court has recently upheld a Commission decision[8] in which it fined 40 producers of *Woodpulp* located in the United States, Canada, Sweden, Finland, Norway, Portugal and Spain for a concerted practice, extending from 1975 to 1981, with regard to prices for bleached sulphate woodpulp sold within the EEC. This was the first occasion on which the Commission fined a collection of enterprises and trade associations all of whom had their headquarters outside the EEC, while doing business on a regular basis within the EEC.

Moreover, the Commission indicated in its 1985 decision on *Aluminium*[9] that it would apply the competition rules of the Treaty equally to foreign undertaking regardless as to whether they are located in free enterprise nations or in State-trading countries. In this instance Eastern bloc producers of aluminium ingot agreed to channel Eastern bloc aluminium through the hands of a consortium of western producers, thus preventing down-stream competitors from obtaining the benefits of lower-priced metal and removing from western markets a major source of price competition. Finally, as regards the Community's competition law jurisdiction, a number of trade agreements concluded with non-Member States[10] contain clauses similar to Articles 85 and 86. However, in each of these trade agreements the Community made unilateral declarations to the effect that it would assess any practices contrary to the competition clauses on the basis of criteria arising from the application of Articles 85, 86 and 90 of the EEC Treaty; in fact, in decisions involving enterprises from countries with which the Community has such trade agreements, the Commission has never referred to the anti-trust provisions of the relevant agreement; see, for example: *Hugin-Liptons*.[11]

Finally, certain provisions of the Treaty make special provision for particular sectors of the economy. For example, Article 42 makes the application of the competition rule to the agricultural sector subject to a decision by the Council. The competition rules presently applicable to the agricultural sector can be found in Regulation 26 of 1962.[12] In *Ministère Public v Asjes*[13] the Court held that as regards the application of the competition rules to sea and air transport, Article 84(2) served merely to suspend the application of the provisions relating to the Common Transport Policy to sea and air transport pending a Council decision on the subject. In the absence of a special provision like Article 42, on agriculture, the Court decided that the Treaty's competition rules are equally applicable to the air and sea transport sectors.

'Undertakings' Both Articles 85 and 86 refer to 'undertakings' as the description of the participants in a restrictive practice or an abuse of a dominant position. This concept has been given the widest interpretation by the Commission and the Court of Justice. It includes individual traders: in *AOIP–Beyrard*[14] the Commission held that the owner of patents relating to components for electric motors was an undertaking because he had commercially exploited his inventions. In short, commercial participation in the marketplace is the sole criterion for classification as an 'undertaking' for the purposes of Articles 85 and 86, but it goes without saying that the vast majority of 'undertakings' are companies and other legal persons.

However, the notion of 'undertakings' does not include entities owned or controlled by a parent company; in these circumstances the Community authorities will 'lift the veil' and will consider the parent and subsidiary companies as part of a single enterprise entity. Because such enterprises are part of the same entity there can be no competition between them and, accordingly, there can be no infringement of Article 85(1) of the Treaty: *Christiani and Neilsen*[15] and *Kodak*.[16] Conversely, the anti-competitive behaviour of a subsidiary company can, on the same principles, be attributed to a parent company: *ICI v EEC Commission*.[17] In this context, it should be noted that the relationship between a principal and his commercial agent or agents is not considered by the Commission to fall within the ambit of Article 85(1): in its Notice on exclusive dealing contracts with commercial agents[18] the Commission indicated that the criterion for distinguishing between a commercial agent properly so-called and an independent trader lay in the assumption of risk in the transaction in question. This issue came up for consideration in a recent decision involving Irish retailers. *Fisher-Price UK*,[19] a division of Quaker Oats Limited, had appointed an exclusive distributor in Dublin for the whole of Ireland. Three Irish retailers became members of Toyco, a purchasing group based in Northern Ireland, and were thus able to buy Fisher-Price toys at far lower prices than those pertaining in Ireland. Fisher-Price UK directed the management of Toyco to cease accepting orders from its Irish members. The result was a prohibition on parallel imports from the United Kingdom to Ireland for approximately 3 years. The Commission imposed a fine of 300,000 ECU on Fisher-Price UK, and did not accept an argument made by that entity to the effect that Toyco acted as the agent for its Irish members, in which capacity it could not have been regarded as an undertaking for the purposes of Article 85(1) of the Treaty; in fact, the

Commission considered that Toyco was best described as a wholesaler in this context.

'Trade between Member States' Both Articles 85 and 86 require, before an infringement can take place, that there be an effect on trade between Member States. Like the concept of 'undertakings' this particular phrase has been extremely widely interpreted by the Commission and the Court of Justice. In *Consten and Grundig v EEC Commission*[20] the Court held that what was particularly important was whether an agreement is capable of constituting a threat, either direct or indirect, actual or potential to freedom of trade between Member States, in a manner which might harm the attainment of objectives of a single market between the Member States. The fact that an agreement might encourage an increase, even a large one, in the volume of trade between States is not sufficient to exclude the possibility that the agreement may 'affect' such trade in the above-mentioned manner. It is also clear that the notion of 'trade' applies not only to transactions in goods but also to the provision of services within the Community: *Gesellschaft zur Verwertung von Leistungsschutzrechten GmbH v EC Commission.*[21] In most instances of infringements of Articles 85 or 86 the participants in restrictive practices or abuses of dominant position, or the victims thereof, are located in more than one Member State. But the fact that a price-fixing arrangement or market sharing agreement is concluded between enterprises located in only one Member State does not preclude an effect on trade between Member States.

In *Vereeniging van Cementhandelaren v EC Commission,*[22] a case involving a price-fixing and market-sharing arrangement between Dutch importers of cement, the Court held that an agreement which extends to the whole of the territory of a Member State has, by its very nature, the effect of consolidating a national partitioning, thus hindering the economic inter-penetration to which the Treaty is directed and ensuring a protection for national production. It is also possible for trade between Member States to be affected by restrictive agreements relating to exports by a Community based undertaking to an enterprise located in a non-Member State; the possibility of such a result is increased where the Community has a trade agreement with the non-Member State concerned: *Junghans.*[23]

1 Case 6/72, [1973] E.C.R. 215.
2 Case 229/83, [1985] E.C.R. 1.
3 Case 127/73, [1974] E.C.R. 51.
4 Joined cases 209–213/84, O.J. L 131, 25.9.1986.
5 O.J. L 195, 7.8.1969.
6 Case 48/69, [1972] E.C.R. 619.
7 See Noel Allen, *The Development of European Economic Community anti trust jurisdiction over alien undertakings*, L.I.E.I. 1974/2.
8 O.J. L 85, 26.3.1985.
9 O.J. L 92, 30.3.1985.
10 See, for example, The agreement with Austria: O.J. (Sp. Ed.) 1972, 31 December, p. 4.
11 O.J. L 22, 25.1.1978.
12 O.J. (Sp. Ed.) 1959–1962, p. 129.
13 Joined cases 209–213/84, O.J. L 131, 25.9.1986.
14 O.J. L 6, 13.1.1976.
15 J.O. L 165, 5.7.1969.
16 J.O. L 147, 7.7.1970.

17 Case 48/69, [1972] E.C.R. 619.
18 J.O. 139, 24.12.1962, p. 2922.
19 O.J. L 49, 23.2.1988.
20 Joined cases 56, 58/64, [1966] E.C.R. 299.
21 O.J. L 370, 28.12.1981.
22 Case 8/72, [1972] E.C.R. 977.
23 O.J. L 30, 2.2.1977.

Article 85(1)

21.6 Article 85(1) prohibits restrictive agreements between undertakings or associations of undertakings which affect trade between Member States and which restrict, distort or prevent competition in the Common Market. We have already examined the notions of 'undertakings' and 'trade between Member States' (*supra* para. 21.5). It is now necessary to examine the other elements of the prohibition contained in Article 85(1).

'Agreements' Article 85(1) prohibits formal contractual arrangements between undertakings which have the negative effects outlined in the Article. A clear instance of this can be seen in the case of *Consten and Grundig v EEC Commission*[1] in which the exclusive distributors of Grundig products were contractually prohibited from selling into the exclusive areas of other Grundig distributors. Therefore, it is clear that Article 85(1) applies to formal written contracts; but it is not essential, for the application of Article 85(1), that the agreement should take the form of a contract having all the elements required by civil law and it is sufficient that one of the parties voluntarily undertakes to limit its freedom of action with regard to the other. This is what occurred in the *Franco-Japanese Ball-bearings Agreement*[2] in which French and Japanese trade associations exchanged letters containing a commitment on the part of the Japanese to raise prices of ball bearings imported into France. The establishment of a new business entity, as in the creation of a joint venture, is also an agreement for the purposes of Article 85(1). In *De Laval-Stork*,[3] an American corporation and a Dutch company agreed to combine their production and marketing activities in respect of turbines and compressors. In *Vlaamse Reisbureaus v Sociale Dienst*[4] an agreement which prevented travel agents from passing on to customers part of the commission they received on the sale of holidays was incorporated into national legislation by a royal decree. The Court of Justice held that the incorporation of what was originally a purely private agreement into legislation gave the arrangement a permanent character in that the parties were no longer free to withdraw from it. The national legislation concerned was incompatible with Article 5 in conjunction with Articles 3(f) and 85 of the EEC Treaty.

'Decisions of Associations of Undertakings' The most common restrictive arrangements are formal contracts concluded between one or more undertakings. However, Article 85(1) also applies to the anti-competitive activities of trade associations and the Commission frequently uncovers market-sharing and price-fixing arrangements concluded by such bodies. A common feature of such practices involves the issuing of 'non-binding recommendations' by the trade association, which is not itself a body carrying out any economic activity. These recommendations cover such matters such as the prohibition of parallel imports, loyalty rebates, price maintenance mechanisms, and market-sharing arrangements. Examples include: the *German Ceramic Tiles Discount Agreement*[5] and *Frubo*.[6]

'Concerted practices' If the prohibition of Article 85(1) applied only to formal written contracts, then undertakings intending to implement anti-competitive practices would be tempted to avoid contractual formalism and engage in 'gentlemen's agreements'. The latter type of activity is captured by the notion of the concerted practice which has been used to condemn some of the classic cartel cases including the *Dye-stuffs*[7] and *Quinine*[8] cartels of the late 1960s and, more recently, the *Polypropylene*[9] cartel. In *ICI v EEC Commission*,[10] in which the plaintiff sought the annulment of that part of the dye-stuff's decision addressed to it, the Court was called upon to define the concept of a concerted practice. It held that in referring to a concerted practice the Treaty intended to bring within the prohibition of Article 85(1)

> '. . . a form of coordination between undertakings which, without having reached the stage where an agreement properly so-called has been concluded, knowingly substitutes practical cooperation between them for the risks of competition. By its very nature, then, a concerted practice does not have all the elements of a contract but may *inter alia* arise out of coordination which becomes apparent from the behaviour of the participants. Although parallel behaviour may not by itself be identified with a concerted practice, it may, however, amount to strong evidence of such practice if it leads to conditions of competition which do not correspond to the normal conditions of the market, having regard to the nature of the products, the size and number of the undertakings, and the volume of the said market.'

In *Compagnie Royale Asturienne des Mines v EC Commission*[11] the Court held that the fact that two competing producers discontinue at the same time deliveries to a certain customer was not in itself sufficient proof of concerted action by the firms concerned: all the circumstances surrounding the case must conclusively point to the existence of a concerted practice. If, on the other hand, the firms managed to adduce and substantiate facts which make a different interpretation of the circumstances appear equally plausible, the allegation that the cartel ban has been infringed is disproved. In this case the Court held that the evidence adduced by the Commission was not sufficient to prove the existence of concerted action by the plaintiff companies.

'Object or effect' An agreement or concerted practice must have as its object or effect the prevention, restriction or distortion of competition within the Common Market. In *LTM v MBU*[12] the Court held that these requirements were alternative rather than cumulative: the precise purpose of the agreement must first be examined and the interference with competition must result from all or some of the clauses of the agreement itself. Where, however, an analysis of the said clauses does not reveal the effect on competition to be sufficiently deleterious, the consequences of the agreement should then be considered and for it to be caught by the prohibition it is then necessary to find that those factors are present which show that competition has in fact been prevented or restricted or distorted to an appreciable extent.

'Prevention, restriction or distortion of competition within the Common Market' In practice, there is no great significance in the three different effects on competition encapsulated by this phrase. The Treaty lists five examples of preventions, restrictions or distortions of competition (*supra* para. 21.1) but this list is non-conclusive. Other examples of restraints of competition include prohibitions on cross-supplies, which prevent authorised dealers from selling contract goods to other authorised dealers, and the control of dealers' advertising campaigns by manufacturers: *Hasselblad v EC Commission*.[13] More recently, the Commission objected a joint venture set up by Gilbeys of Ireland (owned by Grand Metropolitan Plc) and Cantrell & Cochrane (itself a joint venture between Allied Lyons Plc and Guinness Plc) to acquire a controlling interest in Irish Distillers Group using the vehicle of *G C & C* Brands Limited. The Commission objected to the original collusive bid on the grounds that the three most powerful producers of spirits in the EEC were infringing Article 85 of the Treaty by agreeing to take over a competitor and to establish a market-sharing agreement which restricted competition. The parties to the agreement decided to abandon their joint bid after the Commission indicated its intention to impose interim measures ordering G C & C Brands Limited and any company belonging to the same group not to conclude any further agreements for the acquisition of Irish Distillers Group shares unless such agreements were specifically made conditional on the approval of the take-over bid by the Commission.[14]

'Effect on trade between Member States' We have already examined (*supra* para. 21.5) the requirement that trade between Member States be effected by a restrictive agreement or concerted practice. At this point it should be noted that this requirement of Article 85(1) is subject to a *de minimis* rule. In *Volk v Vervaecke*[15] the defendant, in an action for breach of contract, argued that the agreement was null and void pursuant to Article 85(2); the contract at issue involved an exclusive distribution agreement, underpinned by parallel import restraints, involving the importation of approximately 1,000 washing machines per annum. Normally, the parallel import ban would render the agreement prohibited under Article 85(1), but in this case the Court of Justice held that an agreement falls outside the prohibition in Article 85 when it has only an insignificant effect on the market, taking into account the weak position which the persons concerned have on the market of the product in question. Shortly after the Court's decision in *Volk v Vervaecke* the Commission issued a Notice on agreements of minor importance[16] in which it set out to indicate to enterprises those agreements it considered not to fall within the scope of Article 85(1). This Notice has been revised twice[17] and in the current notice the Commission states that, in general, an agreement will not have an appreciable impact on market conditions when the market share of the firms involved does not exceed 5 per cent and where their combined annual turnover does not exceed 200m. ECU. The Notice differs from its predecessor in three respects:

(i) the market share of participating firms is no longer calculated by reference to a 'substantial part of the Common Market' but rather to 'the area within the Community in which the agreement has effect';

(ii) the turnover limit has been increased from 50m. ECU to 200m. ECU;

(iii) the scope of the Notice has been extended to include services.

1 Joined cases 56 and 58/64, [1966] E.C.R. 299.
2 O.J. L 343, 21.12.1974.
3 O.J. L 215, 23.8.1977.
4 Case 311/85, O.J. C 290, 30.10.1987, p. 4.
5 J.O. L 10, 31.1.1971.
6 O.J. L 237, 29.8.1974.
7 J.O. L 195, 7.8.1969.
8 [1969] C.M.L.R. 41.
9 O.J. L 230, 18.8.1986.
10 Case 48/69, [1972] E.C.R. 619.
11 Joined cases 29–30/83, [1984] E.C.R. 1679.
12 Case 56/65, [1966] E.C.R. 235.
13 O.J. L 161, 2.6.1982, p. 18, [1984] ECR 883, ECJ.
14 Commission Press Release I.P. (88) 512, 17.8.1988.
15 Case 5/69, [1969] E.C.R. 295.
16 J.O. L 64, 2.6.1970.
17 O.J. L 313, 29.12.1977; O.J. L 231, 12.9.1986.

Article 85(2)

21.7 Article 85(2) provides simply that any agreement or decision prohibited pursuant to this Article shall be automatically void. In *Brasserie de Haecht v Wilkin-Janssen*[1] the Court held that the nullity provided for in Article 85(2) is of retroactive effect: in other words, it operates *ex tunc* and not *ex nunc*. In *Ciments et Betons v Kerpen and Kerpen*[2] the Court of Justice held that while the nullity pursuant to Article 85(2) is absolute it applies only to the contractual provisions caught by Article 85(1). The effects of this nullity on other parts of the agreement at issue must therefore be assessed under national law, not Community law. This also applies to any orders placed or deliveries carried out under such agreements and to the ensuing payment obligations.

The severity of Article 85(2) has been mitigated to a certain extent by the doctrine of provisional validity.[3] This doctrine was elaborated by the Court of Justice to provide a degree of legal certainty to 'old agreements', that is, agreements concluded before the entry into force of Regulation 17 of 1962 or, in the case of the new Member States, after the entry into force of the relevant Act of Accession. In *Brasserie de Haecht v Wilkin-Janssen*[4] the Court held that in respect of old agreements, particularly agreements which had been notified in accordance with the provisions of Regulation 17, the national court may only declare them automatically void after the Commission had taken a decision by virtue of that Regulation. In *Lancome and Cosparfrance v Etos and Albert Heijn*[5] a national court sought a ruling from the Court of Justice on the effect on provisional validity of a 'comfort letter' issued by the Commission. The first-named plaintiff had notified an agreement in 1963 and had modified its selective distribution system, in accordance with observations made by the Commission, so as to render Article 85(1) inapplicable to it. The Director-General for Competition then sent a letter to Lancome indicating that the Commission was no longer concerned that the agreement was incompatible with Article 85 of the Treaty. However, in subsequent proceedings, the defendants argued that the selective distribution system utilised by Lancome was in breach of Article 85(1) and the national court sought the assistance of the Court of Justice on the provisional validity issue. The Court of Justice held that the comfort letter had the effect of terminating the period of provisional validity in respect of the notified agreement. The opinions expressed in such a letter were not binding on the national court but constituted a factor which the latter could take into consideration in examining whether the agreements were in accordance with the provisions of Article 85.

Although Article 85(2) provides for automatic nullity, the agreement in question will only be void as a whole if it appears that the clauses effected by the prohibition in Article 85(1) are not severable from the agreement itself. Consequently, any other contractual provisions which are not effected by the prohibition, and which therefore do not involve the application of the Treaty, fall outside Community law: *LTM v MBU*.[6]

1 Case 48/77, [1973] E.C.R. 77.
2 Case 319/82, [1983] E.C.R. 4173.
3 See D.J. Gijlstra and D.F. Murphy, *EEC Competition Law after the Haecht II and Sabam cases*, L.I.E.I. 1979/2.
4 Case 48/73, [1973] E.C.R. 77.
5 Case 99/79, [1980] E.C.R. 2511.
6 Case 56/65, [1966] E.C.R. 235.

Article 85(3)

21.8 Any agreement or concerted practice prohibited by Article 85(1) is automatically void according to Article 85(2). However, Article 85(3) allows for the exemption from the prohibition in Article 85(1) and the consequent nullity provided for in Article 85(2) for any agreement or category of agreement or concerted practice or category of concerted practice which fulfils certain conditions: the agreement must

  (1) contribute to improving the production or distribution of goods or the promotion of technical or economic progress;
  (2) while allowing consumers a fair share of the resulting benefits;
  (3) but which does not impose on the undertakings concerned restrictions which are not indispensable to the attainment of these objectives;
  (4) and does not afford such undertakings the possibility of eliminating competition in respect of a substantial part of the products in question.

It will be seen from the above that it is possible to procure either an individual or a category or group exemption from the prohibition in Article

85(1). At present there are six category or group exemption regulations in force and the Commission is currently drafting further group exemption regulations in respect of franchising[1] and know-how licensing agreements;[2] in addition, the Commission is preparing a Notice on its general policy towards joint ventures.[3] The Commission has also been encouraging national courts to apply Articles 85 and 86, along with the group exemption regulations (which, by definition, are directly applicable in the legal orders of the Member States).[4] These various policy initiatives will reduce the burden of notifications with which the Commission's competition Directorate General has to deal; but there will be a need for decisions by the Commission on individual applications for exemption because there will always be the peculiar cases that do not fall within the ambit of any of the group exemption regulations. But the Commission also uses the individual exemption applications as an opportunity to elaborate its policy on particular issues, for example on joint ventures, or as a trial run for a proposed group exemption regulation. Indeed, the basic enabling Council Regulation for most of the group exemption regulations, Council Regulation (EEC) 19/65,[5] specifies in the preamble that the Commission should exercise its delegated group exemption regulation making power '. . . after sufficient experience has been gained in the light of individual decisions . . .'.

The procedure governing applications for individual exemptions is laid down in Council Regulation 17 and in Commission Regulation (EEC) 27/62. This subject is examined later (*infra* para. 21.9). However, the nature of the Commission's powers under Article 85(3) was discussed in *Consten and Grundig v EEC Commission.*[6] In that case the Court held that undertakings are entitled to an appropriate examination by the Commission of their requests for Article 85(3) to be applied. For this purpose the Commission may not confine itself to requiring from undertakings proof of the fulfilment of the requirements for the grant of the exemption but must, as a matter of good administration, play its part, using the means available to it, in ascertaining the relevant facts and circumstances. Furthermore, the exercise of the Commission's powers necessarily implies complex evaluations on economic matters. This latter point, the complex evaluation of economic issues, is the reason why Article 85(3) is not directly effective; it is highly unlikely that national courts or tribunals have available to them the economic materials or analytical skills that are required for the proper evaluation of the four conditions listed in Article 85(3). There is one sense, however, in which Article 85(3) can be said to be directly effective and capable of application by national courts and tribunals: the group exemption regulations are, by definition, directly applicable in each Member State and courts and tribunals may apply the provisions of those regulations, including the automatic exemption granted by each of them, in cases coming before them.

The exemption under Article 85(3), procured either by way of individual application under Regulation 17 or by application of the group exemption regulations, presupposes an infringement of Article 85(1). Accordingly, the duration of the exemption is limited in time. In most individual applications the Commission grants an exemption for a period of 5 years and the exemption can be renewed: *Transocean Marine Paint Association.*[7]

Occasionally, however, because of the nature of the case the Commission grants an exemption for a much longer period; in *De Laval-Stork*[8] the Commission renewed an exemption for a period of 20 years in respect of a joint venture between Dutch and American companies engaged in the manufacture of generators and compressors.

The six group exemption regulations require some explanation. All six regulations are Commission Regulations adopted under powers delegated to it by the Council either under Regulation (EEC) 19/65[9] or Regulation (EEC) 2821/71.[10] The scope of each Regulation is defined in Article 1 which declares Article 85(1) inapplicable to the economic activity in question; for example, Article 1 of Commission Regulation (EEC) 417/85[11] declares Article 85(1) inapplicable to agreements on specialisation whereby, for the duration of the agreement, undertakings accept reciprocal obligations:

(a) not to manufacture certain products or to have them manufactured, but to leave it to other parties to manufacture the products or have them manufactured; *or*
(b) to manufacture certain products or have them manufactured only jointly.

Having outlined the scope of the group exemption available, each of the Regulations outlines

(i) a list of acceptable restraints on competition; and
(ii) A 'black' list of clauses which may, under no circumstances, be included in an agreement if it is to procure an automatic exemption.

Each group exemption regulation also possesses a clause allowing the Commission to withdraw the benefit of the group exemption where it finds that, while an individual case falls within the terms of the relevant regulation, it nevertheless has effects which are incompatible with the provisions of Article 85(3). A novel development, to be found in Article 4 of Commission Regulation (EEC) 2349/84[12] Article 4 of Commission Regulation (EEC) 417/85 and Article 7 of Commission Regulation (EEC) 418/85,[13] is an opposition procedure which allows any undertaking whose agreement falls within the scope of the patent licensing or research and development group exemption regulations, but which contains restraints of competition not mentioned in the relevant 'black' lists, to notify the Commission under Commission Regulation (EEC) 27/62.[14] The benefit of the group exemption provided for in Article 1 of the relevant Regulations will be available to the enterprise if the Commission does not oppose the exemption within a period of 6 months. Amongst other things, this is designed to reduce the backlog of cases pending before the Commission.

1 17th Report on Competition Policy, at point 35.
2 17th Report on Competition Policy, at point 38.
3 17th Report on Competition Policy, at point 48.
4 16th Report on Competition Policy, at points 41 and 42.
5 O.J. (Sp. Ed.) 1965–1966, p. 35.
6 Joined cases 56 and 58/64, [1966] E.C.R. 229.

7 O.J. L 163, 20.7.1967, [1967] CMLR D9.
8 O.J. L 59, 4.3.1988.
9 O.J. (Sp. Ed.) 1965–1966, p. 35.
10 O.J. (Sp. Ed.) 1971, III, p. 1022.
11 O.J. L 53, 22.2.1985.
12 O.J. L 219, 26.8.1984.
13 O.J. L 53, 22.2.1985.
14 O.J. (Sp. Ed.) 1959–1962, p. 132.

Article 86

21.9 At paragraphs 21.2 and 21.5 (*supra*) we noted several similarities and differences between Articles 85 and 86 and also discussed certain features common to both provisions. In the context of Article 86 one further comment should be made about the notion of 'undertakings'. Article 85 is often characterised as being applicable to collusive agreements between undertakings operating at the horizontal level of economic activity; Article 86, on the other hand, is said to apply to the relationship between firms on the vertical axis of the product development scale. Put in another way, Article 85 applies to cartels and Article 86 applies to monopolies. The Court of Justice rejected this categorisation at an early stage: in *LTM v MBU*[1] and in *Consten and Grundig v EEC Commission*[2] the Court held that neither Article 85 nor 86 made any distinction as to whether the parties subject to the relevant prohibitions were at the same level in the economy (so-called horizontal agreements) or at different levels (so-called vertical agreements); no distinction can be made where the Treaty does not make any distinction. Following from this conclusion we can further state that more than one undertaking can be in a dominant position with other enterprises. In *BP-ABG*[3] the Commission held that during the oil crisis in 1973–74 the customers of the oil companies active on the Netherlands market became completely dependent on them for supplies of scarce petroleum products and the suppliers were consequently placed in a collective dominant position *vis-à-vis* their normal customers. In short, Article 86 is not restricted to the behaviour of single monopolistic enterprises.

'Dominant position' Before an undertaking can be subject to the prohibition in Article 86 it must be in a dominant position within the Common Market or a substantial part of it. Ultimately, the existence of a dominant position can be determined only by reference to the relevant geographic and product markets; but the meaning of the phrase 'dominant position' was first defined by the Commission in 1971 and has been utilised by both the Commission and the Court of Justice on many occasions since then. In *Continental Can*[4] the Commission defined 'dominant position' in the following terms:

> 'Undertakings are in a dominant position when they have the power to behave independently, which puts them in a position to act without taking into account their competitors, purchasers or suppliers. That is the position when, because of their share of the market, or of their share of the market combined with the availability of technical knowledge, raw materials or capital, they have the power to determine prices or to control production or distribution for a significant part

of the products in question. This power does not necessarily have to derive from an absolute domination permitting the undertakings which hold it to eliminate all will on the part of their economic partners, but it is enough that they be strong enough as a whole to ensure those undertakings an overall independence of behaviour, even if there are differences in intensity in their influence on the different partial markets.'

It may well be that particular provisions of national legislation confer on a firm or enterprise a privileged provision; this is the case in respect of industrial property rights and other privileges conferred on enterprises by national law. In *Deutsche Grammophon v Metro*[5] the Court of Justice held that the power to exercise an exclusive right analogous to copyright did not in itself amount to a dominant position; it was necessary that the dominant position must extend to a 'substantial part' of the Common Market and that there be an abuse of that dominant position. On the other hand, vehicle conformity and type approval tests, delegated to motor manufacturers by the State, can create dominant positions within the meaning of Article 86 where the approval can only be carried out by the manufacturer or officially appointed authorised agents under conditions fixed unilaterally by the manufacturer: *General Motors Continental v Commission.*[6]

'Dominant position within the Common Market or in a substantial part of it' The existence of a dominant position can be tested only by reference to the market in question; this involves a consideration both of the product market and the geographical market.

(a) *Product market*

In *Continental Can Company*[7] the Commission held that the Company had abused its dominant position by purchasing through its subsidiary, Europemballage Corporation, approximately 80 per cent of the shares in a Dutch company, Thomassen and Drijver-Verblifa, because it already held a dominant position over a substantial part of the Common Market on the market for light packaging for preserved meat, fish and crustacea and on the market in metal caps for glass jars. When the matter came before the Court in *Europemballage and Continental Can v EC Commission*[8] the Court held that the Commission had not taken into account the competition from substitute products, glass and plastic, nor had it demonstrated how the market for light containers for canned meat, for canned seafood and the market for metal closures differed from the general market for light metal containers. Accordingly, it annulled the decision. It may well be that the enterprise accused of abusing a dominant position is the only producer of the product in question; in *ICI and Commercial Solvents Corpn v EC Commission*[9] the plaintiffs sought the annulment of a Commission Decision which accused them of abusing their dominant position on the marketplace for nitropropane and aminobutanol. Both are intermediary products for the manufacture of ethambutol, which is used as an anti-tuberculosis drug. The plaintiff companies (part of the same group) had refused to re-supply a purchaser, Giorgio Zoja SpA, whose attempt to obtain supplies of aminobutanol on the world markets failed. Commercial Solvents was the only significant producer on the world market. The Court rejected the arguments of the applicants that it was not possible to distinguish a market in the raw materials necessary for the manufacture of a product from the market on which the product is sold; an abuse of a dominant position on the market in raw materials could restrict competition in the market on which the derivatives of the raw material were sold. By contrast with the two examples already cited, the product market identified by the Commission in *Hugin-Liptons*[10] concerned spare parts for Hugin cash registers. The majority of parts of Hugin cash registers are made to Hugin designs, with tools belonging to Hugin and are exclusive to Hugin; these parts are not inter-changeable with the parts of other makes of cash registers and cannot otherwise be economically reproduced. Hugin cash registers cannot therefore be properly maintained, repaired or rebuilt without the use of Hugin spare parts. In *Hugin v Commission*[11] the Court of Justice upheld the Commission's statement of the relevant market.

(b) *Geographical market*

Although Article 86 makes it clear that an abuse of a dominant position must take place 'within the Common Market or in a substantial part of it' it fails to define what is meant by a substantial part of the Common Market. In *Continental Can*[12] and *United Brands*[13] the relevant geographical market was considered to be northern Europe. In *British Leyland*[14] the United Kingdom was considered the relevant market. And, even though the separate regulatory and administrative powers of the Member States should not interfere with the operation of the Common Market, it seems that reasons of sovereignty and reasons of State should dictate that each of the Member States must be considered as a substantial part of the Common Market for the purposes of Article 86. Otherwise, Luxembourg—which has a population slightly in excess of 300,000—could hardly be considered to be a substantial part of the Common Market. In two recent Irish cases, *Leanort Ltd v Southern Chemicals Ltd*[15] and *Magee v Ryan*[16] the plaintiffs claimed that the defendants had abused their positions on the relevant markets in Ireland. But in *Cadbury Ltd v Kerry Co-operative Ltd*[17] Barrington J. held that County Kerry could not be considered a substantial part of the Common Market, despite the regal description often given to it.

'Abuse of dominant position' Dominant position is not *per se* prohibited by Article 86; the firm holding a dominant position must abuse it. Article 86 contains a non-conclusive list of abuses (*supra* para. 21.1) and there are many other examples of abuse; refusal to supply or refusal to sell to dependent undertakings: *Polaroid-SSI Europe*;[18] predatory pricing: *ECS-AKZO*;[19] and prevention of parallel imports: *British Leyland*.[20] In *Eurofix-Bauco/Hilti*[21] the Commission imposed a fine of 6m. ECU on Hilti, a Liechtenstein company specialising in the manufacture of fixing equipment, notably nail guns, for the construction industry. The Commission held that Hilti had infringed Article 86 by preventing independent producers of nails for Hilti nail guns from entering the nail market; the abuses identified by the Commission included the following:

— tying the sale of cartridge magazines and nails;
— reducing discounts and other discriminatory practices for orders of cartridge magazines without nails;
— encouraging independent distributors not to fill certain export orders;
— refusing to fill completely the order for cartridge magazines placed by customers or distributors of long-standing, who were likely to re-sell them;
— refusing to honour guarantees without any objective reason;
— applying selective or discriminatory policies against Hilti competitors and their customers;
— unilateral and covert application in the United Kingdom of a policy of differentiated discounts for equipment rental companies and retailers according to whether or not they had favoured-customer status.

In *Continental Can*[22] the Commission held that the purchase of shares in a competitor by an undertaking already in a dominant position amounted to an abuse within the meaning of Article 86. This use of Article 86 to control mergers gave rise to considerable controversy at the time.

Consequences of prohibition   We have already noted (*supra* para. 21.2) that an infringement of Article 86 does not give rise to any consequent nullity nor is there any possibility of exemption from the prohibition. But this does not mean that the prohibition is ineffective. The Commission utilises its 'cease and desist' powers under Article 3 of Regulation 17 to great effect. For example, in *Re Zoja*[23] the Commission ordered ICI and Commercial Solvents to supply to the Zoja enterprise a sufficient quantity of the raw materials necessary to manufacture its products. In *IBM*[24] the Commission reached an amicable settlement with the giant American computer corporation, but made the settlement conditional on an annual reporting requirement concerning interface information requested by competitors for the attachment of their products to IBM System/370 products. The Commission also has the power to take interim measures to protect complainants. A recent example concerns the British manufacturer of musical instruments, *Boosey and Hawkes*,[25] which has a virtual monopoly of supply to the 2,500 or more British bands forming part of the 'brass band movement'; the Commission ordered Boosey and Hawkes to resume supplies provisionally to its principal customer, Gabriel Horn House which had formed a subsidiary with another company to compete with Boosey and Hawkes, which had then cut off supplies to the new subsidiary.

Mergers and concentrations   In *Continental Can*[26] the Commission claimed jurisdiction to control mergers and take-overs on the grounds that the acquiring corporation was already in a dominant position in a substantial part of the Common Market. In other words, a merger or take-over can constitute an abuse of a dominant position within the meaning of Article 86. As we have already seen, the Court of Justice annulled the Commission Decision because it had taken too narrow a view of the relevant product market, but it endorsed the view that the take-over could constitute an abuse of a dominant position. Armed with this precedent the Commission proceeded to draft a Regulation on the control of concentrations; however, the appropriate Council approval was not forthcoming and the draft Regulation was revised in 1982[27] and 1984.[28] The most recent revision of the draft Regulation took place in April 1988[29] and in its present form a concentration is said to exist where two or more undertakings merge or where one or more persons or undertakings acquire, whether by purchase of shares or assets, by contract or by any other means, direct or indirect control of the whole or parts of one or more undertakings (Article 3). If the concentration concerned has a 'Community dimension' it is subject to prior control to determine whether it is compatible with the Common Market (Article 2). It will not be compatible with the Common Market if it gives rise to or strengthens a dominant position but it will be presumed compatible, subject to rebuttal, if the market share of the undertakings concerned in the Common Market or in a substantial part thereof, is less than 20 per cent. According to Article 1, a concentration has a Community dimension if at least two of the undertakings involved have their principal field of Community activities in different Member States or where the enterprises carrying out the concentration have their principal field of Community activity in one Member State but have other activities in other Member States. A concentration will not have a Community dimension where the aggregate worldwide turnover of all the undertakings concerned is less than 1bn. ECU or where the aggregate worldwide turnover exceeds 1bn. ECU but where the aggregate worldwide turnover of the target undertaking is less than 50m. ECU (Article 1). Article 4 requires prior notification of concentrations and Article 6 imposes a two month time limit in which the Commission must decide whether the concentration is compatible with the Common Market; Article 7 prevents the parties to a concentration from putting the concentration into effect until the Commission has taken its decision under Article 6. Article 8 gives the Commission wide powers in relation to notified concentrations: it may decide that a concentration is incompatible with the Common Market and prohibit it, in which case any assets acquired or concentrated must be separated; or it may decide that a concentration is compatible with the Common Market—subject to conditions and obligations which may be attached thereto. Articles 13 and 14 empower the Commission to impose fines and periodic penalty payments in cases where incorrect information has been supplied or the obligation to notify has been infringed.

The lack of support from larger Member States, like the Federal Republic of Germany and the United Kingdom, has not diminished the Commission's determination to exercise control over mergers and the decision of the Court of Justice in *R.J. Reynolds and British American Tobacco Co v EC Commission*[30] has clearly strengthened the Commision's hand. The plaintiffs sought the annulment of unpublished Commission decisions rejecting their complaints that the restructuring of an agreement between Philip Morris (an American tobacco company) and the South African-controlled Rembrandt Group, did not eliminate infringements of the competition rules. Originally, Philip Morris was to take 50 per cent of

Rothmans Tobacco Holdings, a 100 per cent owned subsidiary of the Rembrandt Group, but following Commission objections the Philip Morris shareholding was reduced to 30.8 per cent and the voting rights were reduced to 24.9 per cent. The Court rejected the claim of the plaintiffs but its judgment laid down certain important new principles as to whether and in what circumstances an undertaking's acquisition of a minority shareholding in a competitor could violate Article 85 or Article 86. The Court held that although the acquisition of a shareholding in a competitor was not of itself restrictive of competition, it could be a means of influencing the commercial behaviour of the businesses concerned and thereby of restricting or distorting competition. This would be the case especially where by acquisition of a shareholding or additional clauses in the agreement the investing company gained legal or actual control over the commercial behaviour of the other company or where the agreement provided for economic cooperation between the companies or created a structure which made such cooperation reasonably likely. A restriction of competition was also possible where the agreement opened the way for the investing company to strengthen its position and acquire *de facto* control over the company at a later date. Not only the immediate consequences, but also the potential effects of the agreement had to be considered including the possibility that the agreement was part of a long-term plan. As regards Article 86 the Court held that there was no abuse of dominant position; there could have been an abuse of dominant position under Article 86 only if Philip Morris' acquisition of Rothmans International shares had led to its gaining effective control over the company or at least a position of influence over its commercial behaviour. However, as the examination under Article 85 had shown, this was not the case.

The Commission lost no time in applying these *dicta*: in July 1988 it issued a statement of objections to *G C & C*,[31] a joint venture set up by Gilbeys of Ireland (owned by Grand Metropolitan) and Cantrell and Cochrane (itself a joint venture between Allied Lyons and Guinness) to acquire a controlling interest in Irish Distillers Group, the sole manufacturer of Irish whiskey. The Commission objected to the original collusive bid on the grounds that the three most powerful producers of spirits in the EEC were infringing Article 85 of the Treaty by agreeing to take over a competitor and to establish a market-sharing agreement in relation to the brands owned by that competitor. When the parties to the joint venture agreed to abandon their joint bid for Irish Distillers Group, the Commission decided not to impose interim measures prohibiting G C & C from concluding any further agreements for the acquisition of Irish Distillers Group shares unless such agreements were specifically made conditional on the approval of the take-over bid by the Commission. It also released FII – Fyffes, the Irish fruit importing group, from its previous commitment to sell its 20 per cent stake in Irish Distillers Group to G C & C. The assumption of jurisdiction by the Commission in this case has had some interesting ramifications; one of the implicit consequences in the Commission's action is that it has the power to override decisions of the Take-over panel of the Stock Exchange, and following its action the Take-over panel was said to be considering whether changes in the Take-over code were necessary.[32]

1 Case 56/65, [1966] E.C.R. 235.
2 Joined cases 56 and 58/64, [1966] E.C.R. 299.
3 O.J. L 117, 9.5.1977.
4 J.O. L 7, 25.1.1972.
5 Case 78/70, [1971] E.C.R. 487.
6 Case 26/75, [1975] E.C.R. 1367.
7 J.O. L 7, 25.1.1972.
8 Case 6/72, [1973] E.C.R. 215.
9 Joined cases 6–7/73, [1974] E.C.R. 223.
10 O.J. L 22, 25.1.1978.
11 Case 22/78, [1979] E.C.R. 2869.
12 J.O. L 7, 25.1.1972.
13 O.J. L 95, 9.3.1976.
14 O.J. L 207, 2.8.1984.
15 High Court (1988 No. 5821p), Blaney J., Order of 18 August 1988. Unreported.
16 (1988) Irish Times, 5 October.
17 [1982] I.L.R.M. 77.
18 13th Report on Competition Policy, points 155–157.
19 O.J. L 374, 31.12.1985.
20 O.J. L 207, 2.8.1984.
21 O.J. L 65, 11.3.1988.
22 J.O. L 7, 25.1.1972.
23 J.O. L 299, 31.12.1972.
24 14th Report on Competition Policy, points 94 and 95.
25 O.J. L 286, 9.10.1987.
26 J.O. L 7, 25.1.1972.
27 O.J. L 36. 12.2.1982.
28 O.J. L 51, 23.2.1984.
29 COM(88) 97 final, 25 April 1988.
30 Joined cases 142, 156/84 [1987] 2CMLR 551.
31 Commission Press Release IP(88) 512, 17.8.1988.
32 *Financial Times*, 4.8.1988.

Implementation of Articles 85 and 86

21.10 The enforcement and implementation of Articles 85 and 86 was entrusted by the Council to the Commission in Regulation 17 of 1962;[1] this Regulation further empowered the Commission to adopt implementing measures concerning the form and content of applications for negative clearances and notifications for exemptions, and concerning hearings (Article 24). The principal power conferred on the Commission is the power to terminate infringements of Articles 85 and 86; Article 3 empowers the Commission to require the participating undertakings to bring infringements to an end, either on its own initiative or on foot of a complaint by a Member State or a natural or legal person. This power is extremely wide: in *Continental Can*[2] the Commission ordered the addressee to divest itself of a shareholding purchased in a target company; in *Re Zoja*[3] the Commission ordered an Italian company, ICI and its parent company, Commercial Solvents Corporation, to recommence supply of raw materials to the Zoja firm; in *G C & C*[4] the Commission threatened to make the future purchase of shares in Irish Distillers Group by Grand Metropolitan Plc, Allied-Lyons Plc and Guinness Plc (acting through G C & C) conditional on the approval of the take-over by the Commission. In the event the parties agreed to abandon their collusive bid for Irish Distillers Group. The power to terminate infringements also includes the power to take interim measures: *Cameracare v EC*

Commission.[5] Interim measures can be taken only in cases of proven urgency to avoid serious and irreparable damage to the applicant; the interim measures must be of a temporary and conservatory nature, and must be subject to review by the Court of Justice.

It has been established for some time that complainants under Article 3 of Regulation 17 have a sufficient *locus standi* to seek to have Commission Decisions addressed to a party under investigation, annulled under Article 173 of the Treaty: *Metro v EC Commission.*[6] Moreover, if the Commission proceeds to hold a hearing under Article 19 of Regulation 17 and Commission Regulation 99 of 1963, the Notice informing the complainant that his complaint has been rejected is subject to judicial review by the Court: *Demo-Studio Schmidt v EC Commission;*[7] *CICCE v EC Commission.*[8] But not anybody can ask the Commission to terminate an infringement under Article 3; natural or legal persons must claim a legitimate interest. In *BP/TGWU*[9] the Commission considered that the Transport and General Workers' Union had a legitimate interest in complaining about an alleged concerted practice between BP and Texaco to close down the BP oil refinery at Llandarcy in Wales, but the Commission found that BP had decided unilaterally to close the refinery. A second important function given to the Commission by Regulation 17 is the power to give negative clearances (Article 2) and exemptions (Articles 4 and 5). A negative clearance is a statement by the Commission that it does not consider that Article 85(1) applies to the Agreement in question whereas a notification for an exemption pre-supposes that Article 85(1) is applicable, but requests that the criteria outlined in Article 85(3) be applied to the agreement or concerted practice in question for the purposes of avoiding the automatic nullity of Article 85(2). Two important consequences attach to a notification:

(i) Article 4(1) provides that unless an agreement is notified it cannot be exempted – *Distillers Co v EC Commission;*[10] and

(ii) Article 15(5) provides immunity from fines in respect of acts taking place after notification to the Commission and before its decision in application of Article 85(3).

If, however, after an initial examination of the notified agreement the Commission decides that the agreement is unlikely to benefit from an exemption under Article 85(3) it may remove the immunity from fines: *CBR v EC Commission.*[11] In practice the administrative difference between an application for a negative clearance and a notification for an exemption is not that great because a combined application form, form A/B, is utilised; Commission Regulation (EEC) 27/62[12] on the form and content of such applications and notifications, as amended by Commission Regulation (EEC) 2526/85,[13] sets out the relevant rules and takes into account the opposition procedure which now applies in three of the block exemption Regulations. Three copies of the agreement must be supplied along with thirteen copies of the form (containing a single sheet specifying the names of the undertakings and the purposes of the notification, and a compulsory annex disclosing the legal and economic aspects of the arrangements in accordance with compulsory headings and reference numbers). However, the notification of a standard contract serves to notify other contracts in identical terms entered into by the same undertaking: *Brasserie de Haecht v Wilkin-Janssen*.[14]

Articles 5 and 7 of Regulation 17 made special provision for the notification and exemption of 'old' agreements (concluded before the entry into force of Regulation 17 or the relevant Act of Accession as the case may be). Article 8 allows the Commission to grant an exemption for a specific period and subject to conditions and obligations; under the same Article exemptions may be renewed. Negative clearances and exemptions are given by means of a final Commission Decision but a recent innovation, the 'comfort letter'[15] and the 'provisional letter',[16] have given rise to much the same result without a final decision.

Before taking decisions in connection with the termination of infringements, negative clearances and exemptions, and the imposition of fines and periodical penalty payments, the Commission must give the parties concerned the opportunity of being heard on matters to which the Commission has taken objection; Article 19 of Regulation 17 deals with this issue and extends the right to be heard to third parties who can show a sufficient interest. Third parties are also given the opportunity to comment on possible negative clearances and exemptions because the Commission is obliged to publish, in the Official Journal, a summary of the relevant application and must invite observations from interested parties. The right to be heard has been further developed in Commission Regulation (EEC) 99/65[17] which gives practical effect to the principle *audi alteram partem*. The basic rule is that the Commission must inform the relevant undertakings in writing of the objections raised against them (Article 2). The statement of objections will be sufficient if it indicates the essential facts on which the Commission bases its case: *Europemballage and Continental Can v EC Commission*.[18] The undertaking may then respond to the Commission's objections (Article 3), and in its decision the Commission may deal only with those objections raised against the parties in respect of which they have been afforded the opportunity of making known their views (Article 4). If the Commission is proposing to impose a fine or periodic penalty payment or if an undertaking shows a sufficient interest, the Commission must afford the undertaking in question the opportunity of an oral hearing (Article 7). In order to ensure impartiality the oral hearing is now conducted by a permanent officer known as the Hearings Officer;[19] prior to 1982 the hearing was conducted by an ordinary official who may well have been involved in the investigation. Finally, persons appearing at an oral hearing are entitled to be legally represented (Article 9).

Regulation 17 also empowers the Commission to request information and to carry out investigations (Articles 11 and 14). The latter power is quite extensive and officials of the Commission may enter premises, examine books and records, and take copies; they may be accompanied by officials from the competent national authorities – in Ireland this would be the Director of Consumer Affairs and Fair Trade. It is not open to the undertakings subject to such investigation to assess whether a request for documentation is justified: *FNIC*.[20] Moreover, undertakings can resist the production of documents involving written communication with their legal advisers only if the legal advice has been provided by independent lawyers; in other words, legal privilege does not extend to advice given by in-house lawyers: *Australian Mining and Smelting Europe Ltd v EC Commission*.[21]

The effectiveness of Articles 85 and 86 is underpinned by the power to impose fines and periodic penalty payments; Articles 15 and 16 of Regulation 17 contain the relevant rules. If an undertaking provides misleading information or supplies incomplete records in respect of applications or notifications or investigations, a fine ranging from 100 ECU to 5,000 ECU may be imposed. But where there has been a deliberate or negligent infringement of Articles 85 or 86 or where there has been a breach of conditions attached to exemptions by virtue of Article 8 of Regulation 17, the Commission can impose fines ranging from 1,000 ECU to 1m. ECU or a higher sum not exceeding 10 per cent of the turnover of each of the participating enterprises. Decisions imposing fines are not of a criminal nature (Article 15(4)). Periodic penalty payments varying from 50 ECU to 1,000 ECU per day can be imposed to compel compliance with information obligations or to terminate prohibited practices. As regards fines, the heaviest to date were imposed on 15 petrochemical producers who participated in the *Polypropylene*[22] cartel; in this case the fines amounted to 57.85m. ECU. The Commission adopted a much more stringent fining policy in the late 1970s because it felt that the relatively light fines imposed prior to that point in time had been insufficient to deter deliberate infringements of the competition rules. In assessing a fine, the Commission will take into account all relevant facts of the case such as the gravity and duration of the infringement and whether it was deliberate or merely negligent. The process is not a crude mathematical exercise but involves a legal and economic appraisal of each case; the Commission will also endeavour to observe the principle of proportionality by taking into account the size of the undertaking and its responsibility for the infringement.[23] These principles were upheld by the Court of Justice in *Musique Diffusion Française v EC Commission*[24] although the fine of 6.95m. ECU was reduced to 3.2m. ECU on the merits of the case.

As in all other circumstances where it exercises delegated powers the Commission is assisted by a Committee made up of representatives of the Member States competent in the matter of restrictive practices and monopolies; in this case Article 10 of Regulation 17 establishes an advisory committee on restrictive practices and dominant positions. During 1987 the Committee met six times to consider draft decisions of the Commission in implementation of Articles 85 and 86, and it delivered a total of fifteen opinions.[25]

1 O.J. (Sp. Ed.) 1959–1962, p. 87.
2 J.O. L 7, 25.1.1972.
3 J.O. L 299, 31.12.1972.
4 Commission Press Release IP(88) 512, 17.8.1988.
5 Case 792/79R, [1980] E.C.R. 119.
6 Case 26/76, [1977] E.C.R. 1875.
7 Case 210/81, [1983] E.C.R. 3045.
8 Case 298/83, [1985] E.C.R. 1105.
9 16th Report on Competition Policy at point 43.
10 Case 30/78, [1980] E.C.R. 2229.
11 Joined cases 8–11/66, [1987] E.C.R. 75.

12 O.J. (Sp. Ed.) 1959–1962, p. 132.
13 O.J. L 240, 7.9.1985.
14 Case 48/72, [1973] E.C.R. 77.
15 O.J. C 343, 31.12.1982.
16 O.J. C 295, 2.11.1983, p. 6.
17 O.J. (Sp. Ed.) 1963–1964 p. 47.
18 Case 6/72, [1973] E.C.R. 215.
19 O.J. C 251, 25.9.1982.
20 O.J. L 319, 16.11.82.
21 Case 155/79, [1982] E.C.R. 1575, [1982] 2 C.M.L.R. 309.
22 O.J. L 230, 18.8.1986.
23 13th Report on Competition Policy, points 62–66.
24 Joined cases 100–103/80, [1983] E.C.R. 1825.
25 17th Report on Competition Policy at point 11.

21.11 Regulation 17 applies to most types of economic activity. It covers all aspects of the distribution of goods including selective distribution— *BMW*[1] and franchising—*Pronuptia*.[2] In addition, three group exemption regulations apply to different types of distribution agreements;[3] a fourth, on franchising, is in draft form;[4] and the Notice on exclusive dealing with commercial agents[5] is also concerned with the distribution of goods. In fact, distribution agreements are the most prolific of contracts affected by Community competition rules. In 1987 the Commission estimated (conservatively) that there were 100,000 exclusive distribution agreements and 500,000 exclusive purchasing agreements in existence in the Community.[6] Also falling within the scope of application of Regulation 17 are arrangements concerning technological specialisation, innovation and development. The restrictive use of industrial property rights, such as trade marks, has long been a concern of the Commission: *Consten and Grundig v EEC Commission*,[7] and patent and other licensing agreements have also been subject to scrutiny. In *Nungesser and Eisele v EC Commission*[8] the plaintiffs unsuccessfully sought the anulment of a Commission Decision refusing an exemption to a restrictive licensing agreement concerning maize seed breeders' rights. Also, there are two group exemption Regulations on patent licensing[9] and research and development agreements;[10] a further block exemption Regulation, on know-how agreements is in preparation[11] and specialisation agreements have been the subject of block exemption Regulations since 1972.[12] However, an early Notice on patent licence agreements[13] is widely perceived to be redundant. We have also noted how the Commission has reacted to price fixing and market-sharing agreements: *Dye-stuffs*[14] and *Polypropylene*,[15] and the Commission has also penalised loyalty rebate agreements—*German Ceramic Tiles Discount Agreement*.[16] Other types of collective restrictive behaviour such as collective supply boycotts—*Papiers Peints de Belgique*[17] and voluntary import restraint agreements—*Franco-Japanese Ballbearings*[18] have also been condemned. In the latter context the Commission issued a Notice on the importation of Japanese products, specifying that voluntary import restraints infringed Article 85(1). By contrast, the Commission encourages non-restrictive cooperation between enterprises, particularly small- and medium-sized firms. In its Notice on this subject in 1972 the Commission outlined various types of cooperation that it considered outside the scope of Article 85(1),[19] including joint advertising and joint market research *SOCEMAS.*[20] The Commission is also developing its policy on the application of Articles 85 and 86 to joint ventures—*Bayer-Gist-Brocades*[21]—and to crisis cartels. More recently, the Commission has been extending the application of Articles 85 and 86 to the services sector. In *P & I Clubs*[22] the Commission granted an exemption to an agreement on marine mutual insurance, and in 1985 and 1986 it gave negative clearances to the rules and regulations of nine London-based *Commodity Futures Markets.*[23]

1 O.J. L 27, 3.2.1975.
2 O.J. L 8, 10.1.1987.
3 Regulations 1983 and 1984/83, O.J. L 173, 30.6.1983; Regulations 123/85, O.J. L 15, 18.1.1985.
4 16th Report on Competition Policy, point 31.
5 J.O. 139, 24.12.1962, p. 2921.
6 17th Report on Competition Policy, point 26.
7 Joined cases 56, 58/64, [1966] E.C.R. 229.
8 Case 259/78, [1982] E.C.R. 2015.
9 Regulation 2349/84, O.J. L 219, 26.8.1984.
10 Regulation 418/85, O.J. L 53, 22.2.1985.
11 16th Report on Competition Policy, point 35.
12 Regulation 417/85, O.J. L 53, 22.2.1985.
13 J.O. 139, 24.12.1952, p. 2922.
14 J.O. L 195, 7.8.1969.
15 O.J. L 230, 18.8.1986.
16 J.O. L 10, 13.1.1971.
17 O.J. L 237, 29.8.1974.
18 O.J. L 343, 21.12.1974.
19 J.O. C 75, 29.7.1968.
20 J.O. L 201, 12.8.1968.
21 O.J. L 30, 5.2.1976.
22 O.J. L 376, 31.12.1985.
23 O.J. L 369, 31.12.1985; O.J. L 19, 21.1.1987.

Agriculture and Transport

21.12 In the previous paragraph we attempted to illustrate the breadth of application of Regulation 17 to a variety of commercial activities. There are, however, certain sectors of the economy where Regulation 17 does not apply and the most important of these is the agricultural sector. Article 42 of the Treaty gave the Council the power to determine the extent to which the competition rules applies to the agricultural domain and Regulation 26 of 1962[1] lays down the applicable rules. Briefly, Article 86 applies to the production of and trade in agricultural goods but according to Article 2(1) of Regulation 26, Article 85(1) of the Treaty does not apply to agreements, decisions or practices of farmers or farmers' organisations which form an integral part of a national market organisation, or are necessary for the attainment of the objectives set out in Article 39 of the Treaty. Article 2 of the Regulation provides a simplified exemption/confirmation procedure which has rarely been utilised; although in *New Potatoes*[2] the Commission confirmed that Article 85(1) was not applicable to the agreements and decisions applied by seven regional and economic agricultural committees and their producer groups, which dealt with the production and marketing of new potatoes in France.

Unlike agriculture, which is affected by the rules on competition only to the extent determined by the Council, the transport sector is subject to Articles 85 and 86. However, in 1962, Council Regulation 141[3] declared Articles 85 and 86 inapplicable to transport by air and by sea, and also provided that Regulation 17 should not apply to other transport sectors. Instead, separate implementing regulations have been adopted to regulate restrictive practices in transport services concerning railroad and inland waterways. The latter sectors are governed by Council Regulations (EEC) 1017/68[4] and Commission Regulations (EEC) 1629 and 1630/69,[5] but only one case has arisen in this context. In *EATE*[6] the Commission decided that an agreement between two French trade associations, one representing shipowners and the other representing inland waterway forwarding agents, put foreign inland waterway carriers, who were not party to the agreement, at a competitive disadvantage because levies imposed by all French forwarding agents were distributed to an organisation from which foreign carriers were excluded. In *ANTIB v EC Commission*[7] the decision of the Commission was upheld by the Court.

As far as transport by sea and air are concerned significant developments occurred in 1986 and 1987. In 1986 the Council adopted Regulation (EEC) 4056/86[8] which lays down detailed rules for the application of Articles 85 and 86 to maritime transport and which includes a block exemption in respect of liner conferences. The Regulations came into force on 1 July 1987 but by the end of the year the Commission had already received three complaints and three applications for individual exemptions.[9] In the air transport sector the first significant development came in *Ministère Public v Asjes*[10] where the Court of Justice was asked to rule on the compatibility with the competition rules of the compulsory procedure laid down by French law for air tariffs. It held that Article 84(2) which postpones the application of the Common Transport Policy to air and sea transport, does not preclude the application of the competition rules to the air transport sector; and that the Member States were bound under Article 5(2) of the Treaty, in conjunction with Articles 3(f) and 85, not to adopt or maintain in force any measures which could deprive these provisions of their effectiveness in the field of air transport. This judgment followed the initiation by the Commission in July 1986 of formal proceedings under Article 89(1) of the Treaty against ten Community airlines which it accused of capacity and revenue-sharing arrangements and pricing concertation;[11] in 1987 a further three airlines were included in the Commission's proceedings.[12] The actions against the airlines were resolved in 1987 in the context of the overall package of measures designed to speed up progress towards completion of the internal market in air transport. Two of these measures were Regulations adopted under Article 87 of the Treaty. Council Regulation (EEC) 3975/87[13] lays down the procedure for applying competition rules to air transport; it applies to international air transport between Community airports and is not dissimilar to Regulation 17 in respect of its investigation and enforcement powers but does have a 90-days' opposition procedure concerning the application of Article 85(3). Council Regulation (EEC) 3976/87[14] enables the Commission to adopt block exemption Regulations for certain types of agreements and concerted practices including capacity planning and coordination, revenue sharing, slot allocation and joint purchasing and operation of computer reservation systems.

1 O.J. (Sp. Ed.) 1959–1962, p. 129.
2 O.J. L 59, 4.3.1988.
3 O.J. (Sp. Ed.) 1959–1962, p. 291.
4 O.J. (Sp. Ed.) 1980, I, p. 302.
5 O.J. (Sp. Ed.) 1969, II, pp. 371 and 381.
6 O.J. L 219, 17.8.1985.
7 Case 272/85, O.J. C 169, 26.6.1987.
8 O.J. L 378, 31.12.1986.
9 17th Report on Competition Policy, point 47.
10 Joined cases 209–213/84, O.J. C 131, 25.9.1986.
11 16th Report on Competition Policy, point 36.
12 17th Report on Competition Policy, point 46.
13 O.J. L 374, 31.12.1987.
14 O.J. 374, 31.12.1987.

Public enterprise: Article 90 of the Treaty

21.13 To a greater or lesser extent all of the Member States engage in the ownership or management of commercial enterprises and major public utilities. Article 90(1) of the Treaty makes it clear that in respect of public undertakings and undertakings to which special or exclusive rights have been granted, the Member States must not enact or maintain in force any measure contrary to the rules contained in Articles 85 to 94 of the Treaty. Article 90(2), however, contains an exception to the rule in Article 90(1): this states that undertakings entrusted with the operation of services of general economic interest or having the character of a revenue-producing monopoly are subject to the rules contained in the Treaty, in particular to the rules on competition, insofar as the application of such rules does not obstruct the performance, in law or in fact, of the particular tasks assigned to them. In Ireland enterprises falling into this category include the Electricity Supply Board (ESB), An Post, An Bord Telecom, and the Sugar Company.

The exception in Article 90(2) must be construed strictly: *BRT v Sabam & NV Fonior*.[1] Moreover, in order to benefit from the exception a private undertaking, claiming to have been entrusted with the operation of a service of general economic importance or having the character of a revenue-producing monopoly, must demonstrate that it does so by virtue of some definite official act. It is not sufficient that its activities are merely authorised or approved by the public authorities: *Gesellschaft zur Leistungsschutzrechten*.[2] Finally, it is not sufficient to claim that the application of the Treaty rules to an undertaking entrusted with the operation of a service of general economic importance will make the performance of its tasks more difficult or more complicated; there must be a real obstruction in the performance of its duties: *British Telecom*.[3]

1 Case 127/73, [1974] E.C.R. 51.
2 O.J. L 370, 28.12.1981.
3 O.J. L 360, 21.12.1982.

National competition law and Community law

21.14 A basic principle of Community law is that Community law takes priority over conflicting national laws in any subject in respect of which the Member States have transferred competence to the Community under the Treaty. In the field of competition law, however, the Treaty clearly envisaged the survival of national rules concerning restrictive practices and monopolies. In this regard, Article 87(2) of the Treaty, which enables the Council and the Commission to implement Articles 85 and 86, requires the two Community institutions, *inter alia*

> '(e) to determine the relationship between national laws and the provisions contained in this Section or adopted pursuant to these Articles.'

The Community institutions have not yet adopted special rules to govern the relationship between national law and Community competition law, but the Court of Justice has adopted general rules applicable to conflicts between national and Community competition rules. In *Walt Wilhelm v Bundeskartellamt*[1] the Court ruled that conflicts between rules of the Community and national rules must be resolved by applying the principle that Community law takes precedence. So long as a Regulation adopted pursuant to Article 87(2)(e) of the Treaty has not provided otherwise

> '. . . national authorities may take action against an agreement in accordance with their national competition laws, even when an examination of the agreement from the point of view of its compatibility with Community law is pending before the Commission, subject however, to the condition that the application of national law must not prejudice the full uniform application of Community law or the effects of measures taken to implement it.'

This ruling was reiterated in the 'perfume cases': *Procureur de la République v Giry*.[2] In these cases the Court of Justice was invited by the Commission and by the Danish Government to rule that national law cannot be applied where it would result in an exemption under Article 85(3) being called into question. The Court declined to make such a ruling because a conflict of this type was not at issue in the instant case. However, an application of general principles would tend to suggest that an agreement benefiting from an exemption under Article 85(3), arising out of the application of a block exemption Regulation of the Commission, to be jeopardised by the application of national legislation the effect of which would be to prohibit or nullify that agreement.[3]

In Ireland, competition law is to be found in the Restrictive Practices Act, 1972, as amended in 1987, and the Mergers, Take-overs and Monopolies (Control) Act, 1978. As regards restrictive practices, binding rules only come into operation on the adoption of a ministerial order, so any potential conflict will be between an order prohibiting activities which are permitted or exempted under Community law. The Mergers, Take-overs and Monopolies (Control) Act, 1978 imposes a notification requirement in respect of transactions involving assets in excess of £10m.; title to shares cannot pass until the merger has been approved. This should be contrasted with the notification criteria in the draft concentration

Regulation[4] where the minimum turnover required is 1,000m. ECU. There is obviously scope for conflict if, and when, the Community draft Regulation on concentration comes into force.

1 Case 14/68, [1969] E.C.R. 1, [1969] C.M.L.R. 100.
2 Joined cases 253/78, 1–3/79, [1980] E.C.R. 2327, [1981] 2 C.M.L.R. 99.
3 See also Kurt Markert, *Some Legal and Administrative Problems of the co-existence of Community and National Competition Law in The EEC*, (1974) 11 C.M.L. Rev. 92.; J.-F. Verstrynge, *The relationship between National and Community Anti-Trust Law*, (1981) Nwr. J. Int. L. & Bus. 358.
4 COM(88) 97 final, 25 April, 1988.

The impact of competition law in Ireland

21.15 For some time the Commission has been encouraging national courts to apply Articles 85 and 86 in cases coming before them, with a view to decentralising the enforcement machinery and making the remedial relief more evenly available.[1] It has emphasised that the Court of Justice has confirmed the direct effectiveness of the prohibitions in Articles 85 and 86: *BRT v Sabam and NV Folior*.[2] And because the power to apply Article 85(1) necessarily implies the power to apply Article 85(2), it is for the national court to interpret such nullity in relation to the applicable national law: *Bilger v Jehle*.[3] Likewise, as long as no decision has been taken by the Commission in respect of an agreement notified after Regulation 17 came into force, the parties to an agreement implement it at their own risk; accordingly, national courts can give judgment on the nullity, or otherwise, of an agreement that has been notified to the Commission but in respect of which there has not yet been a decision: *Brasserie de Haecht v Wilkin-Janssen*.[4] In addition, all the block exemption Regulations are directly applicable and may be relied on in domestic courts. But, despite the availability of these remedies to national courts and tribunals, the Commission noted that up to the end of 1986 no damages had been awarded in national courts for infringements of Articles 85 and 86.

In Ireland there have not been many instances of the application of competition rules and doubts have been expressed as to whether Irish firms—and their legal advisers—are making proper use of the competition policy.[5] Indeed, there have been remarkably few notifications of agreements concluded by Irish companies: in the period between 1973 and 1980 there were 129 notifications of which half had been notified in 1973.[6] The adoption of further group exemption Regulations means that fewer, rather than more, notifications will be made, notwithstanding the opposition procedure embodied in three of the block exemption Regulations. There is only one instance of a decision on an application for negative clearance or a notification for an exemption: in *Irish Banks' Standing Committee*[7] the Commission held that the agreements between the Associated Banks (Allied Irish Bank, Bank of Ireland, Northern Bank and Ulster Bank), on opening hours, clearing rules and direct debiting systems, were not in breach of Article 85(1) and granted a negative clearance. There has also been only one case in which a block exemption agreement has been applied by an Irish court: in *Aluminium Distributors Ltd v Alcan Windows Ltd*[8] McWilliam J. applied Commission Regulation (EEC) 67/67,[9] on exclusive distribution agreements, and held that the agreement at issue was invalidated by Article 85(1).

Similarly, there have been few complaints to the Commission by Irish parties. FII Limited was one of a number of enterprises in Europe that complained to the Commission about refusals to supply and discriminatory pricing imposed by United Brands, the banana producer. The complaints led to the imposition of a fine of 1m. ECU.[10] Two other complaints, both connected with Northern Ireland, have led to Commission Decisions in which fines were imposed. In *Re Victor Hassleblad*[11] the Commission imposed a fine of 70,000 ECU on foot of a complaint by Cameracare Limited of Belfast, and in *Fisher-Price UK*[12] three Irish retailers complained that parallel imports by them of Fisher-Price toys, through a Northern Ireland wholesaler, were being improperly restricted by the manufacturer; a fine of 300,000 ECU was imposed.

The surprising feature of Irish case-law on competition is that Article 86 has been utilised much more frequently than Article 85. An early case, *Sugar Distributors Ltd and Thomas Keleghan v Irish Sugar Co*,[13] in which the Sugar Company was accused of abusing its dominant position, was settled during the hearing before the High Court. The decision of Barrington J. in *Cadbury Ltd v Kerry Co-operative Ltd*[14] was most important in that it confirmed that damages could lie for an abuse of a dominant position, although it was held that County Kerry was not a substantial part of the common market for milk. In *RTE v Magill*[15] Costello J. granted an injunction to RTE to prevent Magill magazine producing a rival TV guide. Magill argued that RTE, as the only TV station in the state, had a dominant position on the broadcasting market. This case has recently been the subject of an oral hearing before the Commission. Lastly, in two recent actions, in which final judgment has not yet been given, Article 86 has been relied on by the plaintiffs. In *Leanort Ltd v Southern Chemicals Ltd*,[16] the plaintiffs procured an injunction to restrain the defendants from indulging in predatory pricing in the market for polystyrene insulating panels. And in *Magee v Ryan*,[17] a case that was heard *in camera*, the plaintiff (a shareholder and former managing director of Ryan Air Limited), alleged *inter alia* that Ryan Air and Aer Lingus had jointly engaged in practices in breach of Articles 85 and 86 and that this conspiracy or concerted practice had damaged the value of the plaintiff's shareholding in Ryan Air Limited; accordingly, he sought damages for breach of Articles 85 and 86.

1 Case 127/73, [1974] E.C.R. 51.
2 13th Report on Competition Policy, pt. 217.
3 Case 43/69, [1970] E.C.R. 127.
4 Case 48/72, [1973] E.C.R. 77.
5 See also John Temple Lang *Some consequences of the Internal Market for Irish Lawyers, The Legal Implications of 1992*, Irish Centre for European Law 1988.
6 See Restrictive Practices Commission, Annual Reports 1973–1980.
7 O.J. L 295, 18.10.1986.
8 [1980] J.I.S.E.L. 82.
9 O.J. (Sp. Ed.) 1967, p. 70.
10 O.J. L 95, 9.4.1976.
11 O.J. L 161, 2.6.1982, p. 18, [1982] 2 CMLR 233.
12 O.J. L 49, 23.2.1988.

13 High Court, 1975, Kenny, J.
14 [1982] I.L.R.M. 77.
15 (13 June 1986, unreported) High Court, Costello J.
16 (19 August 1988, unreported) High Court (1988 No. 5821p), Blaney J.
17 (1988) *Irish Times*, 5 October.

Appendix 1

(a) *Council Regulation 17*
O.J. (Sp. Ed.) 1959–1962, p. 87.

Regulation 27
(Form and content of
applications
and notifications)
O.J. (Sp. Ed.) 1959–1962,
p. 132.
as amended by Regulation
2526/85
O.J. L 240, 7.9.1985.

Regulation 99/63
(Hearings)
O.J. (Sp. Ed.) 1963–1964 p. 47.

(b) *Council Regulation 19/65. (Block exemption enabling Regulation)*
O.J. (Sp. Ed.) 1965–1966, p. 35.

Regulation 67/67 (Repealed)
(Exclusive distribution
agreements)
O.J. (Sp. Ed.) 1967, p. 70.

Regulation 1983/83
(Exclusive distribution
agreements)
O.J. L 173, 30.6.1983.

Regulation 1984/83
(Exclusive purchasing
agreements)
O.J. L 173, 30.6.1983.

Regulation 2349/84
(Patent licence agreements)
O.J. L 219, 26.8.1984.

Regulation 123/85
(Motor vehicle distribution
agreements)
O.J. L 15, 18.1.1985.

(c) *Council Regulation 2821/71 (Block exemption enabling Regulation)*
O.J. (Sp. Ed.) 1971 III, p. 1022.

Regulation 2779/72 (Repealed)
O.J. (Sp. Ed.) 1972,
28 Dec. – 30 Dec. p. 80.

Regulation 3604/82 (Repealed)
O.J. L 376, 31.12.1982.

Regulation 417/85	*Regulation 418/85*
(Specialisation agreements)	(Research and Development
O.J. L 53, 22.2.1985.	Cooperation Agreements)
	O.J. L 53, 22.2.1985.

(d) *Draft Regulation on Concentration/Mergers*
O.J. C 92, 31.10.1973.
O.J. C 36, 12.2.1982.
O.J. C 51, 23.2.1984.
COM (88) 97 Final.

(e) *Limitation periods*
Regulation 2988/74
O.J. L 319, 29.11.1974.

(f) *Agriculture*
Regulation 26/62
O.J. (Sp. Ed.) 1959–1962, p. 129.

(g) *Transport by road, rail and inland waterway*
Regulation 1017/68
O.J. (Sp. Ed.) 1968, I p. 302.

Regulation 1629/69
O.J. (Sp. Ed.) 1969, II, p. 371.

Regulation 1630/69
O.J. (Sp. Ed.) 1969, II, p. 381.

(h) *Sea transport*
Regulation 4056/86
O.J. L 378, 31.12.1986.

(i) *Air transport*
Regulation 3975/87
O.J. L 374, 31.12.1987.

Regulation 3976/87
O.J. L 374, 31.12.1987.

Appendix 2

Announcements and Notices

Note: Copies of these Notices and Announcements are available in most
textbooks.

(a) Exclusive dealing with commercial agents, J.O. No. 139, 24.12.1962,
p. 2921.
(b) Patent licensing agreements, J.O. No. 139, 24.12.1962, p. 2922.
(c) Agreements in the field of cooperation between enterprises, J.O. No.
C 75, 29.7.1968, p. 3.
(d) Agreements of minor importance, O.J. C 231, 12.9.1986.
(e) Importation of Japanese products, J.O. C 111, 21.10.1972.
(f) Sub-contracting agreements, O.J. C 1, 3.1.1970.
(g) Hearings officer, O.J. C 251, 25.9.1982.
(h) Comfort letters, O.J. C 343, 31.12.1982.
(i) Provisional letters, O.J. C 295, 2.11.1983.

Chapter 22

The Control of State Aids

22.1 As we have already noted (*supra* para. 21.5) Article 3(f) of the Treaty states that the activities of the Community shall include the institution of a system to ensure that competition in the Common Market is not distorted. Articles 85 and 86, in one sense, counterbalance the prohibitions—directed to the Member States—against erecting barriers to the free movement of goods. These two provisions recognise that the collusive behaviours of enterprises, or the unilateral exercise of immense market power by a firm in a dominant position, can also hinder the establishment of a single market. They presume that the exercise of market forces will be the most efficient means of creating economic growth, of stimulating product innovation and of catering for the needs of consumers. Nonetheless, the economic policies of all of the Member States recognise that there may be peripheral regions of States or branches of industry in which the private sector cannot be tempted to invest, or in which the private sector is reluctant to invest any longer. State intervention thus becomes a necessary instrument of economic policy[1], but unrestricted state assistance could be used as a form of protectionism for domestic industry, provoking retaliatory measures by other Member States and thus distorting trade between Member States.[2] Therefore, a balance had to be struck between the assumption that enterprises enter the marketplace at their own risk and using their own resources, and the recognition of the necessity for state subsidisation in certain circumstances. The Treaty rules on the control of State aids are contained in Articles 92 to 94.[3]

The system of control instituted by the Treaty can be outlined briefly. Article 92(1) declares incompatible with the common market any aid from the State or granted through State resources which: (i) distorts or threatens to distort competition; (ii) by favouring certain undertakings or the production of certain goods; (iii) in so far as it affects trade between Member States. But there are exceptions. Article 92(2) outlines three types of aid which are compatible with the common market, and Article 92(3) outlines four types of aid which may be compatible with the common market. By analogy with Articles 85 and 86, Article 92(1) operates as a prohibition although it is not phrased in such terms. Likewise, Articie 92(3) operates as an exemption system—again not expressly stated—which is administered by the Commission and, to a lesser extent, the

Council under Article 93. The assessment of compatibility with the common market of State aids is carried out mainly by the Commission, and because of the complex considerations to be balanced and determined, the Commission's powers are essentially discretionary; consequently, the Treaty provisions on State aids do not (with one notable exception) produce direct effects. The first paragraph of Article 93 requires the Commission to keep existing systems of aid under review whereas the third paragraph requires Member States to submit new aid schemes to the Commission; in the latter instance the aid may not be initiated or implemented until the Commission has examined it for compatibility with Article 92. If the Commission is not satisfied with the operation of an existing aid or if it considers that a new aid is problematic it may institute the procedure laid down in Article 93(2) which may lead, after the Member State concerned and other interested parties have been heard, to a binding Decision addressed to the State. Should the State fail to comply with the conditions of the Decision, the Commission or any other interested Member State may proceed directly to the Court of Justice to establish the infringement without having to invoke the procedure laid down in Articles 169 and 170 of the Treaty.

Article 93 has considerable ramifications for such a short provision. The requirement to keep existing aids under review is now an important administrative task for the Commission and approximately half of the annual Report submitted by the Commission on Competition Policy, annexed to the Annual Report to the European Parliament, is devoted to the Commission's police work in the State aids sector. The Community policy on State aids receives further publicity when, in utilising the procedure in Article 93(2), the Commission informs interested parties of current investigations by seeking information and comments through notices published in the Official Journal. And, in addition to the novel derogation from Articles 169 and 170, Article 93(2) has also generated a growing use of the Article 173 annulment action by firms and undertakings which stood to benefit from a disputed aid. This is because the Commission's power to order the termination of State aids includes the power to require repayment of unlawful aids.

The framework nature of Articles 92 and 93 is recognised in Article 94 which empowers the Council to adopt Regulations to determine the conditions of application of Articles 92 and 93.

1 Georgio Bernini, 'The rules on competition', in *Thirty Years of Community Law*, at p. 361.
2 Fiona Cownie, *State Aids in the Eighties*, (1982) 12 E.L.Rev, 247, at p. 248
3 For a recent monograph on this subject see: Despina Schina, *State Aids under the EEC Treaty – Articles 92–94* (1987).

22.2 Aid may be granted from State resources for many reasons but the most common example of State assistance occurs when an industry or a sector experiences persistent difficulties or crisis conditions. This has been the case for the coal and steel industries for longer than most other economic activities. The availability of cheap alternative energy resources in the 1950s and the emergence of less costly and more competitive steel producers in developing countries in the 1960s created severe difficulties for the coal and steel industries, and these problems were compounded by the oil crisis of the 1970s and the consequent economic recession.

The ECSC Treaty, drafted during a period of expansion for both industries, treats '. . . subsidies or aids granted by States, in any form whatsoever . . .' in an uncompromising manner. Article 4(c) declares such aids incompatible with the common market and prohibited within the Community. This would appear to allow for no exceptions but in practice the High Authority (Commission), supported by the Court of Justice, has interpreted Article 4(c) in a flexible fashion by distinguishing between aid granted by States on the one hand, and financial assistance granted by the High Authority or expressly permitted by it on the other hand.[1] This also explains why more recent Community measures to deal with the persistent difficulties in the coal and steel sectors have been based on Article 95 of the ECSC Treaty, which is the residual powers provision.

In the steel sector definitive rules were adopted by the Commission in 1980 and modified and extended in 1981 and 1985.[2] The principal objective of this aid code was to allow restructuring of production capacity, provided that surplus capacity was eliminated. Much of the aid, therefore, had to be expended on the social and economic consequences of plant closures and capacity reductions. But by the end of 1985 the Community's steel industry had succeeded in reducing its hot-rolling capacity by 28.6 million tonnes,[3] with further cuts expected in 1986. Thus, the restructuring target of 30–35 million tonnes of reductions had been achieved[4] and in November 1985 the Commission adopted Decision (ECSC) 3484/85[5] which envisaged a return to normal market circumstances and, consequently, a stricter application of Article 4(c) of the ECSC Treaty. By the end of 1987, however, the problem of structural overcapacity was as acute as ever. In any event, aid will be permissible now only for research and development purposes or for environmental protection, and—where additional closures take place—to meet up to 50 per cent of the resulting social costs.[6] In the coal sector the aid code is contained in Commission Decision (ECSC) 2064/86[7] which specifies that aid will be compatible with the common market only if it achieves one of three objectives: the improvement of the competitiveness of the coal industry; the creation of economic viability; or the solution of social or regional problems related to the coal industry.

1 Giorgio Bernini, *op. cit.* at p. 362
2 See: Commission Decision (ECSC) 257/80 O.J. L 29, 6.2.1980 p. 5; Commission Decision (ECSC) 2320/81 O.J. L 228, 13.8.1981 p.14; Commission Decision (ECSC) 1018/85 O.J. L 110, 23.4.1985 p. 5.
3 Fifteenth Report on Competition Policy, at point 180.
4 Idem.
5 O.J. L 340, 18.12.1985 p. 1.
6 Fifteenth Report on Competition Policy, at point 181.
7 O.J. L 177, 1.7.1986 p. 1.

22.3 Although not without importance, the ECSC provisions on aid are of limited sectoral effect whereas Articles 92 to 94 of the EEC Treaty apply to all economic activities. The basic rules are contained in Article 92 and the procedures for controlling and supervising aids are laid down in Article 93.

Article 92(1) declares as incompatible with the common market any financial aid granted by the State or through State resources which affects trade between Member States, favours certain undertakings or the production of certain goods, or threatens to distort competition. As early as 1966[1] the Court of Justice indicated that in the Treaty provisions on State aid only Article 93(3), which requires Member States to notify the Commission of new aid schemes, could produce direct effects. This was confirmed by the Court in *Capolongo v Azienda Agricola Maya*[2] in 1973: Article 93 imposes on the Commission an obligation to keep existing aids under review and to assess new systems of aid for their compatibility with Article 92; an assessment procedure, subject to the review of the Court of Justice, is also provided. Consequently, private parties cannot simply, on the basis of Article 92 alone, challenge State aids before a national court and expect the national tribunal to determine the issue before it. But the national court does possess that right if Article 92 has been applied or implemented by a specific Commission Decision under Article 92(2) or by a general measure provided for in Article 94.[3] In short, as the Court ruled in *Capolongo,* the first paragraph of Article 92 cannot be regarded in isolation, but must be considered within the framework of the scheme of Articles 92 to 94.

The forms taken by State aid are immensely flexible. Examples of aid condemned by the Commission and upheld by the Court of Justice include: the reduction by the State of social charges pertaining to family allowances devolving on employers in the textile sector in Italy;[6] subsidies granted by the State to French fishermen on the basis of their consumption of gas oil;[7] the provision of low interest loans and participation by regional development agencies in the capital of undertakings.[8] It is not necessary, for the purposes of the application of Article 92(1), to distinguish between aid granted directly by the State and aid granted by public or private bodies established or appointed to administer the aid: *Steinike and Weinlig.*[9] Thus, a 'solidarity grant' to farmers, payable by a national agricultural credit fund from its accumulated surpluses, was considered by the Court of Justice as an aid within the meaning of Article 92(1): *EC Commission v France.*[10] In the latter case the Commission had to deal with arguments put forward by the French Government which contended that the surpluses were generated by the management of private funds and did not come from State resources, and that the decision to make the payment was taken by the Fund's governing board on which the State representatives were in a minority. Faced with these arguments the Commission, which considered that the solidarity grant had all the characteristics of a State aid, instituted proceedings under Article 169 rather than Article 93(2), and contended that the French provisions amounted to 'a measure having an effect equivalent to a State aid.' The Court rejected this attempt to extend the scope of Article 92 and held that the measure at issue was a straightforward State aid.

The fact that other Member States provide similar assistance to firms or sectors within their jurisdiction does not justify an infringement of Article 92 by a Member State: *Steinike and Weinlig,* [11] and the fact that a Member State believes that a planned aid is compatible with the Treaty does not relieve it of the obligation to notify the Commission in advance: *EC Commission v Germany.*[12] Nor is it open to a Member State to plead absolute inability to comply with a Commission Decision requiring the abolition of an aid incompatible with the common market as defined in Article 92. In *Deufil v EC Commission*[13] the Belgian Government pleaded inability to recover an aid which took the form of a shareholding in a ceramics firm because the latter had not realised a profit. The Court held that the shareholding/loan could be recouped by the liquidation of the company which could be brought about by the Belgian authorities in their capacity as shareholders or creditors.

The liquidation of an undertaking appears to be a ruthless and extreme means of securing the abolition of a State aid, but such an action is merely a logical consequence of the ruling of the Court of Justice in the 'Kohlgesetz' case: *EC Commission v Germany*. In that case the court held that to be of practical effect a Commission Decision requiring the abolition or modification of an aid may include an obligation to require repayment of aid granted in breach of the Treaty. Consequently, recipients or likely recipients of financial assistance from State resources are on notice that if the Commission considers that Article 92(1) has been infringed, the aid—if already disbursed—will have to be repaid. Therefore, enterprises cannot claim to have a legitimate expectation to aid: *Deufil v EC Commission*; and the Commission has made it clear, in recent decisions, that it will apply the repayment obligation strenuously. In July 1988 it ordered ENI, an Italian State holding company, to repay LIT 260bn (184m. ECU) to the Italian State in respect of illegal aids paid to the clothing subsidiaries of the Lanerossi textile company between 1983 and 1987.[14]

But before the Commission orders the repayment of aid it must demonstrate that aid is capable of distorting or threatening competition and of affecting trade between Member States. The reasoning requirement of Article 190 obliges the Commission to set out these circumstances in the Decision, which should contain information on the position of the recipient undertaking in the relevant market, the pattern of trade between Member States in the products in question and the undertakings exports of those products: *Netherlands and Leeuwarder Papierwarenfabriek v EC Commission*.[15] In this connection Article 92 is not concerned with the causes or aims of State measures, however laudable they might be; it is concerned only with their effects: *Italy v EC Commission*.[16] The Commission is obliged to consider all the legal and factual circumstances surrounding an aid and the aid in question cannot be considered separately from the effects of its method of financing: *France v EC Commission*.[17]

The social or fiscal objectives of a State aid cannot exclude it from the ambit of Article 92, nor does the compatibility of a system of levies with Article 95 (which prohibits discriminatory taxation) absolve the system from the application of Article 92 where the levy is used to finance developments in the domestic textile industry: *France v EC Commission*.[18] Similarly, the conformity of a contested aid with national rules implementing conjunctural policy within the meaning of Article 103 of the Treaty does not exempt it from the application of Article 92: *Deufil v EC Commission*.[19] However, it is also clear that if a measure falls under Article 92 it cannot be subject simultaneously to the prohibitions in Articles 9, 12, 13 or 30 of the Treaty: *Steinike and Weinlig*[20]; *Ianelli and Volpi v Meroni*.[21] This is not to say that elements of an aid system which do not infringe Article 92 cannot fall under other provisions of the Treaty, but they may be so indissolubly linked to the object of the aid that it is impossible to evaluate them separately; the procedure under Article 93 should therefore be used to determine the overall compatibility of the aid.[22]

1 Case 6/64 *Costa v ENEL* [1964] E.C.R. 585, [1964] C.M.L.R. 425.
2 Case 77/72 [1973] E.C.R. 611, [1974] 1 C.M.L.R. 230.
3 See also: Case 74/76 *Ianelli and Volpi v Meroni* [1977] E.C.R. 557, [1977] 2 C.M.L.R. 688; Case 78/76 *Steinike and Weinlig v Bundesamt für Ernährung und Forstwirtschaft* [1977] E.C.R. 595, [1977] 2 C.M.L.R. 688.
4 *Supra* fn. 2
5 Case 93/84 *EC Commission v France* [1985] E.C.R. 829.
6 Case 52/84 *EC Commission v Belgium* [1986] E.C.R. 89, [1987] 1 C.M.L.R. 710.
7 Case 78/76, *Supra*, fn. 3.
8 Case 290/83 *EC Commission v France* [1985] E.C.R. 439, [1986] 2 C.M.L.R. 546.
9 Case 78/76, *Supra*, fn. 3.
10 Case 171/83R. [1983] E.C.R. 2621.
11 Case 78/76, *Supra*, fn. 3.
12 Case 70/72 [1973] E.C.R. 813, [1973] C.M.L.R. 741.
13 Case 310/85 O.J. C 77, 24.3.1977 p. 3.
14 Commission Press Release IP (88) 488; 26.7.1988.
15 Joined cases 296 and 318/82 [1985] E.C.R. 809, [1985] 3 C.M.L.R. 380.
16 Case 173/73 [1974] E.C.R. 709, [1974] 2 C.M.L.R. 593.
17 Case 47/69 [1970] E.C.R. 487, [1970] C.M.L.R. 351.
18 *Idem.*
19 *Supra*, fn. 15.
20 Case 78/76, *Supra*, fn. 3.
21 Case 74/76, *Supra*, fn. 3.
22 *Idem.* at p. 575 and 715 respectively.

22.4 Certain types of aid are or may be compatible with the common market. Article 92(2) sets out three categories of aid which *are* compatible with the common market even if trade between Member States is affected or competition is distorted:

(a) aid having a social character, granted to individual consumers, provided that there is no discrimination concerning the origin of the goods in question;

(b) aid to make good damage caused by natural disasters or exceptional occurrences;

(c) aid granted to certain parts of Germany to ameliorate the economic consequences of the division of the country.

These categories of aid and the reasons for their compatibility are self-explanatory.

Article 92(3) indicates three types of aid that may be declared compatible with the common market and sub-paragraph (d) permits the Council, acting on a proposal from the Commission, to specify other categories of aid to be added to the list. This power has been utilised only in connection with the chronically troubled shipbuilding sector. For almost two decades the Community has provided rules on permissible aids in this sector, but the crisis has persisted and a new strategy has had to be elaborated. The current rules are contained in the Sixth Directive[1] which expires at the end of 1990. This sets an aid ceiling of 28 per cent of the contract value and is designed to '. . . steer Community shipbuilding towards the market segments where it remains most competitive and where the links with subcontractors and supply industries are closest . . .'.[2]

The three categories of possibly compatible aid listed in Article 92(3) are:

(a) aid to promote the economic development of areas where the standard of living is abnormally low or where there is serious underemployment;
(b) aid to promote the execution of an important project of common European interest or to remedy a serious disturbance in the economy of a Member State;
(c) aid to facilitate the development of certain economic activities or of certain economic areas, where such aid does not adversely affect trading conditions to an extent contrary to the common interest.

In effect, these are the criteria against which new systems of aid, notified to the Commission under Article 93(3), are tested and it can be readily appreciated that the Commission—when deciding whether to exempt a notified aid—exercises a discretionary power involving appraisals of an economic and social nature: *Deufil v EC Commission.*[3] For example, in 1983 the Commission approved the plans of the Irish Government to designate the Greater Cork Area for a period of three years; the effect of the designation was to raise aid ceilings in the Cork region from 45 per cent to 50 or 60 per cent in the case of small undertakings. Applying Article 92(3)(a), the Commission did not raise any objection to the plans because of the serious deterioration in the employment situation in Cork (the closures of the Ford and Dunlop factories and the Verolme dockyard) and because of the generally unfavourable socio-economic situation in Ireland.[4]

Over the years the Commission has enunciated a variety of reasons why aid will not be considered as permissible under Article 92(3):

(a) operating aid to cover an undertaking's production costs will rarely bring to the area concerned any lasting benefit by way of increases in income or reduction of unemployment;
(b) aid will not be in the common interest if the industry in question suffers from a Community-wide overcapacity;
(c) aid will not be viewed favourably if its effect is to divert investment away from less well-off Member States;
(d) aid which does not have a compensatory justification will not be permissible, that is if its pursuit of objectives compatible with the community interest do not outweigh the harmful effects of the distortion of competition or the effect on trade between Member States;
(e) aid will not be permissible if the investments in question would be brought about by market forces in any event.[5]

1 Council Directive (EEC) 87/167 O.J. L 69, 12.3.1987 p. 55.
2 Sixteenth Report on Competition Policy, at point 215.
3 *Supra,* fn. 13, para. 22.3.
4 Fourteenth Report on Competition Policy, at point 276.
5 Fiona Cownie, *op. cit.,* fn. 2, para. 22.1.

22.5 Article 92 contains the basic rules on State aids whereas the procedures for assessing aids are laid down in Article 93; a distinction is drawn between existing aids, which the Commission must keep under review (Article 93(1)) and new aids which must be notified to the Commission for prior examination (Article 93(3)). In practice, once a new aid has been approved by the Commission it becomes an existing aid and is kept more or less under permanent scrutiny by the Commission. If the Commission considers that altered conditions require the termination or modification of an aid it will make its views known to the Member State in question in a recommendation (which has no binding force under Article 189). If the Member State does not comply with this request the Commission will then commence the contentious procedure in Article 93(2).

However, most of the Commission's assessment powers are exercised in relation to new systems of aid notified by the Member States. Article 93(3) reads as follows:

'The Commission shall be informed, in sufficient time to enable it to submit its comments, of any plans to grant or alter aid. If it considers that any such plan is not compatible with the common market having regard to Article 92, it shall without delay initiate the procedure provided for in paragraph 2. The Member State concerned shall not put its proposed measures into effect until this procedure has resulted in a final decision.'

The operation of this provision was discussed at length in *Gebrüder Lorenz v Germany and Land Rheinland/Pfalz.*[1] Its object is to give the Commission time to form a *prima facie* opinion on the partial or complete conformity of an aid with the Treaty; Member States cannot unilaterally terminate this period of examination but in the absence of a time limit the Court of Justice considered it appropriate to fix the period, by reference to Articles 173 and 175, at two months; after the expiry of this period the Member State may implement the aid but in the interests of legal certainty the Commission should be informed about this step; the aid then becomes an existing aid subject to continual scrutiny under Article 93(1); if the Commission forms the view that the aid is compatible with the Common Market—using the criteria laid down in Article 92(3)—it is not under an obligation to issue a decision within the meaning of Article 189; the restriction on the implementation of State aid during this preliminary period is directly effective, and if the Commission decides to institute the contentious procedure under Article 93(2) the restriction remains directly effective until a final decision is adopted.

The Commission is empowered by Article 93(3) to take immediate interim measures where necessary: *EC Commission v Germany,*[2] and it is not obliged to specify a time limit for the alteration of a system of aid if it was introduced in contravention of Article 93(3): *EC Commission v Italy.*[3]

Where the Commission has come to the conclusion that an aid is not incompatible with Article 92 it must inform the Member State of its conclusion; if it harbours any doubts on this issue the Commission must initiate immediately the contentious procedure under Article 93(2); but given the urgency of the initial examination by the Commission it is not under an obligation to consult the interested parties (other Member States, competing enterprises) or to solicit their comments: *Germany v EC Commission*.[4] Finally, the obligation to inform the Commission of any new aid applies to the original plan as well as any alterations to that plan: *Heineken v Inspecteur der Vennootschapsbelasting*.[5]

1 Case 120/73 [1973] E.C.R. 1471.
2 *Supra,* para. 3, fn. 12, para. 22.3.
3 *Supra,* para. 3, fn. 16, para. 22.3.
4 Case 84/82, [1984] E.C.R. 1451, [1985] 1 C.M.L.R. 153.
5 Joined cases 91, 127/83 [1984] E.C.R. 3435, [1985] 1 C.M.L.R. 389.

22.6 If Article 93(1) and (3) allow the Commission to keep existing aids under supervision and to scrutinise new aid respectively, Article 93(2) provides it with the power to terminate assistance from State resources and, should a State fail to comply with the decision of the Commission, to proceed directly to the Court of Justice to have the infringement established. Thus, there are two separate stages involved. The first stage commences with the Commission giving notice to the 'parties concerned' and asking them to submit their comments on the aid in dispute, be it an existing aid or a proposed aid. Article 93(2) does not indicate who was envisaged under the rubric of the 'parties concerned' nor does it specify how the Commission is to give them notice. However, the Court of Justice has filled these lacunae: in *Intermills v EC Commission*[1] the Court held that the 'parties concerned' are not only the undertakings receiving aid but also the persons, undertakings or associations whose interests might be affected by the grant of the aid, in particular competing undertakings and trade associations; this means that there is an indeterminate group of persons to whom notice must be given. From this it followed that the Commission could not individually notify all interested parties and, under these circumstances, the publication of a notice in the Official Journal is an appropriate means of informing the parties that a procedure has been initiated and of giving them an opportunity to put forward their arguments. In fact the Commission had adopted this practice at an early stage.[2] The process can be illustrated by an Irish example. In December 1983 the Irish Government informed the Commission of a proposed aid amounting to IR£2.9 million in favour of a producer of polyester yarn located at Letterkenny, Co Donegal.[3] A notice inviting interested parties to submit their comments appeared in the Official Journal in March 1984.[4] The Commission decided that the aid was incompatible with the common market even though there was chronic unemployment in the area. The aid in question would have simply added to capacity underutilisation in the industry and, because the company in question exported virtually all its output, the proposed aid would affect trade in the Community and distort competition, without making a contribution to regional development sufficient to compensate for that distortion.[5]

Originally, the Court considered that the sole aim of the communication provided for in the first sentence of Article 93(2) was to obtain from persons concerned all the information required for the guidance of the Commission with regard to its future action: *EC Commission v Germany.*[6] But by the 1980s the Court had changed its position quite considerably. In *Germany v EC Commission*[7] the Court described the procedure as an essential guarantee to the Member States and to the parties concerned which allows them to make their views known, and in *EC Commission v France*[8] the Court stated that Article 93(2) provided all the parties concerned with guarantees which are specifically adapted to the special problems created by State aid with regard to competition in the common market, and goes much further than the preliminary procedure laid down in the similar remedy created by Article 169 of the Treaty in which only the Commission and the Member State concerned participate. It can hardly be a coincidence that this change of view by the Court has occurred at a time when other Member States and third parties have become much more aggressive in challenging Commission decisions, approving the grant of aid to particular undertakings or sectors of industry, under the annulment procedure set out in Article 173. A connected issue concerns the Member State which is the addressee of a Commission Decision: if the State fails to take issue with the decision within the 2-month challenge period it cannot contest the legality of the decision in subsequent proceedings brought by the Commission before the Court of Justice under Article 93(2): *EC Commission v France;*[9] *EC Commission v Belgium.*[10] Conversely, recipients of aid are directly and individually concerned (within the meaning of the second paragraph of Article 173) by a Commission decision requiring a Member State to abolish that aid: *Intermills v EC Commission.*[11]

Finally, if a Member State fails to abolish or modify the aid in question the Commission or another Member State may go directly to the Court of Justice to have the infringement established. This operates as a derogation from Articles 169 and 170 and the reason is simple enough: it would be a duplication of effort to oblige the Commission to institute the procedure leading to a reasoned opinion under Article 169 when the procedure under Article 93(2) has already allowed for a more wide-ranging exchange of views. However, the Court of Justice has shifted its ground as to whether the Article 169 remedy was equally admissible: *EC Commission v Germany.*[12] By the early 1980s the Court made it clear that the procedural guarantee in Article 93(2) for parties other than Member States required that, while the compatibility of an aid scheme in relation to other Community rules could be assessed under Article 169, the procedure under Article 93(2) had to be utilised if the Commission wants to establish an aid as incompatible with the Common Market: *EC Commission v France.*[13]

---

1 Case 323/82 [1984] E.C.R. 3809, [1986] 1 C.M.L.R. 614.
2 See: Alan Dashwood, *Control of State Aids in the EEC: Prevention and Cure under Article 93;* 12 C.M.L.Rev. 1975 43, at p. 53.
3 Fourteenth Report on Competition Policy, at point 235.
4 O.J. C 90, 31.3.1984 p. 4.
5 Commission Decision (EEC) 84/498 O.J. L 276, 19.10.1984 p. 40.
6 *Supra,* fn. 12, para. 22.3.
7 *Supra,* fn. 4, 22.5.

8 *Supra,* fn. 8, 22.3.
9 *Supra,* fn. 5, para. 22.3.
10 *Supra,* fn. 6, para. 22.3.
11 *Supra,* fn. 1, para. 22.3.
12 *Supra,* fn. 12, para 22.3.
13 *Supra,* fn. 8, para. 22.3.

22.7 Thus far we have been concerned with the roles played by the Commission and the Court of Justice, but the Treaty envisaged that the Council should also take part in controlling State aids. Firstly, Article 94 empowered the Council to adopt Regulations to determine the conditions of application of Articles 92 and 93. The Council has not utilised this power although the Court has often hinted that a procedural Regulation would be desirable, for example to establish the length of the preliminary period of investigation of new aids notified by Member States to the Commission: *Lorenz v Germany and Land Rheinland/Pfalz.*[1]

The Council has another, less Community-orientated power and this is provided in Article 93(2). The third subparagraph of this provision allows the Council, on the application of a Member State, to decide that aid which the Member State intends to grant is compatible with the Common Market. Such a decision has the effect of suspending a Commission investigation of the aid in question. Needless to remark, this power is not often utilised but instances of it can be found comparatively recently.[2]

1 *Supra,* fn. 1, para. 22.5.
2 See: Fifteenth Report on Competition Policy, at point 251.

22.8 A review of Community rules on State aids would not be complete without some reference to the various 'codes', 'guidelines' and 'frameworks' issued by the Commission to explain its policy on the application of Articles 92 and 93. These communications are not binding measures within the meaning of Article 189 of the Treaty but they are important indicators as to what the Commission considers permissible.

We have already noted how the Commission objected to Irish Government plans to grant aid to a producer of synthetic yarn located in Co Donegal (*supra*, para. 22.6). The crisis conditions in the market for synthetic fibres have persisted for more than a decade, and the Community continues to have significant surplus production capacity. These are the circumstances in which Member States are tempted to assist struggling manufacturers, and—whether or not State assistance is forthcoming—the participants in the marketplace are tempted to share the available market between themselves. Where the latter type of behaviour occurs the rules laid down in Articles 85 and 86 of the Treaty are applicable: the *'Polypropylene'* decision of the Commission is a good example.[1] As regards State intervention, the Commission's first statement on the synthetic fibre sector was issued in 1977[2] and this synthetic fibre and yarn 'code' has been extended since then for two-year periods. In view of the industry's chronic overcapacity, the code frowns on State aid for production purposes and encourages diversification out of the synthetic yarn sector.[3]

Other communications outlining Commission policy include Guidelines for the examination of State aids in the fisheries sector[4] published in 1985 and we have already seen how the policy on aids in the shipbuilding sector has been encapsulated in the form of Directives (*supra* para. 22.4). The Commission has also published 'frameworks' for the application of Articles 92 and 93 to horizontal, as opposed to sectoral aids. Investigations carried out by the Commission revealed that by the mid-1980s aid for research and development purposes had become the largest form of government support for industry in many Member States. Consequently, the Commission produced a Community framework for State aid for research and development in 1985.[5] An earlier Commission framework, on aids in environmental matters, was adopted in 1974 and extended and modified in 1980 and 1986.[6]

Another significant Commission statement is the Communication on the coordination of aid granted for the development of certain economic areas. The first such Communication was published in 1971 and the most recent guidelines became effective on 1 January 1979;[7] this Communication was supplemented by a further Communication in August 1988, in which the Commission also set out the methodology employed by it in respect of aids falling within Article 92(3)(a) and (c).[8] The Communication expresses the Commission's attitude towards regional aids in terms either of the net grant equivalent of the initial investment or the cost per job. For central regions, such as parts of Germany or the Netherlands, the total amount that may be awarded by State authorities is limited to 20 per cent of the initial investment. Intermediate regions, such as France or parts of the United Kingdom, are limited to 30 per cent, while in Ireland and other peripheral regions the limit is 75 per cent of the initial investment, and another 25 per cent in other aid may be paid over a minimum of five years.

1 Commission Decision (EEC) 86/398 O.J. L 230, 18.8.1986 p. 1.
2 Seventh Report on Competition Policy, at point 204.
3 Fifteenth Report on Competition Policy, at point 196.
4 O.J. C 268, 19.10.1985 p. 2.
5 O.J. C 83, 11.4.1986 p. 2.
6 Sixteenth Report on Competition Policy, at point 259.
7 O.J. C 31, 3.2.1979 p. 9.
8 O.J. C 212, 12.8.1988 p. 2.

State aids in Ireland

22.9 When the Irish Government was negotiating accession to the Communities in the early 1970s it was concerned to preserve the system of investment incentives that had helped to rejuvenate the Irish economy. The result of its endeavours can be seen in Protocol 30, attached to the Act of Accession. The Protocol is entitled 'Ireland' and in it the Member States recognised that the Irish Government had embarked upon a policy of industrialisation and economic development designed to raise living standards, reduce employment, and eliminate disparities in regional development; that the achievement of the objectives of Irish industrialisation and economic development policy was in the common interest of all the Member States; and, in particular, that these objectives were to be taken into account in the application of Articles 92 and 93 of the Treaty. The Irish Government was well pleased with the Protocol:

'This Protocol is of far reaching importance for our industrial and regional development, and indeed for the future growth of the economy as a whole. We can now proceed with development plans secure in the knowledge that we will be able to operate an adequate system of development aids and supports and that Community resources will be available to us.

We shall be able to honour commitments already undertaken in respect of export tax reliefs and to continue to grant these reliefs to new firms which begin manufacturing for export. Our industrial incentives will be considered in due course by the Commission after our Accession as part of their continuing examination of the whole structure of State aids through the Community'.[1]

It will be observed that government's main preoccupation was with the system of Export Sales Relief—introduced in the Finance (Miscellaneous Provisions) Act, 1956, and extended and amended on numerous occasions thereafter—which was used to attract foreign manufacturers to Ireland. However, the Commission was never convinced that Export Sales Relief was compatible with Article 92 and the government never conceded its incompatibility, particularly in view of the terms of Protocol 30. In the event, a compromise was embodied in the Finance Act, 1980 whereby a new export sales tax of 10%, applicable to all manufacturing enterprises, was introduced and whereby all firms approved by the Industrial Development Authority (IDA) prior to 12 December 1980 will continue to benefit from Export Sales Relief until 1990.

Of equal importance is the view taken by the Commission of the financial incentives granted by the IDA under Part III of the Industrial Development Act, 1986.[2] Sections 22 to 37 of the 1986 Act allow for a variety of financial aids including: grants for fixed assets (section 22); grants for reduction of interest (section 23); loan guarantees (sections 26 and 27); training and research grants (sections 2, 8 and 29); technology acquisition grants (section 30); and grants to secure reduction of factory rents (section 32). Such aids may be awarded for projects established in designated areas (section 4 and third schedule); these areas include the entire Western seaboard (and all of Connaught) as well as other specified areas like inner city Dublin and Cork. This consolidating legislation falls to be considered as existing aid under Article 93 but it is unlikely that it falls outside the context of the Communication on regional aids (referred to *supra* at para. 22.8. Similar considerations apply to aid structures operated by the Shannon Free Airport Development Company Limited (SFADCo)[3] and Udaras na Gaeltachta.[4]

The special incentives underpinning the launch of the Financial Services Centre at the Customs House Dock Site, introduced by provisions of the 1986 and 1987 Finance Acts were submitted for approval to the Commission in 1987 and a favourable response was given.[5]

---

1 Government White Paper 'The Accession of Ireland to the European Communities' Prl. 2064, at 2.27–2.30.
2 For an analysis of this Act see: *Irish Current Law Statutes Annotated 1986*, annotation by Robert Clark.
3 See: Shannon Free Airport Development Company Limited Act, 1959 (as amended).
4 See: Udaras na Gaeltachta Act, 1979.
5 Seventeenth Report on Competition Policy, at point 249.

Chapter 23

The Common Agricultural Policy (CAP)

Introduction

23.1 The Stockholm Convention of 4 January 1960, which established the European Free Trade Area, confines itself to trade in industrial goods; agricultural goods, with minor exceptions, were excluded from the scope of the agreement. Indeed, there were good reasons for this exclusion because in the signatory states there existed profound differences in levels of self-sufficiency and State intervention as well as obvious social, climatic and geographical variations.

Why, then, was agriculture included in the EEC Treaty? Article 9 of the Treaty states that the

'Community shall be based on a customs union which shall cover all trade goods . . .'

This concept is further explained by Article 39(2)(c)

'In the Member States, agriculture constitutes a sector closely linked with the economy as a whole'.

The logic of this particular connection is obvious: if agricultural prices differ from area to area, wages and salaries will also differ accordingly and the prices of goods will be affected. The result will be a distortion of the conditions of competition. Another reason can be found in the need to balance the national interests of the contracting parties. For example, the prospect of enlarged markets in industrial goods must have been foremost in the minds of the West German negotiators, while the French delegation looked forward to increased participation in German agricultural markets, especially in the grain sector. The major reason, however, can be found in the necessity to provide

'. . . a fair standard of living for the agricultural community, in particular by increasing the individual earnings of persons engaged in agriculture'. (Article 39 of the Treaty.)

This provision may sound patronising, but the fact remains that in the time of the Treaty negotiations in 1957, the agricultural community in the Six comprised between 15 and 20 million people.[1] It was also recognised that if the agricultural markets were not organised properly, farmers' incomes were not likely to increase to any appreciable degree.[2] The political necessity to include agriculture in the Treaty must have been clear to all the negotiating States.

Once the political decision to include agriculture had been made, it became necessary to formulate a plan or a policy to overcome the serious problems involved in European agriculture.

1 Second General Report on the Activities of the Communities, p. 136.
2 J. Marsh and C. Ritson, *Agricultural Policy and the Common Market, 1971 at p. 9.*

23.2 Since the turn of the century there had been some form of governmental control in the agricultural sphere in nearly every Western nation. The 'Six' were not an exception. However, it was recognised that if a common market was to be established in agricultural goods, it would require more than conjunctural provisions to achieve that aim.[1] The agricultural problems of Europe were structural, and Article 39(2)(a) of the Treaty required that this fact be taken into account when formulating the agricultural policy.

In contrast to other sectors of the economy, demand and, to a certain extent, supply for agricultural products is inelastic.[2] Increases in production are not always accompanied by higher prices, if only because of the increased use of technology.[3] Price levels are open to pressure on two fronts: external pressure because of world surpluses at deflated prices, and internal pressure because increases in production outstrip increases in demand.

Furthermore, agricultural resources are relatively immobile: unlike producers in other economic sectors, the farmer cannot readily increase the size of his holding, nor does his need for labour grow as production increases. On the contrary, the numbers involved in agriculture dropped by 50 per cent over the 20-year period 1950 to 1970.[4] Finally, there are the regional and social problems involved in the depopulation of certain rural areas due to current economic changes in agriculture. Prosperity tends to visit the farmer who 'rationalises', that is, who dispenses with labour in favour of machinery. In areas where few employment alternatives exist such rationalisation can have disastrous consequences.[5]

1 P. Kapteyn and P. Verloren Van Themaat, *Introduction to European Community Law*, 1973; at p. 302.
2 *Idem* p. 303.
3 *Idem.*
4 Second General Report on the Activities of the Communities, p. 136.
5 J. Marsh and C. Ritson, *Agricultural Policy and the Common Market*, 1971; at p. 28.

Treaty provisions

23.3 It was with these problems in mind that the Treaty drafters set about their task. In Article 3 of the Treaty, the activities of the Community are stated to include, under sub-paragraph (d), the adoption of a common agricultural policy. The objectives of this policy are enumerated in Article 39(1):

(a) to increase agricultural productivity by promoting technical progress and by ensuring the rational development of agricultural production and the optimum utilisation of the factors of production, in particular labour; *in order to*[1]
(b) ensure a fair standard of living to farmers
(c) to stabilise markets
(d) to assure the availability of supplies
(e) to ensure that supplies reach consumers at reasonable prices.

Article 39(2) provides that special account is to be taken of:

(i) The peculiar nature of agricultural activity that is, the social, structural, natural and economic disparities in different regions.
(ii) The need to bring the policy into operation gradually.
(iii) The fact that agriculture is an important part of the economy as a whole.

The Treaty stresses that the Common Agricultural Policy (CAP) must accompany the development of the common market which, according to Article 38(1), extends to trade in agricultural products, including fisheries. In the next sub-paragraph, Article 38(2), the special nature of the agricultural sector is recognised. This provision states that the rules for the establishment of the common market (the abolition of customs duties, abolition of quantitative restrictions, the 'Four Freedoms', and the competition rules) are to apply 'save as otherwise provided in Articles 39 to 46.' Article 42 provides that the Council may determine the extent to which the competition rules shall apply. This article also implicitly empowers the Council to suspend the operation of the rules regarding State aids.

Article 40 of the Treaty provides that the CAP should be developed by degrees and should be in force by the end of the transitional period at the latest. Article 43 provided three steps for the introduction of the CAP.

(1) The Council was obliged to call a conference to compare the policies operative in the Member States.
(2) Following the conference, the Commission, after consulting the Economic and Social Committee was to make proposals for the implementation of the CAP.
(3) The Council was vested with decision-making power to convert Commission proposals into Community legislation.

The basis of the CAP, as can be seen from Article 40(2), was the establishment of common organisations of agricultural markets. Article 40(2) provides that an organisation may be one of three types: common rules on competition, compulsory coordination of the various national market organisations or a European Market organisation. Article 40(3) lays down measures which may be used by common organisations to achieve the objectives set out in Article 39. It mentions price regulation, marketing and production aids, surplus storage and export refunds, all of which have played a big part in the development of the CAP.

Article 40(4) is the basis for the financing of the CAP: it makes provision for the establishment of one or more agricultural guidance and guarantee funds.

Another means of achieving the objectives of Article 39 is Article 41 which provides that measures such as the coordination of vocational training and agricultural research, and product promotions, may be taken within the framework of the CAP. As we have already seen, Article 43 provides the Council with the decision-making power necessary to implement the CAP.

As regards the remaining Treaty articles, Article 44 provides generally for the establishment and maintenance of minimum prices. Article 45 provides for the adaptation of existing import or guaranteed market arrangements to the Community regime. Article 46 allows for contervailing charges wherever the operation of a national market organisation has a discriminatory effect on producers in other Member States. Article 47 provides that the Economic and Social Committee shall hold itself at the disposal of the Commission.

1 It has been argued that (a) and (b) of Article 39(1) were meant to be read together with the result that income improvement was to have been achieved through structural policy and not market policy.

The scope of application of the CAP

23.4 According to Article 38(1) of the Treaty the Common Market extends to trade in agricultural products. Agricultural products are defined as the products of the soil, of stock farming and of fisheries, and the products of first-stage processing directly related to those products. There is a certain inconsistency in the Treaty regarding the definition of the scope of application of the rules relating to agriculture: having defined agricultural products in Article 38(1), Article 38(3) goes on to indicate that a list of the products covered by the title of agriculture is contained in Annex II to the Treaty. When we turn to Annex II we find that it contains a list of Chapter headings taken from the Brussels Nomenclature and there are a number of obvious omissions of items which must be described as products of the soil, or of first-stage processing. In this connection forestry and wool processing are two glaring examples.[1] It was open to the Council, for a period up to two years after entry into force of the Treaty, to add to the list of products contained in Annex II. This power was utilised on only one occasion and gave rise to litigation in due course: *Hauptzollamt Bielefeld v König*[2] In this case the importer disputed a customs classification in respect of alcohol derived from agricultural produce; if the product was classifiable under the common agricultural policy a much higher rate of levy would have applied, but if the product was subject to the ordinary provisions of the Common Customs Tariff a lower rate of duty would apply. The Court held that the addition in December 1959 of the product in question to Annex II by Council Regulation (EEC) 72/61[3] meant that the product was to be classified as an agricultural product to which the higher rate of levy applied. Moreover, the Court held that the meaning of the phrase 'products of first-stage processing' implied a clear economic interdependence between basic products and products resulting from a productive process, irrespective of the number of operations involved therein; where the cost of the original agricultural product was merely marginal in relation to overall processing costs, the final processed product would not be considered an agricultural product for the purposes of Article 38. As regards products such as wool and wood, which are not contained in Annex II of the Treaty, special systems of rules based on Article 235 have been adopted by the Council. These provisions, along with measures relating to products of secondary processing, have tended to mirror the provisions concerning agricultural products included in Annex II of the Treaty.[4]

The territorial scope of the rules on agriculture is no different from that of the provisions of the Treaty: Article 227. But various protocols in the Treaty itself, and in the three acts of Accession, have excluded certain territories and possessions from the scope of the CAP. For example, the CAP does not apply to the Faroe Islands (an autonomous part of the Kingdom of Denmark) nor does it apply to the monastic republic of Mt Athos. In the latest Act of Accession there are special provisions relating to the application of the CAP to Spanish and Portuguese possessions, i.e. the Canary Islands and Madeira. Apart from its effect on the territories of the Member States the CAP also impacts on the economies of the non-Member States. It is axiomatic that European Community farm prices exceed the average price for commodities on the world market by approximately 150 per cent[5] and significant levies are imposed on the importation of agricultural products from outside the Community in order to protect Community producers. The Community's protected markets with subsidised prices for farmers have provoked criticism, particularly from the United States; it is likely that a sustained attack against what is perceived to be Community protectionism will be mounted in the context of the present GATT negotiations, known as the Uruguay Round. But not all of the foreign impact of the CAP is negative: significant concessions to impoverished Third World countries have been made by the Community in respect of the importation of critical agricultural commodities such as sugar and beef, in respect of which there is already an over-supply on the Community Market. Likewise, the Lomé Conventions, which link the African, Caribbean and Pacific countries (ACP) to the Community in a trade and aid relationship, have all contained a system, known as STABEX, for the stabilisation of export earnings derived from the basic staple products.

In one sense the scope and manner of application of the rules relating to the CAP differ from all other economic sectors because Article 38(2) states that the rules for the establishment of the Common Market shall apply to agricultural products save as otherwise provided in Articles 39 to 46. We have already noted that Article 42 provided that the Council was free to determine the extent to which the competition rules were to apply to the agricultural sector. This is the only express departure from the rules for the establishment of the Common Market that one can find in Articles 39 to 46 of the Treaty, but the Court has held that the special position of agriculture within the economy as a whole justifies exceptional treatment: therefore, the rules contained in Articles 39 to 46, including derived or secondary legislation, take priority over the ordinary rules for the establishment of the Common Market wherever these rules conflict: *Pigs Marketing Board (Northern Ireland) v Redmond*[6] however, since these rules form an exception to the general principles of Community law, they must be interpreted restrictively; *EEC Commission v Luxembourg and Belgium*[7]

1 Francis G. Snyder, *Law of the Common Agricultural Policy*, 1985, at p. 17.
2 Case 185/73 [1974] E.C.R. 607.
3 O.J. (Sp. Ed.) 1959–62 p. 68.
4 Francis G. Snyder, *op. cit.* fn. 1, at pp. 17–18.
5 *Financial Times*, 12 August 1988.
6 Case 83/78 [1978] E.C.R. 2347, [1979] 1 C.M.L.R. 177.
7 Joined Cases 2–3/62 [1962] E.C.R. 425, [1963] C.M.L.R. 199.

Institutional structure

23.5 The EEC Treaty contains only ten provisions dealing with agriculture and some of these are transitional in effect. However, the vast bulk of the Community's legislation in any one year is devoted to the Common Agricultural Policy and most of the measures are regulations adopted by the Commission under delegated powers.

The basic decision-making provision is Article 43(2) which assigns to the Commission the function of initiating proposals upon which the opinion of the European Parliament is solicited before being converted into legislation by the Council, which should act by a qualified majority. Although the Parliament has no real input to the content of the legislation it must be consulted, and failure to do so properly constitutes an infringement of an essential procedural requirement for the purposes of Article 173 of the Treaty: *Roquette Frères v EC Council; Maizena v EC Council*[1] Within the Commission agriculture is one of the most important Directorates-General because of the huge budgetary resources devoted to the CAP and because of the amount of legislation generated by it. The Commissioner holding the agriculture portfolio will, as a general rule, be one of the four or five most important Commissioners. He has responsibility for DG VI; when elaborating its proposals DG VI will consult various interest groups including BEUC (an umbrella group for European consumer organisations) and COPA (which includes most of the principal agricultural organisations in the Member States). When working out the political compromises that inevitably form part of the elaboration of the CAP, the Commission consults with the Special Committee on Agriculture which is a variant of COREPER (*supra*, para. 4.17).

The day-to-day implementation of the common agricultural policy is a time-consuming and highly elaborate operation. Consequently, the Council has delegated the function of legislating on specific issues to the Commission but has provided for the supervision of this delegated power by establishing management committees (*supra*, para. 4.48). The validity of the management system of legislating was approved in *Einfuhr- und Vorratsstelle für Getreide und Futtermittel v Köster*.[2] Management Committees are made up of representatives from the Member States, experts in the product area in question; this is logical because in fact the greater part of the implementation of the CAP is carried out by the national authorities, acting on behalf of the Community. In Ireland the European Communities (Common Agricultural Policy) (Market Intervention Regulations)[3] designate the Minister for Agriculture as the appropriate authority; this single statutory instrument is the legislative basis for the implementation in Ireland for the entire corpus of CAP-related legislation.

The implementation by the national authorities of Community legislation can give rise to certain legal problems. For example, is it the Community or the national authorities that are liable for the incorrect implementation of CAP legislation? When this issue has come before the Court of Justice, the Court has proved remarkably reluctant to admit the possibility of Community liability and has insisted that the level and degree of liability, if any, of the national authorities must first be established before an action against the Communities can be initiated. A review of the legality of acts of the institutions in connection with the CAP arises much more frequently in the context of direct actions for annulment, under Article 173, or in requests for preliminary rulings on the interpretation or validity of acts of the institutions, under Article 177. Many of the basic principles for the operation of the CAP have been developed by the Court in such rulings.

1 Cases 138–139/79, [1980] E.C.R. 3333 and 3393.
2 Case 25/70, [1970] E.C.R. 1161, [1972] C.M.L.R. 255.
3 S.I. No. 24 of 1973.

Development of the CAP

23.6 The first step in the implementation of a common agricultural policy was the conference provided for in Article 43(1) held at Stresa in Italy, between national officials and farmers' organisations. Agreement was reached on the following objectives:

(1) Agriculture is an integral part of the economy as well as an essential factor of social life.
(2) Trade in agricultural goods must be increased, between Member States and with the rest of the world.
(3) Close correlation must be established between policy on structural adaptation and market policy;
(4) . . . To achieve a balance between production and potential outlets;
(5) . . . To avoid overproduction;
(6) . . . To eliminate subsidies;
(7) Profitability and growth in agriculture should keep pace with other sectors of the economy.
(8) To preserve the family structure of European farming.
(9) More intensive rural industrialisation.[1]

Soon after Stresa, in November 1959, the Commission presented a series of general proposals, which became known as the 'Mansholt Plan'[2] to the Economic and Social Committee. The next major step was the agreement by the Council to establish common policies for cereals, pigmeat, eggs, poultry, fruit and vegetables, and wine.[3] The second group of regulations organising the CAP were issued in February 1964, in the milk, dairy products, beef and rice sectors.

It has been intended to reduce price differences in the Member States during the transitional stage by two methods:

(a) an automatic customs duties' reduction every year;
(b) an annual decision by the council to reduce 'political prices' so as to reach a common price at the end of the transitional period.[4]

This policy had failed in its non-automatic part (i.e. (b)): as a consequence of this, the Commission proposed the adoption, as quickly as possible, of a common price for cereals. The Member States agreed to this suggestion, but postponed the adoption of such a price until 1 July 1967.[5]

The next development was the request by the Council, in 1965, asking the Commission to submit proposals for the financing of the CAP for the period 1965 to 1967 (the period up to the adoption of a common price in cereals). The Commission produced its proposals in March 1965, and what followed is commonly known as the 'crisis'. Amongst the suggestions put forward by the Commission were:

(1) That customs duties on intra-Community trade be abolished by 1 July 1967; (2½ years before the end of the transitional period).
(2) That the produce from the common external tariff and agricultural levies should go to the Community Budget.
(3) That the powers of the European Parliament should be increased accordingly.

The disagreement that ensued led to the withdrawal of the French delegation from the meetings of the Council. The so-called 'empty chair' policy came to an end in 1966 with the so-called 'Agreement to Disagree'. The plans to strengthen the Parliament were dropped and agreement was reached on the method of financing the Community agricultural policy up to December 1969. Instead of the system of contributions from each Member State, which had been in operation up to July 1967, a new system was substituted. The EAGGF (or FEOGA in French) the European Agricultural Guidance and Guarantee Fund, was to provide the full amount for the Guarantee Section of the Fund, to be paid out of 90 per cent of all import levies on agricultural products. The Federal Republic of Germany, which in the period 1962 to 1968 paid 451 million units of account into the Fund, insisted that the Guidance Section be limited to 285 million units of account per annum. As a result of this settlement, agreement on common prices for other agricultural sectors was possible.

In yet another interim measure, the Member States agreed to finance the cost of the CAP from national budgets for the year 1970. For the period 1971 to 1974 the CAP costs were to be met by a combination of agricultural levies, increased proportions of customs duties on other goods and national contributions. From 1975 onwards, the Community budget was to be finance entirely from its own resources (in accordance with Article 201 of the Treaty), consisting of customs duties and 1 per cent of the then operative VAT systems.

Article 40 of the Treaty required the establishment of the CAP by the end of the transitional period at the latest. Needless to remark, there were some products for which common policies had not been established when the transitional period expired. In *Charmasson v Minister for Economic Affairs and Finance*[6] the Court of Justice considered the legal consequences of this *lacuna* and concluded that pending the adoption of a common policy the Member States were obliged to apply the ordinary rules for the operation of the common market, irrespective of whether a national market organisation was in existence. In the instant case, preferential quota arrangements applicable to banana imports were in breach of the rules on the free movement of goods. By the end of 1986, there were still some products, such as honey and potatoes, for which a common marketing organisation had not been established.[7]

1 First General Report on the Activities of the Community (1958); at pp 74–7.
2 G. Olmi, *The Agricultural Policy of the Community*, 1 C.M.L.Rev (1963) 119.
3 J. Marsh and C. Ritson, *Agricultural Policy and the Common Market*, 1971; at p. 130.
4 G. Olmi, *Common organisation of agricultural markets*, 5 C.M.L.Rev (1967) 366.
5 J. Marsh and C. Ritson, *op. cit.* fn. 3; at p. 130.
6 Case 48/74 [1974] E.C.R. 1383, [1975] 2 C.M.L.R. 208.
7 J.W. Bridge, Chapter 13 'Agriculture', at p. 191; *in* Volume 25, *Law of the European Communities* (Ed. David Vaughan) 1986; These two volumes are also reproduced as volumes 51 and 52 of *Halsbury's Laws of England*, Fourth Edition.

Accession of the new Member States

23.7 All three enlargements of the Community have necessitated adjustments to the existing body of law relating to the CAP. The general principle underlying each enlargement has been that the acceding state must adjust its rules and systems to those of the Community over the transitional period. In the First Act of Accession the transitional period was five years but in the Second and Third Acts of Accession transitional periods of seven years and more have been standard. As far as Ireland was concerned the transitional arrangements were contained in Articles 50 to 103 of the First Act of Accession and the definitive application of the CAP commenced from 1 January 1978.[1]

1 See, generally, J.-P. Dussochet, *The Enlargement of the European Communities*, 1973; G. Olmi, *Agriculture and Fisheries in the Treaty of Brussels of January 22, 1972*, and C.M.L.Rev (27) 293.

Common organisations of the market (COMs)

23.8 Article 40(2) of the Treaty provided that in order to obtain the objectives of Article 39 a common organisation of the agricultural markets had to be established and, depending on the product involved, three different varieties of organisations were envisaged: organisations with common rules on competition; compulsory coordination of national market organisations; or European market organisations. In practice, the Community legislator did not follow this *schema*. Instead, a European market organisation (the third alternative outlined above) exists for virtually all products but the distinction between market organisations is characterised by the level of price support. Some COMs enjoy full price support, some have partial price support and some have no price support at all.[1]

There are now more than twenty COMs but for purposes of illustration we propose to examine one of the most complex – the common organisation of the market in cereals – and one of the least complex – the common organisation of the market in live trees and other plants, bulbs, roots, cut flowers and ornamental foliage.

The common organisation of the market in cereals is presently regulated by Council Regulation (EEC) 2727/75[2] which has been amended on more than fifteen occasions. Regulation 2727/75 replaced Council Regulation (EEC) 120/67[3] which in turn replaced the original market organisation regulation, Council Regulation (EEC) 19/62[4] The regulation establishing the COM for cereals can be described as pivotal; cereals constitute a significant production input for other agricultural products such as poultry, pigmeat, eggs, beef and veal, milk and dairy products. The price of these commodities will reflect to a certain extent the price obtained for the cereal input. We have already noted (*supra*, para. 23.6) that the determination of the first common price for cereals was a constituent factor in the Community constitutional crisis of 1965.

Article 1 of the regulation, by reference to chapter headings in the Common Customs Tariff, defines the scope of application of the COM. It applies to wheat, barley, rye, oats, maize, flour derived from these and certain processed products, i.e. starch and glucose.

Article 3 of the regulation sets out the basic pricing structure for cereals: there are intervention prices, reference prices (applicable to wheat for bread-making purposes) and target prices. The intervention price is calculated by reference to Ormes, in central France, which is situated in the area with the largest surplus of cereals in the Community. The intervention price is the price at which the national intervention authority (in Ireland the Minister for Agriculture) must buy in quantities of cereals when offered by producers. Article 7 of the regulation lays down the principles applicable to intervention purchases: intervention authorities are required to purchase cereals when an offer is made in writing by a producer, subject only to standards concerned with quality and quantity. Intervention stocks can be disposed of by the national authorities by returning them to the Community market, following a tendering procedure, or by sale on the world market. The target price, by contrast, is the price which the Community Legislator expects cereals to attract in the marketing year. The target price is calculated for the period commencing 1 August of each year and ending on 31 July. Target prices are calculated by reference to Duisburg, in the Ruhr, which is the location in the Community with the highest deficit in terms of cereal production. The target price is meant to reflect the intervention price plus a market element or profit added plus the costs of delivering the cereals from Ormes to Duisburg; the prices concerned are in respect of deliveries to wholesalers.

As regards trade with non-Member States Article 12 of the regulation subjects all import or export activity to a licensing requirement; importers and exporters must be in possession of import and export licences respectively. Licences are available as of right, but applicants must lodge a security which will be forfeited if the applicant fails to carry out either entirely or partially the transaction in respect of which the licence was procured. Cereal imports are subject to a levy and the produce of the levy is entered as revenue in the budget of the Community. The levy is equal to the difference between the threshold price (less the c.i.f. price at Duisberg) and the World Market price, calculated by reference to quotations from representative marketplaces. The threshold price mechanism is designed to ensure that deflated prices on the world market will not interfere unduly with the stability of the market in the Community. Article 15 also provides a degree of stability for traders: it is possible to have the levy fixed in advance. Article 16 of the regulation provides for the payment of export refunds wherever a Community produce is sold on the world market. The refund represents the difference between the price in the Community and the price on the world market, and export refunds may be fixed in advance.

The final feature of the trading rules established by Regulation 2727/75 can be found in Articles 21 and 22 which apply to the cereals sector, the rules on the free movement of goods and on State aids. Articles 25, 26 and 27 of the regulation establish a Management Committee for Cereals and provide for the adoption of implementing provisions by the Commission, acting in consultation with the Management Committee.

1 See, J.W. Bridge, *op. cit.* fn. 7, para. 23.6, at p. 191; Michel Melchior, 'The Common Organisation of Agricultural Markets'; in *Thirty Years of Community Law*, 1981; at p. 443.
2 O.J. L 281, 1.11.1975 p. 1.
3 O.J. (Sp. Ed.) 1967 p. 33.
4 O.J. L 30, 20.4.1962 p. 933.

23.9 The common organisation of the market for live trees and other plants etc. was established by Council Regulation (EEC) 234/68.[1] As in the case of the COM regulation for cereals, Article 1 of Regulation 234/68 defines its scope by reference to chapter headings in the CCT. The purpose of the regulation is to promote the rational marketing of 'live plants' and to create stable market conditions. The regulation sets out to achieve these objectives by providing for adoption of the standards concerning quality grading, wrapping and presentation of live plants (Article 3). Implementing legislation has provided that no live plants may be displayed, offered for sale or otherwise marketed unless the marketing is done in compliance with the relevant quality standards. Article 5 provides that the Member States are responsible for the implementation of these quality standards and are to police them by way of quality inspection and controls. Unlike the COM for cereals there is no complex price mechanism applicable to trade in live plants; consequently, there is no need for a complex protective system in respect of trade with non-Member States. Likewise, the provisions of the Common Customs Tariff, rather than special agricultural levies, apply to incoming produce. Article 9 of the regulation provides that the Community legislators may take the necessary measures when serious disturbances in the Community market are caused by imports from particular non-Member States. Finally, Article 13 of the regulation provides that the Commission is empowered to take implementing measures, in consultation with the Management Committee for live plants.

1 O.J. (Sp. Ed.) 1968 (I) p. 26.

23.10 Most of the COMs lie somewhere between the COM on cereals and the COM on live plants in terms of complexity; the common organisation of the market for a particular product is likely to be more complex, and involve a greater degree of price support, where the product concerned is '. . . an important component of farm income and of family farming as a whole'.[1]

Among the more complex COMs the terminology may differ but the essential techniques relating to price support are essentially similar. Thus, the intervention price (the price guaranteed to the producer) is sometimes known as the buying-in price, withdrawal price, or the reference price. Likewise, the optimum price envisaged by the legislator, the target price, is sometimes also known as the guide price or the basic price. Finally, the price by which import levies are determined (to protect intra-Community trade) is variously known as the threshold price, the reference price, and the sluice-gate price.[2]

It has been suggested that an essential feature of the CAP is the 'market principle';[3] the farmer, the primary producer in the agricultural sector, derives his economic returns as a result of prices formed freely on the market. In point of fact, the marketplace for virtually all products subject to a COM is managed or administered by the Community authorities and free price formation plays a relatively minor role. Moreover, '. . . the CAP . . . also incorporates numerous mechanisms which derogate fundamentally from its basic structure . . .'[4]

These measures include storage aids,[5] denaturing premiums,[6] assistance to producer organisations,[7] production aids,[8] production refunds,[9] measures to ensure the compulsory absorption of surpluses[10] and production quotas.[11]

1 Michel Melchior, *op. cit.* fn. 1, para. 23.8, at pp. 442–3.
2 *Idem*, at pp. 441–2.
3 *Idem*, at p. 447.
4 Francis G. Snyder, *Law of the Common Agricultural Policy*, 1985; at p. 105.
5 Michel Melchior, *op. cit.* fn. 1, para. 23.8, at p.449.
6 *Idem*.
7 *Idem*.
8 *Idem*, at p. 450.
9 *Idem*, at pp. 451–2.
10 *Idem*, at p. 451.
11 *Idem*, at p. 451.

The CAP and National legislation

23.11 As in the case of most other sectors, the transfer of competence by the Member States to the Community has had as a corollary the loss, on the part of the Member States, of the power to adopt independent legislative provisions in the agricultural field: *Hauptzollamt Hamburg-Oberelbe v Bollman*.[1] In particular, where a common organisation of the market involves a single price system, as in the case of cereals, the Member States are prohibited from introducing any national measures which will interfere with price formation; but, because the common price system applies only at the wholesale stage, Member States are free to adopt measures which will affect prices at the retail stage: *Galli*.[2] Likewise, the Member States are prohibited from imposing export restrictions or production quotas on products, particularly in the case of COMs where there is no common price system but which involve, in the main, quality, labelling and presentation standards: *Officier van Justitie v Van Haaster*;[3] *Officier van Justitie v Van den Hazel*.[4] There have been a number of Irish cases which illustrate these general principles. In *Pigs and Bacon Commission v McCarren and Co Ltd*.[5] the Court of Justice ruled that levies imposed by the PBC under the Pigs and Bacon Act, 1935 (as amended), were incompatible with Council Regulation (EEC) 2759/75[6] on the common organisation of the pig meat market insofar as the levies were used to finance export bonuses for certain types of bacon only, and insofar as the levy inflicted a financial disadvantage on producers who declined to use the services of the central export marketing agency—the PBC. In *ICMSA v Ireland* and *Martin Doyle v An Toaiseach*[7] the Court of Justice held that national taxation measures—in this case statutory instruments which imposed a 2 per cent levy on the chargeable value of cattle, milk, cereals and sugar—were not incompatible with the common organisations of the market in question, provided that they did not interfere with the mechanisms of price formation. When he came to apply the ruling of the Court of Justice Barrington J., in the High Court, held, in respect of the 2 per cent levy on cattle, that while the levy did not interfere with price formation it did constitute a measure having an effect equivalent to a quantitative restriction on exports within the meaning of Article 34 of the Treaty.[8]

It was apparent at the time of Ireland's accession to the European Communities that a considerable volume of Irish legislation would have to be altered to take account of the regulations establishing common organisations of the market.[9] In fact, there was no attempt by the central government authorities to attack this problem on a comprehensive basis; rather, it was left up to the authorities in charge of each particular market sector to make the necessary changes. This was managed with differing degrees of success. In the dairy sector, always characterised by a high degree of organisation and cooperation, AnBord Bainne (which had enjoyed the exclusive right to market Irish dairy produce abroad) was converted into a cooperative owned by the principal dairy co-ops in the State.[10] The Pigs and Bacon Commission, which had a statutory marketing monopoly under the terms of the Pigs and Bacon Act, 1935 (as amended), did not make the necessary adjustments and its unsuccessful attempt to enforce its levy collection powers, in *Pigs and Bacon Commission v McCarren*,[11] had disastrous consequences: virtually all pig producers stopped paying the levy following the judgment in the case, which effectively emasculated the PBC as a marketing agency. The failure to assess the existing national legislation in terms of Community obligations has had further ramifications, even in the well-organised dairy sector. In *Dublin District Milk Board v Goldenvale Co-operative Creameries Ltd*,[12] which is presently pending before the Court of Justice, the issue concerns the statutory marketing monopoly conferred on the Dublin District Milk Board under the terms of the Milk (Regulation of Supply and Price) Act, 1936.

The agricultural provisions in the Treaty have effects on national law beyond circumstances connected with price formation or marketing considerations. In *Robert Fearon & Co Ltd v Irish Land Commission*[13] the appellant argued that the initiation of the compulsory purchase procedure under Section 35(1) of the Land Act, 1965 was in breach of the right to establishment guaranteed by Article 52 of the EEC Treaty. In *Lawlor v Minister for Agriculture*[14] it was argued on behalf of the plaintiff that Statutory Instrument No. 416 of 1985, which implemented the Community regulations on the milk quota scheme, constituted an unjust attack on the property rights of the plaintiff insofar as it obliged him to transfer a corresponding quantity (milk quota) when selling part of his lands. The plaintiff failed in his action in the High Court and appealed to the Supreme Court; the Supreme Court decided to refer to the European Court of Justice for a preliminary ruling but the parties settled the action before a reference order could be drafted.

1 Case 40/69, [1970] E.C.R. 69, [1970] C.M.L.R. 141.
2 Case 31/74, [1975] E.C.R. 47, [1975] 1 C.M.L.R. 211.
3 Case 190/73, [1974] E.C.R. 1123, [1974] 2 C.M.L.R. 521.
4 Case 111/76, [1977] E.C.R. 901, [1980] 3 C.M.L.R. 12.
5 Case 177/78, [1979] E.C.R. 2161, [1979] 3 C.M.L.R. 389.
6 O.J. L 282, 1.11.75 p. 1.
7 Joined Cases 36 and 71/80 [1981] E.C.R. 735, [1981] 2 C.M.L.R. 455.
8 *Doyle v An Taoiseach*, (26 April 1983, unreported) High Court (Barrington J.).
9 Marcus McInerney; 'Marketing – the adaptation of agricultural legislation,' Chapter 27 in *Legal Problems of an Enlarged European Community*, Eds. Bathurst, Simmons, March Hannings and Welch (1972).
10 Dairy Produce (Miscellaneous Provisions) Act, 1973.
11 [1978] J.I.S.E.L. 87; Case 177/78, *supra*, fn. 3, para. 23.2.
12 (3 April 1987, unreported) High Court (Costello J.).
13 [1982–1983] J.I.S.E.L. 115.
14 (2 October 1987, unreported) High Court (Murphy J.).
16 See, generally Francis G. Snyder, *Law of the Common Agricultural Policy*, 1985; C. Vajda, *Some Aspects of Judicial Review within the Common Agricultural Policy*, (1976) 1 E.L.Rev 244, 341.

Judicial review by the Court of Justice

23.12 Each year the Council and, to a much greater extent, the Commission adopt a huge number of regulations in connection with the CAP. Most of this legislation is highly technical and can best be described, in national terms, as economic administrative law. Consequently, the Court has been obliged to apply to this complex administrative legislation certain general principles of law. First and foremost, the Court has held that the objectives outlined in Article 39 of the Treaty, which were intended to safeguard the interests of both farmers and consumers, may not all be simultaneously and fully attained: *Beus v Hauptzollamt München-Landbergerstrasse.*[1] Moreover, because the implementation of the CAP involves the evaluation of complex economic situations, the

Court will not substitute its decision for that of the Council or Commission but will confine itself to examining whether the legislative act at issue constitutes a misuse of power, or exceeds the bounds of discretion conferred on the Council or the Commission: *Balkan Import Export GmbH v Hauptzollamt Berlin-Packhof.*[2] The Treaty itself contains one general principle which the Court has utilised extensively. Article 40(3) prohibits discrimination between producers and consumers in the implementation of the CAP: unless objectively justified, consumers and producers in identical circumstances may not be treated differently: *Ruckdeschel and Diamalt v Hauptzollamt Hamburg-St Annen and Hauptzollamt Itzehoe.*[3] Other general principles of law applied by the Court of Justice in the interpretation of the CAP include:

(i) Fundamental rights: *Internationale Handelsgesellschaft v Einfuhr-und Vorratsstelle für Getreide und Futtermittel;*[4] *Hauer v Land Rheinland-Pfalz.*[5]
(ii) Equal treatment: *Royal Scholten-Honig and Tunnel Refineries v IBAP.*[6]
(iii) Proportionality: *Bela-Mühle Josef Bergmann v Grows-Farm GmbH.*[7]
(iv) Legitimate expectations: *CNTA v EC Commission.*[8]
(v) Legal certainty: *Töpfer v EC Commission.*[9]

1 Case 5/67, [1968] E.C.R. 83, [1968] C.M.L.R. 131.
2 Case 55/75, [1976] E.C.R. 19.
3 Joined Cases 117/76, 16/77, [1977] E.C.R. 1753, [1979] 2 C.M.L.R. 445.
4 Case 11/70, [1970] E.C.R. 1125, [1970] C.M.L.R. 255.
5 Case 44/79 [1979] E.C.R. 3727, [1980] 3 C.M.L.R. 42.
6 Joined Cases 103, 145/77 [1978] E.C.R. 2037, [1979] 1 C.M.L.R. 675.
7 Case 114/76 [1977] E.C.R. 1211, [1979] 2 C.M.L.R. 83.
8 Case 74/74, [1975] E.C.R. 533, [1977] 1 C.M.L.R. 171.
9 Case 112/77 [1978] E.C.R. 1019.

Structural reform

23.13 It has been argued that the objectives of Article 39 of the Treaty, particularly insofar as they relate to improvement of farmers' incomes, should have been achieved through structural reform rather than through price support policy.[1] However, in terms of legislation and expenditure, structural measures have played a relatively insignificant role in the CAP. The first significant initiative was taken in 1968 with the publication by the Commission of its Memorandum: 'Agriculture 1980' (also known as the Mansholdt Plan).[2] The principal proposals of the Mansholdt Plan were to reduce the amount of money available by way of price subsidisation, to create larger and more profitable farms, to plan production in relation to price policy, to take 5 million hectares of land out of production, to take 5 million people out of agriculture, and to improve the structure of agricultural marketing. These proposals were highly controversial and were not implemented to any great extent.

The first significant structural measures were taken in 1972 when the Council adopted three Directives on the modernisation of farm holdings

(Directive (EEC) 72/159),[3] on the cessation of farming and the reallocation of agricultural land for purposes of structural improvement (Directive (EEC) 72/160),[4] and on socio-economic guidance and training for farmers (Directive (EEC) 72/161).[5] The first two directives were linked insofar as land released by virtue of Directive 72/160 was to be made available for development farmers within the context of Directive 72/159; the latter measure provided certain financial incentives for farmers, engaged in agriculture as their principle activity, to adopt a development plan and to keep accounts. Directive 72/160 provided financial incentives for elderly farmers to retire from agricultural activity and to sell or lease their holdings. Directive 72/161 on socio-economic guidance for farmers required Member States to have educational schemes and courses available for young farmers and potential farmers. In Ireland these directives were implemented mainly by administrative measures rather than legislative provisions, either primary or secondary. It was only in respect of Directive 72/160 on farmer retirement that the State utilised a statutory instrument to implement the directive: European Communities (Retirement of Farmers) Regulations.[6] In *Lee v Minister for Agriculture*[7] the issue arose as to whether payments under the farm modernisation scheme were available in respect of lands which were not wholly utilised for agricultural purposes.

The three Directives of 1972 did not achieve the results that were hoped for.[8] The Community attempted to redress these shortcomings in 1975 with the adoption of Council Directive (EEC) 75/268[9] on mountain and hill farming in certain less-favoured areas; a connected directive, Council Directive (EEC) 72/272[10] applied this scheme to Ireland.

In view of the undertaking given by the Member States, in the Single European Act, to reassess the application of the various structural funds, it is likely that a more comprehensive, integrated approach to structural reform – in agriculture and in other sectors – will be adopted by the Community authorities (*supra*, para. 6.8).

1 P. Kapteyn and P. Verloren Van Themaat, *Introduction to European Community Law*, 1973; at p. 303.
2 Second General Report on the Activities of the Communities, pp.137–8.
3 O.J. (Sp. Ed.) 1972 II p. 324.
4 O.J. (Sp. Ed.) 1972 II p. 332.
5 O.J. (Sp. Ed.) 1972 II p. 339.
6 S.I. 197 of 1983.
7 [1979] J.I.S.E.L. 31; Case 152/79 [1980] E.C.R. 1495, [1980] 2 C.M.L.R. 682.
8 Michel Melchior, in *Thirty Years of Community Law* (1983), p. 46.
9 O.J. L 128, 19.5.1975 p. 1.
10 O.J. L 128, 19.5.1975 p. 68.

Harmonisation of agricultural law

23.14 Apart from rules relating to the marketing of agricultural produce and structural reform, the Community legislature has adopted a considerable number of measures on the harmonisation of law relating to veterinary, phyto-sanitary and foodstuffs legislation.[1] It is likely, however, that the impetus fuelling harmonisation legislation will slacken somewhat as a consequence of the application of Article 100A of the Treaty (as introduced by the Single European Act).

478

1 For a comprehensive survey see J.W. Bridge, Chapter 13, pp. 219–45, in Volume 2, *Law of the European Communities* (Ed. David Vaughan) 1986.

Financing the CAP

23.15 Article 40(4) provides for the establishment of one or more European agricultural guidance or guarantee funds. The operation of the legislation concerning the financing of the CAP is examined elsewhere (*supra*, Chapter 6).

The application of competition rules in the agricultural sector

23.16 Article 42 of the Treaty gave the Council the power to determine the extent to which the competition rules apply to the agricultural sector; the rules are laid down in Regulation 26 of 1962,[1] and these are examined elsewhere (*supra*, para. 21.12).

1 O.J. (Sp. Ed.) 1959–62 p. 129.

Chapter 24

The Common Fisheries Policy (CFP)[1]

Introduction

24.1 Fishery problems, not surprisingly in view of the original membership of the EEC, did not figure prominently in the negotiations leading up to the establishment of the Community. Indeed fishery products were not seen as meriting separate treatment in the Treaty of Rome but were treated as 'agricultural products' and were dealt with under the title in the Treaty reserved for Agriculture (Articles 38 to 47). When the Community began to entertain applications for membership from the United Kingdom, Ireland, Denmark and Norway, however, the traditions and interests of these countries ensured that fishery matters became central issues in the negotiations. The 1972 Accession Treaty dealt with some of those matters in Articles 98 to 99 (guide prices) and Articles 100 to 103 (fishery rights). Stimulated by the interest of the new applicants, the Council began to issue regulations from 1970, dealing with various matters including marketing, structures, conservation, etc.[2] The original Member States perhaps anticipated difficulties on these matters and adopted a rule in 1970 which insisted on the principle of equal access to Community waters for all Community fishermen. The applicant countries were obliged to accept the established Community position on this in 1972 and, on the access issue, negotiations were concerned only with derogations from the general principle for special cases. Two other factors occurred after the establishment of the EEC in 1958 which also increased the importance of fisheries within the Community. First, fishing technology improved dramatically with the result that catches increased to unprecedented levels thereby jeopardising continuing stocks. Over-exploitation endangered not only the stocks themselves but also put at risk the biological resources necessary for a healthy fish industry. Second, pressures outside the Community forced the EEC Member States to extend to 200 miles their exclusive fishery zones. Both of these factors made more urgent the development of a conservation policy, the determination of who has the right to legislate for these new fishing zones (the Community or the Member States) and, finally, consideration as to how the rights to fish in these areas were to be allocated. Until 1983 when a comprehensive common fisheries policy

(CFP) was eventually established, a good deal of uncertainty was generated by these problems and these issues in particular figured prominently in the case-law of the Court of Justice during the period in question.[3]

1 See generally, C.C.H., Common Market Reporter IP 761 *et seq.*; R. Churchill, *Revision of the EEC's Common Fisheries Policy* 5 E.L.R. 3, 95, R. Wainwright *Common Fisheries Policy*, Oxford Yearbook of European Law; The European Community's Fishery Policy, Office for Official Publications of the European Communities, Periodical 1/1985; Farnell and Elles, *In Search of a Common Fisheries Policy*. Gower: 1984; M. Leigh, *European Integration and the Common Fisheries Policy*, Kent: Croom Helm. 1983.

2 See Council Regulations (EEC) 170/83, 171/83 and 174/83 O.J. L 24, 27.1.1983 pp. 1, 14 and 70.

3 The following cases before the Court of Justice dealt with fishery matters. Case 88/77 *Minister for Fisheries v Schonenberg* [1978] E.C.R. 473, [1978] 2 C.M.L.R. 519 and Case 61/77 *EC Commission v Ireland* [1978] E.C.R. 417, [1978] 2 C.M.L.R. 466. (Both of these cases arose out of the same facts. National measures which prohibited larger boats from fishing in Irish waters were held to be *de facto* discriminatory since the criteria used excluded only one boat in the Irish fleet but virtually all the Dutch fleet and half the French fleet); Case 269/80 *R v Tymen* [1981] E.C.R. 3079, [1982] 2 C.M.L.R. 111. (Since 1 January 1979, Community has exclusive powers in relation to conservation matters. Member States no longer have right to exercise powers in these matters except as trustees of the Community interest. Commission's objections stand until clearly withdrawn); See also Case 21/81 *Openbaar Ministerie v Bout* [1982] E.C.R. 381, [1982] 2 C.M.L.R. 371; Case 287/81 *Anklagemyndigheden v Kerr* [1982] E.C.R. 4053, [1983] 2 C.M.L.R. 431. (Permitted national measures relating to conservation (catch quotas) taken before 31 December 1978 provided they complied with proper procedures and were genuine conservation measures); Case 812/79 *A-G v Burgoa* [1980] E.C.R. 2787, [1981] 2 C.M.L.R. 193; Case 181/80 *Procureur Général v Arbelaiz-Emazabel* [1981] E.C.R. 2961. (Rights of Non-Member States (Spain) to fish in Community waters. Treaty obligations of Member States—Article 234. Community replacing Member States in international conventions.) See also Cases No. 180, 266/80 *Tome v Procureur de la République*, *Procureur de la République v Yurrita* [1981] E.C.R. 2997. See also, re Spain, Cases 13–28/82 *Arantzamendi-Osa v Procureur de la République* [1982] E.C.R. 3297; Cases 50–58/82 *Administrateur des Affairs Maritimes, Bayonne v Marina* [1982] E.C.R. 3949. Note also *Pesca Valentia* Case which once more concerned Spanish fishermen in Irish waters. The Spanish fishermen contested the legality of a national requirement that 75 per cent of crew should be EEC nationals. (H. Court, Keane J. 14 May 1986 unreported. Referred to Court of Justice.) Case 124/80 *Officier van Justitie v J van Dam and Zonen* [1981] E.C.R. 1447, [1982] 2 C.M.L.R. 93. (Interim conservation measures taken by Member State in absence of Community action.) See also on this Case 804/79 *EC Commision v United Kingdom* [1981] E.C.R. 1045, [1982] 1 C.M.L.R. 543 and Case 32/79 *EC Commission v United Kingdom* [1980] E.C.R. 2403, [1981] 1 C.M.L.R. 219. Case 141/78 *France v United Kingdom* [1979] E.C.R. 2923, [1980] 1 C.M.L.R. 6. (Member States must, in adopting permitted conservation measures, and in complying with its international obligations, consult with the Commission and observe established procedure.) See also on this Case 32/79 *supra*, Case 21/81, *supra* and Case 63/83, *R v Kirk* [1984] E.C.R. 2689, [1984] 3 C.M.L.R. 522. See *Kirk* case also for non-retroactivity of conservation measure. Cases 3, 4, and 6/76 *Officier van Justitie v Kramer* [1976] E.C.R. 1279, [1976] 2 C.M.L.R. 440; Case 87/82, *Rogers v Darthenay* [1983] E.C.R. 1579, [1984] 1 C.M.L.R. 135. (Community regulation regarding technical conservation measures held to have immediate effects even in the absence of detailed implementing rules.) Case 24/83 *Gewiese and Mehlich v MacKenzie* [1984] E.C.R. 817, [1984] 2 C.M.L.R. 409. (Compatibility of a national conservation measure with Community law.) Case 100/84 *EC Commission v United Kingdom* [1985] 2 C.M.L.R. 199. (Origin of goods. Fish taken from Polish waters in a joint fishing operation between UK and Polish vessels. Were goods of Community origin?) Case 207/84 *De Boer v Produktschap voor Vis en Visprodukten* [1985] E.C.R. 3203, [1987] 2 C.M.L.R. 515.

The role of the Court of Justice

24.2 The role of the Court of Justice in the development and elaboration of the Community's fisheries policy was significant. To appreciate fully the Court's contribution it must be realised that in the period 1970–83 there was a great deal of uncertainty about the law in this area. In the confusion and in the absence of a comprehensive Community fisheries policy Member States began to take unilateral action, the legality of which was sometimes disputed. Fishermen, arrested and brought before national courts for being in breach of such national measures (e.g. fishing without a licence, exceeding catch quotas, using wrong gear and equipment, etc.), contested the legality of these measures and frequently sought a referral under Article 177 of the EEC Treaty to the Court of Justice in Luxembourg.[1] Other times the Commission objected to the national measures and took proceedings, as the Community watchdog, under Article 169 of the EEC Treaty.[2] Still other times the matter surfaced because one Member State prosecuted another Member State under Article 170.[3]

1 See for example, *Kirk, Schonenberg and Burgoa, supra,* fn. 3, para. 24.1. See on the role of the Court of Justice in elaborating the fisheries law Farnell and Elles, *supra* fn. 1, para. 6.1.
2 Case 61/77 *EC Commission v Ireland,* Case 32/79 *EC Commission v United Kingdom,* Case 100/84 *EC Commission v United Kingdom, supra,* fn. 3, para. 24.1.
3 Case 141/78 *France v United Kingdom, supra,* fn. 3, para. 24.1.

24.3 The following questions in particular came before the Court for solution:

(a) What was the capacity and the competence of the Community institutions in relation to both the external and internal aspects of the Community fisheries policy?

(b) Did the Member States retain any authority to act unilaterally on fishery matters in general, or in conservation matters in particular?

(c) If the Member States retained some powers of action what procedures had to be observed before the Member States acted? Did the Commission and the other Member States have to be notified? Did the Commission's objectives have to be complied with, etc.?

(d) Were fishery matters subject to the general provisions of the Treaty such as the duty to cooperate (Article 5) and the duty not to discriminate on the basis of nationality (Article 7)?

(e) Did measures taken by Member States have to comply with the general principles of Community law such as the principle of non-retroactivity or the principle of proportionality?

(f) Apart from the rules established by the Treaty and the Community's secondary legislation, what was the legislative force of other acts which were not mentioned in Article 189 of the EEC Treaty, such as Annex VI of the Hague Resolution?

(g) What was the position with regard to third countries who had treaty arrangements with some or all of the Member States?

24.4 In dealing with those matters the Court was in a difficult position because apart from there being no established Community policy, the legal provisions in the Treaty were not specific and the status of the political response, contained especially in the Hague Resolution, had to be determined. Moreover, the Court had to act in the absence of any relevant legal precedents and in an area which was, in spite of its relative economic insignificance, politically and emotionally very sensitive. Most of the above issues were eventually addressed by the Court and for the most part definite answers were provided by the time a comprehensive policy was adopted in 1983.

Legal basis for CFP

24.5 With regard to the legal bases underlying the CFP the court was particularly concerned with (i) the Treaty provisions on agriculture (Article 3(d) and Articles 38 to 47) as well as the more general Articles such as Articles 5 and 7; (ii) the relevant provisions of the 1972 Treaty of Accession (Articles 98 to 103); (iii) various resolutions passed by the Council of Ministers especially the Hague Resolution of 1976 (and although having no legal basis) the Brussels Resolution of 1980; (iv) the legislative acts (especially the regulations) of the Council and finally (v) the case-law of the European Court of Justice itself as it evolved.

24.6 By 1983 the principal problems relating to fisheries which the Community had then to address included the following:

(i) Since the Court of Justice had established that the Community controls the waters within the jurisdiction of the EEC, how was access by Community fishermen to such waters to be determined. This had become an especially important issue since the establishment of an exclusive 200-mile fishery zone in 1977. Further, it had also to be asked how access to Community water by fishermen from *third countries* was to be determined?

(ii) In view of dwindling stocks and over-exploitation how were *conservation* measures to be formulated, implemented and enforced?

(iii) What measures were to be introduced to stabilise the fish *market* and guarantee a fair livelihood to Community fishermen?

(iv) What *structural* measures should be allowed in respect of the Community fleet?

Before addressing these problems an initial word must be said about the competence of the Commission and the Council to determine the Common Fishery Policy. In short, we may ask whether the Member States have now lost all power of decision in this area?

Competence: Who makes the rules now: the Community or the Member States?

24.7 Since 31 December 1978, the end of the transitional period for the Member States who joined in 1973, the Community now has total and definitive competence in relation to fishery matters.[1] In this respect the transfer of power in fishery matters is no different than the transfer in agricultural matters in general. Accordingly, the Member States must yield to Community initiatives where such initiatives have taken place at Community level. If, however, no Community action has been taken then the Member States may be authorised to adopt national measures so as to avoid an economic or legal vacuum. Such national measures, however, must conform to the general principles of Community law such as, for example, the principle of non-discrimination[2] and the principle of equality.

In the case of *conservation*, however, the transfer of power has been more extensive. In this case because of the effect of Article 102 of the 1972 Act of Accession and decisions of the Court of Justice,[3] Member States, since 1979, no longer have *any national* rights to legislate unilaterally in this matter. It is only in so far as the Community authorises them that Member States can take national measures and then, these must of course be consistent with Community law generally and with the fisheries policy in particular. Moreover, the fact that the Council of Ministers failed to adopt conservation provisions authorised in the Accession Treaty within the period stipulated in Article 102 does not mean that these powers revert to the Member States. Failure by the Council to take appropriate action merely means that the general principles of Community law apply to the situation and this of course would include the principle of equal access and non-discrimination.[4]

Although Member States can no longer exercise *their own powers* on conservation matters the Court does permit Member States to introduce limited measures in certain circumstances and on certain conditions.[5] In effect the Member States are merely acting as trustees for the Community in these circumstances, and in doing so they must be guided by Community policy rather than by national interests. Moreover, such measures, when permitted, have to be genuine conservation measures[6] and have to be non-discriminatory in nature.[7] Further, in taking such measures, Member States must not only undertake detailed consultations with the Commission and seek its approval in good faith, they must also refrain from such measures if the Commission objects.[8] Finally, the national measures permitted in such cases must be publicised and must not be dependent for their operation on the discretion of the authorities.[9]

In *EC Commission v United Kingdom*[10] the Court of Justice summarises the law on this matter with admirable clarity. Having stated that since 1 January 1979, the date on which the transitional period laid down by Article 102 of the Act of Accession expired, power to adopt, as part of the common fisheries policy, measures relating to the conservation of the resources of the sea has *belonged fully and definitively to the Community*, the Court goes on to say:

'Furthermore it should be remembered that in pursuance of Article 7 of the Treaty, Community fishermen must have, subject to the exceptions mentioned above, equal access to the fish stocks coming within the jurisdiction of the Member States. The Council alone has the power to determine the detailed conditions of such access in accordance with the procedures laid down by the third subparagraph of Article 43(2) of the Treaty and Article 102 of the Act of

Accession. This legal situation cannot be modified by measures adopted unilaterally by the Member States.

'As this is a field reserved to the powers of the Community, within which Member States may henceforth act only as trustees of the common interest, a Member State cannot, therefore, in the absence of appropriate action on the part of the Council, bring into force any interim conservation measures which may be required by the situation *except as part of a process of collaboration with the Commission and with due regard to the general task of supervision which Article 155, in conjunction, in this case, with the Decision of 25 June 1979 and the parallel decisions, gives to the Commission.*

'Thus, in a situation characterized by the inaction of the Council and by the maintenance, in principle, of the conservation measures in force at the expiration of the period laid down in Article 102 of the Act of Accession, the Decision of 25 June 1979 and the parallel decisions, as well as the requirements inherent in the safeguard by the Community of the common interest and the integrity of its own powers, imposed upon Member States not only an obligation to undertake detailed consultations with the Commission and to seek its approval in good faith, but also a duty not to lay down national conservation measures in spite of objections, reservations or conditions which might be formulated by the Commission.'[11]

In conclusion, it should also be mentioned that the Court of Justice has held that Member States (at least until 1979) not only have a right, when stocks are being overfished, to adopt measures to protect the biological resources of the sea but also have *a duty* to do so.[12] This obligation stems from Article 5 of the Treaty and again it must be emphasised that when Member States respond to the duty they are not acting unilaterally in a national interest but are fulfilling Community obligations. Consequently, such measures must once more conform to the CFP and to the general principles of Community law.

1 The Community has also replaced Members States in international Conventions: See *Arbeliaz-Emazabel* and *Burgoa*, supra, fn. 3, para. 23.1.
2 *Schonenberg, supra*, fn. 3, para. 24.1.
3 Case 269/80 *Tymen* and case 21/81 *Bout, supra*, fn. 3, para. 24.1.
4 See *Kirk, supra*, fn. 3, para. 24.1. For a case where Council had failed to act and where the Court held that because of procedural defect ('process of cooperation' between Commission and Member States not observed) no Community law within the meaning of Council Regulation (EEC) 729/70, art. 3 existed, see Case 235/85, 15.12.1987. Unreported as yet. Weekly Sheet of Court Proceedings 28/87, p. 1.
5 Case 124/80 *van Dam* and Case 804/79 *EC Commission v United Kingdom, supra*, fn. 3 para. 24.1.
6 *EC Commission v United Kingdom* (*supra* fn. 3, para. 24.1); *R v UK* (*supra* fn. 3 para. 24.1).
7 *Schonenberg supra*, fn. 3, para. 24.1.
8 Article 102 of the 1972 Act of Accession, and subsequent decisions of the Council as interpreted by the Court of Justice in Case 804/79 *EC Commission v United Kingdom* and Case 21/8 *Bout, supra*. But see Case 235/85 *Ireland v EC Commission, supra* fn. 4.
9 Case 32/79 *EC Commission v United Kingdom, supra*, fn. 3, para. 24.1.
10 Case 804/79 *EC Commission v United Kingdom, supra*, fn. 3, para. 24.1.
11 *Idem*, at pp. 1075–6, and 572 respectively. Emphasis added. See also Case 235/85 *Ireland v EC Commission, supra*, fn. 4.
12 Case 32/79 *supra*.

Access

24.8 The problem here was caused by the conflicting claims between, on the one hand, Member States who claimed exclusive rights to their own coastal waters and, on the other hand, the principle of non-discrimination on the basis of nationality which was expressed generally in Article 7 of the EEC Treaty, and more specifically in Council Regulation (EEC) 2141/70 (Article 2). This matter became critical in the first enlargement negotiations and a compromise was reached in the Treaty of Accession in Articles 100 to 103. Basically, what was agreed in these articles was that, while the general principle of equal access was conceded, certain derogations were allowed by the Community on a temporary basis provided certain procedures were observed. In particular new Member States were allowed until 31 December 1982 to restrict fishing in their own waters situated within a limit of six miles to vessels which traditionally fished in those waters and which operated from ports in that geographical coastal area.

After many difficulties and not a little litigation the position on access to Community waters by Community fishermen is now contained in Regulation 170/83. According to this, the system of derogations allowed in the 1972 Treaty of Accession is to continue until 31 December 1992 and the existing regime permits Member States to extend up to 12 nautical miles for all waters under their jurisdiction the earlier 6-mile limits. Moreover, within the 6- to 12-mile zone traditional fishing rights which were still actively pursued were recognised, but, in these circumstances, the legislation detailed the species to be caught and the nationality of the boats permitted in particular locations.[1]

Conservation considerations also caused the Community to introduce restrictions for Community vessels *outside* the 12-mile zone. A special conservation box was created around the Shetland Islands, entry to which was restricted. These restrictions relate especially to larger vessels pursuing edible fish.[2]

By 1992, on the basis of a report by the European Commission on the economic, social and fishing position, it will be decided whether a further ten-year term will run or whether changes or modifications will be introduced.

Access to Community waters by fishermen from third countries, as well as by Community fishermen to waters outside the EEC, are negotiated by the Commission. These agreements contain general regulations on access to the fishing zones, compensation and licence fees (where applicable), cooperation in the region and procedures for settling disputes. The Community also, nowadays, to an increasing extent, represents the Member States in international negotiations and in international organisations.

1 See Regulation 170/83, art. 6 and Annex I.
2 But not industrial stocks. See Regulation 170/83, art. 7 and Annex II.

Conservation

24.9 In January 1983 the Council of the European Communities adopted a new regulation[1] which established a new Community system for the conservation and management of fishery resources. This Regulation, together with regulation 101/76 which it supplements, contains the rules relating to conservation which now prevail in the Community.

We have already seen (*supra*, para. 23.7) that competence to legislate for conservation of fisheries is now exclusively within the Community's domain and that Member States' rights in this matter are severely limited. We will now address ourselves to the Community's new policy on this matter.

The new system includes measures which may involve limitations of the fishing effort, rules for the use of resources, special provisions for in-shore fishing and supervisory provisions.

The limitations of the fishing effort may include the establishment of zones where fishing is prohibited or restricted to certain periods, restrictions as to certain types of vessels, certain types of fishing gear or certain end uses. It may also include the setting of standards for fishing gear, the setting of a minimum fish size or weight per species and the placing of limits on catches (Article 2).[2] The Commission may take immediate action where the conservation of stock is called for.[3]

In the case of strictly local stocks of interest to fishermen of one Member State only, the Member States are authorised to take unilateral action for conservation provided it is compatible with Community law and in conformity with the common fisheries policy. The Commission's agreement must first be sought.[4]

Normally for sensitive species at risk the Community fixes, on an annual basis, quotas, based on scientific evidence, which it considers may be safely taken from the stock in any given year.[5] These total allowable catches (TACs) are then allocated to the Member States in a manner which assures each Member State relative stability of fishing activities for each of the states concerned. Member States may exchange all or part of the quotas allocated to them provided prior notice is given to the Commission. Moreover, it is for the Member States themselves to determine, in accordance with Community provisions, detailed rules as to how the allocated quotas are to be utilised.

Member States may also be allocated quotas by the Council for species outside Community waters which have been negotiated by the Commission with third countries or under international conventions.[6]

---

1 Regulation 170/83, *supra*, fn. 2, para. 23.1
2 See Regulation 171/83, *supra*.
3 See Regulation 171/83, art. 18.
4 See Regulation 171/83, art. 19.
5 See Council Regulation (EEC) 3977/87 O.J. L 375, 31.12.1987 p. 1.
6 See Regulation 174/83, *supra*, fn. 2, para. 24.1 in relation to Canada.

24.10 To ensure that the conservation rules are fully enforced and obeyed the Community also establishes a surveillance system. The new system in operation since June 1982[1] illustrates well the cooperation that is necessary between the Community and the Member States to ensure adequate policing and enforcement of the CFP. Primary responsibility is placed on the Member States to ensure that vessels in their own ports are observing the Community regulations. This involves inspections and regular checks by the Member States using their own inspectorates. When violations are detected the Member States must use whatever legal or administrative weapons are at their disposal to terminate the breaches. Normally this will involve prosecution before the national courts. The national authorities must also keep the Commission regularly informed of its activities in these matters.

Since the end of 1983, the Commission too, has its own inspectors to ensure common interpretation and enforcement of the Community's conservation rules. The Community inspectors, however, are very much observers in the surveillance process since they cannot prosecute individual skippers and can only operate with the national inspectors who remain responsible for the operation at all times. Member States must keep records of all landings at ports within their jurisdiction and skippers are obliged to keep records of all their catches, the dates and locations of such catches, etc. This information enables the Member States to calculate when the national quota has been exhausted.

The cost of patrolling and surveillance has been substantial for Ireland and the Community has allocated 46 million ECU between 1977 and 1982 to enable Ireland properly to discharge its functions in the matter.

1 EC Commission, *op. cit.*, n. 1, p. 47.

Structural policy

24.11 Echoing Article 39 of the EEC Treaty, the objectives of the structural policy of the CFP are as follows: the conservation and management of Community fish stocks, the provision of a fair standard of living for those in the fishing industry, the guaranteeing of regular supplies of fish at reasonable prices and the ensuring that the Community's fishing industry can face up to increasing international competition.

To achieve these ends the Community has since 1983 established programmes and provided finance to support the following:

  (i)   Restructuring, modernising and developing the fishing industry, and in particular supporting modernised storage capacity, energy saving schemes and boat building within the range of 9 to 33 metres boat length;
 (ii)   Fish farming and aquaculture;
(iii)   Scrapping and laying up ('mothballing') Community vessels;
 (iv)   Exploratory voyages in search of new grounds and species; and
  (v)   Joint ventures for new grounds especially in the Mediterranean and off the West Coast of Africa.[1]

1 The Community's policy in this commenced in 1971 but its most recent activities date from October, 1983. Moreover, it should be noted that various support has also been forthcoming under the Social Fund (finance for training programmes in fish farming in Ireland) and under the Regional Fund (support for harbour improvements, research centres and processing factories). On most recent proposals on this, see Proposal for Council Regulation on Community measures to improve and adopt structures in the fisheries and aquaculture sectors O.J. C 279 p. 3, 1986.

Marketing policy

24.12 A market organisation policy was first introduced in 1970 and revised in 1981.[1] To ensure that fishermen get a fair return for their labour, rational marketing in a stable market has been promoted by the adoption of common quality standards at Community level.

Producer organisations are central to the marketing policy of the Community. Although encouraged and aided by the Community these organisations are established on the producer's own initiative, and strive to achieve rational fishing and improved marketing. Generally, members must dispose of their catches through the producers' organisation.

The Commission fixes an official withdrawal price[2] and the producers will not normally sell below this price. Occasionally the producers can fix their own withdrawal price. If the withdrawal price is not reached the members will receive compensation from their producer organisation. The system does not, however, guarantee the producer the full withdrawal price for catches which remain unsold. A sliding scale of compensation exists so that for the first 5 per cent of the catch withdrawn 85 per cent of the withdrawal price is paid, whereas at the other end of the scale, if 15 to 20 per cent is withdrawn only 40 per cent of the withdrawal price is paid for the quantity between 15 and 20 per cent withdrawn. The idea is to encourage producers to sell at reasonable prices while attempting at the same time to provide the fishermen with a reasonable and a somewhat predictable price for their catch. Conditions are also attached to the withdrawal system, the most important of which stipulate that withdrawn fish must not be used for human consumption and its disposal cannot be allowed to interfere with the normal marketing practice.

Guide prices for fish are set by the Council each year and the withdrawal price is fixed by reference to the guide (or target) price. The system is not unlike, in general terms, that which operates for agricultural products.

To cope with the problems caused by differences in the world prices and the Community prices, and which might result in either unwanted imports or exports into or from the Community, provision is made for export refunds and a variety of other measures designed to maintain preference for Community prices.

The principal legislation in Ireland regulating the fishing sector is contained in the Fisheries (Consolidation) Act, No. 14 of 1959 as amended, the most recent collective citation being the Fisheries Acts 1959 to 1987. Most of the Regulations implementing Community policy into Irish law as made under this statutory authority and the most convenient list of this legislation (up to 31 December 1986) is to be found in R.F. Humphrey, *Index to Irish Statutory Instruments*, Vol. 2. These orders and instruments typically now deal with such matters as conservation, rational exploitation and management of fishery resources, prohibitions on fishing for certain stocks, at certain times and in certain areas, licensing arrangements, size of net mesh, etc.

1 Council Regulation (EEC) 3796/81 O.J. L 379, 31.12.1981 p. 1, replacing Regulation (EEC) 100/76 L 20, 28.1.1976 p. 1, which itself replaced Regulation (EEC) 2142/70. O.J. (Sp. Ed.) 1970 (III) p. 707. See, for case on this, Case 207/84 *De Boer*, *supra*, fn. 3, para. 23.1.

2 For system by which Community fixes withdrawal prices, see Council Regulation (EEC), 3796/81 *supra*, n. 1. Detailed rules for calculating withdrawal prices are set out in Commission Regulation (EEC) 3508/82 O.J. L 368, 28.12.1982 p. 18.

Chapter 25

The Community and Labour Law

25.1 There are two separate chapters of the Treaty that are concerned primarily with the welfare of workers. The right of workers to move freely throughout the Community is conferred by Articles 48 to 51, i.e. chapter 1 of Title III of Part Two. This has been dealt with in Chapter 18 of this work. Title III of Part Three of the Treaty contains two chapters, the second of which makes provision for the European Social Fund. The Social Fund is examined in Chapter 6 of this book. Chapter 1 of Title III (Articles 117 to 122) is entitled 'Social Provisions' and there is only one provision in this chapter which imposes an unqualified obligation on the Member States: Article 119 requires the Member States to ensure and maintain the application of the principle that men and women should receive equal pay for equal work. Most of the other provisions are aspirational in tone but are important nonetheless because harmonisation legislation, under, Article 100 or Article 235 or both, has been adopted to give concrete effect to the sentiments expressed therein.

The basic provision is Article 117, according to which the Member States agreed on the need to improve the working conditions and living standards of workers, and expressed the conviction that such improvements would flow from the operation of the common market as well as from the approximation of administrative and legislative measures. With this in mind the Commission was charged, under Article 118, with promoting cooperation between the Member States on the following topics: employment; labour law and working conditions; basic and advanced vocational training; social security; prevention of occupational accidents and diseases; occupational hygiene; and the right of association and collective bargaining between employers and workers. In Article 120 the Member States undertook to endeavour to maintain the existing equivalence between paid holiday schemes. Article 121 empowers the Council to assign further tasks to the Commission, particularly concerning social security for migrant workers, and Article 122 obliges the Commission to include a separate chapter on social developments in the annual report to the European Parliament.

During the 1960s very little was accomplished in the field of social policy; the necessary stimulus for speedy action was given in the final communiqué of the Summit meeting of October 1972 which called for the preparation, before the end of 1973, of a social action programme.[1] The Commission's draft was approved by the Council in January 1974[2] and it called for action to achieve three objectives: full and better employment; improved living and working conditions; and increased participation of both sides of industry in economic and social decisions and of workers in the conduct of firms.

Since 1974 the Community can point to a variety of initiatives designed to implement the Social action programme. The establishment in 1975 of the European Centre for the Development of Vocational Training,[3] located at Berlin, was one of the Community's responses to the task of creating new jobs and alleviating youth unemployment. In 1975 the Council took the first of a series of Decisions authorising the establishment of pilot schemes to combat poverty,[4] and in 1976 the trade union rights of migrant workers were extended by a Council Regulation.[5] Following the establishment by the Council in 1974 of an Advisory Committee on Safety, Hygiene and Health Protection at Work[6] there has been a variety of Directives on safety and working conditions. Examples include Council Directive (EEC) 77/576[7] on safety information at places of work, Council Directive (EEC) 78/610[8] on the exposure of workers to vinyl chloride polymer, Council Directive (EEC) 80/1107[9] on the exposure of workers to chemical, physical and biological agents at work, and Council Directive (EEC) 86/188[10] on the exposure of workers to noise at work. In this regard mention should also be made of the establishment in 1975 of the European Foundation for Living and Working Conditions,[11] which is located at Loughlinstown, Co. Dublin. As regards the participation of both sides of industry in economic and social decisions, the Commission reactivated the Standing Committee on Employment[12] in the mid-1970s and convened regular meetings of the so-called Tripartite Conference,[13] a forum in which representatives of the Member States, the Community, labour and employers discuss the social and economic problems facing the Community.

However, the most significant developments in the past decade or so have taken place in the context of equality of treatment between men and women concerning pay and other conditions of employment and in the consultation of workers and the preservation of their rights in the event of transfers of undertakings, insolvency of employers, and mass redundancies. There have been five Directives on the application of the equal treatment principle and three Directives on the consultation of workers and the preservation of their rights, and these two cognate areas of Community law have had the most profound impact on domestic law. Their implementation has given rise to a new State agency, the Employment Equality Agency, has transformed the activities of two quasi-judicial tribunals—the Labour Court and, to a lesser extent, the Employment Appeals Tribunal—and has generated a significant corpus of Community and domestic jurisprudence, particularly on the doctrine of direct effects. Our starting point for a review of these Directives must be Article 119 of the Treaty.

1 Sixth General Report, point 11.
2 Council Resolution, O.J. C 13, 12.2.1974 p. 1.

3 Council Regulation (EEC) 337/75 O.J. L 39, 13.2.1975 p. 1.
4 Council Decision (EEC) 75/458 O.J. L 199, 30.7.1975 p. 34.
5 Council Regulation (EEC) 312/76 O.J. L 39, 14.2.1976 p. 2.
6 Council Decision (EEC) 74/325 O.J. L 185, 10.7.1974 p. 15.
7 O.J. L 229, 7.9.1977 p. 12.
8 O.J. L 197, 22.7.1978 p. 12.
9 O.J. L 327, 3.12.1980 p. 8.
10 O.J. L 137, 24.5.1986 p. 28.
11 Council Regulation (EEC) 1365/75 O.J. L 139, 30.5.1975 p. 1.
12 Council Decision (EEC) 70/532 O.J. (Sp. Ed.) 1970 (III) p. 863.
13 Ninth General Report, point 199.

Article 119 and the principle of Equal Pay

25.2 Article 119 reads as follows:

> Each Member State shall during the first stage ensure and subsequently maintain the application of the principle that men and women should receive equal pay for equal work.
>
> For the purpose of this Article, 'pay' means the ordinary basic or minimum wage or salary and any other consideration, whether in cash or in kind, which the worker receives, directly or indirectly, in respect of his employment from his employer.
>
> Equal pay without discrimination based on sex means:
> (a) that pay for the same work at piece rates shall be calculated on the basis of the same unit of measurement;
> (b) that pay for work at time rates shall be the same for the same job.

It is clear from the text that the Member States should have taken steps to comply with the obligation expressed in the first sentence by the end of 1961. But the day before the expiry of the first stage of the transitional period the Member States adopted a Resolution delaying the implementation of Article 119 pending the completion of studies into '. . . the material content of the principle of equal pay'. Further deadlines came and went until the Commission, in 1973, threatened proceedings under Article 169 against Member States which had not implemented the obligation in Article 119. This warning did not result in any action from the Commission, and the Council had adopted Directive (EEC) 75/117[1] on the application of the equal pay principle before any legal proceedings were taken. When litigation did commence it was in the Belgian courts and the plaintiff was the redoubtable Gabrielle Defrenne, an air hostess with the Belgian airline SABENA; on no less than three occasions actions initiated by her against SABENA gave rise to references under Article 177. In the second of these cases[2] the Cour du travail in Brussels asked two questions concerning the effect and implementation of Article 119. The Court of Justice ruled that the principle of equal pay for equal work was one of the foundations of the Community, and it could be relied on by citizens before the national courts; it was impossible to base arguments to the contrary on the dilatoriness and resistance which delayed its implementation in the Member States. Article 119 had been directly effective since 1 January 1962 in the original Member States and since 1 January 1973 in the new Member States, and the Resolution of 1961 was ineffective to make any valid modification of the time-limit fixed by the Treaty. However, taking into account the representations of the Irish and British Governments, the Court considered the economic consequences of the (retrospective) application of Article 119 and, while stating that the practical consequences of any judicial decision should not diminish the objectivity of the law and compromise its future application, the Court felt it appropriate to take exceptionally into account the fact that non-compliance with Article 119 had been tolerated by the institutions, if not encouraged. Therefore, since the general level at which pay would have been fixed could not be expressly established '. . . important considerations of legal certainty affecting all the interests involved, both public and private, make it impossible in principle to reopen the question as regards the past'. As a result, Article 119 could be relied on to support equal pay claims prospectively only, except as regards persons who had already instituted proceedings or made an equivalent claim.

The general reaction to the Court's ruling was favourable although that portion of the judgment concerned with the temporal effect of Article 119 was greated with pragmatic cynicism and with regret that while giving vent to high sounding statements of principle the Court '. . . still found its way, in the instant case, to giving priority to purely economic motives'.[3] We have already noted how the Supreme Court utilised the *Defrenne ratio decidendi* in the case of *Murphy v A-G*[4] to limit claims against the State for repayment of income tax unconstitutionally extracted from married taxpayers (*supra*, para. 15.5). But it should be emphasised that the prospective ruling of the Court of Justice in *Defreᴎne v Sabena (No 2)*[5] was exceptional and in a later case, *Worringham v Lloyds Bank*,[6] the Court rejected a request by the defendant bank to limit the temporal effect of Article 119 so that its judgment could not be relied on to support claims concerning pay periods prior to the date of the judgment. The exceptional factors which justified the *Defrenne* decision were not present in the instant case.

The scope of Article 119 has been dealt with in other judgments of the Court. In the third *Defrenne* case, *Defrenne v Sabena (No. 3)*,[7] the Court held that Article 119 constitutes a special rule whose application is linked to precise factors: it cannot be interpreted as prescribing, in addition to equal pay, equality in respect of the other working conditions applicable to men and women. Thus, a discriminatory retirement age for women only did not fall within the field of application of Article 119. However, Article 119 applies directly, and without the need for more detailed implementing measures on the part of the Community or the Member States, to all forms of direct and overt discrimination which may be identified solely with the aid of the criteria of equal work and equal pay: *Macarthys Ltd v Smith*.[8] Thus, a national court would be justified in applying Article 119 to an occupational pension scheme, which would not appear at first glance to fall within the scope of Article 119, if it is clear that benefits paid to employees under the scheme are treated by employer and employee as part of the worker's remuneration in respect of employment: *Bilka-Kaufhaus v von Hartz*.[9]

In recent years the Court has confirmed that certain practices are discriminatory within the meaning of Article 119. In the second *Defrenne* case[10] it was not disputed that an air hostess was paid less than a cabin steward although the work of the hostess and the cabin steward were identical. In *Macarthys Ltd v Smith*[11] the Court held that where men and women receive unequal pay for equal work carried out in the same establishment it is not necessary to certify that the men and women were working contemporaneously; thus Article 119 will apply where a woman has done equal work for the employer but received less pay than a man who was employed prior to the woman's period of employment. In *Worringham v Lloyds Bank*[12] Article 119 was held to apply to the requirement to make contributions to a retirement benefit scheme which applied only to men but where the contributions were actually paid by the employer on behalf of those men by means of an addition to their gross salary. Although the difference in pay between full-time and part-time workers does not normally offend against Article 119 it will be discriminatory if it is in reality merely an indirect way of reducing the level of pay of part-time workers who happen to be composed exclusively or predominantly of women: *Jenkins v Kingsgate (Clothing Productions) Ltd.*[13] The ban on discrimination based on sex will be infringed where an employer provides special travel facilities for former male employees to enjoy after their retirement but does not extend the same facilities to former female employees: *Garland v British Rail Engineering Ltd.*[14] On the other hand, discrimination resulting from the application of social security schemes governed by domestic legislation does not fall within the ambit of Article 119: *Defrenne v Belgium*;[15] neither does discrimination arising from a particular condition of employment, such as a mandatory retirement age for women at a certain age: *Defrenne v Sabena (No 3).*[16] In the latter case the Court held that the elimination of discrimination based on sex was a fundamental personal human right the observance of which the Court had a duty to ensure—but not as regards relationships between employer and employee, which were a matter for national law exclusively. This rule does apply, however, in the relationship between the Community and the men and women employed by it and subject to the Staff Regulations. In this context the scope of the principle of equal treatment was not limited to Article 119 or to the Directives enacted in this area: *Razzouk and Beydoun v EC Commission.*[17] Thus, the provision of two different survivors' pension schemes according to whether the deceased official was male or female was in breach of this principle, as were rules concerning the withdrawal of expatriation allowances from female officials who involuntarily acquired another nationality on marriage: *Airola v EC Commission.*[18]

1 O.J. L 45, 19.2.1975 p. 19.
2 Case 43/75 *Defrenne v Sabena (No 2)* [1976] E.C.R. 453, [1976] 2 C.M.L.R. 98.
3 Catherine A. Crisham, *Annotation on Case 43/75*, 14 C.M.L.R. (1977) 108.
4 [1982] I.R. 241 at 274.
5 *Supra*, fn. 2.
6 Case 69/80 [1981] E.C.R. 767, [1981] 2 C.M.L.R. 1.
7 Case 149/77 [1978] E.C.R. 1365, [1978] 3 C.M.L.R. 312.
8 Case 129/79 [1980] E.C.R. 1275, [1980] 2 C.M.L.R. 205.
9 Case 170/84 [1986] E.C.R. 1607, [1986] 2 C.M.L.R. 701.
10 *Supra*, fn. 2.
11 *Supra*, fn. 8.

12 *Supra*, fn. 6.
13 Case 96/80 [1981] E.C.R. 911, [1981] 2 C.M.L.R. 24.
14 Case 12/81 [1982] E.C.R. 359, [1982] 1 C.M.L.R. 696.
15 Case 80/70 [1971] E.C.R. 445, [1974] 1 C.M.L.R. 494.
16 *Supra*, fn. 7.
17 Joined Cases 75, 117/82 [1984] E.C.R. 1509, [1984] 3 C.M.L.R. 470.
18 Case 21/74 [1975] E.C.R. 221.

Equal Pay: the Directive of 1975

25.3 We have seen how the Member States and the Commission combined to postpone the implementation of the equal pay principle. However, in 1975, the Council enacted Directive (EEC) 75/117[1] on the application of the principle of equal pay for men and women, and the preamble noted the delay consequent on the Resolution of December 1961 and referred to the social action programme in which equal treatment for women was recognised as a priority. In one sense, therefore, the Directive constituted a belated attempt to comply with the obligation laid down in Article 119. In Article 1 the principle of equal pay for men and women outlined in Article 119 of the Treaty is defined as meaning, for the same work or for work to which equal value is attributed, the elimination of all discrimination on grounds of sex with regard to all aspects and conditions of remuneration. If a job classification system is used for determining pay, it must be based on the same criteria for both men and women and so drawn up as to exclude any discrimination on grounds of sex. The first point to note about Article 1 is that the Court has held that it cannot alter the content or scope of the principle of equal pay as defined in Article 119: *Jenkins v Kingsgate (Clothing Productions).*[2] In *EC Commission v Denmark*[3] the Court held that national implementing measures were insufficient (i) because no reference was made to work of equal value when outlining the principle of equal pay; and (ii) implementation was left to management and labour in the first instance; thus, non-unionised workers or sectors not covered by collective agreements would not be adequately protected. If a job classification system is used, the use of values reflecting the average capacity of workers of one sex as a basis for determining the extent to which work makes demands or requires effort or whether it is heavy, constitutes a form of discrimination on grounds of sex, contrary to the directive: *Rummler v Dato-Druck GmbH.*[4] The use of job classification systems is only one method of determining pay for work to which equal value is attributed, so that Member States cannot specify such a system as the sole method of assessing work of equal value; a worker must be able to make a claim for equal pay for work of equal value before an appropriate authority: *EC Commission v United Kingdom.*[5]

Articles 2 to 7 of the Directive deal with promulgation and enforcement. Persons considering themselves wronged by the non-application of the principle of equal pay must have access to a judicial process or another competent authority so as to pursue their claims (Article 2). Member States are obliged to abolish all discrimination contrary to the equal pay principle arising from laws or administrative practices (Article 3), and are also required to ensure that offending clauses in collective agreements may be declared null and void (Article 4). Member States must also protect workers against retaliatory dismissals in reaction to equal pay claims (Article 5), to take the measures necessary to ensure the application of the equal pay principle (Article 6),[6] and to bring the implementing measures to the attention of employees (Article 7).

1 *Supra*, fn. 1, para. 25.2.
2 *Supra*, fn. 13, para. 25.2.
3 Case 143/83 [1985] E.C.R. 427, [1986] 1 C.M.L.R. 44.
4 Case 237/85 [1987] 3 C.M.L.R. 127.
5 Case 61/81 [1982] E.C.R. 2601, [1982] 3 C.M.L.R. 284. In this case the Commission took the unusual step of pointing to Ireland's Anti-Discrimination (Pay) Act, 1974 as an example of how the United Kingdom could comply with its obligations under Directive 75/117; see at pp. 2613 and 289 respectively.
6 See Case 248/83 *EC Commission v Germany* [1985] E.C.R. 1459, [1986] 2 C.M.L.R. 588. In this action under Article 169 the Commission failed to establish that the defendant had failed to implement the Directive fully.

Equal treatment: the Directive of 1976

25.4 In the third *Defrenne* Case[1] the Court held that Article 119 did not apply to discrimination based on sex concerning working conditions other than pay; it was left to the Community's legislative authorities to enact rules designed to achieve equality between men and women in respect of access to work and other conditions of employment. Council Directive (EEC) 76/207,[2] based on Article 235 of the Treaty, is the most important Community measure in this context. In Article 1(1) the purpose of the Directive is stated to be the putting into effect in the Member States of the principle of equal treatment for men and women as regards access to employment (including promotion) and vocational training, and as regards working conditions. Article 2(1) further defines the principle of equal treatment: it involves the prohibition of discrimination on grounds of sex either directly or indirectly by reference in particular to marital or family status. Article 1(1) empowered the Council to enact provisions applying the principle of equal treatment to matters of social security and two separate Directives have been adopted under this rubric (*infra* 25.8 and 25.9). Article 2 permits certain activities to be excluded from the field of application of the Directive: paragraph (2) allows Member States to exclude occupational activities, and the training leading thereto, for which, by reason of their nature or the context in which they are carried out, the sex of the worker constitutes a determining factor. Thus, the non-application of the equality principle to the profession of midwife might be justified in certain circumstances whereas exclusion from the scope of the Directive of employment in private households or in small firms employing not more than five workers would not be justified: *EC Commission v United Kingdom*.[3] Article 2(3) preserves the validity of national measures concerning the protection of women, particularly as regards pregnancy and maternity. But this does not mean that men can claim a right to 'paternity' leave, either in respect of natural children (*Hofmann v Barmer Ersatzkasse*)[4] or adopted children (*EC Commission v Italy*).[5] The difference in treatment between men and women in this regard can be justified by the need to protect the physiological and mental health of women before and after childbirth, and by the need to foster the bonding process between mother and child or, alternatively, the assimilation as far as possible of a child into an adoptive family. Apart from these two exceptions, the principle of equal treatment is not subject to any reservation as regards measures taken for the purpose of protecting national security or of protecting safety or public order: *Johnston v Chief Constable of the RUC.*[6]

Articles 3, 4 and 5 apply the principle of equal treatment to the conditions—including selection criteria—for access to all jobs or posts; to all levels of vocational guidance, vocational training, advanced vocational training and retraining; and to working conditions, including the conditions governing dismissal. In respect of all three areas of application the Member States are obliged to ensure that all laws or administrative practices contrary to the equality principle will be abolished, that provisions in collective agreements infringing the principle of equal treatment may be declared void, and that where laws or administrative practices have been adopted to protect a particular interest they will be revised when the need for protection is no longer justified. Article 5, which applies the principle of equal treatment to working conditions, including the rules relating to dismissals, has generated a considerable body of case-law. As regards its implementation in domestic law, a Member State cannot be criticised for having enacted a number of specific provisions concerning the most important working conditions while confining itself, in relation to all other working conditions, to the adoption of an all-embracing general rule: *EC Commission v Italy.*[7] On questions of substance the dominant issue has been the connection between dismissals and national rules or occupational schemes entitling women to retirement pensions at an earlier age than men. Such rules or schemes do not constitute discrimination within the meaning of Article 5: *Burton v British Railways Board*[8] and *Roberts v Tate and Lyle Industries.*[9] But, while the determination of a minimum pensionable age on a differential basis for men and women does not amount to discrimination, national rules or occupational schemes which oblige women to retire, simply because they have attained the qualifying age for a State pension, infringe the principle: *Marshall v Southampton and South West Hampshire Area Health Authority*[10] and *Beets-Proper v F van Lanschot Bankiers NV.*[11]

Articles 6, 7 and 8 deal with promulgation and enforcement of equal treatment: persons who consider themselves to have been wronged must be able to pursue their claims by judicial process after possible recourse to other competent authorities (Article 6); Member States must implement the measures necessary to protect workers against retaliatory dismissals in reaction to equal treatment claims (Article 7); and they must also ensure that implementing measures are brought to the attention of employees (Article 8). In two decisions of 1984 the Court of Justice underlined the importance of effective implementation of the principle of equal treatment: *Von Colson v Land Nordrhein-Westfalen*[12] and *Harz v Deutsche Tradax GmbH.*[13] In both cases the plaintiffs had sought damages and/or a contract of employment as a remedy for discrimination on grounds of sex. But the Arbeitsgerichte, at Hamm and at Hamburg respectively, considered that German law permitted only the reimbursement of expenses incurred in making the application for employment; these amounted to

DM 7.20 for Von Colson and DM 2.31 for Harz. The requests for preliminary rulings sought to determine whether employers who had infringed the principle of equality in recruitment procedures were obliged to offer contracts of employment to the wronged female applicants, or whether infringement of the principle of equal treatment required an appreciable financial sanction to be available to the victims of discrimination. The Court held that the Directive did not require employers to compensate candidates who had been discriminated against by concluding with them contracts of employment. Similarly, the Directive did not require a specific form of sanction for breach of the prohibition of discrimination. But the sanction must be sufficient to have a real deterrent effect on employers and to guarantee real and effective judicial protection for applicants; compensation must in any event be adequate in relation to the damage sustained and must therefore amount to more than purely nominal compensation such as the reimbursement only of expenses incurred in connection with the application.

Finally, in *Marshall v Southampton and South West Hampshire Area Health Authority*,[14] the Court of Justice was given the opportunity to resolve a long-standing conceptual problem in Community law: can directives produce 'horizontal' direct effects? The Court recalled that in its previous decisions on direct effects it had concluded that if a provision of a directive was clear, precise and unconditional it could be relied on against a State which had failed to implement the directive within the prescribed period or where it failed to implement the directive properly. But it followed from Article 189 of the Treaty, according to which a Directive was binding only in respect of 'each Member State to which it is addressed' that a directive might not be relied on by one individual against another. In the instant case the Court fudged the issue somewhat by holding that the defendant 'State authority' was acting in its capacity as an employer rather than as a legal person or individual, and that Article 5(1) of the Directive which prohibited discrimination in connection with working conditions, including conditions of dismissal, was directly effective.[15]

1 *Supra*, fn. 7 para. 25.2.
2 O.J. L 39, 14.2.1976, p. 40.
3 Case 165/82 [1983] E.C.R. 3431, [1984] 1 C.M.L.R. 44.
4 Case 184/83 [1984] E.C.R. 3047, [1986] 1 C.M.L.R. 242.
5 Case 163/82 [1984] E.C.R. 3273, [1984] 3 C.M.L.R. 169.
6 Case 222/84 [1986] E.C.R. 1651, [1986] 3 C.M.L.R. 240.
7 *Supra*, fn. 5.
8 Case 19/81 [1982] E.C.R. 555, [1982] 2 C.M.L.R. 136.
9 Case 151/84 [1986] E.C.R. 703, [1986] 1 C.M.L.R. 714.
10 Case 152/84 [1986] 1 C.M.L.R. 688.
11 Case 262/84 [1986] E.C.R. 773, [1987] 2 C.M.L.R. 616.
12 Case 14/83 [1984] E.C.R. 1891, [1986] 2 C.M.L.R. 430.
13 Case 79/83 [1984] E.C.R. 1921, [1986] 2 C.M.L.R. 430.
14 *Supra*, fn. 10.
15 *Idem*.

Equal pay and equal treatment in Ireland

25.5 'As a result of our membership of the EC we have seen great changes in the status of women. They owe their present rights of equal pay, access to employment, maternity leave and the general non-acceptance now of discrimination against women in so many areas to the EC.'[1]

The equal pay and equal treatment Directives of 1975 and 1976 have been implemented in Ireland by the Anti-Discrimination (Pay) Act, 1974 and the Employment Equality Act, 1977. Section 56 of the Employment Equality Act provides that the two Acts shall be construed together as one Act; thus, while the substantive provisions on equal pay and equal treatment stand on their own they have an institutional framework in common, and this framework will be briefly outlined before the substantial provisions of the Acts are analysed.

Section 6 of the 1974 Act established equal pay officers to investigate disputes between employers and employees in relation to the existence or operation of an equal pay clause; the Minister for Labour may also refer matters to the officer who may then investigate the dispute and issue a recommendation (section 7). Section 18 of the 1977 Act converted equal pay officers into 'equality officers'; where a dispute relating to the principle of equal treatment arises it may be referred to the Labour Court which may try to settle the dispute through an industrial relations officer or refer the dispute to an equality officer for investigation and recommendation (section 19). Where a recommendation has been issued by an equality officer under section 7 of the 1974 Act or section 19 of the 1977 Act, a party to the dispute may appeal to the Labour Court against the recommendation or appeal to the Labour Court for a determination that the recommendation has not been implemented. Appeals are normally heard in private, and must be lodged within 6 weeks of date of the recommendation (sections 9 of the 1974 Act and 20 of the 1977 Act). When conducting the hearing the Labour Court is bound by the rules of natural justice. If it commissions a special report on work practices for the purposes of an equal pay claim, it must afford the parties to the dispute the possibility of examining its contents and of making submissions in relation to it: *State (Cole) v The Labour Court.*[2] Likewise, if the Labour Court takes legal advice as to whether it has jurisdiction to investigate a dispute, it must afford the parties the opportunity of commenting on the legal submissions made to the Labour Court: *State (Polymark) v The Labour Court.*[3] An appeal may be taken to the High Court, on a point of law, against the determination of the Labour Court. (Section 9(3) of the 1974 Act; section 20(4) of the 1977 Act). This is not a rehearing of the case and the High Court, in an application for relief by way of judicial review, will confine itself to examining whether the Labour Court made its determination without jurisdiction, in excess of jurisdiction, in breach of natural justice, or has made a determination containing an error of law on the face of the record: *State (Casey) v The Labour Court.*[4]

The 1977 Act also established the Employment Equality Agency (EEA) whose general functions are described in section 35: to work towards the elimination of discrimination in employment, to promote equality of opportunity and to keep the 1974 Act under review. The EEA can also undertake and sponsor research (section 37), review legislation (section 38) and carry out investigations (section 39). The EEA may also seek an injunction from the High Court to prevent discrimination (section 33). If in the course of an investigation the EEA is satisfied that discrimination is taking place, it may issue a non-discrimination notice (section 44). An appeal against such a notice may be taken to the Labour Court within 6 weeks of its issue (section 45), but the EEA is empowered to seek the enforcement of non-discrimination notices by applying to the High Court for an injunction (section 46).

The provisions of the 1974 and 1977 Acts have had a considerable impact on contracts of employment and employer/employee relationships.[5] Since 1975 equality officers have issued hundreds of recommendations on equal pay and equal treatment. Requirements of space prevent us from assessing this corpus of decisions but readers are directed to the reviews of cases under the 1974 and 1977 Acts which are prepared from time to time by the Labour Court and are annexed to the Court's annual report.[6]

1 Senator Nuala Fennell, Seanad Debates Vol. 116 at col. 211.
2 [1984] 3 J.I.S.E.L. 128.
3 [1987] I.L.R.M. 357.
4 [1984] 3 J.I.S.E.L. 135.
5 See Deirdre Curtin, *The European Community Right to Sex Equality and its implementation in Irish Labour Law*, (1983) 5 D.U.L.J. 42.
6 (a) Review of cases under the Anti-Discrimination (Pay) Act, 1974.
    i For period from 1.1.76–31.12.81.
    Annual Report 1981, Appendix XII.
    ii For period from 1.1.82–31.12.84. Annual Report 1981, Appendix XIII.
  (b) Review of cases under the Employment Equality Act, 1977.
    i For period from 1.1.78–31.12.82.
    Annual Report 1982, Appendix XI.
    ii For period from 1.1.83–31.12.85. Annual Report 1985, Appendix XII.

Equal pay

25.6 The 1974 Act gives effect to Directive 75/117 on equal pay. The central provision is section 2 which implies into all contracts of employment a term to the effect that a woman employed in any place is entitled to the same rate of remuneration as a man employed in that place by the same employer if both are employed on like work. The implied term also operates in the converse situation i.e. where a man is paid less than a woman doing like work (section 11). Subsection (3) permits an employer to pay employees engaged in like work different rates of remuneration on grounds other than sex. This provision received an extremely narrow interpretation in *Bank of Ireland v Kavanagh*[1] where Costello J. overturned a recommendation of an equality officer and a determination of the Labour Court which had found that the Bank had discriminated against the male respondent by not paying him a marriage gratuity. This gratuity was payable to female officials who had been in the service of the Bank prior to 1974, but not to those employed after that date. Costello J. held that since the gratuity did not benefit *all* women employees, those who did receive it were being remunerated at a higher rate on grounds other than sex.

Section 3 defines 'like work' as follows:

'Two persons shall be regarded as employed on like work—

(a) Where both perform the same work under the same or similar conditions, or where each is in every respect interchangeable with the other in relation to the work,
    or
(b) where the work performed by one is of a similar nature to that performed by the other and any differences between the work performed or the conditions under which it is performed by each occur only infrequently or are of small importance in relation to the work as a whole,
    or
(c) where the work performed by one is equal in value to that performed by the other in terms of the demands it makes in relation to such matters as skill, physical or mental effort, responsibility and working conditions'.

In *Murphy v An Bord Telecom*[2] Keane J. had to consider the correctness of a recommendation of an equality officer, upheld by a determination of the Labour Court. The effect of these decisions was that the plaintiffs were not entitled to pay equal to that received by male colleagues because they were not engaged in 'like work' but in fact performed work superior in value to that of their colleagues. Keane J. did not accept the argument put forward on behalf of the plaintiffs that section 3(c) should be interpreted in the light of Article 119 and Article 1 of the Directive so that the words 'at least' appeared before the words equal in value. This would not result in equal pay for equal work but equal pay for unequal work, and would be doing violence to the words of the legislature to an impermissible extent. It was not possible to pray in aid the provision of the EEC Treaty or the Council Directive in the absence of any ambiguity, patent or latent, in the language used by the legislature. But the judge did agree to refer a series of questions to the Court of Justice as to whether the Community law principle of equal pay applied to claims involving work of higher value to comparable males, and whether Article 1 of Directive 75/117 was directly effective. However, the Court of Justice ruled that if the principle of equal pay forbids workers of one sex engaged in work of equal value to that of workers of the opposite sex to be paid a lower wage than the latter on grounds of sex, *a fortiori* it prohibits such a difference in pay where the lower-paid category of workers is engaged in work of higher value:

> 'To adopt a contrary intention would be tantamount to rendering the principle of equal pay ineffective and nugatory'[3]

When he came to apply the ruling of the Court of Justice Keane J. conceded that his earlier remarks were misleading.[4] It might also be noted that his initial unwillingness to refer to Article 119 or to the Directive in order to aid the interpretation of national implementing measures contrasts with the practice of equality officers and the Labour Court: see for example, the Labour Court's determination in *St Patrick's College, Maynooth v 19 Female employees*.[5]

Section 5 of the Act provides that provisions of collective agreements which stipulate different rates of remuneration on grounds of sex shall be null or void. It is not entirely clear whether an entitlement to equal rates can be waived. In *PMPA v Keenan*[6] Henchy J. in the Supreme Court stated that any compromise of an equal pay entitlement would be unlawful, but Carroll J. in the High Court suggested that a waiver of rights contained in a collective agreement would be effective if supported by adequate consideration.

Finally, sections 9 and 10 deal with cases where employers dismiss women for making claims for equal pay. Section 9 deals with prosecutions; an employer charged with dismissing a woman for making an equal pay claim will be liable on summary conviction to a fine of £100 or to a fine of £1,000 on conviction on indictment. In such a prosecution the burden is on the employer to satisfy the court that the making of the claim was not the principal reason for the dismissal. The court may, if an employer is convicted, impose a further fine equal to the amount a woman would recover in a civil action against the employer for arrears of remuneration and that fine will be paid to the complainant. Section 10 makes similar provisions where a prosecution under section 9 is not instituted but instead the wronged woman complains to the Labour Court. Section 10(1)(d) empowers the Court to order the employer to pay to the woman a sum not exceeding 104 weeks' remuneration by way of compensation, and the Court may recommend her reinstatement.

1 (19 June 1987, unreported) High Court, Costello J.
2 [1986] I.L.R.M. 483.
3 Case 157/86 *Mary Murphy v An Bord Telecom Eireann* [1988] 1 C.M.L.R. 879.
4 *Mary Murphy v An Bord Telecom Eireann* (11 April 1988, unreported), High Court (Keane J.).
5 Labour Court, EP4/1984.
6 [1984] 3 J.I.S.E.L. 122.

Equal treatment

25.7 The substantive provisions of Directive 76/207 have been implemented in Irish law by the Employment Equality Act, 1977. Section 4 implies into all contracts an 'equality clause' which relates to the terms of a contract—other than terms relating to occupational pensions or remuneration—under which a person is employed, and serves to modify or alter the contract to become equivalent to that of a person who does work not materially different from that of the claimant. Section 2 defines discrimination for the purposes of the Act:

(a) where by reason of his sex a person is treated less favourably than a person of the other sex;
(b) where because of his marital status a person is treated less favourably than another person of the same sex;
(c) where because of sex or marital status a person is obliged to comply with a requirement which is not essential for employment or membership of workers' organisations but in respect of which the number of persons of a different sex or different marital status able to comply with the requirement is substantially higher;
(d) where a person is penalised for making a claim under the 1974 or 1977 Acts.

It is clear that where a discrimination claim is made, particularly in connection with (c) above, a recommendation or determination to that effect must be supported by probative evidence: *Northwestern Health Board v Martyn*.[1] Section 3 defines in specific terms discrimination by employers concerning access to employment, conditions of employment, training or experience in relation to employment, promotion or re-grading or classification of posts for employment. In addition to matters directly connected to employment the Act prohibits discrimination in employment-related activities: membership of trade unions or other professional organisations (section 5); vocational training (section 6); employment agencies (section 7); and advertising (section 9).

Certain activities are exempt from the requirements of the Act. Originally, the Act permitted preferential treatment to be given to persons of one sex in respect of access to employment as a midwife or public health nurse (section 11(2)); the Act was inapplicable to employment in the Defence Forces, the Garda Siochana, the prison service, or in a private residence or by a close relative (section 12); and the Act did not apply to any act connected with the employment of a person where the sex of a person was an occupational qualification for the post (for example, where grounds of privacy or decency justified employment of persons of a particular sex) (section 17). However, these three restrictions have been either abolished or amended by statutory instruments adopted by the Minister for Labour under section 3 of the European Communities Act, 1972.[2]

Where an equality officer makes a recommendation, that recommendation may be appealed to the Labour Court. The Court's determination may do one of the following: (a) hold that there was or was not discrimination; (b) recommend a specific course of action; (c) award compensation in accordance with the Act (section 22). Compensation may not exceed 104 weeks' remuneration at the rate the person was receiving when the discrimination occurred (section 23). Finally, sections 24 and 25 make similar provisions concerning dismissals of persons who have made claims for equality pursuant to sections 9 and 10 of the 1974 Act (see above at 25.6).

1 [1985] I.L.R.M. 226.
2 European Communities (Employment Equality) Regulations, 1982, S.I. No. 302 of 1982; European Communities (Employment Equality) Regulations, 1985, S.I. No. 331 of 1985.

Equal treatment in matters of social security

25.8 The next stage in defining the scope of the equal treatment principle was the enactment of Council Directive (EEC) 79/7[1] on the progressive implementation of equal treatment for men and women in matters of social security. The Directive had to be implemented within six years of its notification to the Member States i.e. by 22 December 1984 at the latest. Article 2 defines its scope *ratione personae*: it applies to the working population—including self-employed persons, workers and self-employed persons whose activity has been interrupted by illness, accident or involuntary unemployment and persons seeking employment—and to retired or invalided workers and self-employed persons. Article 3 provides that the Directive applies to statutory schemes (or social assistance) which provide protection against the following risks:

— sickness
— invalidity
— old age
— accidents at work and occupational diseases
— unemployment.

Paragraph (3) empowered the Council to adopt measures extending the equal treatment principle to occupational schemes covering the same risks (see *infra*, para. 25.9). Article 4 defines the principle of equal treatment—no discrimination on grounds of sex either directly or indirectly by reference to marital or family status—and emphasises three circumstances relating to social security schemes where it should apply:

— the scope of the schemes and the conditions of access;
— the obligation to contribute and the calculation of contributions;
— the calculation of benefits including increases due in respect of a spouse and for dependants and the conditions governing the duration and retention of entitlements to benefits.

Article 7 permits the Member States to exclude certain matters from the scope of the Directive such as the determination of pensionable age for the purposes of granting old-age and retirement pensions and the possible consequences for other benefits. According to Article 6 the Member States must provide a means of legal redress for persons alleging injury for failure to apply the equal treatment principle to them; other competent authorities can be nominated to enquire into alleged infringements prior to the commencement of proceedings.

The scope and effect of the Directive have been discussed by the Court of Justice on a number of occasions. In *Drake v Chief Adjudication Officer*[2] the plaintiff gave up work to care for her invalided mother; her application for an invalid care allowance was turned down because she was a married woman. In reply to the Chief Social Security Commissioner the Court made a number of remarks on the scope of the Directive. As regards its application to the 'working population' as defined in Article 2, the Court held that a person whose work has been interrupted by one of the risks referred to in Article 3 is included in that description. Mrs Drake had to give up work because of the invalidity of her mother—a risk listed in Article 3. Article 3 had to be interpreted as including any benefit which in a broad sense forms part of one of the statutory schemes referred to, and the fact that benefit in question was paid to a third party and not to the disabled person did not place it outside the scope of the Directive. In *Netherlands v Federatie Nederlandse Vakbeweging*[3] the respondents had sought a declaration that the Netherlands had infringed the Directive by maintaining in force a provision according to which a married woman could not be considered the head of the household for the purposes of the law on Unemployment Benefit. The Court of Appeal at the Hague asked whether Article 4(1) of the Directive was directly effective after the expiry of the implementation period. The Court considered Article 4(1) to be sufficiently clear, precise and unconditional to be relied on in domestic courts and in the absence of implementing measures women were entitled to be treated in the same way as men according to the provisions of the Directive, which remained the only valid point of reference. The Court has also held that Article 4(1) does not prohibit a scheme in which benefits are calculated, *inter alia*, on marital status and income derived from spouses if the purpose of the scheme is to guarantee that the beneficiary's income is supplemented to take account of the additional burden of a spouse or dependent child, borne by the beneficiary, when compared with single persons.[4] But Article 4(1) does prohibit the extension beyond 22 December 1984 of measures inconsistent with the equal treatment guarantee even if the purpose of the national measure was to ensure that beneficiaries of an old (discriminatory) scheme were automatically entitled to benefit from a new scheme.[5]

Article 4(1) came up for consideration in the High Court in *McDermott and Cotter v Minister for Social Welfare and A-G*.[6] The plaintiffs maintained that the State was in breach of its obligations under the Directive because, subsequent to 22 December 1985, it had maintained in force rules which stipulated that married women were entitled to receive unemployment benefit for 312 days after the initial payment and pay-related benefit for 297 days thereafter. The applicable legislation provided that married or single men and single women were to receive unemployment benefit and pay-related benefit for 390 days and 375 days respectively after the initial payment. The State had not yet taken the measures to apply the Directive in domestic law, so Hamilton P. referred two questions to the Court of Justice. The first question asked whether Article 4(1) was directly effective and the second question (based on the assumption that Article 4(1) did produce direct effects) asked whether married women had enforceable rights of action as and from 23 December 1984. The Court of Justice gave its ruling on 24 March 1987 and repeated its judgment in *Netherlands v Federatie Nederlandse Vakbeweging*[7] to the effect that Article 4(1) was directly effective and, in the absence of implementing measures, the Directive constituted the only valid point of reference for the adjudication of disputes. The President of the High Court, when the matter was referred back to him by the Court of Justice, reserved judgment as to whether rights began to accrue from 23 December 1984. His judgment was delivered on 10 June 1988 and in it Hamilton P. refused the plaintiffs any of the reliefs claimed by them.[8] The logic of the judgment is frequently difficult to follow. For example, in respect of Mrs Cotter's claim for unemployment assistance, the judge found that because the qualifying conditions under the Social Welfare (Consolidation) Act, 1981 were discriminatory against married women she had been precluded from applying for unemployment assistance. However, the 1981 Act allowed the Minister to take the means of an applicant into account, but since Mrs Cotter had not made an application the Minister had not been in a position to decide whether she would have been entitled to unemployment assistance during the relevant period. Accordingly, the judge refused to make any declarations in respect of her claim for unemployment assistance. Furthermore, as noted above, the Court of Justice held that, in the absence of implementing measures, the Directive constituted the only valid point of reference for the adjudication of disputes. But Hamilton P., having already held that the Social Welfare (Consolidation) Act, 1981 infringed Article 4(1) of the Directive by depriving the Plaintiff of various increases in unemployment benefit, went on to apply to the facts of the case a dictum of Henchy J. in *Murphy v A-G*[9] (*supra*, para. 15.5):

> 'It is clear from this judgment that, in deciding whether the Applicant is entitled to any relief in respect of his claim, I am entitled to have regard to what Mr Justice Henchy referred to as "the equity of the case".
>
> The equity of this case requires that she be denied any claim for relief under this heading. It is conceded on behalf of the Applicant that her husband was at all relevant periods not dependent on her and that he was engaged in full-time employment.
>
> In the circumstances, it would be unjust and inequitable to pay to the Applicant an adult dependant increase when the adult concerned, her husband, was not financially dependent on her and it would be unjust and inequitable to require the people of Ireland to pay her such increase. Consequently, I refuse the Applicant any relief in respect of this particular claim.'

Apart from the fact that this element of the judgment ignores completely the ruling of the Court of Justice, to the effect that the directive constituted the *only* valid point of reference for the adjudication of disputes, the decision also ignores the fact that the *Murphy* case was concerned with the *retrospective* application of a ruling that a taxing statute was repugnant to the Constitution; whereas, in this case, the liability of the State was ascertainable from the moment that its failure to implement the Directive commenced i.e. 23 December 1984. In other words, there was no element of restrospectivity in this case at all. Finally, Hamilton P. held that although the Directive was directly effective in Ireland from 23 December 1984 onwards it could not be relied upon to support claims for social security concerning periods prior to the judgment of the Court of Justice except as regards those persons who had brought legal proceedings or made an equivalent claim prior to that date. This is a crude application of the principle in *Defrenne v Sabena (No 2)*,[10] which was relied on by Mr Justice Henchy in *Murphy v A-G*.[11] But it ignores the fact that the prospective ruling of the Court of Justice in *Defrenne* was exceptional and that in a later case, *Worringham v Lloyds Bank*,[12] a case also concerned with the equality principle, the Court rejected a request by the defendant Bank to limit the temporal effect of Article 119 so that its judgment could not be relied upon to support claims concerning pay periods prior to the date of judgment. In short, the *Defrenne* principle applies only in circumstances which are exceptional. It can hardly be said that the circumstances in *McDermott and Cotter v Minister for Social Welfare and A-G*[13] were exceptional. Not surprisingly, the judgment of Hamilton P. has been appealed to the Supreme Court.

The failure of the State to meet the implementation deadline was put right eventually by the enactment of the Social Welfare (No. 2) Act, 1985, the Social Welfare Act, 1986 and a series of statutory instruments adopted in 1986.[14] Unusually for an Irish statute implementing a Directive, the long title of the Social Welfare (No. 2) Act, 1985 makes specific reference to the equal treatment principle.

1 O.J. L 6, 10.1.1979 p. 24. For a detailed analysis of this Directive and its implementation

in Ireland see the papers by Rosheen Callender, Deirdre Curtin and Gerry Whyte in: Gerry Whyte (Ed.), *Sex Equality, Community Rights and Irish Social Welfare Law – The Impact of the Third Equality Directive*, Irish Centre for European Law (1988).
2 Case 150/85 [1986] 3 C.M.L.R. 43.
3 Case 71/85 [1987] 3 C.M.L.R. 767.
4 Case 30/85 *J. W. Teuling v Bedrijfsvereniging voor de Chemische Industrie* O.J. C 181, 9.7.1987 p. 5.
5 Case 384/85 *Clarke v Chief Adjudication Officer* [1987] 3 C.M.L.R. 277.
6 Case 286/85, [1987] I.L.R.M. 324.
7 *Supra*, fn. 3.
8 *Cotter and McDermot v Minister for Social Welfare and A-G*, (10 June 1988, unreported) High Court (Hamilton P.).
9 [1982] I.R. 241.
10 Case 43/75 [1976] E.C.R. 453, [1976] 2 C.M.L.R. 98.
11 [1982] I.R. 241.
12 Case 69/80 [1981] E.C.R. 767, [1981] 2 C.M.L.R. 1.
13 *Supra*, fn. 8.
14 See S.I. No. 173 of 1986; S.I. No. 365 of 1986; S.I. No. 366 of 1986; S.I. No. 368 of 1986; S.I. No. 369 of 1986; S.I. No. 422 of 1986.

Additional implementation of the equal treatment principle

25.9 In 1986 the Council adopted two further Directives to complement the equal pay and equal treatment measures:

— Directive (EEC) 86/378[1] on the implementation of the principle of equal treatment in occupational social security schemes, which had to be complied with by 30 July 1989 at the latest;
— Directive (EEC) 86/613[2] on the application of the principle of equal treatment in self-employed activities (including agriculture), and on the protection of self-employed women during pregnancy and motherhood, which had to be implemented by 30 June 1989 at the latest.

Both directives were based on Articles 100 and 235, and both define the principle of equal treatment as implying '. . . the absence of all discrimination on grounds of sex, either directly or indirectly, by reference in particular to marital or family status' (Article 3 of Directive 86/613, Article 5 of Directive 86/378). In particular, Article 6 of Directive 86/378 lists ten examples of provisions of occupational social security schemes which infringe the principle of equal treatment by using sex or family or marital status as criteria for entitlement, for example: to determine the persons who may participate in an occupational scheme; to fix different retirement ages; or to set different levels of worker contributions.

It will be recalled that Directive 79/7 did not apply to occupational schemes but was limited to statutory social security schemes providing protection against the following risks:

— sickness
— invalidity
— old age, including early retirement
— industrial accidents and occupational diseases
— unemployment.

According to Articles 2 and 4 of Directive 86/378 the principle of equal treatment now applies to any scheme covering such risks which is not covered by Directive 79/7 and whose purpose is to provide workers, whether employees or self-employed, in a company or group or occupational sector, with benefits intended to supplement the benefits provided by statutory social security schemes or to replace them, whether membership of such schemes is compulsory or optional. Article 3 states that the Directive is applicable to the working population (including the self-employed), to retired and disabled workers, to the unemployed, and to persons whose activity is interrupted by illness, maternity or accident. Article 7 requires the Member States to avoid extending administrative or official approval to schemes containing provisions contrary to the equal treatment principle and to declare such provisions null and void where they appear in collective agreements. Finally, Member States are obliged by Article 10 to provide a means of legal redress for persons claiming injury by reason of breach of the equal treatment principle, possibly after bringing the matter before other competent authorities.

According to the Oireachtas Joint Committee on the Secondary Legislation of the European Communities,[3] there are two reasons why women benefit less than men from occupational schemes: (i) such schemes are not common in industries employing mainly women; and (ii) such schemes are rarely applicable to part-time work. These factors—which were unfavourable to women but rarely directly discriminatory—could not be eliminated by direct action aimed at removing discrimination but required broader social protection measures.

Similar considerations applied to Directive 86/613 on the application of the principle of equal treatment to men and women engaged in a self-employed capacity, particularly in an agricultural context. Such women are often engaged in running an enterprise with their spouses but their occupational status, and thus their entitlement to social security, remains unclear and is rarely based on a formal partnership or contract of employment. Moreover, the fact that the basic unit is normally a family unit means that attempts to impose remedies could be problematic.[4] Consequently, the long-term solution to the problem lies in more general social legislation and the remedies available under the Directive are quite limited. According to Article 2 the Directive is applicable to self-employed workers, namely persons pursuing a gainful activity for their own account, including farmers and members of the liberal professions, and to their spouses where they habitually participate in the activities of the self-employed worker and perform the same tasks or ancillary tasks. The difficulty of providing specific remedies for infringement of the principle of equality (defined in Article 3) is recognised implicitly in Article 7, which requires the Member States to examine how the recognition of the work of the spouses of self-employed persons may be encouraged. Nonetheless, Articles 4, 5 and 6 do impose clear requirements on the Member States: discrimination concerning the establishment or extension of a business carried out by self-employed persons must be eliminated; the conditions for the formation of companies by spouses must be made at least as simple as those applicable to unmarried persons; and access to contributory social security schemes must be made available for spouses not covered by the self-employed worker's social security scheme. Lastly, Article 8 requires the Member States to examine how female self-employed workers or spouses of self-employed workers can gain access to such benefits or temporary replacement services during times of pregnancy and maternity. Article 9 obliges the Member States to provide recourse to judicial remedies, possibly after recourse to other competent authorities, for persons feeling aggrieved by failure to apply the principle of equal treatment in self-employed activities.

1 O.J. L 225, 12.8.1986 p. 40.
2 O.J. L 359, 19.12.1986.
3 Fourth Joint Committee, Report No. 4, 'Proposals relating to equality of opportunity (including parental and family leave)', at point 139.
4 *Idem*, at point 35.

Collective redundancies

25.10 Council Directive (EEC) 75/129[1] was enacted so as to eliminate differences between the provisions in force in the Member States concerning the practical arrangements and procedures for collective redundancies and the alleviation of the consequences thereof for workers. The Directive is based on Article 100 of the Treaty but also refers to Article 117 in the preamble; it sets up a system of notification and consultation between employers and workers when mass redundancies are contemplated and it puts a 30-day stay on collective redundancies to allow public authorities to seek solutions to the problems raised by the projected redundancies. In Article 1 of the Directive 'collective redundancies' is defined as meaning the dismissals, for reasons not connected with the employees concerned, over a 30-day period of:

— at least 10 workers in firms usually employing more than 20 and less than 100 workers; or
— at least 10 per cent of the workers normally employed in firms with at least 100 or less than 300 employees; or
— at least 30 in firms normally employing more than 300 workers.

The Member States were given the choice of adopting an alternative meaning in Article 1(1)(b): at least 20 dismissals over a 90-day period. The Directive does not apply to redundancies effected under short-term or specific task contracts, to public servants, to the crews of sea-going vessels, or to workers affected by the termination of a firm's activities brought about by a judicial decision.[2] According to Article 2, an employer must begin consultations with workers' representatives wherever collective redundancies are being contemplated: the consultations must cover means of avoiding or reducing redundancies and workers must be provided with information on the reasons for the redundancies, the numbers to be made redundant and the schedule thereof so as to enable the workers' representatives to make constructive proposals. Copies of this information must be forwarded to the competent national authorities. Article 3 obliges employers to notify the competent public authorities of any projected collective redundancy; the authorities must be sent copies of the consultations with workers' representatives and of the reasons for the redundancies. Article 4 provides for a stay of 30 days on collective redundancies (which can be extended to 60 days by the Member States) so that national authorities can seek solutions to the problems raised by the projected collective redundancies.

The scope of the Directive appears, at first sight, to be quite extensive. However, in *Dansk Metalarbejderforbund v H Nielsen*[3] the Court of Justice exposed some of its limitations. The defendant company experienced financial difficulties in February 1980 and informed its staff representatives accordingly. In March 1980 it filed a statement of bankruptcy which effectively suspended payment of its debts. The two trade unions represented in the company then sought a guarantee for the payment of future wages. When this was not forthcoming they instructed their members to stop work immediately; two weeks later the company was put into liquidation and the workers were notified of their dismissals. The unions then claimed special allowances from the company in liquidation on the grounds that the employer had not given 30 days' notice of projected collective redundancies. Under Danish law the liability to pay such allowances falls on a statutory body, the Wage-earners Guarantee Fund, if the employer has become insolvent. The Danish Supreme Court sought a preliminary ruling on two questions: (i) was termination of employment by workers to be considered as dismissal by the employer for the purposes of the Directive? and (ii) was an employer, by reason of his financial situation, under an obligation to contemplate collective redundancies? In answer to the first question the Court looked at the wording of Article 1 which provides that 'collective redundancies' means dismissals effected by an employer: the Directive could not be extended in scope to cover terminations of employment by workers. As regards the second question, the Court ruled that the employer was required to consult the trade unions only when he was 'contemplating' collective redundancies, whereas he had to inform the public authorities only of 'projected' redundancies. The Directive did not stipulate the circumstances in which the employer must contemplate collective redundancies and in no way affected his discretion as to whether and when he must draw up a plan for collective redundancies.

In Ireland the Directive was implemented by the Protection of Employment Act, 1977. The meaning of 'collective redundancy' is defined in section 6: the numerical standards are reasonably similar to those listed in Article 1 of the Directive but the dismissals can only be effected for five reasons specified in Section 6(2). The exceptions, along the lines envisaged by Article 1(2) of the Directive, are listed in section 7. Section 9 outlines the obligation on employers to consult with worker representatives, and section 10 specifies the information with which they must be supplied. Section 12 obliges employers to notify the Minister for Labour at least 30 days before dismissals take effect and section 14 prohibits collective redundancies from taking effect any earlier than 30 days from the notification of the Minister by the employer. Sections 11, 13 and 15 provide penalties for infringement of the obligations to consult with employees, to notify the Minister and not to initiate collective redundancies earlier than the stipulated 30-day period.

1 O.J. L 48, 22.2.1975 p. 29.
2 See Article 1(2).
3 Case 284/83 [1985] E.C.R. 553, [1986] 1 C.M.L.R. 91.

Safeguarding employees' rights in the event of a transfer of a business or part of a business: 'acquired rights'

25.11 This matter was dealt with by Council Directive (EEC) 77/187[1] In contrast with many other Directives, the implementation of this Directive in Ireland took the form of transposing its provisions, virtually entirely, into a set of Regulations issued under section 3 of the European Communities Act, 1972.[2] The Directive is based on Article 100 of the Treaty but the preamble also refers to the improvement of working conditions and living standards in the context of Article 117. The object of the Directive is to provide protection for employees in the event of a change of employer by ensuring, in particular, that their rights under contracts of employment are safeguarded. According to Article 1, the Directive applies to the transfer of an undertaking, business or part of a business to another employer as a result of a legal transfer or merger. It does not apply to sea-going vessels. However the scope of application of the Directive has already given rise to difficulties. In *Spijkers v Gebroeders Benedik Abbatoir CV*[3] the plaintiff was the assistant manager of an abbatoir which ceased trading in December, 1982. The entire business was purchased by the defendant and reopened as an abbatoir in February, 1983; the plaintiff was the only employee not re-engaged. Was there a transfer of a business for the purposes of Article 1 of the Directive? In answer to the Hoge Raad (Supreme Court of the Netherlands) the Court of Justice held that in determining whether there has been a transfer the decisive criterion was whether the business in question retains its identity; in the present context, that meant considering whether the business was disposed of as a going concern. This would be the case if it is continued in operation by the new owner or, when reactivated, pursues the same or similar economic activities. In *Abels v Bedrijfsvereniging voor de Metaalindustrie en de Electrotechnische Industrie*[4] a more thorny problem arose. The plaintiff had been employed by a company that encountered difficulties and was given leave to suspend payments before being declared insolvent. The business and nearly all the employees were transferred to a new concern but the plaintiff did not receive, either from his former or his new employers, wages, bonuses or holiday pay in respect of his employment by the original owner. In response to the Raad van Beroep (trade and professional court) in Arnhem, the Court held that the Directive did not apply to transfers of undertakings effected in the framework of insolvency proceedings, but the factors militating against the application of the Directive to insolvency proceedings did not apply in relation to proceedings taken at an earlier stage, such as judicial suspension of payments (comparable to a receivership in Irish law). The Court also noted that the different language versions of the Directive revealed disparities such that its scope could not be assessed solely on the basis of an interpretation of the text; the general scheme of the Directive and its objectives had to be taken into account. This teleological approach is of interest for another reason: it has been suggested that the Directive does not apply where the change in ownership occurs by transfers of share capital.[5]

Article 2 of the Directive defines 'transferor' as any natural or legal person who ceases to be the employer in respect of a business by reason of a transfer, and 'transferee' means any person who by virtue of a transfer becomes the employer. It now seems clear that in order to benefit from the substantive provisions of the Directive an employee must possess that status under both transferor and transferee: the Directive is not applicable to an employee of a transferor who becomes a controlling shareholder of a transferee.[6] In Articles 3 to 5 the rights protected by the Directive are outlined. As of the date of transfer the rights and obligations of the transferor arising out of a contract of employment or an employment relationship are transferred to the transferee (Article 3(1)); following the transfer the transferee must observe the terms of any collective agreements until termination or expiry of the collective agreement (Article 3(2)). The transferee is under an obligation to protect the interests of employees and former employees in respect of old-age, invalidity and survivors' benefits under company or inter-company pension schemes outside statutory social security schemes (in Ireland the Social Welfare Acts, 1981 to 1987); but the transferee is not subrogated to the rights and obligations of the transferor in respect of those schemes (Article 3(3)). Nothing in the Directive is to be construed as preventing dismissals for economic, technical or organisational reasons, but the transfer of a business does not in itself constitute grounds for dismissal by the transferor or transferee (Article 4(1)). Specific categories of employees, who are not covered by laws or practices in respect of dismissals, may be excluded from the scope of the Directive (Article 4(2)); but this exemption must be interpreted strictly and will not apply where even a rudimentary protection exists for the worker or category of worker in question.[7]

The Directive also imposes obligations on employers, as transferor and transferee, to inform workers' representatives in good time (i.e. before the transfer) of

(a) the reasons for the transfer;
(b) the legal, economic and social implications for employees;
(c) the measures envisaged in relation to employees.

(Article 6(1)).

If measures are envisaged, consultations must be held with workers' representatives with a view to seeking agreement (Article 6(2)). If the workers are unrepresented, they must be informed in advance that a transfer is to take place: the Irish Regulations stipulate that each worker must receive a statement in writing containing the information required by Article 6(1) and that this information must be displayed prominently in notices located in the workplace (Regulation 7(3)).

The European Communities (Safeguarding of employees' Rights on Transfers of Undertakings) Regulations 1980[8] simply transpose the Directive into Irish law. The only novel elements relate to investigation powers of officials of the Department of Labour (Regulation 8) and offences (Regulations 9 and 10): the latter are prosecutable at the suit of the Minister for Labour, incur a maximum fine on conviction of £500 and may be committed by corporate bodies.

1 O.J. L 61, 5.3.1977 p. 26.
2 European Communities (Safeguarding of Employees' Rights on Transfer of Undertaking) Regulations, 1980; S.I. No 306 of 1980.
3 Case 24/85 [1986] E.C.R. 1119, [1986] 2 C.M.L.R. 296.
4 Case 135/83 [1985] E.C.R. 469, [1987] 2 C.M.L.R. 406.
5 Tony Kerr and Gerry Whyte, *Irish Trade Union Law* (1985), at p. 180.
6 Foreningen af Arbejdsledere i Danmark, representing Case 105/84 *Mikkelsen v Danmols Inventar* [1985] E.C.R. 2639, [1986] 1 C.M.L.R. 316.
7 Case 237/84 *EC Commission v Belgium* [1986] E.C.R. 1247, [1988] 2 C.M.L.R. 865.
8 S.I. No. 306 of 1980.

The protection of employees in the event of the insolvency of their employers

25.12 Council Directive (EEC) 80/987,[1] based on Article 100 of the Treaty, is designed to reduce the differences that remain between the Member States as regards the extent of the protection afforded to employees on the insolvency of their employers, particularly concerning guarantees of payment of outstanding claims. The Directive defines insolvency, requires Member States to ensure that guarantee institutions honour outstanding claims of employees, for a certain minimum period, permits the Member States to limit in time the guarantee of payment, and makes further provision in respect of the non-payment by employers of contributions under national social security schemes or voluntary schemes. The Directive applies, according to Article 1, to employees' claims arising from contracts of employment or employment relationships and existing against employers who are in a state of insolvency. Article 2 states that an employer is deemed to be in a state of insolvency: (a) when a request has been made to open proceedings involving the employer's assets to satisfy collectively the claims of creditors and other outstanding claims including those of employees; and (b) where the competent national authority has decided to open proceedings or has determined that the employer's business has definitively closed down and that the available assets are insufficient to warrant the opening of proceedings. In Article 3(1) the Member States are obliged to ensure that guarantee institutions underwrite the payment of outstanding claims resulting from contracts of employment and relating to pay for the period prior to a given date. The latter date is defined in paragraph (2) and Member States are given the option of selecting as the given date:

— the date of onset of the employer's insolvency;
  or
— the date of receipt of the notice of dismissal occasioned by the employer's insolvency;
  or
— the date of discontinuance of the contract of employment or employment relationship due to the employer's insolvency.

Article 4 permits Member States to limit the liability of guarantee institutions to pay employees and, if Member States choose to do so, Article 4(2) imposes minimum periods of liability. For example, if the Member State has chosen the date of the onset of the employer's insolvency as the relevant date, the guarantee institution must pay claims relating to pay for the last three months of the contract of employment or employment relationship occurring within a period of six months preceding the date of the onset of the employer's insolvency. In Article 5 the Member States were obliged to adopt rules for the organisation and financing of guarantee institutions complying with the following principles: (i) the assets of the institutions must be independent of employer's operating capital; (ii) employers must contribute to the finances of the guarantee institutions; and (iii) the institution's liabilities must not depend on the fulfilment of contribution obligations. Articles 6, 7 and 8 deal with social security contributions; the general principle is that the failure of the employer to make contributions to social insurance schemes or pensioners' schemes should not adversely affect employees' or former employees' entitlements. The Directive was supposed to have been implemented by the Member States before 23 October 1983.

The Directive was implemented in Ireland by the Protection of Employees (Employers' Insolvency) Act, 1984. The guarantee institution nominated to carry out the functions outlined by the Directive was the Redundancy Fund established by section 26 of the Redundancy Payments Act, 1967; henceforth, it will be known as the Redundancy and Employers' Insolvency Fund (section 2). Section 3 states that the Act applies to employees employed in employment which is insurable for all benefits under the Social Welfare Acts, 1981 to 1987. Insolvency is defined in section 1(3) and section 4 establishes when an employer has become insolvent. Section 6 is the important section in that it outlines the employee's rights to payments out of the Redundancy and Employers' Insolvency Fund, which is administered by the Minister for Labour. The Minister will make payments to applicants, who were employed by employers who became insolvent, in respect of debts outlined in subsections (2) and (3). Although the Act was passed by the Oireachtas on 30 November 1984, section 6(1)(b) allows for payments in respect of insolvencies occurring after 22 October 1983 i.e. immediately after the expiry date for the implementation of the Directive. Debts which the Minister will pay out of the Fund include arrears of pay (not exceeding 8 weeks in total), holiday pay or awards under the Minimum Notice and Terms of Employment Act, 1973 or under recommendations under the Anti-Discrimination (Pay) Act, 1974, the Unfair Dismissals Act, 1977 or the Employment Equality Act, 1977. Section 7 permits the Minister to make payments into occupational pension schemes when it appears that employers' contributions to those schemes were not paid. Under section 9 applicants for payments of unpaid wages or holiday pay may complain to the Employment Appeals Tribunal that the Minister has failed to make the payment or that the payment is inadequate. The Minister is also empowered to refer doubtful claims under sections 6 or 7 for the determination of the tribunal. Section 10 in effect subrogates the Minister, when payment of a debt has been effected from the Fund, to the rights and remedies of the employee. The Act also provides for offences in respect of false statements (section 15) but prosecutions can be commenced only with the consent of the Minister (section 14).

In its Annual Report for 1986 the Department of Labour noted that over 9,000 applications were processed by the Department in respect of 387 employers and that payments totalled over £5m.[2]

1 O.J. L 283, 28.10.1980 p. 23, amended by Directive 87/164 O.J. L 66, 11.3.1987 p. 11.
2 Annual Report of the Department of Labour, 1986 at p. 33.

'Mitbestimmung' and the Vredeling proposal

25.13 Apart from equal pay and equal treatment there are two other labour law-related issues which have been on the legislative agenda for some time but whose implementation has been delayed because of fundamental disagreement between the Member States and between the social partners.

'Mitbestimmung' (or worker co-determination) first made its appearance in a Community blueprint in 1970 when the Commission submitted a proposal to the Council for a regulation embodying the Statute for the European Company or SE (*Societas Europaea*). The idea for the creation of a European Company, which was seen as providing an additional type of limited company to operate in an integrating common market rather than as a replacement for national company laws, was conceived in the 1960s by Professor Pieter Sanders of Rotterdam University.[1] The European Company would have three organs of management: the general meeting (of shareholders), the executive board, and the supervisory board. The first of these bodies is familiar enough to common lawyers but the division of the management functions between an executive board, charged with the day-to-day management of the company, and a supervisory board, which exercises control and scrutiny over the permanent managers in the executive board, is a phenomenon more familiar to German, Dutch and French company law. In particular, the election of one third of the supervisory board by employees—as envisaged by Articles 137 to 145 of the Commission proposal—was unknown in British and Irish company law.

In July 1988 the Commission resuscitated the European Company proposal but admitted that the co-determination principle was likely to cause problems, as it had for the fifth Directive on the corporate structure of public limited companies—the first draft of which was published in 1972.[2] The dual board system was included in this latter proposal and, for companies employing more than 500 workers, one third of the members of the supervisory board were to be elected by the employees (Article 4). Although the Commission published a Green Paper on 'Worker participation' and the structure of firms in 1975[3] the dual board system encountered considerable resistance in Britain and, to a lesser extent, in Ireland. In 1983 the Commission published an amended version[4] of the draft fifth directive according to which public companies would be organised on a two-tier basis, but which also introduced the possibility of retaining a unitary board system. But in this latter system supervisory and management functions would be divided between non-executive and executive members of the board with the latter being appointed by the former. In companies with more than 1,000 workers at least one third of the supervisory board (in a two-tier system) would be elected by the workers or at least one-third of the non-executive members of the unitary board would be selected by workers. A further alternative envisaged no employee participation on the board(s) but the employees' representatives were to be given access on a regular basis to information on the administration, progress and prospects of the company, its competitive position, credit situation and investment plans, as well as access to the information available to the supervisory organ or non-executive directors as the case may be. These modified proposals received a lukewarm reception in Ireland[5] even though a limited form of worker participation had been introduced here between the publication of the Commission's Green Paper and the revised draft fifth directive. In the Worker Participation (State Enterprises) Act, 1977 provision was made for the election by the employees of one-third of the board of the following companies: Bord na Mona, Coras Iompair Eireann, the ESB, Aer Lingus, B and I, Comhlucht Sinicre Eireann, and NET. On 10 April 1984 six other entities were added to the list: Aer Rianta, An Foras Forbartha, the VHI, the National Rehabilitation Board, Bord Gais Eireann and Irish Steel.[6]

Insofar as workers would receive considerable information on the activities of the undertaking in which they are employed the draft fifth directive is similar to the 'Vredeling' proposal for a Council Directive on employee information and consultation, which was published by the Commission in 1980[7] and named after the then Commissioner for Social Affairs, Henk Vredeling. A second draft of the proposal was produced in 1983.[8] According to Article 2 it would apply to undertakings employing 1,000 workers or more in the EEC, and parent and subsidiary companies are to be taken together for the purposes of the Directive. Under Article 3 a parent company would be obliged at least once a year to disseminate to its subsidiaries information, intended to give a clear picture of the activities of the corporation, with a view to forwarding this information to the employees. This information would deal with: the structure of the company; its economic and financial situation; the likely development of its business, including production and sales; present and future employ-ment trends; and its investment prospects. In the event that a subsidiary company does not supply information to its workforce, the representatives of the latter would be able to apply directly to the parent company for the information; failure to supply the information in question would be punishable by penalties. In addition, the draft Directive would require parent companies, via their subsidiaries, to communicate information to workers' representatives and enter into consultations with them on topics such as the closure of plants, significant reductions or alterations in the activities or organisation of the undertaking, and measures affecting workers' health and industrial safety. This information would have to indicate the grounds for the decision, the legal, economic and social consequences for employees and the measures planned in respect of such workers (Article 4). However, Article 7 would permit the withholding of confidential business information.

The 'social partners', both in Europe and in Ireland, have taken diametrically-opposed views of the Vredeling proposal. The Irish Congress of Trade Unions considered that proposal was a modest step towards industrial democracy but that it was of great significance to Irish workers employed by multi-national undertakings. The Confederation of Irish Industry believed that the proposal could jeopardise the attractiveness of Ireland in terms of foreign industrial development.[9] In view of these quite different perspectives, progress in reaching agreement on the definitive text of the Directive is likely to be slow.

1 Pieter Sanders, 'Structure and Progress of the European Company', Chapter 5 in Clive M Schmitthoff (Ed) *The Harmonisation of European Company Law*. For text of Statute see: *'Proposed statute for the European Company'* Bull. E.C. Supp 8/70. For the text of the Commission's revised proposal see: COM(88) 320 final.
2 Bull. E.C. Supp 10/72.
3 Bull. E.C. Supp. 8/75.
4 O.J. C 240, 9.9.1983 p. 2.
5 Fourth Oireachtas Joint Committee on the Secondary Legislation of the European Communities, Report no. 20, 'Fifth Company Law Directive', at point 40.
6 *Idem*, at point 19 and Appendix 2.
7 O.J. C 297, 15.11.1980 p. 3.
8 O.J. C 217, 12.8.1983 p. 3.
9 Fourth Oireachtas Joint Committee on the Secondary Legislation of the European Communities, Report no. 19, 'Workers' Consultation and Information Rights (Vredeling Directive)', at points 28–32.

Index

518